Dear Jerry:

Knowing of your interest in the Pacific I hope that you will enjoy this book.

Cheers. Bob.

CULTURES *of the* PACIFIC

Cultures of the Pacific

SELECTED READINGS

EDITED *and with* INTRODUCTIONS BY

Thomas G. Harding

AND

Ben J. Wallace

The Free Press NEW YORK
Collier-Macmillan Limited LONDON

Fp

A Division of The Macmillan Company

Printed in the United States of America

The Free Press
A Division of The Macmillan Company
866 Third Avenue, New York, New York 10022

Collier-Macmillan Canada Ltd., Toronto, Ontario

Library of Congress Catalog Card Number: 70-91883

printing number
1 2 3 4 5 6 7 8 9 10

Preface

Interest in the Pacific area is reflected in the large number of courses and programs of study on the Pacific, or the Pacific and Asia, offered in American colleges and universities. It is with the hope that this interest will continue to grow and mature that we offer this anthology.

Our approach as editors has been guided by the obvious consideration that we are students of Pacific cultures who conduct our studies by means of anthropological methods and concepts. This is inevitably a two-way process. Knowledge of Pacific cultures may be the end, anthropological tools the means, but at the same time, studies of Pacific peoples and their history have contributed to the development and refinement of anthropology's techniques and concepts. Our objectives, therefore, are twofold: to supply concrete information about life in the Pacific as viewed through the anthropologist's eyes and to indicate, wherever possible, how the anthropologist's encounters with Pacific peoples have enlivened and enriched his discipline.

Among social scientists generally, the anthropologist's interests are the least restricted by geographic and temporal boundaries. Indeed, it has been the anthropologist's mission to rescue a host of human societies from the obscurity in which history or geography has placed them. If anthropology as a discipline ranges widely in search of its materials, however, its individual practitioners, for practical and scientific reasons, have been led to specialize. A primary basis of this specialization is geographical, for although the significant problems and methods are universal, the particular forms in which they are presented and applied vary by culture and region. For this reason effective anthropological work depends on many years of study in particular cultures, and this investment of time and effort helps to produce a regionalization of scholarly interests and commitments.

For ethnographers—anthropologists who study live or on-going cultures—the Pacific is an important region. Here, a half-century ago, the modern methods of intensive field work were first developed and applied by such pioneers as Bronislaw Malinowski, W. H. R. Rivers, and A. R. Radcliffe-Brown. Since then, all major fields of anthropological concern—art, religion, economics, political organization, social structure, language, cultural ecology, and cultural change—have been greatly enriched by the labors of Pacific scholars. And today, of course, the Pacific world continues to offer intriguing opportunities for research on variations and change in human culture.

For some anthropologists, "the Pacific" refers to the island cultures of Polynesia, Micronesia, and Melanesia. On the other hand, *Oceania,* one of our principal journals, broadens the area to include indigenous peoples of Australia and New Guinea. Still others wish to think of Indonesia and the Philippines, and perhaps other parts of Southeast Asia, as part of the Pacific.

We favor this more inclusive compass, and we have selected for this anthology a number of essays dealing with Australian Aborigines and the tribal peoples of New Guinea and Island Asia. Our reason for this choice is simple but compelling. A part of the scholarly commitment to the Pacific region is directed to unraveling the history of its peoples and cultures, to understanding its development as a region composed of distinct but related cultures. The historical picture will forever remain fragmentary, the more so as we extend our perspective to include the several thousand years of Pacific history and prehistory. But it is obvious that as we move toward the remote past our attention automatically shifts westward toward Island and mainland Asia, for the ancestors of the Pacific Islanders, New Guineans, and Australian Aborigines were all "men out of Asia." This is not to suggest that the various contemporary tribal peoples of Island Asia necessarily resemble the ancestral populations of long ago; the main clues as to the characteristics of the ancestral cultures will ultimately come from archeological research, not from comparative ethnography. Rather, our objective is to focus attention on the obviously important historical connections between Asia and the Pacific island world.

Historical considerations, then, have partly determined our geographic frame of reference. Of equal relevance, however, are the events of the post-war era: increasingly, Australians, Japanese, Filipinos, Indonesians, New Zealanders, and Malaysians are being drawn together through developing economic, political, and cultural ties. Anthropologists are deeply concerned, both as individuals and as scientists, with the roles that indigenous and formerly colonial peoples will have in this new Asian-Pacific community.

In the main, our selection and organization of the essays have aimed at conveying the methods, problems, and results of anthropological research in Pacific cultures. The essays are arranged by topics, which are in order: culture history, technology and economics, social life, politics and social control, religion, and culture change. The essays introducing the various sections of the book were chosen because they provide insights into method and theory or because of their broad comparative scope. We are confident that the topical orientation will serve equally well the needs of students, non-specialists, and our teaching colleagues. (It is unnecessary to add that in an area so vast, no collection of twenty-eight essays can be genuinely representative of the range of cultural variation or scholarly points of view.)

Most of the articles included have been reprinted in full, with only minor deletions and emendations. The chapter by Firth has been slightly abridged. In addition, four chapters (Freedman, Harding, Lundsgaarde, and Wallace) were written especially for this volume.

Bibliographic references and all substantive annotations of the authors have been retained, and they are arranged by chapter in a final section, "Notes and References."

We are grateful to the editors of The Free Press for their assistance and to the authors and publishers who have allowed us to reprint the essays that previously appeared in books and professional journals. We would also like to thank Kent Wilkinson and Carlos Fernandez, who prepared the illustrations.

T.G.H.

B.J.W.

Contents

Preface v

List of Figures xiii

List of Tables xv

I. *Perspectives on Culture History*

INTRODUCTION 1

1. ISLAND CULTURES *Andrew P. Vayda and Roy A. Rappaport* 5

2. POLYNESIAN NAVIGATION TO DISTANT ISLANDS *Andrew Sharp* 13

3. AUSTRONESIAN LINGUISTICS AND CULTURE HISTORY *George W. Grace* 20

4. THE *Kon-Tiki* MYTH *Robert C. Suggs* 29

5. ORIGINS OF THE MELANESIANS *Mary Elizabeth Shutler and Richard Shutler, Jr.* 39

II. *Technology and Economics*

INTRODUCTION 47

6. THE PRIMITIVE ECONOMICS OF THE TROBRIAND ISLANDERS *Bronislaw Malinowski* 51

7. AGRICULTURAL TECHNOLOGY OF THE PAGAN GADDANG *Ben J. Wallace* 63

8. PRODUCTION, DISTRIBUTION, AND POWER IN A PRIMITIVE SOCIETY *Marshall D. Sahlins* 78

9. PONAPEAN PRESTIGE ECONOMY *William R. Bascom* 85

10. TRADING IN NORTHEAST NEW GUINEA *Thomas G. Harding* 94

III. *Social Life*

INTRODUCTION 113

11. IN PRIMITIVE POLYNESIA *Raymond Firth* 115

12. MALE-FEMALE RELATIONSHIPS IN THE HIGHLANDS OF AUSTRALIAN NEW GUINEA *M. J. Meggitt* 125

13. SOCIOCENTRIC RELATIONSHIP TERMS AND THE AUSTRALIAN CLASS SYSTEM *Elman R. Service* 144

14. SOCIAL ORGANIZATION OF A SIASSI ISLAND COMMUNITY *Michael P. Freedman* 159

15. THE IBAN OF WESTERN BORNEO *Derek Freeman* 180

IV. *Politics and Social Control*

INTRODUCTION 201

16. POOR MAN, RICH MAN, BIG-MAN, CHIEF: POLITICAL TYPES IN MELANESIA AND POLYNESIA *Marshall D. Sahlins* 203

17. A LEADER IN ACTION *Douglas L. Oliver* 216

18. POLITICAL ORGANIZATION, SUPERNATURAL SANCTIONS, AND THE PUNISHMENT FOR INCEST ON YAP *David M. Schneider* 232

19 LAW AND POLITICS ON NONOUTI ISLAND *Henry P. Lundsgaarde* 242

V. *Religion*

INTRODUCTION 265

20. DAUGHTER OF TIME *Peter Lawrence* 267

21. THE NGAING OF THE RAI COAST *Peter Lawrence* 285

22. THE DREAMING *W. E. H. Stanner* 304

23. THE ANALYSIS OF *Mana*: AN EMPIRICAL APPROACH *Raymond Firth* 316

VI. *Aspects of Change*

INTRODUCTION 335

24. SOCIAL STATUS, POLITICAL POWER, AND NATIVE RESPONSES TO EUROPEAN INFLUENCE IN OCEANIA
Charles A. Valentine 337

25. STEEL AXES FOR STONE-AGE AUSTRALIANS
Lauriston Sharp 385

26. THE MILLENARIAN ASPECT OF CONVERSION TO CHRISTIANITY IN THE SOUTH PACIFIC *Jean Guiart* 397

27. PORT TOWN AND HINTERLAND IN THE PACIFIC ISLANDS
Alexander Spoehr 412

28. THE RIGHTS OF PRIMITIVE PEOPLES *Margaret Mead* 419

Notes and References 431

Index 471

List of Figures

Chapter 7

1. Cross-section of Pakak. *65*
2. A Pakak Swidden. *72*

Chapter 10

1. Schematic View of the Siassi Trading Sphere. *95*
2. Production and Exchange from the Point of View of a Siassi Community. *100*

Chapter 13

1. Distribution of Australian Class Systems. *155*

Chapter 14

1. Male Co-gardeners of Garden X, Mandok, 1965–1966. *173*
2. Bush-Clearing Assemblage. *173*
3. Hoeing Assemblage. *174*
4. Representative Fishing Crews. *175*
5. Assemblage of Bridewealth Producers. *176*
6. Assemblage of Bridewealth Recipients. *176*

Chapter 15

1. Iban Kinship Terminology: Cognates. *192*
2. Iban Kinship Terminology: Affines I. *195*
3. Iban Kinship Terminology: Affines II. *196*

Chapter 19

1. Sketch Map of Nonouti Island Showing Village Districts and Islets. *246*
2. Legal and Political Levels. *249*

Chapter 24

1. Boundaries of Polynesia, Micronesia, and Melanesia. *382*

List of Tables

Chapter 7

1. Basic Steps of the Pakak Agricultural Cycle. *67*

Chapter 8

1. Quantities of Major Crops Planted in Gardens of Family Heads, Naroi, 1954. *82*
2. Average Plantings in 1954 by Family Heads in Three Villages. *83*

Chapter 12

1. Schema of Symbolic Classification among the Mae Enga. *140*

Chapter 14

1. Intermarriages among Men's Houses, Mandok Village, ca. 1920–1966. *169*
2. Intermarriages among Maximal Patrilines, Mandok Village, ca. 1920–1966. *169*
3. Genealogical Relationship and Men's-House Affiliation of Male Co-gardeners, Mandok, 1965–1966. *172*

Chapter 24

1. Marriages Registered in the Territory of New Guinea, 1928–1938. *350*
2. Occupations of the Non-indigenous Population in the Territory of New Guinea, 1921. *351*

PART I

Perspectives on Culture History

INTRODUCTION

"Culture history" is the label we give to anthropologists' attempts to reconstruct the history of preliterate societies—that is, societies that have left no written accounts of their activities. From the point of view of the documents-based research of the historian, this may seem a strange and dangerously speculative kind of history. Culture history is impersonal; it deals not with persons and events in discrete societies but with successions of cultural forms in space and time.

Lacking documentary evidence, culture historians must rely on various kinds of indirect evidence. Most important are the archeologists' reconstructions of extinct cultures from the physical traces of past human activities, but it should be noted that in most parts of the Pacific systematic archeological work is in its infancy or has not yet begun. The cultural historical picture becomes less fragmentary, however, when we add the specialist contributions of other scholars. Linguists have devised methods of tracing the history of languages, even to the point of reconstructing "proto-languages," ancestral speech forms that were in use hundreds and thousands of years ago (see Grace's essay in this section). Geologists are able to tell us about the history of land forms, which often suggests possible environmental influences on prehistoric societies. Geography and oceanography aid in a realistic assessment of the geographical possibilities for human migration and intercourse.

Plant geneticists' studies of the diffusion of cultivated plants also supply important clues regarding human movements and contacts. Thus, an historical picture emerges from a variety of facts. The diversity of sources utilized by the culture historian is illustrated in the Shutlers' essay on the "Origins of the Melanesians." Their discussion shows that although the historian's craft may resemble the methods of a Sherlock Holmes, culture history is more like modern detective work which involves the team collaboration of different kinds of technical experts.

The contributions of the ethnologist to culture history are twofold. In the first place, he is able to reconstruct the history of contemporary societies from the period of initial European discovery and contact to the present. In such "ethnohistorical" research he can borrow the ordinary methods of historians, even though the documentary evidence is of a distinctive kind. Thus, although the eighteenth-century Tahitians produced no documents of their own, Captain Cook and other European observers of the Tahitian scene did record pertinent information. To illustrate, Andrew Sharp's assessment of the Polynesians' maritime capabilities (Chapter 2) is based, in part, on a fine-grained analysis of such ethnohistorical sources. Secondly, the ethnologist's concern with process can provide important leads for the prehistorian. For example, Vayda and Rappaport's conclusions regarding the effects of insularity on cultural development apply as much to prehistoric Pacific Island cultures as to the recent societies studied by ethnologists and ethnohistorians.

Whatever the degree of technical refinement, however, culture history remains a highly speculative pursuit. This adds to its fascination, but one must also take account of the rules of the game. Speculative inference is subjected to rigorous standards of proof, some of which underlie Robert Suggs' (Chapter 4) convincing critique of Heyerdahl's *Kon-Tiki* theory.

No compilation of five essays, of course, could display the full range of substantive historical results, but the essays presented here do illustrate some of the principal characteristics of culture-historical reconstruction, such as the use of multiple sources of data, attention to critical details, and reasoning from known processes. This section, then, should not be viewed as a résumé of Pacific culture history—the grand historical synthesis lies far in the future—but rather as an attempt to illustrate the tactics by means of which the historical picture is gradually constructed.

CHAPTER

1

Island Cultures

ANDREW P. VAYDA AND ROY A. RAPPAPORT

What influence do relative isolation and limited territory have upon the evolution and differentiation of cultures? In order to suggest some ways of answering this question, we are dealing in this paper with relatively small dry-land areas, whether islands or island groups, that have human populations whose contacts with other human populations are prevented entirely or greatly restricted by the ocean or by other water barriers.

With large islands, such as New Guinea or the islands of New Zealand, we are little concerned, for in these places the territorial limitations seem to be not too markedly different from those in some continental areas. Nor are we much interested in certain small islands such as Zanzibar or the Maldives west and southwest of Ceylon, since these have long had human populations in regular and frequent contact with other human populations. On the other hand, while centering attention upon relatively isolated and relatively small islands and island groups, we hope also to gain insight into the influence that relative isolation and territorial limitations, here regarded as defining characteristics of insularity, may have upon cultural evolution and differentiation among human populations anywhere. Natural barriers have isolated human populations and have confined them to limited territories not only upon islands but in remote valleys and on mountaintops of large continents. Moreover, there have often been man-made barriers to territorial expansion and to contacts with other populations. A Neolithic village surrounded by hostile neighbors and an ethnic minority living in a ghetto are, to some degree, isolated and confined to limited territories.

I

We ask, first of all, about the influence that insularity may have upon

From *Man's Place in the Island Ecosystem,* F. R. Fosberg, ed. Honolulu: Bishop Museum Press, 1963, pp. 133–142. By permission of the authors and publisher.

the differentiation of one culture from another—that is, the influence upon the founding or establishment of new cultures.

Something like the founder principle discussed by the geneticists (Dobzhansky 1965; Mayr 1954; and Ford 1960) may well be operating not only in biological but also in cultural evolution. That is to say, whatever cultural as well as genetic materials the founders bring with them from their ancestral populations may become distinctive attributes of the new populations as they expand. We state this as a possibility rather than as a firmly established principle, for there have been few studies concerned with establishing the cultural contributions made by the founders of particular insular cultures. A step in the direction of such studies is recommended in effect by Mead (1958:495–496) when she states that human evolution is dependent upon the cultural contributions of individuals and that the locus of human evolution is a "transactional group of individuals . . . who share mankind's universal culture and who share also, *in individual and varying degrees,* the particular system of their society" (italics ours). For most of the insular cultures of the Pacific it is difficult, if not impossible, to specify just what were the cultures of the populations from which particular founders came and to what degree the particular founders shared in those cultures. However, for a few insular cultures in the Pacific, the conditions of settlement are well enough known and sufficient material on the founders should be available to allow for some assessment of the operation of the founder principle in cultural evolution. We have in mind here, particularly, such cultures as those of Pitcairn and Palmerston islands, both of which were founded in the post contact period by combinations of European and Polynesian men and women in small numbers. A comparison of the present-day culture of Pitcairn Island with that of Tristan da Cunha in the south Atlantic might be especially instructive. The cultures were founded at approximately the same time and under somewhat similar environmental conditions and similar circumstances of isolation. The interesting question to ask here is whether differences in the solutions to similar problems of adaptation on the two islands may be due to differences of culture between the original settlers of the two islands. For example, it may be possible to trace the apparently greater degree of collective enterprise in Pitcairn than in Tristan da Cunha (compare Shapiro 1936, with Munch 1946) to the Polynesians among the founders of Pitcairn culture.

The Pacific also offers very recently founded insular cultures. At least two examples come to mind. First, there is the case of the Phoenix Islands, settled by Gilbertese in the late 1930's as part of a colonization scheme that has been described by Maude (1952). There is also the case of some Marshall Islanders who were moved during the postwar years from Bikini Atoll to the island of Kili in the southern Marshalls (Mason 1950, 1957, 1958). Whether these cultures are really, or at least incipiently, new, remains to be demonstrated. It may be that there has been neither sufficient time nor sufficient isolation for the cultures of Phoenix and Kili to differ much from the cultures from which they derived. Yet, the close and continuing observation of such a culture, as has been undertaken by Mason, may be a means of learning a great deal more about the role of founders, the role of isolation, and the various other factors that may be operating in the differentiation of cultures.

For the operation of the founder principle, isolation rather than limited territory seems to be critical. If the migration to an isolated place, whether a small island or a large continent, is by a relatively small group of people who are unable to reproduce in full the culture of the population from which they derived, then the culture in the new place will be immediately different from the culture in the homeland. The degree of difference will depend at the outset upon the extent to which the migrants are able or unable to reproduce the homeland culture. What in the homeland was essentially a subculture, characteristic of a particular class, locality, occupation, or domestic group, may become established in the new setting as a distinctive culture in its own right. Foster (1960:232–234) has indicated that contemporary Hispanic American cultures show a large total of cultural influences stemming specifically from Andalusia and Extremadura. He attributes this to the fact that during the early years of the Spanish colonization of the New World in the sixteenth century, a large proportion of the settlers came from these regions. Separated from the Spaniards of other regions, the settlers drew upon their particular variants of Spanish culture in adapting to New World environments. Foster's study is concerned with the establishment of a new culture not upon an island, but upon a continent; and the situation described by Foster is complicated by the fact that the new culture was being established in a place where there already were human populations, the Indians with their own cultures. Yet, it remains suggestive that the Spanish component of the Hispanic American cultures that eventually developed should to such a large extent have derived from particular regional variants of Spanish culture.

Apart from the question of the founders' influence or, more precisely, the question of the influence of their particular cultural attributes, there are some important matters to be discussed regarding the relation between isolation and the founding or establishment of new cultures. Two populations with a common ancestry but living for some time in isolation from each other will invariably develop at least some cultural differences simply because not all of the innovations made by one population will be independently made by the other. Moreover, isolation may be expected to favor cultural differentiation not only because it implies barriers to the flow of ideas but because it implies barriers to the flow of goods. When the settlers of an island can continue to import materials from their former homelands, the development of special techniques for the utilization of local resources may be inhibited, and certain usages associated with the imported materials may be maintained more effectively than would be the case if there were more complete isolation. It may be suggested, for example, that the development of techniques of making adzes from shell rather than from stone and the abandonment of the kava ceremony would not have taken place in certain Polynesian atolls if the inhabitants had been less isolated and had been more able to import basalt and kava roots from elsewhere.

Granted that isolation implies cultural differentiation, we may still ask about the converse, that is, whether appreciable cultural differences can develop among people only if they are kept from one another by geographical or other barriers. The significance of the question is not confined to the study of oceanic cultures. It has been suggested that even such subcultural differences as those between the classes in some state-organized societies of the Old World originated during a period when the ancestors of members of the different classes constituted separate populations developing their cultures in isolation from one another (Gumplowicz 1899). In the study of linguistics, the suggestion has been made that certain hunting-gathering groups were able to maintain a relatively uniform type of speech over a large continental area because their contacts with one another were not unduly impeded by the terrain or other barriers; more marked linguistic differences are thought to have developed with the advent of agriculture and the establishment of local nuclei of population having limited contacts with other nuclei (Swadesh 1959:33). While it is not part of our task to evaluate suggestions such as these, they are pertinent in the present context as an indication of the fact that the role of isolation in the development of cultural differences may be important also in cultures other than those of islands. We badly need further investigations, not simply to determine whether isolation is a precondition of cultural differentiation but to determine just what kinds and degrees of cultural differentiation may presuppose just what kinds and degrees of isolation.

Island cultures do provide certain special opportunities for studying the role of isolation. Consider the island cultures of Polynesia. The evidence of linguistics, cultural distributions, and traditional history indicates that particular Polynesian coral atolls were settled from particular Polynesian high islands: the Tokelaus from Samoa, the Tuamotus from the Society group, and most of the northern Cooks from the Lower Cook Islands. At the same time, the accounts that we have of Polynesian voyaging and our knowledge of the limitations upon such voyaging in pre-European times (Sharp 1956:14, and *passim*) indicate that the atoll dwellers in the Tokelaus and the northern Cooks were less likely than those in the Tuamotus to have had anything but the most sporadic contacts with the people of the particular high islands where the atoll populations had originated. In all of the atolls under consideration, we can expect to find that there have been some modifications of high island culture in the direction of adaptation to the atoll environments. However, the question of interest in the present context is whether the divergence of the atoll cultures from the related high-island cultures has been significantly greater in the isolated Tokelaus and northern Cooks than in the Tuamotus. Careful comparison of the various atoll and high island cultures as they were at the time of European discovery should help to provide answers to such question.

II

Turning now to the role of territorial limitations in the evolution of island cultures, we may ask about the development of cultural traits affecting the dispersion and size of island populations. Birdsell's analysis (1957) of demographic data from Pitcairn and Tristan da Cunda and also from the isolated islands of the Furneaux group in Bass

Strait between Australia and Tasmania suggests that an island population with simple horticultural techniques may double its numbers in each generation as long as additional land and resources continue to be readily available. If such a rate of increase is maintained by an island population during the early settlement period, it will not be very long before additional land and resources are no longer readily available. Just how much time it will take for land and resource limitations to be felt by the people will depend on the size of the original population and on the size and resources of the particular island or island group. In each of the cases cited by Birdsell, the island population increased in a few generations to a point at which "the food resources of the environment [exerted] a marked depressant effect" (Birdsell 1958:192).

Before measures limiting the increase of population are instituted there will probably be a tendency for island people to utilize more fully the resources available within their limited territory. Efforts in this direction need not be confined to such improvements in the technology and organization of food production as the development of irrigation, craft specialization, the raising of fish in ponds, the drainage of marsh lands, the assignment of production quotas and some of the other special techniques that had become established in some isolated islands or island groups of Polynesia by the time of European discovery (Sahlins 1958:257 ff.). There may also be the development of certain social forms and usages that help to get people to resources and resources to people. For example, in Polynesia the prevalent nonunilineality of land-owning groups (Firth 1957) and the widespread practice of adoption (Firth 1936:588–596, 597) facilitated the movement of people from group to group and from locality to locality according to the availability of resources (Goodenough 1955). Although Polynesians and certain other Pacific islanders are not the only people in the world among whom nonunilineality and adoption were important, it is possible that in some island cultures the traits did develop as adjustments to the limitations of resources and territory that are characteristic of insular conditions. What may have developed as another adjustment to such limitations, another way of getting people to resources and resources to people, is the organization of the people of Pukapuka Atoll into three land-owning villages whose members could annually transfer their affiliation from one village to another; village-owned land in Pukapuka was either worked communally or redistributed annually among village members (Vayda 1959a:127 ff.). We must also note here the attempt made by Sahlins (1957, 1958) to show that the distributions of goods were facilitated in Polynesia by the development of stratified social hierarchies in the high islands and of intricate systems of interlocking social groups in the coral atolls.

There are, of course, limits to any people's ability to improve their utilization of resources within a finite territory. On any island, ways may eventually have to be found to check the increase of population. Lorimer *et al.* (1954:105) have posed the following questions:

> Did the relative isolation of primitive societies in the Pacific afford opportunity for the development of cultural institutions that include specific motives and means for the adjustment of population to resources? Even where this was

> not so, did island population tend to develop types of social organization with less emphasis on high fertility than those of the dominant African and Asiatic societies?

Along with Lorimer, we find some evidence in support of an affirmative answer to these questions. For example, the previously discussed nonunilineality and adoption in Polynesia made it relatively easy for any particular social unit to maintain itself and to get specific jobs done, even if particular men or women belonging to it were the biological parents of few children or of none at all. Accordingly, the motivation for having children in order to maintain the household or lineage or some other group and to maintain its ability to use and defend its land and other resources might well have been smaller among Polynesians than among unilineally organized people having groups whose perpetuation depended largely upon the numbers of children born to members.

Regardless of the nature and strength of the motives that Pacific islanders may have had for either increasing or not increasing their numbers, there remains the question of just what devices for limiting population growth were developed in the island cultures. One device employed in many of the islands by the time of European discovery was abortion, most commonly, according to Danielsson (1956:162–164), by means of herbal decoctions, massages, and violent bodily movements. Infanticide was also practiced in some islands, especially in the Hawaiian and Society groups (Danielsson 1956:159–165; Williamson 1939:193–198). In the Polynesian outlier of Tikopia there existed such additional checks upon population growth as celibacy of junior males in large families, the practice of coitus interruptus by both married and unmarried persons, the often fatal overseas voyaging of young men, and the expulsion or slaughter of people in war (Firth 1936:414–415, 490–493, and 1939:42–45, 48). According to Firth (1939:43), some of these devices were consciously resorted to by the Tikopians as "a reflex of the population situation" and others, such as the oversea voyages, were not. However, even the overseas voyaging, apparently motivated by a conscious desire for adventure rather than by any desire to solve demographic problems, may have varied in its incidence according to the degree of population pressure upon the land. It may be that young men were increasingly inclined to get away and to seek adventure on the high seas when the population pressure in Tikopia was growing and a diminishing food supply was heightening domestic frustrations and other intracommunity tensions. From other islands in the Pacific, such as the Marquesas and Tahiti, there are indications that the incidence of overseas voyages, especially voyages of exile, and of such population-reducing activities as warfare may have fluctuated with the degree of population pressure (Sharp 1956:48; Vayda 1958:328). To be able to demonstrate such correlations rather than merely to see them as possibilities, we would need more data on pre-European demography and culture in the islands than are available to us now or, unfortunately, are ever likely to become available.

In any event, we would not want to assert or even to hypothesize that all the population-limiting devices that developed in island cultures worked unfailingly to effect nice adjustments of the numbers of people to their resources.

On the Micronesian island of Yap a custom of self-induced abortion developed among the young women during what apparently was a period of either ample population or even overpopulation. This custom, which probably helped to keep down the birth rate, became an integral part of a psychologically gratifying behavioral pattern involving youthful love affairs and nonresponsible early adulthood. The result, according to Schneider (1955), has been the young women's persistent practice of self-induced abortion even while underpopulation has become a dominant problem. Wagley (1951) reports a comparable persistence of customs of infanticide among a continental people undergoing severe depopulation, the Tapirapé Indians of central Brazil. It may be that the Tikopians' previously cited practice of consciously adjusting their use of coitus interuptus, infanticide, and similar devices to the available resources ("measuring them according to the food," writes Firth 1939:43) is indeed, as Lorimer *et al.* (1954:109) say, very unusual, if not unique.

One may ask not only about the variations from one time to another in the extent to which cultural devices for limiting population were employed on any one island but about the variations in the extent of their employment from one island to another. The data available are meager; but there are indications of a tendency for devices such as infanticide (Danielsson 1956:164–165) to have become established more firmly in such fairly large and populous islands as Tahiti than in the small coral atolls that were often densely settled. Possibly the fact that the small, low, and exposed atolls were generally more subject than the high islands to recurrent droughts, cyclones, and other disasters (Vayda 1959b:820–821) contributed to comparatively high death rates in coral atolls and obviated the need to institute elaborate cultural devices limiting population (Fischer and Fischer 1957:81–82, and Fischer 1958:22).

III

There remain to be discussed the rate of change in island cultures and their receptivity to outside influences when isolation is not complete. The questions posed are numerous and complex. Are innovations in the ways of doing things less frequent in more or less isolated and small populations because there are not many people interacting with one another and making new combinations of acts and ideas? Or do such innovations as occur tend to spread among the members of a population more quickly and to become established in the culture more readily when the population is small and isolated? Might cultural change, therefore, be rapid in such a population despite a low incidence of innovations? Is it true, as suggested elsewhere by Vayda (1959b), that small insular populations are particularly receptive to outside influences as well? Is receptivity of island cultures to outside influences affected significantly by the presence or absence of a pattern of hostilities between competing social groups within the local population? Do the smallest and most isolated insular populations, lacking competing social groups and deficient, therefore, in cultural devices for defining group boundaries and for enhancing group solidarity, have an especially marked inability to defend themselves and their cultures against the intrusions of outsiders when isolation is broken down?

These questions and many similar ones are of obvious importance for determining how cultural evolution is influenced by relative isolation and territorial limitations. Unfortunately, the systematic collection of data on island cultures has not supplied enough information for us to give confident answers at the present time. Perhaps further research, guided by an awareness of the questions, will enable us to provide answers before too long.

CHAPTER

2

Polynesian Navigation to Distant Islands

ANDREW SHARP

In a book entitled *Ancient Voyagers in the Pacific,* which was published by the Polynesian Society in 1956 and reprinted by Penguin Books in 1957,[1] I argued that deliberate navigation to and from remote ocean islands was impossible in the days before the plotting of courses with precision instruments, and that in prehistoric times neither the Polynesians nor any other people in the Pacific performed the feats of deliberate long voyaging and colonization with which they have been credited. I cited world-wide evidence in support of Captain Cook's theory that the detached ocean islands of the world in general, and the Pacific in particular, were settled by accident,[2] and applied this theory to a re-examination of the prehistoric Pacific migrations.

Since then a number of writers have continued, as I see it, to confuse myth with history on these themes. Prominent among them, because of his expertise in modern navigation, was the late Harold Gatty, who in his book *Nature is Your Guide*[3] repeated with modifications the theories of Polynesian long navigation given in his previous publication *The Raft Book*.[4] Roger Duff, a New Zealand ethnologist, in a recent article,[5] stated that he was impressed by Gatty's theory that the Polynesians sailed to distant islands by bringing stars overhead which were known from previous contacts to be overhead at those islands at a given time of the night and a given time of the year. While Duff did not come out unreservedly in this article for the Polynesian deliberate settlement of New Zealand, he thought the New Zealand Maori traditions of a Tahitian colonizing fleet contained evidence of fairly accurate navigation, because most of the fleet canoes were described as arriving on the same part of New Zea-

From *Journal of the Polynesian Society,* 70(2):221–226, 1961 (Wellington, New Zealand: The Polynesian Society). By permission of the author and publisher.

land's coast. Robert C. Suggs, an American archaeologist, in his book *The Island Civilizations of Polynesia,*[6] similarly crossed swords with me over what I regard as peripheral and inconclusive issues, but failed to get to grips with the fundamental navigational issues which are the crux of the whole matter.

I cannot in an article repeat the world-wide evidence of the character and range of early navigation without precision instruments, which I cited in my book. What I can do is prove to any perceptive mind that the statements of Polynesian long navigation by Gatty and other deliberate voyage theorists are fallacious, and in particular that the deliberate settlement of Hawaii and New Zealand by the Tahitians or other Polynesians was impossible. Everybody is interested in the prehistoric Polynesian migrations to Hawaii and New Zealand because of the thousands of miles which separate them from Tahiti and the other islands of Eastern Polynesia, and because of the importance of Hawaii and New Zealand as centres of Eastern Polynesian culture.

Before proceeding to demonstrate the specific fallacies of the theories on Polynesian long navigation of Gatty and others who share such views, let me mention five facts which have an important bearing on the matters at issue, and which one does not ordinarily hear of from the deliberate voyage theorists.

The first of these facts is that the idea of deliberate settlement implies at least three voyages, two of them navigated ones—an initial voyage of discovery, a navigated voyage back to the home islands, and a navigated voyage of settlement back again to the discovery. The crucial voyage would therefore be the return one from Hawaii or New Zealand to report the discovery, following on which a further navigated voyage on the outward leg would be required to complete the picture implied by the deliberate settlement theory.

The second fact is the variable and unknowable character of the ocean currents on these supposed long journeys. In the case of Hawaii the voyagers would have had to pass through three separate belts of currents operating across their path, each characterized by marked local variations in width, direction and speed. In the case of New Zealand the voyagers would have had to negotiate the zone of the South Equatorial Current extending for hundreds of miles across their path on both legs of the supposed journeys, as well as a zone of variable currents extending for hundreds of miles round New Zealand. Such currents are imperceptible out of sight of land without the pin-pointing of courses by precision instruments, because the whole body of water surrounding a vessel which is being influenced by them moves with the vessel. The speed with which the Pacific currents move rafts, bottles, and other floating objects is well known and remarkable. The action of currents on vessels is known as *set.* The phenomenon of set, therefore, is a major issue in a consideration of Polynesian navigation.

The third fact is the variable character of winds on the supposed long journeys. In the case of Hawaii, the voyagers would, on the leg from Hawaii to Tahiti, have had to buck the southeast trade wind which blows for 1,200 miles and more north of Tahiti and the other central islands of Polynesia. They would also have had to pass through the equatorial doldrums on both legs, not to mention the northeast trade wind round

Hawaii itself. In the case of New Zealand, the voyagers would have had to pass through the belt of the southeast trade wind as well as an area of variable winds extending for hundreds of miles round New Zealand on both legs of the supposed journeys. In such circumstances the accurate calculation of drift or leeway with the wind was and is impracticable. Unknown drift of considerable dimensions was inevitable on the supposed journeys.

The fourth fact is that set and drift are independent variables, set continuing whether the wind is blowing or not.

The fifth fact is the relatively small target offered by remote islands as compared with islands near at hand. New Zealand, the largest land mass in the Pacific Islands, with a generous margin of 75 miles (Gatty's figure) for visibility or other natural homing aids on either side, occupies only one sixth of the south-to-west quarter of the compass in relation to Tahiti. Hawaii is less again, as are the central groups of Polynesia on the return leg. A comparatively small error in the course to these objectives, therefore, would result in their being missed, as a glance at a map will show. For this reason the local Tahitian voyages of several hundred miles in the trade wind zone where set and drift were relatively predictable bear no relationship to the supposed two-way contacts over 4,000 miles and more of variable currents and winds. Putting on a golf green is a deliberate art because the hole offers a relatively large target. Holing out from a golf tee is achieved only occasionally and with luck, and is a one-way affair.

We are now in a position to consider the specific fallacies of the theories of Gatty and others, and the lack of any valid theory of Polynesian long navigation.

Gatty's main statement of Polynesian long navigation is that the voyagers came within 50 to 75 miles of a distant objective by bringing stars overhead which were supposedly known from previous probes to be overhead at the objective at a given time of the night and a given time of the year. It was this theory of Gatty's which impressed Duff. The time of night, however, is a relative and local phenomenon, because of the apparent constant motion of the sun. The local times of night at which a star is overhead at various points as it passes across the celestial sphere at a given time of the year are all within a few minutes of one another. It is not possible, therefore, to differentiate between one point and another where a star is overhead by judging the time of night at a given time of the year. The problem of longitude cannot be solved so easily. The range of positions on the surface of the Pacific Ocean where a star appears to be overhead at a given time of the night and a given time of the year is, therefore, limited only by the western and eastern sides of the Pacific Ocean itself. The margin of error in Gatty's theory, therefore, is not 75 miles, but 8,000.

The reason why the time of night when a star is overhead is not specific to locality is because the stars and sun follow one another round the celestial sphere during a rotation of the earth, and the time of night and day is determined in relation to the sun. If, therefore, it is four hours after sunset or eleven hours after high noon at one point on the earth's surface where a star is overhead during a rotation of the earth, it will be four hours after sunset or eleven hours after high noon at every other point where the star is overhead as it completes its apparent circuit, apart from the negligible difference arising from the variation between sidereal and mean solar time.

In view of these facts, Gatty's argument that the voyagers, having come within 50 to 75 miles of their objective, used natural homing aids to make their final landfall, is beside the point. Gatty, in any case, like many others, exaggerates the applicability of these aids. Cloud effects over islands are not always present, and are frequently simulated over tracts of ocean where no land exists. The smell of land is discernible only when one is close to land, and only when the wind is blowing off shore. Releasing tropic birds is no use if one has no way of knowing whether or not one is closer to Australia or Norfolk Island than to New Zealand, or to the Marshalls or Gilberts than Hawaii. Concentrations of sea birds are not always present near land, and are detectable only in the vicinity when they are. The mountains of Savaii in Samoa are visible at 70-odd miles. Most of the Pacific Islands are visible at 50 to 15 miles.

The further theory of Gatty and others that the Polynesians followed migratory birds is subject to the fatal defect that to keep in touch with the birds in the face of set and drift it would be necessary to see some birds every hour or two. In the hours of darkness at sea, however, birds are invisible, and are heard only intermittently, if at all, particularly in winds. It would therefore have been something of a miracle if the birds were still in sight after the first night, let alone the many nights required for the supposed long journeys. Furthermore, whereas migratory bird flights last two or three weeks, Captain Cook, when he made the first historical voyage from New Zealand to the Cooks, took five weeks to get there, and was still 600 miles short of Tahiti.[7]

The reserve theory of Gatty that the Polynesians, having made a southing or northing to the latitude of their objective, then moved west or east along a line of latitude to their objective, is subject to the inherent defect that the voyagers had no way of knowing whether they were thousands of miles west of their objective while still thinking themselves east, or thousands of miles east while still thinking themselves west. (The reasons for this will be strengthened when the following two paragraphs have been read.) The chances of the voyagers' turning in the right direction on both legs of each supposed visit were, therefore, four to one against.

The time-honoured theory of Polynesian navigation, put forward by Teuira Henry,[8] Percy Smith[9] and many others, including Gatty himself in his earlier publication *The Raft Book*,[10] is that the Polynesians sailed toward guiding stars which were supposedly known from previous explorations to be in line with the desired objective. There are, however, no stable guiding stars on voyages to or from Hawaii, New Zealand or other remote Polynesian islands, and the stars do not shine during the day. Even if a theoretically ideal horizon star were to shine by night and by day beyond these distant objectives, the voyagers, as they sailed toward this beacon, would have no way of knowing if, because of set and drift, they had missed their objective by hundreds of miles on either side. This method of navigation is practicable only over short distances in areas where set and drift are predictable and can be allowed for. Even then it is only as good as the voyagers' dead reckoning of set and drift, as the observations of Thomas Gladwin, cited later in this article, show. Over courses of thousands of miles to and from New Zealand and Hawaii the method was useless, because of the changing bearings of the stars and the lateral displacements caused by set and drift.

The same defect applies to courses by bearings on the cardinal points, such as southwest, or north-northwest, or "a little to the left of the setting sun." Again the voyagers would have no way of knowing whether they were off course as the result of set and drift, because their vessels, as they passed their objectives on one side or the other, would still be aligned to the southwest, or north-northwest, or "a little to the left of the setting sun," as the case might be. This is the well-known defect of compass bearings also.

At bottom the techniques of sailing toward a point on the horizon marked by guiding stars and of sailing by a bearing on the cardinal points as determined by the stars including the sun are closely akin. In order to achieve anything like accuracy on voyages to and from Hawaii and New Zealand by such methods, it would have been necessary to have calculated and allowed for lateral displacement as the result of set and drift, which the Polynesians had no means of doing.

Horizon stars give no clue to lateral displacement because the objective is relatively near at hand but the stars are at a very great distance, so that the true course and all the possible false courses arising from lateral displacement all the way round the world are in effect parallel. Thus the widest separation between two possible courses is equivalent to the diameter of the earth, but the stars are astronomical distances away.

A *reductio ad absurdum* of theories of finding remote ocean islands by sailing toward guiding stars, aiming to bring stars overhead, and/or setting courses by bearings in relation to the cardinal points is given by applying these notions to courses toward the North Pole by sailing toward the Pole Star. The Pole Star, being almost in line with the axis on which the earth rotates, is relatively stable in its bearings in relation to all points in the northern hemisphere. It is unique in the heavens, there being no visible pole star in the southern hemisphere. If a number of amphibious vessels spaced across the Pacific at the equator were to sail toward the Pole Star, they would all at one and the same time be using the Pole Star as a guiding star, aiming to bring the Pole Star overhead, and sailing by a bearing on the north. Eventually in theory they would all come together at the North Pole with the Pole Star overhead. They would, however, have no idea of what their intervening courses had been, within the limits of 8,000 miles set by the west and east sides of the Pacific, nor what islands they might happen on, nor how far west or east of the direct course they might have wandered as the result of the inevitable vagaries of set and drift. The reason for this is that, wherever they were, they would at all times be sailing toward the Pole Star, aiming to bring the Pole Star overhead, and sailing by a bearing on the north. The North Pole is the only distant objective on the globe which there is any assurance of finding by sailing toward horizon stars, aiming to bring stars overhead, and/or sailing by bearings on the cardinal points. The Polynesians, however, did not live at the North Pole.

It has been pointed out earlier that the concept of the deliberate settlement of Hawaii or New Zealand or of other remote islands implies of necessity that the discoverers got back by deliberate navigation to the home islands. Let us suppose that after Hawaii or New Zealand was discovered by its original settlers, or rediscovered by later ones, some navigators set out on an attempted journey back to the central islands of Eastern Polynesia. That such attempts were in fact made is well within the bounds of possibility. Let us also assume that the navigators had carefully noted their courses on the sun, stars, and cardinal points on the inital voyage of discovery, and that they set out for home at the beginning of the migratory season of the plovers or long-tailed cuckoos, so as to use them as an auxiliary navigation aid. The voyagers set sail, and after about 50 miles the coast behind them sinks beneath the waves. For the remaining hours of daylight the voyagers follow the remembered bearing on the sun's east-west path, as well as the birds. Then darkness falls. The birds, being independent of the set and drift which push the voyagers hither and yon, keep on course, invisible to the voyagers. The remembered courses on the stars, for the reasons given earlier, afford the pilots no clue whatever as to the influence of currents and winds in putting the vessels off course. Already, therefore, before the voyagers are more than a hundred miles or so on their journey of twenty times that distance, a concept of deliberate navigation ceases to have any reality. If by chance the navigators were still on course after the early part of their journey was completed, they would have no way knowing where the westward set of the South Equatorial Current, extending for two thousand miles or more both north and south of the home islands, became dominant, nor the local changes of direction and speed within it.

What do these fundamental navigational issues add up to? Simply this, that the potential margin of error in navigation between Hawaii or New Zealand and the Tahiti area or anywhere else in Eastern Polynesia in any form of sailing or paddling vessel in the days before the plotting of courses with precision instruments was a great distance of hundreds or thousands of miles on either side of the objective on each and every leg of the supposed long journeys, with no way of knowing what the actual error was at any time. Deliberate long voyaging and colonization in such circumstances were impossible. Hawaii, New Zealand and the other detached islands in the Pacific were each settled by one or more accidental one-way voyages of waifs of the storm or exiles hoping to find new land. The evidence of design and planned transfer which Duff[11] and Suggs[12] think they see in the diffusion of artifacts, food plants, livestock, and other cultural items to the peripheral islands can be explained by the seting forth of exiles with these items and their accidental arrival on these islands, or by the piecemeal diffusion of the items in several vessels over a period of time, or by both these types of transfer. Not only is it needless to think that the Polynesians first discovered distant islands, then returned to their home islands by deliberate navigation, and then set out once more on navigated voyages of settlement to explain to cultural facts, but also the facts of physical geography are such that there were no valid techniques of long navigation whereby this needless concept of deliberate long voyaging and colonization can be sustained. Accidental settlement by exiles who had made preparations and set out in the hope of finding new land, and by waifs of storms, could have achieved the peopling of the peripheral islands of Eastern Polynesia within a few centuries of the peopling of the central islands, since the winds and currents are relatively favourable to such voyages on the outward legs, although not on the return ones.[13]

At the time when I was writing my own book, Thomas Gladwin, an American ethnologist, was independently writing up his own observations of voyaging in the Truk Islands,[14] where the Trukese voyagers still sail their outrigger sailing canoes without precision instruments. Gladwin's conclusions were the same as my own, namely that the inherent defect in such navigation was that it was fundamentally a dead reckoning system dependent on calculating and allowing for set and drift, and that when errors or failures in dead reckoning occurred, the voyagers were powerless to detect or correct them, in which case the landfalls were missed. Gladwin's observations were in due course published in the *American Anthropologist*.[15]

Another formidable authority to the same effect is Bret Hilder, a captain of Burns Philp vessels with over thirty years' experience of Pacific navigation. In an article in a navigation journal,[16] he endorsed the view that deliberate navigation to and from remote islands in the Pacific in native vessels did not occur because of the mobility of currents and the difficulty of determining drift with winds.

Why do so many people hanker so determinedly after the notion that the Polynesians sailed to and from remote islands by deliberate navigation? After innumerable discussions I am driven to the conclusion that most people who cherish this belief do so for unconscious emotional rather than scientific reasons. These reasons are that the belief appeals to their romanticism, that it was taught to them at school, that it is flattering to the modern Polynesians, that many people have propounded it in the past, and that the modern believers have said it or written it.

CHAPTER

3

Austronesian Linguistics and Culture History

GEORGE W. GRACE

This paper is concerned with culture-historical inferences from Austronesian (Malayo-Polynesian) linguistics. There are numerous kinds of linguistic information which can be relevant to culture-historical problems, but that of the greatest interest in the first instance is the classification of the languages involved. In the case of Austronesian, of course, we are dealing with a single language family, and therefore the problem of classification becomes that of subgrouping. Most of the discussion of specific culture-historical points will be in terms of Austronesian subgroups. That fact, since there is some divergence of opinion as to how subgroups may be discovered, seems to require some preliminary discussion of the methodological problem. Therefore there are two parts to this paper. The first of these is a brief discussion of the nature of the problem of discovering linguistic subgroups. The second treats some aspects of the linguistic situation of Oceania in their relation to the culture history of that area.

Methods for Discovering Subgroups

Since change is constantly going on in all languages, any appreciably large period of time in the history of any language should leave some marks—the marks of the changes which occurred during that period. The evidence which indicates to us the existence of a subgroup consists of those changes which occurred during the period of common history of the members of the group. Any of the features of a language which are subject to observation are also subject to change. There is

From *American Anthropologist,* 63:359–368, 1961. Reproduced by permission of the author and the American Anthropological Association.

phonetic change: phonemes come to be pronounced differently. This might or might not involve the development of different pronunciations in different linguistic environments—i.e., allophones. There can be phonemic change: a change in the number of elements in the sound system or in their constituency. This can occur through a phoneme's simply ceasing to be pronounced, through a new phoneme's being introduced, or through reallocation of the allophones. There can be changes in the stock of morphemes or idioms, and in the circumstances, both linguistic and nonlinguistic, in which they may occur. There are, in short, a great variety of changes which may occur in a given period in the history of a language. It is these changes which provide the clues that two or more languages have participated in the same historical developments, that is, that their historical unity extends through that period.

The problem with which we are concerned is to infer what has actually happened. There are a number of disciplines concerned with determining what has happened within the domains of their own subject matter. The disciplines of geology, or history itself, are examples. Collingwood (1956:266–268) describes the method of the historian as resembling that of a detective—seeking clues, posing questions, piecing together bit by bit a coherent picture of what has actually happened. It is possible to approach problems of subgrouping in an analogous fashion: simply to search for clues and attempt to piece together the scheme of historical relations. For convenience, I will refer to such a procedure as the "historical method."

This procedure has the advantages of taking all kinds of evidence into account and of being applicable even where the available data do not measure up to exacting standards. The principal disadvantage seems to be that the range of facts considered, and the differential weighings accorded them, make the bases of decision too complex to be systematically explained. It is impossible within reasonable compass to give a full explanation of the grounds for the decisions.

Many linguists feel that more rigorous methods of subgrouping are required. There are two techniques available which might serve as the basis for a rigorous subgrouping method. The first is what is known as the "comparative method." This method is designed to reconstruct the features of the parent language from which a group of languages is descended. Obviously, if we can reconstruct the proto-language, we can then work out the changes which have occurred in the daughter languages, and determine which of the languages have undergone like changes.

Should we regard reconstruction as a methodological prerequisite to the consideration of problems of subgrouping? There would be difficulties in this. One such difficulty is the amount of work involved. For a language family such as Austronesian, composed of several hundred languages, working out the comparisons for every language would involve much time and effort. Moreover, descriptive data for the majority of languages is completely lacking or inadequate for more than the most sketchy comparisons. A large number of new descriptive studies would be required before a thorough comparative job could be done. For Austronesian and many other language families this would probably postpone attention to subgrouping problems to some remote future time.

However, there is a more serious obstacle to reconstructing before we subgroup; namely, the fact that no serious reconstruction is possible which does not involve assumptions about subgrouping. Each time we reconstruct a morpheme for the proto-language, this involves the assumption that those languages which provide evidence for that morpheme do not belong to a common subgroup. This becomes a serious concern when the evidence comes from a number of languages substantially smaller than the total number of languages of the family. Even the reconstruction of phonemes is not immune to this problem. We can scarcely reconstruct a phoneme for the proto-language unless we have some grounds for believing there was at least one morpheme of the proto-language in which it appeared.

What I am attempting to show is that subgrouping and reconstruction are interrelated problems. For any given language family, neither reconstruction nor subgrouping can be regarded as completed until both are completed. In fact, I do not really conceive of my "historical method" for subgrouping as distinct from the comparative method of reconstruction, but rather as the same methodological tool applied to a differently defined problem. The subgrouping method of which I speak consists simply in attemping to identify those particular reconstructable features which are relevant to the problem of subgrouping —that is, those reconstructable features which we are not justified in reconstructing for the proto-language of the entire family.

Another method which might be used as a basis for a rigorous subgrouping method is lexicostatistics. It has the advantage of relative simplicity and of quantitative results. However, there are certain difficulties. First, the standard retention rate used is an average. Some languages show higher retention rates, some lower. The range so far attested is not sufficient to produce serious distortion over short periods, but after three or four milennia the effects could be quite serious. As yet, we simply do not have enough information to assess this problem.

Further difficulties arise in the application of the method. An error is introduced if we fail to find the correct equivalent for each item on the test list for each of the languages being tested. In fact there are likely to be errors in any case where the language is not well known to the compiler. How serious the effects of this error may be is hard to estimate.

An error is likewise introduced if we fail to make the correct decision as to whether or not items are cognate. If the sound correspondences between the two languages being compared are known in detail, errors from this source will be at a minimum. If not, they will be increased.

I do not intend to suggest that lexicostatistics should be abandoned, or even that it should not be applied to problems of subgrouping. It is only through its application that we will be able to learn its potentialities. I do wish to point out, however, that at present there are serious quesions about the point at which differences in the percentages produced in a lexicostatistical study become significant.

It is possible to distinguish two different manners in which either lexicostatistics or comparative reconstruction might be used in subgrouping. First, they might simply be used as guides. After the percentages were calculated or the reconstructions made, the investigator might then proceed, on the basis of whatever considerations appeared relevant to him, to elaborate a hypothesis of subgrouping. This, however, would be only a special case of what I have called the "historical method."

However, the point which concerns us here is that the same methods might also be used in a rigorous fashion. This could be done by stating explicitly certain conditions, such that, when these conditions were found with regard to a set of languages, those languages would be said to constitute a subgroup. The method thus defined would automatically produce subgroupings. This has the advantage of making it clear what the investigator has done. However, it should be made clear that such a procedure involves a redefinition of "subgroup." A "subgroup" now is defined as that which the method produces.

A rigorous subgrouping method of a trivial sort would be easy to formulate, of course. The difficulty increases in the measure that accuracy is required. By "accuracy" I mean approximation to the true historical relations among the languages involved.

The crucial question is not, in fact, how a classification was arrived at, but how accurate it is. And it seems likely that a requirement of rigorous formulation of the discovery procedure must necessarily impose limits on the accuracy of the results. Such a procedure will probably be forced to disregard some kinds of evidence if it is not to become overly complicated. In the case of lexicostatistics, of course, the evidence usually considered relevant is not given any attention as such.

Historical facts are not directly discoverable by any method. What we must in fact seek to discover is the pattern of historical relations which would produce the known facts with the greatest probability. That is, we seek to formulate a family tree such that the set of all similarities among any of the languages concerned would occur with greater probability in language families whose relations conformed to that family tree than in families conforming to any conflicting family tree. More succinctly, we can only seek that classification which best accounts for all of the facts.

Obviously, precise calculation of the probabilities is impossible. We can only base our judgments on a rough estimate of the order of magnitude of the probabilities involved.

A somewhat clearer statement can now be made of the difficulties involved in devising a discovery procedure which is rigorous and still produces interesting results. A rigorous procedure, as I conceive of it, involves the instruction that, when certain conditions are present, the existence of a particular subgroup is to be asserted. In so doing, it in fact undertakes to guarantee the support of probabilities of a sufficient order of magnitude.

For the subgroups produced by the method to be interesting, it appears that two requirements must be met. First, it should be able to discover subgroups which are not obvious on inspection. This points to an upper limit to the quantity of evidence which could be required for the assertion of a subgroup. Secondly, the groupings produced must be reliable. That is, we must be able to feel confidence that in each instance where a subgroup is proposed by the method, the odds are good that such a subgroup actually exists. This poses a lower limit to the quantity of evidence which could be required.

However, as was indicated, a rigorous procedure of the sort envisaged here would almost certainly restrict itself to a limited subset of those facts which are actually relevant to the problem of subgrouping. This implies that to ensure reliability, the standards of proof must be set sufficiently high to compensate for the possibility that there are facts beyond the purview of the method which are unfavorable to the hypothesis. To establish standards of proof sufficiently flexible to meet the first requirement and at the same time sufficiently stringent to meet the second would appear to be difficult.

In sum, I see no prospect for a new method which will automatically produce interesting linguistic classifications. On the other hand, I do believe that the most significant groupings are accessible to a linguist who understands the comparative method and who is willing to make a careful and objective examination of the data. There are recent indications of an increased interest in subgrouping problems. This should lead to a better formulation of the rules of evidence and to more and more reliable results.

Historical Inferences from Austronesian Linguistics

The external relations of the Austronesian family do not fall within the scope of this paper. It will be sufficient to note that they seem to indicate that the original Austronesian language was spoken in or near Southeast Asia. As regards the internal relations, I am not able to offer a complete classification. However, it is possible as of now to identify certain subgroupings and to consider their historical implications.

EASTERN AUSTRONESIAN

One well-established point is the existence of an Eastern subgroup of Austronesian. The evidence for such a subgroup consists primarily in an impressive array of shared phonological innovations. First, all word-final consonants have been lost. Secondly, a number of unifications of Proto-Austronesian consonant phonemes had occurred in the proto-language of the Eastern group. In all, fifteen Proto-Austronesian consonants were involved, while the number of Proto-Eastern phonemes resulting from those fifteen was only six. Thirdly, all diphthongs of Proto-Austronesian become unit vowel phonemes in Proto-Eastern. In addition, a number of Proto-Austronesian consonant clusters have become unit phonemes in many Eastern languages. However, it is not certain that they were not still clusters in Proto-Eastern.

Although the existence of the Eastern Austronesian subgroup is clearly established, its precise membership is not certain. It is certain that all of the languages of Polynesia are included. It likewise seems certain that all of the languages of Micronesia except two—Palauan and Chamorro—are included and equally certain that Palauan and Chamorro are excluded. It now seems that all of the Austronesian languages of Melanesia are probably included, except for a few languages on the west coast of New Guinea. There is also some question about some of the languages of Geelvink Bay in Dutch New Guinea. However, if these are not members of the Eastern subgroup, they are closely related to it.

It would be of interest to culture history to know where Proto-Eastern was spoken. There is at the moment no certain answer to that. However, it would appear that it was in Melanesia, rather than in Polynesia or Micronesia, since both the Polynesian languages and those Micronesian languages which belong to the Eastern subgroup seem to represent recent movements from Melanesia. Since the spread of the Austronesian languages appears to have been from west to east, we would expect to find that the parent language of the Eastern group was spoken in the western part of the area. This would suggest the environs of New Guinea. The best guess at present appears to be that it was somewhere in the area including the north coast of New Guinea, New Britain, and the Admiralty and Western Islands. The languages of this area are not well known, but the diversity appears to be considerable. Still, for the present we can only conjecture.

POLYNESIA AND MICRONESIA

One obvious, and long-recognized, subgroup within Eastern Austronesian is Polynesian. This includes not only the languages of geographical Polynesia but a number of languages of Melanesia and Micronesia as well—the so-called "Polynesian outliers." This grouping is obviously recent. I have attempted elsewhere (Grace 1959) to show the existence of a larger grouping composed of Polynesian and the languages of Fiji and Rotuma. A still larger grouping can be distinguished which consists of these languages (i.e., Polynesian, Rotuman, and Fijian) and certain languages of the New Hebrides. The New Hebrides languages involved are Tongoa, Sesake, Makura, Nguna, and all of the languages of the islands of Efate and Epi.

Another distinguishable subgroup consists of all of those languages of Micronesia which are Eastern Austronesian and are *not* Polynesian (i.e., all of the languages of Micronesia except Palauan, Chamorro, Nukuoro, and Kapingamarangi). I am increasingly convinced that this Micronesian subgroup has its closest linguistic affiliations with languages of the New Hebrides. There does not, however, appear to be a closer relationship with those *particular* New Hebrides languages which are closest to Fijian, Rotuman, and Polynesian than with other New Hebrides languages.

This suggests that for some time all of the Eastern Austronesian languages were spoken in Melanesia. Then, at a later time, certain of these languages moved into Micronesia and Polynesia and came to be known as "Micronesian" and "Polynesian" languages.

What does this imply as to the long-disputed question of Polynesian origins? First, it is clear that the Polynesian languages are simply continuations of a single earlier Melanesian language. As far as the linguistic data are concerned, either the Polynesians came from Melanesia or they came from somewhere else and acquired a Melanesian language. If they came from somewhere else—i.e., if we are to assume a non-Melanesian component in their ancestry—the linguistic evidence provides not the slightest clue as to the source of that component. If they came from Melanesia, it would be difficult to maintain that their ancestors in Melanesia were physically distinguishable from their contemporaries whose descendants remained in Melanesia.

MELANESIA

The third major geographical area in which Eastern Austronesian languages are spoken is Melanesia. The Eastern Austronesian languages of Melanesia show much greater diversity than those of Micronesia or Polynesia (cf. Grace 1955). They can in no sense be thought of as representing a subgroup as opposed to Micronesian and Polynesian. The Melanesian linguistic picture is further complicated by the presence of several hundred non-Austronesian languages, the so-called "Papuan" languages.

In the works of some scholars the influence of Papuan languages seems to be assumed as virtually the sole source of all linguistic change in the Austronesian languages of Melanesia. This notion is dubious at best, but it is particularly puzzling when the changes appear to be recent changes occurring in areas geographically remote from any contemporary Papuan languages. However, the assumption seems frequently to be made that Papuan languages were once spoken throughout Melanesia. In fact, it is frequently said that the Austronesian languages regularly are found along seacoasts—either on small islands or on the coasts of larger ones—and that Papuan languages regularly are found in the interiors. The implication seems to be that throughout Melanesia, Austronesian speakers have occupied the coasts of already settled islands and only gradually, if at all, spread to the interior.

This seems questionable. It appears to me that the statement that Austronesian languages are found along the coasts and Papuan languages in the interior is really valid for only one island—New Guinea—although one might argue that Bougainville shows some tendencies in that direction. There are no Papuan languages at all in New Caledonia, the Loyalty Islands, Fiji, or the New Hebrides. There are only four in the Solomon Islands east of Bougainville. Each of these four is spoken on a small island. In the interior of the larger islands only Austronesian languages are found, and there are certain of these island interiors which are rugged enough to have been easy to defend against invaders (e.g., Guadalcanal, Espiritu Santo). In short, there are no good linguistic grounds for assuming that any of the islands east of Bougainville were occupied in pre-Austronesian times.

This question assumes particular interest with respect to the languages of New Caledonia. These languages have always been regarded as exceptionally aberrant Austronesian languages, and it is certainly true that only a small number of cognates shared with other Austronesian languages can be identified with confidence. It has been suggested that this aberrant nature is due to the influence of Papuan languages. However, as has been pointed out, there is no evidence that there have ever been Papuan languages in that part of Melanesia.

Moreover, New Caledonia is a long, narrow island. The languages at one end of the island are sufficiently different from those at the other that this fact also requires explanation. For example, in the case of the Kapone language at the extreme southern end of the island we must ask not only why it appears so different from Austronesian languages on other islands, but also why it appears almost equally different from, say, the Yalasu language at the extreme northern end of New Caledonia. The possibility that Papuan influence can somehow serve as an explanation, therefore, becomes more remote since it appears that not one, but several Papuan languages would need to be involved.

The linguistic situation described for New Caledonia would also be explained by the assumption that linguistic differentiation had been going on for a longer period of time in New Caledonia than in other Austronesian-speaking areas. That is, we might assume that New Caledonia was the original homeland of Austronesian, and that the other Austronesian languages derived ultimately from New Caledonia at a time when some linguistic differentiation had already occurred there.

However, such an assumption presents some difficulties. First, on geographical grounds it is difficult to reconcile with the fact that Austronesian belongs to a larger family, the other members of which are all found in Southeast Asia. Secondly, this would mean that all of the major subgroups of Austronesian had had New Caledonian members. I can see no indication of this at present, nor any indication that any non-New Caledonian language has a particularly close relationship with any particular New Caledonian language.

Moreover, it is quite clear that the closest relations of each individual New Caledonian language are with other New Caledonian languages. In fact, the entire island comprises a single network of languages, each of which is closely related to its neighbors. In view of these facts, it is very difficult not to regard the languages of New Caledonia as constituting a single subgroup of Austronesian. However, the length of the island is sufficient to make it possible for the most remote members of the network to differ strikingly.

It is apparent that there are unsolved problems in the case of the New Caledonian languages. However, theirs is not an isolated case. There are languages in various parts of Melanesia which show few recognizable cognates with most other Austronesian languages. We cannot explain this fact at present, and I do not believe that any conclusive explanation will be possible until we know more of the phonological history of the languages in question.

Most of the Eastern Austronesian languages which have been best studied from the comparative point of view appear to have undergone remarkably few conditioned sound changes. It is natural that in such cases the cognates will be easily identifiable. In some cases that is probably one reason why those particular languages were chosen for the comparative studies. However, as is shown by Isidore Dyen's (1949) excellent study of the history of the vowel system of Trukese, we cannot expect that all of the Eastern Austronesian languages will have been so immune to conditioned sound changes. Consequently, I do not believe that, at present, we are justified in assuming either outside influences or exceptionally long periods of isolation simply on the basis of a paucity of readily identifiable Austronesian etyma.

Summary

The linguistic data known to me suggest the following historical outline. The Proto-Austronesian language was probably spoken in or near Southeast Asia. At a considerably later date a language was spoken, most probably on or near the north coast of New Guinea, which became the proto-language of the Eastern Austronesian subgroup. At some time after the breakup of this language, Eastern Austronesian languages spread to the Territory of Papua and to the Solomons and New Hebrides (the geographical relations suggest that the latter spread also included the Santa Cruz Islands, the Loyalty Islands, and New Caledonia—however, the precise relations of the languages of these places are too unclear either to support or oppose such an hypothesis). It is possible that most of eastern Melanesia was uninhabited before the spread of Austronesian languages into the area.

It seems indicated that the Eastern Austronesian languages had approximately their present geographical distribution in Melanesia for some time before their spread to Fiji, Rotuma, Polynesia, and Micronesia. Eventually, however, a language moved from the New Hebrides to Micronesia and subsequently spread to most of the Micronesian Islands. It should be recalled, however, that Austronesian languages also moved into Micronesia (at least to the Marianas and Palau) from Malaysia. The relative times of these two movements into Micronesia is not clear at present.

At perhaps about the same time, languages moved from the area of Efate and Epi, in the New Hebrides, into the Central Pacific. Perhaps the original movement was to Fiji, whence, after a short time, settlements occurred on Rotuma and in some part of Western Polynesia. The number of distinctive features shared by the Polynesian languages would suggest that a considerable period of time ensued before the breakup of Proto-Polynesian and the spread of the Polynesian languages both to the west and to the east.

It should be emphasized that this outline is intended as nothing more than a working hypothesis. Much of it is speculative, and much of it would not find general consent among linguists. It offers no explanation of the vexing physical diversity among the populations of Oceania because the linguistic evidence suggests no explanation. It is based solely on linguistic (and to some extent, geographical) considerations. However, I feel that it shows an encouraging compatibility with the few radiocarbon dates now available and with Andrew Sharp's (1956) proposal that settlement took place primarily through accidental voyaging.

CHAPTER

4

The Kon-Tiki *Myth*

ROBERT C. SUGGS

The natives of the atoll of Raroia in the Tuamotu Archipelago of French Oceania were quite surprised one day to see a strange sail appear on the horizon. Gradually the sail approached, bringing into view a most unusual-looking sea craft, far different from the copra schooners and trim cutters that usually plied their trade among those islands. The vessel supporting the sail was riding low in the water, the waves almost level with her deck. A flimsy house of leaves, like a matchbox on a plank, stood on the deck behind a mast that supported a large sail bearing a strange emblem. As the Raroians watched with interset, the odd craft kept its heading, coming ever nearer to the vicious reef that encircled the island without displaying any attempts to escape the crashing surf that heaved against the jagged coral rampart. The crew-men of the sailing raft were obviously unable to control their vessel with any degree of precision, and the raft, moving closer to the reef, was finally caught by a swell and heaved upon the coral, tumbling occupants, canned food, radio equipment, and other gear in every direction. At last it settled in the shallows behind the reef crest in a heap of wreckage. The five occupants of the raft, tall, tanned, bearded, and fortunately unhurt, picked themselves up gingerly and began to collect their belongings from among the spiny sea urchins and sea slugs on the floor of the tidal shallows.

For Thor Heyerdahl, the leader of this group of hardened mariners, this day was memorable in more than one respect. He and his companions had just completed a voyage of 101 days from the coast of South America aboard the now half-wrecked balsa-log raft *Kon-Tiki,* and their arrival on Raroia wrote *finis* to a voyage of hardship and danger. More important, however, was

---

From *The Island Civilizations of Polynesia* by Robert C. Suggs. New York: The New American Library, 1960, pp. 212–224.

the fact that Heyerdahl, in successfully drifting on the raft between South America and Polynesia, had secured additional proof for a theory for which he had long tried unsuccessfully to win scientific acceptance among the anthropologists of the world.

Heyerdahl's theory, familiar to many laymen through the popular account of the *Kon-Tiki* voyage,[1] concerned the origin of the Polynesian race. Differing with the anthropologists, Heyerdahl believed that the Polynesians did not come from Asia, but were rather American Indians who had sailed from the coast of the New World, which was admittedly much closer to the Polynesian triangle than the coast of Asia. Such a theory was by no means new. It had first been developed in 1803 by a Spanish missionary in the Philippines, Father Joacquin M. de Zuñiga in his book *Historia de las Islas Philipinas,* who proposed an American origin for the natives of those islands. The theory attracted the Polynesia scholar-missionary, William Ellis, who could not completely accept it as applicable to the Polynesians. In more recent times the possibility of Polynesian-Peruvian relationships has been resurrected on several occasions, but it has never received any serious consideration.

According to Heyerdahl's hypothesis, two separate groups of Indians were involved in this population of the islands of Polynesia. First, a group of Peruvian Indians *drifted* out on their rafts from the coast of Peru into the islands of Eastern Polynesia, touching Easter Island and subsequently moving westward through the Marquesas and the Societies right to the western border of Polynesia. Secondly, a group of Indians from the Pacific Northwest of the United States and Canada forsook their cedar trees and totem poles and paddled to Hawaii in their dugouts, after which they gradually filtered into the southern islands of the Polynesian triangle, mingling with the Peruvians who were already dwelling in that area. This obviously presupposes an advanced muscular development for the paddling arms of Northwest Coast Indians, but such strength is certainly no more remarkable than the lengthy patience displayed by the undersized Peruvians on their drifting itinerary through the islands.

The foundations of this theory are somewhat heterogeneous and even include some scientific observations and facts, the most significant of which are the prevailing southeasterly winds and currents in Polynesia, the remote possibility of Peruvian origin of the sweet potato (which is unconditionally accepted by Heyerdahl), and the similarity of Polynesian and Peruvian blood-type distributions.

Heyerdahl pointed out that the winds and currents are mostly against any voyages from Asia to Polynesia, but that the same winds and currents would aid voyages from South America to Polynesia. Therefore it would have been simpler to have populated the Polynesian triangle from the Peruvian coast. But this is not proof that such a migration did occur, for prevailing southeasters do not in any way present an obstacle to sailing canoes or other sailed vessels. Tacking and laying close to the wind were both possible in a Polynesian canoe. The fact that the trade winds quite frequently reverse themselves for long periods is further overlooked by Heyerdahl, and the possibility of using the eastward-flowing equatorial countercurrent is not discussed. Both of these are obviously major factors in attempting to prove the impossibility of eastward voyages in Polynesia.

High on the list of Polynesian-Peruvian parallels is the now-famous sweet potato which bears, both in Peru and in Polynesia, the name *Kumara* or some derivation thereof. We have already had an opportunity to discuss the controversy concerning the sweet potato in the chapter on Polynesian environment and have indicated that the plant and the name are probably of Old World origin and may have been introduced into Peru by Polynesian voyagers before the Spanish Conquest or by Spaniards themselves in the colonial period.

Another major prop for the Heyerdahlian theory is the similarity between the blood types of the Peruvians and the Eastern Polynesians. We have noted in a previous chapter that very disparate races may have similar blood-type frequencies and that blood typing alone is meaningless for a comparison of two groups of people, if their morphological characteristics are dissimilar to begin with. There is little resemblance between the short, coppery, barrel-chested Peruvian with round head, straight hair, and slightly hooked nose and the tall, brown, stocky Polynesian with a wide range of head shape, wavy black hair, and a rather flat, wide nose.

Heyerdahl has unwittingly provided in his own work some of the most telling evidence against the use of blood types for determination of racial connections. In the course of the work of his Norwegian Expedition on Easter Island and elsewhere in Eastern Polynesia[2] blood samples were collected for typing from supposedly selected natives on all the islands visited. On the island of Nuku Hiva, where I was residing at the time, the selection of donors was not very rigorous, consisting merely in rounding up of the available Marquesans in the vicinity of the Taiohae Valley dispensary—some twenty-four in number. The results of the serological studies done on these samples indicate that the tested Marquesan group resembles those of the other islands of Eastern Polynesia quite closely.

This seemingly innocuous fact becomes suddenly inexplicable in light of the fact that none but possibly two of Heyerdahl's Marquesan blood donors were of pure Polynesian ancestry.

In over a year of residence on Nuku Hiva, I learned the native language and got to know a large number of the 980 inhabitants. I had an opportunity to examine old church documents that go back to the beginning of French occupation of the island, recording marriages of natives and Europeans, deaths and births. My wife also collected a number of reproductive histories from native women, obtaining further information about genealogies in this fashion. On the basis of my knowledge of these people, there are only 4 individuals out of the 980 who can claim pure Polynesian ancestry with some degree of assurance. Of these 4, only 2 were available for Heyerdahl's tests, the others being in remote parts of the island. There are some 13 other individuals who have made claims to an untainted Polynesian genetic heritage, but their immediate Asian or European ancestry is too well known to their neighbors to remain a secret for long.

One specific "pure Polynesian" who contributed to the blood-type study that day in Taiohae was the wife of my head workman, Tahiaei Puhetini. Dear Tahia went along for the ride, so to speak, and gave a cc. or two of vital fluid to science. It would be difficult to describe her actual ancestry in a brief fashion. She is the granddaughter of a Castilian Spaniard, Alvarado by name, who jumped ship in the Marquesas to live out his life there, and left behind a sizable number of progeny and a wicked reputation. Her father, half Marquesan, married a woman who was also a half-breed herself, with the result that Tahia and her sisters were endowed with a light skin and completely European features. If her blood type resembles that of any pure Polynesian, it does so by sheer chance, because she is genetically and physically half European. The others who contributed their blood were also of mixed racial ancestry. The amount of racial crossing which has gone on in Taiohae and on the island of Nuku Hiva in general can be shown by a brief sketch of Taiohae history since European contact.

The population of Nuku Hiva, particularly of Taiohae Valley on that island, has been exposed to European genetic admixture since the late eighteenth century, when sailors from early whaling vessels went ashore there. Later, in 1813, an American Navy squadron arrived and stayed at Taiohae for fifteen months, during which time an additional increment of Caucasoid genes was introduced into the population. Further deserters from whaling ships formed a large element in the population in 1840 when the French occupied the island and placed a military garrison, backed by a naval force, at Taiohae. The French troops remained for many years, during which time a considerable amount of miscegenation naturally took place between French and Marquesans. In the late nineteenth and early twentieth centuries, Chinese laborers were brought in, many of whom married native women. Martiniquan Negroes were also used as laborers on one plantation for a period, as a result of which a few half-Negro children were born.

During all this time, of course, foreign ships were always present, bringing sailors who were always looking for female companionship. It is obvious that anyone who wishes to find a true Marquesan in such a polyglot group is going to have to do more than merely ask for all Marquesans to step forward, or ask the local French doctor who does not speak a word of the native language and may have only been there a short time himself. Even to ask the missionaries to name the true Marquesans is most foolish, for they, of all people, know least about who *really* sired the Polynesian babies they baptize.

Thus, it is plain that blood-type distribution studies are not always reliable as proof of racial connections and that a racially mixed group may often resemble the type distributions of another possibly pure group. In this case it is of course doubtful whether any of the groups sampled in the entire blood-type program are even close to 100 per cent pure Polynesian in their structure, and the resemblance between the various groups may actually be a result of the fact that they all have a fairly equal amount of foreign blood, especially Caucasoid and Mongoloid admixture. The above incident shows clearly how far afield it is possible to wander using blood types alone in attempts to prove racial connections. It is further an object lesson in the use of stringent controls for any scientific study. Whatever the subject involved may be, if it is worth study, then data-collection techniques merit the closest of controls. Without such controls experiments are merely wasted effort, no matter how pleasing the results may be to partisans of particular views.

In addition to these main points discussed above, Heyerdahl has adduced a large number of cultural "resemblances" between the cultures of Peru and Polynesia, which he claims as further evidence that the Polynesians are actually American Indians. A few of these resemblances actually do exist, but they are nonsignificant and generally involve traits found all over the world. Other causes of this similarity may also be due to the fact that both the Polynesians and the American Indians are of general Asiatic origin, although the earliest Indians in the New World may have departed from Asia to cross the Bering Straits as many as 25,000 years ago. Heyerdahl is quite enthusiastic over the fact that the Polynesians, the Peruvians, and other American Indians all formerly marked the summer and winter solstices[3] (as an aid to regulating their agricultural calendars). This is supposed to be an extremely important fact in showing a definite relationship between Polynesian culture and that of the New World. The resemblance crumbles immediately, however, when it is recalled that observance of the summer and winter solstices was found universally in the ancient and primitive cultures of Asia, Africa, the Mediterranean, and Europe. The fact that solstices were marked in Polynesian and Peruvian societies is no more an indication of the later connection of those two cultures than it is an indication of their relationships with any of the other cultures of the world.

Most of the other numerous "resemblances" between Peru and Polynesia, however, are far less credible than even the above example. Facts are taken and artistically presented to serve the purpose of showing Polynesian-Peruvian relationships, when in truth the opposite is the case. A few examples of this will show the technique quite clearly. Speaking of the Polynesian water craft, in an attempt to prove that Polynesians used rafts instead of canoes (rafts being a unique Peruvian trait, of course!), Heyerdahl says: "The Tahitian name for a raft-ship was *pahi*. . . ."[4] Actually, however, the Tahitians had no "raft-ships" as a matter of record, and the word *pahi* really means "double canoe" and has also been applied in modern times to the European type of ships.

Again, in the field of language we are told[5] that the Marquesans have a predilection for beginning their valley names with the prefix *hana,* such as Hanamenu, Hanahei, and so on. *Hana,* by a "well-known Polynesian sound change," is supposedly related to the Quechuan word *sana,* which means "paradise." This therefore purports to demonstrate once again a relationship between Peru and Polynesia. The word *hana* is actually the southeastern dialect equivalent of a word which appears elsewhere in the Marquesan archipelago as *haka, hanga,* and *ha'a.* It means "bay," referring specifically to the body of water rather than the land surrounding the water. It has no relation to any word for "paradise" and there is no "Polynesian sound change" that would produce *sana* from *hanga, ha'a,* or *hana.* A change from *h* to *s* exists in the Samoan dialect, however, but is strictly a regional dialect variation, not characteristic of all Polynesian languages.

Evidence against the Peruvian origin of the Polynesians is naturally quite voluminous; but evidently Heyerdahl has not read many contrary arguments, for they are seldom mentioned. Thus, in trying to convince his readers that Polynesian is not an Asiatic language, Heyerdahl states: ". . . the Polynesian language was only remotely related to the Malay tongues."[6] Nowhere in the extensive bibliography which he included in his *American Indians* volume is there any reference to the numerous works on the Polynesian languages and their genetic affiliations with Malay. Dempwolff, Dyen, Schmidt, and other Polynesian linguists are completely ignored as though they did not exist.

One could devote several volumes the size of Heyerdahl's single "scientific" tome to a cataloguing of his gratuitous uses of scientific data. There is, however, little value in being more exhaustive than is necessary to give a brief indication of the "methodological approach" characteristic of the *Kon-Tiki* theory. The above examples suffice to show what sort of evidence was utilized in formulating the theory.

Let us pause briefly to examine the *Kon-Tiki* raft itself, however. Did not Heyerdahl really prove by his voyage that Peruvian Indians could have reached Polynesia on such rafts? The answer is, flatly, negative.[7] The *Kon-Tiki* raft is a type of craft developed by the Peruvians *after* the Spanish brought the use of the sail to them. Although the Peruvians did use rafts to voyage off their coast long before the white men ever came, such rafts did not use sails, but were propelled by paddles. Sailing rafts of the *Kon-Tiki* type were never used by prehistoric Indians. Furthermore, the Peruvian Indians, whether using sails or paddles, or just drifting, never had the benefits of canned foods, modern solar stills to make drinking water from the sea, radios, maps, and navigation instruments, and a knowledge of where they were going. All these were used by the *Kon-Tiki* crew, and it must be said that without them the voyage would have quickly ended in tragedy. When the *Kon-Tiki* ran afoul of Raroia's reef there were 1,500 cans of food[8] still aboard her. Therefore, one presumes that for the crew life was not possible, sustained on what the sea yielded alone. Why should it then have been possible for the less well-equipped, sail-less Indians?

In sum, the *Kon-Tiki* voyage was not a fair test of the sailing ability of the ancient Peruvians by any means and proved only this: that by using a modern, Post-European-contact type of sail-raft with navigation aids and modern survival equipment, men can survive a 101-day voyage between Peru and Polynesia.

It is needless to say that when the Heyerdahl theory hit the press, the reaction of the scientific community was uniformly negative. The same thesis had been raised a few times before, as I have previously noted, and Heyerdahl's version was the same old story, decked out in newer trappings and backed by a high tide of sensational publicity. The manner in which fact had been fitted to the Procrustean bed of the Peruvian migration theory failed to win Heyerdahl any followers among scientists, who are accustomed to demanding a high degree of objectivity from themselves as well as their colleagues. A few scientists devoted some effort[9] to pointing out in scientific journals various of the numerous inconsistencies and shortcomings of the theory and the evidence upon which it was based. The publication of the *Kon-Tiki* theory did stimulate further scientific work in the area of Polynesian anthropology, which of course resulted rather in an increase in the evidence marshaled against the theory than contributed to its support. The public, completely unaware of the detailed literature of Polynesian and American Indian anthropology, was quite willing to accept the hypothesis as it was presented in the numerous popular publications concerning the raft voyage. The glamour of such an undertaking, the undeniable hardships imposed upon the crew, and their great courage in opposing the mighty Pacific on such a flimsy craft obviously added to the attraction of the theory, if it was not indeed the main cause for its popularity.

After the initial burst of popular enthusiasm immediately following the voyage, public interest tapered off gradually while scientists continued their labors, occasionally pausing to punch a few more holes in the theory which had never been more than Swiss cheese, anyway.

Heyerdahl, however, was not resting, and in 1956 he led the Norwegian Expedition to Polynesia. (We have already had occasion to discuss their work on Easter Island.) The expedition's purpose was to delve into the prehistory of Eastern Polynesia, concentrating on Easter Island in particular. That information lending support to the *Kon-Tiki* theory should be found by such an expedition was, naturally, not too much to expect. The most recent Heyerdahl opus, entitled *Aku-Aku,* is a result of this work, serving as our main source of knowledge of the work of the expedition members on Easter Island and elsewhere. *Aku-Aku* is of the same tradition as the previous works, differing only in that it is more extreme in its position. The general style of the work was set long ago by such hoary favorites of the travel-thriller devotees as *Green Hell* and *All the Rivers Ran East.* The aura of mystery surrounding Easter Island is built up to a fantastic extent with practically no references being made to any of the first-class anthropological studies which have been carried out on Easter by Métraux, Lavachéry, Routledge, and others. Although Heyerdahl avoids mentioning such sources, he obviously is acquainted with them, as anyone who has read Métraux's works will note upon perusal of *Aku-Aku.*

Having thus established for the uninformed reader that Easter Island and its culture are *terra incognita* to the anthropological world, Heyerdahl proceeds to tell what *he* was able to find out by his own special methods during the expedition's five-month sojourn. The Easter Islanders, of course, regurgitated the sum total of their esoterica for this impressive visitor, and he was shown all manner of secrets heretofore hidden from the eyes of white men. These included ancestral caves, reached only by perilous routes deep beneath the island surface, crowded with odd sculpture of *aku-aku* or demons; the secrets of how the great statues were moved and raised; the secret of the Easter Island script; and a number of other outstanding firsts. As a matter of fact, one would gather the impression that the Easter Island natives had done an Ed Sullivan type of spectacle for Heyerdahl, staging the "History of Easter Island" with the original cast and a score by Tiomkin.

Amidst all these accomplishments are some rather disturbing features. The stone sculptures discovered[10] deep in the ancestral caves are the crudest of frauds of a type made every day by Easter Islanders for sale to tourists and sailors. The poor proportions, the abominable sculptural technique, and the obviously contrived forms of these "masterpieces" mark them as bogus even in a photograph. Compared to the fine, delicate woodcarving from the pagan past of the "Navel of the World," these stone figures are monstrosities. It is heartening, however, to see that the natives of Easter Island recognized so quickly the possibilities for pulling such a stunt, and one is impressed by the creativity of their imagination in this as well as some of the other "secrets" which they revealed.

As to the secret of the Easter Island script, Dr. T. Barthel's work on Easter Island after the departure of the Norwegian Expedition has indicated the true nature of the system of signs used on the *rongorongo* boards. The results of this work, as pointed out in a previous chapter, indicate that the script was brought to Easter Island by the earliest settlers and is of Polynesian origin.

Aside from the interludes of excitement and suspense, the book contains the usual sort of statements. For instance, Heyerdahl credits himself with doing the first archaeology ever done in the Marquesas.[11] He was some thirty-seven years too late. Ralph Linton took that honor in 1919, and I personally was doing the first stratigraphic excavation on Nuku Hiva a month before Heyerdahl's ship dropped anchor in Taiohae Bay. The honor of "first" should be and is truly meaningless, anyway; there are far more desirable adjectives, but not so easily won.

Heyerdahl goes on to claim to be the first white man to see the well-known two-headed statue in the valley of Taipivai, Nuku Hiva.[12] Actually, this statue was first seen by Karl von den Steinen, the famous German ethnographer, in 1898, and duly noted in his volume on Marquesan art. Von den Steinen was unfortunately prevented from photographing it by the superstitious fear of his native guide.

Again Heyerdahl claims discovery on the large fort of Morongo Uta on Rapa Iti.[13] This site was mapped and well studied by J. G. Stokes of the Bernice Bishop Museum in the 1920's, but the report was never published. No attempt was ever made by the museum officials to hide the fact that Stokes worked there.

The general picture of Easter Island prehistory imparted in *Aku-Aku* is that the islands were first settled by Peruvian Indians and later invaded by Polynesians (who were in actuality Northwest Coast Indians) at the very end of the prehistoric period. Borrowing from an old Easter Island legend of warfare between two factions who were called, respectively, the Long Ears and the Short Ears, Heyerdahl identifies the Long Ears as the Peruvians and the Short Ears as Polynesians. He shows a few pictures of supposedly pure Long Ears still living on Easter Island—who, I might add, are remarkably Caucasoid in appearance. He attributes this to the fact that the Peruvian conquerors were not really Indians after all, but white men with red hair. (Is there a Nordic hypothesis hidden here?) The fact that no prehistoric Caucasoid population is evident in Peru anywhere is of course immaterial to the theory. The sudden appearance of white men in the Heyerdahl theory is most confusing as Heyerdahl has tried so desperately to show that Polynesian blood is similar to American Indian blood in type distributions.

What racial relationships do these whites have to the Indians, then? Do they possess the same blood types as the Indians? If so, then blood type and physical phenotype certainly do not go together, which contradicts his theory.

The date of settlement of Easter Island is set at A.D. 380 by a radiocarbon date of completely unspecified context, already discussed above. The culture of the Peruvian settlers is, according to Heyerdahl, that of the epoch known to South American archeologists as the Tiahuanaco period. The Tiahuanaco culture, however, arose in the highlands of Bolivia (near Lake Titicaca) at approximately A.D. 750; thus the Peruvians arriving at Easter Island brought the Tiahuanaco culture some 400 years before it even existed, a great feat even for the fabulous Peruvians! What is even more astonishing, however, is the fact that these Peruvians brought with them the technique of building fitted masonry walls which did not appear in Peru until even later, in approximately A.D. 1500.

Although possessing this remarkably developed (and absolutely anachronistic) stone-working technique, the Tiahuanaco discoverers of Easter Island were strangely lacking in all things typically Tiahuanaco. The Tiahuanaco period is characterized by an abundance of beautiful pottery bearing elaborately painted decorations of felines, anthropomorphic deities, and buzzards. No pottery was found on Easter Island, however. On the Tiahuanaco site itself in Bolivia are the ruins of large buildings and several large statues. There is no resemblance whatsoever between the Easter Island statues, portraying nearly naked human beings, and those of Tiahuanaco, representing anthropomorphic cat-fanged beings heavily clothed in elaborate raiment. The statues of Easter and Tiahuanaco are both of stone, however, but surely this is not very significant.

As to the buildings of Tiahuanaco, they do not resemble in the least the Easter Island *ahu,* which are puny by comparison with the immense rectangular Akapana by Lake Titicaca and its huge, neatly carved monoliths held together with poured copper cleats.

Further characteristics of the Tiahuanaco culture are its beautifully woven fabrics produced from a variety of plants with many techniques. No such things have ever been found on Easter Island.

The migration which carried this paradoxically non-Tiahuanaco group of Tiahuanaco Indians to Easter Island was supposedly led by the great god Viracocha, to whose name Heyerdahl has obligingly prefixed the title "Kon-Tiki." Actually, worship of Viracocha, a creator high-god, may date back as far as A.D. 750 in Peru, but this is uncertain. Viracocha was apparently an Inca deity who rose to importance only when the Inca empire developed after A.D. 1500,[14] and may even be a tribal deity limited to the Inca alone. Certainly there is no evidence that he was a real man, any more than Apollo or Zeus is believed to have been real.

Heyerdahl's Peruvians must have availed themselves of that classical device of science fiction, the time machine, for they showed up off Easter Island in A.D. 380, led by a post- A.D. 750 Incan god-hero, with an A.D. 750 Tiahuanaco material culture featuring A.D. 1500 Incan walls, and not one thing characteristic of the Tiahuanaco period in Peru and Bolivia. This is equivalent to saying that America was discovered in the last days of the Roman Empire by King Henry the Eighth, who brought the Ford Falcon to the benighted aborigines.

Such a nimble use of Einstein's fourth dimension is only one of the many facets of *Aku-Aku* that cause concern to anthropologists, but there is no value in discussing the book at further length here. As to the other side of the coin, the reader by this point has some indication of the nature and amplitude of the scientific evidence that constitutes the basis of the current scientific opinion on the origin of the Polynesians. The bibliography of this work will give only a small sample of what literature awaits a student of Polynesia, and anyone interested is invited to read the original sources for himself.

In conclusion, the *Kon-Tiki* theory is seen as a *revenant* from the past, clothed in a more attractive shroud. Its basis is mainly the success of a modern raft voyage that could not even hope to prove anything concerning ancient Peruvian navigation. The meager scientific evidence for the theory is weak, even in the few instances where it is completely acceptable. Otherwise, the similarities which are purported to show Polynesian-Peruvian relationships are completely equivocal. The *Kon-Tiki* theory is about as plausible as the tales of Atlantis, Mu, and "Children of the Sun." Like most such theories it makes exciting light reading, but as an example of scientific method it fares quite poorly.

CHAPTER

5

Origins of the Melanesians

MARY ELIZABETH SHUTLER AND RICHARD SHUTLER, JR.

Attempts to trace the prehistory of the Melanesians have followed a number of different lines. Examinations of the people themselves and of their fossil remains have cast some light upon the racial affinities of the earliest inhabitants of Melanesia and their subsequent physical change. Studies of Pacific languages, their probable relationships and ages have added other data. Analyses of customs, artifacts and food plants have suggested possible migration routes. Archaeological investigations through controlled surveys of surface remains and stratigraphic excavations have as yet been few in Melanesia and the yields scanty, though the prospects for more archaeological work in the future are promising.

At this time, before much archaeological field work has been undertaken in Melanesia, it seems profitable to review the hypotheses concerning the origins of the Melanesians that modern workers in physical anthropology, linguistics, ethnology, and human ecology have devised. Such a review should be useful in drawing up programs of archaeological research to provide the sorts of data needed to tell the story of the origins and development of Melanesian peoples and cultures.

An inquiry into the origins of the Melanesians must concern itself not only with evidence from their present island homes, but also with evidence from the continents of Asia and Australia and from islands further to the east. The history of the Melanesians has been bound to the history of the people of Southeast Asia, Australia and all the other Pacific islands.

Physical Anthropology

Two quite recent appraisals of the pertinent literature offer hypotheses on the origins of the physical types found

From *Archaeology and Physical Anthropology in Oceania,* 2(2):91–99, 1967. By permission of the authors and the Editor, A. P. Elkin.

in Melanesia, one by Coon (1965) and the other by Macintosh (1965).

Coon's summary of the evidence derived from study of archaeological remains and the physical characteristics of the living people suggests to him that the inhabitants of Australia and of the Pacific Islands are representatives of the same human group which he calls the Australoid subspecies. This group evolved from the Pithecanthropoids of Southeast Asia. Before the end of the Pleistocene, Australoids had migrated to New Guinea and Australia. Later in the Mesolithic and Neolithic periods of Southeast Asia four racial types can be discerned: The Australoids, who represent the unmixed descendants of the late Pleistocene inhabitants of the region; the Mongoloids, who were invading the area from the north; the Melanesians, who represent a mixture between Australoids or Negritos or both and the invading Mongoloids; and the Negritos, who are dwarfed Australoids or in some cases a dwarfed Australoid-Mongoloid people.

Neolithic sea-faring people of mixed Australoid-Mongoloid ancestry moved out into the Pacific to settle the islands of Micronesia and Polynesia, others moved into Melanesia where they mixed again with the descendants of the late Pleistocene inhabitants whom they found in New Guinea and spread out already as far as New Caledonia to form the modern Melanesians. The Negrito people of Melanesia may have evolved their small stature in the islands. The variety of physical characteristics found today in Melanesia is explained by different histories of hybridization, isolation and responses to different environmental situations.

Macintosh's (1965) summary is concerned with the Australian Aborigines but necessarily considers much of the evidence describing what he calls the "Papuo-Melanesians." He feels that the Australian Aborigines and the Papuo-Melanesians do not represent a single group but two quite different patterns. Both arose in Southeast Asia and may have been somewhat hybridized there before migrating to Oceania in late Pleistocene times. He sees no evidence of Australian Aborigines in island New Guinea.

Linguistics

Languages of the Melanesian islands have been divided into two groups: Austronesian, represented by numerous Melanesian languages and some scattered communities of Polynesian speakers, and Papuan, or more properly non-Austronesian because these latter form a very diverse group and many of them are probably unrelated to others in the group. The non-Austronesian languages cluster in Western Melanesia, in New Guinea, New Britain, and the western Solomon Islands. It is presumed by most investigators that these languages were introduced by very early settlers to Melanesia coming from the Asiatic mainland and spreading out over the eastern islands of Melanesia.

The problem of the origin and spread of the Austronesian languages has been dealt with in three recent papers.

Capell (1962) derives the Austronesian languages from the Asiatic mainland. From original Austronesian, proto-Indonesian, proto-Melanesian, and proto-Polynesian developed, the latter perhaps by differentiation from the Melanesian languages, or by independent differentiation from the Austronesian stock and migration to Oceania.

Alternatively, Western Indonesia may be a modern form of original Austronesian which gave rise to Micronesian, Melanesian, and Polynesian at an early date. Capell seems inclined towards the position that, at different times, different groups of Austronesian speaking people left the Asiatic mainland. The Melanesian language arose as a result of mixture with non-Austronesian languages. The Polynesian languages are the result of a later movement of people through Melanesia and out into the islands to the east. He sees the Polynesian outliers in Melanesia as colonies left behind in this eastward migration unlike most students who regard them as colonies settled by westward migrations from Western Polynesia.

Grace (1964) agrees that the original homeland of the Austronesian languages was Southeast Asia where they differentiated from the Kadai languages. This split was followed by a separation of Austronesian speakers into at least two groups and considerable movement of Austronesian speakers, so that by 1500 B.C. Austronesian languages were distributed throughout Indonesia, the Philippines, Taiwan and Melanesia. Subsequently Fijian-Rotuman-Polynesian differentiated from the languages of the Efate-Epi area of the central New Hebrides and there was probably a movement of Austronesian speakers into Fiji. The Austronesian settlement of Fiji was followed by the differentiation of Fijian, Rotuman and Polynesian from one another and the first migration into the Polynesian islands. At about A.D. 1 there was a differentiation of the Polynesian languages. Excepting Palauan and Chamoro, Grace suggests that the Micronesian languages represent a group whose closest relations are languages of the central New Hebrides, although not those particular languages related to Fijian-Rotuman-Polynesian. A movement of people from the central New Hebrides to the north may have taken place before A.D. 1, perhaps considerably before.

Dyen's classification of the Austronesian languages (Dyen 1965) as recently presented by Murdock (1964) suggests a quite different pattern of movements of languages in the Pacific. Dyen groups about three quarters of all the Austronesian languages into a single Malayo-Polynesian family. Other Austronesian languages represent isolated languages or small groups which are, potentially at least, to be regarded as independent families. He concludes that the Malayo-Polynesian languages originated somewhere in Melanesia (Murdock suggests the area of the Banks and New Hebrides Islands). From the Melanesian centre a series of migrations distributed the Malayo-Polynesian languages: a migration into Polynesia probably by way of Fiji; a movement of the Carolionian language west through Micronesia; a migration westward through the Solomons to the Bismarcks and coastal New Guinea; a movement of Moluccan-speakers through eastern Indonesia to Flores and Sumba; a migration of Hesperonesian-speakers through the Celebes to the Philippines and Borneo and thence to Madagascar, the Greater Sunda Islands and the mainland of Southeast Asia. Elsewhere Dyen (1962: 46) indicated that the spread of the Malayo-Polynesian languages possibly began well before 2500 B.C.

Ethnobotany

Studies of plant distributions and uses indicate that the first inhabitants of

Melanesia were nonagricultural (Oliver 1961; Bulmer and Bulmer 1964). Murdock (1964) assumes that even the first Austronesian-speakers based their economy upon shell-fish collecting, fishing and gathering wild foods. Barrau (1965) points out that the modern use of some wild or only occasionally cultivated crops may be an indication of former rather different economic patterns. The earliest European explorers in Melanesia found the inhabitants growing a number of root and tree cultigens which, with the exception of the sweet potato, derived ultimately from the Indo-Malaysian area. Cultivation of rice reached only the western Micronesian islands of the Pacific and did not spread into Melanesia. The domestic pig and fowl were also introduced to the Melanesian islands from the Indo-Malaysian area and were found to be widely spread by the time of European contact. The change from food collecting to intensive cultivation of root crops seems to have been a slow and halting process in Melanesia. Watson (1964), for example, suggests that intermittent or supplementary horticulture persisted in the Central Highlands of New Guinea until the introduction of the sweet potato after Europeans had reached the Southwest Pacific.

Ethnology

Early students of Pacific people frequently attempted by means of studies of the modern distribution of cultural traits to reconstruct past migrations of people. Though a number of theories have been discarded, two more recent studies of this tradition have remained current in discussions of Pacific migrations.

Heine-Geldern (1932) postulated an early spread of part of the *Walzenbeil* Culture from Asia down into New Guinea and adjacent parts of Melanesia. This migration brought to the Pacific "round" adzes (that is, adzes having a more or less oval outline and an oval or lenticular cross section), plank-built boats lacking an outrigger, ring-built pottery, and probably some of the non-Austronesion languages. This culture greatly influenced even earlier cultures already established in northwestern Melanesia. About 1500 B.C. there was a spread of the *Vierkanterbeil* culture from China into Southeast Asia. This culture was related to the Neolithic Yangshao and brought to Southeast Asia the quadrangular adze, cultivation of rice, the pig, horse and cattle, pit-houses, megaliths, a simple form of the outrigger canoe, possibly bark cloth and the Austronesian languages. Ultimate penetration of these people to Melanesia and mixture there with the former inhabitants produced the Melanesians. The Polynesians were formed independently by a mixture, in the vicinity of Formosa and the Philippines and north Celebes, of the *Vierkanterbeil* culture and the *Schulterbeil* culture. The latter is characterized by shouldered adzes, Austroasiatic speech, and Mongoloid race.

Speiser's studies of Pacific cultures led him to postulate two great migrations of Austronesian speakers into the Pacific (Speiser 1946). An early group having quadrangular adzes migrated along the northern coast of New Guinea and into northwest Melanesia. Mixture with previous inhabitants using round adzes produced an Austro-Melanid group associated with people of predominately Negroid race and Austronesian language. People of this mixed tradition then penetrated the previously uninhabited islands of southern Melanesia and Polynesia. A second migration of Austronesian speakers using quadrangular adzes with grips entered Polynesia through Micronesia and, by themselves mixing with the Austro-Melanid people they found in Polynesia, produced the Polynesians.

More recently Solheim (1964) has analysed the distribution of Neolithic and Iron Age pottery in Southeast Asia with results significant to the understanding of Melanesian origins. He distinguishes three traditions of pottery-making in Southeast Asia, two of them with resemblances to Melanesian Pottery. Pottery of the Bau-Malay tradition he first identifies in South China, where it is called geometric pottery, beginning by 1500 B.C. The pottery is paddle and anvil finished, carved paddles are used, forms are commonly spherical with rounded bottoms. In some areas appliqué decorations are found. This tradition became extremely widespread in Southeast Asia and ultimately penetrated into Melanesia. The Sa-Huynh-Kalanay pottery tradition is characterized by well-made paddle and anvil-finished pottery showing some use of a slow wheel. A variety of forms were produced by different combinations of cylindrical, conical, and spherical parts. Decoration by cord-wrapped or basket-woven paddles is early. Carved paddles were used; later a variety of polished, painted, incised, and impressed designs is found as well. This pottery is also widely distributed in Southeast Asia. The radiocarbon dates available for this pottery tradition range from 750 B.C. to A.D. 200, though Solheim indicates that it may be as old as 1000 B.C. and have lasted in some areas to A.D. 1000. Solheim feels that the pottery excavated from archaeological sites on Fiji and New Caledonia shows similarities to both of these traditions. The distinctive Lapita pottery bearing intricate impressed designs reported from several areas of Melanesia Solheim assigns to the Sa-Huynh-Kalanay tradition or possibly to earlier Japanese pottery-making traditions.

Archaeology

There is now reasonably sound archaeological evidence for the late Pleistocene occupation of Australia and New Guinea. The dates for the human occupation of Australia extend back as far as 16,000 B.C. (Mulvaney 1964). The earliest evidence for the occupation of Melanesia comes from the Eastern Highlands district, Australian New Guinea. A radiocarbon date from Kiowa Rockshelter of about 8,400 B.C. is associated with waterworn pebble tools or flakes from pebbles having a working edge on the end or side or on two sides converging to form a point. From about 4000 B.C. the people camping at the shelter used polished adzes of lenticular crosssection and waisted blades (flake blades with a notch on each side to facilitate hafting). From 3000 B.C. to historic times planilateral (rounded with straight sides) adzes are found and pottery. The Yuku site in the Western Highlands has waisted blades at its lowest levels together with pebble and flake tools. But here too polished lenticular adzes precede planilateral ones (Bulmer 1964; Bulmer and Bulmer 1964).

The Bulmers postulate three phases of Highland prehistory from these excavations. The first phase is characterized by flaked tools and a hunting and gathering economy. The second phase sees a change in economy to horticulture suggested by the polished lenticular adzes (for forest clearing), waisted blades (possibly hoes), and the use of the pestle and mortar. The last phase is marked by the planilateral adze and pottery manufacture, possibly brought together with new crops by people from the coast.

Little archaeological information is available from New Britain, New Ireland, Bougainville, and nearby smaller islands. Some flake tools and waisted blades have been collected from the surface in New Britain (Goodale 1966). These are undated. The flakes, struck from river cobbles, bearing an unifacial or bifacial working edge, resemble some of the Patjitanian tools of Pleistocene Java; the waisted blades resemble those excavated from Highland New Guinea. Finds of this assemblage *in situ* might provide much information on late Pleistocene migration from Southeast Asia.

Some pottery sherds collected from the surface on Bougainville have been described. Again these are undated and unassociated with other artifacts. They are not dissimilar to the pottery taken from archaeological sites in Fiji, the New Hebrides and New Caledonia and to pottery reported ethnographically from many parts of Melanesia (Shutler and Shutler 1964). Similar surface finds of pottery have been reported from New Guinea (Solheim 1958) and the Solomons (Kraus 1945).

Other archaeological data are lacking from the Solomon and Loyalty Islands.

Archaeological excavations in New Caledonia (Gifford and Shutler 1956) suggest that the historic cultural patterns of the inhabitants extend back in time until at least A.D. 150. There is evidence throughout this period of gardening people who also relied on shell-fish collecting and fishing. The pottery is paddle and anvil finished and bears incised decorations of lines, gouges and gashes, relief nubbins, ribs, cross-hatching and ridges, and appliquéd elements. The pottery is similar to that made in historic times in New Caledonia Shell artifacts, *Arca* net sinkers, *Placostylus,* fishhooks, *Trochus* and *Conus* bracelets, shell paring knives, and disc-shaped *Conus* beads resemble objects made in modern times. A few flakes and cores modified slightly for use as tools were found. The evidence for ground-stone tools came mainly from surface finds and the examination of private collections in New Caledonia. Few of these artifacts were found *in situ*. Adzes, axes, chisels, hi-pointed sling stones, flat disclike ceremonial maces, and beads were made of ground stone. The adzes and axes all have a lenticular or oval cross section. No quadrangular or planilateral adzes were observed.

At the Lapita site on the Foué Peninsula, a different kind of pottery from that described above was encountered. This Lapita pottery is a well-made ware paddle and anvil finished, characterized by complicated incised decoration of continuous or dotted lines arranged in geometric patterns, sometimes occurring on the interior of bowls as well as the exterior. Evidence of more variety of vessel form is provided by sherds showing gambreled shoulders, flat bottoms, and decorative flanges below the rim. The pottery is quite distinctive from other pottery found in Melanesia both in the skill of execution it exhibits and in the intricacy and variety of decoration. Pottery of this type had been previously noted on Watom Island (Casey 1936) and on the Ile des Pins off New Caledonia (Lenormand

1948; Avias 1950). The Lapita site had been used as a yam field and the deposit turned over and mixed as a result of cultivation so that the pottery was found mixed with the usual Melanesian pottery. Subsequent examination of the area by the present writers showed in places a stratum bearing only Lapita sherds. A radiocarbon date from the Lapita site of 847 B.C. shows the Lapita pottery to be at least that old. Lapita pottery has since been recognized on Efate in the New Hebrides (Hébert 1965); among Gifford's collection from Sigatoka, Viti Levu, Fiji, where further excavations have dated it at 510 B.C. (*British Newsletter* 1967); from Tongatabu in the Tonga Islands where it dates at 430 B.C. (Golson, personal communication).

Archaeological surface surveys and excavations being undertaken in the New Hebrides have already begun to produce results. Going down the chain from north to south, a recent survey by the writers showed the Banks and Torres Islands to have lacked pottery in prehistoric times; archaeological sites are few and shallow. The larger islands of the Northern Group have numerous archaeological remains. Pottery is found similar to pottery described elsewhere in Melanesia but exhibiting local variations, especially in decorative elements.

In the Shepherd Group of the Central New Hebrides a two-phase cultural sequence has been demonstrated (Garanger 1966). On the island of Makura at two sites Garanger found a buried midden separated by a sterile zone from an upper midden deposit. In both sites the upper midden contained only a little pottery, some internally incised, and stone and shell artifacts similar to those found elsewhere in the New Hebrides. The buried midden lacked the stone and shell but did contain abundant pottery of a more richly decorated style, some bearing relief or appliquéd designs. The bottom midden of the Lapua site on Makura has a radiocarbon date of 590 B.C. The latter style of pottery Garanger also found on the island of Tongoa in beds underlying a stratum of volcanic ash, witness of a great eruption. A buried layer from Enta on Tongoa yielded a date of 400 B.C.; one from Mangarissu, also on Tongoa, a date of 905 B.C. These dates indicate the presence in Melanesia, at an early date, of at least one other pottery-making tradition distinct from the Lapita. The island of Efate in the Central New Hebrides appears to have some sites with pottery of the usual Melanesian type and some which lack pottery. A site from Fila Island in Vila Harbour bears a radiocarbon date of A.D. 860 (Shutler and Shutler 1965).

In the Southern Group of the New Hebrides on Erromango, Tanna, Aniwa, Futuna, and Aneityum, no pottery at all was seen (Shutler and Shutler 1965). Radiocarbon dates from this group show that Tanna was occupied by at least 420 B.C.; Futuna, a Polynesian outlier, by A.D. 300; and Aneityum by at least A.D. 1100.

Stone and shell artifacts so far revealed by excavations in the New Hebrides show much similarity from island to island. Polished stone axes and adzes are uniformly of oval or lenticular cross section with an oval or subtriangular outline; abraders and rubbing stones are found; long cylindrical ground clubs are typical of Tanna and Futuna; a variety of shell artifacts are known: *Tridacna* and *Conus* adzes, choppers and scrapers made of heavy shell, vegetable peelers made of several different kinds of shell, *Terebra* and *Mitra* gouges, and a variety of shell beads, pendants, and bracelets. The artifacts which come from areas in which Melanesian languages are spoken today are indistinguishable from those found on Polynesian outliers. The shell artifacts found to date in the New Hebrides are closely similar to those reported from a number of islands in Micronesia (Gifford and Gifford 1959; Spoehr 1957).

The remains from the New Hebrides indicate a long occupation by a people having the pig, dog, and fowl, and practising shifting cultivation supplemented on the coasts by intensive shellfish collecting.

Following excavation on Viti Levu in the Fiji Islands Gifford (1951) proposed a three-phase cultural sequence. His periods were based on the types of designs found on pot sherds and on the presence or absence of shell in the midden. His Early Period was characterized by relief-decorated pottery and an absence of shell in the midden. The Middle Period, only tentatively proposed by Gifford, had a predominance of plain pottery. The Late Period was defined by the presence of incised pottery in a shell midden.

Green (1963) has since elaborated this sequence. Subsequent work under the direction of Palmer has greatly supplemented Gifford's early efforts. Green's sequence begins with the provisional Sigatoka Phase ending at about 250 B.C. and beginning at an as yet unknown period. The Sigatoka Phase is characterized by Lapita pottery as well as the more usual Melanesian incised and relief pottery. This Lapita pottery from Sigatoka dates back to at least 510 B.C. (*British Newsletter* 1697). The Navatu Phase corresponds to Gifford's Early Period and dates from between 100 B.C. and the eighth to eleventh century A.D. Plain and relief decorated sherds occur in about equal quantities, wavy relief beginning to be especially abundant. In the following Vunda Phase (Middle Period) plain sherds are overwhelmingly predominant. This phase lasts to A.D. 1643. The final Ra Phase (Late Period) sees an increase of incised pottery but plain sherds remain most numerous.

A review of Melanesian studies makes it abundantly clear that Melanesian origins can not be sought at a particular place nor at a particular time in history. Rather the people of Melanesia are the result of an extremely ancient and long-lasting flow of people from the Asiatic mainland into the islands of the Southwest Pacific. During the latter part of their history they have in addition maintained sporadic contact with people inhabiting island groups to the north and east. From time to time and from place to place new movements of people bring changes in the gene pools, in the languages and customs, and subsistence patterns of the people of the Melanesian islands. New ways of exploiting island environments give impetus to fresh movements within the island groups themselves and modify further the life of the people. Shifting patterns of contact and isolation have brought and continue to bring other changes. Our aims for future research must not be therefore to find the origin of the Melanesians but rather a fuller understanding of the mechanisms of the continuing evolution of the people of the Melanesian Islands.

PART II
Technology and Economics

INTRODUCTION

Geography impresses its stamp upon various branches of anthropological knowledge insofar as concepts, theories, and methods issue from a dialogue with ethnographic data, i.e., information concerning regionally delimited cultures. In this respect economic anthropology is no exception. Thus, "reciprocity," that pervasive feature of daily economic and social life in Melanesian societies, which was first described in detail by Malinowski, became a theoretical construct—an "ideal type"—in the discussions of such comparative theorists as Marcel Mauss and Karl Polanyi. The debt that economic anthropology owes to studies of Pacific cultures is illustrated by the list of basic books for college libraries on technology and economics recently compiled under the auspices of the American Anthropological Association. Over half (six of eleven) of the monographic studies listed describe the economic organization of societies in the Pacific area. These include two "classics": Malinowski's *Argonauts of the Western Pacific* (1922) and Raymond Firth's *Economics of the New Zealand Maori* (second edition, 1959; originally published in 1929). It is from these works that the comparative study of non-Western economic forms received its initial impetus.

It is appropriate that this section begins with Malinowski's "The Primitive Economics of the Trobriand Islanders." In a real sense, this essay announced the discovery of "tribal economy." It argues that the economic life of primitive societies is worthy of serious scientific investigation, that the analysis of non-Western economic concepts and institutions "opens a new vista of economic research" affording a deeper understanding of indigenous cultures.

In recent years, however, the "new vista" promised by Malinowski has been somewhat clouded by a polarization of opinion among anthropologists concerning the appropriate methods and objectives of economic anthropology. One group, the so-called "substantivists," following Malinowski's lead, would describe and analyze the economic systems of Pacific and other non-Western societies in their sociocultural context. After all, in such simple or unspecialized societies, "economy" emerges largely as an aspect of various social institutions. Therefore, one may expect that the principles governing economic life will turn out to be corollaries of more general sociological principles.

The second group, the "formalists," would have us consider the Pacific Islander version of the Economic Man. The focus should be the process of economizing, the allocative choices or economic decisions of individuals and groups. From this perspective many of the concepts developed by economists for the study of Western market economies appear to be relevant.

In assuming our task of selecting essays illustrating the forms of economic life characteristic of indigenous Pacific communities, we considered it unnecessary to espouse one view or another on the strategy of economic anthropology. Rather, we call the reader's attention to the fact that a controversy exists and that studies of Pacific cultures are as relevant now as they were when the anthropological inquiry into economic life began. It should be admitted, however, that as ethnographers who have worked in societies only slightly affected by intrusive Western economic practices, we are naturally predisposed to the Malinowskian view. Thus, although an explicit theoretical position has not served as a criterion of selection, it happens that the essays of this section are more or less representative of the "substantivist" approach to primitive economics.

Wallace's essay on a culturally marginal group of dry-rice cultivators in northern Luzon affords insight into the interrelations of environments, technology, and economy. Sahlins and Bascom explore the relationships of economic distribution to power and prestige in Fiji and Ponape, respectively. In the final selection on New Guinea, Harding describes a regional economic network of a type that was typical of the islands of the Western Pacific.

CHAPTER

6

The Primitive Economics of the Trobriand Islanders

BRONISLAW MALINOWSKI

Only a very slight acquaintance with ethnological literature is needed to convince us that little attention has been paid so far to the problems of economics among primitive races. A certain amount of speculation has been devoted to origins of economic institutions—more especially to origins of property, to the stages of economic development, and to certain questions of exchange, "primitive money," and rudimentary forms of division of labour. As a rule, however, small results have been achieved, because the amount of serious consideration given by theoretical writers to economic problems is in no way proportional to their complexity and importance, and the field observations extant are scanty. Again, the lack of inspiration from theoretical work has reacted detrimentally on ethnographic field work, and a careful survey of the best records of savage life reveals little or nothing that might be of value to the economist.

A student of economics, in possession of a systematic theory, might be naturally tempted to inquire how far, if at all, his conclusions can be applied to a type of society entirely different from our own. He would attempt in vain, however, to answer this question on the basis of the ethnological data extant, or, if he did, his results could not be correct. In fact, the question has been set forth and an attempt at its solution made by C. Buecher in his *Industrial Evolution*. His conclusions are, in my opinion, a failure not owing to imperfect reasoning or method, but rather to the defective material on which they are formed. Buecher comes to the conclusion that the savages—he includes among them races as highly developed

---

From *The Economic Journal,* 31:1–16, 1921. By permission of Valetta Malinowska and the publisher.

as the Polynesians—have no economic organisation, and that they are in a pre-economic stage—the lowest in that of the individual search for food, the higher ones in the stage of self-sufficient household economy.

In this article I shall try to present some data referring to the economic life of the Trobriand Islanders, a community living on a coral archipelago off the northeast coast of New Guinea. These natives, typical South Sea Islanders of the Melanesian stock, with a developed institution of chieftainship, great ability in various crafts, and a fine decorative art, certainly are not at the lower end of savagery. In their general level of culture, however, they may be taken as representative of the majority of the savage races now in existence, and they are less developed culturally than the Polynesians, the bulk of North American Indians, of Africans, and of Indonesians. If we find, therefore, distinct forms of economic organisation among them we are safe in assuming that even among the lowest savages we might expect to find more facts of economic interest than have been hitherto recorded.

I shall first give an outline of the natural resources of the Trobrianders and a broad survey of the manner in which these are utilised. The natives live on flat coral islands, covered with rich, heavy soil, very well suited for the cultivation of yams and taro, and they also enjoy a good regular rainfall. The coast is surrounded in parts with a fringing reef, in parts it encloses a big, shallow lagoon, teeming with fish. Having such excellent natural inducements, the natives are splendid tillers of the soil and first-rate fishermen, efficient and hard-working in both pursuits. These in turn reward them with a perennial abundance of food, sufficient to support a population very dense, as compared with other tribes of that part of the world. In gardening the natives obtain their fine results in spite of using only the most primitive implement—a pointed stick, made and discarded every time they go to work. In fishing they use big nets, also traps, fish-hooks and poison. As manufacturers they excel in wood-carving, basket-weaving, and the production of highly valued shell ornaments. On the other hand, through lack of material, they have to rely on the importation from other tribes of stone implements and pottery, as, of course, neither hard stone nor clay are obtainable on a coral island. I have begun by giving this general outline of their resources, pursuits, and crafts, in order to indicate the narrow frame within which the current accounts of economics are encompassed. The data would there, no doubt, be given with a much greater wealth of detail—especially in the technological aspect—but it would be mainly the successive description of the various activities, connected with the quest for food and the manufacture of objects, without any attempt being made at a discussion of the more complex problems, referring to organisation of production, apportionment, and to the mechanism of tribal life in its economic aspect.

This will be done here, beginning with production, and taking agriculture as an example.

The questions before us are, first, the important problem of land tenure; next, the less obvious problems of the organisation of production. Is the work in the gardens carried out by each family, or each person individually and independently? Or is there any general coordination of this work, any social organisation of their efforts, and, if so, how is it done, and by whom? Are the successive stages of the work integrated into any organic whole, by any supervision, by any personal guidance, or any social or psychological force?

Land tenure among the Trobriand natives is rather complex, and it shows well the difficulties of solving ethnographic field problems of this type and the dangers of being misled into some inadequate approximation. When I began to inquire into this subject, I first received from my native informant a series of general statements, such as that the chief is the owner of all land, or that each garden plot has its owner, or that all the men of a village community own the land jointly. Then I tried to answer the question by the method of concrete investigation: taking a definite plot, I inquired successively, from several independent informants, who was the owner of it. In some cases I had mentioned to me successively as many as five different "owners" to one plot—each answer, as I found out later on, containing part of the truth, but none being correct by itself. It was only after I had drawn up complete plans of the garden land of several village communities, and inquired successively into the details, not only of each separate garden unit, but also into the details of each of the alleged forms of "ownership," that I was able to reach a satisfactory conclusion. The main difficulty in this, as in ever so many similar questions, lies in our giving our own meaning of *ownership* to the corresponding native word. In doing this we overlook the fact that to the natives the word *ownership* not only has a different significance, but that they use one word to denote several legal and economic relationships, between which it is absolutely necessary for us to distinguish.

The chief (*Guya'u*) has in the Trobriands a definite over-right over all the garden land within the district. This consists in the title of "master" or "owner" (*Toli*), and in the exercise of certain ceremonial rights and privileges, such as the decision on which lands the gardens are to be made, arbitration in garden disputes, and several minor privileges. The garden magician (*Towosi*) also calls himself the "master of the garden" and is considered as such, in virtue of his complex magical and other functions, fulfilled in the course of gardening. Again, in certain cases, and over certain portions of the land, the same title is given to notables or subchiefs, who carry out certain minor offices in connection with it. Finally, each garden plot belongs to some individual or other in the village community, and, when the gardens are made on this particular land, this owner either uses his plot himself or leases it to someone else under a rather complicated system of payment. The chief, the magician, and the notables also own individually a number of garden plots each, independently of their general over-rights.

Now the reason why an economist cannot ignore such over-rights and complications is that the natives value them extremely, and, what is more important, that such over-rights carry with them definite functions and wield definite influences of economic importance.

Thus the complex conditions of land tenure, the not infrequent quarrels about gardening, and the need for summoning and maintaining communal labour require a social authority, and this is supplied by the chief with the assistance of the notables. On the other hand, the

Towosi, the hereditary garden magician of each village community, has to a great extent the control over the initiative in the more detailed proceedings of the work. Each stage of gardening is inaugurated by a magical rite performed by him. He also orders the work to be done, looks after the way in which it is carried out, and imposes the periods of taboo, which punctuate it.

The proceedings of gardening are opened by a conference, summoned by the chief and held in front of the magician's house, at which all arrangements and the allotment of garden plots are decide upon. Immediately after that, the members of the village community bring a gift of selected food to the garden magician, who at night sacrificially offers a portion of it to the ancestral spirits, with an invocation, and at the same time utters a lengthy spell over some special leaves. Next morning, the magician repairs to the garden, accompanied by the men of the village, each of whom carries an axe with the charmed leaves wrapped around its blade. While the villagers stand around, the *Towosi* (magician) strikes the ground with a ceremonial staff, uttering a formula. This he does on each garden plot successively, and on each the men cut a few saplings with their axes. After that, for a month or so, the scrub is cut in the prospective gardens by men only, and communal labour is often resorted to. The *Towosi* has to decide when the next stage, the burning of scrub and the clearing of soil, has to begin. When he thinks that the cut scrub is sufficiently dry, he imposes a taboo on garden work, so that any belated cutting has to be suspended. In a series of rites, lasting, as a rule, for about three days, he inaugurates the work of clearing the garden plot; this afterwards is carried on by men and women jointly, working in families, each on its own plot, without the help of communal labour. The planting of yams is inaugurated by a very elaborate ceremony, also extending over a few days, during which no further garden work is done at all. A magical rite of its own inaugurates each further stage, the erection of supports for the yam vine; the weeding of the gardens, done by female communal labour; the cleaning of the yam roots and tubers; the preliminary harvest of early yams; and finally the main harvest of late yams.

When the plants begin to grow a series of magical rites, parallel with the inaugural ones, is performed, in which the magician is supposed to give an impulse to the growth and development of the plant at each of its successive stages. Thus, one rite is performed to make the seed tuber sprout; another drives up the sprouting shoot; another lifts it out of the ground; yet another makes it twine round the support; then, with yet other rites, the leaves are made to bud, to open, to expand, respectively.

The *Towosi* (garden magician) always performs a rite first on one of the four garden plots selected for the purpose each season, and called *Leywota*. In certain ceremonies he afterwards carries the magic on into each garden plot, in others the magic is performed on the selected plots only. The *Leywota* are important from the economic point of view, because the owner of such a plot is bound to keep pace with the progress of magic, that is, he may not lag behind with his work. Also, the *Leywota* plots are always worked with a special care, and they are kept up to a very high standard of gardening.

Thus, both in the regularity and in the quality of the work done, these plots set a definite pattern to all the others.

Besides the indirect influence which the *Towosi* exercises on garden work by giving the initiative and inaugurating the successive stages, by imposing taboos, and by setting the standard by means of the *Leywota* plots, he also directly supervises certain activities of general importance to all the gardens. Thus, for example, he keeps his eye on the work done in fencing round the garden. All the plots are placed within a common enclosing fence, of which everyone has to make his share, corresponding to his plot or plots. Thus, the neglect of one careless individual might result in a damage to all, for bush pigs or wallabies might find their way in and destroy the new crops. If this happens, the garden magician gets up in front of his house in the evening and harangues the village, often mentioning the culprit by name and heaping blame on him—a proceeding which seldom fails to take effect.

It is easy to see that the magician performs manifold and complex functions, and that his claim to be the "master of the garden" is not an empty one! What is now the economic importance of his functions? The natives believe deeply that through his magic the *Towosi* controls the forces of Nature, and they also believe that he ought to control the work of man. To start a new stage of gardening without a magical inauguration is, for them, unthinkable. Thus, his magical power, exercised side by side with their work, his magical cooperation, so to speak, inspires them with confidence in success and gives them a powerful impulse to work. Their implicit belief in magic also supplies them with a leader, whose initiative and command they are ready to accept in all matters, where it is needed. It is obvious that the series of magical rites—punctuating the progress of activities at regular intervals, imposing a series of rest periods, and, in the institution of standard plots (*Leywota*), establishing a model to the whole community—is of extreme importance. It acts as a psychological force, making for a more highly organised system of work, than it would be possible to achieve at this stage of culture by an appeal to force or to reason.

Thus, we can answer the questions, referring to the organisation of production, by summing up our results, and saying that the authority of the chief, the belief in magic, and the prestige of the magician are the social and psychological forces which regulate and organise production; that this latter, far from being just the sum of uncorrelated individual efforts, is a complex and organically united tribal enterprise.

Finally, a few words must be said about the character of native labour in the Trobriands. We would see their economic activities in an entirely wrong perspective if we were to imagine that these natives are temperamentally lazy and can work only under some outside pressure. They have a keen interest in their gardens, work with spirit, and can do sustained and efficient work, both when they do it individually and communally. There are different systems of communal work on various scales; sometimes the several village communities join together, sometimes the whole community, sometimes a few households. Distinctive native names are given to the various kinds of communal work, and payment in food also differs. In the more extensive kinds of work, it is the chief's duty to feed the workers.

An interesting institution of ceremonial enterprise deserves special attention. This is known as the *Kayasa*, and might be described as a period when all activities, whether gardening, fishing, industrial or even merely tribal sports and merrymaking, are carried out with special intensity. When the season is good, and the time is felt by the whole community to be propitious, the chief announces the *Kayasa*, and inaugurates it by giving a big feast. The whole period of the *Kayasa* is punctuated by other feasts, also provided for by the chief, and everyone who takes part is under an implicit obligation to do his best, and work his hardest, so that the *Kayasa* may be a success.

We have discussed their production on the example of gardening. The same conclusions, however, could have been drawn from a discussion of fishing, building of houses or canoes, or from a description of their big trading expeditions. All these activities are dependent upon the social power of the chief and the influence of the respective magicians. In all of them the quantity of the produce, the nature of the work and the manner in which it is carried out—all of which are essentially economic features—are highly modified by the social organisation of the tribe and by their magical belief. Customary and legal norms, magical and mythological ideas, introduce system into their economic efforts and organise them on a social basis. On the other hand, it is clear that if an ethnologist proposes to describe any aspect of tribal life, without approaching it also from the economic point of view, his account would be bound to be a failure.

This will be still more evident after a description of the manner in which they apportion the produce and utilise it in what could be called the financing of tribal enterprise. Here, again, I shall speak, for simplicity's sake, mainly of the garden produce. As each man has allotted to him for each season one or several garden plots, we might expect that, following the principle of "closed household economy," each family would by themselves consume the results of their labour. As a matter of fact, the apportionment or distribution, far from following such a simple scheme, is again full of intricacies and presents many economically interesting features. Of these the two most important are: the obligations, imposed by rules of kinship and relationship-in-law, and the dues and tributes paid to the chief.

The first-named obligations involve a very complex redistribution of garden produce, resulting in a state of things in which everybody is working for somebody else. The main rule is that a man is obliged to distribute almost all his garden produce among his sisters; in fact, to maintain his sisters and their families. I must pass over all the complications and consequences implied by this system, and only notice that it means an enormous amount of additional labour in handling and transporting the produce, and that it enmeshes the whole community into a network of reciprocal obligations and dues, one constant flow of gift and counter-gift.

This constant economic undertow to all public and private activities—this materialistic streak which runs through all their doings—gives a special and unexpected colour to the existence of the natives, and shows the immense importance to them of the economic aspect of everything. Economic considerations pervade their social life, economic difficulties constantly face them. Whenever the native moves—to a feast, to an expedition, or in warfare—he will have to deal with the problems of giving and counter-giving. The detailed analysis of this state of affairs would lead us to interesting results, but it would be a side issue from our main theme—the public economy of the tribe.

To return to this, we must first consider, what part of the whole tribal income is apportioned to the chief. By various channels, by dues and tributes, and especially through the effect of polygamy, with its resulting obligations of his relatives-in-law, about 30 per cent of the whole food production of his district finds its way into the large, finely decorated yam houses of the chief. Now to the natives the possession and display of food are of immense value and importance in themselves. Pride in possessing abundant food is one of their leading characteristics. One of the greatest insults that can be uttered is to call someone "Man with no food," and it would be bitterly resented, and probably a quarrel would ensue. To be able to boast of having food is one of their chief glories and ambitions. Their whole conduct, in the matter of eating in public, is guided by the rule that no suspicion of scarcity of food can possibly be attached to the eater. For example, to eat publicly in a strange village would be considered humiliating and is never done.

Their ambitions in this direction are also shown by the keen interest taken in the display of food. On all possible occasions—at harvest time, when there is an interchange of gifts, or when the enormous food distributions (*Sagali*) take place—the display of the food is one of the main features of interest. And there are even special food exhibitions, in which two villages compete against each other, and which in the old days used to be taken so seriously that often war was the result.

The chief is the only person who owns a big yam house, which is made with open interstices between the beams so that all may look through and admire the yams, of which the finest are always placed to the front. The chief is, as a matter of fact, also the only person who can accumulate, and, as a matter of privilege, the only one who is allowed to own and display large quantities. This gives him a definite status, is a sign of high rank, and satisfies his ambition. Finally, it enhances his power, broadly speaking, in the same manner as possession of wealth does with us.

Another important privilege of the chief, is his power to transform food into objects of permanent wealth. Here again, he is the only man rich enough to do it, but he also jealously guards his right, and would punish anyone who might attempt to emulate him, even on a small scale.

The *Vaygua*—objects or tokens of wealth—consist of several classes of highly valued articles, mainly big ceremonial axe-blades, necklaces of red shell discs, and armshells of the *conus millepunctatus* shell. These objects are hardly ever put to any real use, but they are extremely highly valued in themselves by the natives. The material of which they are made is rare and difficult to obtain, and much time and labour must be spent in working it. Once made, however, the objects are very durable, almost indestructible. Their main economic function is to be owned as signs of wealth, and consequently of power, and from time to time to change hands as ceremonial gifts. As such, they are the foundation of certain kinds of native trade, and they constitute an indispensable element of the social organisation of the natives. For, as mentioned above, all their social life is accompanied by gift and counter-gift. These are, as a rule, arranged so that one party has to give a substantial present of food, when the other offers one of the tokens of wealth.

The chief, as said, has the means and the customary privilege of producing these objects. He also, in definite circumstances, frequently acquires them in exchange for food. In any case, about 80 per cent of these objects remain in his possession (or at least this was the proportion before the chief's power and all their tribal law had been undermined by white man's influence). This acquisition of valuables, side by side with possession of food, is the basis of his power and a mark of his dignity and rank.

The chief finally is (or, more correctly, in olden days was) the owner of about three quarters of all the pigs, coconuts, and betel nuts in the district. By a system of *métayage*, there are in the various villages certain people who look after his right over these three classes of things; they also receive their share, but have to bring him the bulk of the produce.

Thus, the possession of the beautiful yam houses, always ready to receive the crops, and often filled with them; the acquisition of a large amount of *Vaygua* (tokens of wealth), and of the greater part of the pigs, coconuts, and betel nuts, give the chief a static basis of power, prestige, and rank. But also the control over all these classes of wealth allows him to exercise his power dynamically.

For in a society where everything has to be accompanied by gift and payment, even the chief, the highest and most powerful individual in the community, though, according to customary rule, he can command the services of all, still must pay for them. He enjoys many personal services, such as being carried about on his journeys, sending people on errands, having all forms of magic performed for him. For such services, rendered by retainers and picked specialists, a chief must pay immediately, sometimes in *Vaygua*, sometimes in food, more especially in pigs, coconuts, and betel nuts.

The essential of power is, of course, the possibility of enforcing orders and commanding obedience by means of punishment. The chief has special henchmen to carry out his verdicts directly by inflicting capital punishment, and they must be paid by *Vaygua*. More often, however, the punishment is meted out by means of evil magic. How often the sorcerers in the Trobriands use poison, it would be difficult to say. But the enormous dread of them, and the deep belief in their power, renders their magic efficient enough. And if the chief were known to have given a *Vaygua* to a powerful sorcerer in order to kill a man, I should say that man was doomed.

Even more important than the exercise of personal power is the command, already mentioned once or twice, which wealth gives the chief over the organisation of tribal enterprises. The chief has the power of initiative, the customary right to organise all big tribal affairs and conduct them in the character of master of ceremonies. But there are two conditions incidental to the role he has to play. The leading men, such as the headmen of dependent villages, the main performers, the always indispensable magicians, the technical specalists, have all to be paid, and are, as usual, paid in objects of wealth, and the bulk of the participants have to be fed.

Both these conditions can be fulfilled by the chief in virtue of his control over a considerable portion of the consumable and condensed wealth of the tribe.

As a concrete example of big tribal affairs, organised and financed by the chief, we can quote first of all the above-mentioned *Kayasa*, a term embracing several kinds of ceremonial enterprises. In these, as we saw, the chief, by means of gifts, imposes a binding obligation on the participants to carry out the undertaking, and by means of periodical distributions he keeps everyone going during the time of dancing, merry-making, or communal working. In former times during war, when the inhabitants of two hostile districts used to foregather in their respective chiefs' villages, the chief had to summon his vassal headmen by gifts of *Vaygua*. Then at an initial ceremonial gathering, there would be a distribution of food, in particular the specially coveted pig's flesh, coconuts, and betel nuts. And, later on, when during the progress of hostilities large numbers had to camp in or near the chief's village, his yam houses would be severely taxed in order to keep the warriors provided with food. Again, there is an important feature of their tribal life—the *Sagali*, or ceremonial distributions of food from one clan to another, associated with their mortuary ritual. In these the chief's wealth often had to be called upon to a considerable extent if the nominal giver of the feast had any claim on him as his kinsman, clansman, or relative-in-law.

We see, therefore, that in following up the various channels through which produce flows, and in studying the transformations it undergoes, we find a new and extremely interesting field for ethnological and economic interest. The chief's economic role in public life can be pointedly described as that of "tribal banker," without, of course, giving this term its literal meaning. His position, his privileges, allow him to collect a considerable portion of tribal yield and to store it, also to transform part of it into permanent condensed wealth, by the accumulation of which he gives himself a still bigger fund of power. Thus, on the one hand, the chief's economic function is to create objects of wealth, and to accumulate provisions for tribal use, thus making big tribal enterprises possible. On the other hand, in doing so he enhances his prestige and influence, which he also exercises through economic means.

It would be idle to generalise from one example, or to draw strained parallels—to speak of the chief as "capitalist" or to use the expression "tribal banker" in any but the most unpretentious way. If we had more accounts of native economics similar to this—that is, going more into detail and giving an economic synthesis of facts—we might be able to arrive, by comparative treatment, at some interesting results. We might be able to grasp the nature of the economic mechanism of savage life, and incidentally we might be able to answer many questions referring to the origins and development of economic institutions. Again, nothing stimulates and broadens our views so much as wide comparison and sharp contrast, and the study of extremely primitive economic institutions would no doubt prove very refreshing and fertilising to theory.

It is necessary to point out that, in such a short article, where the broad outline of the institutions and customs has to be given with a few strokes, I have had to summarise certain things. Thus I speak of "the chief," whereas in a more detailed account I would have shown that there are several chieftainships in the tribe with a varying range and amount of power. In each case the economic, as well as the other social conditions, are slightly different, and to these differences I have not been able to do justice in this article. I have tried to present the general features which, in a manner, are common to all the districts of Kiriwina. A greater wealth of detail, though it might blur certain outlines and certainly would make things look less simple, would have allowed us to draw our conclusions even more forcibly and convincingly.

To sum up the results so far obtained, we may say that both the production and its apportionment in the native communities are by no means as simple as is usually assumed. They are both based on a special form of organisation, both are intertwined with other tribal aspects, depending and reacting on other social and psychological forces.

Through the institution of chieftainship and the belief in magic, their production is integrated into a systematic effort of the whole community. By this a considerable amount of consumable wealth is produced, a great part of which is controlled by the chief, who transforms some of it into permanent wealth and keeps the rest in store. This, again, coupled with the natives' regard for wealth, and the importance of material give-and-take in their social institutions, allows the chief to wield his power to organise and finance tribal life.

We have not spoken of exchange yet, and, indeed, it is such a vast subject in the Trobriands—that is, if treated in the light of a more precise analysis—that in this paper I shall not attempt to deal with it exhaustively. There is, however, one point to which I want to draw attention. The tokens of wealth have often been called "money." It is at first sight evident that "money" in our sense cannot exist among the Trobrianders. The word *currency*—differentiated from *money* in that it is an object of use as well as a means of exchange—does not help us much here, as the articles in question are not utilities. Any article which can be classed as "money" or "currency" must fulfil certain essential conditions; it must function as a medium of exchange and as a common measure of value, and it must be the instrument of condensing wealth, the means by which value can be accumulated. Money also, as a rule, serves as the standard of deferred payments. It is obvious at once that in economic conditions such as obtain among the Trobrianders, there can be no question of a standard of deferred payments, as payments are never deferred. It is equally clear that the *Vaygua* do serve as a means of condensing wealth—in fact, that this is their essential role.

The questions of a common measure of value and a measure of exchange require, however, some consideration. Exchange of useful articles against one another does exist in Kiriwina, both in internal and external trade. Indeed, barter among the natives is very well developed. Their exchange sometimes takes the form of free gift and following counter-gift—always repaid according to definite rules of equivalence. Sometimes it is real barter (for which they have a term—*Gimwali*), where one article is traded against another, with direct assessment of equivalence and even with haggling.

But in all cases trade follows customary rules, which determine what and how much shall be exchanged for any given article. Thus the villagers of Bwoitalu are the professional carvers in hard wood and produce excellent carved dishes. They are, on the other hand, in need of coconuts and yam food, and they like to acquire certain ornaments. Whenever one of them has a few dishes of certain dimensions on hand, he knows that in the village of Oburaku he can get about forty coconuts for one grade, twenty for another, ten for another, and so on; in the central villages of Kiriwina, he can obtain a definite number of yam baskets; in some other villages, he can get a few red shell discs or turtle-shell earrings. Again, some coastal villages need a special kind of strong creeper for lashing their canoes. This they know can be obtained from villages near swamps for a definite payment—that is, one coil of creeper for one coconut or betel nut, or ten coils for a small basketful of yams.

All the trade is carried on in exactly the same way—given the article, and the communities between which it is traded, anyone would know its equivalent, rigidly prescribed by custom. In fact, the narrow range of exchangeable articles and the inertia of custom leave no room for any free exchange, in which there would be a need for comparing a number of articles by means of a common measure. Still less is there a need for a medium of exchange, since, whenever something changes hands, it does so always because the barterers directly require the other article.

This leads us first of all to the conclusion that we cannot think of *Vaygua* in terms of "money." Moreover, what is more important still, we see that in Kiriwina the character of the exchange does not admit of any article becoming money. Certain things, no doubt, more especially basketsful of yams, bundles of taro, and coconuts are very frequently exchanged, and against a wide range of other articles, and in economic considerations they may serve us as measures of value, but they are not regarded or purposely used as such by the natives.

When reading ethnological accounts about native "money"—such, for example, as those about the *diwarra* shells in New Britain or about the big stones in the Carolines—the statements appear to me singularly unconvincing. Unless it is shown that the mechanism of exchange among the natives there requires or even allows of the existence of an article, used as a common measure of value or medium of exchange, all the data given about an article, however much they might lend it a superficial resemblance to money, must be considered worthless. Of course, when a savage community comes into commercial relations with a higher culture—as in Africa, where trading between Arabs and Europeans has long taken place—then money can and even must exist. Some forms of the so-called South Sea "money" may have acquired this character recently under European influence, and the *diwarra* may possibly be a case in point.

The discussion of the problem of money among primitive peoples shows very clearly how necessary it is in ethnology to analyse the economic background of the conditions indispensable to the existence of certain complex phenomena. The existence of "money" or "currency" so easily assumed, so glibly introduced by the use of these terms, proves with close analysis to be an hypothesis extremely bold and probably equally misleading.

One further function of the tokens

of value should be mentioned here, that is, their exchange in the form of circular trading, called by the natives *Kula*, which takes place over a wide area amongst the islands and coasts of this part of British New Guinea. This peculiar form of circular trade presents many interesting economic features, but as it has been described elsewhere I shall not enter into the subject now.

All the facts adduced in this article lead us to the conclusion that primitive economics are not by any means the simple matter we are generally led to suppose. In savage societies national economy certainly does not exist, if we mean by the term a system of free competitive exchange of goods and services, with the interplay of supply and demand determining value and regulating all economic life. But there is a long step between this and Buecher's assumption that the only alternative is a pre-economic stage, where an individual person or a single household satisfy their primary wants as best they can, without any more elaborate mechanism than division of labour according to sex, and an occasional spasmodic bit of barter. Instead, we find a state of affairs where production, exchange, and consumption are socially organised and regulated by custom, and where a special system of traditional economic values governs their activities and spurs them on to efforts. This state of affairs might be called—as a new conception requires a new term—*tribal economy*.

The analysis of the natives' own economic conceptions of value, ownership, equivalence, commercial honour, and morals opens a new vista of economic research, indispensable for any deeper understanding of a native community. Economic elements enter into tribal life in all its aspects—social, customary, legal and magicoreligious—and are in turn controlled by these. It is not for the observer in the field to answer or to contemplate the metaphysical question as to what is the cause and effect—the economic or the other aspects. To study their interplay and correlation is, however, his duty. For to overlook the relation between two or several aspects of native life is as much an error of omission as to overlook any one aspect.

CHAPTER

7

Agricultural Technology of the Pagan Gaddang

BEN J. WALLACE

Introduction

This chapter describes the annual production cycle of the Pagan Gaddang of the Philippine Islands. In general, my analysis centers on the Pagan Gaddang of the Cagayan Valley who number about 2,000 and, in particular, those who reside on the Gaddang settlement of Pakak. A more detailed description of the Gaddang economic system has been presented elsewhere (Wallace 1767b). The agricultural technology of the Pakak Gaddang is representative of that found among other southern Pagan Gaddang where shifting cultivation methods are used in farming. Because the habitat characteristics of Pakak differ from the Gaddang area farther north where there is much more forest land, however, generalizations concerning crop yield and ecosystem equilibrium are applicable only to the region of the southern Pagan Gaddang.[1]

The Pagan Gaddang have maintained a culture of their own, not having significantly adopted the ways of the lowland Filipinos. The so-called Christian Gaddang of Isabela and Nueva Vizcaya, on the other hand, practice a lowland Filipino way of life and should not be confused with the Pagan Gaddang (see Lambrecht 1959, 1960; Galang 1935; Wallace 1968). The Pagan Gaddang, as viewed by the Christian Gaddang and other lowlanders, are not Gaddang; they are "Kalinga." They are considered to be wild and dangerous people who live

---

An earlier version of this paper was published in the *Philippine Sociological Review* (Wallace 1967a). Field work among the Pagan Gaddang was carried out in 1965–1966 and in the summer of 1968. The research was supported by the Midwest Universities Consortium for International Activities, Inc., the Wenner-Gren Foundation for Anthropological Research, and Agricultural Development Council, Inc. I would like to express my appreciation to Milton L. Barnett and William W. Elmendorf for their helpful and critical comments on earlier versions of this paper.

in the forest. In short, the Christian Gaddang have joined the mainstream of rural Filipino life while the Pagan Gaddang have maintained their ethnic identity.

In 1965–1966 the Gaddang settlement at Pakak consisted of thirty-three people, occupying eight houses. The houses, situated in a small forest, were located at an elevation of about 700 feet in the foothills of the eastern slopes of the *Cordillera Central* in Ifugao. The habitat of the Pakak area conforms to what is generally termed a "monsoon forest" (see Dobby 1954; Huke 1963; Wernstedt and Spencer 1967). Importantly, there is a short dry season of two or three months. During these months the trails are covered with dust, and cracks can be seen in the soil of most areas not protected by vegetation. There is less plant diversity in the area than is found in a rain forest. It is a region of alternating stretches of forest and grassland. Pakak is part of a forest that follows both sides of a winding river from the lowlands to its headwaters in the mountains, a distance of around 40 kilometers. But, as the forest is seldom more than a kilometer wide at any one point and the banks of the river are very precipitous, the actual land available for cultivation is much less than it might appear. The lack of arable land is compounded by the fact that the forest is banked on both sides by *cogon grass, Imperata cylindrica.* Figure 1 is a schematic representation depicting a cross-section of Pakak.

The overall appearance of a Gaddang swidden (or farm site) depends upon the season and the number of years the land has been cultivated.[2] For example, a first year swidden, by the month of October, is a lush growth of ripening rice grain and an assortment of maturing beans, peas, tomatoes, squashes, and other vegetables. By February, which is part of the dry season, the same swidden appears barren and dull in color because the principal crop is tobacco. It is important to remember that a Gaddang swidden does not house a single crop. Throughout the year it will contain many different cultigens. In general, the people of the southern Gaddang area live a more marginal agricultural existence than the Gaddang living farther north. Their swiddens are less productive because, among other things, there is more grassland than usable forest land in their area.

Settlement, Labor, and Equipment

Among the Gaddang, the *tabalayan* ("one house") is primarily responsible for the preparation, cultivation, and harvesting of its swidden. The most common type of household is comprised of a nuclear family, consisting of husband and wife (polygyny is rare) and all unmarried children. But a household may also consist of a man and wife without offspring, a divorced or widowed person with or without offspring, or an adult celibate. Each household is an independent and self-sufficient economic unity. For example, there is very little labor cooperation between households, and the occasional surplus is not shared with other families but is used instead to obtain prestige goods and tools. As Geddes (1954:42) notes for the Land Dayak of Borneo, "A household is not only a distinct unit, but one which minds its own business." When felling large trees or during a rice harvest people do find it necessary to cooperate, and they do so on a contract basis. Kinship is an important part of Gaddang social organization, but economic cooperation is generally based on other factors. Except for a unique form of temporary "kinship" involving spouse exchange (see Wallace 1969), economic cooperation is more often than not based on friendship and sociability. I have observed cases among the southern Gaddang where old women maintain their own household, cultivate their own swidden, and assume full responsibility for their economic welfare. Neighbors and relatives assist them only when the job to be done is beyond their physical capability.

The members of each household occupy a single dwelling. If possible, a Gaddang family will construct its house in forested areas along hilltops. Such a location affords a degree of privacy, convenient access to swiddens, and a good vantage point for observing the surrounding countryside. There is considerable variation in the size and shape of Gaddang houses, the smallest house in Pakak having a floor space of 40 square feet, and the largest a floor space of 150 square feet. The houses average approximately 75 square feet in floor space. They are constructed on upright posts or trees serving as posts with the floor a yard or as much as three yards above the ground.[3] The walls may be of split bamboo, plaited bamboo, upright bamboo, a variety of grasses, or a combination of two or more of these. This assortment of building products found in the forest contributes to a variety of house types. House variation appears to be one of many expressions of the individuality of Gaddang households. There are no interior partitions and there is a single hearth area. The roof is of *cogon* thatching and the floor is of split bamboo. As a rule, very small houses are considered temporary residences while the family is preparing a new swidden. In actuality, many Gaddang never construct a larger and more durable type of house.

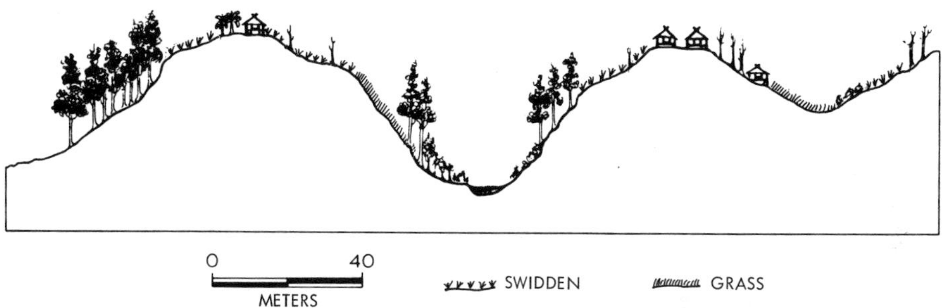

Gaddang households and settlements are small. At Pakak there is an average of four persons in each house, the largest three households consisting of six people and the smallest one person. There are fifteen houses at Pakak, eight of which are occupied, the others having been abandoned during the last six years. Although there are examples of close kin building homes near one another, there are no cultural prescriptions as to where a house must be situated within a settlement. Gaddang houses have no durable value and are abandoned when the new swidden is sufficiently distant to warrant the construction of a new house.

The only other semipermanent structure found around Gaddang settlements are granaries. They are more or less standard in size and shape. Roughly rectangular, with a floor area measuring about 30 square feet, the granary is built on four support posts and the floor is about one yard off the ground. The roof, arching downward from a central horizontal beam and extending almost to the level of the floor, is of *cogon* thatching. The walls are made of plaited bamboo and the floor is of closely aligned split bamboo. About a foot below the floor, circling the support posts, are round wooden disks which serve to keep rats and mice from climbing up the posts and entering the granary. A small ritually blessed bead is tied to the door to ward off intruders from the spirit world.

Because the rice granary is as important to a family as the dwelling house, great care is exercised in building it, and it is often better constructed than the house. Food is difficult to obtain in the Gaddang area, and the family supplies are carefully protected from weather, rodents, thieves, and supernatural agents.

Bushknives, axes, and digging sticks are the basic tools used by the Gaddang in clearing, planting, and cultivating. More elaborate forms of equipment are, however, used to protect the crops from animals. For example, watching shelters are constructed within the fields. The shelters have thatched roofs, are open on the sides, and the floors are one to two yards above the ground. The floor areas measure one to two square yards. Small lookouts are also placed in trees that have been pruned in a manner that leaves three or four outward projecting branches on which a floor can be easily constructed. A small grass or banana-leaf canopy is placed overhead. At Pakak there are two tree lookouts, the highest one being about three yards above the ground. A member of the household (often a child) goes to the watching shelter each morning during the rice season and watches the swidden until dark. Birds are a more serious threat to the rice than wild pigs or monkeys. At Pakak monkeys and wild pigs have seriously damaged a rice swidden only twice in recent years. Domesticated animals are no serious problem because they can be easily controlled.

Besides the obvious techniques of shouting and throwing sticks and stones to warn off intruders, noise-making devices and grass scarecrows are used. The noise-making devices are elaborately made, effective instruments. At the far edge of the swidden from the watching shelter, three-yard long pieces of bamboo are placed upright in the ground. In an area of 400 square yards there are eight to ten of these, spaced about three yards apart. The upright bamboo are notched at the top so that another equally long piece of bamboo may be horizontally attached, thus forming a T-shaped apparatus. The bar of the "T," however, is free to rock back and forth on a wooden cotter pin. As the "T" bar is always off center, it rests parallel to the upright. Each horizontal bamboo is attached to a long piece of rattan that runs to the watching shelter. The man in the watching shelter pulls two or three strings of rattan if he wants to lift the horizontal bamboo to form the "T." When he releases the rattan, the "T" bar drops against the upright making a clapping noise, and this, coupled with the movement of the many rattan strings that cross the swidden, functions as an effective means of frightening birds and other intruders away.

The Agricultural Cycle

The Pagan Gaddang living in Pakak divide the agricultural year into two seasons, the "rice-growing" (*abafini*) and the "other domesticated plant-growing" (*mamula*) seasons, the former lasting from about July to December and the latter from January to July. *Mamula* means "planting all cultigens other than rice." To refer to the non-rice season a Gaddang might say, *mamula si uma*, "cultigens, other than rice, growing in the swidden." The year begins with rice planting, and events are often associated with reference to a particular rice season. The basic steps of the Pakak agricultural cycle are presented in Table 1. It should be noted that informants do not consider fallowing an integral step in farming. The Gaddang have two terms pertaining to fallowing, *baratbat*, "to reclear a swidden," and *balat*, "to recultivate an old swidden," but, as will be shown later, fallowing and refarming are seldom practiced at Pakak.[4]

When a new swidden site is needed, the head of the household generally makes his selection during February or March. The common practice is to prepare a new site after farming the current one for three years. A new site may be cleared sooner if the current one needs enlarging or is unproductive. A poor yield one year will occasionally, though not always, prompt a person to enlarge his swidden the following year. In selecting it, all land is considered cultivatable except areas where *cogon* is present. Because almost all terrain in the area is either covered by *cogon* or forest, the primary consideration in se-

Table 1

Basic Steps of the Pakak Agricultural Cycle

Gaddang Term	Month	Activity
1. **busing**	February	Site selection and preliminary cutting.
2. **pidwana busing**	March	The second cutting.
a. **mataraw**		Trimming the trees.
b. **nauma**		The site is cut.
c. **magangu**		The felled materials are drying.
3. **sikulan**	May	Burning the debris.
a. **makat**		Piling the unburned debris for reburning.
4. **malandak**	June	Pulling the weeds from the site.
5. **makamel**	July	Cleaning the site.
6. **mimunaw**		A rice rite.
7. **mabini**	July	Planting the rice.
8. **mamula**		Planting other cultigens.
9. **amuwawan**	September	Protecting the swidden.
10. **mimunaw**	November	A rice rite.
11. **magani**	December	Harvesting the rice.
a. **mamilag**		Drying the rice.
b. **madot**		Tying the rice in bundles.
c. **minudu**		The rice is safely placed in the granary.
12. **mamula**	January	Planting other cultigens.

lecting a future farming plot is that the area be heavily wooded. The people of Pakak, then, select those areas which are potentially most productive to support their crops.

Little consideration is given to soils, drainage, stones in the soil, or the slope of the land. There are sites at Pakak characterized by poor soils, high erosion, numerous stones, and slopes of 60 degrees. Few slopes appear to be too steep for a swidden. Ideally, however, soils and the slope of the site are considered. There are three types of slope soils: (1) *murung*, "loam-like on flat land"; (2) *ḳarab*, "clay-like on hill slopes"; and (3) *ḳulud*, "clay-like on tops of hills." The most common type of slope soil at Pakak is *ḳarab*. Informants say, however, that if it were available in sufficient quantity, they would prefer *murung*.

The only cultural factor that prohibits a household from using a particular piece of land for a swidden, other than that the site already belongs to another household, is an encounter with a bad omen when the area is first visited for the specific purpose of surveying it as a potential farming plot. Informants agree that there are five kinds of these omens. If a man sees a snake hanging from a tree, if a kingfisher crosses his path, or if he hears a deer calling, a lizard chirping, or a child sneezing at the site, he will have to abandon his plans and go elsewhere. If he were not to do this, illness would surely befall his house. One family's misfortune, however, does not prevent another Gaddang from working the area. If the man sees no omens and he decides he wants the area for a swidden, he will cut some of the bush or perhaps a small tree. The cutting is more symbolic than functional. It marks the termination of the *busing,* that is, the site has been selected and the cutting has begun.

Conflicts over the selection of sites seldom occur. This can be attributed to the fact that Pakak is small and it is necessary to respect the needs and wishes of the other households to maintain harmony within the settlement. Once a man makes it known that he has chosen a particular site, his claim to the site is respected. No devices other than natural landmarks are used in defining the area. A Gaddang will let it be known that he will clear between, perhaps, a certain acacia tree and an outcropping of rocks. If a person were not to honor the swidden rights of another household, informants say he would be publicly ostracized and ultimately forced to leave the community. But, as noted, swidden disputes are uncommon. I was aware in 1965–1966 of only one dispute over a swidden in which a person was forced to leave the community.[5]

For purposes of convenience and economy of labor, a new swidden is located near an older one whenever possible. Informants say that if the new site is more than one-half hour walking distance from the old, a new house ought to be constructed. A swidden may be completely irregular in outline, the shape depending largely on the slope and general terrain while the size depends upon the needs of the household. The largest swidden area at Pakak farmed by a single household was 6,500 square yards and the smallest 200 square yards. A household may farm one or more plots. Sometimes the fields are contiguous and other times they are not. As in house size, the size of the swidden does not necessarily depend upon the number of people in the household. For example, the largest is farmed by only three people, while the smallest plot is farmed by a household of six. For the most part, in selecting a site a man considers the productivity of his present swidden and alternative sources of income, such as working in the lowlands, selling bamboo, rattan, or other forest products to lowlanders, or renting water buffalo (see Wallace 1967b).

The people of Pakak realize that they do not own, but rather have rights of usufruct to, the land they farm. The land is the property of the Philippine government, though in local practice the household has exclusive rights to its land and produce, even if the swidden is no longer under cultivation. That is, in order for a household to farm a swidden that has already been abandoned by another household, or for that matter to take a banana from it, they should obtain permission from the previous owners. Ideally, the occupants of Pakak pay a small land-use tax to the municipality to which Pakak belongs. Currently, however, only one man makes the five-hour hike to a nearby town to pay his tax.

Land clearing by means of utilizing bush knives and occasionally a digging bar and axe begins during the month of March. This work is the primary responsibility of the male head of the household, although he may occasionally be assisted by a neighbor or by older children. If there is no male in the household, a relative or neighbor will be called upon to help. Generally, the only time the aid of a neighbor or relative is needed is when felling trees sufficiently large to require cutting from a scaffold. Because reciprocity is the basis of economic cooperation, it is understood that if a man requests aid, he will also give aid. Cutting the site may take one day or a month, depending upon its size, the growth, and the speed at which a man chooses to work.

In clearing, a man starts with the bushes and grasses, gradually working up to the larger trees. The smaller trees and saplings are cut anywhere from a few inches to eight to ten feet above the ground. Large trees are generally left standing, but are frequently topped and their branches removed. There are two primary reasons why the large trees are pruned: (1) it is necessary to leave a few stripped trees standing to accommodate the climbing plants to be planted later, and (2) rice cannot tolerate shade. The critical feature in cutting a site is that it be completed about one month before burning so that the felled trees and bushes may dry. A recently cut swidden site is in appearance a scattered stand of naked trees projecting upward from a mass of cut grass, bushes, trees, and general debris, which is left as it fell and allowed to dry.

Informants say that a good burning of a new site is necessary for the healthy growth of their crops. That is, the debris in the site should be reduced to ash or well charred by the fire. Large trees and logs are, of course, more scorched than charred. A good burning then accelerates the process of decay and increases the amount of energy available for utilization by their domesticated plants, despite the fact that a considerable amount of nitrogen is lost in the burning. During April or May, aware that the heavy afternoon rains will soon commence, the farmer burns his swidden site. As in the preliminary steps in farming preparation, burning is done without any form of ritual, and assistance is not needed. Few preparations are made for controlling the fire. Unless their current swiddens or house structures are in imminent danger, the people of Pakak see no harm in the fire spreading beyond the designated burning area. The lack of concern for the control of fire is further illustrated by the random burning of *cogon* during the dry months of February and March. *Cogon* is burned so that after regeneration, fresh and more tender grass is available for water-buffalo grazing. The fires occasionally spread into the forest and destroy potential swidden sites.

If there is no strong wind, the site is burned from all sides. In cases of uneven burning, the smaller bushes and trees are thrown into piles and new fires are begun, or, in some cases, the debris is thrown into the forest. Stumps, trees, and large logs are not refired and lie among the ashes. For the next month the burned site, covered with ashes, charred materials, scorched logs, and general debris remains untouched by man, and the regeneration process brings forth new life.

In late June, new plants, drawing energy from the ashes and decomposed materials and nourished by the afternoon showers, begin to appear in the site. The appearance of this ground cover signals the people of Pakak that it is time to clean the site and prepare for the planting of their most important crop, dry rice. At this time, the members of the household carefully clear the ground of all new plants. Only stumps, large logs, trees, and stones are left intact. The site is then swept clear of all debris with a bamboo rake and transformed into a manicured swidden plot.

Two or three days before the planting of the rice, the members of each household gather in their house to perform the *mimunaw,* in this case a rice-planting rite. The ceremony is exclusively a household affair, and, except for a priest-medium—generally an old woman—it is not elaborate. It consists of little more than the cooking and eating of rice by all and the utterance of a prayer by the old woman asking that the rice be protected from disease, insects, and predatory animals.

Adults and older children do the planting, and occasionally two households will work together. The workers are generally related in some way or are working nearby fields. Whether the work is done by one household or more, the labor force is generally around five persons. During the planting, which takes about one day, the owner of the swidden expresses his appreciation to his helpers by having on hand food and drink for their midday and evening meals.

The mechanics of planting are relatively simple. Working together, the work force punch small holes in the ground, a few inches deep and about one to two feet apart, with a stick having a sharpened end. About ten rice grains are dropped into each hole. Little effort is made to plant straight rows, but the logistics of several people working in the small confined area brings order to the planting because the workers tend to work in rows. Rice is planted around stumps, trees, logs, and large rocks. The grain is not covered, and the area must be carefully watched to keep the birds away until there is a heavy rain to cover the seed.

As soon as the people of Pakak finish planting the rice, they immediately turn to planting other crops. As noted, all cultigens other than rice are classed by the Gaddang as *mula.* It is, however, permissible to say *tobaku* or *mula si tobaku,* both meaning "tobacco." At times, informants choose not to be specific about their cultigens and say *mula si natung*. The nearest English equivalent of *natung* is "vegetable." For example, squash, tomato, eggplant, beans, and peas. There is no term for fruit in Gaddang, as it is understood in English. It is necessary to use a specific term, for example, *mula si abat* (banana) or *mula si pinya* (pineapple).

Two of the important cultigens at Pakak planted during August are the lima bean and the wing bean or Goa bean. These annual vines are planted around the base of ten or more stripped trees in the swidden and climb up to three or four yards. As the fruits appear they are eaten regularly until they are gone. Some of the seeds are dried and saved for planting the following year. In addition, eggplant, cassava, and pineapple can be seen growing in the Pakak swiddens at this time. Eggplant is an important crop, and most of the households at Pakak plant about ten bushes each year. Cassava and pineapple, on the other hand, are relatively unimportant crops. Informants say that in the past, however, cassava was a Gaddang staple, but this is not currently the case. Only one man grows pineapples. (About fifty were planted, most of which produced small fruit. The fruits are eaten mainly by children between meals. They were planted along the edge of the swidden, and their spiny, thick, upward-projecting leaves served as a relatively good fence.)

By the time the other crops associated with the rice season have been planted, the swidden is dotted with immature rice plants. The plot is then placed under close surveillance to protect it from domesticated animals, wild pigs, monkeys, and birds. The people at Pakak are aware that lowlanders protect their rice from insects and disease with commercial insecticides, but they do not use them. Informants say they do not have the needed equipment and cannot afford to purchase the chemical solution. Unless the swidden is near a path frequently used by people or water buffalo, it is not protected by a fence. The one fence in Pakak borders the side of a swidden that is adjacent to the main path entering the settlement. As noted, the people of Pakak sit in shelters of bamboo and timber or tree lookouts while watching the swiddens during the rice season.

By late November the rice is mature and it is ready for harvesting. The day before the harvest a brief harvesting rite is held similar to that held at the time of the planting. Again, it is a household affair in which rice is eaten and a priest-medium utters a short prayer of appreciation.

Each household harvests its own rice crop. It is cut with a small hand tool and tied into small bundles. At the point of tying, just below the grain, the bundle is about two inches in diameter. One bundle is a *ta tak̜*, literally one *tak̜*. Eight small bundles are then tied together to form a *ta rot*, or one *rot*. There are approximately eight *rot* in one cavan or 2.13 bushels of rice. The Gaddang tie the rice for convenience in handling and storage. When available, a family of five will eat from six to eight *tak̜* of rice each day.

Because most of the members of a household share in the work, harvesting the rice takes an average of three or four days. The bundles of grain are carried to a nearby cage-like structure where they are left for two to three weeks for drying, after which they are removed to a granary. Two *rot* are placed in the corner of the granary and will not be touched, even if there is no rice to eat, until they are used at the rice-planting ritual the following year.

In 1965 the people of Pakak devoted approximately 20,000 square yards, about two hectares (one hectare=2.5 acres) of land, to rice. The individual swiddens ranged in size from about 800 to 6,500 square yards. One household planted rice in two swiddens, the others in only one. The yield from the total area cultivated was 125 *rot,* or roughly 64 *rot* per hectare. That is, the people of Pakak harvested an average of 8 cavans of rice per hectare, a very low figure. For example, Yengoyan (1960, and cited in Geertz, 1963) reports from 10 to 70 cavans per hectare for the Mandaya of the southern Philippines. Conklin (1957) reports up to and over 53 cavans per hectare for the Hanunóo of the Philippines, and Freeman (1955) notes about 33 to 44 cavans per hectare for the Iban of Sarawak. This variation in yields is not surprising considering the variation in technology and ecology found throughout Southeast Asia. The low yield at Pakak in 1965 is, at least in part, a result of the fact that the rice was afflicted with the stemborer. In 1964 the people of Pakak harvested about 28 cavans per hectare and in 1963 about 33 cavans per hectare. During these years the swiddens were relatively new, and informants say the crop was generally free of insects and disease.

I would estimate rice yields from first-, second-, and third-year swiddens at Pakak to be as follows: first year, 20 to 50 cavans per hectare; second year, 15 to 30 cavans per hectare; and third year, 10 to 20 cavans per hectare. (It should be emphasized that my estimate is only as reliable as the memory of my informants.)

Figure 2. A Pakak Swidden.

It is not feasible to plant rice four years in succession at Pakak. By the third or fourth year the fertility of the soil is insufficient to support the crop, and the *cogon* has almost completely taken control of the area. A household, therefore, needs to prepare a new swidden every three or four years. If suitable land is available, it is located near the old one, and if not it becomes necessary to move to a new forest. The people at Pakak had moved to their present location when their previous habitat became unsuitable for swidden farming.

After the rice harvest the rice stems are cut and left covering the ground for one month. During this time the bacteria and fungi go to work on the stems, bringing new fertility to the soil. The people at Pakak also begin to reclear the swiddens and prepare for the planting of their most important crop of the non-rice season, tobacco. They are also gathering on a day-to-day basis the cultigens planted along with the rice and planting new food crops. The crops planted at this time are sweet potato, mung bean, cowpea, sponge gourd, garlic, tomato, and millet. The complexity of the swidden increases as the year progresses. Figure 2 is a drawing of a Pakak swidden after the rice harvest.

Most of the people plant some sweet potatoes, although they are not a staple food crop. They are planted along the edge of the swidden, generally in the same area where the cassava was planted some months before. As the hairy vine grows, its dark green leaves spread and cover the ground.

Mung beans and cowpeas are often planted together. Although these plants will climb, at Pakak they are placed in small open areas and tend to trail along the ground. The long linear pods of the mung and the short pods of the cowpea are harvested in February. The largest area devoted to this crop at Pakak in 1966 amounted to 36 square yards.

Sponge gourds, garlic, and tomatoes are not economically important crops at Pakak, but each household attempts to grow a few of these. The sponge gourd is planted at the edge of the swidden, the crawling vine reaching a length of about ten yards and producing a rather bitter fruit. Garlic is planted in small plots of about one yard by two yards in size and is an important Gaddang condiment. Small bushes of tomatoes are scattered throughout the swidden, and the fruits are also used as a condiment.

Informants say that less than a generation ago millet was the important non-rice-season crop, second only to rice as a staple; only one household planted it in 1966. Millet demands a larger portion of a swidden, and the people at Pakak would rather devote the space to tobacco. It is planted, harvested, dried, stored, and cooked much like rice. The household that planted millet harvested a little less than one cavan from about 400 square yards of land.

Besides the cultigens already discussed, the following can also be found growing at different times of the year in some of the swiddens at Pakak: bananas, yams, taro, biter melon, swamp cabbage, spineless amaranth, leaf mustard, red pepper, papaya, and sugar cane, but often in small amounts. The most important of these is the banana. Grown near the houses or at the edges of swiddens, the Gaddang recognize twelve different types of banana, and as these perennials grow throughout the year some type of banana is always available as food. Yams and taro have potential economic importance, but few people at Pakak grow them and then only in very small numbers. Sugar cane is grown for the purpose of making wine.

It is noteworthy that betel and coconut palm are not grown at Pakak. Because they do not bear fruit until several years after planting, the people consider them an unproductive endeavor. They do not own the land they cultivate, and few expect to be in the area long enough to reap the fruits of many seasons.

Supplementary Income

Pakak and other southern Gaddang settlements under similar environmental conditions do not produce enough food to subsist for a full year. To supplement their basic rice and vegetable-growing economy, they grow tobacco; hunt and fish; work in the lowlands as day laborers during wet rice planting and harvesting; sell bamboo, rattan, and other forest products to lowlanders; and rent their water buffalo. On occasion they were seen stealing corn from lowland fields or acting as gleaners after the wet rice harvest.

Tobacco is the one cash crop at Pakak. Each year, in March, the flowers of the tobacco are cut and dried and the seeds removed and put aside until after the rice planting. The soil for tobacco seedling plots must be high in organic matter and free of *cogon,* otherwise the sensitive seedlings will develop poorly. Ideally, each household makes a seedling plot, but in 1965–1966 some households at Pakak did not, choosing rather to trade a part of their future harvest for the needed seedlings. The plots, carefully tilled with a digging bar, are about one by three or four yards in size. Planting is by broadcasting and a plot can produce several thousand plants. While the seedlings mature the bed is frequently weeded and the small plants are protected from animals and the weather with a fence and a grass canopy. By January they are ready to be transplanted.

A household spends two to four days preparing the swidden for tobacco planting, removing the rice stems and carefully weeding. Planting the seedlings is a slow process, and a household may spend a week or more accomplishing the task. Seven to ten days after planting the swiddens are checked, and the seedlings that did not take are replaced with new ones.

The leaves are hand primed over a period of two to three months, and special equipment is needed for harvesting and curing. A rack must be built on which to dry the tobacco. This rack, constructed of bamboo and timber, is about five yards square, a yard above the ground, and not enclosed. By February the lower leaves are pulled and "sticked." A one-inch piece of bamboo about a yard long is inserted through the proximal end of each tobacco leaf after it is pulled. It takes a man a month, working on and off, to make the sticks, and 1,000 leaves can be "sticked" in two days of consistent work. As the sticks are filled with tobacco leaves they are placed on the drying racks, and after about two weeks they are removed to the houses and stacked. Tobacco is pulled four or five times, and by late March or early April the flowers are cut and the seeds removed for the seedling plots of the following year. Besides working the tobacco fields, each household is also planting new crops and daily harvesting the existing cultigens.

Tobacco is sold by the bale. Each bale weighs approximately 125 kilograms, and the selling price in the lowland area near Pakak in 1966 was ₱ 90.00 (US $22.00) per bale. The people of Pakak took their tobacco down to the lowlands where a Cagayan Valley buyer set up a temporary buying station.

Approximately 1.6 hectares were devoted at Pakak to tobacco in 1966, the swiddens for this crop ranging from about 800 to 5,000 square yards. The yield from the total area farmed was eight bales, roughly 970 kilograms, or 625 kilograms per hectare. The national average native tobacco yield per hectare is 800 kilograms (Reed 1963:365). An important cause for the relatively low yield at Pakak is that the soils are not well suited for tobacco, and the technical knowledge and money required to achieve good yields are lacking. "In tobacco farming, every stage of cultivation must be carried out with the utmost care if satisfactory results are to be achieved" (Reed 1963:359).

In addition to growing tobacco, fishing, and, to a lesser degree, hunting, selling forest products, and working in the lowlands are important secondary economic activities. Fish are plentiful in the streams and a diligent fisherman can catch more than his family will consume. A large carp, for example, will bring enough rice in trade for three meals. The demand for bamboo in the lowlands, where most houses are constructed of bamboo, exceeds the supply, so the Gaddang cut bamboo in the forest where it is plentiful and float it down river for sale. A hundred sticks of quality bamboo will bring sufficient cash to purchase rice for one month. More remunerative, however, is the hiring out of water buffalo owned by many of the Gaddang. Water buffalo are of no use in swidden farming, but to the Gaddang they are highly valued because the more water buffalo a man has the more feasts he can give and the greater his wealth and status. Water buffalo are rented to lowlanders for 4 to 6 cavans of rice, sufficient to feed a household for four to six months. It must be emphasized, however, that not all Gaddang own water buffalo, work for wages, or trade in the lowlands. The extent to which a man actively engages in these secondary economic activities depends upon the productivity of his swidden, the needs of his family, and his desire to acquire wealth.

Summary and Discussion

Gaddang swiddens are an important feature of a complex ecosystem. Because the crops are planted at different times during the year, and because their maturation is not uniform, a swidden, with its intercropping and boundary cropping, is a mixture of foodstuffs for most of the year (see Conklin 1957:147). Ideal swiddens at Pakak, drawn and described by informants, contain about fifteen cultigens, but in actuality it is uncommon for more than ten different food plants to be growing at any one time. Ten to fifteen are less than the number cultivated by many other Southeast Asian peoples, but nonetheless swidden farming at Pakak is basically crop intensive.

Crop-intensive farming will not necessarily bring imbalance to an ecosystem, but at Pakak this is what happened. When I returned there eighteen months after my 1965–1966 study, I found the settlement abandoned.[6] Instead of rice and other crops, I found scrubby secondary growth and, more importantly, *cogon* in the gardens. With their technology the Pakak Gaddang modified their habitat to the point that the existing cultigens and other flora were replaced with *cogon*. Before leaving the field in 1966, I suggested that the Pakak ecosystem was in imbalance but moving toward a new equilibrium with *cogon* becoming the dominant vegetation (Wallace 1967a:122). My data led me to believe that the planting of a swidden three years in succession at Pakak could lead to a decline in soil fertility which would encourage the spread of *cogon*. As noted, it is impossible to successfully practice swidden cultivation on *cogon*-covered terrain. The people at Pakak overcultivated their land, which led to soil infertility and erosion, the spread of *cogon*, and ultimately to the necessity of abandoning the settlement.

The Pakak Gaddang were no less knowledgeable of the technological and ecological factors that allow for a more stable form of swidden farming than other Pagan Gaddang and other Southeast Asian peoples. They had reasonably good knowledge of soils, climate, burning and clearing techniques, planting, protection, and plant maturation. The Pakak Gaddang, however, were unaware of the need for controlled fallowing or failed to accept it as a necessary step in the agricultural cycle. Prior to arriving in Pakak, every household there had moved (usually a distance of 5 to 10 kilometers) an average of once every five years for the past fifteen years. When I asked an informant why he moved so often, he replied very simply, "There is always *cogon*." This is a truism, but it is not the complete picture. If the reader will allow me some speculation, I would like to suggest that the Pagan Gaddang move about periodically, or are truly shifting cultivators, because of the time-honored expectation that there will always be a new forest to cultivate. The Pakak Gaddang in particular and the Pagan Gaddang in general are running out of new forest lands. It appears that they will soon have to adjust their system of cultivation to meet the conditions of the existing forests, or abandon their traditional way of life and adopt a new technology based on the use of draft animals and the plow.

It may be added that Pagan Gaddang have found it increasingly necessary to abandon their traditional way of life for plow agriculture. In 1965–1966, I had the opportunity to study a Pagan Gaddang community, Cabanuangan, which had recently made the change-over. Because of technological and ecological factors similar to those I have described for Pakak, the Cabanuangan forest was replaced with grass. The Gaddang living there were confronted with the choice of either abandoning their traditional slash-and-burn system of farming for the water buffalo and the plow, or moving to a new forest where swidden cultivation could be practiced with success. Part of the population moved to Pakak, the others stayed in Cabanuangan. As those remaining in Cabanuangan turned to plow agriculture their total economic system underwent drastic change. Growing corn and tobacco, both cash crops, became the basis of agricultural activity at Cabanuangan. The abandonment of subsistence farming for cash farming forced them into a market-cash economy, and the new technology demanded new forms of cooperative labor arrangements. All these factors stimulated changes in social organization and religious beliefs (see Wallace 1967b).

It remains to be seen whether the Cabanuangan Gaddang will be able to adjust to their new technology and become productive Filipino farmers. My personal belief is that they will be able to make the transition from primitive to peasant, but in so doing they will lose their ethnic identity.

CHAPTER

8

Production, Distribution, and Power in a Primitive Society

MARSHALL D. SAHLINS

This paper proposes to examine the relationship between certain features of production, goods distribution, and political power in a kin-organized society, that of the island of Moala in the southeast of Fiji. The ethnographic materials to be utilized were collected by the author doing more than ten months of field work in 1954 and 1955. Moala is an island 24 square miles in area with a population of approximately 1,200 (all Fijian), settled in eight villages. The major units of social organization are patrilineal descent groups, various segments of which are localized in the villages. Leaders of certain descent-group segments operate as territorial chiefs within the unified, island-wide polity. Principal subsistence activities are growing root crops by swidden agriculture and raising wet taro. The culture has been subject to European influences. Involvement in the colony's monetary economy has been increasing of late. But thanks to British indirect rule, the native political and economic organizations are still operative, and their interrelationship is clear.

It will be shown that in Moala the ability of chiefs to exercise authority depends markedly on their ability to utilize prevailing distributive forms in order to dispense goods liberally in the community. Since strict reciprocity is not characteristic of these forms, those who play dominant roles in distribution are thereby impoverished rather than enriched. Furthermore, the possession and consumption of vital goods tends to be equalized rather than unequalized. While this result is paradoxical from a modern viewpoint, in

---

From *Men and Cultures, Selected Papers of the Fifth International Congress of Anthropological and Ethnological Sciences,* A. F. C. Wallace, ed. Philadelphia: University of Pennsylvania Press, 1960, pp. 495–500.

Moala it is adaptive and advantageous. For production in the local environment regularly and expectably engenders large and critical differences in the quantities of such essentials as foods acquired by individuals, families, and villages. Thus at the same time the system of distribution is a basis of political authority, it also constitutes an adjustment to local ecological circumstances.

Outside of the simple pooling of resources within households, the predominant method of goods distribution in Moala is known as *kerekere*. To kerekere is to solicit an item from a relative. Almost any type of goods, *viz.* food, money, mats, tools, clothes, tobacco, canoes, and so forth, can be requested by kerekere. One may also solicit labor services, such as help in garden work, or the services of the several types of part-time specialists. It is possible to kerekere usufructory rights to land from relatives in patrilineal descent groups (the land-holding units) other than one's own.

There are two critical characteristics of kerekere. The first is that the person making the request and the potential donor should be kinsmen. This does not actually restrict the operation of kerekere, for the existing classificatory kin terminology permits very widespread extension of kin ties. The avenues of kerekere open to any individual encompass just about everyone he meets. But always the ethic of mutual aid and solidarity inherent in kin relations rationalizes its practice. The second critical characteristic is that one should solicit a good or service only if there is a genuine need. One should not and usually does not ask for something in pursuit of greedy desires (*kothokotho*). By the same token, the only legitimate reason for refusing a request—except lack of the solicited item—is that the donor, by giving, would place himself in need. Even in that case a refusal is sometimes difficult and is usually awkward.

In a few forms of kerekere there is direct reciprocation for solicited items. This occurs primarily by way of recompense for solicited services rendered, or where goods have been specifically requested for short-time use only and then returned. But in most instances of kerekere, especially of goods, there is not even an implicit understanding that the recipient will return the goods or their equivalent by his own initiative. It is only implied that said recipient is bound (in the vague future) to honor any request made by the donor if the latter chooses to kerekere in return. An obligation to reciprocate merely exists insofar as the recipient of an item is made more accessible than otherwise to a future request by the donor. Should the donor kerekere in return, he will not ask for things equivalent to what he gave—only for that of which he is in need. The obligation to reciprocate is fulfilled whether or not the items secured by the original donor in a return kerekere are equal, greater, or less in value to that which he gave in the first instance.

Reciprocity may not occur at all. The donor of a thing might choose not to kerekere from the person to whom he has given something. Strict reciprocity is in fact not encouraged by an implication of prestige which attends the giving of a thing and an implication of inferiority attending soliciting a thing. To give is to indicate "strength," productive ability, while to ask is to admit "weakness," inability to produce sufficient for one's needs. A man usually humbles himself before a donor in making a request, while the latter assumes a dominant, patronizing posture. Moreover, it is not necessary for a man who has received a good from another to reciprocate (through the donor's kerekere) before requesting something else from the same person.[1] There may be a continuous series of one-way transactions between two people which tends to differentiate them in terms of social superiority. This, as will be shortly described, is the aspect of kerekere which lends itself to political manipulation. At this point, I would note that being based on considerations of need and allowing for a one-way goods flow, kerekere functions to equalize consumption in the face of possible differences in production.

Goods distribution has a specific relationship to chieftainship, the nature of which tends to strengthen chiefly authority. The greatest moral obligation incumbent on a chief is that of giving material aid to his people. Chiefs of villages and particularly the island paramount in the ranking village, Naroi, therefore become subject to a great deal of kerekere. But there is a critical difference between kerekere from a chief and kerekere from others. For a chief almost never solicits goods in the way of return for goods given by him; it would be a sign of "weakness" on the chief's part. How then is a chief able to satisfy the numerous requests which come from his inferiors? The answer is, primarily through the productive labor of himself and members of his extended family. The chief's family must work mightily to insure that the reserve on hand is sufficient to allow the chief to function adequately in his distributive capacity. If these resources should fail, the chief may send to a subordinate chief or to close relatives for the items required to satisfy a kerekere. Although identical in effect, chiefly demand is not considered kerekere—nor is it delivered as such—rather it is a request for what is his inherent due. So from household resources and occasionally from goods procured outside the household, chiefs honor the requests of those who come to them when in need. In return, chiefs reap the rewards of giving: the prestige, the acknowledged superiority, and the loyalty and continued support of the people. Thus political position is reinforced by a measure of economic control.

Succession to office may be influenced by the distributive role which a chief should perform. The primary qualification for succession to a chieftainship is high rank according to seniority of descent within the patrilineal group traditionally filling the position. But senior men descending in the line of first sons of former chiefs are sometimes passed over in selecting a successor because they lack productive ability or lack a large household—in short, because there is doubt that they could fulfill the economic obligations of chieftainship. A man of junior status having these qualifications may accede. Thereby is born a conflict between high rank and high office. Rivalry for power grows between the descendants of the ousted senior line and the offspring of a chief of junior rank, and this rivalry may continue over many generations. Every high chieftainship in the island polity is the center of a controversy of this sort. The rivalry is only intensified if the higher-ranking group manages to recapture leadership. The group out of power at the moment will repeatedly fail to comply with chiefly wishes and neglect to give the chief the proper forms of respect. At the same time, the chief and his nearest relatives hesitate to take suppressive action. In fact to take any measures that may be construed as oppressive would merely serve to arouse, possibly to violent action, those around the chief who are hostile to his rule.

An even more direct debilitating influence on chiefly power arises from the character of the distributive system. It is critical to note that distributing goods widely by kerekere is not a chiefly prerogative; anyone capable of doing it can and will.[2] Non-chiefly families, especially large ones, are often able to accumulate ample reserves of vital goods. They become subject to kerekere by less fortunate relatives, but with large reserves it is unnecessary to kerekere in return. The leader of such a family gradually accumulates prestige through his distributive activities. Moreover, he weans loyalties and support away from the local chief, since to some degree the chief is not given the opportunity to distribute goods. The chief's authority is challenged and weakened, for his distributive function has been usurped. Again power rivalries arise, and they are just as intense as those created by a succession of a person of inferior status to a chieftainship—in fact, they may lead to such a succession. There is mutual hostility between chiefs and those who challenge their distributive position, accompanied by widespread disinclination to acknowledge the status or even the rule of the chief. The degree of autocratic control that the chief might otherwise exercise is thereby checked.

We have seen the ways by which the system of goods distribution may both reinforce and limit political power. I shall now deal with an aspect of the cultural ecology which helps to account for the predominance of kerekere as a distributive mechanism. It is not implied that features of vital production in the local environment come first in an historical sense and the method of distribution developed in Moala as a response thereto. Certainly social, ideological, and other factors—even the distributive system itself—influence the manner of adaptation to the environment. It is irrelevant, however, in this context how one accounts for the methods of technological activity. Given the environment and the way in which it is exploited, certain characteristics of production result to which the remaining aspects of culture are and must be adjusted.

An outstanding aspect of food production in Moala is that there are large differences in the quantities of food raised by different individuals and families. *In a given village these variations amount to the difference between surpluses in some or all foods in certain households and food scarcities in others.* I am unable to state with precision the degree to which surpluses and scarcities exist, but the accompanying table of quantity differences in the major foods planted in the gardens of nuclear heads in Naroi in 1954 will give some indication. (The figures are not exact. Most men keep close track of the amount of food they plant, at least in round numbers, but I was able to check only a few of the numbers reported to me. Therefore, I would be unwilling to use these figures more than to indicate in crude terms the range of variation in planting. The figures are based in most cases on a sample of 30 of the nearly 50 nuclear family heads in the village. The sweet potato and dry taro amounts are based on a sample of 29.)

A variety of factors account for these differences in production. First, it should be noted that despite relatively dense population (50 per square mile), land available for swidden agriculture is not cultivated to its potential extent, and large families are easily able to expand their cultivations. The higher land of the island, relatively distant from the coastally located settlements, is usually covered with long reverted forests. Yet this is fertile land, and many are able to clear and plant there. Moreover, soil analyses undertaken by the Fiji Agricultural Department with samples I collected show that, even in areas closer to the villages, the usual period of reversion after cultivation is much longer than the minimum period necessary for soil recuperation. The land tenure rules are of sufficient flexibility to accommodate productive expansion. Lands at higher elevation are free to all comers. And if land nearer the village is insufficient for a large family or undesirable, it is an easy matter to kerekere usufructory rights from relatives.

As just implied, the available manpower in a family is a significant determinant of total household reserves. Some of the differences in Table 1 are due to the fact that certain of the men have mature sons whose labors considerably increase familial output. (Women do not take part in agriculture.) As a general rule, families with many male workers, few females, and immature children are able to accumulate larger reserves than families with fewer workers and more nonworkers—for in the latter case less is produced and more of that is consumed. Other factors contributing to differences in production include: variable fertility of planting sites due to soil and climatic conditions, differential occurrence of incapacitating illnesses, and differences in age, strength, agricultural skill, and personal motivation. (Such motivation, incidentally, derives partially from the rewards offered by kerekere—either the reward through dispensing aid or that of being able to garner a food supply through solicitation rather than production.)

A second feature of production to which I call attention is regional varia-

Table 1

Quantities of Major Crops Planted in Gardens of Family Heads, Naroi, 1954

	Yams (Mounds planted)	Wet Taro (Corms)	Cassava (Mounds)	Xanthosoma (Corms)	Sweet Potato (Mounds)	Dry Taro (Corms)
Total range in plantings per man	200–3400	0–4000	0–3000	0–1005	0–500	0–600
Interquartile range (middle 50% of cases)	400–700	400–1300	150–500	150–500	130–300	0–200
Mean planted per man	734	1000	428	369	213	165

tion in the quantities of various types of food produced. In different locales, variations in rainfall and sunlight, and of waters and topography necessary for irrigation, produce different potentials for growing the several types of crops. The Moalans are aware of the conditions required by their crops and plant accordingly. As a result, different villages tend to produce more of certain crops, one village more yams, one more wet taro and so forth. Table 2, indicating averages of the planting per family heads in three different villages, describes the nature of regional variation in production. The villages are Naroi in the extreme northeast of the island, Keteria on a deep bay in the eastern or windward coast, and Nuku on the westernmost point of Moala.

Regional, individual and familial variations in quantity of food production are key characteristics of the Moalan economy which help account for the predominance of kerekere as a distributive mechanism. Food scarcity is a daily possibility in any number of houses in a village, while at the same time other families may have a surfeit of food. Moreover, a family abundantly supplied one day may run short on the next. But kerekere, being predicated on need and operating through widespread networks of kin relationship, is an effective means for alleviating these innumerable crises and potential crises. Kerekere may easily be invoked on a moment's notice to procure food (or other vital goods) from any available source. Similarly, kerekere as it is invoked between members of different villages spreads the consumption of regionally diverse produce. Through kerekere individual and local differences in production become contributions to the general welfare in a material sense, while large-scale producers derive nonmaterial compensations for their efforts. Kerekere is a simple, efficient, and advantageous means of goods distribution when one takes into account the method and results of vital production in the local environment.

In summary, production, distribution, and political power comprise a functionally related system. The predominant form of distribution, kerekere, is an effective mechanism for adjusting inequalities occasioned in the produc-

Table 2

Average Plantings in 1954 by Family Heads in Three Villages

	Naroi (sample as above)	Nuku (N=13, all family heads)	Keteira (N=16, all but two family heads)
Yams (mounds)	734	371	371
Wet taro (corms)	1000	3200	1875
Cassava (mounds)	428	219	354
Xanthosoma (corms)	369	175	47
Sweet potato (mounds)	213	19[a]	52
Dry taro (corms)	165	117	293

[a] Time usually given to planting occupied by building new village water-supply outlets in 1954.

tive exploitation of the environment. Dispensing goods widely by kerekere contributes markedly to a person's prestige; hence, chiefs attempt to engage in the system on a large scale as a means of reinforcing their standing and extending their authority. But because such manipulation of the distributive system cannot be solely restricted to chiefs, kerekere may foster a type of rivalry which debilitates the power structure and produces an atmosphere of militant egalitarianism.

If there is one outstanding implication of this study, it is that a crucial investigation is yet to be made into the types of distributive systems of the primitive world, their bases in production, and the measure of economic control they bring to the prevailing power structure. This analysis provides the hope that such an investigation might permit formulation of broad propositions relating economic and political development in kin-organized societies.

Addendum

In conversation subsequent to the presentation of this paper, Professor Raymond Firth suggested that explicit mention be made of the problems raised by kerekere in conjunction with the introduction of a monetary economy. In concurrence with the suggestion, I would point out that kerekere, while adaptive under traditional conditions, is an impediment to the transition to a monetary economy. The difficulty is occasioned by the multitudinous claims laid through kerekere on the hard-earned goods procured by individuals through copra production. Accumulation of capital is thereby discouraged despite many economic and social pressures, having the opposite effect.

CHAPTER

9

Ponapean Prestige Economy

WILLIAM R. BASCOM

The inhabitants of Ponape,[1] second largest of the Caroline Islands in Micronesia, have a system of prestige competition reminiscent in some ways of the potlatch of the American Indians of the Northwest Coast, but with a distinctive character deriving from the Ponapean pattern of modesty. Instead of the distribution and destruction of property that marks the potlatch, contributions of certain foods to community feasts are the traditional means of achieving status.

For the purposes of analysis it is useful to distinguish between the subsistence economy, the commercial economy, and the prestige economy. The first concerns food, clothing, and other subsistence commodities which are consumed locally, generally by the household which produces them. The second relates to the commodities produced for export and sold to obtain money with which to purchase clothing, hardware, and a variety of imported goods for which Ponape has become dependent upon the outside world since contact. The prestige economy involves the goods through which social approval and social status are gained; as in the case of subsistence goods, these are consumed locally, but they are shared with other households within the Section.[2] Although, as might be expected, there is some overlapping, most goods fall clearly within one or another of these three categories as far as their primary function is concerned.[3] The foods consumed at feasts contribute to the Ponapean diet, but those which are important in prestige competition are set apart from subsistence foods by

From *Southwestern Journal of Anthropology,* 4:211–221, 1948. By permission of the author and publisher. Read, in part, before the American Anthropological Association in Albuquerque, New Mexico, December 28, 1947. Field work on Ponape during the four months of May through August was carried on in 1946 as a part of the US Commercial Company's Economic Survey of the Trust Territory. Further details are available in microfilm at the Library of Congress in W. R. Bascom, *Ponape: a Pacific Economy in Transition,* which is being used in the preparation of a handbook on the Eastern Carolines by Felix Keesing and his staff.

the objectives which motivate their production as well as by the patterns which surround their consumption.

Yams, pit breadfruit, kava, and pigs are the basis of the prestige economy associated with feasting, Ponape's commercial economy, on the other hand, is based on copra, while in the subsistence economy fresh breadfruit is more important than either yams or breadfruit which has been preserved in leaf-lined pits.[4] Neither coconuts, nor fresh breadfruit, nor the variety of seafoods which are essential to the Ponapean diet, enter into the traditional prestige economy. Nor can the Ponapean's interest in yams be explained in terms of their importance in either the commercial or the subsistence economy.

The characteristic love of the Ponapean for his own farmstead and his reluctance to leave his own land to seek wage labor, which led the Japanese to import labor from other islands before the war and to resort to forced labor during the war, are related to his interest in growing yams for competition. His motivations and attitudes towards work cannot be explained simply in terms of a desire to earn enough money to purchase necessary imports and to produce enough food to keep himself and his family from hunger. Not infrequently families go hungry at home when they have large yams in their farms ready for harvest. Only small yams are used at home for subsistence purposes; prize yams are saved for feasts. Each family is said to grow about fifty yams each year solely for the purposes of feasting.

The feasts (*ḳamatipw*) about which competition centers usually take place from September to December while yams are being harvested. This season is opened and closed by two large feasts given for the District chief's by each Section. Until late in the German period of administration (about 1912) these two feasts were among the various forms of tribute required from commoners in return for the use of the land, which was owned by the District chiefs. When the Germans issued private titles to individual land holdings, the number of required feasts for the chiefs was limited by the government to one a year; but the intermediate feats, which were voluntary and which were the most common occasion of prestige competition, were not restricted. Under the Japanese the prohibited feasts were revived and all forms of feasting seem to have flourished until the war.

No large feast can be given without kava and one or more pigs. The prestige earned by the host through giving a feast is related to the number of pigs and kava plants which he provides, the size of the pigs, and the length of their tusks. Yams and pit breadfruit may be contributed by any member of the host's section. Pit breadfruit are important contributions, but they are not as commonly used at feasts as yams, which seem to be the basis of active and continuing prestige competition. Rarely are more than one or two pit breadfruit brought to a feast. It is only if an exceptionally large and important feast is being arranged that each member of a section agrees to contribute a pit breadfruit, and none at all is brought to most feasts.

Each head of a farmstead contributes a yam, in addition to other food, when a section feast is given. Everyone present examines and compares the yams as they are brought into the feast house, and praises the largest yam for its size and quality. They go up to the man who, in their opinion, brought the best yam to tell him that he is "Number One." The commoners praise him for his skill and ability as a farmer; the chief praises him for his generosity.

As far as any standards of generosity are concerned, the rules of competition are artificial and arbitrary. Contributions of fresh breadfruit, fish and other seafood, coconuts, taro, bananas, and other foods do not count. It is the size of the individual yam, and not the quantity of yams that is important. A man cannot win prestige by bringing a large number of small yams to a feast. Each yam, furthermore, must have only a single vine, even if it grew from a single cutting; otherwise it is regarded as several small yams.

In the case of pit breadfruit, it is age rather than size that counts. Just as Ponapeans respect a host who serves his guests left-over food, so they praise a man for having kept a pit breadfruit for many years without having eaten it. Both show the abundance of food he has provided. Pit breadfruit (*ma:r*) is not brought to a feast until it is at least ten years old. It will keep almost indefinitely as long as its leaf wrapping is changed annually, and its flavor improves with age. One pit breadfruit on Ponape is said to date from before the small pox epidemic of 1853, almost 100 years ago. Portions of pit breadfruit may be removed and used for subsistence purposes, and the pit breadfruit may be replenished by adding fresh breadfruit to it when it is rewrapped. In such cases, as in the case of blended whiskey, its age for competition purposes is dated from the oldest portion. Pieces of pit breadfruit which are cut off and taken to feasts count for no more than contributions of bananas or fresh breadfruit. In order to count in competition, the pit must be emptied. The entire pit breadfruit, leaf wrapping and all, is taken out of the ground and carried to the feast house slung in a "nest" (*pă:s*) between two poles borne by four to twenty men, with one to five men at each corner. Pit breadfruit are said to contain from 3,000 to 10,000 breadfruit and to be from four to six feet thick and six to nine feet in diameter.

Yams (*ķă:p*) are classified according to size by the number of men required to carry them. The largest size is known as pă:s from the "nest" or sling between two poles in which it is carried, like pit breadfruit, by four to twelve men. If two men are required the size is *ķă:i* and the yam is suspended from a single pole between their shoulders. A yam which one man can carry is known as *ķă:ptăwăn*.

On the basis of shape the native varieties of yams grown on Ponape can be classified into five types: (A) single yams, which are long and slender, and often three to twelve inches in diameter and two to ten feet in length; (B) bunches of long slender yams, similar to those in the first group, which are attached to each other at the top, giving an overall diameter of several feet for the bunch; (C) "branchy" yams, which have many "branches" or roots coming out irregularly in all directions from a central core, giving an overall diameter of several feet; (D) single spherical yams about twelve inches in diameter; and (E) groups of separate, unattached yams about six inches in diameter growing from a single vine.

Although it is size and not quantity that counts in prestige competition, the shape or variety of the yam is taken into consideration. A very large single yam of type A, which requires only two men to carry it, may be judged best at a particular feast rather than a larger, but not really outstanding bunch of type B, which is always carried by four men. The yams most highly prized for feasting are varieties of these two types, although occasionally "branchy" yams of type C have been acknowledged as the largest. Type D, which is too small to be "good for feasting," and type E are both cultivated but not used in competition. The roots of type E count as several yams even though they have a single vine. On the other hand, if there is a single vine, a bunch of type B counts as a single yam because the roots are attached together at the top.

That Ponapeans are able to grow yams of enormous size cannot be doubted. Their reputation has spread at least as far as Truk, where yams are of minor importance. It is said that yams of the best-liked variety, of type B, have reached as much as nine or ten feet in length and three feet in overall diameter, with the individual roots which make up the bunch each about three inches in diameter. Several varieties of yams which ordinarily grow to about six feet on Ponape, may reach ten, twelve, and even fifteen feet if grown with special care in steep places on the side of a hill. A reliable informant told of having seen a yam weighed on a scale at 100 kilograms, or 220 pounds. This was not a competition yam, but one which was being sold to a Japanese for food purposes. First-hand weights and measures of prize yams could not be obtained because of the season during which field work was done, and because of the secrecy which surrounds yam farming.

Success in prestige competition is regarded as evidence not only of a man's ability, industry, and generosity, but also of his love and respect for his superiors. The latter is most important as a qualification for holding a title in the eyes of the section and district chiefs who appoint and promote those beneath them. Devotion to the chiefs may be shown in other ways as well, but the accepted pattern through which it is formally expressed is by giving feasts in honor of the chiefs and by contributing large yams and old pit breadfruit to the feasts given by others.

Each Section chief watches to see which men consistently bring the largest yams and chooses them to fill Section titles which are vacant or, if they already have a title, promotes them to higher rank. When the Section chief is not present at a feast, his people tell him who brought the largest yam. The Section chief in turn reports to the District chief, so that a man who consistently brings large yams may be appointed to fill a vacant District title for which he is eligible by virtue of his hereditary or ascribed status. Within the limits set for him by his membership in one of the twenty-three matrilineal clans, he may thus win actual status as well as praise and social approval.

However much personal satisfaction a man may derive from the praise he receives when he contributes a very large yam or a very old pit breadfruit, he must not show his pleasure unduly. He must not act proudly or boast openly about his achievement. When others discuss the merits of his yam, he pretends not to listen. When they come up to tell him that his yam is the largest, he protests that it really isn't. He points to the next largest yam, claiming that it is better than his own. He goes over to its owner and tells him that *he* is "Number One." The latter, of course, also protests. A man who shows his pride openly is talked about and laughed at, and his prestige is turned to shame.

Modesty and sensitivity to ridicule are important aspects of the Ponapean personality. There are few situations in which a Ponapean can show pride in his accomplishments or his possessions without fear of criticism for pretentiousness or "acting big" (*a:ḳilapalap*). Fear of unfavorable comment and gossip is sufficiently strong to enforce what to the outsider seems to be a pattern of exaggerated modesty and humility that pervades most social situations. A Ponapean who approaches an employer in search of work, without waiting to be asked, is considered forward. Ponapeans regard it as boasting to state their qualifications for a job even when they have been asked to apply for it. The best carpenter on the island may deny that he can build a house, or that he is a carpenter. If asked where to find one, he would probably reply, "Oh, I am sorry. There are no good carpenters on Ponape." This is but one of many occassions when Ponapeans deprecate their personal abilities and possessions.

In the case of prestige competition, this pattern of modesty is enforced not only by the desire to avoid ridicule for pretentious behavior, but also by fear of being shown up in the future. The man who is acclaimed "Number One" does not dare to ridicule or laugh at the man with the second largest yam, or even the man who has brought the smallest one, for fear that they may bring larger yams than he does to the next feast. The assumption is that no one ever brings his largest yam or his oldest breadfruit to a feast, but keeps it in reserve in case someone challenges him. A man who is challenged may actually bring several very large yams to the following feast and demand of his challenger, "So you said I couldn't grow any large yams?" and if the challenger has not brought larger yams himself, he is publicly shamed. A comment which is commonly made while praising a man who has brought a pit breadfruit to a feast is "And what about the other one?" referring to the one which is kept in reserve and which is certain to be even older than the one he has brought.

While most forms of property are apologized for unnecessarily, they are displayed openly. Yams, pit breadfruit, and kava, however, are matters of great secrecy. Answers to questions about their number, or about the age of a man's pit breadfruit and the varieties of his yams are evaded or deliberately falsified. A man may try to ignore such questions or reply that he has planted only a few yams or none at all, or he may lie about the size and the age of his pit breadfruit. Information of this kind is concealed in the hopes that the element of surprise may enable the owner to surpass his neighbors at future feasts. In a way such questions are comparable to those asked of an automobile manufacturer by a competitor about his production goals, the details of his next year's model, or other information which is generally accepted as a trade secret.

It is impolite to look at another man's yams, and anyone caught doing so will feel the shame of gossip and ridicule. When visiting another man's house, a Ponapean pretends to ignore even the yams growing near the house, although yams planted so openly are for subsistence rather than for prestige competition. The best and largest yams are grown in parts of the farmstead which are as far away from the house and any paths as possible, and often heavily overgrown with bush. Breadfruit pits and kava plants are also hidden away in remote and inaccessible parts of the farmstead. Members of the household or the clan, male and female, cooperate in making pit breadfruit, but the growing of yams is an individual affair which a man does by himself.

Yam planting was formerly carried on in as much secrecy as football practice or spring training among ourselves. A farmer got up at two or three in the morning to plant his yams or tie their vines. Working in the dark so that no one could see him, he finished before dawn. Only a few old men take this much trouble today, but yam planting is still secret. When they were interned by the Japanese during the war the two Belgian families on Ponape found that, in spite of the urgency of their need for food, they could not get their servant to grow yams in the yard because he did not want them to see how it was done. After 1921 cooperative work groups became very popular on Ponape, but they never helped a man in farming yams or even in harvesting breadfruit, under which yams are commonly planted.

Whereas fertilizer is used for taro throughout most of Micronesia, on Ponape it is used only in growing yams. Very large yams, such as are desired in competition, can be produced only by selecting a good variety of yam, good soil in a good location, the correct time for planting and harvesting, and in addition by digging very large holes, preparing them correctly with alternating layers of earth and leaves or grass, using large enough cuttings, trimming and training the vines properly, and protecting them effectively from pigs, cows, and other animals. The labor expended in growing prize yams is far greater than would be necessary to produce the same quantity of foodstuff from a larger number of smaller yams of the same variety. Ponapeans can, if they are willing, describe in detail the best way to grow large yams, but questions about the yield per acre or total production in relation to the amount used as seed have little meaning since the objective is size and not quantity.

The social importance of yams is reflected in the skill and care used in growing them, and also in the interest in yam varieties and their characteristics and histories. At one sitting an informant was able to name ninety-nine varieties of yams. It is doubted that many corn farmers from Iowa, wheat farmers from the Dakotas, or apple growers from Washington could do better with the crops on which they are economically dependent. Without by any means exhausting the subject, one hundred fifty-six native varieties of yams were recorded, together with their shape, size, color, and other characteristics, and in many cases the periods when they were first planted on Ponape, the names of the men who first planted them, and the districts and sections in which this was done. A striking contrast is furnished in the case of bananas, which are important in the subsistence economy but to which no prestige is attached. In spite of the fact that all three of the worm-resistant varieties which everyone uses today were introduced recently, in the Japanese period, the informants questioned could not name any of the men who introduced them. Interest is shown in all varieties of yams, old or new, even when these are too small to be used in competition. This interest is not distinctive of yams, but rather is characteristic of the Ponapean pattern of agriculture, and is to be seen in the continued attempts to grow the older native varieties of bananas, all of which have been rendered practically useless by the recent introduction of the banana worm.

The appearance of new varieties is dated in terms of the Japanese (1914–1945), German (1899–1914), and Spanish (1886–1899) administrations, the period between first outside contact and the establishment of Spanish rule (1826–1886), and the period before contact (before 1826). Before contact, if informants today are correct, few varieties of yams were grown on Ponape. Most of the current varieties date from the pre-Spanish period. Ponapeans were eager to experiment with the new varieties from South America and the Pacific islands which they obtained from the early whaling and trading vessels. Other new varieties were brought back by Ponapeans who visited New Guinea and less distant places.

New varieties of yams are also discovered locally when known varieties that have been planted grow into yams with different characteristics. These local variants (*ḳi:ěwěḳ* or *ḳilimanip*) may differ from the parent variety in the shape or color of the root, leaves, or vine, and these changes are stable, reappearing year after year. To take a specific variety as an example, *Kunuḳuntha* or *ḳi:ěwěḳ ěn Tamwěroi* was discovered locally in the Japanese period by the uncle of the wife of the present chief (Nanikěn) of Nět District, who acted as informant. It was named for the chief's daughter (Kunukuntha), because it was discovered on the day she was born. Its alternate name refers to the fact that it is a local variant discovered in Tamwěroi Section of Nět District. The new variety has white flesh and consists of bunches of two or three roots, each about six inches in diameter, giving an overall diameter of about twelve inches, and is about two feet long. The cutting from which it grew came from a variety (*ḳǎpin Na:npe:lam*) with reddish flesh and a single root about twelve inches in diameter and five feet in length, which was first grown on Na:npe:lom farmstead on Lǎngǎr Island in Nět District in the Spanish period.

The appearance of a new variety of yam is an important event. When one is first brought to a feast there is great excitement. Everyone gathers about it to examine its shape, its color, and its skin texture, and to measure its size in hopes that they may later raise a larger one of the same variety. They also gather about the man who brought it, asking what he has named it, what kind of a vine it has, what it tastes like, when he planted it, how long it takes to grow, and to try to buy cuttings from him. The man in turn is pleased by the interest shown in his yam and their desire to plant it. He gains more prestige than whoever may have happened to bring the largest yam to the feast.

Prestige from the introduction of a new variety of yam extends beyond the boundaries of his section. As the news spreads, people from all parts of the island come to him to ask for cuttings, hoping to be the first to introduce it into their own District or Section. He has the privilege of naming the new variety, and if it is one of which he can be proud, he usually gives it his own name. Whatever name he chooses, he is known wherever he goes as the man who introduced it. When he is a guest at a feast in which the largest yam is one of his own variety, he receives more praise and personal satisfaction than the man who actually grew it.

A new variety of yam is not immediately presented at a feast. In one case a variety (*Na:liklapalap*) which had been given to a chief (Na:liklapalap) of Kiti District by Mr. Grey, an American missionary, in the early part of the German period, was not introduced publicly until the Japanese period, at the very least seven years later. A man who finds or introduces a new variety always waits for several years until he has grown about a hundred yams from it. He would be ashamed if he had to refuse requests for cuttings because he did not have enough. He plants the new variety in the most secret parts of his farmstead and in the meantime he may let the news of his discovery be known so that people may speculate about it. Word of this kind spreads rapidly over the whole island, so that everyone is discussing the new yam years before it is shown to anyone. An announcement of the discovery of a new variety of yam which had not yet been introduced or given a name was made in my presence on Ponape in 1946 by a chief (*Na:ni:thlapalap*) of Kiti District. Although it was made in a casual and offhand manner in keeping with the Ponapean pattern of modesty, it was apparent that he was concealing his pleasure with difficulty.

In conclusion, economic goods in the form of the yams and pit breadfruit contributed to feasts by the participants, and the pigs and kava provided by the hosts, are the basis of prestige and achieved status on Ponape. Contributions of other foods are not socially significant. Although subsistence foods may be consumed at feasts, they do not count in prestige competition. With the exception of kava, which commoners were fobidden to drink except at feasts, the prestige foods may be used by individual households for subsistence purposes, but in this case only small yams, young pigs, and portions of pit breadfruit are consumed. Prestige foods are distinguished from subsistence foods by the attitudes and behavior associated with their production and consumption, in particular by the secrecy surrounding and the objectives motivating the production of kava, pit breadfruit, and large yams. Secrecy is lacking only in relation to pigs, which forage for food much as they please.

The distinction between subsistence and prestige economies has been made previously.[5] The additional category of commercial economies, suggested here, should prove equally useful,[6] particularly in acculturation studies and possibly also in dealing with cultures, such as those of West Africa, with a money economy and considerable inter- and intratribal trade.

Contributions of prestige foods to feasts are arbitrary as measures of generosity, in terms of which they are judged by the chiefs. They are, however, related to an individual's skill in farming, to his industry, and to his ability to produce more food than he requires for subsistence purposes. The production of yams of the size suitable for feasting, in particular, requires both skill and industry to a degree that cannot be explained in terms of the subsistence or the commercial economy alone. Industry is likewise required in the preparation of pit breadfruit for feasting, and also in the production of sufficient quantities of other foods so that the breadfruit pits do not have to be emptied for subsistence purposes.

The overproduction of food, as a basis

of achieved status, has Melanesian parallels, but there is no evidence of the conspicuous waste of food comparable to eating to the point of vomiting at a feast, or allowing yams to rot in front of the house. Food that is not consumed at Ponapean feasts is shared according to rank and taken home to be eaten later. The public display of a yam harvest is incompatible with the pattern of secrecy. Yams are left in the ground where no one can see them until they are consumed. Parallels to Polynesia are to be seen in the institution of chieftainship, and the emphasis on lineage affiliations as a basis of ascribed status. In other aspects of culture also, parallels to both areas are to be found.

Yams which are left in the ground eventually sprout again—most varieties at the beginning of the rains in the spring. Some of the largest yams are produced by allowing them to grow for five or ten years, transplanting them annually to new holes. For several months after they sprout they are "rotten" and cannot be harvested. As a result of their desire for secrecy, Ponapeans cannot enjoy their favorite vegetable food as often as they would like during this season. Nevertheless the social advantages of the Ponapean pattern of prestige competition are readily apparent. The value of production beyond foreseeable subsistence needs is emphasized and industry is rewarded. This emphasis is reflected in the Ponapean's interest in agriculture and in his own land. It has meant that, in a favorable environment, Ponapeans have seldom experienced serious shortages of food. Pit breadfruit and yams, neither of which are destroyed by the tropical storms of the Pacific, constitute important food reserves against periods of shortage, particularly in view of the limited number of ways in which food is preserved on Ponape. Typhoons, which may destroy a year's crop of breadfruit and which frequently produce starvation conditions on neighboring islands, have little effect, by comparison, on Ponape, where the traditional famine foods of the Pacific are relatively unimportant.

From the sociopsychological point of view, the Ponapean data underscore an important point: that competition is not necessarily associated with aggressive behavior. The retiring modesty of the Ponapeans, even in comparison with the peoples of neighboring islands of Micronesia, could have been more fully documented than has been possible in this article.[7] Yet it is coupled with a system of winning prestige and status which is almost as competitive as that of the "Dionysian" Kwakiutl.

CHAPTER

10

Trading in Northeast New Guinea

THOMAS G. HARDING

Broadly speaking, there are two ways in which the benefits of specialization of labor may be realized: exchange of goods among the specialist producers, and redistributive allocation by a central agency. The redistributive role of chiefs was a prominent aspect of the regional economic organization of many Polynesian and Micronesian societies, but in Melanesia the exchange mode was dominant.

This chapter is concerned with Melanesian patterns of exchange as seen among village communities in northeastern New Guinea. This was one among a number of Melanesian subareas in which regional exchange systems developed on an elaborate scale. A principal task will be to describe, concisely, the exchange system's dimensions, components, and operations. Additional aspects of trading, such as the impact of trade on local economy, have been chosen for separate analysis. The discussion depends implicitly, at times explicitly, on comparisons with patterns of regional exchange found elsewhere in Melanesia, particularly in the well-known *kula* ring of Papua (see Chapter 6). Although trading achieved a distinctive configuration in northeastern New Guinea, numerous features are paralleled in other regional systems.

The Trade System of the Vitiaz Strait

Regional trading in the Vitiaz (pronounced vit-ee-ahs′) Strait persists in

---

Field work in northeastern New Guinea in 1963–1964 was supported by a grant from the National Science Foundation and a Research Training Fellowship awarded by the Social Science Research Council. Field work in the winter of 1968 was made possible by grants from the National Science Foundation and the University of California at Santa Barbara.

In writing this chapter I have benefited from past discussions with Michael P. Freedman, who studied the Siassi community of Mandok.

semitraditional form despite over eighty years of Western cultural influence. However, because my interest in the present context is the aboriginal system, I have elected to speak in the past tense even though many of the features described were observed, in pretty much traditional form, in the 1960's (see Harding 1967a).

The trade system enclosed an extensive land-and-sea area: the mainland of northeastern New Guinea from modern Bogia, northwest of Madang, to Finschhafen and around the Huon Gulf to Morobe Harbor in the southeast, together with a portion of the Bismarck Archipelago (western New Britain and neighboring islands). Mainland and archipelago are separated by the Vitiaz Strait, a passage about 200 miles long and 30 to 40 miles wide, which forms the main waterway for overseas trade. Several hundred communities, ranging in size from less than 100 to nearly 1,000 persons, participated to varying degrees in exchange. The total population of the region was about 150,000.

It is not possible here to examine the specialized subregions and actual geographical patterns of exchange, although the main types of communities and larger units composing the system, and their spatial interrelationships, can be described in schematic fashion (see Figure 1). The system was centered on three groups of overseas traders: the Bilibili Islanders in the western part of the Strait, the Tami Islanders in the southeast who had the Huon Gulf as their special preserve, and the centrally situated and largest group, the Siassi Islanders. The regular voyages of these trading peoples, in large twin-masted canoes of uniform design, linked the various communities and subregions in an embracing trade system. Their fields

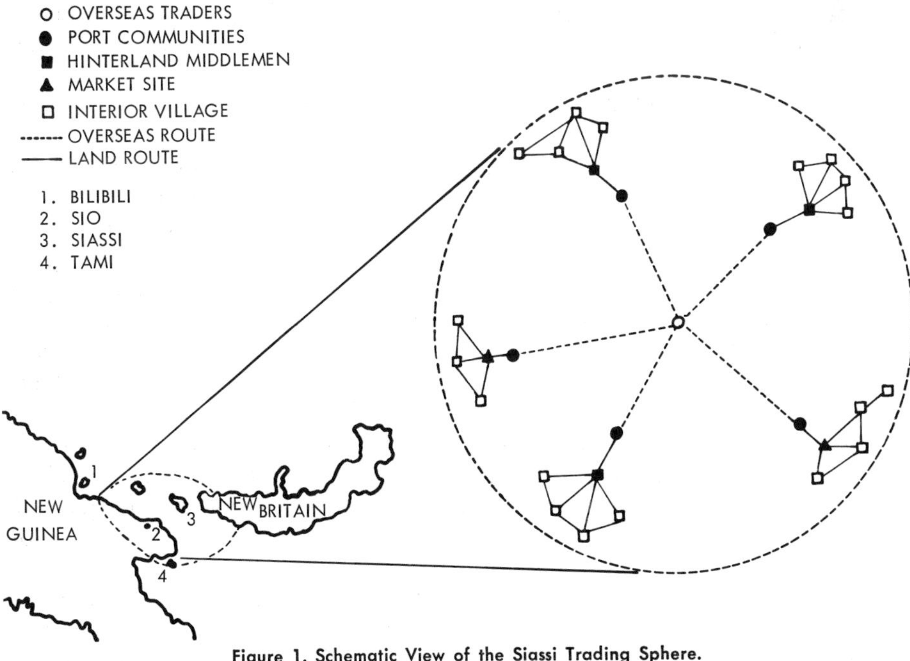

Figure 1. Schematic View of the Siassi Trading Sphere.

of operation overlapped, those of the Siassis and Bilibilis along a 100-mile stretch of the Rai Coast, those of the Tamis and Siassis along the coast of the Huon Peninsula and in southern New Britain. Relations between the Siassis and Tamis, in particular, were frequent and cordial. Although monopolies on productive specialities were actively asserted and vigorously defended in various communities, there was no hint of competition among the main groups of overseas traders and, so far as is known, no attempt at the formation of trading monopolies (see Hanneman 1949; Harding 1967).

Connected to the maritime trading centers by overseas trade routes were dozens of coastal villages, the ports of the canoe traders. The coastal ports, in turn, were linked to the communities of the interior through direct relations with one or more groups of hinterland middlemen. In some areas middlemen were absent, and coastal peoples deal directly with inland villages.

A port community, with its hinterland, formed a local trading sphere. The people of the ports thought of their hinterlands less in terms of bounded territories than in terms of proprietary interests in economic relations with a number of interior communities. The numerous local trading spheres making up the larger system varied in size and population (although averaging a few thousand villagers), and they varied also with regard to items traded and the urgency of exchange (e.g., some coastal ports depended on the interior for imports of food). The Siassi traders had a local trade sphere of their own, by which they were closely linked with the tribal groups who inhabited the neighboring high volcanic island of Umboi.

The mode of exchange varied between the different types of communities. Most exchange between the maritime centers and the coastal ports was conducted among trade friends. Trade partnerships were enduring, heritable relationships, based usually on putative kinship, and were associated with a definite code that stipulates rules of hospitality and exchange between partners. Trade between coastal ports and hinterland communities was effected both through the reciprocal visiting of trade friends and at periodic or seasonal markets. Among the interior groups themselves, much of the exchange flowed through channels based on kinship and intermarriage. In some of the local trade spheres markets predominated, in others trade friendship. Market exchange tended to be associated with short overland distances, trade partnership with longer distances. The type of goods traded also had a bearing on the mode of exchange. Highly valued wealth objects, for example, were not exchanged at markets.

The boundaries of the trading system have to be delimited in rather arbitrary fashion, by using the central groups of maritime traders as points of reference. The outer boundary would be formed by those communities that either have direct links with the port communities, or whose relations with the coast are mediated by an intervening group, and hence are three links removed from one of the three maritime centers. Geographical barriers—open ocean and mountainous terrain—help define boundaries in some quarters. For example, much of the southern border is formed by a continuous series of mountain ridges reaching altitudes of over 13,000 feet. But in fact this montane barrier only served to make more conspicuous the trade routes that extended across it at fairly regular intervals. Still, if only for practical reasons, it is useful to delimit the Vitiaz Strait region as a field of economic relations.

To these remarks on boundaries I should add that the "folk view" of the indigenous traders did not begin to embrace the regional system as a whole, nor did it resemble my suggestion of a radial or wheellike pattern in which the linked series of port communities, hinterland middlemen, and interior villages (the "spokes") were connected to maritime centers. Rather, there was a tendency for each community to regard its own role in exchange as a central one. Of course, many of the port communities were themselves important trading-manufacturing centers. But even the central and most important group of overseas traders—the Siassi Islanders—had only a partial and selective notion of the regional system. Briefly, each Siassi trader had his own egocentric view (his "roads"), a network that did not extend beyond the ports-of-call, and included only some of those.

Communication for purposes of trade is properly viewed against the regional linguistic situation. Northeastern New Guinea exhibits as much and probably more linguistic diversity than other areas of comparable size in the Western Pacific. There are communities here that have regular commercial and other forms of contact, but whose languages appear to be more closely allied with those of such distant places as Fiji and Palau than they are with each other (see Murdock 1964). Compounding the diversity, however, is that in addition to the numerous distinct Melanesian (Austronesian) languages, the majority of the people of the region—the interior groups—speak various non-Austronesian languages.

This extreme fragmentation of local speech communities was partly overcome in aboriginal times by means of a trade jargon—specifically, a pidgin form of the Siassi language in the central portion of the Strait. The Siassi pidgin was employed by the overseas traders in their dealings with the coastal ports, and to some extent it was used between members of different port villages. In addition, bi- or multilingualism was characteristic of the area. Generally, knowledge of the Melanesian speech of the port communities spread to the non-Melanesian-speaking interior peoples. In post-European times (since 1884), Neo-Melanesian (a type of pidgin English) has become the language of trade and of intergroup relations generally. The indigenous Siassi pidgin has passed out of existence, although elder informants recall its use, while at the same time multilingualism of the traditional sort persists.

A distinguishing feature of the Vitiaz Strait system is its radical or centralized pattern of exchange. "Centralized" in this context refers to the dominant pattern of movement, and does not imply the existence of hierarchically organized political relations. Nor did trade ever assume the form of tributary relations based on political dominance. Even though imbalances in exchange could develop, the system remained acephalous, a "horizontal" network of linked communities.

An essential attribute of centralization emerges, first of all, in the fact that overseas trade routes converged in the Siassi group (and in the other overseas trading groups in their respective areas). The economic flow was thus centralized, the voyages of the Siassi traders effecting a redistribution of goods among the port communities and hence throughout the region.

A second aspect of centralization is that the central trading groups, as the main carriers, regulated the volume of exchange. Ultimately the cargoes carried in Siassi canoes helped to determine the volume and composition of trade in areas far beyond the Siassi sphere of operations.

The center of the system consisted of the home base of the maritime traders. This was a point for the storage and transshipment of goods, but it is important to realize that the center was not itself a trading site. Rather, the various port communities, peripheral to the center, were the principal sites of exchange. Thus, unlike a peasant region dominated by a central periodic market, the transactions here were both territorially and temporally dispersed.

As far as the physical loci of exchange were concerned, the trading system was multicentered. All groups of producers, suppliers, and consumers did not meet for exchange. More than that, it was a rare occasion when members of port communities visited Siassi. This meant that there was a centralized flow of information relating to production methods, labor costs, exchange ratios, and local supply-demand conditions that was almost exclusively under the control of the overseas traders. It appears, too, that the interests of the latter were best served by curtailing the flow of information between the various parts of the system, and at times it appears they disseminated false information in support of their trading position. It was only in modern times that people generally were made aware of the substantial discrepancies of value that had developed between regions, that clay pots commanded many times the amount of garden produce in the archipelago as compared with the mainland, or that obsidian and ochre, scarce and high-priced on the mainland, were superabundant in the archipelago.

Apart from the arrangement of port communities and regional trading units around a center, the southern or mainland communities on the one hand, and the northern or archipelago communities on the floor, formed opposite halves or sides. To some extent the two sides of the Strait were differentiated in terms of resources and specialist production. For example, red ochre and obsidian, carried to the mainland in Siassi canoes, originated from single localities in the archipelago. Clay pots, palm wood bows, and woven net bags, on the other hand, were manufactured exclusively on the mainland, and reached the archipelago communities by way of Siassi. In addition, the two sides were linked by a set of complementary movements that were not based on the distribution of resources or on factors of supply. These movements involved the highly valued wealth objects—dogs, pigs, dogs' teeth ornaments, and curved boars' tusks. Boars' tusks and dogs from the archipelago were transmitted to the mainland, while dogs' teeth and pigs traveled in the opposite direction.

Thus far I have dwelt on regional patterns of exchange while saying little about the content of economic relations and the motives for trading. The size and complexity of the system, however, requires selectivity. To round out the present discussion, I will describe the economic operations of the principal maritime groups—the Siassi Islanders. [Supplementary information on Siassi, as well as material on other participating communities, will be found in Chapter 14 of this volume and in Freedman (1967) and Harding (1967a).] It should be realized, however, that had I chosen one of the other overseas trading groups, one of the port communities, or an inland community, the component operations would be different. To some degree, the role in exchange of each of the hundreds of participating communities was unique. Unlike the *kula* ring of Papua, no single type of transaction ran through the entire system.

Siassi, one of the three maritime trading centers and the only center operating in modern times, is composed of four island villages. Two of these, the outer groups of Malai and Tuam, are situated far out in the Strait and were most committed to overseas voyaging. The inner groups, Mandok and Aramot, are situated close to the south shore of Umboi Island, where the islanders traveled every two or three days to exchange fish for supplies of taro and other vegetable food. The outer islanders, too distant to visit the frequent food markets, practiced limited horticulture on their small islands, while the inner islanders relied almost wholly on trade for their daily provisions.

Apart from food, the Umboi villages produced or procured all of the raw materials required by the Siassis for the manufacture of their sailing canoes. The Mandoks and Aramots, close to the sources of supply, were the canoe-builders; most of the canoes they manufactured were sold to the outer islanders for pigs and other goods. For their own annual voyages, the inner islanders often hired or rented craft from their Tuam and Malai customers.

In the Siassi Archipelago and Umboi Island, then, there was a complicated pattern of economic interdependence. On one side the inner islanders were linked to the Umboi communities producing food and raw materials, and on the other to the outer islanders, who paid for sailing canoes with imports from overseas. Doubtlessly because of this interdependence, there appears to have been no competition among the Siassi groups or attempts to monopolize trading privileges in particular regions or port communities. Indeed, the overseas contacts of the maritime traders exhibited considerable overlap.

In addition to their activities as sailors and traders the Siassis were expert craftsmen and industrious fishermen. Their archipelago of coral islets, sandbanks, and reefs offered very limited scope for agriculture. Most available land was reserved for coconuts, on the production of which Siassi maintained a near-monopoly (in pre-European times). Because the Siassis were not agriculturalists, neither were they breeders of pigs. But in Siassi, no less than in other Melanesian societies, pigs were of the supreme value, the essential ingredient of politicoceremonial life. It was primarily to amass large quantities of pigs that the Siassis made extensive voyages. A man who was successful in trading abroad invested his profits in a political career at home, in the distributions of wealth on which superior social position depended. Successful traders, then, became prominent local leaders, or "big-men."

The complex interrelation of production and exchange by which the profits of trade were realized in the desired forms is shown schematically in Figure 2. Some of the transactional sequences entailed multiple overseas voyages and might require months or even years to complete. A typical sequence might have begun with various low-value goods, some of which, like coconuts and pandanus mats, were produced locally, while others, such as red ochre and sago, were acquired in exchange with Umboi communities. The low-value goods—that is, goods low in value at their point of origin—were then converted into high-value items—clay pots, ornate wooden bowls, dogs, and ornaments of teeth and shell. Thus, mats were exchanged for pots on the New Guinea mainland, the pots being exchanged later on for pigs, for example, in New Britain. Bowls, pots, dogs, and ornaments were exchanged for pigs at various localities, and some additional pigs were received in payment for services as ceremonial dancers, services the Siassis performed at the invitation of prominent leaders of the port communities. Many of the incoming pigs were reserved for ceremonious distribution. As shown in Figure 2, however, a substantial fraction was invested in capital equipment, such as canoes and bark fiber for fish nets. Some pigs were occasionally reinvested in trade (e.g., to secure red ochre), and some were exchanged for taro, the essential vegetable ingredient of feasts (most taro for ceremonial purposes was received from Umboi Island producers in return for such goods as pots and bowls; fish were traded for taro to meet daily subsistence needs).

When a number of pigs and large quantities of taro were assembled, the stage was set for the trader-turned-big-man. Each of the Siassi communities was composed of a number of men's club-house groups, which were the functioning units in ceremonial life (see Chapter 16). The essential ritual of social climbing in Siassi involved the public distribution of pigs and taro puddings among the various men's houses. Further, a competitive or potlatching element was introduced in a

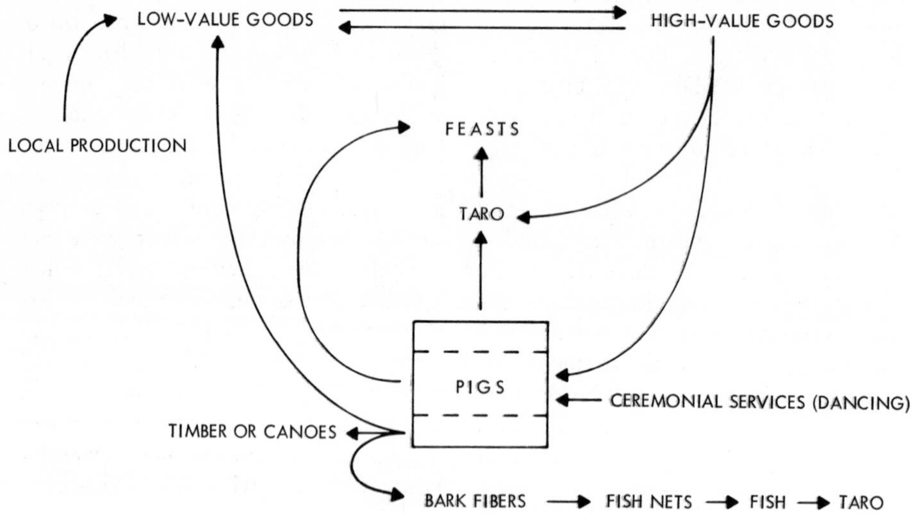

Figure 2. Production and Exchange from the Point of View of a Siassi Community.

special exchange institution termed *atam*. When a man, with the assistance of his group, finally assembled pigs and taro for distribution, he turned everything over to his *atam* or exchange partner, who made the presentations in his own name. Then, if the atam were to maintain his own status, he had to reciprocate with an equal or larger amount of pigs and taro on a subsequent occasion. Thus were the gains of Siassi trading periodically consumed in ceremonious distributions.

In common with neighboring peoples, the Siassi traders invested considerable wealth, as well as their productive and managerial efforts in politicoceremonial life, in the local big-man system. Unlike agricultural communities, however, for whom surplus production of vegetable food and pigs was comparatively easy, the Siassis labored long and hard, and with considerable risk, to accumulate small disposable surpluses. In consequence, according to Freedman (1967), their political system achieved only the level of a "mini-man" system. Of course, one can hardly gainsay the technological and economic ingenuity by means of which they transformed an unpromising island habitat into the central base of operations of a farflung economic network.

The Siassis were not the only ones to benefit. Once a number of communities were linked in exchange there was the possibility of expansion both territorially and in the volume and variety of goods traded. Opportunities for nonparticipants to enter the system were comparatively easy to realize and would involve, typically, taking advantage of a favorable geographical position, developing minor craft specialities, or stepping up production of some home product for export.

It is apparent, however, that to a major extent the developmental potential of the Vitiaz Strait system hinged upon sociocultural in addition to technological specialization, and upon diversification of local political and ceremonial institutions. These included bridewealth and ceremonial exchange among affinal groups, potlatching or competitive distributions among male club-house associations, mortuary distributions, and others. Often associated with these politicoceremonial complexes was a demand for specific kinds of imported goods. To the extent that imports played a role in internal payments, trade would increase as internal transactions expanded, for example, in the form of bigger bridewealth payments or more frequent potlatching. The status rivalries of local big-men, who took prominent roles in internal payments and distributions, would tend to insure some degree of escalation, and this would entail increasing "exotic" imports.

The Kovai peoples of Umboi Island, for example, had so escalated bridewealth payments that men lamented that "we never finish paying for our wives." Major payments to wife's kin, which included imported clay pots, were required from the time a woman was betrothed until her death. As a result the demand for pottery was probably ten times what it would have been supposing that pots were used for utilitarian purposes alone. To satisfy the demand the Kovai produced taro for the pot-importers—the Siassis—who required taro in large amounts for their own politicoceremonial system.

From the point of view of the development of trade, it mattered very little what local sociocultural forms were elaborated so long as the scale of internal payments was increased and the demand for imports of the various communities remained somewhat specialized. Many communities, for example, elaborated bridewealth while maintaining distinctive preferences for type of payment. Thus, the Tami Islanders, who produced carved wooden bowls, required imported boars' tusks for bridewealth payments, while a host of communities used imported Tami bowls in their own payments. Umboi Islanders and some New Britain peoples insisted upon clay pots to make up bridewealth payments, whereas the pottery producers themselves preferred such goods as dogs' teeth, bowls, and pigs. As it developed, then, the pattern of specialized demand was linked to local productive specialties in wood carving, pot making, manufacture of ornaments, taro growing, and so on.

In sum, it may be said that regional exchange in the Vitiaz Strait rested on three distinct but interconnected levels of specialization. There is first the *environmental* level, which includes the distribution of natural resources, differences in agricultural potential from region to region, and the advantages in trade conferred by geographic location. The second level is *technological*, which refers to the local differences in knowledge and skills underlying specialized production of exchangeable goods and services. The third type of specialization is *sociocultural*, which entails the diversified demand patterns stemming from culturally acquired needs.

Village communities combined these kinds of specialization in various ways. Thus, Sio, a large mainland village in the central part of the system, may be described as a food-importing industrial port community. The Siassis, on the other hand, in compensating for poverty in environmental resources by means of technological specialization in sailing and manufacturing, evolved the unique sociocultural type of overseas traders.

The Impact of Trade on Local Economy

Trading in the Vitiaz Strait is comparable in scale to the trading of ancient and preindustrial societies. Neither, of course, would resemble modern international trade in scope and complexity. Finley, for example, relates that "In the fifth century B.C. Athens supplied much of the fine pottery for the whole Greek world and for the Etruscans, and the total production at any one time was the work of about 125 painters working with a still smaller number of shapers and assistants" (1965:42). When the pottery trade died in the next century, Athens' economy was not visibly affected. Proportionately, the production of pottery for export played a larger role in certain Vitiaz Strait communities than it did in ancient Athens. But even though in Sio, for example, surplus pottery was used to make up recurrent food deficits, it seems doubtful that a breakdown of trade in pottery would have drastically affected Sio livelihood or caused a reorganization of the local economy. The fact that scholars have, at times, greatly overemphasized the role of ancient export trade serves to warn against similar errors of exaggeration when we come to discuss the economic importance of primitive trading. As we will see, however, there has been a tendency in some anthropological quarters to err in the opposite direction, to ignore the economic functions of primitive exchange.

With the exception of the three

groups of trading peoples, none of the few hundred communities of the Vitiaz Strait was absolutely dependent upon trade. In other words, communities had not specialized to the point of sacrificing self-sufficiency; specialization of effort was a means of material enrichment, not the necessary means of survival.

As already indicated, the bases of participation in regional exchange varied. Typically, a community offered some specialty produce such as pots, bark cloth, or bows, or perhaps high-quality versions of products that were widely manufactured, such as the expertly carved drums and betel mortars of the Arop Inlanders. Some communities took advantage of their geographical positions to serve as carriers and middlemen, while still others benefited because of the availability of some locally restricted resource, such as ochre and obsidian. The role of the overseas trading communities depended upon a combination of the production of specialty articles, geographical position, trading-carrying, and maritime skills.

With the exception of stone axe blades, which were imported into most parts of the Vitiaz Strait region, self-sufficiency in the production of basic necessities, especially food, was the rule. But apart from the obvious fact of local production of specialty articles for export, trade appears to have affected village economies in other significant, though indirect, ways. Wherever trade friendship and commitment to exchange resulted in stable, peaceful intergroup relations, agricultural pursuits were promoted because of the freedom from attack and security of land tenure. Also, the regional circulation of wealth objects was connected with the status-achieving activities of local leaders or big-men. I discuss first the impact of trade on subsistence agriculture.

Associated with the type of slash-and-burn production of root crops characteristic of tropical areas were varying degrees of community stability, ranging from complete sedentariness to high mobility. Often the degree of mobility would be less a function of physical factors—such as soil depletion—than of social environment. Mobility was both a measure of military insecurity and a means of defense against attack; sedentariness, on the other hand, was a measure of security. Associated with community stability or sedentariness was the likelihood of greater dependence on agriculture as opposed to extractive pursuits. By contrast, hunting-collecting-fishing activities were apt to remain an important part of the adaptive repertoire of highly mobile or "shifting" communities. Not only a consideration of local conditions (see Harding 1967b), but comparative evidence as well, suggests a correlation between the degree of geographical mobility, military security, and intensity of agriculture.

Trade, however, is a fourth factor to be added to the mobility-warfare-production formula. Regional exchange took place through a network of intercommunity social links, the latter consisting primarily of trade friendship. Insofar as these remained effective, and as the value of trade itself was conducive to the maintenance of peace, life was made more secure. Even when hostilities erupted, as they often did, trade friendship played a role in limiting the destructiveness of violence. Warfare typically followed a pattern of surprise attack: the ambush of small parties of gardeners or predawn attacks on sleeping villages aimed at total annihilation. But often in traditional accounts of warfare, trade friends sounded an early warning, thus allowing the community under attack to take refuge or marshall its defenses.

It seems reasonable to suggest as an hypothesis that reliance on agriculture, at the expense of extractive aspects of production, was promoted to the degree that the "peace of the trade" enhanced security. It is a matter of record, of course, that the effective peace established by Europeans, in combination with steel tools, resulted in a marked expansion and intensification of agricultural production in these same communities.

The second indirect effect of trade, like the effects on horticulture, depends upon the interaction of a number of factors. The use of imported wealth objects, such as wooden bowls, pots, pigs, dogs, the shell and teeth valuables in transactions of bridewealth, and other important social payments contributed directly to the capacity of local leaders—big-men—to mobilize wealth for prestige-building distributions. The character and frequency of such distributions or "feasts of merit" determined, in turn, the sponsoring big-man's status, including his ability to act as an economic manager. For example, the Kovai leaders who gained prominence in the intravillage exchanges of imported pots and bowls were also the men who were able to call up gangs of laborers to cut and drag to the beach the large cedar logs purchased by the Siassis for canoe hulls.

A big-man's claims to the goods and services of others depended partly on the obligations explicitly created by strategic payments of wealth objects—for example, contributions to the bridewealth payments of junior kinsmen. It was in this sense that such goods as pigs, dogs' teeth, bowls, pots, etc., formed a kind of political currency. The big-man's superior control of the flow of such valuables allowed him to augment and maintain a fund of obligation and indebtedness. The size of this "fund" and the leader's managerial effectiveness were directly correlated. The economic organization of a village community utterly lacking in big-man leadership would consist of little more than household units linked by ties of kinship and neighborhood and occasionally joined in cooperative endeavor. In other words, in the absence of the big-man's prestige-seeking and managerial activities, the local economy would have been less effectively organized at the suprahousehold level and less productive.

Profits and the Specificity of Trade

The fact that the same products—such as clay pots—received markedly different valuations in different parts of the region, as well as the centralized flow of information mentioned earlier, suggests that trading offered considerable opportunity for profit, at least for the overseas traders and perhaps also for the less mobile middlemen. Even so, it is not possible to speak of profit in the market sense in the absence of all-purpose money and money pricing.

The difficulties of calculating gains and losses in exchange are heightened because all goods were not exchanged against all others (at particular places certain combinations of goods were traded), and there are substantial variations in size and quality within particular classes of goods. If all of the fifty[1] or so types of goods were interexchangeable, this would require, in the absence of an accepted standard of value, 1,225 pairs of exchange ratios or equivalencies (ignoring for the moment variations in size and quality; a large wooden bowl, for example, has twenty times the value of a small one). Such a multiplicity of ratios would clearly be unworkable, a fact which economists have in mind when discussing the disadvantages of "barter" or moneyless exchange. At any particular locale, however, all types of goods did not change hands, and although the overseas traders operated in terms of a multiplicity of ratios or "prices," trading was their specialty—their lives depended on it. In any case, it is not known with any degree of certainty how the exchange ratios were established or how they changed (but see Sahlins 1965), nor is it known precisely what role the various customary exchange ratios elicited from informants had in actual trading. This means that although the locally variable exchange ratios or equivalencies suggest possibilities for gain, they cannot by themselves serve as a basis for calculating profits.

In addition to the difficulties already mentioned, although the data are sufficient to show the actual and possible transactions and transactional sequences, they are not sufficient for estimating the frequencies of particular kinds of transactions between given points (in overseas trade) or for estimating total volume. The problem of estimating gains and losses must be approached along different lines.

Apparently promising in this connection would be a comparison of costs of labor associated with different products and services. Labor time offers a unidimensional criterion of value, but, perhaps equally important, indigenous traders appear to make use of a similar concept. It is apparent from discussions with Siassi traders, for example, that they regarded the returns of trade as a just price for the "hard work" of sailing. In the Siassi view, as Freedman points out, "they deal in a service. They do not buy cheap and sell dear; the differential between purchase and sales prices is a portage fee or, as one Mandok put it, 'the pay for breaking the Vitiaz Strait' " (1967:171). Although it is relatively easy to estimate on the basis of observational data the labor costs of pot making, canoe manufacture, taro growing, and so on, how does one estimate the value of the Siassi sailing-carrying service? In particular, how is one to calculate the possible loss of canoes, cargoes, and crews in terms of labor time?

Similar problems of incommensurability arise in examining local trade. The Komba mountaineers incurred the main costs of transport in their trade with the coastal Sios, but the Sios assumed the burden of providing hospitality, often precisely at the times they could least afford it. The etiquette and the language of partnership trade clearly militated against the explicit comparison or matching of costs of transport on the one hand, and of hospitality and protection on the other. Trade partners were "friends" and "relatives"; they offered and received gifts; they did not pay for goods and services; they did not engage in buying and selling. Trade friends assumed an obligation to satisfy the needs and wants of their partner, no matter what the inconvenience or temporary imbalance in exchange.

Ultimately, the concept of profit appeared irrelevant because the objectives of trade for any participant community were highly specific. The Siassis counted the returns of trade in pigs and vegetable food which could be reserved for the "feasts of merit" staged by local leaders. The Komba mountaineers were drawn to Sio because "they smelled the grease of our coconuts," "they were hungry for fish and salt." Because of these specific objectives, transactions that might be judged unprofitable as measured by comparative inputs of labor time were desirable nonetheless. Indeed, for the overseas traders whose entire way of life was trade-dependent they were vital.

The "Peace of the Trade"

There is a seeming paradox in the fact that regional trading systems developed on such an elaborate scale in Melanesia where, in pre-European times, intergroup violence and sorcery were pandemic. It is from this vantage point that one can appreciate Reo Fortune's characterization of the overseas trade of the *kula* ring as an annually repeated miracle. Nevertheless, in every major island group of Melanesia there is evidence of widespread trade.

In attempting to account for the maintenance of peaceful exchange under such unfavorable conditions, Fortune suggested that the ceremonial exchange of nonutilitarian goods (the *kula* valuables) be viewed as an elaboration of normal exchange that has peace-maintaining functions: ". . . in such a place as the *kula* ring, where suspicion of the black art of strange people runs rife, where enmity is likely to flare up easily, the over-development of exchange is a very good counter against the over-development of international enmity" (1963:207). Peace, in this view, was the outcome of the elaboration or "over-development" of the trading itself—the "useless" unnecessary "exchange for exchange's sake" of valuables on which the traders' attentions were concentrated, while trade in vital utilitarian goods was conducted as a "side issue." This "latent-function" interpretation may be restated succinctly as follows: the exchange of nonutilitarian objects deflected attention from trade in utilities, and thereby reduced the probability that conflict would arise to disrupt the flow of vital goods. Thus, the function or effect of ceremonial or nonutilitarian exchange was to maintain the trade in goods which served human biophysical needs.

Without pretending to offer a systematic critique of the latent-function hypothesis, which would require another chapter, one may make the following observations based on consideration of the Vitiaz Strait system. First, the above hypothesis rests on an ethnocentric distinction between ceremonial and utilitarian exchange, between "useless" and useful goods. This distinction either oversimplifies or is not consonant with Melanesian categorizations of exchangeable goods, but, more important, it presupposes discontinuities in exchange that do not exist (see Figure 2). As we have seen, it is essential—for the overseas traders and for the system as a whole—that low-value ("utilitarian") goods be converted into high-value ("nonutilitarian," "ceremonial") objects. Goods that might be thought of as "utilitarian" in one context—e.g., Sio exchanges of pottery for Siassi mats—are "ceremonial" in others—e.g., the same clay pots in Kovai bridewealth payments. If this had not been the case the overseas traders would have been out of business.

Secondly, as to the peace-maintaining function of "nonutilitarian" trade, it is probable that exchanges of high-value goods were more apt to generate conflict than the exchange of low-value utilities. Although the characteristically delayed reciprocity of transactions involving valuables required a degree of mutual trust, it probably also provided fertile ground for the most intense antagonisms. As Freedman points out (1968), the threat of sorcery always hung over delayed exchange between Siassi and Umboi partners, and it is no surprise that in modern times defaulting in transactions involving high-value goods has led people to seek a remedy in formal litigation. Similarly, in the *kula* ring Trobrianders resented their Dobuan partners "milking the *kula,*" that is, withdrawing armshells for use in internal payments. Thus it appears that the elaboration of exchanges of ornaments or valuables—what Fortune referred to as "overdevelopment"—creates numerous possibilities for conflict.

Clearly, in the Vitiaz Strait region the physical hazards of trading were ever present and constituted so many limitations on the conduct and development of trade. The Komba mountaineers made forced marches to Sio, taking circuitous routes in order to avoid contact with enemy groups. A coastal group, such as the Sios, could turn a prearranged meeting at a market site into an ambush. Lone visitors to alien communities might too often be made the scapegoat for a local sorcery killing. And the Siassis, braving the elements in their incessant voyaging, faced graver hazards if forced to land on enemy shores.

Semiannually the grand entrance of the Siassi traders into Sio was accompanied by a martial display of spear-brandishing. This performance really underscored the fact that on any such occasion the Sio hosts could easily have overpowered their visitors and seized their canoes together with their valuable cargoes. The stay-at-home Sios were rarely placed in such a potentially disadvantageous position. At the same time, they viewed the home areas of certain foreign traders as sources of supernatural danger. Graveside vigils were required to protect their newly buried dead from the depredations of the dread flying ghouls who lived in the mountains near Siassi. Most dangerous of all in the Sio view, however, were the Komba sorcerers of the Puleng Valley, the hinterland area with which Sio was most closely linked in coastal inland trading.

This indicates that apart from the pledge of protection and safe conduct afforded by trade friendship, the sublimation of hostility is ritualized performances and the transference of distrust to the supernatural realm, evident in Sio beliefs, played some role in maintaining peaceful relations. Ultimately, however, the peace of the trade was contingent upon an uncertain balance of forces in which the implied threat of reprisal through attack or suspension of trading and the temptation to gain by means of force were counterposed.

It should be pointed out that an opposition of interests was inherent in trade-friendship exchange, no less than in modern market exchange. The incidence of conflict, however, as well as the usual means of resolving or channeling it, differ as betwen the two modes of exchange. In market exchange people potentially involved in three types of conflictual behavior: buyer versus seller, buyer versus buyer, and seller versus seller. Conflict is resolved in the case of buyer and seller through bargaining, among buyers by means of competitive bidding, and among sellers through underbidding (as in "price wars").

Although conflicts of this type were implicit in trade-friendship exchange, they were rarely allowed to rise to the surface. The predominantly private dealing among partners had the effect of insulating individual exchange circuits. This prevented comparison of offers and returns, thus ruling out competitive bidding or undercutting. Bargaining or haggling among partners was specifically eliminated as a breach of trading etiquette, as a violation of the social ethic guiding partnership exchange. Even in the dealing among comparative strangers at markets competitive bidding was largely curtailed by the fact that inland and coastal traders paired off before the commencement of trading (there remained, however, some scope for bargaining between the several pairs of traders). Through solicitory overtures or gifts, people might seek to "steal" the partners of fellow villagers. Perhaps this might be regarded as a type of competitive bidding, but it could also be dangerous to the extent that it was successful. In the old days, informants relate, a man who lost a trade friend in this way would attempt to kill both the interloper and his errant partner.

The dynamics of partnership trade limited the scope for economic maneuver by restricting the number of one's partners and to the extent that continued relations among "friends" and "kinsmen" (as partners are usually described) could not tolerate unscrupulous dealings. At the same time, trade friendship provided the most effective safeguard for peaceful relations. Under conditions of stateless anarchy, "trade follows trade friendship." Where such cross-community bonds were absent exchange was at best an uncertain proposition.

Economic Significance of Melanesian Exchange

It comes as a surprise to find that a number of anthropologists have regarded Melanesian exchange systems (the *kula* ring in particular) as noneconomic in character, or, at least, they have emphasized their social, ritual, or political aspects while underplaying the economic significance of regional trading. A brief examination of some representative noneconomic interpretations of the *kula* may help to bring into focus the basis of the contrary view that regional trading systems—in the *kula* region, the Vitiaz Strait, and elsewhere—are best understood in an economic context.

Evans-Pritchard, for example, writes that "the most significant feature of the *kula* [is] the bringing together, through the acceptance of common ritual values, of politically autonomous communities" (1951:95). By "most significant" Evans-Pritchard apparently means that the political-integrative effect of *kula* exchange seems most interesting from the "structuralist" viewpoint, but this, of course, is a limited perspective. The exchange of *kula* valuables was a part of the trade-friendship relationship, in one of its aspects a social instrumentality, a means to an end. The communities participating in the *kula* ring remained politically autonomous, their members coming together periodically for limited purposes, mainly to trade.

Leaving aside the so-called "subsidiary" trade in a variety of goods, the exchange of *kula* valuables had an economic in addition to the social-integrative aspect. From this vantage point, what should be emphasized were the different uses of *kula* ornaments in the various Massim communities, and the resulting *differential* values. In the Vitiaz Strait local differences in valuation of such wealth objects as pigs, dogs, wooden bowls, clay pots, and teeth and shell ornaments formed a principal basis of trading, and the ethnographic reports of Seligman (1910), Malinowski (1922), Fortune (1963), and Belshaw (1955) indicate that a similar situation existed in the *kula* region.

Similar to Evans-Pritchard's view is that of Firth: ". . . what the *kula,* sociologically, does seem to offer above all is a means through the use and exchange of symbolic objects, of expressing, maintaining and building up status relations on a scale not possible in any single Massim community" (1957:224). This notion of the *kula* ring as a political association finds its fullest exposition in Uberoi's *Politics of the Kula Ring.* However, that Uberoi has greatly exaggerated the political significance of the *kula* is indicated in Powell's critical observation that the main function of the *kula* is "to motivate and maintain inter-island and inter-district cultural and especially economic exchanges, and to stimulate economic activities within the major communities" (1965:98). This appraisal applies equally well to the Vitiaz Strait system, centered a few hundred miles to the northwest. Powell adds that "Kula partnership . . . gave safe conduct to participants in otherwise hostile areas, and thus made possible a degree of continuing economic exchange which was of more or less importance to different districts; but this hardly amounts to the making of political alliances" (*ibid.*).

Parenthetically, it should be noted that Firth's assessment seems to fit best such regional systems as the *moka* of the New Guinea highlands. The *moka* did represent an extension of exchange-based competitive politics to the inter-group level, the development of big-man politics on a regional scale (see Bulmer 1960). By contrast, in the Vitiaz Strait, and as Powell affirms for the *kula* ring, trade-partner exchange never served as an adequate basis for organizing intercommunity political relationships.

If Evans-Pritchard and Firth have implicitly de-emphasized the economic aspect of regional exchange, Leslie White's interpretation of the *kula* is an explicit denial of economic functions:

> The kula is a sociopsychological game. Arm bands are exchanged for strings of beads in a formal, ritual manner. . . . To participate is a privilege; to hold one of the articles of exchange is an honor. Here . . . we have a game the purpose of which is to confer honor and distinction, a way of making life pleasant and interesting. The shells and necklaces are merely instruments with which the game is played. They are the visible, tangible expression of a game of make-believe . . . kula elements . . . as counters in a social game . . . are not economic elements (1959:241–42).

Here again is a partial and misleading view. One could similarly abstract particular classes of transactions from the total pattern of trade in the Vitiaz Strait in order to highlight the "game" aspect of trading. For example, the exchange of boars' tusk pendants for dogs' teeth necklaces (similar to the *kula* exchange of armshells and necklaces) between Siassi and Sio partners may be regarded as a social ritual, an annually repeated game of tit for tat.

On a wider view, however, the social significance of this stereotyped transaction leads to a consideration of additional motives and purposes. In the first place, the ornaments themselves, the pendants and necklaces, were among the most highly valued goods used in social payments such as bridewealth and compensation, and they also figured in subsequent external exchanges. Then there is the matter of the partnership which was defined and sustained in part by the regular boars' tusk–dogs' teeth transaction. Apart from such goods as pigs, bark cloth, woven net bags, pottery, and bows, the Siassi looked to his Sio partner for protection, hospitality, and—when needed—materials and assistance in repairing his craft. In return, the Sio partner was supplied with pandanus mats, obsidian, dogs, sailing canoes, and other items. In other words, the partnership itself was an economic good—a "utility," in Weber's sense of "social relationships which are valued as a potential source of present or future disposal over utilities" (1947:165). The traders did not exchange objects as part of a game, although obviously fulfilling social obligations to one's partner may have been intrinsically gratifying. Rather, they engaged in social rituals of exchange as a means of acquiring valued need-serving goods. In exchanging tusks for teeth they were no more involved in social make-believe and no less attuned to material considerations than business associates who exchange silk ties at Christmas-time.

Regional trading systems are, of course, complex affairs that may be appropriately treated in a number of relevant contexts: ecological, economic, ritual, political, game-theoretical, and so on. Take, for example, the political aspects of the Vitiaz Strait system. Aboriginally, trading was linked in important ways to *local* politics; trade paid off for the Siassi traders in terms of political status when they could devote the hard-won gains of trade to "feasts of merit" and certain imported goods played a role in the political life of other communities as well. In the context of modern election politics, the regional social system based on trade friendship has important implications for political recruitment and communication (Harding and Lawrence n.d.).

On the other hand, one does not want to confuse the part with the whole, the components of a system with the system itself. To say that trading is a "social ritual"—the same might be said about any interpersonal behavior—should not be taken to deny its economic *raison d'être*. An exchange system is no more a ceremonial system or political association because it is composed, in part, of political and ceremonial behaviors than a molecule of H_2O is an atom because it is composed of atoms. The *kula* ring, like the Vitiaz Strait system, represented a set of rules, practices, and values by which groups of people cooperated in making, trading, and using a variety of goods. The economic context is of primary significance.

Regional trading has an obvious bearing on our appreciation of the economic ingenuity of Melanesian peoples. By developing institutions that linked individuals and groups in a regional economy, the Vitiaz Strait villagers acquired means of coping more effectively with survival problems, of utilizing the environment more fully, and of enhancing the material side of life. In the process they enriched the technical, artistic, and political aspects of their cultures. This engagement in a wider field of relations and its consequences is a far cry from the traditional anthropological portrayal of the "primitive isolate," the small neolithic village subsisting on its own resources. It remains true, however, that Melanesian societies were unable to sustain political integration much beyond the village community. Intercommunity trade ties produced, at best, an ephemeral sort of political association. For successful experiments in regional polity and political economy one must look elsewhere in the Pacific, particularly to the high-island chiefdoms of Polynesia.

PART III
Social Life

INTRODUCTION

Since Rivers' and Malinowski's pioneering contributions to ethnographic methods, developed in the course of their work in Melanesian societies, the analysis of interpersonal relations in small communities and groups has been the basis of the ethnographic study of institutions. Substantively, the focus has most often been on kin group structure, particularly in societies possessing unilineal descent groups (corporate groups whose members are related by common descent through the male or female line). The essays presented here, following Firth's discussion of aspects of the ethnographer's role in the field work situation, exhibit the interests of social anthropology in a wider variety of institutions.

M. J. Meggitt documents in an illuminating way the distinctive cultural definitions of sexual roles and categories characterizing societies in the Highlands of New Guinea.

In the third selection, Elman Service provides a sensible, real-world interpretation of Australian section and subsection systems, which have often been regarded as peculiarly complicated by anthropologists and their students. By placing the section systems in the larger class of "sociocentric" status systems, Service shows that they are structurally simple solutions to the problem of organizing intergroup relations.

In the final essays, Michael Freedman and Derek Freeman describe the organization of two societies that lack unilineal descent groups. In both cases, features of these societies may be related to their particular adaptive problems. The Siassi Islanders described by Freedman are maritime traders (see also Chapter 10), while the Iban of Borneo treated by Freeman are a highly mobile group of slash-and-burn agriculturalists. In describing the organization of these societies both authors introduce novel concepts.

CHAPTER

11

In Primitive Polynesia

RAYMOND FIRTH

In the cool of the early morning, just before sunrise, the bow of the *Southern Cross* headed towards the eastern horizon, on which a tiny dark blue outline was faintly visible. Slowly it grew into a rugged mountain mass, standing up sheer from the ocean; then as we approached within a few miles it revealed around its base a narrow ring of low, flat land, thick with vegetation. The sullen grey day with its lowering clouds strengthened my grim impression of a solitary peak, wild and stormy, upthrust in a waste of waters.

In an hour or so we were close inshore, and could see canoes coming round from the south, outside the reef, on which the tide was low. The outrigger-fitted craft drew near, the men in them bare to the waist, girdled with bark cloth, large fans stuck in the backs of their belts, tortoise-shell rings or rolls of leaf in the ear lobes and nose, bearded, and with long hair flowing loosely over their shoulders. Some plied the rough heavy paddles, some had finely plaited pandanus-leaf mats resting on the thwarts beside them, some had large clubs or spears in their hands. The ship anchored on a short cable in the open bay off the coral reef. Almost before the chain was down the natives began to scramble aboard, coming over the side by any means that offered, shouting fiercely to each other and to us in a tongue of which not a word was understood by the Mota-speaking folk of the mission vessel. I wondered how such turbulent human material could ever be induced to submit to scientific study.

Vahihaloa, my "boy," looked over the side from the upper deck. "My word, me fright too much," he said with a quavering laugh. "Me tink this fella man him he savvy kaikai me." *Kaikai* is the pidgin-English term for "eat." For the first time, perhaps, he began to doubt the wisdom of having left what was to him the civilization of

Abridged from *We, the Tikopia.* London: Allen and Unwin, 1936, pp. 1–11. By permission of the author and publisher.

Tulagi, the seat of government four hundred miles away, in order to stay with me for a year in this far-off spot among such wild-looking savages. Feeling none too certain myself of the reception that awaited us—though I knew that it would stop short of cannibalism—I reassured him, and we began to get out the stores. Later we went ashore in one of the canoes. As we came to the edge of the reef our craft halted on account of the falling tide. We slipped overboard on to the coral rock and began to wade ashore hand in hand with our hosts, like children at a party, exchanging smiles in lieu of anything more intelligible or tangible at the moment. We were surrounded by crowds of naked chattering youngsters, with their pleasant light-brown velvet skins and straight hair, so different from the Melanesians we had left behind. They darted about splashing like a shoal of fish, some of them falling bodily into pools in their enthusiasm. At last the long wade ended, we climbed up the steeply shelving beach, crossed the soft, dry sand strewn with the brown needles of the Casuarina trees—a homelike touch, it was like a pine avenue—and were led to an old chief, clad with great dignity in a white coat and a loin cloth, who awaited us on his stool under a large shady tree.

Even with the pages of my diary before me it is difficult to reconstruct the impressions of that first day ashore—to depersonalize the people I later came to know so well and view them as merely a part of the tawny surging crowd; to put back again into that unreal perspective, events which afterwards took on such different values. In his early experiences in the field the anthropologist is constantly grappling with the intangible. The reality of the native life is going on all around him, but he himself is not yet in focus to see it. He knows that most of what he records at first will be useless: it will be either definitely incorrect, or so inadequate that it must later be discarded. Yet he must make a beginning somewhere. He realizes that at this stage he is incapable of separating the pattern of custom from the accidentals of individual behaviour, he wonders if each slight gesture does not hold some meaning which is hidden from him, he aches to be able to catch and retain some of the flood of talk he hears on all sides, and he is consumed with envy of the children who are able to toss about so lightly that speech which he must so painfully acquire. He is conscious of good material running to waste before him moment by moment; he is impressed by the vastness of the task that lies before him and of his own feeble equipment for it; in the face of a language and custom to which he has not the key, he feels that he is acting like a moron before the natives. At the same time he is experiencing the delights of discovery, he is gaining an inkling of what is in store; like a gourmet walking round a feast that is spread, he savours in anticipation the quality of what he will later appreciate in full.

The Background to Anthropological Work

It is a matter of common agreement among modern anthropological field workers that an account of the institutions of a native people should contain some description of the methods by which the information was obtained. This is in accordance with the recognized logical position that even the simplest record of what purports to be the "facts" of a native culture has involved a considerable amount of interpretation, and every generalization about what the people do has meant a selection from the immeasurably wide field of their activity, a comparison of items of individual behavior. The conditions of the selection—that is, the situation of the observer in regard to the material—should therefore be indicated. In terms of anthropology, it is desirable to make clear such points as the relation of the investigator to other folk of his own culture, whether isolated from them or in daily contact; the linguistic medium of communication with the natives, whether the vernacular, a "pidgin" or other *lingua franca,* or translation by interpreters; the economic and social medium—payment, in money or kind, services rendered, goodwill, or simple gossip and conversational exchange; the nature of the record, whether accounts of eye witnesses, or hearsay evidence, or personal observation of the investigator himself; whether what is described is current practice or is now obsolete; and the range of instances relied upon for generalization. Elaborate documentation of every single statement is impossible in the space available, but some general reference is necessary. In the following pages details of this kind are given. They are not in tabular form but are set out as a running account, which is less of a tax on the reader's patience and allows of a realization of the flavour of scientific work in a remote community.

Rarely visited by Europeans and with no white residents, Tikopia lies in the extreme east of the British Solomon Islands Protectorate, and is inhabited by twelve hundred healthy and vigorous natives. Homogeneous in speech and culture, they are a unit of what may be termed the "Polynesian fringe" in Melanesia, their closest affinities being not with the people of the Solomons region but with those of Samoa, Tonga and even more distant groups to the east.

Almost untouched by the outside world the people of Tikopia manage their own affairs, are governed by their chiefs, and are proud of themselves and their culture. They are primitive in the sense that the level of their material technical achievement is not high and they have been affected in only a few externals by Western civilization; at the same time they have an elaborate code of etiquette, a clear-cut systematic social organization, and they have developed very strongly the ceremonial side of their life. They still wear only their simple bark cloth, they live in plain sago-leaf thatch huts, they carry out the traditional forms of mourning, marriage, and initiation. *Mirabile dictu,* a large section of them still worship their ancient gods with full panoply of ritual, a condition almost unique in the Polynesia of today.

A brief reference to the religious condition of the people is necessary in order to give some idea of the setting in which my work was carried out.

A section of the Tikopia are ostensibly Christian, the mission vessel calls on the average once a year, and there is a native teacher from the Melanesian community of Motlav in the Banks group living on the island. He, however, is married to a Tikopia woman, and conforms in most respects to the customs of what has been for twenty years his home. He uses the Tikopia language alone, except in church services, he moves freely among the people, his children go through the normal ceremonies of youth, and he makes the appropriate exchanges at funerals and other social occasions. He has no ground of his own but works his wife's land in native style, and when a canoe is manned takes his place among the crew in the ordinary way. In so far as he conforms to native custom his position is that of a man of influence in Tikopia society. On the other hand, he regulates church affairs with several Tikopia teachers under him, is strict regarding the observance of the *aso tapu,* the Sabbath, and endeavours to maintain morality by deprecating free sexual association of young people (an old Tikopia institution) urging marriage on those who sin, and debarring from church young men who attend the heathen festivals. He takes advantage of his position, too, to rally even the heathen among his wife's kin to assist him in large-scale gardening, initiation, and other important affairs. A man of strong personality, he pursues the aims of the Church and his own advancement as parallel activities, and with equal zeal; he is calculating but generous; and he interprets the Christian teaching with force, in an essentially native manner.

The baptized Tikopia comprise about half the population, and though of the four churches two are on the eastern side of the island the majority of the Christians live in the district of Faea, on the western or lee side. Here is the only convenient anchorage for vessels. This has been one of the predisposing factors in the conversion of the local people. The traditional rivalry between the districts, the character of the chief of the dominant clan of Faea—a strong-willed old man with a distinct eye to the main chance—and the system of payment to mission teachers in European goods, which are greatly coveted by the natives, are other elements in the situation. The equivalent of even £1 or £1, 10s. per annum in calico, fish hooks, knives, and other articles—the salary of a Tikopia teacher—is a prodigious amount of wealth to a native family; the equivalent of the £7, 10s. which is given to the Motlav man each year contributes in a very large measure to his power and prestige. It has not been entirely accident that two of the teachers are sons of the old chief, and another is his brother's son, while the Motlav man is settled in the chief's village.

In many respects the Christianity of the Tikopia is only superficial. That the old gods still exist is never questioned by the chief or his people; they are merely latent, and from time to time make their presence felt with startling effect. The old chief has abandoned the essence of his kava ritual—the pouring of libations to ancestors and gods with invocations for fruitfulness and health to the land. But he retains an emasculated version of it by throwing food offerings daily to his ancestors before meals. He also conducts the making of turmeric with most of the ancient ritual, especially in observance of taboos. When he fell ill during my stay, as the result of his dramatic attempt to coerce his old gods, it was by the intervention of a heathen chief with these deities that he was cured.

The heathen constitute the district of Raveŋa, and number among them three chiefs, including the principal of all, the Ariki Kafika. This man and his eldest son, Pa Fenuatara, were two of my most regular and valuable informants. Among others were the Christian chief, the Ariki Tafua, and his eldest son, Pa Raŋifuri, the Ariki Taumako, Pae Sao, Pa Teva, Seremata, Kavakiua,

Pa Motuata, Pa Raŋimaseke, Pa Tekaumata, Pa Taraoro and Afirua. They were drawn without distinction from heathen and Christian, from all districts and clans, from married and unmarried. . . .

As I moved about freely among the people of the whole island, however, most of my data were gathered not from selected individuals in set interviews but in the course of the ordinary affairs of their daily life. In particular I gained a great deal while reclining for hours at a time in the native houses during the intervals of ceremonies, or when food was cooking, when conversation flowed easily and without haste.

I spent just twelve months on Tikopia, from July 1928 to July 1929, and in that time received one visit from the mission vessel—an extra call by courtesy—in October 1928, bringing a second supply of stores and trade goods. For the ensuing nine months I saw no white man. The outer world seemed dim and far away, the only events of interest were those happening in Tikopia, and when the *Southern Cross* finally arrived I can honestly say that the colour of white faces seemed less pleasant than that of brown, and that my chief desire was for the letters of friends rather than for the company of Europeans as such. And this in no way is to impugn the hospitality of the Melanesian Mission and the officers of the *Southern Cross,* from whom I received kindness much more than ordinary courtesy demanded, most generously given.

During practically all my stay I used only the native language, my initial medium of conversation—a mixture of Moari and pidgin-English—being abandoned entirely after the first three weeks. At no time did I have a regular interpreter. Naturally, I recorded as much material in the Tikopia tongue as possible. But apart from taking down the statements of informants in the ordinary way, I made a practice of jotting down verbatim on the spot scraps of what I overheard, conversations between people, comments on behaviour, observations made during the progress of work, and the like. These often give a more intimate insight into the human relationships involved than a long dictated text on the same theme, and I regard this type of material as among the most valuable of my records. The comparatively simple orthography needed for the language, and a fortunate rapidity of handwriting, enabled me to get down all such material immediately.

Of money I had no need, for the Tikopia do not understand its use. They know of the existence of this thing called *mane,* and that by its aid one may walk into a *fare ḳoroa,* a house where goods are stored, and secure what one desires. From visiting vessels they have even received stray coins, but of their relative values they know nothing. Pa Fenuatara brought me a florin one day and said: "Friend, is this a pound?"

"No," I said.

"What is its value?"

"It is worth a knife, not a knife of the size for clearing the cultivations, but a knife so long—" (indicating a 10-inch blade).

"*A,* so that is it." And after deliberation he gave it to me as a keepsake, since, though he himself had no use for it, it was obviously a thing of value.

Another brought me a halfpenny, and said, "Friend, this is money?"

"Yes."

"What it is?"

I replied that it was worth five small

fish hooks for *api* and *nefumefu,* or two of the *tau kurakura* size—the only method of indicating its worth.

Others being given pence by sailors on board a warship in payment for coconuts and bananas threw them overboard on their way back to shore, exclaiming: "Useless bits of iron!"

All my transactions took place through the medium of trade goods. Thus for the building of my house I paid Fakasiŋetevasa and his assistants the sum of one axe, two plane irons, five knives, six pipes, five sticks of tobacco, and fifty fish hooks, with douceur of rice, meat, and tobacco to other people who helped to make the thatch. For the purchase and repair of my small canoe I handed over goods of about the same kind and amount, though they were received with rather bad grace, as an adze was desired instead.

This absence of money in Tikopia has a bearing on several situations. It is an index of the barrier that lies at present between the Tikopia and the economic forces which are at their door; it was one of the conditioning factors in my relationship to my informants, since any equivalent which I gave them had to be in objects desired for their own sake, not as tokens of value; it offers a point of comparison with the culture of other Polynesian peoples, practically all of whom now know and use money even among themselves.

At first I had the greatest difficulty in resisting the acceptance of presents, mainly of pandanus mats in exchange for my goods; later these were implemented by invitations to meals, which it would have been discourteous to decline. Gradually, however, I made my would-be hosts understand that my goods were intended primarily not for purchase of specimens, but as gifts to those who assisted me in recording language and customs. And, in conformity with the native attitude, for the chiefs were reserved the choicest items, of which they early received a selection as an earnest. My system was to make good gifts to those who contributed valuable material and let this principle be known. In my experience the old anthropologist's maxim never to pay for information is not applicable in a community where individual or family privileges are jealously conserved. The only feasible method is to pay, but with discretion, and to rely on one's system of checks to ensure accuracy. As every field worker who knows a native community well will probably agree, one can always find other people with some knowledge of the matter desired from the expert, and by cautious probing, by challenging his accuracy, by suggestion of his ignorance or of matters withheld by him, or by studied reticence oneself and implication of one's own foreknowledge, one may check very accurately the information given by the real authority. I myself knew for four months the secret name of the principal god of the Ariki Kafika and much subsidiary data before, his confidence won in the meanwhile, he whispered it to me himself, and unconsciously thus proved his own veracity. He never knew that I had forestalled him in this, though he suspected that some lesser "official secrets" were being disclosed by others of his clan. In such a closely knit community as that of Tikopia, where every chief and elder has links with the ritual of the others, it is comparatively simple, once one has made the first steps, to exercise fairly complete control even of esoteric material.

To make the first breach in the barrier, however, is no easy matter. When I arrived in the island my motives were of course suspect, and though outwardly very friendly and hospitable the people were really greatly disturbed. As I learnt much later, the chiefs gave orders that I was to be told nothing about their gods and ritual practices, and, such is still the solidarity against the stranger, Christian and heathen alike down to the smallest child continued to obey, and to preserve silence on such matters. Shortly after I settled in Matautu I had occasion to ask the sons of the Ariki Tafua, among whom were two Christian teachers, for the beginnings of the genealogy of their family. As one man they assured me with every appearance of sincerity that they did not remember the names of their ancestors, that even the old people did not know who their forefathers were. Surprised at finding such ignorance among a Polynesian folk, usually so proud of their descent, I let the matter pass for the time being. Months later of course they acknowledge their own deceit with a laugh, but when one realizes how in their belief the invocation of the names of their ancestors lies at the core of their safety and prosperity, one can well understand the attempt to mislead the stranger in the interests of the community. Gradually, however, I began to get an inkling of the facts. A fishing formula appealing to ancestors, the existence of the term *atua* (spirit), a disclosure by an informant who went further than he intended, a comparison with Maori custom, and the like all served to prise open the door. Even then, however, the majority remained aloof in such matters, and intensely suspicious of any people with whom I had private sessions. Even the man on whose ground I had built my house had incurred the anger of his fellow villagers, and had been cursed by them for his acquiescence. In an atmosphere of distrust, spying, and reticence in all but overt social affairs I lived for some months, every step to establish a foothold being a struggle. Later I found that during the first few weeks of my stay a whole cycle of ceremonies of the "Work of the Gods" had taken place day after day in Raveŋa, and not a soul, not even the Motlav teacher, had told me a word about it. Men, women, and even children preserved absolute reticence. A canoe ceremony of the Ariki Taumako I indeed attended as a guest, by invitation, and also went through the ritual of the five days of the turmeric-making of the Ariki Tafua, keeping its taboos, but in neither case was I allowed to realize that what I saw was merely a part of a long intricate scheme of systematic activities which marked the turn of the year. Towards the end of 1928, however, I had learned the significance of this cycle, and managed to make up the deficiency by attending the ritual of the following two seasons at the express invitation of the chiefs. And before this, mainly through the agency of one man of rank, a perversely honest rough-tongued elder, who after declaring on the beach on the day of my arrival his intention of boycotting me, later received me hospitably, performed for me his kava, and constituted himself one of my most trustworthy advisers and informants, I had obtained some insight into the real meaning of Tikopia ritual. Later again as I attended their ceremonies, behaved circumspectly, ate their food, conformed to the tapu, took part in the system of exchanges and, above all, spoke in approval of what I saw, chiefs and elders opened their stores of knowledge.

Most of all, as an inmate of the houses of Kafika and Tafua, spending long days under their roofs, I began to feel the pulse of the real native life.

This was not without its reaction. When I fell ill after the ritual cycle of the monsoon season, gossip had it that the chiefs, fearful of my use of what they had disclosed, had sought my death through supernatural means. As I recovered it was said that, fearing vengeance from the white men if I died on Tikopia, they had changed their plan, and intended that I should go and die in my own land. Other responsibilities came too. The Ariki Kafika himself said to me: "Friend, I have told you the secrets of my kava; my *ora* (life) and that of my people and this land Tikopia will go with you. I shall sit here and watch; if evil comes to this land then I shall know that it is through your doing."

More than any other scientist the anthropologist is dependent on the confidence of his human material, and must be always faced by the quandary of how far he is betraying this trust by the publication of what he has learned. To withhold some sections of his data means distorting the picture he is trying to give.

Here I would like to express a personal feeling. What I have set down in this book, and what will appear in subsequent publications I have tried to make an exact and scientific record, keeping back nothing that I learned, and documenting opinions in order that as accurate an estimate as possible may be formed of the institutions and ways of life of these people. Much that was told me, especially in matters of religion, was given in confidence on the understanding that it would be made known only to taŋata poto, to adepts, to persons of wisdom. I publish it in the belief that this is being done. Should there be among the readers of this book any who may visit Tikopia, in a professional capacity or otherwise, I trust that the knowledge they may gain from it may give them an understanding and a respect for the native custom and belief, and that nothing which they find herein will be used to the discomfiture of the people or as a lever to disturb their mode of life, whatever be the motive. If this is observed I will have made no breach of faith.

As personal servant I took with me Vahihaloa, a lad of Ontong Java; to secure a Tikopia who knew white men's ways was impossible. I had wished therefore for a boy who was trained, but a Polynesian, because of his ability to fit into the speech and culture of the Tikopia. Vahihaloa—Vasieloa, as they called him—was admirable in this role. With a native shrewdness was combined a quick wit and a capacity for making friends, and his flair for organizing the youth of the village to assist him in domestic duties and for attending to the proper distribution of the volume of food which flowed into our household was extremely useful to an anthropologist. His love story, a curious mixture of calculation and desire, of magic secretly practised and attraction openly disavowed, was an interesting and rather touching lesson to me in native mentality. I have since learned that tuberculosis has claimed him.

Vahihaloa soon recovered from his tremors on the day of our landing. After a month or so he began to consort with the young people, he became enamoured of the native dance, let his hair grow long, and bleached it in Tikopia style. . . .

For about a month we lived in the

fare sul, the mission school hut kindly placed at my disposal by Bishop Steward. Then we moved to a house built for me nearby, and named Otara, after my New Zealand home. Midway through my stay I went over to Raveŋa to live, partly to become more closely acquainted with other sections of the people and partly to be near the scene of the season's religious ceremonies. There I occupied Tuaraŋi, an old house lent by the Resiake family, with father and grandfather of the owners lying buried beneath the floor, as is the common Tikopia practice. In both Faea and Raveŋa I lived in the villages, with neighbours within a few yards, so that I was able to observe a great deal of their domestic affairs with ease.

I give this somewhat egoistic recital not because I think that anthropology should be made light reading—though with a little more clarity of thought much of it might be made lighter than it is—but because some account of the relations of the anthropologist to his people is relevant to the nature of his results. It is an index to their social digestion—some folk cannot stomach an outsider, others absorb him easily. The student of human societies is in a different position from most scientists; the active reactions of his material to him, the character of the association between them, determines to an important degree the quality of his data. The social or institutional digestion of the Tikopia, once induced to begin, is of a vigorous character. Conformity to their customs they take not so much as a compliment as a natural adaptation; in a specific ceremony they can conceive only of participants, not of observers. At such a time one cannot be outside the group, one must be of it. There are limits, of course. One has a notebook, for writing is one's habit; one does not wail at funerals, for it is recognized that Europeans are dry fountains; but one must be of this party or that, one must keep the prescribed taboos of sitting or eating, one must make and receive the normal economic contributions.

At the same time the fact that one wears different clothing, usually sleeps in one's own house and normally takes at least the evening meal there, and acts in so many things as an independent unit, not as a member of a group, always prevents complete absorption into one's native surroundings.

Like most anthropologists I regard with scepticism the claim of any European writer that he has "been accepted by the natives as one of themselves." Leaving out of account the question of self-inflation, such a claim is usually founded upon a misapprehension of native politeness or of a momentary emotional verbal identification with themselves of a person who shares their sympathies. I myself have been assured a number of times that I was "just like a Tikopia" because I conformed in some particulars to the economic and social habits of their people, as in dancing with them and observing the etiquette of (pseudo-) kinship, or because I espoused their point of view on some problem of contact with civilization. But this I regarded as a compliment of much the same order as a reference to "our" canoe or "our" orchard ("yours and mine") by one of my courtesy brothers, which did mean certain concrete privileges, but not a share in real ownership. This problem of identification with the native culture is not merely an academic one. Europeans who allege that they "have become a member of the tribe," or "are regarded by the natives as one of themselves," are prone to lay claim to knowing what the native thinks, to being qualified to represent the native point of view. On a particular issue this may be in substance true, but too often dogmatic statements about ideas are substituted for detailed evidence of observed behaviour. . . .

* * *

CHAPTER

12

Male-Female Relationships in the Highlands of Australian New Guinea

M. J. MEGGITT

I

In 1954, Read surveyed the ethnographic evidence from the Highlands of Australian New Guinea and Papua and not only delineated the general features of the Highlands cultures, but also indicated areas and problems that would repay intensive field work. He noted that the people (now known to number some 750,000) everywhere possess much the same kinds of social organization and material culture.[1] They are sedentary horticulturalists, employing in most cases gardening techniques that support populations dense by Melanesian standards. There is commonly a great emphasis on the acquistion and circulation of valuables such as pigs and shells, whose public distributions enhance the prestige of individuals and of groups. Moreover, the vigorous oratory that accompanies such transactions is a particular expression of the prevailing aggressiveness of the Highlanders. It is not simply that the people are by nature individually quarrelsome or tend to intergroup belligerence; in addition there is in most significant social relationships an unmistakable component of bellicose competitiveness.

Read further asserted that an important and widespread manifestation of this aggressiveness is an antagonism pervading intersexual encounters. At one level this is reflected in the pan-Highlands rule of residence which separates men from their wives and takes

From *New Guinea: The Central Higlands,* James B. Watson, ed., pp. 204–224. Special publication of the *American Anthropologist,* Vol. 66, Part 2, No. 4, 1964. Reproduced by permission of the author and the American Anthropological Association.

boys early from the company of women, including their mothers. Often connected with this domiciliary demarcation is some form of male initiation and seclusion intended to strengthen and purify the growing youth, who is regarded as liable to pollution or injury through contact with women.

At the time Read wrote, little comparative material had been published on the subject of male-female relationships in the Highlands, and he had to rely largely on his own field data from the Asaro valley. He was able to show that there, among the Gahuku-Gama, "the female principle is in itself considered to be inimical to men, and care has to be exercised to see that youths have as little contact with it as possible, at least until they reach physical maturity" (1952:14). Male initiation rites "express unmistakably the rigid sex dichotomy of the culture, the community of male interests and their essential opposition to the sphere of women . . ." (1952:11). "At the conclusion of initiation ceremonies, crowds of women armed with bows and arrows, sticks and stones, dressed in male decorations attack the returning procession of men and boys. Similar fights are staged at marriages when characteristically enough, a man is required to shoot an arrow into the thigh of his wife" (1954:23). Read also suggested that the instability of Gahuku-Gama marriages is related to this antagonism.

Although Read argued that male-female hostility would be found throughout the Highlands, he did not simply extrapolate from Gahuku-Gama data and assume that everywhere it would take precisely the same form. Indeed, he pointed out that the evidence then available indicated a significant division between the cultures of the Eastern and Western Highlands. For this reason, he said, we should expect to discover consistent regional differences in the pattern of relationships between men and women.

Since 1954, anthropologists working in the Highlands have provided a great deal more information about individual societies and cultures. It is true that not all of them have been concerned to describe local features of male-female interaction, but none of the material so far published upsets the general proposition that, in the Highlands, relations between the sexes exhibit to a greater or lesser degree elements of tension or antagonism.

Thus, Berndt, writing of the Kamano and their neighbors who live southeast of the Gahuku-Gama, says: "There is then a current idea that women are potentially dangerous to men, apart from any consideration of interpersonal relations and lineage affiliations (1962:56) . . . sex demarcation is strictly observed (in the festivals). The rituals and ceremonies associated with the flutes, as symbols of male dominance, accentuate it. Men apparently feel that they must exert this pressure, continually reassuring themselves that they are superior to women (p. 67) . . . we speak of men's dominant ritual status—their desire to hide certain knowledge from women, their power . . . to enforce their opinion and retain their position through force and fear" (p. 72). It seems also that among the Siane the relationship between men and women displays features analogous to those Read noted for the neighboring Gahuku-Gama. Salisbury (n.d.) has remarked, for instance, that a dualistic opposition of male and female is an important theme in Siane religion.

Turning to peoples further west we

are reminded that earlier Nilles said of the Kuman of Chimbu: "The women's sex as such is considered by men as dangerous; and the woman as a person because of her sex is thought mentally inferior to men" (1950:48). More significant in this context, however, is Marie Reay's account of the Kuma of the Wahgi valley: "Relations between men and the women they seek by ritual and practical means are characterized by a fundamental antagonism . . . men say, 'women are nothing,' and women retaliate, 'men are no good' . . . the marriage relationship is fraught with tension" (1959:161–62). Furthermore, although hostility of this order may not be usual among the Medlpa of Mount Hagen, there is evidence that to some extent men in this society fear women's supernaturally derived sexuality and prevent them from participating in the most important rituals (see Vicedom and Tischner 1943/48, Vol. 2). Similarly, among the Kyaka of the Baiyer valley—northern neighbors of the Medlpa—Bulmer (n.d.) reports the emphatic exclusion of women from the major cults, one of whose functions is to protect men from the unclean women, especially from menstrual pollution, and to keep the latter in their place. Finally, there are the Huli of the Tari basin, southwest of Mount Hagen, of whom Glasse (n.d.) writes that a significant characteristic of their culture is the belief that males may suffer ill health as a result of feminine influence. Consequently, in their anxiety to avoid harm, men try to keep to a minimum their social contacts with all women, and some men actually refuse to marry at all.

As this brief survey shows, the available ethnographies not only confirm in a general way Read's assertion that relations between men and women in the New Guinea highlands are commonly tense or hostile; they also indicate that there are significant local or regional variations in both the form and the content of the relationship. But so far nobody has attempted a systematic study of such differences or tried to relate them to observed differences in other variables.

In this paper I want to clear the ground for such an investigation. First I shall augment the ethnographic evidence wtih an account of male-female relations and of bachelors' rituals among the Mae Enga of the Western Highlands. Then I shall show that the Mae phenomena are part of a nexus of social attitudes and practices which, although common to a number of Western Highlands peoples, differs significantly from its Central highlands analogue.[2] Moreover, the latter complex in turn differs from that in the Eastern Highlands. I suggest that these variations are correlated with the presence or absence of particular kinds of men's purificatory cults, with differences in the social status of women in everyday life, and with the degree of hostility existing between affinally related groups. I do not, however, make explicit assertions about the direction of causal sequences or the relative efficacy of particular factors; these questions cannot be taken up until many more Highlands data have been reported.

II

Most of the Enga-speaking people, who today number about 100,000, live west of the Hagen Range in the Wabaga and Lagaipu subdistricts of the Western Highlands district of the Australian Territory of New Guinea.[3] The 30,000 or so Mae Enga form a cultural subdivision of the central Enga, whose population density averages about 120 per square mile and in places exceeds 250. They are sedentary horticulturists and also keep pigs and fowls. Hunting is unimportant. Sweet potatoes, grown under an efficient system of long fallowing and composting, are the staple crop.

The significant sociopolitical entity is the named, exogamous and localized patriclan of about 350 members. Groups of contiguous clans comprise named phrotries. A clan has several named subclans, each of which is composed of named patrilineages. Patrilineages are made up of elementary and composite families which are the basic gardening units. There are no villages; houses or homesteads are scattered about the clan territory, whose average area is between one and two square miles.[4]

Men and women generally live in separate houses. The men's house is primarily a secular meeting and sleeping place; it is not the focus of any important ritual activities. Ideally its occupants are males of one patrilineage or one subclan, over seven or eight years of age. In fact, about 40 per cent of the houses deviate from this norm, mainly because men may stay for long periods with friends in parallel subclans. As a rule, the wives connected with a men's house live in its vicinity. A married woman is expected to share her house only with her unmarried daughters and infant sons, and about 70 per cent do live thus. In a survey of three clan territories, I found that 256 men and 53 boys (under about 15 years) dwelt in 57 men's houses. In the 155 women's houses associated with these, lived 235 women, 266 children, and 9 men. Of the 9 men, 7 were married and 2 widowed; all were elderly or poor, and their behavior was thought to be eccentric.

This residential separation not only provides the anthropologist with an initial insight into the Mae relationship between the sexes; it is also the basis of the local chidren's introduction to the subject. That is to say, when a boy is about five years old, his father and brothers begin to warn him of the undesirability of being too much in the company of women, and they (and his mother) encourage him to spend more time in the men's house and in herding pigs with older lads. The boy, alarmed by these admonitions, is eager to associate with the men and within a year or so regularly sleeps in their house. In the unusual event of a boy's wanting to remain with his mother, his kinsmen ridicule him and his father beats him and orders him to move.

As the lad grows older, his clansmen give him more explicit reasons for not staying with women. Females, they say, are basically different from males, for their flesh is laid "vertically" along their bones and not "horizontally" across them; thus they mature more quickly than do males and are ready for marriage earlier.[5] Whereas youths are still vulnerable because they are not yet fully adult,[6] adolescent girls have already acquired through the menarche their most dangerous attribute, the ability to pollute males.[7] Young men should therefore employ magic to hasten their own growth and to protect themselves from the perils of contamination. Above all, they must recognize the need to avoid unnecessary encounters with women, including their own mothers and sisters.

Moreover, the lad learns that such

pollution implies something more serious than mere uncleanliness. Men regard menstrual blood as truly dangerous. They believe that contact with it or a menstruating woman will, in the absence of counter-magic, sicken a man and cause persistent vomiting, turn his blood black, corrupt his vital juices so that his skin darkens and wrinkles as his flesh wastes, permanently dull his wits, and eventually lead to a slow decline and death. Menstrual blood introduced into a man's food, they say, quickly kills him, and young women crossed in love sometimes seek their revenge in this way. Menstrual blood dropped on the bog-iris plants (*Acorus calamus*) that men use in wealth-, pig-, and war-magic destroys them; and a man would divorce, and perhaps kill, the wife concerned.[8]

It is not surprising that men refer to a woman during her menstrual period as "she with the evil eyes" and require her to remain in seclusion. In some localities she retires to a small hut used only for this purpose; in others she stays in the rear cubicle of her house, the room that a man never enters; everywhere she withdraws from the sight of men for four days from the onset of her menses.

During this time the woman has her own fire and may prepare food for herself alone. She can collect food at night, but may harvest only mature "female" crops such as sweet potato, setaria, or crucifer, those which women normally cultivate. Should she enter plots containing "male" (-tended) plants such as taro, ginger, or sugar cane, these would die. Similarly, she must not walk among any young plants lest they wilt and those who eat them fall ill. She may feed pigs, for these are usually in her care and are therefore "female," but not dogs or cassowaries, as these are "male" and would lose their condition. She must not eat game, for this too is "male" and the hunter concerned would never again be successful.

On the fifth morning the woman cleanses herself before emerging from seclusion. Because an unmarried woman is by definition chaste, she is less dangerous than a married woman and need take fewer precautions. She spits on white clay, recites a spell taught her by her mother, and draws a line from navel to vulva and an arc under each eye. A married woman, however, also receives from her husband (through a daughter or sister) a package of leaves (*Evodia* sp.) which he has collected and bespelled. She bites off the ends of the leaves before placing them in the gable of her house, an action intended to neutralize the effects of blood remaining in her uterus when next her husband copulates with her. Meanwhile, she hides in the forest the soft moss used as menstrual pads[9]; the moss is not simply thrown away lest a pig eat it and die, and men then eat the contaminated pork.

The Mae also identify the placenta with menstrual blood, so that a woman during parturition is regarded as unclean and remains secluded for four days after the birth. On the fifth morning her husband sends her bespelled leaves to cleanse her. She may now look after pigs and work in the gardens, but she should not prepare food for males for another month. Because of the baby's intimate association with her uterine blood, it remains polluted for two or three months, during which the father refused to view it. If he did so, his power as a warrior would kill the delicate child and then dissipate, to leave him vulnerable in battle. Moreover, should a male child be born with "blood" (or contusions so interpreted) on his skin or in his mouth, the mother severs one of his finger-tips to release this dangerous female blood. Otherwise he would remain physically stunted and mentally deficient.

In addition to such dramatic responses to the climactic occurrences of menstruation and childbirth, there are the continuing consequences of the cultural definition of femininity—the enduring complex of beliefs, attitudes, and usages connected with the assumption that women are intrinsically unclean. These reactions range from the apparently trivial to those with significant implications for whole social groups.

For instance, men debar women from cooking meat on public occasions and from eating meat prepared at the clan cult-house.[10] There is also a total prohibition on females entering men's houses, although a few old men actually live in women's houses. Normally a man keeps his valuables in his wife's or mother's house, but his visits, although regular, are brief and for specific purposes, such as the discussion of domestic economy, and he never enters the rear sleeping cubicle which, because it is used for menstrual seclusion, is charged with femininity.[11]

Men also believe that a woman's genitals contaminate her skirts (of *Elaeocharis* sp. leaves), so that contact with the skirt is almost as damaging as with menstrual blood.[12] Consequently, a number of rules prohibit a woman from stepping over objects or touching them with her skirts. She must not climb on the roof of a house lest a male be seated inside. She must never walk over a boy's hair clippings or else he will become stunted and stupid; his hair should be placed in a pandanus seedling so that he will grow tall as the tree does.[13] More important, a woman should not step across the legs of a seated man (for without the proper counter-magic his blood will "die"), across his weapons (they will lose their efficacy), or across food (it will spoil and poison any male who eats it). To prevent inadvertent infringements of the prohibitions when a crowd gathers at a woman's house—for instance, during a wedding—the living room and the adjoining courtyard are divided in two. The right hand side—looking into the house—is reserved for men; here they may sit, store their equipment, and make ovens on public occasions. Even when men are absent, women prefer to keep to the left-hand side of the living room.

I should note here that the Mae distinction between right and left hand appears also in the structural opposition of agnates and maternal kin/affines, as well as of male and female. To summarize, the people believe that maternal blood "makes" the child's body, whereas paternal spirit animates it. Henceforth in the person's lifetime his agnatic spirits and ghosts stand opposed and inimical to his maternal flesh and blood, just as semen and mother's milk stand as antithetical forms of the vital fluid that resides in the skin of men and women.[14] Most deaths are attributed ultimately to attacks by agnatic ghosts, for which the deceased's maternal kin are entitled to receive heavy compensation in pigs. In the case of a sudden or inexplicable death an autopsy is performed; the presence of black marks in the righthand lung or ventricle of the heart places the blame on agnatic ghosts or sorcery, whereas marks on the left-hand side indicate that maternal kin or ghosts are responsible.[15]

III

Given their beliefs about the essential nature of women, it is hardly surprising that the attitudes of most Mae men towards sexuality reflect unease and anxiety. Men rarely mention sexual matters, menstruation, or childbirth among themselves and would be ashamed to discuss them in mixed company. Compatible with this restraint is the infrequent use of obscenities in everyday speech. Such expressions exist in the form of insults (for instance, "feces-eater," "eater of your sister's menstrual blood," "mother-copulator") but cut too deeply to be used outside serious quarrels. The only more or less accepted utterance of obscenities occurs on certain public occasions, as when men haul logs to build a bridge. The young women aim insulting songs at the men, who reply in kind (for instance, girls: "No wonder that log defies your efforts—you cannot even raise your own tiny penes!" Men: "Stand aside or close your legs lest our huge logs burst your dragging vulvas").

But despite their vainglorious responses, the men do not accept the invitations in the women's taunts. Their reluctance does not stem only from the assumption that women are unclean and that, therefore, each act of coitus increases a man's chances of being contaminated; there is also the fear that copulation is in itself detrimental to male well-being. Men believe that the vital fluid residing in a man's skin makes it sound and handsome, a condition that determines and reflects his mental vigor and self-confidence. This fluid also manifests itself as his semen. Hence, every ejaculation depletes his vitality, and overindulgence must dull his mind and leave his body permanently exhausted and withered. It is true that when a man marries he can buy spells to protect him in his conjugal relations both from menstrual pollution and from uncontrollable discharge of his dermal juices. But, although he may conscientiously employ his new magic before every act of intercourse, an element of uncertainty remains, so that he is likely to experience disquiet rather than pleasure in his marital exercises. Even after using magic he should not enter his gardens on the day he copulates, lest the female secretions adhering to him blight his crops, or try to cook meat lest it spoil. As a result the ordinary husband copulates with his wife only as often as he thinks necessary to beget children and, naturally enough, regards with abhorrence any erotic preliminaries to the sexual act.

It is understandable that most bachelors believe sexual abstinence to be the best safeguard against pollution, enervation, and deterioration of appearance. Some so fear these dangers that they try to postpone marriage, and their elders have to tell them it is their duty to wed and to produce heirs to strengthen the clan.[16] Nevertheless, in everyday life even the most cautious young men must come into contact with women; consequently, bachelors as a category seek a generalized protection from females. They find this in the intermittent performance of *sanggai,* rituals intended not only to cleanse and strengthen the actors but also to promote their growth and make them comely. Thus, the more effective this magic is, the more attractive to young women the bachelors become, so that ultimately it procures wives for them and ensures that they will beget children for the clan.

The term *sanggai* ("that which is hidden") refers to the actual period of seclusion, to the purificatory rituals which the clan bachelors as a group then undertake, to the bachelors at that time, and to the bog-iris leaves used in the rituals.

Usually the seclusion houses of a clan are situated in a part of its forest domain that few people enter, although men in search of timber or stray pigs may occasionally go there; once the sanggai is mooted, the area is closed to all but the bachelors. Within the reserve, the seclusion house of each subclan—a large subclan may have several—stands in a fenced clearing reached by a track that winds through several gateways decorated with asplenium ferns. A stream in the vicinity is dammed to form shaded, shallow pools in which the bachelors bathe. Beside each pool is a screen of branches through which spouts made of pandanus leaves channel spring water.

The seclusion house is a smaller version of the men's house, and a lean-to shelters the earth-oven outside. Carefully concealed in the forest nearby is a strongly fenced plot, in which grow the iris plants needed for the rituals. Ideally the plot, which belongs to the subclan that built the house, should contain a scion of the plant used by the founder of the subclan, but some irises are known to have replaced plants that died. Moreover, individual bachelors buy from extraclan acquaintances irises with great reputations to add to the plot. Such a plant belongs to the purchaser until he weds and passes it on to a bachelor in his patrilineage; then it is regarded as the property of the patrilineage. Before long, however, this distinction fades and it becomes part of the subclan heritage.

In each subclan two or three of the oldest bachelors active in the sanggai (men aged about 28 to 30 years) are custodians of the irises. Only they may handle the plants, and they visit the plot at intervals to weed it and to repair the fence. When a bachelor from the subclan marries, the caretakers transplant all the irises to a new plot to prevent their injury by the man's change of status. The senior bachelors of all the subclans in the clan also decide together when the young men should go into seclusion, although the subclans in big clans may act independently. Normally, the four-day seclusion occurs after the northwest monsoon at any time from about March to June, so that the interval between ceremonies may vary from about 9 to 21 months.[17]

A lad participates in his first sanggai when he is about 15 or 16 years old.[18] Only then can he don the long apron worn by men and safely join in the ceremonies through which men communicate with domestic and clan ghosts. Once in the sanggai, he has the right to attend all performances until he marries. A man who has not found a wife when all his coevals have wed, however, may give up the rituals after a time and privately persuade a married clansman to sell him protective magic.

A young man pays no fee to join the bachelors, but he should scrupulously observe certain prohibitions. The most important concern copulation and the taking of food from women's hands, for these are two sure avenues of feminine contagion. In addition, he should not eat particular foods, including liver, belly fat and intestines, the leaves of a solanum often cooked with meat, and certain grasshoppers; otherwise his skin would become wrinkled and greasy (like the guts), slimy and green (like solanum juice), or riddled with lesions (like leaves attacked by grasshoppers). Moreover, a bachelor who breaks the rules also strikes at the welfare of his peers. Not only his own body but also the iris plants of his subclan will reflect the consequences of his self-indulgence, so that the protective powers of the irises are diminished, if not entirely lost. Consequently, the individual bachelor is morally obliged to eschew temptation and so secure his comrades' safety, and the senior bachelors should be ready to apply sanctions to the rare defaulter. Thus, if gossip suggests that one of the group is a philanderer, the custodians watch his physical appearance for "proof" that he is copulating or accepting food from women. At the same time they inspect the iris plants for evidence of his behavior. Once the monitors are convinced of the young man's guilt, they inform the other bachelors in the subclan and all of them descend on the offender. They berate him, strike him, and demand payment of a pig as compensation for the injury he has done them.

The bachelors go to these lengths only when fairly sure of their ground, so that usually the culprit apologizes and pays up without demur; indeed, unasked, he may confess and offer a pig. But if a condemned man refuses to give up a pig, his peers seize one of his or his father's herd—an action likely to provoke bitter quarrels. However the bachelors obtain the pig, they cook and eat it at their seclusion house and, to mark their forgiveness and to reaggregate the offender to the group, invite him to join in the feast. Meanwhile, the senior bachelors determine whether the irises need replacement. If necessary, they exact one valuable from each member of the group towards the purchase of a new plant and spell from the bachelors of another clan.[19]

When the senior bachelors decide to hold a sanggai ritual, they set a date weeks ahead to allow for adequate preparation. All the young men clear the tracks to the seclusion houses, repair the fences and gateways, and hang up fern leaves that taboo the area to outsiders. Some men renovate and decorate the houses; others reconstruct the screens beside the pools. Everyone helps to cut and store firewood in the houses; this wood comes from trees uncontaminated by women's gaze. The forest buzzes with activity by day, and, despite their exertions, the young men enjoy little rest by night. Instead, they visit neighboring clans to ensure that people will attend the festival marking the bachelor's emergence from seclusion, for the larger the crowd the greater will be the prestige of the hosts. In particular the bachelors, in subclan groups, call at the houses of girls to whom they are betrothed or whom they know well in order to sing to them and persuade them to come to the festival.[20] The girls prepare food and invite other girls of their acquaintance to join them. Chaperoned by their mothers and aunts, they listen to the slow, interminable songs of the bachelors. I should emphasize that these drearily proper gatherings, which are typical of Mae courtship, have none of the gay licence of analogous assemblies elsewhere in the Highlands. Only the older bachelors can sustain easy conversations with the girls; younger men simply lapse into glassy-eyed embarrassment. This social activity reaches a climax on the night before the exhausted bachelors go to the seclusion houses, and they may visit several clans in succession.

Next evening each man fills a net bag with sweet potatoes from his parents' garden and carries it to his seclusion house to add to the common store.[21] The young men then beat tapa from *Ficus dammaropsis* to make into caps and plait cordyline leaves into waist cinctures. After this they spend their first restful night in weeks.

The custodians rouse them early and the period of seclusion begins; for the next four days the young men are under the control of the senior bachelors and have to observe a number of additional prohibitions, which aim at completely shielding them from femininity, sexuality, and impurity. Thus, not only must they avoid women but also they may not use anything already polluted by women's viewing. Each man removes and hides his everyday apparel, then rubs his body with red earth before donning a voluminous skirt of cordyline leaves and a tapa cap. For the rest of the seclusion period, the bachelors may not see each other's hair, armpits, pudenda, buttocks, thighs or soles of the feet, for these are unclean. They may not refer to sexual or natural functions and, as far as possible, should not think of such matters but only of the benefits the rituals will confer.

Pork is forbidden them, for women have tended the pigs; the only food permitted comprises tubers harvested at night and game and pandanus nuts taken from the forest. During such excursions the men should not look at the ground lest they see human or porcine feces or women's footprints. Food is cooked at night to hide the smoke from the eyes of the distant women; otherwise it would be contaminated. The men may smoke tobacco grown at the seclusion house but must wrap it in forest leaves, which women have not seen. Infraction of these rules nullifies the effects of the rituals, which must be performed anew after the bachelors have again cleansed themselves.

On the first morning, the senior bachelors produce sweet potatoes that their mothers have cooked for them. They give each man a piece, telling him to swallow it quickly without chewing, but he chokes on the sticky substance. The custodians announce that this demonstrates the polluting influence of women which the men must remove. The bachelors repair to the pool, which lies dark and cold under the trees. Two of them plunge into the shallow water and scrub each other with leaves (*Medinilla* sp.) while the others softly chant spells to reinforce the purifying effects of the washing.[22] The shivering men then kneel before the screen so that water from the spouts strikes their eyeballs. To the accompaniment of the singing, they vigorously rub their eyes with conus-shell discs and medinilla leaves until they are bloodshot, so as to rid them of impurity. Then, blue and chilled, they join the singers and two other men take their places in the pool. When everyone in the group has washed, they indulge in horseplay to warm themselves; and youths whose past behavior has offended are seized and plunged headfirst into the mud. The senior bachelors, however, remain in control and, as tempers fray, they order everyone to the houseyard. When the sun has warmed them, they all return for more washing. Periods of warming and washing alternate until late afternoon, when the tired men gather at the seclusion house to eat.

The custodians go to the iris plot and pluck a leaf for each bachelor; they give it his name and wrap it in a cordyline leaf. The men stand in a row at the house to receive their leaves, which they hold in their left hands[23] and lightly rub against their hair and skin for about half an hour while singing the spells.[24] They go indoors and each tucks his leaf in the rafters above his sleeping place so that its emanations continue to strengthen him and induce significant dreams.

Inside the house the men build up a blazing fire and sit around it, sweating and sunk in contemplation of their mental and physical well-being. From time to time they sing sanggai spells. Should a man wish to go outside to relieve himself, he warns the others to close their eyes in case he uncovers his private parts as he stands. Occasionally, if the moon is bright, the men hunt small game in the forest and place part of the catch on the roofs of their fathers' houses for patrilineage "brothers" to share.

The tired men salute the dawn with a round of singing and a meal, then sleep until afternoon. When they wake, they recount their dreams and try to interpret them. Not all dreams are taken to be significant, but some are thought to illuminate current events or to foretell individual misfortunes.

This pattern of activity continues for another two days, but the initial washing is not repeated unless some chance pollution occurs. On the last afternoon, however, preparations begin outside the seclusion area for the festival to mark the bachelors' emergence. Their married male agnates bring bundles of finery for them to wear, which they place outside the fence after warning the bachelors to hide. Afterwards the bachelors put the gear inside, then produce their iris leaves for the final rubbing, which they conclude by throwing the leaves into the forest. They go indoors and sing for the rest of the night.

Before dawn the senior bachelors douse the fire and lead the men into the yard, where they sing lustily "to wake the birds." Then each undresses and carefully cleans himself with moistened leaves (*Caly carpa* sp.) before donning new belts and aprons. The young men re-enter the darkened house and stand silently by the fireplace. The senior bachelors throw dry wood on the coals and the sudden blaze illumines the clean, shining bodies of "the new men." Delighted with their handsome appearance, they congratulate each other and praise the sanggai ritual. Then they sing happily as they await the sunrise and the arrival of clansmen to help them decorate.

Meanwhile, their earlier visits to neighboring clans have borne results. Throughout the preceding afternoon parties of girls arrive, and the mothers and sisters of the bachelors offer them hospitality. At dusk the girls assemble in groups on the danceground, and those who have sweethearts or friends among the bachelors lead the singing, which refers indelicately to the young men's attributes. For instance: "My man is short and his nose (=penis) is short, too. No matter, we can cut our skirts short to accommodate him." "My man's penis is a tiny mushroom that merely teases me and makes me scratch my vulva." "We come to sing at your festival, but you men do not speak fair to us. Very well, we shall rub our skirts (=vulvas) on your mouths."

These songs greatly embarrass the married men, who ostentatiously leave the danceground. Before long, however, bands of young men of other clans arrive to sing aggressively at the girls, decrying the host bachelors and extolling their own merits. Eventually as many as 200 to 300 young people, in 20 or 30 groups, are present and sing independently for several hours; the cacophony generates a tremendous excitement among them. The girls retire to the houses of their chaperones, and for the rest of the night the groups of young men visit them in turn to drone their songs of flattery. As the men sing indoors, rival groups stamp around the houseyards, chanting challenges and demanding that the singers leave to make room for them. Sometimes newcomers crowd into a house only to encounter classificatory "sisters" whom they must not court; then there is an undignified scramble for the door.

Eventually the visiting men go home to sleep. At dawn the girls gather on the danceground and, still chanting, set off for the seclusion area. There they all sing by the outer gateway, then those who fancy particular bachelors sing at the inner gateways of the seclusion houses. Warned by the noise, the junior bachelors stay indoors, while the others take firesticks and stealthily approach the gateway, hiding behind hedges lest the girls see them and nullify the effects of the ritual washing. As each girl calls the name of her choice, he indicates his interest in her by silently tossing a fire-brand in her direction. A girl who fails to elicit a response is humiliated and, dreading the gibes of her companions, hurries home.[25] The other girls return to the danceground to sing.

After the girls leave the seclusion area, the clansmen of the bachelors arrive to help them decorate. Two or three men attend each bachelor and take several hours to complete their task; they croon spells throughout to enhance the effect of the finery. They rub his skin and hair with palm oil and pig fat, blacken his face with soot and whiten his eyes, tease out his huge plate-shaped wig and blacken it with salvia juice; they adjust his many net aprons and cane belts and armlets; they bedeck him with shell pendants, necklets, and headbands; they pin cassowary plumes on his wig; and they arm him with a splendid stone axe and a black palm spear or bow. Novices who have not yet attended their third sanggai are adorned less elaborately.

When the dressing is completed, the groups assemble on a promontory overlooking the clan territory. The bachelors stand in a row flanked by the heavily armed but unadorned married men, and all chant lustily. The songs magnify the clan's strength and wealth or, by recounting sanggai dreams, touch on interclan disputes. Thus: "We have divided and redivided our iris plants, but still they are too few for the many bachelors in our clan." "We dreamed we walked on (=occupied) the land of clan so-and-so; were we dreaming, or will this come to pass?" The men halt and sing many times on their meandering path down to the danceground.

In the meantime, hundreds of visitors on the danceground await the appearance of the bachelors and the subsequent distribution of food. Young men stand in clan groups and resume their aggressive singing of the night before. For instance: "Clearly our hosts have no food to spare; their hungry bachelors do well to stay in seclusion." "Why do these men bother to visit their sanggai plants? We all know they have copulated too often to benefit from this!" At the same time the group of girls sings of their young men, thus: "We have visited the seclusion houses and received many firesticks." "Oh, where are our bachelors? We wish to seize their penes!"

The conflicting songs are deafening and the danceground seethes with activity. Visiting men exchange news, discuss disputes and negotiate business deals, while married women, enjoying a holiday from the round of gardening, gossip happily. The older men and married women among the hosts are still in their houses, cooking sweet potatoes, taro, corn, and pandanus nuts for the distribution that will follow.

Towards midday the songs of the bachelors become louder, and the phalanx of armed men marches down the hillside to make an impressive entry onto the danceground. The ground fairly shakes as they stamp round and round, chanting and brandishing weapons. Eventually the married men fall out and instruct the bachelors to sing at one end of the danceground. Orations by government headmen and other important men punctuate the songs; they concern plans for ceremonial distributions of valuables, disputes over land and pigs, the latest edicts of the Australian administration. Then the older men withdraw to discuss these matters and the bachelors resume their singing.

The visiting girls now link arms and form small clan or subclan groups that face the bachelors and sing independently. Every few minutes a girl leads her group in a hopping dance towards a bachelor she favors. She seizes his right hand,[23] her friends grab at his belts and, shrieking and laughing, they try to draw the embarrassed man along the danceground. Both the girl and the onlookers can gauge the degree of the victim's interest by the ease with which he allows himself to be led away. It he merely holds back, the girls may dance off with his axe, so that he must follow to retrieve it; but if he resists strongly, they quickly turn to another man. Should two girls try to seize the same man, they may argue and come to blows. The bachelor's following of a girl, however, is not a form of betrothal; it is simply a sign that he is willing to pursue an acquaintance with her.

After an hour or two, the women of the host clan carry bags of food onto the danceground, and "big-men" among the hosts call for silence. They make speeches about the reason for the gathering and then hand the food to important visitors to distribute among their own clansmen. When everyone has eaten, the sanggai bachelors take up their singing. Older people begin to drift home, but most of the visiting bachelors remain. They stand in clan groups and sing rudely in opposition. This is a potentially explosive period as the songs on all sides become more and more biting and aggressive. Men of the host clan stand by watchfully, clutching their weapons and ready to join in any fighting. Eventually wiser men decide to act before blood is shed, and they order the visitors to leave.

For the next four days, the armed and decorated bachelors perambulate the territories of their own and neighboring clans to show off their "new skins" and their finery. They halt frequently to chant topical songs and at night sleep in men's houses wherever they are visiting; they must not enter women's houses or accept food from women. On the last morning they go back to the seclusion houses to remove their ornaments and change into ordinary dress. Then they cook and share a meal of pork or fowl before returning to everyday life where, strengthened by the rituals, they face once more the insidious influence of unclean women.

In this way the Mae bachelor protects from women until he marries, when he must acquire a stronger defense against pollution. Once the wedding negotiations begin, he dons for the last time his sanggai apparel, which he wears until he consummates the union. After the wedding pigs are slaughtered and the marriage is ratified, the groom's father tells him to give a netbag of pork to a married kinsmen whose appearance testifies to the efficacy of his personal magic. In return, this man spends the next month teaching him the forms of magic to use before copulating and when his wife menstruates.

When his older agnates are satisfied that the groom knows the magic, they tell him to take his bride (whom he has so far avoided) into the clan forest for intercourse. The embarrassed and apprehensive man reluctantly does as he is bid and, after several such visits to the forest, doffs his finery and settles down to everyday married life. His bride also removes her decorations and begins work in his gardens.

IV

I do not intend to discuss here the "social functions" of the practices I have described, for I feel they are obvious enough: for instance, the bachelors' association provides alternative satisfactions for men who are politically impotent and economically beholden to their married elders, and the emergence festival enables the host clan to vaunt its size, strength, and solidarity in the presence of rival groups. But before I compare the Mae data with those from elsewhere in the Highlands, I want to examine briefly the way in which the people extended the distinction between right hand and left hand.

It has lately been fashionable not only to discover such oppositions among the symbols employed by various peoples but also to associate them with particular social usage or even total social structure.[26] Thus Needham, in writing of the Aimol, says: "In a prescriptive system corporate lineal descent groups are related by affinal alliance . . . and with the relations of affinal alliance are commonly found a characteristic system of prestations and a symbolic classification concordant with the structural divisions of the social order . . . [The social order and the symbolic order] will be found ultimately to exhibit a radically common structure, a mode of ordering phenomena of all kinds within a single scheme of relations by a structural principle of complete generality" (1960a:81). Needham generalizes further in his paper on the Meru: ". . . in societies based on descent such symbolic representations may be expected to correlate with the type of descent system. Roughly, in cognatic societies the relation of symbolic to social order may be indefinite or minimal; in lineal systems the relationship may be discernible in a limited range of particulars but not commonly in a comprehensive manner; and in lineal system with prescriptive affinal alliance there is usually a correspondence of structure between the two orders such that one may speak of a single scheme of classification under which both are subsumed" (1960b:21–22).

Now, although the Mae are not given to subtle elaboration of their cosmological or religious beliefs, in their dogmatic exigeses they frequently assert that fundamental differences exist between certain kinds of phenomena, and they express these in a consistent manner. On this basis it is possible to draw up a paradigmatic list of paired contrarieties among Mae concepts in the form A:B::C:D.

Such a schema, it seems to me, differs little from those reported for "societies based on prescriptive alliance"; its distinctions are as sharp and as wide-ranging. Nevertheless, the Mae not only lack any kind of prescriptive marriage rules; they do not even emphasize marriage preferences. The only unequivocal rules are those which prohibit unions with certain clearly defined categories of people. Consequently, I cannot believe that the presence of prescriptive alliance is *necessary* for the formulation of dualistic symbolic classifications. Moreover, field work among the Walbiri of Central Australia has persuaded me that the presence of a system of prescriptive alliance is not in itself *sufficient* to generate or maintain a thoroughgoing dualistic classification.[27] These people, who possess both matrilineal and patrilineal descent groups, not only prescribe marriage with classificatory "mother's mother's brother's daughter's daughter" but also in practice adhere closely to the norm. Yet it would be wrong to attribute to them any elaborate pattern of symbolic oppositions beyond noting that, like most Australian Aboriginies, they associate patrilineal recruitment with religious activities and matrilineal recruitment with secular activities.[28]

Clearly, we need some other explanation of the arrangement of the terms in Table 1, and, as a beginning, we might look briefly at the politics of Mae patriclan organization. Until recently clans fought constantly over scarce land resources, pig thefts and failure to meet debts; and in any given clan most of the men lost in battle have been killed by its immediate neighbors. At the same time, because of the rugged mountainous terrain, propinquity has been a significant variable in determining actual marriage choices. Thus there is a relatively high correlation (= +.65) between interclan marriage and homicide frequencies with regard to the nearness of clans. The Mae recognize this concomitance in a crude way when they say: "We marry the people we fight."

Typically, then, a man's wife and his mother come from those clans which are perennial enemies of his own clan and which are responsible for most of the deaths of his clansmen. But because the rule of clan exogamy disperses his female agnates at an early age, the only adult women with whom the man is in close regular contact and who exemplify for him the peculiarly feminine characteristics of menstruation and parturition are his own and his "brothers'" wives and mothers—the women drawn from hostile groups. Here is a possible reason for the Mae equation of femininity, sexuality, and peril—and, by extension, one way of interpreting the dual oppositions denoted in Table 1. That is, a chain of homologues can be traced from extraclan military threat versus intraclan military protection to feminine pollution versus masculine purity.[29]

At this point we may return to Read's earlier postulation of regional differences in the pattern of intersexual relations, especially antagonisms, in the Highlands cultures. My suggestion that male-female tensions among the Mae express, in part, oppositions connected with enduring but specific political conditions implies also that there should be predictable intersocietal variations. We might expect, therefore, to find the notion of feminine pollution emphasized in societies where affinal groups are seen —for whatever reason—as inimical to one's own group, but absent or of little significance where marriages usually occur between friendly groups. Moreover, as a logical extension of this argument, associations devoted to male purification, seclusion, or initiation should be more sharply defined among the former. Finally, it follows that where male-female hostility exists in societies in the second category—those favoring intermarriage among friendly groups—it will differ markedly from that of the first category.

If Mae culture exemplifies that constellation of traits which includes fear of sexuality and of pollution, emphasis on a male cult and frequent conflict between affinally connected groups, then the culture of the Kuma of the central Highlands might well stand as its opposite. Marie Reay's account makes it clear that Kuma men have little or no fear of contamination by women; although separate residence is the norm, many men sleep in their wives' houses, and "only the wealtheir men (=polygynists) practise taboos including the avoidance of sexual relations with their wives while children are still breast-fed

Table 1

Schema of Symbolic Classification among the Mae Enga

Inferiority	Superiority
Nonentity ("rubbish man")	Leader ("big-man")
Neighbors/affines	Clansmen
Matrilateral kin	Patrilateral kin
Mother's agnates	Father's agnates
Mother	Father
Female	Male
"Vertical" flesh	"Horizontal" flesh
Flesh and blood	Spirit
Milk	Semen
Sexuality	Chastity
Pollution	Purity
Married man	Bachelor
Domestic life	Ritual seclusion
"Female" crops	"Male" crops
Pigs	Game
Secular dwelling house	Ancestral cult house
Woman's (=mother's) house	Man's (=father's) house
Woman's side of house and yard	Man's (=oven) side of house and yard
Left hand	Right hand
Matrilateral ghost or sorcery	Patrilateral ghost or sorcery
Left side of thorax	Right side of thorax
Moon	Sun
Earth dwellers	Sky dwellers
Dark (brown) skin	Light (red) skin
Mortals	Immortals
Forest (=demons)	Settlement (=kinsmen)
Danger	Security

or their wives are menstruating" (1959: 84). Premarital sexual intercourse is common and uncondemned; married men, to their wives' annoyance, enjoy "sanctioned promiscuity" (162), and "sexual attractiveness . . . is closely associated with prestige" (161). Sexuality and fertility are basic themes of the major pig and nut ceremonials. The initiation of boys is also associated with the pig festival, but both occur infrequently (every fifteen years or so) and a number of men do not bother to offer their sons as candidates. As Reay says: "Kuma initiation affects only a handful of boys at long intervals" (170). Moreover, although in one respect such initiation symbolizes the separation of the lads from the mothers, its purpose is primarily didactic—the inculcation of clan values. "Lecturers instruct the novices to cooperate in work with clansmen; to marry and have sons to continue their line; to be strong and defeat the clan's enemies, avenge the death of a clansman, and prevent the clan from being destroyed. In short, they must do as their fathers did" (172). Finally, as we should predict, Kuma do not attribute enduring hostility to affines. ". . . A man is prohibited from marrying . . . his own clan's traditional enemies. Hostility between clans is strictly incompatible with inter-marriage, and when asked whether marriage is possible with a certain clan, the natives answer, 'No, we fight,' if the clan named is a traditional enemy. Warfare between previously friendly clans prevented further inter-marriage until after the payment of compensation for deaths and the ensuing peace-making ceremonies" (59).

The Kuma data support the hypothesis that, in Highlands societies, where there is no persisting animosity between affinally connected groups, there is also little or no fear of feminine pollution and sexuality. Nevertheless, there exists among the Kuma "a deep-rooted antagonism between the sexes" which emerges in various contexts. Men continually strive to dominate women, and the latter "obstruct men's aims by exercising choices the men try to deny them" (237). Women who have experienced the pleasure of premarital freedom have no desire to submit to the constant demands of domestic drudgery, and they fight hard to assert their independence after marriage. In consequence Kuma men's main concern is not to avoid hypothetical perils of psychosexual pollution but rather to combat those expressions of feminine "unreliability" that would undermine male pretensions to superiority. They are not always successful in this, so that in many respects Kuma women enjoy a relatively high social status.[30]

Now this is very different from the Mae situation. There we see no sharp competition between the sexes; the men have won their battle and have relegated women to an inferior position. In jural terms, for instance, a woman remains throughout her life a minor (the ward of her father, brother, husband, or son) denied any title to valuable property. She rarely participates in public affairs except to provide food for men or to give evidence in court cases. For the rest, she should simply look on passively and keep her opinions to herself. Indeed, men are apt to discourage their wives from attending such gatherings, on the ground that their proper place is in the garden or at home tending the pigs. Hence, women are less mobile than men and maintain a much narrower range of social relationships. In short, Mae men expect, and in general receive, deference from their women, even to the extent that the latter should turn aside and lower their eyes whenever they encounter men walking on the same track. And in the sexual field, women proceed from a restricted and perforce chaste adolescence to a similarly constrained marital condition, for not only do bachelors shun sexuality but married men also fear for their "skins" and are rarely given to erotic adventuring.

On the basis of this comparison, then, I suggest that in Highlands ethnography we must discriminate between at least two kinds of intersexual conflict or opposition—the Mae type and the Kuma type.[31] The one reflects the anxiety of prudes to protect themselves from contamination by women, the other the aggressive determination of lechers to assert their control over recalcitrant woman. Moreover, it is possible, despite the paucity of relevant published data, to make a tentative geographical distinction between the two complexes. The Mae syndrome appears to flourish in the Western and Southwestern Highlands, among the various Enga groups, the Ipili and the Huli, whereas the Kuma syndrome is a Central Highlands phenomenon, appearing also among the Medlpa, the Chimbu and, perhaps, the Siane. I am still doubtful about the status of the Kyaka and Mendi, but incline towards placing them in the Mae category.

Finally, I should remark that some other societies, apparently only those in the Eastern Highlands, display both sets of characteristics simultaneously or in parallel. Berndt has documented this in detail for the Kamano and their neighbors. Here hostile groups commonly intermarry. "Marriage and close relationship in this region are intimately correlated with warfare . . . the conventional local warning (is) 'Don't trust an affine.' There is expectation of dissension, and this is reflected in real situations" (1962:234). "The assumption is often made . . . that the districts most often and most bitterly at enmity with one's own are those with which its members have contracted the greatest number of marriages . . ." (411). Women, especially when menstruating, are thought to be unclean and dangerous; and older men warn bachelors to abstain from sexual intercourse and from accepting food from women's hands lest their strength be sapped. Youths are also inducted into male associations which practice rites of blood-letting in order to cleanse the participants of female influences. But despite such prohibitions and admonitions, most men, married or single, are engaged in a constant sexual struggle with women as they endeavor to demonstrate their superiority and virility. "Through sexual activity a man justifies his status as a male; and the more he engages in this activity, the more highly are his strength and powers assessed. His sexual relations with women are regarded as a kind of armed combat" (129). As we might expect, the position of women in these societies is ambiguous. In some contexts their actions are sharply restricted, their opinions ignored and their status obviously depressed; yet, as the prize sought by sexually competing males, they also enjoy considerable sexual freedom and actual physical mobility.

Broadly speaking, then, the position of women in the Eastern Highlands falls somewhere between that of women of the Central Highlands and that of women of the Western Highlands. It is significant that women's status is highest in those societies which do not sharply conceptualize long-term hostility between affinally related groups and do not stress the initiation of youths into male associations.

V

In this paper I have described the pattern of male-female relationships among the Mae Enga in an attempt to compare the available material concerning such intersexual oppositions reported from societies of the Highlands of Australian New Guinea. I believe that my analysis has demonstrated the presence of two basically distinct kinds of syndromes (complexes which are largely geographically separate), and I have tried to relate these differences to variations in other social phenomena. No doubt the publication of fuller accounts of these and other Highlands societies will necessitate some modification of the argument, but for the present, at any rate, the generalizations appear to subsume adequately the data so far reported.

CHAPTER

13

Sociocentric Relationship Terms and the Australian Class System

ELMAN R. SERVICE

In any human society individuals occupy social positions which have significance in interpersonal conduct. When the names of these positions are used in address or reference, they may be called status terms. Kinship nomenclature is a worldwide and well-known example of this terminology, but it is by no means the only one. Status terms in general can be divided into two distinct types, egocentric and sociocentric, and this division can be useful in the study of social organization. The problems of the Australian class system will be discussed as a rather extended illustration of the utility of this dichotomy.

Egocentric and Sociocentric Status Terms

Every human society has relationship terms which specify kinds of social categories of persons or groups relative to others. The category of any individual depends on who the speaker (Ego) is. That is, someone may be "mother" to one Ego and "aunt," "cousin," or "grandmother" to others. Such terms may be called *egocentric*. But there are other terms which are not egocentric. A person occupies a named position and status, or is a member of a recognized group, no matter who is addressing or referring to him. These categories are, in a sense, objective, and the reference point is the structure of the society itself rather than another person. We may call such terms *sociocentric*. A person is an "Eaglehawk"—of Eaglehawk moiety—and not a "Crow." Clan names, locality names, personal names, named generations, occupations, and even nationality and racial terms, are other examples of sociocentric nomenclature.

From *Essays in the Science of Culture in Honor of Leslie A. White,* Gertrude Dole and Robert Carneiro, eds. New York: Thomas Y. Crowell, 1960, pp. 416–436.

I am grateful to Robert Carneiro, Gertrude Dole, Morton Fried, A. Kimball Romney, Marshall Sahlins, Gerald Weiss, and Leslie A. White for helpful comments.

Sometimes sociocentric terms are derived from egocentric kinship terms, and may even be the same words, but the distinction can still be made. Thus, "*my* grandfather" designates someone in the egocentric pattern, but a person may also be said to be "*a* grandfather," and this is sociocentric, referring to a socially significant generation grade of the society. A boy may be "son" to anyone of the older generation, and an older person may be "father" or "uncle" to any member of the younger generation. But each person is also "son," "father," or "uncle" in the egocentric set of kinship terms.

Conversely, there are terms which are not derived from the kinship system which are both egocentric and sociocentric. "My Lord" (in reference or address) is egocentric. But "He is *a lord*" refers to the status held in the society, no matter who is speaking. "Boss," "comrade," "captain," "husband," "wife" —a near infinity of examples come to mind.

Two persons can relate better, that is, more precisely, to each other if they can trace an egocentric genealogical relationship between themselves, particularly in a primitive society which stresses familial bonds. But lacking this knowledge, if each can be named as *a* something— an "elder," an "in-law," a "relative," a "stranger," a "nobleman," and so on— relationships of a certain character can be initiated. Suggested in this last sentence is a further and very important difference between the two kinds of terms—the context or occasion for their use.

Egocentric terms are used in small face-to-face groups which have a high degree of stability. A family is the most obvious and undoubtedly the most typical example of such a group; hence, familial relationship terms (kinship terms) form the most common egocentric nomenclature of social relationship. In a family, any member knows a great deal about everyone else, and therefore a great number of things relevant to social position do not need to be specified. At the same time, because all of the social relations are close, consistent, and quite permanent, the system of nomenclature can have considerable complexity; the terms can refer to the relationship of any person or number of persons in the group to any particular Ego. It becomes a cumbersome system, however, if the society is large and numbers of the people do not have frequent and continuing social contacts. Familial relationship ties become attenuated, and some relationships become insignificant and infrequent. On the other hand, familial terms may have to be metaphorically extended to include relationships which are significant in daily social behavior, but which are not truly familial.

It is in such larger complex societies that sociocentric terms have their greatest utility, particularly because of the frequency of contact between strangers. In such cases, broad categories are established first: One is a Rotarian, a midwesterner, a used car dealer; the other an Elk, a Californian, and a chiropractor. As the relationship continues, finer distinctions become specified. But as everyone knows from experience, certain things may be so manifest that they do not need to be stated; that one is a male or female is (usually) readily apparent, as is relative age if the disparity is great. Strength, wealth, and wisdom, for example, may or may not be obvious, depending on the culture and the circumstances. At any rate, one endeavors to place a stranger in a class or a series of classes and subclasses which are relevant to social status. The most important statuses may be designated by brief titles in formal usage, such as "Doctor," "Sir," "Professor," "Madame," "Lord," and so on.

In primitive life the family is such a basic part of society, and suprafamilial institutions are so rare, that all or nearly all social relations are formalized in terms of statuses which are in fact either directly familial or are derivatively or metaphorically so. To the extent that sociocentric nomenclatures exist, they typically refer to kinship categories. Probably the most common are moiety and clan names, and generation terms. And because the sociocentric terms are often kinship-relevant, the basic difference between egocentric and sociocentric categories is easily lost sight of by the ethnographer—both kinds are included in descriptions of "the kinship system."

The Australian aborigines have several sociocentric terms of relationship as well as egocentric familial terms.[1] There are locality names, totemic "clan" names, and names for whole linguistic divisions. In addition, there are categories of kindred once called "marriage classes," more recently called by Radcliffe-Brown "moieties," "sections," and "subsections," depending on whether the society has two, four, or eight of these divisions. As a generic term for these groupings, I shall use "class," intending it to be synonymous with "category," with no implication of socio-economic status or suggestion as to its function in marriage.

If the Australian classes are seen as examples of sociocentric nomenclature, then we may assume that, as elsewhere, they function, not in the context of the internal order of a given social group, but in the meeting of people who do not know each other's egocentric kinship positions. And also, because Australian culture is a very primitive one, it follows that because sociocentric terms express the most significant characteristics of a person's position in the structure of his own society, the class terms will be derived from the kinship order.

These interpretations can be supported by statements from ethnologists of wide experience in Australia. A. R. Radcliffe-Brown once put it this way:

> The relationships between one person and another in the kinship system are individual relationships. In deciding what they are appeal is always made to actual genealogical connection. Thus in Western Australia the first questions always asked of a stranger is "who is your father's father?" Similarly in all discussions as to the suitability of a proposed marriage it is the genealogical connection between the two persons that is considered. *It is true that when the genealogical connection is too remote to be traced the natives fall back on a consideration of the section or subsection or the clan to which an individual belongs* [italics mine], but this does not alter the fact that in the minds of the natives themselves they are dealing, throughout all the ramifications of the kinship system, with real genealogical relations of parent and child or sibling and sibling (Radcliffe-Brown 1930–1931:436).

A. P. Elkin has stated several times that as guides to social behavior the class terms are used among people who are *not* continuously associated with each other, rather than among members of the same kinship group:

> This is especially true in inter-tribal meetings. It is much easier for one group to learn the other's subsection

> system than to bother about all its kinship terms, and so mutual behavior during the gatherings is largely controlled by the subsection grouping, but only, of course, because fundamentally this is a grouping of kinship relations (Elkin 1954:101).

And again:

> If different tribes are to meet together, and they do, they must understand their various methods of grouping relatives so that mutual behavior can be organized and respected during the time of meeting. . . . (Elkin 1954:32). The meeting of tribes for ceremonial purposes, and nowadays, too, the mixing of members of different tribes in white employ, facilitates and encourages the spread of such systems of summarizing kinship. They are naturally of very great value at intertribal gatherings, enabling camping, social activities, and marriages to be readily arranged, whereas the labour of comparing and adjusting the actual relationship through kinship terms alone in different languages, would be a very difficult process indeed (Elkin 1932: 325).

If sociocentric class names function predominantly in a society's external, rather than internal, relations, and if they express the most fundamental categories of the egocentric kinship system, we wonder what those categories may be. There has been disagreement among students of Australian customs as to what the causes and purposes of the class system are, with a resulting variation in their ideas of the basic elements in its composition.

The Components of the Australian Class System

The many analyses and explanations of Australian class nomenclature can be reduced to three general types. One of the earliest was propounded by Lewis H. Morgan and his disciples, Fison and Howitt. In its essentials, it consisted of the assumption that the named categories, which they called "marriage classes," were survivals of a previous custom of group marriage. This theory has long since been discredited and has no support today; hence, it may be ignored for the purpose of this paper.

Another early explanation is apparently accepted by most modern anthropologists, possibly because it has been presented so convincingly by G. P. Murdock in his influential work *Social Structure* (1949:51) and elsewhere (Murdock 1940). The essentials of this view were first argued by Francis Galton (1889) and later by Emile Durkheim (1897). A. B. Deacon, A. R. Radcliffe-Brown, and Brenda Seligman, all in the same volume of the *Journal of the Royal Anthropological Institute* (1927), proposed it again. In 1937, W. E. Lawrence made a thorough review of the literature and revised the explanation.

Galton and Durkheim felt that the four-class system was caused by the intersection of male and female descent lines, and that the purpose of the naming of the categories was to regulate marriage or prevent incest. Seligman also said that "bilateral descent," the recognition of both father's and mother's descent lines, is the cause, and the purpose is to regulate marriage (1927: 375). Radcliffe-Brown (1930–31:55–58) put it this way: "The patrilineal lines of descent (I and II) constitute a pair of patrilineal moieties. The matrilineal lines of descent (X and Y) constitute a pair of matrilineal moieties. The system of four sections is constituted by the crossing of patrilineal moieties and matrilineal moieties giving four divisions in all." He further suggests that the subsection system of eight classes is caused by the presence of four patrilineal lines or "semi-moieties" instead of two. Lawrence (1937) also considers the four-class system (Radcliffe-Brown's "sections") to be formed by an intersection of two lines of descent, the patrilineal line formed by the patrilineal local group, and a matrilineal moiety. Eight classes are formed when the mother's patrilineal line is also recognized in order to prevent marriage with these relatives.

One of the characteristics of the four- and eight-class systems is that children do not belong to the class of either of the parents, but belong instead to the class of the father's father and mother's mother in the four-class system, and to the class of the father's father in the eight-class system. This characteristic has been phrased as "indirect descent," or as "alternating generations." But it is seen by Murdock, Lawrence, and their predecessors to be a result of the intersection of descent lines, and not as one of the basic and original components of the class system. And truly enough, if one draws a genealogy and assigns each person in it to a named category depending on the combination of descent lines, the same class names do reappear only in alternating generations.

This version of the components of the class system is particularly convincing if one assumes that the purpose of naming the groups is to regulate marriage, or as Durkheim put it, to "prevent incest." There is no doubt that most primitive societies do endeavor to prevent marriages with some relatives and to foster them with a certain few others. If this is the purpose of the class system, then the alternation of generations might well be merely a by-product of the intersection of descent lines. All of those mentioned as proponents of the "descent-lines" explanation state in one way or another that the regulation of marriage is the purpose of the naming of classes, and they seem to regard the distinctions between generations as insignificant and functionless, as indeed they would be in the context of marriage rules.

But there are some ethnological facts which contradict this interpretation. Radcliffe-Brown (1913:192 and 1930–1931:58–59), Elkin (1954:90, 92), and W. L. Warner (1937:122–123) observed ethnographically that marriages are arranged in terms of the kinship system, not the class system. A further comment was made by Radcliffe-Brown (1951:42): "marriage systems and 'class' systems of Australia are not co-variant but vary independently. . . . Thus tribes with four 'classes' have marriage systems of any of the four types mentioned, and all four types are equally to be found in tribes that do not have four 'classes.' "

There is still another unsatisfying aspect to the "descent-lines" functional analysis; it doesn't explain very much. Some Australian tribes have no named classes, others two, four, or eight. They all have patrilineal descent[2] and are remarkably similar in most other aspects of social organization. Why do they not all use class nomenclatures? Why do the southern Arunta have four named classes and the northern Arunta eight, when they are otherwise identical? How can the diffusion of the system be explained, if its presence is caused by some strong local social function or need? These facts, particularly the well-documented cases of modern diffusion of the class nomenclature, properly impressed A. L. Kroeber (1952), and led him to describe the classes as "secondary" and "epiphenomenal" institutions, products of "play," rather than basic ones, and to suggest that there is no functional reason at all for things of that kind. Considering the distinction between egocentric and sociocentric nomenclatures, I would agree with Kroeber that the class terms have no important functional determinants within a group's *internal* order. But I would argue that there are important uses for it in a group's *external* social relations.

Radcliffe-Brown (who here contradicts one of his earlier quoted statements), Warner, and Elkin have said many times that the class terms have the same purpose as the kinship terms: They are convenient signposts for kinds of social conduct. As Elkin (1954:100–101) put it, "This makes the system a very useful method of summarizing the twenty classes of relations that an individual possesses. . . . It also makes the system a very useful guide to social behavior." And here we ought to be reminded again of the statements of Radcliffe-Brown and Elkin that the occasion for the use of class nomenclature is in the personal relations of people who do not belong to the same intimate social group. That is, the social context of the use of class names is that which is normal to sociocentric nomenclature.

More plausible than the theory which considers the class nomenclature to be a result of isolating descent lines specifically for the purpose of regulating marriage, then, would be an analysis which included as the basic components of the class system those aspects of the kinship system which are most significant for general social conduct or etiquette, particularly when the individuals cannot establish their specific kin relationship. Such an analysis has been suggested by three people, Radcliffe-Brown, Warner, and Elkin. Each proposed it so succinctly and without argument or embellishment that it has not made much of an impression in anthropology.

Radcliffe-Brown's latest statement on the subject reads:

> Both endogamous moieties (alternating generation divisions) and exogamous patrilineal moieties which divide the local groups into two intermarrying sets, are widespread. Where they exist together, there inevitably results a fourfold kinship division. If we call the generation divisions M and N, and the patrilineal moieties I and II, the four divisions are MI, MII, NI, and NII. The generation division may be regarded as "horizontal" and the moiety division as "vertical," since these two divisions cut across each other (1951:39).

Inasmuch as Radcliffe-Brown makes the above statement specifically in opposition to Lawrence, we assume that this is a final and considered judgment, and that he had given up or forgotten his earlier statement supporting the descent-lines theory. Curiously, he does not say anything about the causal or functional significance of his later interpretation.

Warner (1937:177) very briefly states a similar notion. The class system "regroups" and "generalizes" the kinship system. The first significant determinant of the groups is the separation of adjacent generations. The second is the moiety principle, making four groups. Eight classes "are achieved by dividing each kinship personality into two."

Elkin (1954:96) has offered the same

idea, but phrased a little differently. He sees the separation of generations as one important function of the four-class system and the separation of cross cousins as the other. This latter function is essentially the same as that of Radcliffe-Brown's "exogamous moiety," for the effect of a moiety is to separate cross cousins (and other actual and potential in-laws). Eight subsections are formed when first cross cousins are separated from second cross cousins (p. 99).

This last point, incidentally, has long been accepted by field workers in Australia. Spencer and Gillen first noted it (1899:70–75). The eight-class system is associated with tribes whose kinship system and marriage customs do in fact separate first from second cross cousins, prohibiting marriage with the former. It should be noted, however, that not all of the tribes that specify second cross-cousin marriage have an eight-class system.

At this point, the above descriptions of the class system seem preferable to the descent-lines theory in certain respects. The class system is described as functioning in the context of generalized social behavior, particularly in intersocietal contacts, which is exactly what is to be expected of sociocentric nomenclature. Marriage customs are relevant to the formation of classes, but are not specifically and solely the determinants; nor is the function of the classes merely to regulate marriage. Marriage rules are significant aspects of the social structure and affect social behavior, but so do other kinds of rules and conditions. The regulation of marriage and the prevention of incest are universal problems and are typically dealt with, in Australia as elsewhere, in the context of egocentric kin systems or genealogies. The class system is seen by Radcliffe-Brown, Warner, and Elkin as having a much broader and more generalized social function. They have, in fact, *witnessed* its function, in large part; this is not a "viewpoint" but a matter of ethnographic fact. And because the class terms are guides to social behavior, the distinction they create between adjacent generations is seen as one of the basic and purposeful features of the system rather than as an insignificant consequence of the recognition of intersecting lines of descent.

No one argues that exogamous moieties are not one of the basic components of the class system. In much of the primitive world, relatives are regarded as consisting of two distinct kinds, "other" and "own."[3] Social behavior is always strongly influenced by this general dichotomy and in very many primitive societies this exogamous division exists as two named moieties; that is, a sociocentric terminology is applied. In Australia, it appears that all tribes have this division, whether named or not. Many Australian tribes have a two-class system which consists of two named intermarrying divisions. Named moieties are thus very familiar to anthropologists, and it is not difficult to see them as an ingredient in four- and eight-class systems. Their relation to marriage rules is a subordinate one, however. They do not "regulate marriage," but exist, rather, *because of* a rule of marriage which creates two intermarrying groups in the society; that is, marriage and moiety are two aspects of the same thing. Individual marriages are arranged much more specifically with particular relatives and are not affected by the presence or the absence of named moieties. Exogamous moieties separate *all* of the people into two groups, rather than being relevant merely to the position of the small proportion of people who are about to be married. It should be apparent that marriage customs are not, therefore, to be discounted as factors in the formation of moieties and further subdivisions. But the classes receive names because of certain conditions in wide, usually intertribal, social and ceremonial relations. The names merely *reflect* marriage customs, among other things.

But it would seem that generational distinctions are also significant. All anthropologists are familiar with a common form of primitive kinship terminology which uses so-called "self-reciprocal" terms between grandparents' generation and grandchildren's. But another way of putting it is to say that the kin terms distinguish parent-child generations, but not the second ascending and second descending generations. And this form of nomenclature can occur both in egocentric and in kinship-derived sociocentric systems. This should not be too unexpected if we assume that relationship terms name categories which are important in social behavior. In all human families the two adjacent generations have distinct statuses relative to each other.

In Australia, social distinctions between members of adjacent generations are very strong, and these distinctions are reflected in the kinship terminology. However, the ways anthropologists describe such systems conceal this point. The expressions "alternating generations" and "self-reciprocal terminology" focus on the fact that the class membership and kinship terms of grandparent and grandchild are the same. But the social significance is that adjacent generations are separated. Radcliffe-Brown's term "endogamous moieties" puts the emphasis on the fact that one marries within his or her own generation, but again, the most important point is that the two generations are separated terminologically.

Some Australian tribes have a two-class sociocentric nomenclature which is no more than the use of only two terms, like "M" and "N," successively, separating adjacent generations but leaving the third or alternate generations undistinguished from each other. The fact that this kind of two-class system, and the previously mentioned two-class system of exogamous moieties each exist separately around the periphery of the four- and eight-class area is, incidentally, another strong indication that these two kinds of divisions are the components of the four-class system.

A further point concerning the matter of generations may be made. Our emphasis is on the fact that adjacent generations are separated by the class terminology. But a more usual perspective, consistent with the phrasing "alternating generations," is that the alternate generations are lumped together. This view suggests that merging these generations in terminology is peculiar and must be explained. The typical explanation is that the social behavior of grandchildren with grandparents is somehow equivalent, equal, or symmetrical. As Radcliffe-Brown (1952: 48–49) put it, "There is, in fact, a generalized relation of ascendancy and subordination between the two generations (that is, parent-child). This is usually accompanied by a relation of friendly equality between a person and his relatives of the second ascending generation." This seems peculiar, when it has been noted time and again in Australia, as well as in many other societies in the world, that although grandparents may be indulgent toward grandchildren, the two social statuses are the most unequal in the society, old people holding the very highest status, and children the lowest.

Instead of wondering why alternate generations are merged in terminology, it could just as well be said that those generations are left undistinguished from each other—not distinguished because there is no need to do so. As we have defined them, sociocentric terms specify some status or significant characteristic of a person when it would otherwise be unknown, or at least not readily apparent. The difference between persons separated by two generations is so obvious that there is no need to specify the difference in status. To be sure, through time a considerable disparity may arise between a person's actual chronological age and the age normal for his generation, but such a disjunction would not be usual enough and great enough to affect the scheme. But there is another reason, perhaps more important, why alternate generations need not be distinguished. By the time a person is fully adult in a society as primitive as that of the Australians, with its early aging and low life expectancy, people of the grandparental generation have died, with perhaps a few exceptions. And, of course, relationship terms are based on usual or normally expected situations, not on exceptions.

It is quite a different matter when adults of more nearly the same age meet. If they cannot avail themselves of the more precise egocentric or genealogical knowledge, the one apparently somewhat older might be of either the other's own generation or of his parents' generation, just as in a family it is possible to have a cousin or brother of nearly the same age as one's uncle. But the difference in social behavior is supposed to be considerable, even if the disparity in chronological age is not great. Thus, in a sociocentric context it is useful to have membership in one of the two adjacent contemporaneous generations defined.

A four-class system, then, is nothing more than four names for categories, each of which includes two socially significant attributes. A person is of one side or the other of the intermarrying moieties, and his is the ascendant or subordinate one of the two generations which are present among the active adults at any given period. These categories are socially significant in many primitive societies. They are, in fact, the major distinctions drawn in the widespread "classificatory system" of kinship nomenclature. A. M. Hocart, in speaking of the point of view of Fijian natives toward establishing the relationship of one person to another, said:

> In short, what we seek most is the next of kin, and so we run up and down the family tree. The Fijians (and the Australian aborigines, and the rest) do not, because there is no point in doing so. All they want is such information as will enable them to place each man on the correct side in the right generation. An inquiry proceeds thus: "How are you related?" "Of the same side and generation." "Why?" "Because our fathers were of the same side and generation." Or else: "We belong to successive generations on opposite sides, because he is of my mother's side and generation" (1955:193).

Any family, anywhere, has these distinctions implicit in its organization. The question, though, is whether they will remain only implicit in the egocentric kinship pattern of terms, or whether objective sociocentric groups will be named from the distinctions drawn in the kinship system. Two-class sociocentric systems, consisting of exogamous moieties (the naming of father's and mother's "sides"), are very common in the primitive world. Separating adjacent generations by giving them sociocentric terms is perhaps less common, but still not unusual. The four-class system, composed of both these distinctions, has been considered as primarily an Australian phenomenon, though a few instances of its occurrence elsewhere have been pointed out. The eight-class system, which includes a further subdivision of the exogamous moieties by separating first from second cross cousins, is still more unusual, having only a limited distribution even in Australia.

The fact that an argument has been presented here to establish the usage, purpose, and components of the class divisions does not mean that all important questions have been discussed. We still want to know why some tribes have class terms while others have not, and how the distribution of the various two-, four-, and eight-class systems can be explained. Can their origin, development, and diffusion be inferred? A review of the distribution of the various kinds of class nomenclatures is indicated in order to discover whether the perspective taken so far in this paper has any further utility in relation to the several questions which arise from the distribution pattern of the class systems.

Distributional Problems

In various places located on the coastal periphery of Australia there are tribes which have been described as having no class system. To be more consistent with the point of view taken here, we should say that they are one-class tribes, for without doubt every social order has a sociocentric term, frequently the name of a locality, by which it may be distinguished as a totality from other societies. But one class or none, the important features of the distribution of these groups are that they are infrequent, discontinuous, and marginal; yet they exist in the continent's most productive and densely settled areas, the coastal regions.

More widely scattered and more frequent are tribes with two classes. As mentioned earlier, they are of two distinct kinds. One is the named moiety, a division of the society into intermarrying halves. A person's membership in a moiety may be taken from the mother in some tribes and in others from the father, but the effect is the same: two exogamous groups are formed; cross relatives are separated from parallel relatives; mother's own kin are distinguished from father's; and a generalized kind of behavior characteristic of the relations of affines rather than consanguines corresponds to the delineation. The egocentric kinship terms make these distinctions too, of course, but named moieties objectify, generalize, and extend the distinctions. The other kind of two-class system is created by the separation of the two adjacent generations.

As Radcliffe-Brown describes it, the division which distinguishes the two generations is "horizontal" and the moiety division is "vertical." When both distinctions are made and the resulting groups are named, the society is separated into four compartments. This system has the widest geographical distribution in Australia, and the tribes that have it are contiguous except where the eight-class system has overlaid it.

There is another kind of four-class system, limited and peripheral to the above, which has been called a system of "semimoieties." It is merely the ordinary named exogamous moieties, but with each divided into two parts by the separation of first from second cross cousins of any Ego. It exists only when the marriage rule prescribes second cross-cousin marriage rather than first cross-cousin marriage. Affinals, potential or actual, are thus defined in a more restricted way. This distinction is not a difficult one for the Australians to make and adhere to, because postmarital residence rules cause second cross cousins to be members of different local groups from first cross cousins.

The eight-class system is simply the above form of semimoieties bifurcated by generation. Stated another way, it is the other more usual four-class system of generation and moiety divisions with the moieties subdivided between first and second cross cousins. As in the system of semimoieties, second cross-cousin marriage is not caused by the system, but, rather, the rule of second cross-cousin marriage is a necessary antecedent condition.

Both N. W. Thomas (1906) and D. S. Davidson (1926, 1928) felt that the distribution of these systems was significant. With one-class tribes the most marginal and scattered, two-class tribes less so, four-class systems contiguous and widespread, and with eight classes limited, but contiguous and central, something is suggested about their origin and development. The implied development could be represented by the diagram accompanying the distribution map in Figure 1.

A logically permissible conclusion from these data is Davidson's judgment (1928) that once there were no classes (or one), that two classes appeared and became widely distributed, that four classes appeared next out of two, and eight later, out of the four-class systems. I add to this only the reminder that there are two kinds of two-class systems, the named adjacent generations as well as the named exogamous moieties. The usual four-class system appeared when these two kinds came together. The eight-class system of semimoieties combined with the separation of adjacent generations appeared more recently and diffused rapidly.

Why are the compound systems later and central? It is helpful, as remarked earlier, to see each one as dependent on a previous, simpler system. From this perspective we can see more clearly what the components are. But something else can be inferred from their distribution. The map reveals, in a very general way, that one- and two-class systems occur in the coastal areas where the population density tends to be greatest, and where the camps do not travel so extensively or distantly in search of food. The arid regions of least population density, where local groups must travel most widely, are in central Australia, where the four-class system, and finally the eight, originated and spread. A. W. Howitt (1889:34) commented on this ecological fact long ago, but reached the conclusion that the no-class groups represent an evolutionary advance over the four- and eight-class groups, because he regarded the classes as survivals of earlier group-marriage customs.

Elkin has made several observations

which aid in understanding the distribution of the eight-class system. "Generally speaking it is in the drier and arid regions where this organization is more clear cut. In them, the foraging groups must be comparatively small and be separated by miles, often for weeks at a time, otherwise the sources of food would soon fail" (Elkin 1954:47). If we follow the implications of the view that class nomenclature, being sociocentric, is most useful among people who meet only sporadically and infrequently, it becomes more comprehensible why the compound systems tend to be centrally located in the arid

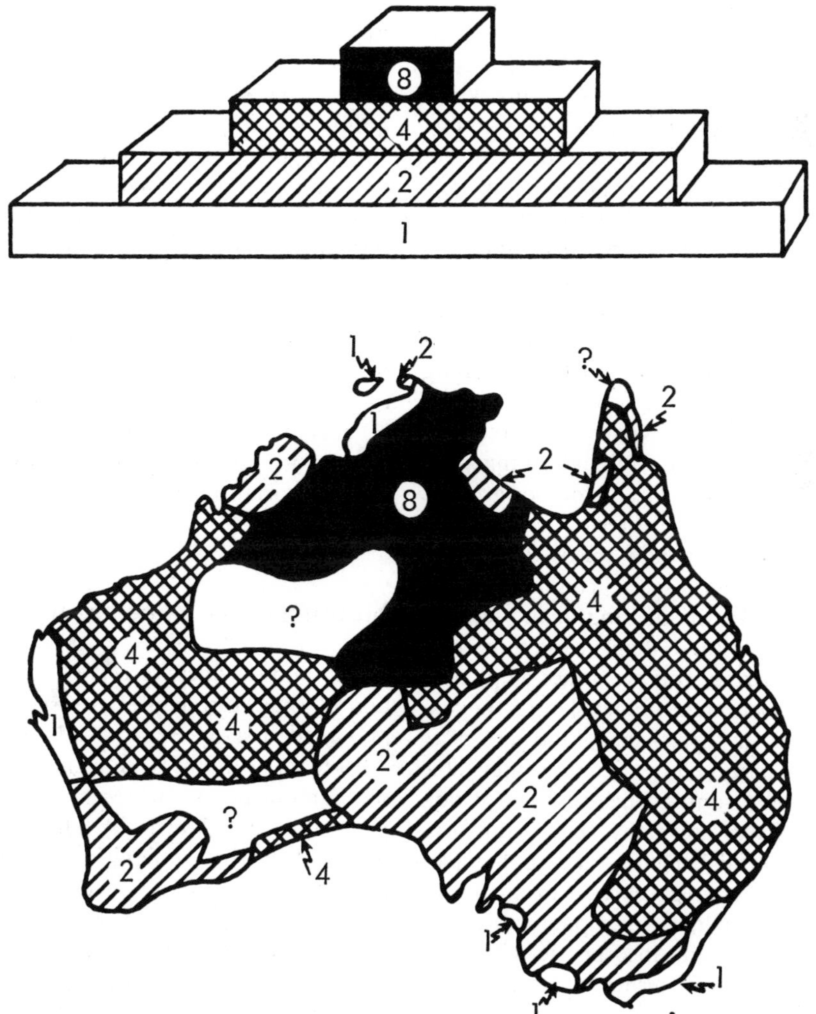

Figure 1. Distribution of Australian Class Systems. The distribution map follows Lawrence (1937:348, Map A). I have simplified it by noting only *named* classes, and I have not distinguished the two kinds of two-class and four-class systems. (Drawn by Edwin Ferdon, Jr.)

regions. Again, Elkin (1954:101) states, "There is little doubt that the practical usefulness of the system at meetings of an intertribal character is the cause of its spread. . . ."

The points made so far agree with Elkin's scattered statements, but it would seem that a more positive conclusion than Elkin's is justified. The practical usefulness of class nomenclature at meetings of an intertribal character is not only the "cause of its spread," but is also the stimulus which led to its origin. Discriminations among people of a social group in terms of generation differences and in-law relationships are not particularly useful among people who see each other frequently; the egocentric kinship system is sufficient and preferable. The four-part distinctions are implicit in their social order but the need for naming them sociocentrically does not exist.

Where meetings are less frequent, and the people are relative strangers to each other, the need for sociocentric terminology is greater—a stimulus is present. This would mean that in inland Australia social conditions exist which make the naming of the sections more likely there than in the more productive areas. But we must emphasize that sociocentric nomenclature in general, or any particular kind of sociocentric terminology, is not an inevitable functional consequence of these conditions. There are many ways people can codify social behavior, and it is apparent that even egocentric kinship terms can be extended—metaphorically, and by adoption—to incorporate strangers. But sociocentric terms do come about; and it is easier to understand a development of this kind when we see its utility.

The fact that sociocentric terms are used in intertribal meetings means that one system has to be used by the diverse groups that meet. If each one of the language groups had its own special system, only confusion would result. The invention of a class system, in a sense, must be something like a cooperative venture between at least two groups, with others acquiring it as its utility is manifested. As described by Elkin (1950), the eight-class system spreads at the expense of simpler ones, because, we may suppose, of its greater utility in intertribal relations. This intertribal use also has resulted in the diffusion of the system from areas where it is most useful, and where it presumably originated, to areas such as coastal Arnhem Land, where it would be less useful. This occurs because there is a belt of contiguous tribes having social relations from the former to the latter areas. The presence of a compound system in one group dictates its acquisition by the adjacent ones if social relations obtain among them.

Summary and Conclusion

The most widely accepted explanation of the Australian class system was presented first by Francis Galton, then Durkheim and others, and finally, with some refinements, in recent years by Lawrence and Murdock. This theory holds that the recognition of both matrilineal and patrilineal descent lines creates four groups which are named in order to regulate marriage. Eight classes are formed when Ego's mother's patrilineal line is also isolated by certain marriage rules. A terminological distinction between parents' and children's generations results from the intersection of the descent lines, and is not seen as an original and fundamental part of the class system.

Another theory, briefly set forth by Radcliffe-Brown, Warner, and Elkin, describes the components of the class system as (1) a division of the society into two intermarrying halves (moieties); (2) a distinction between adjacent generations, parents' and children's. This makes four basic compartments in the society. Eight classes are created when each of the intermarrying moieties is divided into semimoieties, separating any Ego's first cross cousins from second cross cousins.

Both of these explanations are logical and coherent, and both propose a "purpose" to the class divisions. The purpose of naming groups formed by the intersection of descent lines is to regulate marriage; the purpose of the moiety-generational distinctions would seem to be a more generalized one, that of summarizing and simplifying the kinship nomenclature in the context of intertribal social meetings. On the face of it, there seems to be little to choose between the two views.

The distinctions drawn in the present paper between egocentric and sociocentric status terms, however, permit us to make a clear choice between the two arguments. Egocentric terms specify the social position of a person relative to a particular ego. Kinship nomenclature is the best known example of this type. Sociocentric terms, on the other hand, express a person's membership in a component category of the society itself; the term is therefore applied no matter who the Ego is addressing, or who is referring to him. The Australian class system is sociocentric by definition, and we find by reanalyzing the problem with this characteristic in mind that there are several reasons for rejecting the Lawrence-Murdock theory in favor of the presentation of Radcliffe-Brown, Warner, and Elkin.

Sociocentric status terms, in any society, differ from egocentric terms not only with respect to their point of reference—the society rather than individual persons—but also in the social context of their use. Sociocentric terms are used in the interaction of people whose meetings are sporadic and rare, people who do not know the finer and more complex status characteristics of each other, but who do need to know the most significant and gross characteristics in order to initiate an ephemeral social relationship. This expectation, based on theory, is substantiated by ethnographic descriptions of the use of the class system; it is described as functioning largely in intertribal gatherings. For this reason alone, it is reasonable to expect that the components of the class system are the generational and moiety divisions proposed by Radcliffe-Brown, Warner, and Elkin, for these are the two most important aspects of the Australian kinship order, as they are in a great many other primitive societies. The distinction drawn between egocentric and sociocentric nomenclatures reveals that the kinship system and the class system are merely two terminological facets of one social organization. The context of the use of the terms is different, but the social organization itself is a usual primitive one based on familial ties, in no way complex or unusual.[4]

So far as the purpose of the class nomenclature is concerned, then, it is the same as that of the kinship terminology. Both are systems of *status* terms, having to do with social behavior, and not merely the regulation of marriage. Marriage rules are not precisely irrelevant to either the formation of class nomenclature or its subsequent utility; they bear the same relationship to the classes as they do to the kinship system, for the class terms and the kinship terms are both determined by the social organization in general, of which marriage is only one aspect among many. The Murdock-Lawrence assumption that the purpose of the class system is to regulate marriage can be shown to be wrong also on other grounds, namely ethnographic fact. Marriages have been described as arranged in terms of the kinship system, not the class system. Furthermore, kinds of marriage rules do not co-vary with kinds of class systems.

A further test of the utility of the egocentric-sociocentric dichotomy is made by testing its value in accounting for the distribution of the various class systems in Australia. The simplest systems exist marginally and sporadically in the coastal areas. The two-class systems may be inferred, for this reason, to be the oldest of the multiple-class systems. Four-class systems exist mostly in the interior of the continent and are contiguous to each other and widespread. Eight-class systems are a limited central block. This suggests that the eight-class system is the latest and that it includes the components of the simpler systems. Interestingly enough, we find that there are two kinds of two-class systems: one of named exogamous moieties; the other of named alternating generations. The four-class system is merely composed of both generational and moiety distinctions. Eight classes appear when each moiety is subdivided to separate first from second cousins.

The distribution of the class systems corresponds roughly to distinct ecological zones. The simplest systems occur in the coastal regions, which are the richest and most densely populated areas. The four- and finally the eight-class systems are in progressively poorer and less settled areas. The character of the social gatherings in these different zones reflects the ecological variation; in the arid interior "the foraging groups must be comparatively small and be separated by miles, often for weeks at a time, otherwise the sources of food would soon fail" (Elkin 1954:47). The use of class nomenclature, as described by ethnologists in Australia, is found among people who meet only sporadically and infrequently, just as should be expected from the general character of sociocentric relationship terms. It is therefore comprehensible why the compound systems first developed in the interior of Australia.

It should be remarked at this final point that the main purpose of this paper has not been to show that one view of the Australian class system is correct and another one wrong. The theoretical distinction between egocentric and sociocentric relationship terms, however simple and obvious it may be, is much more important. It is this idea which makes possible a choice between the two views by presenting a new kind of supporting argument for one of them, and it suggests answers to a wider variety of questions than either of the two views could supply alone.

CHAPTER

14

Social Organization of a Siassi Island Community

MICHAEL P. FREEDMAN

Students of Melanesian social organization have in the past decade discovered, described, and discussed a rapidly increasing number of "loosely structured" societies. Under one term or another they have been identified in West Irian, the Highlands, coastal New Guinea, as well as in other locations in Melanesia.[1]

What anthropologists confront in New Guinea is more than simply a difference between *ideal* unilineal organization and *de facto* cognatic grouping. What appears to render the elegant definition of "loose structure" so elusive is the fact that individuals in such societies often tend to form action and residential groups in a somewhat random way—on the basis of agnatic ties, through links of affinity, because of ritual asociations, etc. It would be difficult to epitomize the composition of the groups. Furthermore, there is often little discrepancy between their *composition* (*de facto* grouping) and their *constitution* or ideal organization. Such "loose groupings," moreover, may occur in societies with relatively well-defined unilineal or cognatic kin groups—that is, groups whose membership share a common ancestor traceable in the male or female line or, as in the case of cognatic groups, without regard to either line.

In the following pages I propose to identify and elucidate a particular form of "loose" social structure that I observed in the course of field work in the Siassi Islands, New Guinea. Clearly defined and explicitly recognized kin groups *do* exist there; they are not, however, normally relevant to the organization of most social activities, including production, trade, warfare, or ritual celebration. Thus, with respect to these units Siassi social organization seems to display a certain looseness. What, then, is the societal function of Siassi kin groups? How are they related to the loose organization? What are the structural underpinnings of this apparent looseness, and what are the adaptive benefits of such social organization in the Siassi setting?

Siassi Society

The Siassi Islands form a series of tiny coral islets south of volcanic Umboi in the Vitiaz Strait. Six of these islets are inhabited and each comprises a single village of 50 to 450 individuals. Only two, comprising the Outer Islands, are sufficiently large (about one-half square mile) to allow gardening. Like the Manus of the Admiralties, the Siassis support themselves through fishing and trade. They are important middlemen, conveying goods between the northeastern littoral of New Guinea and the opposite coast of New Britain as far east as Arawe. Divided into a daily or weekly local trade and a seasonal overseas trade, Siassi commerce includes a fish-for-vegetable exchange with nearby Umboi communities and a considerably more diversified ex-exchange with distant ports in New Guinea and New Britain. The range of goods Siassis convey extends from "domestically" produced pandanus mats, coconuts, and trochus armlets through "foreign" goods such as clay pots, Tami Islands bowls, net bags, obsidian, ochre, bows and arrows, cowrie shells, pigs' tusks, dogs' teeth, dogs, and pigs, plus numerous other items of less importance.

Siassi social structure may be divided into three levels: the village, the men's house, and the household. These are units of social organization that are explicitly recognized and indeed precisely defined by Siassis.

THE VILLAGE

Geographically separate, each island village is named and socially distinct. Permanent residents identify themselves and are identified by outsiders as belonging to a certain community. Sometimes vocalized as boastful claims, at other times evidenced in the suspicion and denigration of neighboring communities, village distinctiveness is fostered by ethnocentric prejudice and preserved by high rates of local intramarriage. (Since around 1920, 85 per cent of the females and 100 per cent of the males resident in the Siassi village of Mandok have been natal members. Fewer than one tenth of all native Mandoks born after 1900 emigrated from their island community.)

Siassi villagers collectively comprise a corporate land-owning unit. Although land that has been cultivated or that serves as a house site typically is regarded as household property, uncut growth is held in public tenure by the village at large. Such land and its wild resources are closed to outsiders but freely accessible to all village members. Beginning with the German administration (1885), Siassis residing on the smaller islets have made use of garden land on the opposite coast of Umboi, and the practice continues today. Village land includes, in addition, the island and village site, a restricted "men's area," and small islets or sandbanks used aboriginally for pig pasturage and more recently for coconut plantings. Village property further includes special buildings for storing ritual paraphernalia, pig enclosures, adjacent coral reefs, and nowadays a copra drier, latrines, and quarters for government officials on patrol.

The village in Siassi constitutes the maximal unit of production and the widest extent of distribution. Occasionally nearly all the men of the community may participate collectively in a fishing expedition, in the construction or repair of some village-owned edifice (storage shed for ritual masks and such, copra drier, wind screen, pig stockade) or—in round robin fashion—in the manufacture of long fishing seines. On the whole, the village is seldom a productive unit either in the statistical sense that most villagers cooperate in a given undertaking or in the corporate sense that some enterprise is conducted in the name of the village. Villagewide food distributions occur throughout the year, typically as the material side of rites of passage, but also in conjunction with corporately sponsored harvest ceremonies and competitive, renown-building feasts.

Each Siassi village forms a more-or-less distinct cultural entity. Dialect differences tend to distinguish one Siassi community from another, as do personal names, artistic motifs, insignia, and designs. Because many spirits are "localized" in a particular whirlpool or weirdly deformed tree, the pantheons of Siassi communities tend to be distinctive.

What most significantly marks the village as a level of Siassi social organization is that it is an administrative and jural unit. Indeed, it remains the most inclusive level of political activity in Siassi. Recognized by the Australian Administration as an electoral ward and (within limits) as a self-governing community, the Siassi village is not the contrivance of Western colonial administration. It had, prior to European contact, its own headman (*maron*), its own means for settling disputes and effecting collective decisions. What appears to be the product of European control is the nucleated *form* of settlement—particularly on the larger islands.

Formerly, hamlets of three to five dwellings, separated by gardens and fallow plots, checkered the islands. Each local aggregate was identified with a patrilineal group. It is not clear whether several such units exclusively comprised a single men's house or men's house organization crosscut the local kin groups so that one patrilineage was represented in a number of men's houses. In any case, linked through affinal ties and common membership in a men's house, hamlets jointly participated in ritual celebration and feasting. At times they are reported to have attacked one another; but violence, Siassis aver, was "unknown" within the agnatic kin group. The meager evidence available suggests that these attacks were primarily between kin groups, that supporters from other hamlets participated on the strength of a close kinship bond now and then, but that local groups never formed military alliances. In effect, these hostile acts constituted "breaches of the peace" and, I believe, may be usefully regarded as "feuds" rather than "wars." The hamlets are identified in the vernacular as *panu gegeo,* which conveys at once the notion of "small" and "constituent" settlements.

Each village aboriginally recognized a single elder male as headman or *maron* of the entire community. The office, although hereditary in theory, fell in practice to the man whom village consensus informally elected. In the larger islands, where horticulture was practiced, the *maron* apparently set the time for the yam harvest. Apart from this the *maron* enjoyed no special privilege. Since contact, Government-appointed *luluais* and *tultuls* have usually provided formal leadership. In actuality, however, leadership has been diffusely exercised by a number of prestigious and influential men within the community. These—the "big-men" of the village—have distinguished themselves by their industry, wealth, generosity, oratory, and wise counsel. Although their rhetoric may have been persuasive, their power over other villagers was never coercive. Through informal and sustained conversations the islanders continue to pose problems, air their differences, and arrive at collective decisions, which on rare occasions receive public enunciation in a formally convened meeting of the village men.

Disputes, arising chiefly from the theft of garden crops, pigs, and women (i.e., adultery and related offenses), or from the illicit appropriation of garden land, were seldom if ever settled by the *maron* or any other village leader. For example, Siassis tell of an Outer Island gardener, born in the last half of the nineteenth century, who expropriated some adjoining garden land by clandestinely replanting the boundary-marking shrubs. The men involved were not related; they addressed each other by name and never used kin terms. Upon discovering his loss the wronged man publicly accused the other. The latter's denial of shifting the boundary markers led to a fight. The contest ended when the expropriator cut the brow of his antagonist with a knife, previously concealed in his garments, while the villagers watched without physically taking sides. The wounded man retired from the arena, having lost the contest and a portion of his garden land. In this instance no one else joined in the conflict nor interceded to effect a settlement, for reasons informants no longer remember. Nevertheless, the violence committed was slight, and the possibility of containing the fight or separating the disputants was always at hand.

Individuals might publicly bemoan the loss of some harvested garden crops and hope that a guilty conscience would prompt the thief to return them. More serious offenses moved Siassis to employ the services of an Umboi sorcerer to divine and punish the guilty party. Competitive feasting, often prompted by theft, slander, and adultery, was yet another alternative antagonists traditionally resorted to short of outright feuding.

Chagrined by his wife's infidelity and her paramour's ridicule, a renowned Siassi big-man (now dead) is remembered to have retaliated by pressing upon his adversary—with great ostentation—a costly pig, the focus of a lavish banquet, which at once honored the donor and humiliated the recipient. Thus shamed into a "one-upmanship" rivalry, the philanderer produced a pair of swine, and many months thereafter the competition ended when the initiator humbled his rival with a presentation of five pigs.

Only when confronted with extraordinary or chronically repeated offenses did the villagers as a corporate group exact penalties. Either several male villagers, anonymously disguised as supernatural beings, stoned the offender's house and demanded a pig in compensation, or perhaps close kinsmen might agree to kill the reprobate in the interests of the village. The latter course, Siassis recognize, was practiced to forestall feuding. What is pertinent in the present context is that the village as a level of organization, as a unit of activity, rarely materialized around disputes. Neither the *maron* nor other big-men, *qua* village leaders, characteristically sought to mediate, much less adjudicate, disputes. And these observations appear to be generally valid today. Seldom do feuds physically engage more than a handful of villagers. Feuds in Siassi do not crystallize component subunits; they could never trigger even the ephemeral disintegration of village society into constituent clans, wards, or moieties. Most transgressions are viewed simply as acts against individuals, which therefore compel the persons concerned to rally the support of their friends and close kinsmen. Yet the fact that the village corporately does not respond to feuding should not obscure the constraints it imposes on the expression of interpersonal aggression.

Intravillage violence, if not negligible, was restricted. Feuding was reportedly seldom sanguinary. Prominent villagers and senior kinsmen commonly exerted informal influence upon both parties to exchange tokens of goodwill and cease hostilities. Indeed, the parties themselves, under the vague press of public opinion and a common village morality, often arrested their own hostilities before grave injury could be inflicted. An example of such self-imposed restraint occurred in the early years of the German administration. A dispute arose between the *tultul*-and-former-*maron* of Mandok and the ruling *luluai*. The former had taken the wife of the *luluai* to the bush. The aggrieved husband insisted on a spear duel in the central plaza where he, together with his younger brother, hurled spears at the *tultul* and his junior sibling. The spears were dodged and the fighting terminated when the offender declared, "I am the cause of this trouble. I cannot throw my spear at you." An older classificatory brother of the two combatants then intervened and shortly thereafter the protagonists exchanged a single span of beads to symbolize the peace settlement.

Village corporateness, as I observed earlier, is further manifest in the custom of channeling private differences within the community into economic contests that serve public interests. Furthermore—and most importantly—intravillage aggression could never escalate beyond modest limits. The coherence, integrity, and solidarity of the village was preserved, as we shall see, precisely because intravillage groups were never set against each other; indeed, barring the men's house, individual antagonists had no discrete groups to fall back upon.

By contrast, warfare—that is, intercommunity violence—involved the corporate village just because it could *potentially* mobilize a determinate and enduring social body, namely, the village itself. Warfare (before it was outlawed) pertained to the village level of organization not because it necessarily enlisted the joint cooperation of most of the community's men, but because the rationale for participation was common membership in the community, co-residence in the neighborhood.

The Malais relate an incident that followed the death of a local big-man, supposedly the victim of a Siassi sorcerer from Aramot village. The version I heard continues as follows:

> Now the men of Malai agreed to avenge the death of their fellow villager and kill Sopol (the alleged culprit). They left Malai at night and reached Aramot Island just before dawn. So

> many Malais joined the expedition that they completely surrounded the island with their canoes.
>
> One Aramot *lapun* [old man] got up to urinate and noticed the Malai fleet. "Oh, you men sleep," wailed the *lapun* to his comrades, "while a mountain of canoes has sailed here." All Aramot was speechless. But Sopol realized instantly that the Malais had come to fight and ran to the men's house where he hid with his spear.
>
> The Malais entered the center of the village. They wished no harm to the Aramots. Thye inquired where Sopol was hiding. The Aramots answered, "We don't know; you find him." But already one *lapun* of Malai observed Sopol in the men's house. He said hello to him and took him outside. The Malais fired away at him, but he dodged the spears and arrows. Then one spear hit him in the leg. All the Malais stood next to him and speared him until he died. Afterwards his head was smashed with a wooden sword, which is the way our ancestors killed sorcerers.

Although perhaps more violent than local feuding, Siassi warfare—or better, raiding—was seldom destructive of life or property. Only one exception came to my attention. Three or four generations ago the Mandoks aided one distant Umboi village in laying waste to its neighbor. What prompted the devastation and motivated so atypical an alliance is no longer remembered.

There was no special organization for offense or defense. There were no specialized warriors, no men trained to fight or responsible for the security of the village. As with any skill, of course, some men excelled in fighting. Anecdotes revealingly recount the Siassi warrior's preference for the bow and arrow or spear rather than the sword, a weapon restricted to close-in combat. They also suggest that hostilities ceased with the first bloodshed—at least within Siassi.

Aboriginal warfare in Siassi appears to be related neither to securing booty nor to capturing trophies. There is little evidence tying its occurrence to systematic economic pressures, although in historic times, spurred on by the profits of cash cropping and commercial shell fishing, rival claims to land and reef have developed which the administration has been forced to arbitrate. A government anthropologist surveying the area in 1926 wrote of a defunct Aramot refuge on adjacent Umboi, which reportedly those Islanders had established as a precaution against the raids of other Siassis. When and why these attacks were perpetrated remains unknown, and to judge from the few accounts of warfare retailed in Siassi, one may conclude that its incidence was low and its effect nil. It appears that warfare, like feuding, erupted sporadically and was often the outgrowth of interpersonal antagonisms, which, in the absence of a recognized authority, could not be otherwise mediated.

Warfare could surely appeal to a wider community of interests than feuding, while being less dampened by an embracing morality. Yet I suspect it commonly, perhaps typically, involved the village not as an organic whole, a corporate entity, a state, but as an aggregation of individuals, collectively supporting the one among them who instigated the campaign or in whose interests it was conducted. In this respect it differs from feuding only in the basis for recruiting support.

What is important to note here is that the external relations of Siassi villages are composed of numerous individual relationships, principally trading partner ships and bonds of adoption and affinity. The village as such does not trade; the village has no foreign policy. Except for some military expeditions and occasional ceremonial performances which Island villages stage in mainland and sister communities, the village never acts externally as a unit. Its external relations must be otherwise induced from the extralocal relations of its members. To understand the organization of Siassi society we thus must appreciate the central role individual households play in the conduct of daily life.

THE HOUSEHOLD

The lowest, least inclusive level of Siassi social organization and the most fundamental unit in daily activity is the household. As a rule, the household and conjugal family coincide. Sometimes the former includes widowed parents, orphaned nephews and nieces, or junior siblings in addition to the nuclear family. Less often the household comprises children plus a widowed father or mother. Commonly households occupy their own quarters exclusively, and when two families share a single dwelling, each inhabits a separate apartment, equipped with a private entrance. Indeed, it is not the house but the hearth that symbolizes the independence and the integrity of the household. As the household constitutes the daily commensal unit, it possesses its own hearth and provides its own fare.

Gardening, collecting, manufacturing, and often fishing, which are daily activities, center around the members of the household, and although long-distance sailing is always a collective undertaking, trade is characteristically carried out between private individuals. Not only is it the primary unit relevant to consumption, the household in Siassi constitutes the principal unit of production and distribution. Given the complementarity of men's and women's roles, the Siassi household is quite stable and self-sufficient.

Furthermore, it is the major proprietary unit. Possession of garden land, fallow land, fruit trees, crops, livestock, canoes, nets, household effects as well as the house itself is normally vested in the household or one of its adult members. Ownership of material property may devolve jointly on a set of blood brothers, but more often the first-born child or eldest son inherits the paternal "estate," a portion of which he holds in trust for the junior siblings until they reach maturity. Ideally, land and other wealth is equitably—if not equally—divided among all offspring. In practice, however, garden land and fruit trees are typically inherited by sons.

Aboriginally, only the Outer Islanders engaged in horticulture; since the nineteenth century all Siassis have gardened and most—even from the Outer Islands—have utilized unoccupied Umboi land. Consequently, it is uncertain how closely contemporary tenure customs correspond with precontact practices. Older informants agree that garden land was never owned by the whole village corporately. Some assert that such property was jointly held by a localized agnatic family; others claim it was in the past, as it is today, the private possession of individual households. Yet, surely then as now, if the right of disposal and preferential access were prerogatives of the conjugal family, implicit usufructory privileges nevertheless extended to close kindred and intimate friends. Data from Malai (an Outer Island) indicate that not infrequently a man and his son-in-law operated a plot together, and somewhat less often a daughter and her husband inherited the plot, which they eventually bequeathed to one or more of their sons. Far more often, however, a man inherited a share of either his father's or adopted father's estate.

An example from Mandok (an Inner Island) may clarify the nature of tenure, inheritance, and joint operation. Before an old big-man died, some twenty years ago, he divided his estate between his two sons (half-brothers on their father's side). One stretch of fallow land, which supported coconut and betel-nut groves, a few sago palms, three breadfruit trees, and a mango tree, was given to the elder brother along with a small parcel some distance away. The younger brother inherited a large fallow tract without many fruit trees. Greater size compensated for the substantially fewer fruit trees. The brothers never worked a garden together. Their tracts of land are not contiguous.

In 1965, with the help of two maternal half-brothers, the younger man opened up some primary forest bordering on his old garden. His half-brothers utilized a portion of this new area as well as another garden situated in fallow land a quarter mile away. Rights to the new strip of garden land belong to all three men. However, each one actually operated small, separate plots within the garden. They cooperated in certain tasks such as clearing and fence mending; otherwise, each worked independently with the aid of his wife and children.

As there is a sexual division of production, there is a functional division of inheritance by sex. Fathers typically apportion their personal possessions among their sons, as mothers do among their daughters. Thus, the sons inherit woodworking tools; the daughters, cooking utensils. If a man dies a widower, his house is likely to fall to his eldest son or his neediest son. As with virtually all facets of Siassi social organization, there are few stated rules, and those that exist are never rigidly applied. Traditionally, heirlooms and other valuables have been divided among all the siblings upon the death of the surviving parent.

In the past, it is said that a man's debts were inherited by his children, because the scorcery employed against him by his creditor extended to them. The administration has prohibited debt inheritance as a means of curtailing sorcery. It is no longer possible to determine to what extent sons repaid their deceased fathers' debts. Besides moral persuasion and the fear of sorcery, there was nothing in the traditional culture that could compel them to honor the debts of their fathers.

Knowledge of magic and sorcery—unlike material possessions—was inherited outside as well as within the nuclear family. Special aptitude apparently carried greater significance in the transmission of esoteric and ritual information than it did in the inheritance of corporeal property, and Mandoks report that at times brothers' sons and sisters' sons were trained in preference to one's own son.

A closing remark concerning private property and ownership seems warranted. The exclusiveness of rights implied, if not denoted, by the legal concept "private property" is not strictly appropriate to traditional Siassi custom. I have used the term here to convey two kinds of relationship between persons with respect to things: one moral, the other statistical. Possession denotes an automatic right to use and dispose of things. But it does not denote an exclusive right, because close kinsmen in need have a moral claim to usufruct. Although etiquette requires that they secure prior permission from the owner, the latter is morally impelled to grant it. Refusal would ordinarily subject him to scorn and opprobrium. The more distant the relationship between individuals, however, the less likely an individual will seek permission to use another's property. The petitioner feels uncomfortable asking favors from distant kinsmen, and he risks being embarrassed by a denial. Normally, he has a circle of intimate comrades and relatives he can approach instead. As the tie between persons grows tenuous, the ethic of kinship responsibility loses its force.

Possession further means a differential access to goods, and in a society in which production is largely geared to household needs, a moral claim to the use of certain property will often be superseded by an outright claim of ownership. In effect, a man's brother may use his canoe anytime—except when he himself needs it.

Household property, then, is not a conscious principle or a proscriptive law, but a custom, a statistical norm, a patterned rule of conduct derived from moral imperatives. It is primarily a relationship governing usufruct.

THE MEN'S HOUSE

A named, exogamous, localized kin group, the Siassi men's house, stands formally between the least and most enclaving levels of Siassi social structure. Its membership nowadays is largely composed of kinsmen related to one another through their fathers. In earlier decades matrilineally related persons may have more regularly affiliated, and adoption then was practiced more systematically, particularly in order to maintain numerical parity among the men's houses within each village. The *raison d'être* of the men's house, Siassis explain, is to provide an expedient instrument for distributing pork, fish, and vegetable foods throughout the village on ceremonial occasions. Following the initial, equal division to every men's house, each then redivides the produce among its constitutent households. Usually the domestic shares are prepared and consumed separately, in the privacy of the family dwelling.

As a ritual group, the men's house is identified with distinctive designs and motifs, some of which the male members incise or paint on their canoes. The men's house also owns certain personal names.

The men's house appears to have little pertinence to other facets of Siassi life. At least since the turn of the century, the men's house *per se* has not engaged in productive tasks nor actively served political ends; it has owned no corporeal property, nor have its members regularly fraternized as men's house brothers.

The ancient character of the Siassi men's house is impossible to conjure up today. At present, it resembles a ritual descent group, but membership depends neither on a demonstrated nor stipulated pedigree. The men's house has no explicitly lineal tradition, although Siassis are not in agreement on this point; it unquestionably lacks eponymous ancestors. In fact, the men's house is not an ancestor-based group. Men's house composition, as I have said, is at present strongly patrilineal and suggests therefore the existence of agnatic lineages. I was told that aboriginally the men's houses on the larger islands comprised several shallow, localized lineages; perhaps, in the absence of good documentation, it is preferable to call them "patrilines," and thus eliminate denotations of incorporation and descent reckoning. In any event, so long as the men's houses were kept at about the same population size the membership composition would have had to be highly cognatic—that is, include kinsmen whose mutual relation is not traceable exclusively through males or through females. Genealogies offer evidence that in the past brothers affiliated with different men's houses; older informants affirm that such a practice was customary even as recently as 1930. Ideally the adoption of every other child by some avuncular kinsman helped produce the desired distribution of offspring among varied men's houses. But with the deterioration of men's house organization, particularly in the Outer Islands, the requisite data are no longer available to determine how closely the ideal was approximated. The best data I have (from Mandok) suggest that roughly 13 per cent of the offspring (who reached maturity) were adopted, one seventh of whom remained in the same men's house and two sevenths of whom remained in the same patriline (though not necessarily in the same men's house). No marked sex preference is indicated. Presumably, adoption in the Outer Islands helped equalize the distribution of land rights. However, Siassis do not view adoption in those terms, and in the absence of detailed information this hypothesis must remain conjectural.

If in the precontact period men's houses assumed corporate functions, contemporary Siassis are unable to confirm it. In sum, the Siassi men's house is a recognized institution for expediting the equitable apportionment of ceremonial food and for regulating the choice of marriage partners.

But it is more. By permitting marriages to occur randomly among equal-sized, exogamous units, men's house organization effectively scrambles affinal bonds throughout the community and thereby forestalls the formation of enduring intravillage blocs. Thus ideally men's houses display uniformity in the breadth and intensity of their respective alliances. There is negligible variation among men's houses in the number of connubial links that join any two units and in the number of sister units with which anyone is tied (see Table 1).

Were marriages contracted wittingly between patrilines, were patrilines overt elements of Siassi social structure, then, because of the vagaries of population growth in small groups, considerable variation would be manifest among parallel units in the scope and intensity of their peculiar affinal bonds. Inevitably, intravillage factions would emerge as a consequence of differential size and secondarily in response to an uneven distribution of marital alliances (see Table 2).

However, Siassi patrilines, as I have stressed, are not indigenously perceived. If Siassis know the personnel of their own patrilines, they are not mindful of which co-villagers comprise the membership of coordinate units. Patriline confreres hardly ever marry one another —an observation that holds true even when the sodality is defined as broadly as genealogical knowledge allows; yet the leagues of patrilines joined by exogamous unions, although statistically demonstrable, lack social significance. Unnamed and untermed, the patriline seems to be eclipsed by the men's house. One may even argue that the contempo-

Table 1

Intermarriages among Men's Houses, Mandok Village (ca. 1920–1966)

Husband's Men's House	Wife's Father's Men's House							
	Man.	Tabob.	Pandan.	Tapugu	Sim.	Bed.	Pan.	Total
Mandogsala	2	1	2	1	3	4	2	15
Tabobpugu	4	0	5	1	3	1	1	15
Pandanpugu	1	4	2	1	2	3	1	14
Tapugu	1	2	3	0	3	2	0	11
Simban	5	3	0	4	0	1	1	14
Bedbedang	4	2	2	2	2	0	3	15
Panuboga	3	2	2	0	0	1	0	8
Total	20	14	16	9	13	12	8	92[a]

[a]Two men (from Tabobpugu and Tapugu) married women of uncertain men's-house affiliation and are therefore not included in the matrix.

rary Siassi patriline is merely an ethnographic artifice. The men's house, it appears, has assumed the functions of a ritual lineage. But more than a structure or level of organization, the men's house is an important *mechanism* of organization. Where lineages, clans, age-grades, secret societies, and wards coalesce individuals into higher-order units, the men's house in Siassi—although itself a group—latently and importantly checks the formation of emergent entities within the community.

The Organization of Social Action

Activities arise that demand collective participation—overseas sailing, net fishing, bridewealth production, feuding. Other undertakings commonly involve

Table 2

Intermarriages among Maximal Patrilines, Mandok Village (ca. 1920–1966)

Husband's Patriline	Wife's Patriline										
	1	2	3	4	5	6	7	8	9	10	Total
1		5		3	2					1	11
2	5		1	4	1				1	1	13
3				3		1			1		5
4	7	2	2	1	5	5		2	1	3	25
5	4	3	1	7				1			19
6		1	1				1				3
7		1		3		1					5
8			1				1				2
9			1		1						2
10	1	1		2	3		2				9
Total	17	13	7	23	12	7	4	3	3	5	94

a task force also, although the inherent need for cooperation is less evident. If there are not practical, standing groups in Siassi larger than the household yet smaller than the village, what are these social units which emerge frequently to execute certain collective tasks and lessen the monotony of other, solitary chores?

In a word, they are "assemblages"—that is, *ad hoc* gatherings of relatives and friends impermanently united to assist some Ego, about whom this congregation materializes and in whose interest—if not at whose instigation—the group carries out a defined job. Assemblages constitute mosaics of kinsmen, related in one way or another to Ego, although not necessarily to one another. Statistically, these groupings display a centripetal tendency and an agnatic bias. In other words, Ego is more likely to call first upon close rather than distant kinsmen, and he will sooner seek the aid of a father's brother than a maternal uncle. This is, of course, trivial. What is more useful is that Siassi assemblages normally comprise a *majority* of rather distant kinsmen with reference to the pivotal figure. That is, although an assemblage predictably contains a few very close agnates (brother, father/son, perhaps a father's brother/brother's son), most of the composition includes more remote kin. Still more significant, I think, is the Siassis' *expectation* that such task forces will comprise a variety of kith and kin, whose particular genealogical pathway to Ego is of no importance.

Over the years a person develops a number of relationships which, although biased by genealogical relatedness, are profoundly affected by the selective influence of personality. The stamp of kinship is not inexorable. There are brothers who do not cooperate and remote kin who maintain intimate relations. All kinds of relationships—agnatic, matrilineal, cognatic, affinal, demonstrable, and putative—are knowingly exploited.

Siassis construe the meaning of "kinsman" broadly and without rigor. Defined strictly, affines cannot be included within the "kindred," for they and Ego do not share common ancestry; they are not "one blood." Yet operationally and in ordinary parlance Siassis treat in-laws as kinsmen. Again, the particular form of kinship link joining Ego to his in-law matters little. What matters most to the energetic and ambitious Siassi is that he have a reservoir of dependable kinsmen that he can tap.

Consider overseas voyaging, for example. Does the men's house or patriline form the nucleus of Siassi sailing parties? Or, are expeditions organized upon some other foundation? Interviewing informants from all over the archipelago proved indecisive: a majority denied that sailing crews are explicitly composed of agnates or the members of a single men's house, but a significant minority dissented from that view. Often a set of brothers (who nowadays most probably belong to one men's house) form the crew's core. But this hardly proves that the patriline or men's house acts pivotally in the staffing of overseas expeditions.

To better gauge the possibly masked presence of the men's house in overseas voyages, I analyzed 100 different expeditions with respect to crew composition. Most of the voyages occurred after 1945; a few predate the War by five to ten years. The data were culled from Mandok informants—who, of all Siassis, remain most faithful to traditional practices. There seems no reason to doubt the general applicability of these findings to the whole area.

An individual men's house contributed at least half the personnel to 58 out of 100 expeditions. In another two, a pair of men's houses each comprised 50 per cent of the crew. But those 58 voyages dominated by a single men's house exhibited a relatively small crew size—5.55 men; in contrast, the remaining 42 expeditions averaged a crew of 10.95. Particularly in small populations the ability of one men's house to provide half the crew declines sharply as crew size increases. Whether sailing crews are initially recruited from the membership of a single men's house, or whether men's house representation is a probable outcome of chance combinations in small populations, the figures suggest that the men's house cannot systematically furnish the framework around which overseas voyaging is organized.

As one would expect in a small population without a developed division of labor, the tendency for the same individuals to journey together repeatedly is not very pronounced. Eighty-three per cent of the average Siassi's fellow travelers accompany him only once or twice. Of those who sail with him three or more times—Ego's circle of "consistent" co-voyagers—no more than 4, and on the average 2.7, join him at any one time. As a rule, the more actively a Siassi engages in overseas voyaging, the fewer the number of "consistent" companions who undertake any one expedition with him. My figures indicate they accompany him on anywhere from 22 to 88 per cent of his expeditions. The median is 50 per cent. Thus, it is apparent that ordinarily a crew is composed of Ego, two or three of his "Consistent" co-voyagers, and four or more villagers who are available. Clearly the data show that most of any given Ego's "consistent" co-voyagers are his patrilineal kin—chiefly brothers, fathers, paternal uncles, and father's brother's sons. The evidence also indicates that normally the bulk of any crew is not patrilineally related to any given Ego. Indeed, its organizing principle, it seems to me, neither relates specifically to the men's house nor to the patriline; the organization of sailing parties is simply that of the assemblage.

If overseas voyaging calls into question the relevance of the men's house and patriline to collective activities in Siassi, the organization of gardening confirms their utter nonpertinence. The most comprehensive data I have comes from Mandok, but they do not appear to conflict with the isolated accounts I obtained elsewhere in the archipelago. Table 3 summarizes the genealogical relationship of co-gardeners in Mandok, 1965–1966, and notes parenthetically their men's-house affiliation. By "co-gardeners" is understood individuals who in one year systematically work the same garden that bears the crops they consume. Many people help with certain gardening chores, but this alone does not make them "co-gardeners." Women garden too, of course, but usually they do not inherit land nor engage in those activities (heavy clearing) that confer gardening rights. On the whole, relationships between female co-gardeners are more remote genealogically than those between males.

The intricately interconnected webs of kin relations that ephemerally crystallize as assemblages resist succinct characterization. It is doubtful that a meticulous analysis of a great many assemblages would reveal substantially more about their heterogeneous and indeterminate constitution than a few diagrams of typical Siassi action groups. I therefore present, without further comment, some graphic depictions (Figures 1 through 6) of actual assemblages related to garden work, fishing, bridewealth production, and bridewealth distribution.

A form of productive and commercial unit, called simply by its pidgin term *Kombani,* was organized by a Mandok villager, recently returned from New Britain, who learned that his trade partner in a certain Umboi village was prepared to repay an outstanding debt in the form of seven "sticks" (logs) of sago. If the Mandok villager had had

Table 3

Genealogical Relationship and Men's-House Affiliation of Male Co-gardeners, Mandok (1965–1966)

Garden	Primary Bush Cut by	Ego's Co-gardeners
A	Ego's F(T)	None
B	Ego(T)	WS, by previous marriage (B)
C	Ego (N)	DH(M); FFBDSS(P)
D	Jointly by 2 matriparallel cousins, (W) and (T)	
E	Ego's F(N)	B(W)
F	Ego(M) and F(M)	S(M)
G	Jointly by 2 brothers, (W) and (M)	S(W); B(P)
H	Ego(N)	BS(N); WZH=FBS(M)
I	Ego(N)	MBS(P)
J	Ego(T) and F(T)	B(T); B(W); BS(T)
K	Jointly by Ego(S) and ZS(W)	$\bar{S}$(S); BS(S)
L–R	Jointly by 3 half-brothers, (W), (N), and (S)	
M	Ego's F(W)	$\bar{B}$(W); MB(N); $\bar{F}B\bar{S}$(P); $\bar{F}B\bar{S}$WB(M)
N	Ego's(N) WF(W)	None
O	Ego(N)	None
P	Ego(N)	WB(B)
Q	Ego(N)	DH(B)
S_1	Ego's F(S)	None
S_2	Ego's F(S)	None
T–U	Ego's F(M) and FF$\bar{B}$S(M)	FF$\bar{B}$SS(M)
V	Ego(T) and B(T)	S(T)
W	Ego(B)	$\hat{B}$(B); $\hat{B}$(B); $\hat{Z}$H(B); $\hat{Z}$S(B)
X	Collectively by the co-gardeners (see Figure 1)	

KEY:

F—Father
M—Mother
B—Brother
Z—Sister

S—Son
D—Daughter
H—Husband
W—Wife

$\bar{F}$, $\bar{B}$, $\bar{S}$—Adopted father, brother, son, etc.
$\hat{B}$, $\hat{Z}$—Step-brother, step-sister, etc.

Men's houses:

(B) Bedbedang
(M) Mandogsala
(N) Pandanpugu
(P) Panuboga
(S) Simban
(T) Tapugu
(W) Tabobpugu

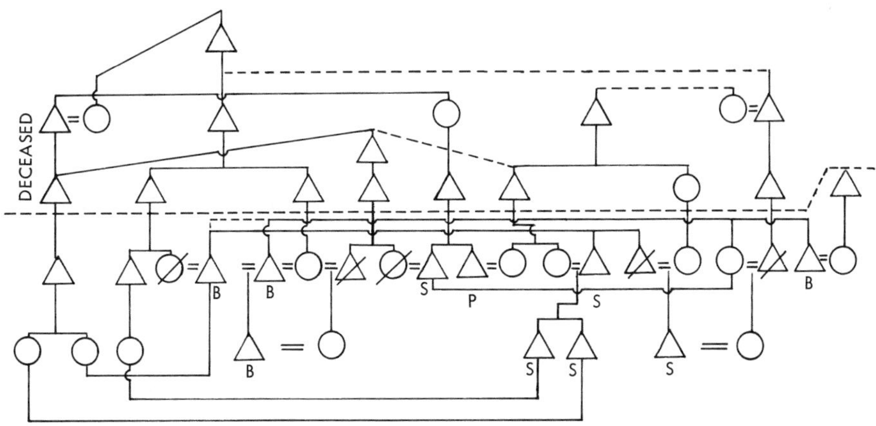

Figure 1. Male Co-gardeners of Garden X, Mandok, 1965–1966. Men's house of co-gardeners indicated as follows: B=Bedbedang; P=Panubog; S=Simban; T=Tapugu. Scored lines indicate adopted sibling ties; slash=deceased.

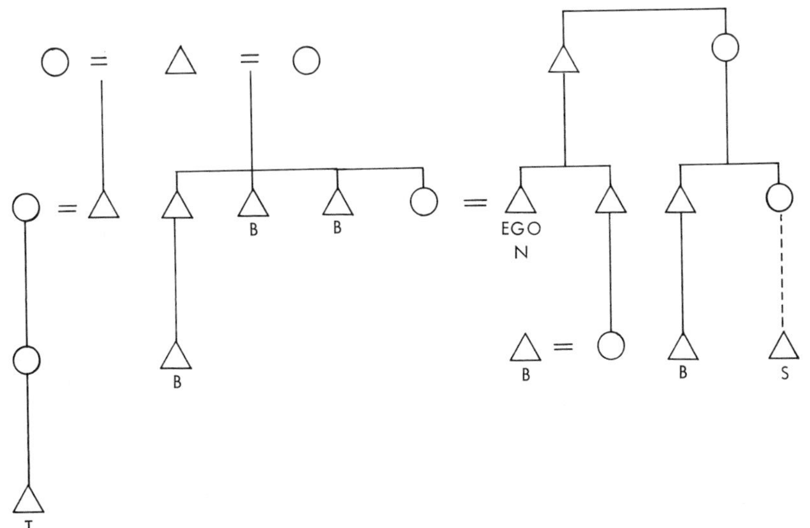

Figure 2. Bush-Clearing Assemblage. Men's-house affiliation of relevant men indicated. Scored vertical line indicates adopted offspring. Ego owns garden "P" (see Table 3).

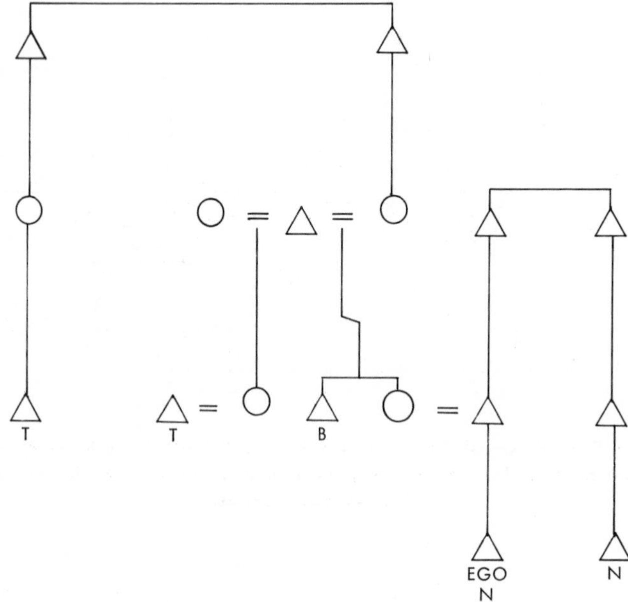

Figure 3. Hoeing Assemblage. Men's-house affiliation of relevant men indicated. Ego owns garden "N" (see Table 3).

a sufficient store of food, he would have "hired" fellow villagers to help him process the sago into flour. However, since he was unable to subsidize the necessary labor, he formed a temporary association with his brothers, cousin, and affines who contributed their labor for a more or less equal share of the produce.

The man's elder brother had an important trading partner in New Britain who notified Mandok that, because of a drought, villagers there were eager to trade for sago. The elder brother possessed no sago of his own at this time and was, therefore, particularly anxious to cooperate in the *kombani.* The two men called upon their youngest brother, an agnatic classificatory brother, and a couple of villagers who were matrilateral cousins of the two brothers and affines to the central figure of this venture. The six men represented three different men's houses.

Siassis have surrendered the right of collective retaliation since Europeans have exercised power in the area. Villagers are prohibited from avenging wrongs committed against them. Vengeance units no longer exist. Most serious crimes come to the attention of the administration; however, kinsmen provide mutual aid in other ways and assume a degree of responsibility for one another.

A case in point occurred in 1966, when the Mandoks, advised by an Aramot traveler that a local man accused of adultery was hiding on a nearby islet, dispatched three young men to apprehend him. One of the three was his adopted brother, another was his father's

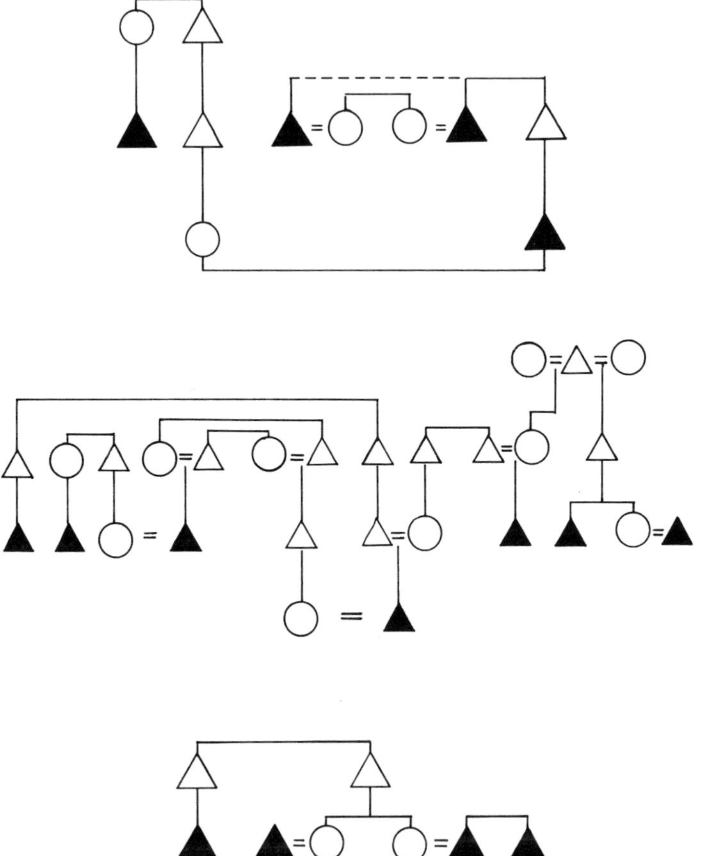

Figure 4. Representative Fishing Crews. Fishing crew indicated by solid triangles.

sister's son, and the third was the son of the man's maternal aunt. Each belonged to a different men's house.

Later, when the man returned home from a two-month jail sentence, he paid out approximately 400 pounds of manioc to the village "to buy back his honor." He had no living older brothers to assist him in this public distribution, but received material support from his maternal uncle and his father's mother's brother's son. These two individuals—important members of the community—also belonged to two different men's houses. The significance of the mother's brother is more apparent here than real. The man's father had no brothers and his father's father came from New Britain.

Assemblages come into existence to perform tasks, not to fulfill continuing needs. Once the forest is felled, the fish caught, the feud settled, the assemblage dissolves into so many persons. Its constitution follows no perceived formula, no inferable pattern that I am aware

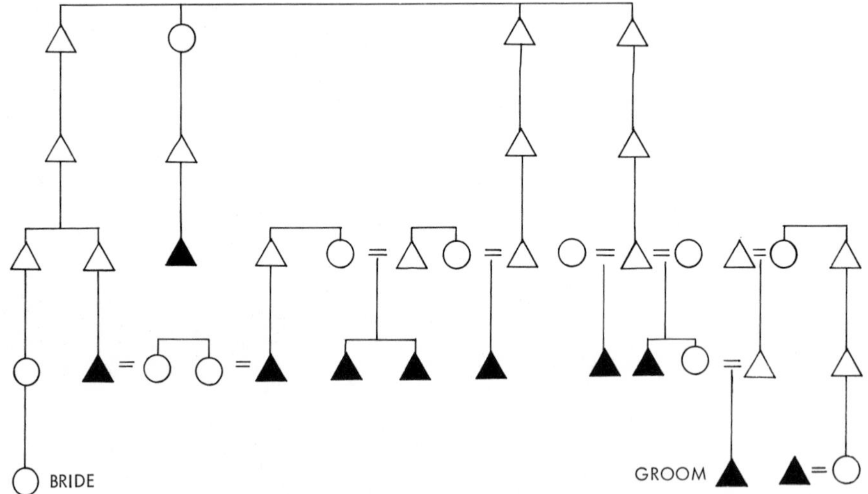

Figure 5. Assemblage of Bridewealth Producers.

cousins or second cousins once removed. of—except the very general rule I offered at the beginning of this section.

But if a particular assemblage is short-lived, the institution—the concept of a throng of kinsmen cooperating in some given venture—persists indefinitely. And, consciously or otherwise, Siassis continually sculpt these fleeting action groups out of the clay of kinship. Now engaging one kind of relation, now another, Siassis rely on numerous

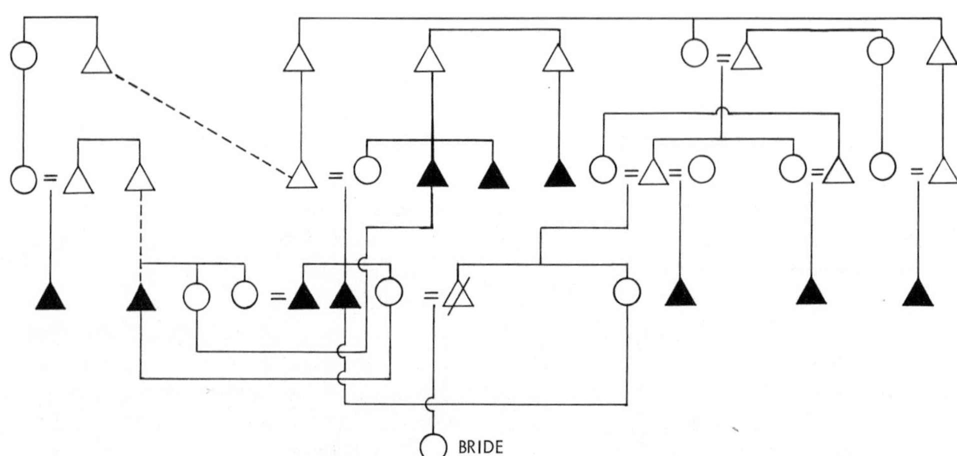

Figure 6. Assemblage of Bridewealth Recipients.

kinsmen and a wide variety of genealogical relationships.

MARRIAGE

Marriage creates kinsmen. It is the principal instrument for converting strangers into relatives and distant into near kin. For men who have few brothers, a probable situation in small populations, marriage ties are apt to be crucial; however, they are regularly exploited by nearly all Siassis.

In the island villages of Siassi, marriages are in practice locally endogamous, yet seldom do they join persons more closely related than second cousin. Of 114 marriages contracted in Mandok village between around 1920 and 1966, only 18 (16 per cent) were with nonlocal women. During this period, which saw the population grow from around 140 to just under 400, only 45 (39 per cent) marriages occurred between persons for whom one could demonstrate (through blood, adoption, or stepparentage) a common ancestor. Two thirds of these are unions between a male ego and some patri*lateral* kinswoman; however, Siassis articulate no preference for the male over the distaff side, and in general marriages appear predicated less on laterality than on consanguinity.

Tradition forbids marriages between kinsmen closer than second cousin (or first cousin once removed)—a custom that Siassis appear to have honored through the present. Most of the "consanguineous" unions studied—36 out of 45—occurred between either third cousins or second cousins once removed. Thus, minimal descent lines cannot perpetuate their affinal alliances across adjacent generations. In other words, the children of two sibling sets, united through one or more marriages, are barred from marrying one another. If aboriginally men's-house composition was cognatic, then the taboo on first-cousin marriage would effectively prevent the sons of brothers, distributed in different men's houses, from marrying one another's sisters. The regulations governing the choice of spouse at once militate against the formation of institutionalized, intravillage affinal factions and, through preferred local endogamy, ensure individuals of a potential corps of helpmates in their affines.

Lattice Structure

Analyzed as an instance of descent group organization, Siassi social structure would seem to be highly fluid, extremely "loose," and rather enigmatic. For instance, even if we imbue the patriline with group status, neither it nor the men's house appears singularly relevant to most economic and political affairs, as I have outlined earlier. Moreover, although the latter explicitly and the former statistically regulate marriage choices in the village, Siassis express an additional rule prohibiting first-cousin unions. Clearly, the men's house and the patriline *alone* do not regulate marriage. Even the men's house, which *is* a group, seems peculiarly devoid of group functions, except insofar as it distributes the village population evenly and permits consequently the scrambling of marital alliances throughout the community.

Thus Siassi society displays two levels that have practical bearing on most aspects of social life: the household and the village. Viewed from the individual's standpoint, society is a composite of overlapping egocentric kindreds. Viewed societally, the community may be likened in its structure to a crystal whose lattice of diversified kinship ties bond together the basic molecules—the households—into an emergent entity—the village. The lattice model draws attention to the constituent units, the total aggregate body, and the connecting linkages. Unlike a segmentary system erected on a nesting principle, lattice structure evidences no intermediate political or economic units. Unlike cognatic descent groups, proprietary rights are vested in the household, and collective activities are prosecuted by *ad hoc* cognatic groupings.

Annually new households emerge while others dissolve. To the householder the web of ties he has with other nuclear families remains relatively stable, although surely the intensity with which he exploits cerain lines fluctuates in response to the kind of assistance he seeks, the availability of helpmates, and the status of his varied friendships. But seen as the cohesive force of the village, the pattern of interhousehold ties continually alters and reforms itself in an unpatterned sequence of interfamily relations.

Conceivably, lattice organization might materialize in locally exogamous communities that are not internally segmented by clans, wards, associations, etc. However, under such conditions, but for the nexus of friendship any given household would be coupled to others only by unilateral consanguineal ties. The engineering of lattice organization is appreciably more complex when marriages occur within the community with significant regularity.

Where the selective forces operating on a culture have placed a premium on the integrity of the village, on the unity of the community, the absence of institutionalized factions within the local society is desirable. It forestalls intergroup rivalries and disruptive competition. But endogamous marriages in tribal society necessarily establish potential alliances and therefore potential lines of cleavage. Family sizes naturally vary, so that even if marriages are contracted randomly, demographic imbalances will inadvertently but unavoidably create latent affinal groupings. The problem in engineering lattice organization, then, is to prevent these latent sets of affines from surfacing as operant blocs.

To that end, as I have explained, the design of lattice structure includes a device for scrambling marriages among co-resident and related families. This entails (1) random connubium—the nonsystematic movement of women in marriage; (2) "familial exogamy"—the prohibition of unions between persons closer than second cousin; and (3) the maintenance of numerical parity among exogamous units. Inasmuch as family size is likely to be variable, an artificial means of maintaining equivalence must be employed. In Siassi, as noted earlier, this artifice is the men's house.

If lattice structure integrates the community, it also tends to isolate producers, atomize proprietorship, and abort the formation of politically meaningful corporations. What, in adaptive terms, is the utility of such a social system?

Sustained by trade, Siassi society has evolved a means of compensating for infertile soils and insufficient space. Imports do not merely furnish dietary needs in Siassi; they enhance life. Were the ownership of produce corporate and the right of disposal collective, the idle could batten on the labor of the industrious. Atomized propretorship, however, prevents the leveling of differentials in household production. Surpluses produced are preserved—and are thus exportable. The wherewithal to trade is safeguarded, and needed imports consequently can be secured.

In the absence of strong counterforces promoting the establishment of corporate groups around garden land, fishing sites, or capital equipment, the selective pressures of trade have pared down the size of proprietary units in Siassi to the level of the household. Even on the larger islands, where gardening was practiced aboriginally, trade in foodstuffs as well as other items seems to have been important if not imperative. Siassi reefs do not yield seasonal fish "harvests," and such durable products as dwellings, nets, and canoes seldom last a decade. There is, in other words, little reason for corporate groups to arise and considerable advantage gained from their absence.

Yet the need for collective action occurs repeatedly. Groups are indispensable in overseas sailing, some kinds of fishing, and defense. They expedite most forms of production and ease the burden of hosting public banquets or amassing respectable bridewealth payments. Lattice structure, a series of interdigited kindreds, provides householders with a matrix from which they can readily recruit an *ad hoc* task force. Thus, lattice structure reconciles the demands of maintaining the household's commercial independence without compromising its reliance on larger units for assistance in production and support in distress.

CHAPTER

15

The Iban of Western Borneo

DEREK FREEMAN

The Iban, or Sea Dayaks,[1] are a Proto-Malay people of western Borneo. Today, most of them live in Sarawak, where they are the predominant element in a heterogeneous population. The total population of Sarawak, as computed in the census of 1947, was 546,385, of whom 190,326, or 34.8 per cent, were Iban. Sarawak, like all the countries of Southeast Asia, has a plural society. Along the coast, among the deltaic swamps and in the low-lying country bordering the tidal reaches of the rivers, are the main centers of Malay, Chinese, and Melanua settlement. Farther inland, in broken country covered with tropical rainforest and drained by fast-flowing rivers, live the indigenous hill peoples: the Land Dayaks, the Iban, the Kayan, the Kenyah, the Kajang, and others, all with subsistence economies based on the shifting cultivation of dry rice. Other Iban tribes inhabit the headwaters of the great Kapuas River of what is now Kalimantan, or Indonesian Borneo, but on these information is scant and reliable population estimates are not available.

The people with whom the present account is primarily concerned are the Ulu Ai Iban of the Baleh River in the Third Division of Sarawak. The Baleh enters the great Rejang River from the west at a point about 170 miles from the sea, and along its banks and those of its many tributaries (the Sut, Mujong, Gat, and Merirai being the most important) are scattered some 130 Iban communities with a total population of about 11,500. Almost all of these people are the descendants of migrants from the interior of the Second Division of Sarawak (particularly the Ulu Ai, or Upper Lupar River) and from parts of the Kanyau, a tributary of the Kapuas. Leaving these areas in the early decades

---

Reprinted by permission of Quadrangle Books from *Social Structure in Southeast Asia,* pp. 65–87, edited by George P. Murdock, copyright © 1960 by the Wenner-Gren Foundation for Anthropological Research.

of the nineteenth century, they moved intermittently forward by way of the Katibas and Rejang rivers, cultivating the hillsides in their path, and reached the primeval forests of the Baleh about 1880. During the years that followed the Iban were several times expelled from the Baleh, a number of punitive expeditions being sent against them by the Brooke government because of their recalcitrant addiction to headhunting, and not until 1922 was permanent settlement achieved. Today the Baleh is an exclusively Iban area.

The field work on which my findings are based was carried out during two different periods: the first from February 1949, to January 1951, and the second from December 1957, to March 1958.[2] During the former period the Iban of the Baleh region were a pagan and preliterate people whose *adat* and way of life had been little influenced by the outside world. Since then governmental and missionary activities have brought about various kinds of cultural change. To date, however, at least within the Baleh, there have been no significant departures from the traditional kinship system described in this paper. Moreover, such comparative data as are available to me (mainly in the form of inquiries which I have made in other parts of the Third Division, and in the Second Division during a two months' survey in 1951) suggest that the system here described is the traditional system of all the Iban tribes of Sarawak.

A more detailed account of the Iban family and the kinds of residence and descent associated with it has been published elsewhere.[3] In the present paper I shall direct attention to the wider cognatic social structure of the Iban and their system of kinship and affinity.

The Bilek Family

The Iban of the Baleh all live in long-houses, each consisting of a series of separate family apartments occupied by small family groups. Later I shall have something to say of the general kinship structure of the long-house community. First, however, because of its relevance to the understanding of the Iban system of kinship terminology, I would like to make brief reference to some of the salient characteristics of the family units of which a long-house is composed—*bilek*[4] families, as the Iban call them.

Every Iban *bilek* family is an autonomous corporate group. This fundamental fact is expressed in several ways. For example, the *bilek* family is always a local group owning and occupying a single long-house apartment. Again, it is always an independent entity economically, its members constituting a single household and providing for their subsistence by the cultivation of hill rice and other crops. Likewise, it is always an allodial unit possessing both land (including tree crops) and valued heirloom property in its own right. Finally, in ritual matters every *bilek* family is a distinct group performing its own rites (*gawai*) and possessing its own magical charms (*pengaroh*), its own special kind of sacred rice (*padi pun*), and its own set of ritual prohibitions (*pemali*).

Typically a *bilek* family contains three generations, consisting of a pair of grandparents, a son or daughter and his or her spouse, and grandchildren. Stem families of this type usually have about six or seven members. Such families are perpetuated as corporate groups by a simple expedient: at least one of the children of the family, when he (or she) reaches maturity and marries, remains permanently in the ancestral *bilek*. All the other children of the family may marry out, and so become members of other units, but one (either a son or a daughter) always stays in the natal *bilek*. In this way an Iban *bilek* family achieves continuity through time as, from one generation to the next, one elementary family grows out of and succeeds another in an unbroken sequence. This means that every *bilek* family is (in theory) a perennial corporation aggregate. In other words, although birth, adoption, marriage, and death result in regular changes in its personnel, a *bilek* persists through time as a jurally defined entity—an estate in land and property which, at any moment, is always held in common ownership by a group of coexisting family members.

To achieve continuity in this way a *bilek* family, generation by generation, must produce the children one of whom will, in due course, succeed his (or her) parents as a manager of the family estate. This requires that the parents in each generation should be joined in a productive and ideally a stable marriage.[5] Further, as the *bilek* family is a strictly exogamous unit, it must in each generation recruit to its membership at least one affinal member. As we have already seen, the individual who remains a resident of the ancestral *bilek* may be either a son or a daughter. In actual fact, sons remain in the parental *bilek* to approximately the same extent as do daughters, and, similarly, sons and daughters marry out of their natal *bilek* to about the same extent. In other words, the in-married affine of a *bilek* is just as likely to be a husband as a wife.

The significance of marriage for the *bilek* is shown in the fact that affines acquire full membership in the family into which they marry, while relinquishing all parcenary rights in their natal *bilek*.[6] Further, affinal members frequently come to play a dominant role in the management of a *bilek* family's affairs. In Iban society, then, the conjugal tie is of great importance; indeed, it can be shown in certain respects and contexts to matter more than does the relationship between siblings.

Residence and Filiation

From the foregoing it will be seen that marriage among the Iban is of a kind that may be called utrolocal,[7] meaning by this term a system of marriage in which either virilocal or uxorilocal residence may be followed and in which rules of kinship and inheritance result in no special preference for either form of domicile. In fact, virilocal and uxorilocal residence occur with nearly equal incidence; for an extensive series of marriages of Baleh Iban, 51 per cent were instances of uxorilocal and 49 per cent of virilocal residence.

Every individual in Iban society is born into one particular *bilek*, and the system of marital residence just described means that this is just as likely, in general, to be the *bilek* of the child's mother as it is to be the *bilek* of the child's father. Further, the *bilek* in which a child is born and grows up is the only *bilek* in which he (or she) jurally possesses parcenary rights, for rights may not be held in more than one *bilek* at a time. These rights over the *bilek* estate are relinquished only by adoption into another *bilek*, by outmarriage, or by death. Filiation among the Iban is thus of a special kind which I have called *utrolateral*,[8] meaning by this term a system of filiation in which an individual can possess membership in either his father's or his mother's corporate birth group (i.e., the *bilek* family among the Iban), but not in both at the same time. In practice, both types of filiation occur to an approximately equal extent.

Among the Iban, then, filiation takes the form of attachment to a local family estate, principles of both descent and residence being involved. In other words, it is filial consanguinity and local residence acting together which establish the jural rights of the natal members of any *bilek* family. In practicing this type of filiation to a local family estate the Iban have solved the problem of establishing a system of corporations without resort to any unilineal reckoning of succession.[9] It is one of the virtues of the Iban system that it defines the rights of *bilek* members without ambiguity, and in this respect it can be said to be just as efficient as a family system based on unilineal descent. The *bilek* family assumes great importance among the Iban, for it is the principal corporate group of their society.

Siblings and Partition

Within a *bilek* family, siblings are parceners; there is no differentiation of rights between older and younger members, between the sexes, or between natural and adopted children. In other words, co-resident siblings hold equal rights jurally over the family estate. This equivalence of siblings in the structure of the *bilek* is one of the basic principles of Iban society. Unmarried siblings, we may say, are joined by a common interest in their family estate. In the course of time, however, when siblings marry, affines enter the *bilek*, and children are born, the situation is changed by the intrusion of rival loyalties. The *bilek* family is now no longer a simple group, for it contains within its boundaries two different elementary families, and when two such families emerge within the confines of the same apartment there is a very strong tendency for their interests to diverge. The recognized course in such circumstances (and here we are dealing with one of the basic values of Iban society) is for one of the siblings to claim his (or her) share of the family estate, secede from the ancestral *bilek*, and set up a separate domestic unit. This process of family partition is, in fact, a common occurrence. It is important to note, however, that partition occurs only when the seceding sibling is already married, or has established an elementary family of his (or her) own, and, moreover, that in about 80 per cent of the cases there are two married siblings and their spouses in the *bilek* immediately prior to partition.

Thus, whereas prior to partition the solidarity of a *bilek* family depends on the sibling tie, after this event the solidarity of each independent section rests primarily on a conjugal tie. These two forms of relationship—the sibling tie and the conjugal tie—are, I would argue, the most important in the kinship structure of Iban society. As already indicated in part, the two ties assume importance at all the main stages in the developmental cycle of the *bilek* family. They are also of cardinal significance beyond the *bilek*. Immediately before or during partition siblings within a *bilek* frequently quarrel. After partition, however, the siblings concerned stand at the head of autonomous *bilek* families, and in these changed circumstances it is usual for their solidarity to be gradually reestablished, though in more diffuse terms. That is, while no longer possessing a common interest in a family estate, they behave toward one another with the same kind of general affection and helpfulness that normally exist between siblings of the same *bilek*. It should be noted, however, that the same kind of relationship exists between the affinal spouse of a *bilek* and his (or her) siblings, wherever they may be. Indeed this remark may be extended to the general statement that a *bilek* family normally maintains the same kind of friendly relationships with the cognates of both its natal and its affinal members.

The Long-House Community

Bilek families are grouped together in long-house communities. These communities vary considerably in size: from as few as 4 to as many as 50 *bilek* families, the average size being about 14. Of a sample of 61 houses in the Baleh region,[10] 25 per cent contained fewer that 10 *bilek* families, only 13 per cent comprised more than 20 *bilek* families, and 62 per cent consisted of from 10 to 20 *bilek* families.

In the Baleh region all Iban long-houses are situated on the banks of rivers or streams navigable by dugout canoes. Their dispersal along the banks of these rivers is irregular, and the distance between houses may vary from a few hundred yards to four or five river miles. Nowhere in the Baleh are there clusters of houses such as occur among the Land Dayaks of the First Division of the Iban of the Rejang delta. The universal rule is that each long-house constitutes a single community; in other words, the village and the long-house coincide. Moreover, traditionally each long-house community is an autonomous entity not subject to the control of any other group.

Every long-house is situated on part of a specified tract of land, and between long-houses there are always recognized boundaries, consisting in the main of easily distinguishable natural features such as streams or ridges. A long-house, then, is the domicile of an independent community of families situated on the bank of a river that runs through a specified territory over which these families have either rights of access or ownership.[11]

Most of the families making up a long-house community are related to one another cognatically. It is important to realize, however, that, despite the high degree of interrelatedness that may exist among its component families, a long-house holds no property of any consequence in common ownership, nor is there collective ownership of swiddens. Again, there is an absence of economic activity by the long-house community as a corporate group. Nonetheless, membership in a long-house does impose upon a *bilek* family many duties and obligations, for it is universally accepted that the well-being of any community is dependent upon its ritual state, and for the maintenance of this all are responsible. Thus, joining a long-house always involves ritual incorporation.

General responsibility for preserving the ritual well-being of a long-house rests with its *tuai burong,* or augur, who also performs the important task of taking auguries for the community as a whole. Every long-house also has a *tuai rumah,* or headman, whose principal duty is the safeguarding and administering of the customary law, the *adat*. Today the *tuai rumah* is accepted as the official intermediary between his community and the British colonial administration, which has conferred upon him limited magisterial powers. Thus, in jural as well as ritual matters the long-house is a conditional corporate group, for all its *bilek* families willingly place themselves under the jurisdiction of their *tuai rumah*. For the offices of neither house augur nor house headman is there any rigid dogma of succession; any male cognate may succeed to either.

The Kindred

In Iban society there is no semblance of any sort of unilineal descent groups of the type usually described as a lineage or clan. Instead, Iban social structure is based on purely cognatic principles. Let us begin our analysis of these principles with an examination of the main categories of relationship which the Iban themselves recognize, considering first the term *kaban*. In its widest connotation, this term refers not only to an individual's cognates and affines but also to all of his (or her) friends and acquaintances. In this connotation the term *kaban* refers to the same social category as the Old English phrase "kith and kin."[12] The extension of the term *kaban* to cover this broad field may be seen as an expression of the fact that in Iban society, with full bilateral recognition of all relatives, almost all of those persons with whom an individual associates are, in some degree, either his (or her) cognatic or affinal kin.

There is, moreover, a general assumption that most if not all the members of a tribe are kinsfolk, even though their exact relationships to one another can no longer be traced. This can be discerned in such assertions as *itong se kaban magang kami Iban* ("We Iban, it may be said, are all kin of one kind or another") and *se ribu kaban tu kaban magang magang, enda olib kria* ("One's kin [cognatic and agnatic] run into thousands; all, all are kin, they can not be counted"). The Iban are also well aware, as the second of these assertions implies, that because of the widely ramifying nature of their cognatic system many kinsfolk become forgotten to one another in each generation. Furthermore, this forgetting is frequently erratic and one-sided, so that it is by no means an unusual experience for an Iban to be hailed as a kinsman by a tribesman whom he himself does not recognize. The term of address used within the category of kith and kin, where there is no knowledge of the generational relation of the two persons concerned, is *wai*. This term may be used of and by both sexes and all ages. In its widest sense it is best translated as "friend," but in many contexts it carries the general implication of "to whom I am probably related."

Within the broad category of kith and kin three main distinctions are made, namely: (a) *kaban mandal:* cognatic kin; (b) *kaban tampil:* affinal kin; (c) *orang bukai:* other people.

The adjective *mandal* has the primary meaning of near or close, as in the sentence: *umai aku mandal amat* ("My swidden is very near at hand"). The phrase *kaban mandal* is used to designate an individual's cognates, i.e., all of his (or her) known consanguineal kin, tracing descent through both males and females. The word *tampil* has the primary meaning of joined together, as in the sentence: *iya nampil ka brang kalambi iya* ("She is joining on the sleeves of her jacket"). The phrase *kaban tampil* is used to refer to all of an individual's affinal kin, including both the cognates of his (or her) spouse and the affines of his (or her) cognates. In these phrases the distinction between cognatic and affinal kin is made semantically clear. However, as we shall see, the Iban custom of marriage between close cognates, e.g., between second cousins, results in a frequent overlapping of the two categories.

Those within the pervasive category *kaban* who cannot be shown to be cognates or affines are said to be *orang bukai,* or other people. This does not contradict the assumption mentioned earlier that such people may perhaps be one's relatives; indeed, a common statement among Iban is that if cognates do not intermarry they will eventually become *orang bukai,* or strangers, to one another.

For any individual the category *kaban mandal* is identical with his (or her) personal kindred. In recent years some anthropologists[13] have extended the term "kindred" to include affinal as well as cognatic kin. For my part, I see no justification for this tinkering with an ancient and concise term, and in this account I shall continue to employ kindred in its long-established sense of the category which embraces all of an individual's father's kin and all of his (or her) mother's kin, or, to put it more succinctly, all of an individual's cognates.[14]

As has long been recognized by those engaged in the study of Germanic societies, strictly speaking no two individuals have precisely the same kindred.[15] However, if the relationships between themselves are excepted, and assuming they have not produced children of their own, the members of the same sibling group do have the same kindred. Looked at in this way, a kindred is seen as radiating out bilaterally from the children of an elementary family to include all those persons to whom relationship can be traced consanguineally through both male and female links.

The point of reference in a personal kindred is the individual at its center who in reckoning its membership must trace his (or her) relationship to collateral kin through one or more ascending generations. Looked at synoptically, however, a kindred is made up of a series of affinally related cognatic groupings, which, it should be noted, are in no sense corporate groups. A child is directly a member of two cognatic groupings: those of his father and of his mother. Similarly, each parent is directly a member of two cognatic groupings, to all of which the child also belongs, making four in all. The number of cognatic groupings to which an individual belongs thus doubles with each additional ascending generation that is taken into account. It becomes an essential task, therefore, in the analysis of cognatic societies like that of the Iban, to establish the extent to which bilateral relationships are in fact reckoned. As we shall presently see, the average Iban is able genealogically to trace bilateral relationships only as far as the second ascending generation, i.e., to the siblings of his (or her) grandparents and their descendants.

In a kindred of this range four cognatic stocks are represented, namely, those stemming from the sibling groups of father's father, father's mother, mother's father, and mother's mother. While from the point of reference of the individual at the center of the kindred the members of all these four groupings are cognates, a number of them are ordinarily not cognatically related to one another. In other words, at ascending generation levels the cognatic groupings of which a kindred is composed are often linked primarily by a conjugal tie between two of their members.[16] Indeed, in a genetic sense all kindreds are brought into being by a succession of marriages through the generations; thus the four unions of a man's great-grandparents produce the four individuals whose two marriages produced his parents. In short, affinal kin (*kaban tampil*) in one generation become cognatic kin (*kaban mandal*) in the next. It can thus be said that the conjugal tie is of great importance in the general kinship structure of Iban society, just as it is within the *bilek* family.

Let us next consider briefly the average range of an individual's personal kindred, or *kaban mandal*. An obvious criterion to use in attempting to establish the range of the kindred is the extent to which the average Iban adult can bilaterally trace his (or her) genealogical relationships. According to this criterion, it can be said that the normal range of a personal kindred is two generations (alternatively, it can be described as of second-cousin range); that is, it extends as far as an individual's four grandparents, the siblings of these grandparents, and their descendants. Within this range an individual's cognates often number more than a hundred, and further they are commonly dispersed over a wide area. To take an example, the second-cousin-range kindred of Kubu, a man of Rumah Nyala, Sungai Sut, aged about 57 years in 1957, numbered 120 and were living in more than twenty different long-houses scattered over several hundred river miles, mainly in the Baleh and its tributaries, the Rejang and the Katibas.

The plotting of genealogical knowledge is an essential first stage in the exploration of an individual's kindred, but in all the cases I have investigated (and I am confident that this is quite a general phenomenon) an individual recognizes many cognates beyond the second-cousin range which we have just been discussing. While the exact genealogical details of their relationship may be forgotten, cognates commonly know that two or more of their grandparents were cousins. The usual limit to the identification of cognates in this manner is fourth cousinship, i.e., where a pair of individuals know that two of their grandparents were second cousins. Very occasionally the limit may extend to fifth cousinship. A typical Iban utterance on this point runs as follows: *agi empat sarak agi damping itong kaban mandal, ngilah empat sarak enda alab tusut nyau nyadi kaban jaub* ("Up to four generations kin are still close and are reckoned as cognates, but beyond four generations relationships can no longer be established; cognates become lost and turn into distant kin"). Another informant likened the network of cognatic relationships under discussion to an Iban *jala,* or casting-net, which, when finished, is conical in shape and weighted around its circumference by iron rings or small lumps of lead. At the commencement, a casting-net is a very small cone, but as the knotting proceeds and one circle of mesh is succeeded by the next it increases in size until its final circumference is measured not in inches but in fathoms. In the same way, said my informant, cognates grow farther and farther apart, generation by generation, until in the end they no longer know that they are kin.

As these examples indicate, the kindred is an uncircumscribed cognatic category which the Iban think of as extending indefinitely outwards. The total number of cognates which any individual Iban recognizes obviously varies from person to person, depending on such factors as age, memory, and domicile, but they are always numerous. Kubu, the genealogical composition of whose kindred has already been cited, estimated that altogether his *kaban mandal* (i.e., all of his cognates known to him) would number from two to three hundred. And this, I believe, is probably typical of the personal kindreds of elderly and prominent men, of whom Kubu is one.

It will be obvious that an individual's *kaban mandal* do not in any sense constitute a group. But it can also be said that these cognates do make up an important part of the social field within which activity is organized. Indeed, one of the most significant characteristics of bilateral societies like that of the Iban is the broad scope which they offer for the organization of activity among kinfolk. Among the Iban, for example, work groups (for hunting, the gathering of jungle produce, etc.) are largely composed of cognates, who may be drawn from both sides of the leader's kindred. However, such groups also commonly contain affinal kin, or *kaban tampil,* the category next to be discussed.

Marriage and Affines

Iban marriage rules are predominantly concerned with alliances between cognates. There is no objection to marriage with an unrelated individual (*orang bukai*) as long as it is known that he (or she) has no hereditary taint of the evil eye (*tau tepang*) and is not descended from a slave (*ulun*). Such marriages are not favored, however, and are infrequent; instead, it is the marriage of cognates which is the norm, both preferred and actual.

For cognates the rules governing marriage are strictly formulated. In summary, sexual relations are forbidden as incestuous (*jadi mali*) between (a) all cognates of the same *bilek* family; (b) siblings (both full and half), even though they may be members of different *bilek* families; (c) all close cognates (i.e., within a kindred of second-cousin range) who are not on the same generation level.

The most stringent of these incest prohibitions are those which apply to relationships within the elementary family, and they hold with the same force whether or not the individuals concerned are members of the same *bilek*. In the majority of cases, of course, the members of an elementary family are all members of one *bilek,* but it is significant that the Iban have extended these prohibitions (though with lessened stringency) to all cognates living in the same household, thereby making the natal members of a *bilek* family an exogamous group. Thus the union of first cousins, though normally a permissible form of marriage, is interdicted if they are members of the same *bilek* family on the ground that, having grown up in the same *bilek,* it is as though the cousins concerned were siblings.

Beyond the *bilek* and elementary family, incest prohibitions apply exclusively to relations between cognates on different generation levels. Particular emphasis is placed on the avoidence of sexual relations and marriage between individuals of adjacent generations; *adat* prescribes that within a kindred of second-cousin range individuals in adjacent generations must never marry. Breaches of this rule do sometimes occur at the outer limits, e.g., in the case of a man marrying the daughter of his second cousin, but in all instances known to me severe action was taken, e.g., the infliction of a fine and expulsion from the community where the offense occurred.

It is significant, I think, that it should be the kindred of second-cousin range that marks the generally enforced limit of marital prohibitions among the Iban, for, as already noted, the second-cousin kindred also marks the extent to which the average Iban is able to trace genealogical relationships. Beyond the second-cousin range it is possible, provided certain sacrificial and placatory rites are performed, for cognates on adjacent generation levels to marry; thus, if he first performs the required rites, a man may marry the daughter of his third cousin. By following a similar course it is also possible for a man to marry the granddaughter of his first cousin. Beyond these limits the rites lessen in magnitude as the relationships involved become more attenuated, but the appropriate rites are always insisted upon by the cognates concerned when it is known that those entering upon a marriage belong to different generation levels.[17]

On the other hand, if cognates belong to the same generation level there are no objections to their marrying as long as they are not siblings or do not belong to the same *bilek*. Thus, if they belong to different *bilek* families, it is fully permissible for cousins of the first, second, third, or any other degree to marry if they so desire; and those of the first degree may be either parallel or cross-cousins. Indeed, the marriage of cousins is strongly preferred in Iban society; about 75 per cent of marriages are between individuals who are *kaban mandal,* and of these the majority are *petunggal,* or cousins of some degree.

The Iban, as has presumably become apparent, are a monogamous people. Moreover, marriage is not accompanied by any kind of substantial bride-price or dowry. This, I would argue, is correlated with the absence of any large-scale corporate kin groups and with the fact that marriage among the Iban is very much a matter of personal predilection. Beyond the limits of the prohibited categories mentioned above, Iban men and women please themselves whom they marry. For parents, the main concern is with where the couple are to live. It is a common occurrence for each set of parents to be strongly opposed to losing one of their children in out-marriage, and there is often serious disagreement and quarreling between *bilek* families before a solution, i.e., a decision as between virilocal or uxorilocal residence, is reached. Neolocal residence is never practiced.

The dissolution of a marriage may be achieved without difficulty. According to the *adat* of the Third Division Iban, any married couple is permitted to divorce at any time by mutual consent, and a partner who discards his (or her) spouse is liable to little more that a nominal fine.[18] Under these conditions any husband or wife can easily terminate a marriage if this be desired, and divorce is a common occurrence. There is a marked tendency, however, for divorces to be confined to young men and women under 35 years of age. By the time they have reached the age of 35 years or thereabouts most men have settled down to a stable and lasting marriage. This, it is significant, is the age at which men usually become responsible for managing the *bilek* estate, and there is widespread realization that the successful preservation and advancement of a *bilek* family, as well as the attainment of wealth, prestige, and the other goals valued by the Iban, depend on the successful maintenance of a marriage.

In almost all such settled marriages husband and wife are joined in a relationship which each finds congenial. In the course of time a married couple become linked by intimate ties of both sentiment and material interest, and it is commonly said by the Iban, in discussing marriage and the *bilek,* that the relationship between husband and wife is closer than that which exists between siblings (*laki bini itong damping agi ari menyadi tampong pala*). In a successful marriage, it is pointed out, a husband and wife share equally in the most important undertakings of life: the bringing up of children, the cultivation of rice, and the custody of the *bilek* estate (*ngimpun anak, ngimpun bilek, enggau turun*). The conjugal tie, it may be said, is basic to the structure of the *bilek* family.

This leads back to the category of affinal kin, or *kuban tampil.* A husband and wife, should there be no cognatic relationship between them, possess entirely separate personal kindreds, each of which becomes part of the personal kindred of their children. For the husband and wife, however, the relationship between their personal kindreds is purely affinal, the cognates (*kaban mandal*) of one spouse being the affinal kin (*kaban tampil*) of the other. In practice, however, about 75 per cent of marriages are between cognates, and it is thus usual for the categories of *kaban mandal* and *kaban tampil* to coincide to at least some extent; when close cousins marry the overlap may be considerable.[19] Here we are confronted with one of the most important features of Iban society: the intermarriage of cousins constantly reinforces the network of cognatic ties linking individual Iban, and kin that might otherwise have become dispersed are brought together again.

Community Structure

Having briefly adumbrated the cognatic basis of the Iban kinship system we are now in a position to give a summary account of the social structure of the long-house. Within every long-house community there is a core group of *bilek* families linked by close ties of cognatic kinship. These families are commonly those of the founders of the community, and their apartments are usually side by side in the center of the long-house. For example, in Rumah Nyala (of the Sungai Sut), which contained twenty-five apartments in 1950, there was a compact block of eight *bilek* whose families were all joined by relationships which were, for the most part, between siblings, or first or second cousins. Moreover, each of the other seventeen *bilek* was related to one or more of this central block of eight families, which therefore constituted a kind of core around which the rest of the long-house was grouped. A similar sort of structure is found in most Iban communities, though occassionally there may be two distinct core groups. It is important to note, however, that while each family is always related to at least one other family, it seldom if ever occurs (except in small houses of under ten apartments) that there is complete interrelatedness among the families of a community. Again, while the linkage of *bilek* families in a community is chiefly in the form of cognatic ties between the natal members of these families, it does happen in an appreciable number of cases that the linkage of a *bilek* to others in the long-house is traced either predominantly or exclusively through an in-married member.[20] We may say, then, that a long-house community is a local confederation, based on cognatic kinship, of a series of autonomous family corporations.

It should be stressed, however, that an Iban long-house community is an open and not a closed group, for its component *bilek* families are joined in free association from which withdrawal is always possible. Each *bilek* family always possesses cognatic kin in a number of other long-houses, and may join any of these other settlements should its members so desire.[21] There is, indeed, a good deal of movement from one long-house to another. In pioneer regions like the Baleh, where land is still in fairly abundant supply, few long-houses maintain the same combination of *bilek* families for more than a year or two at a time. In general the core group is stable, but it occasionally happens in cases of serious dispute that a long-house breaks up completely, its component families dispersing to a number of separate and often widely scattered destinations. Such cases of community disintegration offer striking evidence of the conditional nature of group formation at the long-house level.

When a *bilek* family does change its place of abode it always seeks out a long-house in which kinsfolk are already established. Usually there are many different possibilities, for, as we have seen, the basis of long-house organization is cognatic kinship, and it is recognized that all cognatic ties, whether they be traced from natal, adopted, or affinal members of the *bilek* family, are equally available for purposes of affiliation. This means that a family is free to join any long-house in which there are cognates of either husband or wife, or of both.

The kinship network we have been considering was formerly also the basis of the Iban tribe. The tribe was a diffuse territorial grouping of long-house communities dispersed along the banks of a major river and its tributaries. Throughout the entire tribe there extended an intricate network of cognatic and affinal relationships linking its various members, all of whom recognized one another as *kaban,* kith or kin. Although the Iban tribe entirely lacked any sort of overall political organization, it did provide an area within which disputes could usually be settled, i.e., through the mechanisms of kinship. Furthermore, it was endogamous, and its members did not take one another's heads. Today, however, with the establishment of colonial government, the tribe—always a diffuse and inconsiderable entity—has been almost entirely superseded by a series of administrative districts under officially appointed Iban leaders called *pengulu.*

Kinship Terminology

COGNATES

Having sketched some of the salient features of Iban society I shall now turn to a brief discussion of the system of kinship terminology. In this discussion I shall be chiefly concerned with an examination of some of the ways in which the kinship terminology of the Iban reflects or is functionally consistent with the more important relationships and distinctions of their social structure. This approach to kinship terminologies is by no means a new one,[22] and its cogency has been amply demonstrated in recent decades by Radcliffe-Brown and others. Most of these studies, however, have been concerned with unilineal societies. The modern literature on kinship in purely cognatic societies is a sparse one, and there is thus some ground for looking at the Iban system from this point of view.

The main terms of reference for cognats are shown in Figure 1. The first point I would like to note is that there are no distinctions in terminology based on the sex of the speaker.[23] This, I would argue, is consistent with the fact that in all matters of property, inheritence, and the like, both within the family and beyond it, males and females have equivalent jural rights.

Next, I would like to direct attention to an important general feature of the Iban system of kinship terminology. The whole system, it will be observed, is bilaterally symmetrical. In other words, none of the relationships traced through one's mother and distinguished terminologically from homologous relationships traced through one's father. Thus father's sister and mother's sister are both referred to by the term *ibo;* father's brother and mother's brother are both referred to by the term *aya;* and all first cousins (both parallel and cross, and on both sides) are referred to by the term *petunggal.*[24]

In all these instances it can be shown that the relationships referred to by the same term have, in general, the same structural significance. In the absence of any unilineal principle of descent, father's siblings do not assume any differential significance, either jurally or

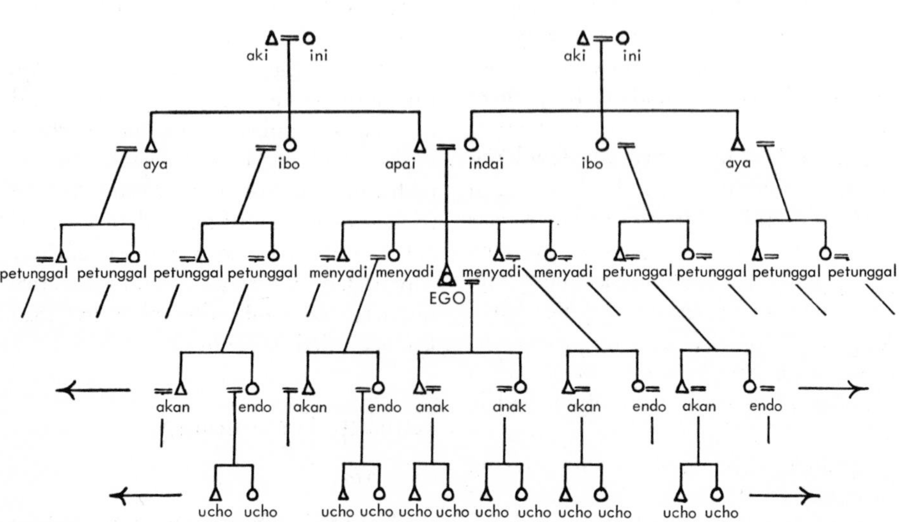

Figure 1. Iban Kinship Terminology: Cognates.

in any other way, as against mother's siblings. Both are equally available to Ego should he wish to seek assistance, and both are equally expected to give such assistance should it be sought. Similarly, at rituals held by Ego (or for him after his death) father's siblings and mother's siblings are equally entitled to shares of property distributed to cognates. The same considerations apply to all of an individual's first cousins (and beyond to second and remoter cousins). All these cousins, moreover, if they are of opposite sex to Ego, are equally available as partners in marriage. It is possible, then, to make the generalization that, beyond the *bilek*, rights and duties within the personal kindred are so balanced as to be bilaterally symmetrical.[25]

The Iban, with an attention to detail that delights the ethnographer, have symbolized this in one of their more important personal rites, the *gawai tusok*, which is concerned with the ritual piercing of a child's ear lobes. This operation is an event of moment in the life of an individual, for it is believed that on its proper performance will depend his (or her) subsequent health and welfare. The rites are elaborate, involving the invocation of tutelary gods and the employment of special charms and magical materials. The culmination of the *gawai* is the actual piercing of the ears with a small steel augur. It is common practice to have the lobe of one ear pierced by a cognate of the father and that of the other by a cognate of the mother, thus symbolizing the child's equal dependence on both sides of his (or her) personal kindred.

An individual's siblings, it will be noted, are all referred to by the same term, *menyadi*. In other words, brothers are not distinguished from sisters, and, furthermore, the term *menyadi* is applied to all brothers and sisters irrespective of seniority within the sibling group. Similarly, no distinction is made by either parent in respect of his (or her) children; both sons and daughters, and whatever their birth order, are referred to by the same term, *anak*. These usages also illustrate the reflection of basic jural rites in kinship terminology, for, as noted earlier, sons and daughters irrespective of age possess full and equal rights over the family estate.[26]

From the facts cited it will be seen that the Iban system of kinship terminology (in its terms of reference) is of the type called Eskimo by Murdock (1949: 233). That is, cross-cousins are referred to by the same term (*petunggal*) as parallel cousins, and both are distinguished from siblings, who are referred to as *menyadi*.[27]

Another feature of the Iban system of kinship terminology is the clear demarcation of kin by generation. No term is used in more than one generation level; there are no intergeneration reciprocals. This leads us to a principal regularity in Iban kinship behavior, namely, that all cognates at any generation level stand in a subordinate relationship to all those of the immediate senior generation and in a superordinate relationship to all those of the immediately junior generation. This is expressed most clearly in the relationship between parent and child. It is the duty of parents to care for their children and to instruct them in the traditional ways of the Iban. In these as in other matters they have authority over their children, who are expected to show them deference and respect. For example, there should be no undue levity between child and parent, and a child must not address a parent by his (or her) personal name, nor by the familiar term *wai*.[28]

The terms *apai* (father) and *indai* (mother) as terms of reference apply only to an individual's own parents; as terms of address, however, *apai* and *indai* are extended within the personal kindred to embrace all males and females of the parental generation. It is common practice, for example, to address uncles on both sides of the kindred as *apai,* and aunts as *indai;* and the same practice holds for the cousins of both parents. Similarly, all cognates on the same generation as one's children may be addressed as *anak*. The general superordination-subordination relationship of parent and child is also extended to all of these classificatory categories, though its force diminishes as genealogical distance increases. It can be said, therefore, that the classificatory terms of address *apai, indai,* and *anak* serve as indicators of kinship behavior. This is seen most clearly in the regulation of sexual relations between cognates. The prohibition of such relations between siblings and between members of the same *bilek* is made so obvious as a child grows up as to be taken for granted. The prohibition of sexual relations between cognates who are not on the same generation level is a pervasive rule applying, in theory, to all such cognatic kin. Parents make no attempt to nominate for their children all of the individuals in this prohibited category; instead, as they grow up, children are told that they may not *jadi* (marry) anyone they address as *apai, indai,* or *anak*. In this way the prohibition is unequivocally expressed and in a readily comprehensible way.

In contrast to the authority-respect relationship between members of adjacent generations, that which prevails between members of alternate geerations is of the kind usually described as a joking relationship. Although grandparents are expected to help in the education of their grandchildren and to this end may exercise discipline over them, grandchildren are nevertheless treated in general with great affection and indulgence. By custom, moreover, grandchildren are licensed to joke (*tau nundi*) with their grandparents. The terms for grandmother (*ini*) and grandfather (*aki*) are extended both in reference and in address to include all collateral cognates of the same generation; similiarly the term *ucho* (grandchild of either sex) is applied to all collateral descendants on the same generation level as one's own grandchildren.[29]

The rationale of the Iban kinship system for cognates will now have become apparent. In the absence of unilineal descent groups of any kind there is no need in Iban society to distinguish, unilaterally, different sets of collateral kin or specific unilateral kinship roles; instead, at each generation level all collaterals are seen as homologous. In its essentials the whole system may be looked on as a simple extension of the relationships existing within the three-generation stem family, which, as we have seen, is a modal form of the *bilek* family. Thus, in respect of general kinship behavior, collateral cognates are viewed in approximately the same way as lineal kin of the stem family. For example, beyond the *bilek:*

a. all cousins are viewed like siblings, and are addressed by the same classificatory term, *menyadi;*
b. all collaterals of the first ascending

generation are viewed as being like parents, and are addressed by the same classificatory terms, *apai* and *indai;*

c. all collaterals of the second ascending generation are viewed as grandparents, and are addressed by the same classificatory terms, *aḳi* and *ini;*
d. all collaterals of the first descending generation are viewed as children, and are addressed by the same classificatory term, *anaḳ;*

for cognates. Thus the whole system is bilaterally symmetrical, both for the cognates of Ego's spouse and for the affines of Ego's cognates. For example, both the patrilateral and matrilateral aunts and uncles of Ego's spouse are known as *entua mata ari,* and both parents-in-law as *entua.* Again, all of a spouse's cousins on both sides of his (or her) kindred are called *ipar,* the same term as for spouse's siblings. Similarly, with the affines of Ego's cognates,

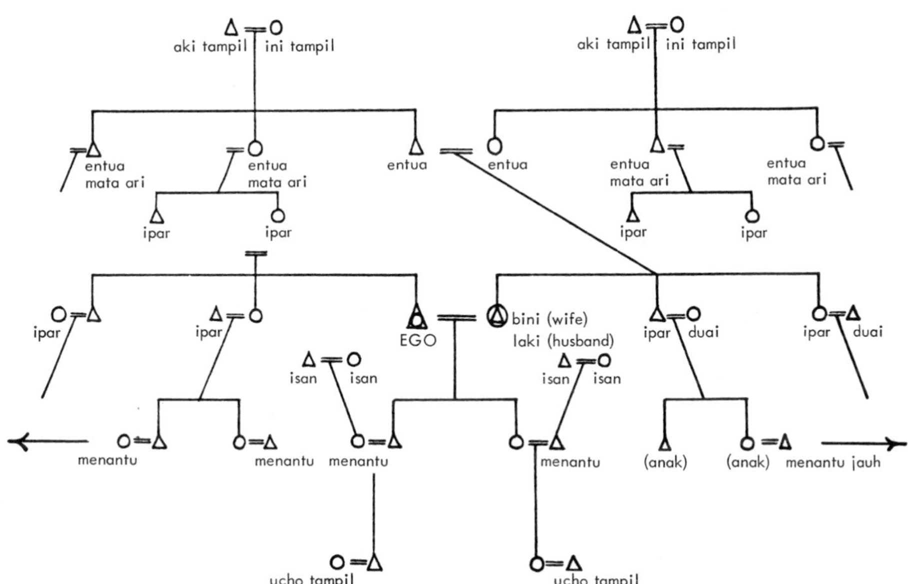

Figure 2. Iban Kinship Terminology: Affines I.

e. all collaterals of the second descending generation are viewed as grandchildren, and are addressed by the same classificatory term, *ucho.*

AFFINES

The Iban system of terminology for affines (see Figures 2 and 3) exhibits the same general characteristics as that

the wives of both patrilateral and matrilateral uncles are termed *ibo,* and the husbands of both patrilateral and matrilateral aunts are called *aya.* As in the case of cognates, this symmetry in terminology reflects structural equivalence.

Affinal kin are also clearly demarcated on a generational basis. Particularly noteworthy is the avoidance relationship which exists between a *menantu* (child-in-law) and *tntua* (parent-in-law). Here, as with parent and child, the *entua* is superordinate and the *menantu* subordinate. Sexual relations between them are severely prohibited, and all familiarity and joking are interdicted. These aspects of the relationship are expressed in a strong prohibition (with supernatural sanctions) against a *menantu* uttering the personal name of his (or her) *entua.* Those prohibitions also to have known from infancy. These affines are called *aya* or *ibo,* and are not regarded as *entua.* As the survival of a *bilek* depends very largely on the maintenance of proper relations between *entua* and *menantu* it can be seen that the ritual prohibitions associated with this affinal tie serve an important social function.

The relations between affines of alternate generations also closely resemble

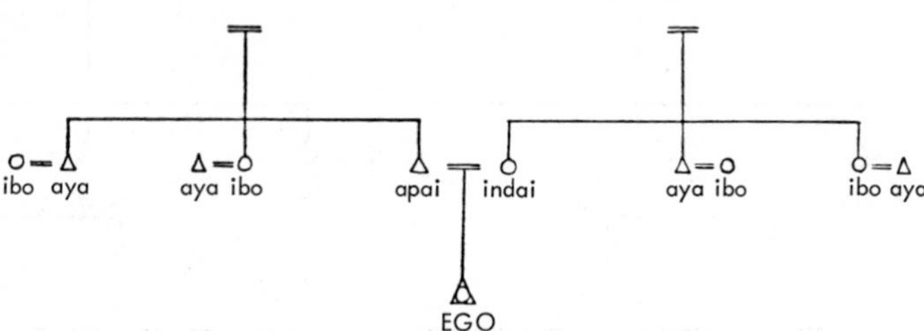

Figure 3. Iban Kinship Terminology: Affines II.

apply to all the siblings of both parents-in-law, i.e., to all of an individual's *entua mata ari.* I would argue that the ritual prohibitions associated with the relationship of *menantu* and *entua* have the primary purpose of precluding the possibility of sexual relations between them. Whereas the moral sentiments which interdict incestuous behavior between child and parent (and parents' siblings) are adequately internalized in the process of socialization, this does not happen for an *entua,* whose identity is not known until a marriage takes place. It is significant to note, for example, that there is no comparably severe attitude of avoidance between a male child and the wives of his uncles, or a female child and the husbands of her aunts, all of whom a child is likely those existing between cognatic kin. Thus the spouse of a grandchild is, in general, treated in the same way as a grandchild. Similarly, between affines on the same generation level, i.e., *ipar* and *duai,*[30] there are relations of familiarity and solidarity resembling those which exist between siblings and cousins.

An affinal term which deserves special mention is *isan,* used reciprocally by parents whose children marry one another. At the time a marriage is contracted there is almost always disagreement between the two sets of parents over the selection of the place of marital residence, but after the resolution of this difficulty resentments are usually forgotten, and where marriages are stable and productive the relationship between *isan* becomes one of mutual helpfulness and friendliness. It will be noted that when children are born of a marriage, both sets of *isan* become members of the personal kindreds of these children. Again, because the *bilek* is an exogamous group the *isan* relationship never occurs within the same *bilek* family; instead, it is always a link between *bilek* and is, therefore, of importance in the wider social structure.

As indicated previously, affinal kin are of great consequence in the kinship structure of Iban society. In the *bilek*, for example, affinal ties have an importance fully comparable to that of ties between natal members. Furthermore, it can be shown that all affinal relationships (with the exception of that linking *isan*) closely resemble in their functions the homologous cognatic ties. This point is well appreciated by the Iban themselves, who when asked to explain the significance of affinal relationships commonly compare them directly to relationships existing between cognates. For example, it is said that the relationship between *ipar* (siblings-in-law, etc.) is like that between *menyadi* (siblings) and *petunggal* (cousins). Again, *entua* are often described as being virtually equivalent to father and mother (*itong apai indai*), and *menantu* as nearly the same as sons and daughters (*runding anak*). As noted earlier, a *menantu* acquires full membership in the *bilek* into which he (or she) marries. This jural incorporation, moreover, is accompanied by a gradual phychological absorption until a *menantu* does become virtually "a child of the family." This process is nicely illustrated in the Iban custom whereby a *menantu* who has become a widow or widower may be ritually transformed into a son or daughter (*anak*). In such cases there is an adjustment of kinship terms, and the new son or daughter is free to marry again, although it is usually insisted that such an adopted affine should remain resident in the *bilek* of his (or her) adoption. In general terms, then, affinal relationships may be said to reduplicate in their significance the basic cognatic relationships of Iban society.[31]

Finally, we may comment briefly on the most important affinal relationship of all, that of husband and wife. The conjugal tie, as already noted, is basic to the structure of the *bilek* family and is of crucial significance to the kinship system as a whole. Monogamy is reflected in the fact that the terms *laki* (husband) and *bini* (wife) can be applied to only one person at a time. Between husband and wife there is no clearly structured pattern of superordination-subordination; although there is a sharply demarcated sexual division of labor, and a differentiation of ritual and other roles, a husband and wife, in their family life, are equals. Again, marriage among the Iban rests not on status, class, clan membership, or any other kind of prescriptive structural consideration but on the affection and regard which a husband and wife have for one another. It is understandable, therefore, that the bond between husband and wife is ideally, in the opinion of the Iban, closer than that between siblings.

A husband and wife always live together as members of the same household; indeed, the conjugal tie is the only relationship, affinal or cognatic, which invariably occurs within the confines of the *bilek* family. The conjugal tie may be looked on, then, as the keystone of the *bilek* family. In particular, it is important to realize that a *bilek* family in the arrangement of its affairs has available to it the cognates and affines of all its members. From the point of view of the senior natal members of a *bilek*, the cognates of an in-married member are *kaban tampil*, or affines, but to the children of the marriage they are part of these children's personal kindreds, or *kaban mandal*. In this way, as generation succeeds generation, affinal relationships become cognatic relationships and part of the network that forms the wider kinship structure of Iban society.

Concluding Remarks

Social structure theory, as it has been developed over recent years, has been predominantly concerned with societies having unilineal descent groups, and in this field valuable results have been attained. In comparison, our understanding of cognatic or bilateral societies, which are not very much less numerous,[32] is lamentable. Preoccupation with unilineal descent systems can lead to dangerously lop-sided views of social structure in general, as, for example, in the assertion by Radcliffe-Brown (1952: 8) that "unilineal institutions in some form are almost, if not entirely, a necessity in any ordered social system." Although thorough studies may still be sparse, we do know enough about some of the hundreds of bilateral societies still in existence to be able to demonstrate that there are a number of solutions alternative to unilineal descent all of which result in ordered social systems. The Iban solution, in which family corporations are perpetuated by a system of utrolateral filiation, is one of them. This type of family, supported as it is by the ramifying cognatic kinship structure of the Iban, does result, beyond any question, in an ordered social system. Furthermore, if the expansion of the Iban people during the past 150 years of their history be any criterion, it is also an efficient system.

It would be of the greatest interest for social anthropological theory if a detailed comparative study of the morphology of bilateral kinship systems could be undertaken. Unfortunately, the dearth of modern structural analyses prevents this. Many of the world's bilateral societies are to be found in Southeast Asia and the Insular Pacific. It is to be hoped that research in these regions during the coming years will provide the materials for a comparative analysis of bilateral social structures of the kind already achieved for the unilineal systems of Africa.[33]

Appendix—List of Kinship Terms

The terms listed below are to be understood as used in both reference and address except where particular referents are followed by the letters R or A in parentheses indicating that for these referents the term is used, respectively, only in reference or in address.

1. *aki:* Grandfather, either maternal or paternal; grandfather's brother or male cousin; spouse's grandfather (A); parent-in-law's uncle (A).

   aki tampil: Spouse's grandfather (R); parent-in-law's uncle (R).

2. *ini:* Grandmother, either maternal or paternal; grandmother's sister or female cousin; spouse's grandmother (A); parent-in-law's aunt (A).

   ini tampil: Spouse's grandmother (R); parent-in-law's aunt (R).

3. *apai:* Father; parent's brother or male cousin (A); spouse's father (A); spouse's parent's brother or male cousin (A); father's sister's husband (A); mother's sister's husband (A).
4. *indai:* Mother; parent's sister or female cousin (A); spouse's mother (A); spouse's parent's sister or female cousin (A); father's brother's wife (A); mother's brother's wife (A).
5. *aya:* Father's brother or male cousin; mother's brother or male cousin; father's, sister's husband; mother's sister's husband; spouse's father (A); spouse's parent's brother or male cousin (A).
6. *ibo:* Father's sister or female cousin; mother's sister or female cousin; father's brother's wife; mother's brother's wife; spouse's mother (A); spouse's parent's sister or female cousin (A).
7. *menyadi:* Sibling, either brother or sister; cousin of any degree and of either sex on the same generation level as Ego (A).
8. *aka:* Elder brother or sister (A); cousin of any degree and of either sex older than Ego but on the same generation level (A).
9. *adi:* Younger brother or sister (A); cousin of any degree and of either sex younger than Ego but on the same generation level (A); spouse's younger sibling or younger cousin (A); sibling's spouse if younger than Ego (A); spouse's sibling's spouse if older than spouse (A).
10. *petunggal:* Cousin of any degree and of either sex on the same generation level as Ego.
11. *anak:* Child, either son or daughter; sibling's child (A); cousin's child (A); son's wife (A); daughter's husband (A); nephew's wife (A); niece's husband (A).
12. *akan:* Nephew, i.e., sibling's son; cousin's son.
13. *endo:* Niece, i.e., sibling's daughter; cousin's daughter; son's wife (A); nephew's wife (A).
14. *ucho:* Grandchild of either sex; sibling's grandchild; cousin's grandchild; grandchild's spouse (A); sibling's grandchild's spouse (A); great-grandchild (A); sibling's great-grandchild (A); cousin's great-grandchild (A).

    ucho tampil: Grandchild's spouse (R); sibling's grandchild's spouse (R).
15. *ichit:* Great-grandchild (R); sibling's great-grandchild (R); cousin's great-grandchild (R).
16. *entua:* Spouse's parent of either sex (R).

    entua mata ari: Spouse's parent's sibling or cousin (R).
17. *laki:* Husband (R). In address, a spouse is called *wai,* or by his (or her) personal name, or by a teknonym.
18. *bini:* Wife (R). For usage in address, see above under *laki*.
19. *ipar:* Spouse's sibling or cousin of either sex; sibling's spouse; cousin's spouse.
20. *ika:* Spouse's elder sibling or cousin (A); sibling's spouse if older than Ego (A); spouse's sibling's spouse if older than spouse (A).
21. *duai:* Spouse's sibling's spouse.

22. *isan:* Child's spouse's parent; child's spouse's uncle or aunt.
23. *menantu:* Son's wife (R); daughter's husband (R); nephew's wife (R); niece's husband (R).
24. *igat:* Daughter's husband (A); niece's husband (A).
25. *wai:* Relative (A). This term may be used in addressing a kinsman of unknown generational level, of Ego's own generation, or of the second ascending or descending generations, but not one of an adjacent generation.

PART IV
Politics and Social Control

INTRODUCTION

Although political anthropology and the anthropology of law have only recently emerged as distinct subdisciplines, interest in the study of power and conflict, of law and social control, goes back to the beginning of anthropological inquiry. In the Pacific such scholars as Barton, Goodenough, Hogbin, Pospisil, and Oliver have made trail-breaking investigations of law or political life that have not only deepened our knowledge of Pacific societies but have also extended our comparative understanding of politics and law. Yet the presence of a variety of indigenous nonstate polities in the Pacific, ranging from the small-scale Australian band societies to the complex Polynesian chiefdoms—and not to mention the varied historical impact of colonial rule on indigenous political and legal systems—indicates that there remains much to be learned.

In the lead essay Sahlins contrasts two major historic variants: the egalitarian and competitive "big-man" systems characteristic of Melanesia and the hierarchically organized polities of the Polynesian high islands. In the second selection Oliver describes in rich detail the rise to prominence of a Solomon Island politician.

The focus of the third and fourth selections is on law or social control rather than politics. Schneider's inquiry concerns the nature of punishment in the Micronesian society of Yap, and Lundsgaarde describes the contemporary legal system of a Gilbert Island community that has resulted from the mutual adaptation of British and indigenous law-ways.

CHAPTER

16

Poor Man, Rich Man, Big-Man, Chief: Political Types in Melanesia and Polynesia[1]

MARSHALL D. SAHLINS

With an eye to their own life goals, the native peoples of Pacific Islands unwittingly present to anthropologists a generous scientific gift: an extended series of experiments in cultural adaptation and evolutionary development. They have compressed their institutions within the confines of infertile coral atolls, expanded them on volcanic islands, created with the means history gave them cultures adapted to the deserts of Australia, the mountains and warm coasts of New Guinea, the rain forests of the Solomon Islands. From the Australian Aborigines, whose hunting and gathering existence duplicates in outline the cultural life of the later Paleolithic, to the great chiefdoms of Hawaii, where society approached the formative levels of the old Fertile Crescent civilizations, almost every general phase in the progress of primitive culture is exemplified.

Where culture so experiments, anthropology finds its laboratories—makes its comparisons.[2]

In the southern and eastern Pacific two contrasting cultural provinces have long evoked anthropological interest: *Melanesia,* including New Guinea, the Bismarks, Solomons, and island groups east to Fiji; and *Polynesia,* consisting in its main portion of the triangular constellation of lands between New Zealand, Easter Island, and the Hawaiian Islands. In and around Fiji, Melanesia and Polynesia intergrade culturally, but west and east of their intersection the two provinces pose broad contrasts in several sectors: in religion, art, kinship groupings, eco-

From *Comparative Studies in Society and History,* 5:285–303, 1963. By permission of the author and Cambridge University Press.

nomics, political organization. The differences are the more notable for the underlying similarities from which they emerge. Melanesia and Polynesia are both agricultural regions in which many of the same crops—such as yams, taro, breadfruit, bananas, and coconuts—have long been cultivated by many similar techniques. Some recently presented linguistic and archaeological studies indeed suggest that Polynesian cultures originated from an eastern Melanesian hearth during the first millenium B.C.[3] Yet in anthropological annals the Polynesians were to become famous for elaborate forms of rank and chieftainship, whereas most Melanesian societies broke off advance on this front at more rudimentary levels.

It is obviously imprecise, however, to make out the political contrast in broad culture-area terms. Within Polynesia, certain of the islands, such as Hawaii, the Society Islands, and Tonga, developed unparalled political momentum. And not all Melanesian polities, on the other side, were constrained and truncated in their evolution. In New Guinea and nearby areas of western Melanesia, small and loosely ordered political groupings are numerous, but in eastern Melanesia, New Caledonia and Fiji, for example, political approximations of the Polynesian condition become common. There is more of an upward west-to-east slope in political development in the southern Pacific than a step-like, quantum progression.[4] It is quite revealing, however, to compare the extremes of this continuum, the western Melanesian underdevelopment against the greater Polynesian chiefdoms. While such comparison does not exhaust the evolutionary variations, it fairly establishes the scope of overall political achievement in this Pacific phylum of cultures.

Measurable along several dimensions, the contrast between developed Polynesian and underdeveloped Melanesian polities is immediately striking for differences in scale. H. Ian Hogbin and Camilla Wedgwood concluded from a survey of Melanesian (mostly western Melanesian) societies that ordered, independent political bodies in the region typically include seventy to three hundred persons; more recent work in the New Guinea Highlands suggests political groupings of up to a thousand, occasionally a few thousand, people.[5] But in Polynesia sovereignties of two thousand or three thousand are run-of-the-mill, and the most advanced chiefdoms, as in Tonga or Hawaii, might claim ten thousand, even tens of thousands.[6] Varying step by step with such differences in size of the polity are differences in territorial extent: from a few square miles in western Melanesia to tens or even hundreds of square miles in Polynesia.

The Polynesian advance in political scale was supported by advance over Melanesia in political structure. Melanesia presents a great array of social-political forms: here political organization is based upon patrilineal descent groups, there on cognatic groups, or men's club-houses recruiting neighborhood memberships, on a secret ceremonial society, or perhaps on some combination of these structural principles. Yet a general plan can be discerned. The characteristic western Melanesian "tribe," that is, the ethnic-cultural entity, consists of many autonomous kinship-residential group. Amounting on the ground to a small village or a local cluster of hamlets, each of these is a copy of the others in organization, each tends to be economically self-governing, and each is the equal of the others in political status. The tribal plan is one of politically unintegrated segments—segmental. But the political geometry in Polynesia is pyramidal. Local groups of the order of self-governing Melanesian communities appear in Polynesia as subdivisions of a more inclusive political body. Smaller units are integrated into larger through a system of intergroup ranking, and the network of representative chiefs of the subdivisions amounts to a coordinating political structure. So instead of the Melanesian scheme of small, separate, and equal political blocs, the Polynesian polity is an extensive pyramid of groups capped by the family and following of a paramount chief. (This Polynesian political upshot is omten, although not always, facilitated by the development of ranked lineages. Called *conical clan* by Kirchoff, at one time *ramage* by Firth, and *status lineage* by Goldman, the Polynesian-ranked lineage is the same in principle as the so-called *obok* system widely distributed in Central Asia, and it is at least analogous to the Scottish clan, the Chinese clan, certain Central African Bantu lineage systems, the house groups of Northwest Coast Indians, perhaps even the "tribes" of the Israelites.[7] Genealogical ranking is its distinctive feature: members of the same descent unit are ranked by genealogical distance from the common ancestor; lines of the same group become senior and cadet branches on this principle; related corporate lineages are relatively ranked, again by genealogical priority.)

Here is another criterion of Polynesian political advance: historical performance. Almost all of the native peoples of the South Pacific were brought up against intense European cultural pressure in the late eighteenth and the nineteenth centuries. Yet only the Hawaiians, Tahitians, Tongans, and to a lesser extent the Fijians, successfully defended themselves by evolving countervailing, native-controlled states. Complete with public governments and public law, monarchs and taxes, ministers and minions, these nineteenth-century states are testimony to the native Polynesian political genius, to the level and the potential of indigenous political accomplishments.

Embedded within the grand differences in political scale, structure, and performance is a more personal contrast, one in quality of leadership. An historically particular type of leader-figure, the "big-man" as he is often locally styled, appears in the underdeveloped settings of Melanesia. Another type, a chief properly so-called, is associated with the Polynesian advance.[8] Now these are distinct sociological types, that is to say, differences in the powers, privileges, rights, duties, and obligations of Melanesian big-men and Polynesian chiefs are given by the divergent societal contexts in which they operate. Yet the institutional distinctions cannot help but be manifest also in differences in bearing and character, appearance and manner—in a word, personality. It may be a good way to begin the more rigorous sociological comparison of leadership with a more impressionistic sketch of the contrast in the human dimension. Here I find it useful to apply characterizations—or is it caricature?—from our own history to big-men and chiefs, however much injustice this does to the historically incomparable backgrounds of the Melanesians and Polynesians. The Melanesian big-man seems so thoroughly *bourgeois,* so reminiscent of the free-enterprising rugged individual of our own heritage. He combines with an ostensible interest in the general welfare a more profound measure of self-interested cunning and economic calculation. His gaze, as Veblen might have put it, is fixed unswervingly to the main chance. His every public action is designed to make a competitive and invidious comparison with others, to show a standing above the masses that is product of his own personal manufacture. The historical caricature of the Polynesian chief, however, is feudal rather than capitalist. His appearance, his bearing is almost regal; very likely he just *is* a big man— "'Can't you see he is a chief? See how big he is?'"[9] In his every public action is a display of the refinements of breeding, in his manner always that *noblesse oblige* of true pedigree and an incontestable right of rule. With his standing not so much a personal achievement as a just social due, he can afford to be, and he is, every inch a chief.

In the several Melanesian tribes in which big-men have come under anthropological scrutiny, local cultural differences modify the expression of their personal powers.[10] But the indicative quality of big-man authority is everywhere the same: it is *personal* power. Big-men do not come to office; they do not succeed to, nor are they installed in, existing positions of leadership over political groups. The attainment of big-man status is rather the outcome of a series of acts which elevate a person above the common herd and attract about him a coterie of loyal, lesser men. It is not accurate to speak of "big-man" as a political title, for it is but an acknowledged standing in interpersonal relations—a "prince among men" so to speak as opposed to "the Prince of Danes." In particular Melanesian tribes the phrase might be "man of importance" or "man of renown," "generous rich-man," or "center-man," as well as "big-man."

A kind of two-sidedness in authority is implied in this series of phrases, a division of the big-man's field of influence into two distinct sectors. "Center-man" particularly connotes a cluster of followers gathered about an influential pivot. It socially implies the division of the tribe into political in-groups dominated by outstanding personalities. To the in-group, the big-man presents this sort of picture:

> The place of the leader in the district group [in northern Malaita] is well summed up by his title, which might be translated as "centre-man". . . . He was like a banyan, the natives explain, which, though the biggest and tallest in the forest, is still a tree like the rest. But, just because it exceeds all others, the banyan gives support to more lianas and creepers, provides more food for the birds, and gives better protection against sun and rain.[11]

But "man of reknown" connotes a broader tribal field in which a man is not so much a leader as he is some sort of hero. This is the side of the big-man facing outward from his own faction, his status among some or all of the other political clusters of the tribe. The political sphere of the big-man divides itself into a small internal sector composed of his personal satellites—rarely over eighty men—and a much larger external sector, the tribal galaxy consisting of many similar constellations.

As it crosses over from the internal into the external sector, a big-man's power undergoes qualitative change. Within his faction a Melanesian leader has true command ability, outside of it only fame and indirect influence. It is not that the center-man rules his faction by physical force, but his followers do feel obliged to obey him, and he can usually get what he wants by haranguing them—public verbal suasion is indeed so often employed by center-men that they have been styled "harangue-utans." The orbits of outsiders, however, are set by their own center-men. "'Do it yourself. I'm not *your* fool,'" would be the characteristic response to an order issued by a center-man to an outsider among the Siuai.[12] This fragmentation of true authority presents special political difficulties, particularly in organizing large masses of people for the prosecution of such collective ends as warfare or ceremony. Big-men do instigate mass action, but only by establishing both extensive renown and special personal relations of compulsion or reciprocity with other center-men.

Politics is in the main personal politiking in these Melanesian societies, and the size of a leader's faction as well as the extent of his renown are normally set by competition with other ambitious men. Little or no authority is given by social ascription: leadership is a creation—a creation of followership. "Followers," as it is written of the Kapauku of New Guinea, "stand in various relations to the leader. Their obedience to the headman's decisions is caused by motivations which reflect their particular relations to the leader."[13] So a man must be prepared to demonstrate that he possesses the kinds of skills that command respect—magical powers, gardening prowess, mastery of oratorical style, perhaps bravery in war and feud.[14] Typically decisive is the deployment of one's skills and efforts in a certain direction: towards amassing goods, most often pigs, shell monies, and vegetable foods, and distributing them in ways which build a name for cavalier generosity, if not for compassion. A faction is developed by informal private assistance to people of a locale. Tribal rank and renown are developed by great public giveaways sponsored by the rising big-man, often on behalf of his faction as well as himself. In different Melanesian tribes, the renown-making public distribution may appear as one side of a delayed exchange of pigs between corporate kinship groups; a marital consideration given a bride's kinfolk; a set of feasts connected with the erection of a big-man's dwelling, or of a clubhouse for himself and his faction, or with the purchase of higher grades of rank in secret societies; the sponsorship of a religious ceremony; a payment of subsidies and blood compensations to military allies; or perhaps the giveaway is a ceremonial challenge bestowed on another leader in the attempt to outgive and thus outrank him (a potlatch).

The making of the faction, however, is the true making of the Melanesian big-man. It is essential to establish relations of loyalty and obligation on the part of a number of people such that their production can be mobilized for renown building external distribution: The bigger the faction the greater the renown; once momentum in external distribution has been generated the opposite can also be true. Any ambitious man who can gather a following can launch a societal career. The rising big-man necessarily depends initially on a small core of followers, principally his own household and his closest relatives. Upon these people he can prevail economically: he capitalizes in the first instance on kinship dues and by finessing the relation of reciprocity appropriate among close kinsmen. Often it becomes necessary at an early phase to enlarge one's household. The rising leader goes out of his way to incorporate within his family "strays" of various sorts, people without familial support themselves, such as widows and orphans. Additional wives are especially useful. The more wives a man has the more pigs he has. The relation here is functional, not identical: with more women gardening there will be more food for pigs and more swineherds. A Kiwai Papuan picturesquely put to an anthropologist in pidgin the advantages, economic and political, of polygamy: "'Another woman go garden, another woman go take firewood, another woman go catch fish, another woman cook him—husband he sing out plenty people come *kaikai* [i.e., come to eat].'"[15] Each new marriage, incidentally, creates for the big-man an additional set of in-laws from whom he can exact economic favors. Finally, a leader's career sustains its upward climb when he is able to link other men and their families to his faction, harnessing their production to his ambition. This is done by calculated generosities, by placing others in gratitude and obligation through helping them in some big way. A common technique is payment of bridewealth on behalf of young men seeking wives.

The great Malinowski used a phrase in analyzing primitive political economy that felicitously describes just what the big-man is doing; amassing a "fund of power." A big-man is one who can create and use social relations which give him leverage on others' production and the ability to siphon off an excess product—or sometimes he can cut down their consumption in the interest of the siphon. Now although his attention may be given primarily to short-term personal interests, from an objective standpoint the leader acts to promote long-term societal interests. The fund of power provisions activities that involve other groups of the society at large. In the greater perspective of that society at large, big-men are indispensable means of creating supralocal organization: in tribes normally fragmented into small independent groups, big-men at least temporarily widen the sphere of ceremony, recreation and art, economic collaboration, of war too. Yet always this greater societal organization depends on the lesser factional organization, particularly on the ceilings on economic mobilizations set by relations between center-men and followers. The limits and the weaknesses of the political order in general are the limits and weaknesses of the factional ingroups.

And the personal quality of subordination to a center-man is a serious weakness in factional structure. A personal loyalty has to be made and continually reinforced; if there is discontent it may well be severed. Merely to create a faction takes time and effort, and to hold it, still more effort. The potential rupture of personal links in the factional chain is at the heart of two broad evolutionary shortcomings of western Melanesian political orders. First, a comparative instability. Shifting dispositions and magnetisms of ambitious men in a region may induce fluctuations in factions, perhaps some overlapping of them, and fluctuations also in the extent of different renowns.

The death of a center-man can become a regional political trauma: the death undermines the personally cemented faction, the group dissolves in whole or in part, and the people regroup finally around rising pivotal big-men. Although particular tribal structures in places cushion the disorganization, the big-man political system is generally unstable over short terms: in its superstructure it is a flux of rising and falling leaders, in its substructure of enlarging and contracting factions. Secondly, the personal political bond contributes to the containment of evolutionary advance. The possibility of their desertion, it is clear, often inhibits a leader's ability to forcibly push up his followers' output, thereby placing constraints on higher political organization, but there is more to it than that. If it is to generate great momentum, a big-man's quest for the summits of renown is likely to bring out a contradiction in his relations to followers, so that he finds himself encouraging defection—or worse, an egalitarian rebellion—by encouraging production.

One side of the Melanesian contradiction is the initial economic reciprocity between a center-man and his followers. For his help they give their help, and for goods going out through his hands other goods (often from outside factions) flow back to his followers by the same path. The other side is that a cumulative build-up of renown forces center-men into economic extortion of the faction. Here it is important that not merely his own status, but the standing and perhaps the military security of his people depend on the big-man's achievements in public distribution. Established at the head of a sizeable faction faction, a center-man comes under increasing pressure to extract goods from his followers, to delay reciprocities owing them, and to deflect incoming goods back into external circulation. Success in competition with other big-men particularly undermines internal-factional reciprocities: such success is precisely measurable by the ability to give outsiders more than they can possibly reciprocate. In well delineated big-man polities, we find leaders negating the reciprocal obligations upon which their following had been predicated. Substituting extraction for reciprocity, they must compel their people to "eat the leader's renown," as one Solomon Island group puts it, in return for productive efforts. Some center-men appear more able than others to dam the inevitable tide of discontent that mounts within their factions, perhaps because of charismatic personalities, perhaps because of the particular social organizations in which they operate.[16] But paradoxically the ultimate defense of the center-man's position is some slackening of his drive to enlarge the funds of power. The alternative is much worse. In the anthropological record there are not merely instances of big-man chicanery and of material deprivation of the faction in the interests of renown, but some also of overloading of social relations with followers: the generation of antagonisms, defections, and in extreme cases the violent liquidation of the center-man.[17] Developing internal constraints, the Melanesian big-man political order brakes evolutionary advance at a certain level. It sets ceilings on the intensification of political authority, on the intensification of household production by political means, and on the diversion of household outputs in support of wider political organization. But in Polynesia these constraints were breached, and although Polynesian chiefdoms also found their developmental plateau, it was not before political evolution had been carried above the Melanesian ceilings. The fundamental defects of the Melanesian plan were overcome in Polynesia. The division between small internal and larger external political sectors, upon which all big-man politics hinged, was suppressed in Polynesia by the growth of an enclaving chiefdom-at-large. A chain of command subordinating lesser chiefs and groups to greater, on the basis of inherent societal rank, made local blocs or personal followings (such as were independent in Melanesia) merely dependent parts of the larger Polynesian chiefdom. So the nexus of the Polynesian chiefdom became an extensive set of offices, a pyramid of higher and lower chiefs holding sway over larger and smaller sections of the polity. Indeed the system of ranked and subdivided lineages (conical clan system), upon which the pyramid was characteristically established, might build up through several orders of inclusion and encompass the whole of an island or group of islands. While the island or the archipelago would normally be divided into several independent chiefdoms, high-order lineage connections between them, as well as kinship ties between their paramount chiefs, provided structural avenues for at least temporary expansion of political scale, for consolidation of great into even greater chiefdoms.[18]

The pivotal paramount chief as well as the chieftains controlling parts of a chiefdom were true office holders and title holders. They were not, like Melanesian big-men, fishers of men: they held positions of authority over permanent groups. The honorifics of Polynesian chiefs likewise did not refer to a standing in interpersonal relations, but to their leadership of political divisions—here "the Prince of Danes" *not* "the prince among men". In western Melanesia the personal superiorities and inferiorities arising in the intercourse of particular men largely defined the political bodies. In Polynesia there emerged suprapersonal structures of leadership and followership, organizations that continued independently of the particular men who occupied positions in them for brief mortal spans.

And these Polynesian chiefs did not make their positions in society—they were installed in societal positions. In several of the islands, men did struggle to office against the will and stratagems of rival aspirants. But then they came *to* power. Power resided in the office; it was not made by the demostration of personal superiority. In other islands, Tahiti was famous for it, succession to chieftainship was tightly controlled by inherent rank. The chiefly lineage ruled by virtue of its genealogical connections with divinity, and chiefs were succeeded by first sons, who carried "in the blood" the attributes of leadership. The important comparative point is this: the qualities of command that had to reside in men in Melanesia, that had to be personally demonstrated in order to attract loyal followers, were in Polynesia socially assigned to office and rank. In Polynesia, people of high rank and office *ipso facto* were leaders, and by the same token the qualities of leadership were automatically lacking—theirs was not to question why—among the underlying population. Magical powers such as a Melanesian big-man might acquire to sustain his position, a Polynesian high chief inherited by divine descent as the *mana* which sanctified his rule and protected his person against the hands of the commonalty. The productive ability the big-man laboriously had to demonstrate was effortlessly given Polynesian chiefs as religious control over agricultural fertility, and upon the ceremonial implementation of it the rest of the people were conceived dependent. Where a Melanesian leader had to master the compelling oratorical style, Polynesian paramounts often had trained "talking chiefs" whose voice was the chiefly command.

In the Polynesian view, a chiefly personage was in the nature of things powerful. But this merely implies the objective observation that his power was of the group rather than of himself. His authority came from the organization, from an organized acquiescence in his privileges and organized means of sustaining them. A kind of paradox resides in evolutionary developments which detach the exercise of authority from the necessity to demonstrate personal superiority: organizational power actually extends the role of personal decision and conscious planning, gives it greater scope, impact, and effectiveness. The growth of a political system such as the Polynesian constitutes advance over Melanesian orders of interpersonal dominance in the human control of human affairs. Especially significant for society at large were privileges accorded Polynesian chiefs which made them greater architects of funds of power than ever was any Melanesian big-man.

Masters of their people and "owners" in a titular sense of group resources, Polynesian chiefs had rights of call upon the labor and agricultural produce of households within their domains. Economic mobilization did not depend on, as it necessarily had for Melanesian big-men, the *de novo* creation by the leader of personal loyalties and economic obligations. A chief need not stoop to obligate this man or that man, need not by a series of individual acts of generosity induce others to support him, for economic leverage over a group was the inherent chiefly due. Consider the implications for the fund of power of the widespread chiefly privilege, related to titular "ownership" of land, of placing an interdiction, a tabu, on the harvest of some crop by way of reserving its use for a collective project. By means of the tabu the chief directs the course of production in a general way: households of his domain must turn to some other means of subsistence. He delivers a stimulus to household production: in the absence of the tabu further labors would not have been necessary. Most significantly, he has generated a politically utilizable agricultural surplus. A subsequent call on this surplus floats chieftainship as a going concern, capitalizes the fund of power. In certain islands, Polynesian chiefs controlled great storehouses which held the goods congealed by chiefly pressures on the commonalty. David Malo, one of the great native custodians of old Hawaiian lore, felicitously catches the political significance of the chiefly magazine in his well-known *Hawaiian Antiquities:*

> It was the practice for kings [i.e., paramount chiefs of individual islands] to build store-houses in which to collect food, fish, *tapas* [bark cloth], *malos* [men's loin cloths], *pa-us* [women's loin skirts], and all sorts of goods. These store-houses were designed by the Kalaimoku [the chief's principal executive] as a means of keeping the people contented, so they would not desert the king. They were like the baskets that were used to entrap the *hinalea* fish. The *hinalea* thought there was something good within the basket, and he

> hung round the outside of it. In the same way the people thought there was food in the store-houses, and they kept their eyes on the king. As the rat will not desert the pantry . . . where he thinks food is, so the people will not desert the king while they think there is food in his store-house.[19]

Redistribution of the fund of power was the supreme art of Polynesian politics. By well-planned *noblesse oblige* the large domain of a paramount chief was held together, organized at times for massive projects, protected against other chiefdoms, even further enriched. Uses of the chiefly fund included lavish hospitality and entertainments for outside chiefs and for the chief's own people, and succor of individuals or the underlying population at large in times of scarcities—bread and circuses. Chiefs subsidized craft production, promoting in Polynesia a division of technical labor unparalleled in extent and expertise in most of the Pacific. They supported also great technical construction, as of irrigation complexes, the further returns to which swelled the chiefly fund. They initiated large-scale religious construction too, subsidized the great ceremonies, and organized logistic support for extensive military campaigns. Larger and more easily replenished than their western Melanesian counterparts, Polynesian funds of power permitted greater political regulation of a greater range of social activities on greater scale.

In the most advanced Polynesian chiefdoms, as in Hawaii and Tahiti, a significant part of the chiefly fund was deflected away from general redistribution towards the upkeep of the institution of chieftainship. The fund was siphoned for the support of a permanent administrative establishment. In some measure, goods and services contributed by the people precipitated out as the grand houses, assembly places, and temple platforms of chiefly precincts. In another measure, they were appropriated for the livelihood of circles of retainers, many of them close kinsmen of the chief, who clustered about the powerful paramounts. These were not all useless hangers-on. They were political cadres: supervisors of the stores, talking chiefs, ceremonial attendants, high priests who were intimately involved in political rule, envoys to transmit directives through the chiefdom. There were men in these chiefly retinues — in Tahiti and perhaps Hawaii, specialized warrior corps — whose force could be directed internally as a buttress against fragmenting or rebellious elements of the chiefdom. A Tahitian or Hawaiian high chief had more compelling sanctions than the harangue. He controlled a ready physical force, an armed body of excutioners, which gave him mastery particularly over the lesser people of the community. While it looks a lot like the big-man's faction again, the differences in functioning of the great Polynesian chief's retinue are more significant than the superficial similarities in appearance. The chief's coterie, for one thing, is economically dependent upon him rather than he upon them. And in deploying the cadres politically in various sections of the chiefdom, or against the lower orders, the great Polynesian chiefs sustained command where the Melanesian big-man, in his external sector, had at best renown.

This is not to say that the advanced Polynesian chiefdoms were free of internal defect, of potential or actual malfunctioning. The large political-military apparatus indicates something of the opposite. So does the recent work of Irving Goldman[20] on the intensity of "status rivalry" in Polynesia, especially when it is considered that much of the status rivalry in developed chiefdoms, as the Hawaiian, amounted to popular rebellion against chiefly despotism rather than mere contest for position within the ruling stratum. This suggests that Polynesian chiefdoms, just as Melanesian big man orders, generate along with evolutionary development countervailing anti-authority pressures, and that the weight of the latter may ultimately impede further development.

The Polynesian contradiction seems clear enough. On one side, chieftainship is never detached from kinship moorings and kinship economic ethics. Even the greatest Polynesian chiefs were conceived superior kinsmen to the masses, fathers of their people, and generosity was morally incumbent upon them. On the other side, the major Polynesian paramounts seemed inclined to "eat the power of the government too much," as the Tahitians put it, to divert an undue proportion of the general wealth toward the chiefly establishment.[21] The diversion could be accomplished by lowering the customary level of general redistribution, lessening the material returns of chieftainship to the community at large—tradition attributes the great rebellion of Mangarevan commoners to such cause.[22] Or the diversion might—and I suspect more commonly did—consist in greater and more forceful exactions from lesser chiefs and people, increasing returns to the chiefly apparatus without necessarily affecting the level of general redistribution. In either case, the well developed chiefdom creates for itself the dampening paradox of stoking rebellion by funding its authority.[23]

In Hawaii and other islands cycles of political centralization and decentralization may be abstracted from traditional histories. That is, larger chiefdoms periodically fragmented into smaller and then were later reconstituted. Here would be more evidence of a tendency to overtax the political structure. But how to explain the emergence of a developmental stymie, of an inability to sustain political advance beyond a certain level? To point to a chiefly propensity to consume or a Polynesian propensity to rebel is not enough: such propensities are promoted by the very advance of chiefdoms. There is reason to hazard instead that Parkinson's notable law is behind it all: that progressive expansion in political scale entailed more-than-proportionate accretion in the ruling apparatus, unbalancing the flow of wealth in favor of the apparatus. The ensuing unrest then curbs the chiefly impositions, sometimes by reducing chiefdom scale to the nadir of the periodic cycle. Comparison of the requirements of administration in small and large Polynesian chiefdoms helps make the point.

A lesser chiefdom, confined say as in the Marquesas Islands to a narrow valley, could be almost personally ruled by a headman in frequent contact with the relatively small population. Melville's partly romanticized—also for its ethnographic details, partly cribbed—account in *Typee* makes this clear enough.[24] But the great Polynesian chiefs had to rule much larger, spatially dispersed, internally organized populations. Hawaii, an island over four thousand square miles with an aboriginal population approaching one hundred thousand, was at times a single chiefdom, at other times divided into two to six independent chiefdoms, and at all times each chiefdom was composed of large subdivisions under powerful subchiefs. Sometimes a chiefdom in the Hawaiian group extended beyond the confines of one of the islands, incorporating part of another through conquest. Now, such extensive chiefdoms would have to be coordinated; they would have to be centrally tapped for a fund of power, buttressed against internal disruption, sometimes massed for distant, perhaps overseas, military engagements. All of this to be implemented by means of communication still at the level of word-of-mouth, and means of transportation consisting of human bodies and canoes. (The extent of certain larger chieftainships, coupled with the limitations of communication and transportation, incidentally suggests another possible source of political unrest: that the burden of provisioning the governing apparatus would tend to fall disproportionately on groups within easiest access of the paramount.[25]) A tendency for the developed chiefdom to proliferate in executive cadres, to grow top-heavy, seems in these circumstances altogether functional, even though the ensuing drain on wealth proves the chiefdom's undoing. Functional also, and likewise a material drain on the chiefdom at large, would be widening distinctions between chiefs and people in style of life. Palatial housing, ornamentation and luxury, finery and ceremony, in brief, conspicuous consumption, however much it seems mere self-interest always has a more decisive social significance. It creates those invidious distinctions between rulers and ruled so conducive to a passive—hence quite economical!—acceptance of authority. Throughout history, inherently more powerful political organizations than the Polynesian, with more assured logistics of rule, have turned to it—including in our time some ostensibly revolutionary and proletarian governments, despite every prerevolutionary protestation of solidarity with the masses and equality for the classes.

In Polynesia then, as in Melanesia, political evolution is eventually short-circuited by an overload on the relations between leaders and their people. The Polynesian tragedy, however, was somewhat the opposite of the Melanesian. In Polynesia, the evolutionary ceiling was set by extraction from the population at large in favor of the chiefly faction, in Melanesia by extraction from the big-man's faction in favor of distribution to the population at large. Most importantly, the Polynesian ceiling was higher. Melanesian big-men and Polynesian chiefs not only reflect different varieties and levels of political evolution, they display in different degrees the capacity to generate and to sustain political progress.

Especially emerging from their juxtaposition is the more decisive impact of Polynesian chiefs on the economy, the chiefs' greater leverage on the output of the several households of society. The success of any primitive political organization is decided here, in the control that can be developed over household economies. For the household is not merely the principal productive unit in primitive societies, it is often quite capable of autonomous direction of its own production, and it is oriented towards production for its own, not societal consumption. The greater potential of Polynesian chieftainship is precisely the greater pressure it could exert on household output, its capacity both to generate a surplus and to deploy it out of the household towards a broader division of labor, cooperative construction, and massive ceremonial and military action. Polynesian chiefs were the more effective means of societal collaboration on economic, political, indeed all cultural fronts. Perhaps we have been too long accustomed to perceive rank and rule from the standpoint of the individuals involved, rather than from the perspective of the total society, as if the secret of the subordination of man to man lay in the personal satisfactions of power. And then the breakdowns too, or the evolutionary limits, have been searched out in men, in "weak" kings or megalomaniacal dictators—always, "who is the matter?" An excursion into the field of primitive politics suggests the more fruitful conception that the gains of political developments accrue more decisively to society than to individuals, and the failings as well are of structure not men.

CHAPTER

17

A Leader in Action[1]

DOUGLAS L. OLIVER

Now, to exemplify the general statements of the preceding chapters, there will be presented an account of the career of a high-ranking leader, Soŋi, of Turuŋom village. Soŋi's career began before warfare was outlawed, and reached a peak during our stay in Siuai. It was our good fortune to reside in Turuŋom village during the very months when Soŋi's feast-giving activities were most intensive, when he carried out plans for consolidating his position as the most renowned man of Siuai. Soŋi's case is necessarily somewhat atypical—only one man at a time can rise to the very top; but it nevertheless indicates how one exceptional individual makes effective use of his culture's means to achieve nearly universally desired cultural goals.

Historical Setting[2]

The northern three quarters of northeast Siuai is known throughout Siuai as the region of the *Rataiku,* "hillmen." When used by outsiders "hillman" has a derogatory meaning, connoting the scorn of the lowlander for the more isolated and conservative highlander. Nevertheless, the latter have accepted the term and now apply it to themselves and their region. Rataiku is bordered on the east and north by miles of uninhabited rain forest; its western borders are also marked by long stretches of forest. On the other hand, its southern border, abutting the region known as Mokakaru, is marked by social and political boundaries.

Judging by genealogies and myths, Rataiku has long been numerically dominated by members of the Tree-rat, Hornbill, and Kingfisher sibs, with only small enclaves of Parrots and Cranes and a scattering of natives belonging to other sibs. It is claimed that the Tree-rats (Left-behinds subdivision) also formerly dominated the

Reprinted by permission of the publishers from Douglas L. Oliver, *A Solomon Island Society*. Cambridge, Mass.: Harvard University Press, Copyright 1955, by the President and Fellows of Harvard College, pp. 422–439.

present inhabited part of Mokakaru but were superseded there by fairly recent intrusions of Eagles (from Ruhuaku region) and of Cockatoos and Iguanas (from Terei).[3]

At the present time Tree-rats, Hornbills, and Kingfishers are scattered throughout Rataiku in numerous matrilineages which own most of the land. Of these three, Tree-rats are most numerous, most extensively subdivided, and weathiest in land and shell money. It is impossible to determine who were the *original* residents of specific places —even myths conflict here; the farthest our evidence will carry us is five or six generations beyond the oldest persons now living.

Reliable political history is equally shallow but we can describe with some confidence the circumstances as they were three decades ago. At that time Hiniŋ, a Tree-rat man (Rukaruinai subdivision) of Maisua, was highest-ranking mumi of all the northern part of Rataiku; Moki, a Tree-rat (Hanoŋnai subdivision) of Moronei, ranked highest among the southeastern Rataiku; and Tokura, a Kingfisher (Legs-apart subdivision) of Jeku, ranked highest among the southwestern Rataiku. Some fighting took place among these three mumis but they eventually banded together against the Mokakaruans and Ruhuakuans to the south. This was also the situation later on when Australian control was becoming established.

It has already been reported how the Mokakaru mumi, Konsei, induced the Australian authorities to punish the Rataiku for alleged feuding.[4] In the process, the mumi Tokura was arrested and soon died in jail. Hiniŋ's adherents were scattered and he too died shortly thereafter. Only Moki, the Moronei mumi, survived this onslaught, living until about 1934. This left the Paramount Chief, Konsei, officially in charge of Mokakaru and most of Rataiku until his death in 1936. Konsei, however, was never able to win the support of the Rataiku.

Meanwhile, with fighting outlawed and new concepts of authority being introduced by the Australians, the traditional type of political authority underwent far-reaching change.[5] Native-style leaders lost their powers of physical coercion to the new administrative-appointed Hat-men. Some of the former, it is true, became officials in the new regime, but even in these instances the new-style force was dependent upon outside powers and not entirely upon the personal effectiveness of the mumis themselves. The mumi, Moki, seems to have adjusted to the new circumstances without much loss of authority or influence—his having been a renowned war-maker added to his luster as a feast-giver. However, among the new generation of ambitious men renown had to be founded on feast-giving alone. Foremost among this emerging new generation was Soŋi of Turuŋom.

The Rise of Soŋi

Soŋi was born around 1893 in Turuŋom; his mother was a Rukaruinai Tree-rat, his father a Whistler Kingfisher; both parents were also born in Turuŋom and their marriage conformed to a long-standing local tradition of "straight" cross-cousin intermarriage between local Rukaruinais and Whistlers. Soŋi was orphaned during early childhood, and for the next few years he was cared for by his own maternal uncle. Later on one of Soŋi's own paternal uncles took over the job of sponsoring Soŋi's rise to mumihood —the young man having begun to show promise at an early age. Meanwhile Soŋi slept about in the houses of several kinsmen and was provided with food by a matrilineage *sister* of his deceased father.

In terms of material possessions the young Soŋi was comparatively well off. His own matrilineage, the Turuŋonai brach of Rukaruinai Tree-rats, had settled in Turuŋom several generations previously and acquired much land in the course of time; it also possed a large hoard of heirlooms. In addition, Soŋi had access to the resources of his father's matrilineage, much of whose property had become practically combined with his own matrilineage's through the many cross-cousin marriages that had taken place between members of the two units. Moreover, enough inheritance was left over from his father's private capital (pure) to start his accumulation of pigs. Soŋi purchased a few small pigs and turned them over to his sponsoring paternal uncle to fatten for sale. The uncle also solicited the aid of neighboring kinsmen, telling them: "Let us all help this boy Soŋi become a mumi. He has the ambition and industriousness but is an orphan and hence cannot depend on his father for help. Let us all make pots and sell them, then give (?) the money to Soŋj for buying pigs." Several men did as the uncle suggested, even fattening the pigs that were purchased with the money earned for Soŋi.

Then, when Soŋi was about fifteen, his uncle mobilized all the men in Turuŋom to help build a small clubhouse for the boy, and thus he was launched on his feast-giving career. It should be mentioned that the paternal uncle had a son of his own about Soŋi's age, but that individual showed no promise of becoming a mumi and hence received no special assistance from his father or others. This man later moved to a neighboring settlement and although he appears to harbor no resentment against Soŋi, neither has he assisted him in any way.

Another event cleared the way for Soŋi's continued advance. The maternal uncle who cared for Soŋi during the latter's early childhood was then the most prominent man in Turuŋom itself. The latter's son, Koŋkoma, was several years older than Soŋi, showed fair promise, and was beginning to be pushed ahead by his father until an interruption occurred. A resident of nearby Hiuannai died and divination singled out a Turuŋom native, Ham, as responsible for the death. The Hiuannai mumi then paid Koŋkoma's father to kill Ham, which he did. The only thing wrong with this action was that Ham happened to be a kinsman of the great Jeku mumi, Tokura, and when Tokura heard of the murder he set out with a few followers to kill Koŋkoma's father. The latter received ample warning and escaped with Koŋkoma to a distant settlement where kinsmen provided haven for them until Tukura died many years later. This episode left the field open for Soŋi's advance, there having been no other young man in Turuŋom with comparable promise or support. (Later, when Koŋkoma returned to Turuŋom Soŋi was already firmly established as highest-ranking leader there. Koŋkoma was jealous and angered by what he considered to be Soŋi's usurpation, but could do nothing about it. On one occasion when Soŋi had just completed a new club-house. Koŋkoma cleared a new path so as to make a wide detour around the club-house, hoping thus to deflect some of the traffic. This tactic backfired, causing Koŋkoma much embarrassment; Soŋi called the new path "empty-stomach trail," signifying that people who traveled along Koŋkoma's pathway would miss being fed at Soŋi's frequent club-house feasts. Eventually Koŋkoma contracted what appears to be tuberculosis, and now is a frail old widower dependent upon relatives for food and shelter.)

Soŋi consolidated his preeminence in Turuŋom by building, successively, two large club-houses and filling them with gongs, thereby keeping his neighbors actively working on his behalf and rewarding them with numerous pork banquets—pork, it should be added, which they themselves helped to fatten for him. Natives still tell of Soŋi's readiness, during that period, to contribute generously at the baptisms of their children and the funerals of their kinsmen. When the Patrol Officer wished to appoint a Headman for Turuŋom Soŋi was offered the position, but he would have no truck with the new regime and arranged for the Hat to be given to his elder matrilineage mate, Siham.

Soŋi has reportedly given scores of feasts but his adherents single out fourteen of these as having been especially large and significant for his sociopolitical career. The first seven of these were given to reward leaders of neighboring settlements for their assistance in building Soŋi's club-houses and carrying slit gongs. For the seventh, Soŋi had intended asking his rival, Konsei, the Paramount Chief, to assist in carrying his largest gong from an old club-house to a new one, but Konsei rejected the bid, terming it insolent. ("That Turuŋom is a place of no consequence. If they want me to honor them with my presence they will have to pay me in shell money.") On hearing this Soŋi redoubled his efforts and prepared a huge feast to which he invited all of Rataiku and none of Mokakaru. This episode served to publicize Soŋi's name throughout Siuai and caused him to be identified with Rataiku sentiment against the hated Konsei.

The four subsequent feasts were mumi-honoring affairs (muminai) given for neighboring Rataiku leaders. Two of these leaders reciprocated, while making it clear that they did not wish to compete further. The two others did not even attempt to repay and accepted defeat philosophically. Thanks to Soŋi's tact, all four of these erstwhile rivals became Soŋi's faithful allies. Later, on the death of Moki, the last of the great war-making mumis, Soŋi became tacitly recognized as highest-ranking leader of Rataiku and he began to prepare to extend his activities beyond Rataiku.

Mokakaru was the logical place to begin, but after Konsei's death there was no one left in Mokakaru to offer suitable competition. Soŋi disposed of Konsei's Chief Interpreter, the opportunistic U'ta[6] (who, by the way, is, like Soŋi, a Rukaruinai Tree-rat), with a feast which U'ta could never hope to repay; but Soŋi did this more as an amusement than as a serious social-climbing tactic. U'ta is universally disliked on account of his conceit and officiousness, and Rataikuans make a great joke of him by imitating his exaggerated salutes and his insistence upon giving orders in pidgin English. They dub him "the *kou,*" in reference to a long-necked, supercilious looking bird,[7] which is described in a folk tale as acting as if all feasts it attended were being given in its honor. Nor was young Tomo, Konsei's successor as Paramount Chief, a suitable rival for Soŋi to compete with;[8] hence Soŋi turned towards central Siuai for the next stage of his career. It was at this point that we moved to his village and were thus on hand to witness his most ambitious enterprise.

Turuŋom Village

The consolidated line village of Turuŋom is fairly typical though slightly larger than the average Siuai line village.[9] It is divided into two lines: Turuŋom proper, the larger, and Ohinnai. Hamlet houses of Turuŋom villagers are scattered around the surrounding countryside in the following hamlets (households are identified by the names of their heads):

Mitapukori and West Ohinnai: Haiju, Opisa
Kupariri: Soŋi
North Turuŋom: Koura, Kepina
South Turuŋom: To'osi
West Pirui: Asinara, Tahiŋ, Tamaŋ, Siham
East Pirui: Naru, Tanari, Nakao, Pana
East Ohinnai: Pitaino, Koiri
Noveina: Ho'oma, Ronsa, Tampa

Among other Turuŋom household heads, Kukerei, Orim, and Maria do not posses hamlet houses; while Asinara and Tanari do not have line houses of their own. One resident, Pinako, has his hamlet house near Jeku village, his wife's home. Finally, there are two old men, Koŋkoma[10] and Kanasai, who live with kinsmen, having no houses of their own.

Turuŋom is located between two creeks, the Miraka and the Reraka.[11] The land verbally identified with Turuŋom does not ordinarily extend beyond these creeks even though various groups of Turuŋom residents own tracts outside that area. Several generations ago this Turuŋom area was "owned" by four matrilineages: a Komma matrilineage (subdivision of Kingfisher) in the north, a Left-behind matrilineage (Tree-rats) in the west, a Belly-fat matrilineage (Tree-rats) in the east, and a Legs-apart matrilineage (Kingfishers) in the south. Presumably, some members of these matrilineages resided here. Since then some land titles have passed to members of other matrilineages and now the Turuŋonai (Rukaruinai Belly-fats) are the biggest landholders.

The present residents of Turuŋom fall into the following extended families:

1. The senile Kanasai, his sons (Opisa, Haiju), his daughters (including Apavo, wife of Maria), and their spouses and offspring reside in Ohinnai on Kanasai's matrilineage land.

2. The most prominent extended family consists of members of the Turuŋonai[12] including Soŋi, Siham, Arapa, and their spouses, offspring, offspring's spouses, and the latter's children. They are descended from sisters who moved to Turuŋom after marrying Turuŋom men. The hamlet houses of these natives are somewhat scattered but their village houses are all together at the northern end of the line. All the women and children of this group are frequently together, either sitting under one of their houses, gossiping and nursing their infants, or trooping off to the

gardens, or down to the spring. Sometimes they pool their food resources and cook in the same pot. When their menfolk are in the village they likewise join in. These Turuŋonai are an exclusive lot; other villagers almost never loiter near their houses. Other children may wander up to take part in some game, but the little Northenders nearly always send the small Southenders home crying.

3. Several generations ago some Komma men married Whistler women and took them to Turuŋom to live. The matrilineal descendants of these women are Pana, Pitaino, Koiri, Tanari, Nakao, Ho'oma, Pinako, and Koura; they and their spouses and offspring comprise the largest extended family in Turuŋom. Their hamlet and line houses are somewhat scattered and they are not as well-knit as the preceding ones.

4. Ronsa, his brother's son, Tampa, and their dependents constitute an impoverished extended-family of refugees, Ronsa having left his home farther east and sought haven in Turuŋom during fighting times.

Koŋkoma, now sick and old, lives alone in Koura's village house; the latter resides entirely in his hamlet house. Kepina, Kukerei, and Tahiŋ live more or less separate domestic lives, having no close extended-family affiliations in Turuŋom. Orim, whose real home is Hanuŋ village, resides in Ohinnai by virtue of being the Methodist catechist there; also he is married to Siham's daughter. To'osi, also an outsider, is married to one of the Rukaruinai women and has become a member of that extended-family.

Many kinship ties form links between these families, and in addition most residents have close kinship ties with natives scattered throughout Rataiku.

Ohinnai residents are Methodist: the catechist, Orim, holds daily services there. Most adults in Turuŋom proper have been "converted" to Catholicism, but there is no chapel in the village and few bother to attend services elsewhere. Soŋi himself has remained aloof from the missions and this helps account for his neighbors' indifference.

Soŋi's matrilineage mate, Siham, is village Headman and sees to it that the villagers remain "straight," leaving Soŋi free to concentrate upon his political career. Opisa makes a loud but rather ineffectual interpreter, Pitaino a completely useless medical orderly.

Five Turuŋom men own club-houses (Soŋi, Koura, Pana, Opisa, Ho'oma) but Soŋi's is the center of activity. All Turuŋom men except ailing Koŋkoma and senile Kanasai cooperate actively in Soŋi's feast-giving enterprises; in terms of interaction criteria they were arranged in the following hierarchy at the beginning of our residence there: (1) Soŋi; (2) Siham; (3) Opisa, Koura, Maimoi,[13] Pana, Pitaino, Haiju, To'osi, Asinara, Tahiŋ, Naru, Ho'oma, Tampa, Orim, Koiri; (4) Tamaŋ, Ronsa, Pinoko, Siha, Tanari, Nakao, and Ho'oma's two sons, Kaiai and Minsipi.

Soŋi the Man

And now for Soŋi himself. He is about forty-five years old, of medium height, and slender. He usually wears a conical fiber hat (ohkuna) and a dirty, ragged calico loincloth, seldom troubling to bathe—in fact, he is rather contemptuous of the fastidiousness of his Methodist neighbors. His manner is usually solemn, without appearing unfriendly, and his rare smiles are benign and infectious. His voice is high-pitched but he seldom speaks loudly. Occasionally his anger flares up, but manifests itself in masterfully worded sarcasm rather than in shouts or threats.

Soŋi has no intimate friends. Aside from his quest for renown the joy of his life is his two young sons by his first wife. This wife died in childbirth when the younger son was still an infant and Soŋi has lavished care and affection on the two little boys, explaining that he pities them because they have no mother. Soŋi's third wife also died in childbirth during our stay there, leaving only his second wife, with her young son and infant daughter. Because of the nature of the deaths of these two wives, Soŋi appears convinced that some envious man has carried out tao sorcery,[14] and often speaks of moving away from Turuŋom in order to escape this evil and thus be able to sire more children without risking their mothers' lives. It is often suggested to Soŋi that he take measures to divine the identity of the tao sorcerer, but he refuses, saying that his enemies would have him jailed if they learned of it, and that even if he learned the man's identity the Australian regime would not permit him to punish him.

While other men gad about visiting kinsmen or attending ceremonies and court hearings, Soŋi remains in his club-house or pottery shed, restringing shell money or making pottery. Now and then he disappears to his hamlet house and remains secluded there with his wife and children for days at a time. Few people visit him at his village house and even fewer venture near his hamlet house.

Soŋi is a mikai-magician and states candidly that he practices mainly in order to earn money. A few years back his services were in considerable demand but when his failures multiplied, clients dropped away. Now, Koura is considered a more skillful mikai than Soŋi by his Turuŋom neighbors. Soŋi's spirit-familiar is the ghost of his younger brother (and only sibling), Mokekui, who died in infancy. Mokekui's ghost walks around with Soŋi and is given regular food offerings. Soŋi asserts that Mokekui's tender age may account for his run of failures as a mikai, and talks of acquiring a more effective familiar. Soŋi's club-house demon is said to have resided in the Turuŋom area for a long time, but prior to Soŋi it was unattached to any individual for as far back as informants can recall. This demon spends most of its time in Soŋi's club-house but occasionally appears (to Soŋi) at the latter's village house demanding food. Soŋi usually prevails upon the demon to return to the club-house by staging there a small pork feast for his adherents, with the essence of the pig's blood going to the demon. (It is, of course, a danger to women and children for the demon to lurk near the place where they stay.)

Soŋi's Muminai Feast

The first overt action signalizing the preparations for Soŋi's new muminai feast occurred when he tabooed his coconut trees. This event took place in February 1938, and was described to us by a Turuŋom resident: "Soŋi slaughtered a pig, placed some of the pork in a pot along with a banana leaf and cooked them. When the stew was done he removed the leaf and fastened it around the trunk of one of his coconut palms, saying: 'Hey, there, you horomorun. Smell this food I offer you and look out for my coconuts. If a thief steals any of them, kill him.' "

After this, Soŋi began to formulate plans for financing the feast and obtaining a record number of pigs. First of all, in late October, he mobilized his hand-money men (aŋuraranopo), telling Tamaŋ, Maimoi, Asinara, Pitaino, Koiri, Tampa, Ronsa, Tahiŋ, and To'osi to pen up the pigs he had farmed out to them and hold them ready for the feast. "The hand-money payment," he told them, "will come later." (Afterwards Maimoi told me: "The only hand-money we ever get is the smell of the cooking pig.")

Farming out pigs was one of the simplest methods used by Soŋi to accumulate animals for his feast. Some of his transactions were far more complex, as illustrated by the following example.

In May 1938, Soŋi said to Koura: "I am going to single you out as one of my principal mouhes (supporters) at the next feast. So you give to me now the pig which you would eventually give when I honor you." Koura went to Opisa and asked him to repay a pig lent to him months previously. Koura then gave this pig to Soŋi, who in turn presented it to Pitaino for slaughtering on the occasion of the baptism ceremony of Pitaino's infant daughter. Pitaino owned a fine tusker pig which Soŋi coveted. When Soŋi began to collect pigs for his own feast he turned to Pitaino and asked for the tusker in return for his earlier (coercive) gift. This tusker was then sent to Kaopa, leader of Noronai village, to induce him to lend Soŋi several hundred spans of shell money. Here is the actual record of these negotiations with Kaopa.

November 21: Soŋi sent for Siham and Opisa and took them along with him to see Kaopa. Soŋi and Siham waited in Kaopa's club-house while Opisa went to find Kaopa. After about two hours Kaopa arrived—he had been in his hamlet house. They all joined together in chewing betel nut, then Soŋi told Kaopa that he wanted to give him a large pig and make him principal *Defender*[15] at his big feast. He also told him that he would like to borrow 500 spans of shell money Kaopa thought this over for a while and went to find three of his followers. They conferred, and Kaopa told Soŋi that he probably could could raise it. More betel nut, and the Turuŋom natives returned home.

November 26: Today Soŋi sent Siham, To'osi, Tamaŋ, Tampa, Pitaino, and Ho'oma to Noronai. With them they carried the pig (the one given to Soŋi by Pitaino), which Soŋi gave to Kaopa, who in turn presented Soŋi with a small pig—"betel nut" he called it, "to pay for your trip"—together with 400 of the 500 spans of shell money requested by Soŋi. Soŋi and his company returned home but I remained in Noronai and learned how Kaopa had raised the money: Kaopa had ordered several of his adherents to repay sums owed to him, and by this method he collected 350 spans; Kaopa himself added the other 50.

Later on, Soŋi officially named Kaopa principal resident-defender for the feast.

Soŋi also sent messages to his taovu partners throughout Siuai that he wished to buy their largest pigs, some of which had already been promised him. (One noteworthy aspect of all these events was that no transactions took place with the residents of nearby Mataras village, the place where Soŋi's arch enemy, Konsei, used to reside.) In one instance negotiations led to the temporary dissolution of a taovu partnership. Soŋi had long had his heart set on obtaining a prize tusker pig belonging to his taovu, Maosiŋ, of Rapauru village, but when the time came to collect it Maosiŋ put the price at 200 spans. Soŋi refused to pay this, saying that no pig is worth so much, and announcing that he and Maosiŋ were no longer taovu: "Maosiŋ does not know how great mumis should act towards one another." Later, Maosiŋ relented and offered to sell the pig for 100, and the two met, exchanged expressions of mutual esteem, and resumed their partnership.

Most of the pigs and shell money needed for his feast Soŋi was able to procure from his own adherents, either from their own resources or by sending them out to canvass their friends and kinsmen. The methods he employed were quite direct, as the following diary entries indicate.

> Today (November 2) Soŋi sent Siham and Opisa to round up all the male villagers. After an hour they began to straggle into the club-house; everyone came except Koŋkoma, who is ill. Soŋi asked Maimoi and Ho'oma for the loan of some shell money with which to buy pigs. And he told Pana, Pitaino, Opisa, and Haiju to pay back in pigs the equivalent of money he had previously lent them. Then he sent Koiri and Tamaŋ to round up his (Soŋi's) own pigs and put them in a pen. Then Soŋi left and went to his house. Maimoi grumbled a bit and told Ho'oma that he would be a rich man if Soŋi paid him back all the money he had lent him. Ho'oma replied that a mumi's ways are not like those of other men.

As far as Opisa was concerned, this was a surprise move. A few days later he told me about his experiences in trying to comply with Soŋi's order.

> November 20: This morning Opisa told me that he had had a lot of trouble over the pig Soŋi wanted. He said, that it was true—he did owe Soŋi money, but he had made no plans for repayment. But finally Soŋi had transferred the debt to Pinoko, whereupon Pinoko began to pester him (Opisa) for a pig, much to Opisa's embarrassment. The latter said: "Soŋi shamed me by causing a menial (moŋo) like Pinoko to demand payment. My heart became hot and I went to my mother's brother in Hanoŋ to try and induce him and his son to lend me a pig so that I could repay Pinoko and finish with the whole matter." But in Hanoŋ he also had difficulties, in fact, it had caused a row in his uncle's family. The uncle's son had wanted to sell the pig for 50 spans of mauai. He wanted to use this money to make a final bride-payment to his fiancée's father. When Opisa's uncle finally overruled his son and gave the pig to Opisa, the son became very angry and left home. "He has gone to the coast to work on a plantation. He says he will never come back," said Opisa. "The boy's mother gave her husband and me a good tongue lashing and said that we thought more of Soŋi than we did of our own relatives. Her anger surprised us. She's always been a hot-tempered woman and used to rail at her son all the time; but she had never flared up at her husband before. He would have beaten her if she had!"

Widespread ramifications like these were common features of Siuai feast preparations.

Among all Soŋi's adherents, Koura was most heavily indebted to him for past loans, and Soŋi asked him to repay his debt of five pigs so that they could be used at the big feast. Koura, who is one of Soŋi's most ambitious adherents, decided to make the loan repayment into something of a renown-winning occasion. He invited residents of several neighboring hamlets to attend a feast and help him transfer a fine old gong from his old abandoned club-house to his new one. This feast was held in January, only a few days before the big feast, and Soŋi was requested to attend and receive his pigs. The other guests received four small pigs for their help in carrying the gong. Soŋi expressed mixed feelings about this affair of Koura's. On the one hand, he was somewhat annoyed at Koura for using up pigs which might have been saved for the big feast to come. On the other hand, he was pleased to have an adherent of his put on a feast and thereby increase both the adherent's and, indirectly, his own renown—but in this connection Soŋi complained that the four pigs distributed among the guests were inadequate and did not reflect enough renown upon Turuŋom.

After Soŋi had made initial preparations for collecting pigs he decided to go hunting opossums. He sent word to every able-bodied adult male in the village and set a date for starting out.

On the preceding night Siha-the-Cripple dreamt that a man fell from a tree. He told several villagers of his dream and warned them not to go opossum-hunting. Opisa, Pitaino, and Tamaŋ were sitting in the club-house discussing the advisability of hunting in the face of Siha's warning, when Soŋi arrived and said, very angrily: "You are a crowd of women, all of you. True, Siha is a dream prophet but who cares about his dreams? If I dream, that's different, that's something real." That night they all set out as scheduled, with Siha included.

As soon as they had arrived in the forest, Ho'oma went off alone in the direction of the Mivo River; he was armed with hunting spears and took his dogs with him. "He wants to taste pork," I was told. "He's a real bush demon, that one; and he will surely bring back a wild pig." Sure enough, three days later after all the men had returned loaded down with opossums, Ho'oma stalked in with the carcass of a wild pig slung across his back.

"Now," he said, "I'm going to have *my* feast." Whereupon he sent Ronsa, Pitaino, and Tampa off to get firewood, Siha and Ţo'osi to get cooking pots, and Koiai to take out some taro from his garden. Meanwhile, he singed and butchered the pig, and joked about himself: "I've become a mumi now, a mumi with one pig!"

When everyone had returned, Ho'oma supervised the cooking. For my benefit he swaggered around in imitation of an officious administration appointee, and enjoyed his joke immensely. Then he invited all men in the village to come and eat. When a crowd had gathered he distributed the pork—it was a typically thin wild pig, and didn't go far—and jokingly told his guests: "Just try and surpass my feast!"

When the materials were being assembled for his feast Soŋi commissioned a talented musician from Mokorino village to compose a eulogy to be sung and piped at the feast by the hosts and defenders. Soŋi provided the theme, a lament which he himself had earlier composed in the form of a complaint against an ulcer which had malformed one of his feet; in substance:

> You sore, demon, if you were a man I would rise and slay you and place your skull in the club-house. But alas, you are only a sore, and I can only look at you and weep from pain. (Meaning: I am a powerful warrior and a club-house owner and can work my will on mortal men, but against a little sore I too am powerless.

The composer elaborated somewhat on the theme and adapted it to music. He chose a panpipe of five reeds, cutting them in lengths to suit the required tones. Then he passed around his master panpipe for copying by Soŋi's adherents and by Kaopa's co-defenders.

Prior to this, in mid-October, preparations for the feast were temporarily interrupted when Soŋi's third wife died in childbirth. Soŋi was visibly and probably sincerely grieved by her death, but he was also annoyed by its untimeliness and resolved not to allow it to interfere with his feast preparations.[16] As he said: "People here are always dying and causing me to use up my resources on funeral feasts. That's why my other feasts were not as large as I wanted them to be." He did, however, taboo sounding the gongs in his club-house for a while. Then, in mid-December, he held a *tureko* feast to celebrate the re-beating of his gongs, and to this feast he invited the male residents from all his tuhias, asking them to bring along their panpipes to practice singing and dancing the song intended for the big feast. He butchered seven small pigs and distributed baskets containing stone-baked pork, taro, sweet potatoes, and cooked greens among all the guests, giving one large basket to the leader of each contingent. After the food had been consumed two of the mikai magicians present removed the taboo by beating each gong with coconuts, which were then broken open and eaten. Then hosts and guests joined together in panpipe practice.

After this, practice sessions were held at several club-houses. The Siuai show tireless enthusiasm when actually performing at a feast, but become very bored and tired when learning and practicing, as the following incident illustrates:

> December 4: At about nine in the evening while the village was quiet, Soŋi stalked in, evidently very angry, and cried: "Hey, you good-for-nothings. This is no way to prepare for a feast. You should all be in the club-house so that you could hear what work I've planned for you tomorrow. The time is short now, and all of you do nothing. You slip away to your houses and sleep with your wives when you should be all together in the club-house where men belong. You should be singing or playing on your pipes."
>
> Two or three men crept out of their houses and turned toward the club-house. A few minutes later Pitaino began to blow on the conch shell and there was a little singing and playing, but this lapsed after a while. Tamaŋ walked around in the dancing ground feeling very sorry for himself and trying to rouse somebody to sing; Soŋi sat in the club-house by the small fire and shouted out for someone to sing.
>
> Siha the Cripple joined Tamaŋ, as did Peuru,[17] and they began to sing Terei songs. They were cold, miserable, tired, and not in the least humor for singing; but were afraid to displease Soŋi. Peuru was the only spirited one there.
>
> I left after an hour of this miserable business. All night, at infrequent intervals, the singing would break out again and continue for half an hour. During the early morning a small group from Morokaimoro and Maisua joined in and swelled the noise somewhat. The whole performance was as pathetic as could be imagined. No one wanted to sing. Least of all did they want to stay up all night after a hard day's work, and with the prospects of another day's work on Saturday.

Next, the time arrived for preparing puddings, but before this could be done Soŋi had to remove the taboo placed earlier on his coconut palms. He secured a live opossum for a scapegoat, and forced it to climb into one of the palms. Then he called out to his club-house demon: "Go away now." The opossum was then recaptured, killed, and cooked, and its essence was offered to the club-house demon. In explanation of this event an informant stated: "The club-house demon seized the soul of the opossum, and perceiving that it is no longer necesary to guard the palms, the demon called off all his demon followers."

It was decided to make *anitapu* (sago and almond) and *kihanu* (taro and coconut) puddings for the big feast. First of all, sago had to be secured.

During the second week of December Soŋi sent for Ronsa and Maimoi to arrange for cutting sago palms. Ronsa, it transpired, had none ripe enough, so Soŋi "bought" two from Maimoi, and promised to pay later. Then Soŋi set a date for the tree-felling and sent To'osi and Opisa to get some helpers. To'osi engaged the "shredders," while Opisa engaged the "washers." Maimoi—they were his palms and his job to fell them—asked Tampa, Siha, Ho'oma, and Ronsa to assist him with the felling. When the palms had been felled, Maimoi reported to Soŋi, who passed the word on to the "shredders." Early the following morning the "shredders" removed the bark from one side of the palms and began to chop away the pith. Soŋi sent Ho'oma to beat a gong to summon the "washers." Soon they all appeared with Opisa, and when the shredders gave them a signal they set about washing the shredded sago pith. When the "washers," had finished the job they called out to several "packers," who joined them and compressed the starch into leaf packages. When they had finished with this, Soŋi directed them to store the packages in the club-house and in their own houses.

Even though the adult males of the village were busily employed preparing food for the feast, the ordinary affairs of everyday life had to drone on, but with this difference: women had to perform much of the work ordinarily done by men. Such differences were evident in many families and resulted in some temporary changes in the relationships among family members. The case of Ho'oma is informative.

Ho'oma is a faithful subject of Soŋi's and at the same time is generally regarded as a good family man. He usually works very hard in the garden, even assisting his wife with planting and weeding, a task which most men consider undignified. His wife, Pirume, is a regular Xanthippe, but she was once overheard telling a group of women that her husband, Ho'oma, is a good husband: "He is unselfish; he divides his pork among us all."

The men of Turuŋom like Ho'oma—they always laugh at his buffoonery—but they do not have much respect for him. Younger men would not hesitate to send him on errands, and Ho'oma—anxious to please—generally does as he is told. As one would expect, Soŋi began to depend more and more upon him when preparing for his feast. By December 7, Soŋi was referring directly to Ho'oma whenever he wanted some important task done. He started conferring with Siham and Ho'oma preliminary to starting a job and left much of the business of preparation to them; consequently, Ho'oma began to give orders to other natives. At the same time he slept more often at the club-house and returned to his own home only for meals.

This behavior obviously annoyed Pirume because she railed at Ho'oma whenever he appeared, screaming to him to "try sounding wood (cutting down trees) in his garden rather than waste time sounding wood (beating wooden gongs) in Soŋi's club-house." After one of these squabbles Ho'oma stayed away from home for a week, during which time Pirume forced her lazy sons, Koiai and Minsipi, to do more work than was their custom.[18]

In spite of the redoubled efforts of men like Ho'oma, in mid-December it became obvious to the Turuŋom natives that there were not enough local laborers to carry out all the work of food preparation. Thereupon Soŋi acted as he had on many previous occasions and sent word to Tukem, leader of Rennu village to assist. Hitherto Soŋi and Tuken used to meet in each other's club-house and make arrangements for exchanging pigs or money. Each treated the other with greatest deference, addressing each other as "friend" (*ŋonosim*) and sharing betel nut. Tukem and his Rennu villagers stood in the same relationship to Soŋi and Turuŋom villagers as Kaopa and his Noronai adherents, and many other leaders and their adherents. When Soŋi, acting in his capacity as the leader of Turuŋom village, wanted outside assistance, he went directly to the leader of another village. Not even in his most expansive mood had he seriously attempted to usurp authority in another village. This situation is aptly illustrated by an incident that occurred in Rennu.

One of Tukem's old followers has, as a result of an old feud, borne a grudge against Soŋi since boyhood and he has always resented Soŋi's visits to Rennu. Once while Soŋi was there, he addressed the old fellow and his son and jokingly asked them to contribute a pig for the coming feast. The old man remained stolidly silent, not even bothering to look in Soŋi's direction. After Soŋi left, Tukem asked the ancient why he had not spoken to Soŋi, and the old man replied: "I'm not his fool. One mumi's enough for me." Later Tukem suggested to Soŋi: "I will ask the ancient stone-heart for a pig, perhaps he will give it to me." Soŋi replied: "Never mind, if I had really wanted his pig, I would have asked you in the first place." And there the matter rested.

After Soŋi had received Tukem's assurance that Rennu villagers would assist in the food preparations, he turned to Siham and asked him to supervise. Siham is the most knowledgeable cook in Turuŋom. Besides knowing all the recipes, he controls a large number of magical techniques which insure successful baking and boiling. The cooking lasted for six days. During this time nearly every adult male from the two villages was on hand, even decrepit Kanasai and Koŋkoma. Only the bitter old man of Rennu remained at home, sulking.

Finally the time came for making sago-almond pudding. Siham set various individuals to do certain things, and the work proceeded apace. Stone-heaters called out to sago- and almond-grinders when the oven was prepared. Grinders, working with mortar and pestle, reduced, mixed, and thinned the ingredients, and passed on the mash to packers. Packers poured it into leaf-lined frames; then placed the pudding in the oven. Meanwhile Siham supervised nearly every step, regulating the speed and pointing out deficiencies. Soŋi also hovered around, and on several occasions sent numbers of Turuŋom and Rennu men to get more firewood and to refill the bamboos with water. This change in relations surprised me but, apparently, not the Rennu villagers. Having become so accustomed to the formality and restraint between Soŋi and those natives, I was not prepared to see the former order the Rennu villagers about as if they were his own adherents.

From this time on, Rennu villagers frequented Soŋi's club-house and aided Turuŋom natives with all their communal tasks.[19]

The first striking evidence of the "political" merger of Rennu with Turuŋom occurred just before the social-climbing feast, when Soŋi deputized Ho'oma to direct the construction of a display platform. Tukem complained that he had expected to supervise that job himself; and spent the rest of the day at his hamlet house, disappointed and sulky.[20]

But Tukem or no Tukem, the display platform was finished under Ho'oma's direction, and was decorated with food. The completion of these events was a signal for the feast invitation to be sent.

As early as September it was rumored about that "all the big leaders in Siuai are nervous over Soŋi's choice of a guest of honor for his feast; they would all be shamed by so much generosity." Soŋi appeared to enjoy the suspense he was creating, then, one day just after the display platform had been decorated with coconuts, he announced that he had made his choice, and without recourse to divination. This was the news the Siuai had been waiting for.

"Siham," ordered Soŋi, "collect as many men as you need and carry invitation pigs to Sipisoŋ of Kinirui."

This was a great surprise to the curious natives; that is, until they realized the significance of the gesture. Earlier, while Soŋi was making arrangements to collect pigs for his feast, he had a bitter quarrel with this Sipisoŋ, an administration appointee of little renown. Soŋi had been frustrated in his effort to secure one of Sipisoŋ's great tuskers and obviously wished to humiliate him. Soŋi knew that to refuse an invitation to a muminai is to suffer contempt, but to accept without hope of reciprocating is to court even worse disaster. His move was successful. Siham returned with the invitation pigs and recounted how humiliated Sipisoŋ had been: "He felt so much shame that he vowed he would never again set foot in Turuŋom" (Nor did he—until the feast, which he attended and seemed to enjoy thoroughly!).

After having rebuked Sipisoŋ, Soŋi conducted divination and sent the invitation pigs to Kope, most influential leader and Paramount Chief of central Siuai. Wisacres claimed they knew that he was going to be the choice from the beginning. Kope accepted and they agreed on a date. Messages passed to and fro, with Soŋi begging Kope's pardon for the presumption shown by inviting such a great man to so modest a repast; and with Kope expressing gratitude that a mumi as big as Soŋi would deign to notice him, and prophesying that he would never be able to reciprocate such a bountiful gift.

Kope slaughtered the invitation pigs sent to him by Soŋi, cut them in strips, and sent the strips around to all the leaders of central, southern, and western Siuai, as well as to a few leaders from the neighboring ethnic areas of Banoni and Nagovisis. They were invited to attend the feast with Kope, who designated them as his *allies* and urged them to join in the *attack* on Turuŋom.

While this was going on, Soŋi sent out other invitation pigs to Kaopa of Noronai and some other Rataiku natives designated to be his defenders. Kaopa, in turn, invited many other leaders to attend with their adherents as his co-defenders. He invited all Siuai leaders and Hat-men not directly asked by Soŋi or Kope, including Moŋko of Kupiŋku, the Paramount Chief and highest-ranking leader of northwest Siuai; Tomo, the Paramount Chief of northeast Siuai; and even some leaders from Terei.

In other words, this was to be not only a whole tribal affair and probably the first such ever given, but was also intended to reach out beyond the borders of Siuai.

Now there remained only one decision to make. Should or should not Soŋi appear at the feast and be seen by his guests? Hitherto on several occasions he had made all preparations for his feasts and then retired to his hamlet house in order to hide from envious sorcerers. The matter was not decided until Kope himself sent a message saying that "he would only come to the feast—Turuŋom is so far away!—provided he could be assured of seeing his renowned host." Soŋi decided to remain and he was assured that every device known to his followers would be used to protect him.

All was in readiness. The curious and excited Defenders strolled in hours before dawn on January 10, 1939, and took part in the final *pig-counting*. Koura claimed he saw Soŋi's horomorun dancing along the ridgepole, vastly pleased with the noise and the smell of food. Women huddled together around minute fires in the village and discussed the great event with animation; some of the bolder ones actually stole up to the edge of the dancing ground and peered through the reeds at the drummers.

The morning was spent by all the men applying cosmetics and decorating weapons, preparing themselves as if they were making ready for war. Spears were oiled and bows restrung and polished. Faces and torsos were painted both with powdered lime, sign of invulnerability in battle, and with red ochre, sign of warfare and festivity. Protective charms were distributed about the body to guard against sorcery.

By noon all the Defenders had massed around the front of the club-house and were straining to hear the faraway shouts that announced the approach of the Attackers. While some of the tardier ones quickly applied ochre and lime there was a last minute consultation to reconsider whether Soŋi should remain or hide. He remained, and sat upon his largest wooden gong alongside the spot believed to be occupied by his horomorun.

Then, like a shot, a single spearman rushed into the clearing, ran up to the front of the club-house, threatened the natives lined up there, and retired. A second followed suit, then a third, and so on until scores of howling natives had rused in brandishing their spears and axes and twanging arrows against bowstrings. More men entered at a run carrying pigs, for the guest must reciprocate the invitation pigs previously sent to him.

The rush then slackened off and the Attackers began to mill around the southern end of the dancing ground, while the Defenders formed a revolving circle nearer the club-house. Then the piping began. Every native performed so strenuously that he could not hear the rival melody above the din of his own. The Turuŋom natives discovered that their song, the lament for Soŋi's sore, now seemed too complicated and slow, so after halting along with it for a while they abandoned it for a more spirited tune.

The music went on for an hour before the guests began to move gradually in the direction of the club-house. As they pressed forward the Defenders thinned out in order to give the guests a chance to see their host. Soŋi reluctantly slid down from his perch and stood upright while his guests stared at him.

Then, at a signal from Soŋi, some of his men rushed to the pens and dragged in the squealing pigs. Others climbed the display platform, whisked away with bundles of leaves the demons guarding it, and began to hand down baskets of food.

After the pigs and puddings had been lined up on the ground, Soŋi motioned to Kope to accept them. This was the signal for a stampede. Puddings were ripped into, drinking nuts broken open. Meanwhile Kope recorded on a fern frond tally the value of the pigs, and distributed them among his allies. The pigs were quickly strangled and tied to poles, and the whole company of Attackers and Defenders moved off. The exit was as sudden and dramatic as the entry. The whole affair had lasted only two hours.

Some 1100 natives attended the feast and received 32 pigs, distributed as follows: 17 pigs worth a total of 1070 spans of mauai to Kopec; 7 pigs worth a total of 450 spans to Koapa;[21] 4 pigs worth a total of 220 spans to those Rataiku leaders who were directly invited; 3 pigs worth 160 spans given directly to Soŋi's principal taovu partners; and one pig worth 20 spans given to the Australian Patrol Officer, whom Soŋi invited in order to show him "how *Siuai* leaders act."

Every Turuŋom native seemed to sense the depression of anticlimax. A few of them strolled around the dancing ground, now red with betel juice. Some of them kept up a disconsolate piping. No pudding remaind for them —"We shall eat Soŋi's renown for a day or two"—so the only thing left to them was talk about the feast, particularly about the number of guests who had been present. And of course by nightfall these numbers had been exaggerated to legendary proportions, as had accounts of everything else concerned with the feast.

"Now we shall rest," To'osi told me hopefully. "Now we can attend our gardens." I agreed with him, just as hopefully, and went away to sleep.

Yet early the next morning the wooden gongs boomed out again and they seemed louder than ever, probably because the noise was so unexpected. A few sleepy natives strolled in the direction of the club-house and heard Soŋi storm out:

> Hiding in your houses again; copulating day and night while there's work to be done! Why, if it were left up to you, you would spend the rest of your lives smelling yesterday's pig. But I tell you, yesterday's feast was nothing. The next one will be really big. Siham, I want you to arrange with Konnu for his largest pig; and you, Maimoi, go to Mokakaru and find a pig for Uremu; . . . [etc.]

Opisa turned to me and whispered: *"That's* the fashion of a mumi!"

CHAPTER

18

Political Organization, Supernatural Sanctions, and the Punishment for Incest on Yap

DAVID M. SCHNEIDER

I will enquire here into the nature and severity of the punishment for incest on Yap. Such an enquiry might well entail an extended analysis of a multitude of factors and yield a volume of intimidating proportions, but I will confine myself to one problem among the many which bear on the nature of punishment—the problem of the relationship between political organization and the nature and severity of the punishment for incest. I do not thereby deny the relevance of other factors, but simply set aside their consideration. My intention is merely to demonstrate the relevance of the question of who has the right to inflict punishment to an understanding of the nature and severity of the punishment inflicted.

The exposition which follows proceeds by a method of successive approximations. I will begin with a brief outline of the Yap incest regulations and of the punishment when those regulations are not observed, and follow this with a first approximation of the relationship between political organization and punishment in general terms. I will then analyze the empirical material more fully to see how well the generalizations apply to the data, and will continue to balance generalization against data until I believe that I have developed a set of precisely defined generalizations which apply to these Yap data. I make no pretense of presenting a full and complete theory of punishment.

The incest taboo on Yap, a high island in the West Carolines, Micro-

From *American Anthropologist,* 59: 791–800, 1957. Reproduced by permission of the author and The American Anthropological Association.

nesia, applies to members of the nuclear family, the patrilineal lineage, and the matrilineal clan. The prohibition on sexual relations among members of these groups applies to all and any, regardless of genealogical distance (Schneider 1953).

Diffuse sanctions in the form of disapproval and shunning are applied if incest should occur, but these are actually mild. The guilty pair are not ostracized, but only whispered about and held to have behaved like animals. In the cases which I observed, as well as in reports of other cases, no one seemed severely embarrassed or emotionally upset, and in a few of these cases the relationship was sustained over a long period. The diffuse sanctions certainly did not break up the relationship.

No organized sanctions are ever applied. The events are held to be no one's concern except the kin group of the participants.

Consequences of incest are of two sorts. Where incest occurs between brother and sister, who should normally practice a mild avoidance and respect relationship which is explicitly phrased in terms of minimizing sexual interest in each other, the consequence is automatic and "immediate." The patrilineage ghosts are offended and cause the death of some member of the patrilineage (it may or may not be one of the incestuous pair) within about two months. Usually an illness precedes the death. However, death may come from any source, such as a supernaturally determined accident. A man may be climbing a coconut tree and fall and be killed. The fall will have been caused by the ancestral ghosts.

If the brother and sister are of different patrilineages but of the same matrilineal clan, the spirits of the matrilineal clan cause some member of that clan to die. Here again, since clansmen are siblings, the consequence is automatic and limited in time. It will happen within about two months. But here, too, the offenders themselves may or may not be the ones to die.

If, however, incest occurs between kinsmen who are not classed as siblings, the supernatural consequence is essentially the same except that it may happen at any time. It can happen within two months, but usually it does not. It may be two years, or twenty years, but eventually some member of the patrilineage will die because of the incest, since the ancestral ghosts of the patrilineage have been offended.

It is especially noteworthy that the group is responsible for the incestuous acts of any of its members, and that any member of the group is liable to die as a result of the incest committed by some other member. The group is thus collectively responsible for the occurrence of incest, just as it is collectively responsible for any other transgression.

The group takes no formal action against the transgressors. There may be sharp words and ill feeling, but these are kept well under control and are not expressed in the presence of outsiders. This is, of course, exactly how the group behaves when two of its members commit any other transgression against each other, be it fratricide, theft, or insult.

The group does take action in cases of incest to prevent the punishment from occurring. The head of the lineage divines to discover a happy ancestral ghost, and divines again to find out what sort of *biul* or gift this ghost will accept in order to enlist his good offices in prevailing on the other ghosts to stay their hand. If the divination is successful, if a happy ancestral ghost is found (and one always is), and if a suitable arrangement can be made with this ghost (one always is), and if this ghost is successful in prevailing on the other ghost (this is where the difficulty lies; sometimes he is, sometimes he is not), then no one need die for the incest. The head of the lineage does what can be done, and beyond that it is up to the ghosts. But some action must be taken as soon as possible, otherwise there is no chance at all of forestalling the punishment.

My informants viewed incest as essentially impractical because of the risk of death. Informants invariably asserted that incest was "wrong" and "bad," but their assertions had about the same quality and tone as their essertions of most other "wrong" or "bad" things. They regarded incest as the sort of thing animals, not humans, do. But I was never given to understand, nor did their actions convey in any way, the depth of horror or revulsion which has been reported as the attitude of other peoples. My informants were quite willing to discuss it in the abstract or to discuss concrete cases.

An attempt to explain the kind and severity of a punishment might well begin by distinguishing the punishment from the definition of a particular act as "right" or "wrong." An act defined as "wrong" may or may not be punished. If it is punished, there is then the separate question of "what punishment." I am only concerned here with why incest is punished as it is, not with why it is prohibited. Although the grounds for its prohibition may well bear on the nature of the punishment, these are not my concern here.

If incest is prohibited it will necessarily have some negative emotional quality attached to it. But no society can permit its members to express their emotions in perfectly free and unencumbered ways. This is particularly true where the emotions are of an aggressive nature, and punishment is a form of aggression. Every society must specify when, where, how, and by whom aggression may be expressed and punishment applied.

The socially regulated use of force, or aggression, is essentially political activity. The right to use force under specified conditions is distributed among the groups and statuses of a society. Which social unit holds the right to punish whom and under what circumstances is an aspect of its political organization.

Incest is an intra-kin group offense. The role of the kin group as a political unit of the social structure is thus a critical variable. Where the kin group is an autonomous, self-regulating unit it has a monopoly on the use of force in regulating its internal affairs. No agency outside the kin group can impose punishment on any of its members for intragroup offenses.

If an intra-kin group wrong is to be punished when the kin group is autonomous and self-regulating, there are two alternatives or some combination of these open. Either living members punish the offender, or the punishment is left to supernatural agencies.

These seem to be reasonable formulations, but how do they fit the Yap data?

Incest is prohibited on Yap and clearly negative emotional attitudes are associated with it. The fact that mild diffuse sanctions are expressed makes it clear that these attitudes are not merely neutral but entail attitudes of condemnation and aggression. If the Yap people really felt that incest was no one's business other than the kin group of the concerned couple, they would not whisper and shun the offenders. But a sharp line is drawn between this very diffuse expression of judgment and actually doing something about it. Others may have the right to feel that a wrong has been committed, but only the kin group of the offenders has the right to do anything about wrongs committed within that group.

The Yap patrilineage appears to be an autonomous and self-regulating unit. If a member commits a crime against another member of his patrilineage, no outsider can automatically interfere. This is true of incest, fratricide, petty theft, insult, and so forth.

Units outside the patrilineage may take action under two conditions. First, where the father's sister's children have been neglected, insulted, or where food which should be reserved for them has not been set aside and kept for them, or where any very serious breach of custom occurs, the father's sister's children have the right to drive the entire patrilineage from its land, or such members of it as they feel to be especially at fault. However, there is grave reluctance to take such action. My informants could not cite a single instance of such an event in their memory. All they could say was that they believed that this had happened long ago.

Second, where patricide or an assault on a father occurs, the heads of the patrilineages of the village may assemble and, if the assaulted father asks them to, or if the father is dead and they deem it necessary, they can force the offending son to leave the village. Here again the right of the assembled heads of the patrilineages to take action was clearly asserted by all informants, but although assaults on fathers were by no means unknown, and patricide had occurred, there was such grave reluctance to take this action that it had never occurred so far as my oldest informants could remember. But again they insisted that in the distant past it certainly had happened.

In discussing fratricide my informants stated that any further action by the father or the surviving brothers would disrupt the patrilineage still more and was therefore not undertaken since the patrilineage should be maintained as an indivisible unit at any cost. Moreover, they argued, it was wrong for brother to attack brother, for brothers should stand together. It would therefore compound the evil should a surviving brother punish the offending brother. What happens, they explained, is that the ancestral ghosts take note of the action and are indignant. But they too feel that the patrilineage must remain intact, so they confine themselves to remaining inattentive to prayers on behalf of the offender. They punish him by not helping him when he needs help and so eventually he dies for his fratricide, for he will one day need them desperately. When they see that it cannot hurt the patrilineage to let him die, they do so.

The offense of fratricide, as the Yaps see it, is an offense against the solidarity of the lineage. But the essential structure of the lineage is that it is the core of a series of linked nuclear families, and the critical relationship is that of father and son. The solidarity of siblings is important, but without a father or father surrogate, according to the Yap view, there can be no lineage.

The role of the son and brother is

confined to intralineage activity. He plays no part in the affairs of the lineage as they relate with other lineages or with the village. It is the father who is head of the lineage, and it is the head of the lineage who represents it to other lineages, and to the village. His is the status which articulates the lineage with the rest of the elaborate political structure of Yap.

Fratricide is thus very different from patricide in terms of its effect on lineage structure in particular and the political system in general. When one brother kills another, the father-son relationship may still be maintained. When a son kills his father, or assaults him, the necessary link between the lineage and the community is broken. This offense is not merely against lineage solidarity, but is in addition an offense against the village. This follows from the Yap view that when a man acts as "father" he relates himself to members of his lineage; when he acts as "head of the lineage" he is acting toward the outside—toward the village or other lineages. The village is thus directly concerned with delicts against the head of the lineage; it has no concern with sons who are brothers.

Two difficulties with the initial formulation are now apparent. The first centers on the fact that a particular delict cannot be assumed to be purely intra-kin group in nature merely from knowing the kinship categories of those involved. Although at first glance patricide would appear to be a purely intra-kin group offense, this is definitely not the case on Yap. Patricide is in part an offense against the lineage by one of its members, but in part it is an offense against the village. The matter is further complicated by the fact that despite the clear right of the village to act in cases of patricide or asault on the father, there is an equally clear tendency to treat this particular offense as if it were an intra-kin group matter. That is, the village has consistently left the matter in the hands of the kin group and has never taken the action to which it would be entitled.

The second difficulty is closely related to the first. In the case of the patrilineal lineage, the statement that it is autonomous and self-regulating is limited by the fact that it is part of a larger political structure and articulated with it. Its affairs, in certain respects, are the affairs of other lineages and of the village. Hence it is not completely or perfectly autonomous, though it closely approximates this.

The other kinship group on Yap is the matrilineal clan. This is a territorially diffuse unit without corporate organization, internal differentiation, or authority structure. The matrilineal clan requires exogamy, provides for hospitality and help in case of need, and sanctuary in case of war. There is no way of enforcing these obligations beyond expressions of indignation.

The matrilineal clan is autonomous and self-regulating in the sense that members of one clan do not interfere in the affairs of another clan. But the clan's affairs are so limited in scope and the clan is so lacking in internal structure that it is self-regulating more by default than by design. Yet the fact remains that outsiders have no right to take action with respect to events internal to the unit.

The matrilineal clan and the patrilineal lineage approximate autonomous and self-regulating units, but whereas the lineage has a clear authority structure, the clan does not. It is difficult to see how the clan could take action against a member for any delict which might occur within, since it lacks a differentiated authority structure. The fact that supernaturals and not the living people act in cases of incest thus makes good sense in these terms. But this reasoning cannot apply to the lineage. The mere presence of an authority structure may thus be a necessary but by no means sufficient condition for certain members of a self-regulating kin group to undertake punitive action against offending members.

The comparison between the general formulation and the Yap data can now be continued. The comparison of incest with other offenses provides further correction of the general formulation.

The Yaps see incest as an offense against the ancestral ghosts, who are treated as if they were a separate unit and in return treat the lineage as a corporate unit. In cases of incest the lineage has collective responsibility. Neither in fratricide nor patricide is any notion of collective responsibility involved.

The ancestral ghosts have formal dealings with the lineage through its representative, the lineage head. When they are offended they retaliate against the lineage through any of its members, but treating any one member as the equivalent of any other. Ordinarily no one prays to the lineage ghosts except the head of the lineage, and he does so on behalf of the lineage, just as he deals with the village on its behalf. When he asks for the help of the ancestral ghosts he does so on behalf of the lineage as a whole, not for the personal benefit of one of its members. It is true that he may pray that one member may not die, or that one member may recover from an illness, or that one member may have children. But the recovery or the children are for the lineage, not for the person alone. If an individual wishes to enlist supernatural aid purely on his own behalf he does so through magical manipulations, not through his ancestral ghosts.

The responsibility of the lineage for the incest of its members is not connected with any mystical notions of ritual pollution or contamination or contagion that I could discover.

Incest is thus seen by the Yaps as essentially sacrilegious in nature. But why it is sacrilegious, why the ghosts are offended, was never made clear to me. Although there was no reluctance to discuss the matter, the whole attitude seemed to center on a kind of simple empirical generalization: incest offends the ancestral ghosts who retaliate for the offense unless properly placated.

If a man from one lineage assaults a man from another lineage within his village, the head of the offender's lineage hastens to bring an appropriate gift and apology to the head of the victim's lineage. If the gift and apology are not promptly tendered, the lineage of the offended person has the right to retaliate by force against the lineage of the offender. In such a case, someone —and it can be anyone—in the offender's lineage may be wounded or killed.

The pattern is thus essentially the same in the case of the ghosts as in the case of any extralineage delict: a wrong invites retaliation unless an appropriate gift and apology are proffered promptly. Retaliation is by injury or death to any member of the offending lineage.

One significant difference between any other lineage and the ancestral ghosts lies in the fact that when a delict has been committed against a living person, the head of his lineage is always well known and can be approached directly. If the head of the offended person's lineage deems the gift and apology unsuitable, he can make this known and a more suitable gift may promptly be substituted. But the proper representative of the ancestral ghosts must be discovered on each occasion by divination, as must the propriety of the gift and apology. Divination is openly admitted to be subject to error, but there is no certain way of establishing this error until it is too late.

Again two difficulties in the original formulation become evident. The first is the question of whether the consequences of incest can properly be viewed as punishment or whether they are more accurately described in simple cause and effect terms. The distinction between the consequences of a particular act and punishment rests on the fact that punishment implies moral transgression of some sort. In one case the consequences are inherent in the nature of the act itself, while punishment is not a necessary concomitant of the nature of the act but only of the value placed on it. It is true that the Yaps are not given to elaborate emotional expressions of moral indignation uttered in pious phrases. They allocate more concern to practical consequences and dwell less on good and evil, but this does not mean that they fail to distinguish between immoral and impractical acts. Both are ill-advised, both have unpleasant consequences; but the consequences of an immoral act follow from its immorality, the consequences of a foolish act follow from the nature of the act itself and no more. For the Yap, the consequences of incest are punishment in this sense.

The second difficulty again centers on the problem of just what constitutes an intra-kin group offense. Although I defined incest as an intra-kin group offense, the Yaps see it as an offense against the ancestral ghosts and treat it as if it were of the same order as any other extralineage offense, namely, that the offended unit has the right to retaliate unless placating gifts and apologies are promptly made. Retaliation is in the form of injury or death.

Lineage ghosts are dead members of the lineage who once stood and continue to stand in a parental position with respect to the living lineage, and they represent the only channel through which the lineage as a unit can influence the supernatural. Although various supernatural beings are distinguished, each having a domain and an area of concern—one with the sea, another with the fruit-bearing trees and plants, another with the clouds—they are collectively referred to as "the spirits" (*kan*). It is the spirits who, long ago, established the social and moral regulations which govern Yap life, who originally forbade incest, and who take action against it when it occurs. The spirits are therefore seen as the source of morality and the locus of ultimate authority.

However, the spirits are amenable to the influence of the ancestral ghosts, who can forestall their retribution or enlist their support for a worthy cause. Although the spirits are the ultimate source of morality and authority, the crucial figures are the ancestral ghosts because it is only through them that the lineage can influence the spirits and because their influence on the acts of the spirits is decisive. It is thus in this narrower sense that incest is seen as an offense against the ghosts; it is really an offense against the spirits.

There are, of course, various ways in which the relationship between moral norms and the acts of the living can be phrased. It is possible to see morality as a part of the self, deified to a degree, but essentially operating as a form of self-regulation. It is possible to see morality as the concrete acts of concrete beings who can see, hear, and discover what human beings do no matter where or when they do it. These beings may be beneficient, punitive, dictatorial, capricious.

The Yap view is that the moral regulations governing intralineage relations emanate from concrete beings, spirits, while the decisive control over the acts of the spirits is personified in the form of the ghosts. This image of the relationship between moral norms and the acts of the living is congruent with the organization of the lineage. It is, after all, the fundamental social unit in which solidarity and unity are the cardinal conditions for its maintenance in that form. That it ought never to be rent by conflict must be balanced against the human beings of which it is composed. Yaps recognize the gap between what people ought to do and the persistent tendency to do wrong. Where unity and solidarity are cardinal conditions of existence, as well as clearly expressed values, the problem is to limit wrongs to a minimum, not to compound them.

But different wrongs have different effects, as well as different frequencies of occurrence. Although the right to punish incest is ultimately in the hands of the spirits and immediately in the hands of the ghosts, the father of a small disobedient child does not depend on the ghosts alone; he reprimands the child or he strikes it, though, of course, his right to do so is clearly delegated to him by the spirits through the ghosts. Nor does the father of a grown, persistently disobedient son depend on the ghosts alone; he may exclude his son from lineage membership and thus deprive him of his rights in land. So, too, the father who has been assaulted has the right, given him by the spirits and backed by the ghosts, to terminate the father-son relationship, thereby excluding the son from lineage membership and terminating his rights in land.

Incest is thus different from an assault on the father by the son, or from disobedience on the part of a son. It might be suggested that in this particular case the gravity of the offense depends in part on the probability of its occurrence and in part on the immediacy of the disruptive effects of the crime. Incest does not rend a lineage apart; the failure of a son to perform his role as it is prescribed does so rend it. In the latter case immediate action by members of the kin group is required to maintain the lineage, in the former no such immediate action is required.

But what about the punishment? Is death a more severe penalty than disinheritance? Or does the nature of the punishment depend on still other considerations?

If punishment is allocated to supernatural agencies, then certain conditions inherent in this alternative bear on the nature of the punishment. A supernatural sanction which specifies that the criminal's left arm will fall off at high noon on the third day following the crime cannot be maintained for long except for such crimes as are practically never committed. This is because the probability of anybody's arm falling off at high noon is very, very low. But a supernatural sanction which specifies that someone will die can be maintained because the probability that someone will die is equivalent to certainty. The events which can be counted on to occur in the natural world are the events which must be used as supernatural punishments where the crime is committed with any frequency sufficient to put the matter to test. The crime which is never committed may be linked with a supernatural punishment that could never happen only because that linkage cannot be tested. The crime which is committed with discernible frequency must be linked with a punishment that is very likely to occur if the punishment is to be regarded as supernaturally caused. the only qualification on this generalization is in the case of an effective counter-spell or neutralizing magic. Here, obviously, the efficiency of the counter-spell depends entirely on the probability of the occurrence of the punishing event.

Illness and death are the sorts of events which human beings the world over can count on to occur. They are therefore precisely the sorts of events which can be regarded as supernatural punishment. On Yap the punishment for incest is death.

A man who returns to Yap from a long overseas voyage and has sexual intercourse during the next three-month period, during which time it is prohibited (by the spirit of the sea), may fall ill unless he has successfully sought the intervention of his lineage ghosts. But such a man is not expected to die of his illness. In one case which I saw, ringworm developed on the man's buttock. With prayer and propitiating gifts to the spirit, as well as an ointment and numerous food taboos, he recovered.

Illness, death, and bad luck are precisely the sorts of events which human beings can count on to occur and can be expected as supernatural punishments. But within the framework of the kinds of punishments which can be seen as supernatural, there are different degrees of severity of punishment and crimes of different gravity. Both incest and the breach of the taboo on intercourse after an overseas journey are sexual crimes, but the former is the graver offense in the eyes of the Yaps.

In sum, because the Yap kin groups are practically autonomous and self-regulating, no outside agency has the right to punish intra-kin group offenses, and just for this reason any punishment which is administered must be carried out by the kin group itself. Yet the Yap lineage concretizes and personifies authority in its spirits, which are controlled by lineage ghosts, and separates these from its living members. It treats these ghosts as a corporate body and conceives of itself as a corporate body in relation to the ghosts. Although the observer can see incest as an intra-kin group offense, the Yap view is that it is of essentially the same order as inter-lineage offenses. The punishment for incest is therefore consistent with the punishment for any serious interlineage offense; it is the retaliation by force by the offended group, the consequences of which are injury (equivalent to illness) and death. But another set of conditions limits the kind of punishment which is possible for incest. Since the punishment is carried out by supernaturals, it must be such that supernaturals can be credited with effecting it. Death is precisely the kind of event which occurs with unfailing regularity in the natural order of things, and it is therefore the kind of event which can be viewed as supernaturally determined.

Discussion

The Yap data suggest that it may be useful to separate the problem of why an act is deemed wrong from the question of what is done about it and by whom. It seems that what is done about a particular crime depends very much on who has the right to do something about it. This is essentially a political question and depends on the manner in which the right to use force is distributed throughout the social structure. In the case of Yap, the kin group is practically autonomous and self-regulating and therefore is responsible for the acts of its members and the application of sanctions against them.

I have by-passed the question of what happens when the kin group is not autonomous and self-regulating since this is not the case on Yap. But the question is an important one and any general theory of punishment must cope with it. It may very well be that kin groups are easier on their own members than impartial courts or councils or other kin groups.

I suggest that where the kin group is autonomous it has the choice of applying sanctions against its own members or delegating this responsibility to supernatural agencies. Various considerations bear on whether the responsibility for carrying out punishment is delegated to supernaturals or living members of the group. Among these are the frequency with which the crime occurs and the degree to which it is immediately disruptive. Although this is a very important question in any general theory of punishment, there was no need to go into it here since the critical question is only that of whether humans or supernaturals execute the punishment. It seems sufficient to note here that incest is neither very frequent nor, when it occurs, immediately disrupting on Yap, and that the delegation of responsibility for applying sanctions to the patrilineage ghosts seems congruent with the value of maintaining lineage solidarity at any cost.

CHAPTER

19

Law and Politics on Nonouti Island

HENRY P. LUNDSGAARDE

The purpose of this paper is to combine some of the empirical strengths of ethnology with the conceptual tools of jurisprudence. I shall attempt to test a specific hypothesis about the relationship between legal phenomena and the concept of law in a small island society and to explore the problem of cross-cultural comparisons. I will outline some of my assumptions about law and define a few essential concepts, and these will then be applied to the analysis of Gilbertese legal and political phenomena. The concluding section of the paper re-evaluates the basic propositions developed in the following paragraphs.

The concept of law is like that of culture in that both concepts refer to a variety of distinctively human activities. Although the latter is believed to be a universal concept applicable to all human societies, there is considerable disagreement about the universality of law as a phenomenon. Acceptance of law as a universal depends to a large extent on the inclusiveness of the concept and the explanatory yields gained through its application. If, for example, law is restricted to the activities of courts and legislatures one automatically eliminates law from most of the preliterate societies studied by anthropologists. If we define all acts of social control as law, we have unnecessarily opened the range of the concept to include almost any norm, sanction, or custom in society (see Redfield 1967:3–24).

I subscribe to Gluckman's (1965:183) suggestion that ". . . we continue to use the word 'law' itself loosely . . ." so that we can operationally specify the circumstances to which the concept of law may be applied. Thus, when Gluckman describes what he calls "the process of adjudication" as ". . . the process which, in African tribes with courts,

Fieldwork in the Gilbert Islands during 1963–1964 was generously financed by the Woodrow Wilson Foundation and the National Science Foundation. Additional support from the National Institute of Mental Health (Grant No. MH-13042) and the University of California at Santa Barbara allowed me to revisit the Gilberts during the summer in 1965 and to prepare the data for publication.

judges take and assess the evidence, examine what they regard as the facts, and come to a decision in favor of one party rather than another . . ." he has, in fact, provided a workable definition of modern Gilbertese law.

Two additional problems remain. First, we somehow have to isolate legal from other social customs affecting social control. I do so by drawing a distinction between interpersonal relations founded on reciprocity and those based on the recognition of legal obligations, or by distinguishing legal from other kinds of social sanctions. It may also be necessary to draw a boundary line between legal authority and political power. Second, it is important to provide an accurate interpretation of "exotic" ethnographic data without either distorting or oversimplifying such data to suit comparative or analytical ends.

Can such general western legal concepts as "obligation," "ownership," or "contract" be applied to the analysis of Gilbertese law, or should the native legal system be analyzed from "within" or in terms of native categories? The elevation of native categories (i.e., "folk concepts") to analytical concepts is, in my opinion, scientifically indefensible because it precludes comparative analysis and generalization.

It is nevertheless important to heed the cautious advice of Vansina who, in reference to the traditional law ways of the Kuba of Africa, explicitly voices his support for the "ethnoscientific" position as follows:

> Kuba law is . . . very different from any European legal system, and to try to define it in terms of European legal concepts is like trying to fit a Bantu grammar into a Latin model of grammatical categories, something that actually was done until descriptive linguistics taught us better. Insofar as possible, Kuba law should be analyzed on its own terms. One can analyze it on a broad basis by examining the existence and the use of legal vocabulary, by investigating the legal formulas, if there are more than one, and by exploring the structural and institutional features of the system itself (Vansina 1965:117).

Vansina's point, from an ethnographic and methodological perspective, is indeed well taken. I do not think, however, the methodological parallels between a linguistic analysis of a particular language and a juristic analysis of a non-Western legal system should be carried so far. The linguist or the jurist must adapt any preconceived theories to accommodate new facts and both should ideally welcome any new facts which may challenge the existing theory. It may also be noted that despite the vigor with which descriptive linguists attack the "theoretical truths" of their pre- or post-Chomskiam colleagues, they have in no way supplanted the steady output of useful, if "unsophisticated," grammars and dictionaries of exotic languages written by various missionaries who often work on the basis of a Latin-derived model of language structure.

The comparative analysis of legal systems (exemplified in the writings of Barton, Bohannan, Gluckman, Hoebel, Llewellyn, Malinowski, Radcliffe-Brown, Redfield, and many others) has yet to reach the methodological achievements of descriptive linguistics. It may also be said that whereas linguists seem to have reached some agreement about the nature of language, it is clear why students of comparative law, given the theoretical problems, have yet to develop a cross-cultural paradigm of legal phenomena.

Although progress in comparative jurisprudence has been slow it does seem that Pospisil's efforts (1952 and 1958) to create a universalistic paradigm of legal phenomena holds much promise. The three most significant elements of his contribution to a theory of law (which by no means has gone unchallenged) consists of (1) the separation of law and custom, (2) the analysis of legal phenomena through a matrix of four distinctive dimensions (e.g., "authority," "intention of universal application," *"obligatio,"* and "sanction"), and a general hypothesis which states that ". . . law is not limited to the society as a whole . . ." but that ". . . every functioning subgroup of . . . society has its own legal system which is necessarily different in some respects from those of . . . other subgroups . . ." (Pospisil 1958:272). I will attempt to apply this theoretical framework to the data on Gilbertese law, expanding where possible, on Pospisil's notion of law as a constellation of four attributes (see Pospisil 1958:257–272).

These attributes of law may be defined briefly in the context of Gilbertese law as follows:

1. *The attribute of authority.* A person, or group, invested with the legitimate power to make decisions in matters relating to common or collective interests has authority. In the Gilbertese situation, authority is an attribute highly correlated with social status, rank, or with the extent of political power invested in a social group. For example, an *unimane* or "Old Man" has more status and authority than females and his juniors; a land-owner, whether male or female, has more authority than a landless or a custodial person. An island magistrate through his formal political position has more authority than all nonoffice holders. Similarly, we can observe that the head of a household has more authority than the members of his household, the *maneaba* assembly can exercise more authority than individual persons, and the Island Council has greater authority than hamlet or Village District representatives.

2. *The attribute of intention of universal application.* "This attribute . . . *if applicable* as a criterion of law demands that the authority in making a decision intends it to be applied to all similar or 'identical' situations in the future" (Pospisil 1958:262, italics mine). This is the most subjective and problematic of the four attributes. It is doubtful whether the Gilbertese magistrate adjudicates a case before the Lands Court or the Native Court on the basis of "rule recognition" (e.g., a thief is convicted and sentenced in accordance with the Native Law, which defines degrees of theft and corresponding degrees of punishment). It is also questionable whether the western concept of *precedent* (and its most prominent form in *Stare decisis*) is a significant attribute of Gilbertese law. Court proceedings and rulings on various cases by the Nonouti magistrate suggest that Gilbertese legal decisions are most often made on an *ad hoc* basis. For example, the Magistrate has been observed to decide a particular case on the basis of such factors as a litigant's age, sex, social status, or public opinion surrounding the case. He is, in other words, very much influenced by a wide set of public and political pressures of the moment and less influenced by what might be called "formal rule recognition" (see Hart 1961).

3. *The attribute of obligation.* Pospisil

employs the Roman concept of *obligatio* to call attention to the inadequacy of the familiar concept of "obligation" that only incorporates the notion of "duty" and omits the opposite notion of "right." The distinction between *obligatio* and "obligation," however, seems rather pedantic. Obligation, for our purposes, denotes any part of an authority's decision that spells out the respective rights and duties of two parties. Legal decisions involving obligation are particularly important in all matters pertaining to Gilbertese "civil law," e.g., in disputes involving torts, equity, or contracts.

4. *The attribute of sanction.* I will define *legal sanctions*—as opposed to all other kinds of social sanctions—as those negative sanctions imposed by a recognized authority (see Radcliffe-Brown 1952:205, 211). It should also be mentioned that positive sanctions (which are usually ignored by writers on this subject) play a significant part in the legal system. Positive sanctions, or acts of approval, may significantly determine how legal decisions are made and, in fact, whether a particular decision is to be made at all. The island magistrate must continually validate his authority in the eyes of fellow islanders by sustaining public support for his actions. The activities of the Nonouti Island Magistrate, examined in detail below, clearly illustrate how positive sanctions serve as feedback mechanisms which legitimatize the Magistrate's role as a judicial authority.

The Setting

The Gilbert Islands archipelago consists of sixteen coral islands which straddle the equator between 172°E and 178°E longitude and from 4°N to 3°S latitude. The islands were incorporated as a British Protectorate in 1892 and, together with the adjacent Ellice Islands archipelago, became part of the Gilbert and Ellice Islands Colony in 1916. The official government census of 1963 reported a total of 36,423 Gilbertese inhabitants (McArthur and McCaig 1964). The Gilbertese people are on the whole a tough and energetic people, perhaps because of the many physical difficulties imposed by their habitat. Most of the southern Gilbertese suffer from periodic shortages of good drinking water, and the majority of people still subsist on a traditional diet of fish, coconut, pandanus, and taro. Imported rice, flour, sugar, and twist tobacco have increasingly come to be regarded as necessities.

Although the formal judicial system of the colony is controlled by British officials, who have focused attention on the codification of native laws, legislation, and adjudication of serious criminal offenses, the basic legal machinery is staffed and run by the Gilbertese people themselves. Because I have dealt elsewhere with the changes in the Gilbertese legal system resulting from contacts with the British government (Lundsgaarde 1968b:n.d.), I will here emphasize the structure of the legal system as it exists on the local island level. To avoid overgeneralization, however, I have limited the discussion to an overview of the legal system on Nonouti (No-Noose) Islands as observed in 1964 (Figure 1). It should be noted that parts of this system (Figure 2, levels 4 and 5) were changed after my first visit to the Gilberts in the year 1963–1964. Most of the changes have been in the area of statutory revisions pertaining to the administration of local island courts and the creation of "Island Executive Officers" who, in some ways, have superseded the legal authority exercised by island magistrates (GEIC 1965; Barwick 1965).

Nonouti Island is an atoll which is located at 0°40′S latitude and 174°27′E longitude. The island forms a long 25-mile protective crescent-shaped barrier around some 143 square miles of lagoon. The actual land area does not amount to much more than 9.83 square miles, which is broken up into a number of islets (see Figure 1). Many of these

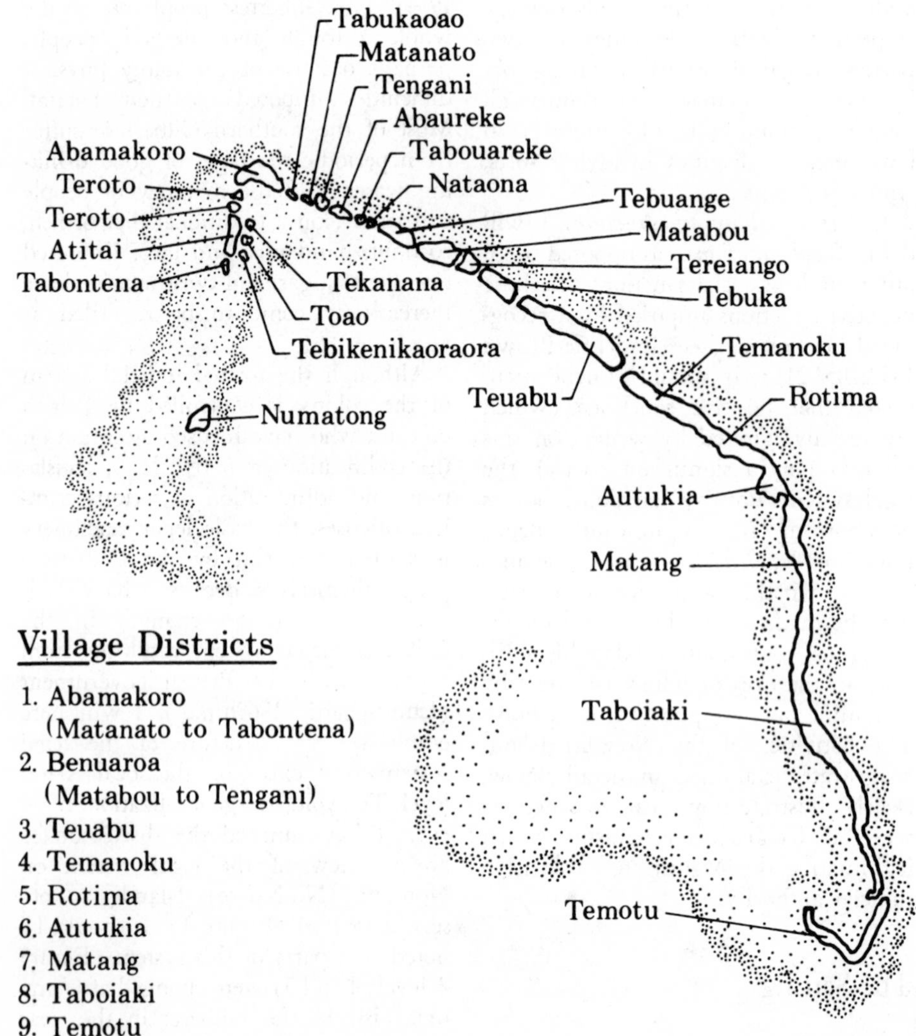

Figure 1. Sketch Map of Nonouti Island Showing Village Districts and Islets.

islets, particularly in the northern part of the island, are uninhabitable for any length of time. Extreme sandiness of "soils," the lack of reliable fresh water supplies, and a relatively sparse growth of coconut trees has in the past precluded any large and permanent village settlements north of the Teuabu Village district.

As of 1964 there were some 2,220 Nonouti residents (1,075 males and 1,145 females) who were unevenly distributed among 427 households with an average of 4.98 members per household. The greatest population densities are found in the Taboiaki Village district and the lowest, as noted above, in the Abamakoro and Benuaroa settlements in the extreme north. Of the total population some 531 adults reportedly belong to the Protestant London Missionary Society, while 459 profess adherence to the Catholic Sacred Heart Mission. A small religious minority (six residents) belong to the Seventh Day Adventist church. The bipolar distribution of the populace into Protestant and Catholic religious groupings is a common and continuous source of friction among Nonoutians.

Most households on Nonouti Island cluster together in small hamlets. These hamlets are often grouped so closely together that they comprise one continuous village settlement. There are approximately thirty-nine such distinctive settlement clusters on the island, and these in turn are grouped into nine Village Districts. Each hamlet has its own local government organization centered around a *maneaba*, or public meeting house. Membership and affiliation in the hamlet *maneaba* organization is founded on the formal recognition of both descent and residence rules. A person is allowed to sit in the *maneaba* assembly on the basis of his kinship relationship to a *boti* (a special seating location within the *maneaba*) founder or if his spouse can claim such a relationship. At the hamlet level of organization, however, residence alone commonly suffices as a criterion for membership in the hamlet *maneaba*.

The hamlet *maneaba* organization is analogous to what might be termed a neighborhood organization. The *maneaba* building is regarded as public area, and any member can sleep, eat, rest, or participate in *maneaba* events at his own leisure. When islanders visit relatives who reside in a different district they are accommodated in the *maneaba*. When visitors are not present or when there are no special community events to be celebrated, the *maneaba* serves as a focal meeting place for elders who are exempt from primary economic duties. On an average day, therefore, one can find a group of elder men and women gather in the *maneaba* for no other purpose than to enjoy the conversation, perhaps to play a game of cards, or to discuss forthcoming events of community interest (e.g., a marriage, a feast, or a visit by outsiders).

The relative informality of hamlet *maneaba* activities contrasts with the degree of formality observed in the Village District *maneaba*. The Village District *maneaba*, although it also may serve as a community center for feasts and public celebrations, is the exclusive domain of the Village District Assembly. This assembly (*te ḳabowi n unimane*, or "the assembly of Old Men") is composed of politically influential elders who are charged, by virtue of their high social status in the society, with responsibility of overseeing the day-to-day affairs in their own district. The assembly serves its constituents in a number of ways. It may select and send delegate representatives to serve in the Island Council (which meets in the Nonouti Island *maneaba* located at Matang) to formulate or ratify island policies, debate new legislative measures proposed by the colony government, or perhaps propose new ordinances or regulations to be considered for legislation.

The Island Council thus serves as the voice of the Nonouti people in all matters related to their government and public welfare. Before the advent of British rule the island *maneaba* council constituted the highest legal authority in southern Gilbertese society. The Island Council originally was organized to maintain peaceful relations among islanders and, if necessary, to plan and wage war against neighboring island societies. Nonouti Island, like all the other islands in the southern Gilberts, was "a nation unto itself" until Europeans imposed a centralized or federal governmental structure over all the islands.

The imposition of this federal officialdom, however, has not eradicated the traditional and local forms of *maneaba* organization. As illustrated in Figure 2, the colonial authority has simply created two additional levels on which matters of law and politics can be settled. The modern native administration is involved with three distinct political bodies: the Island Council, the native courts, and the colonial administration. Gilbertese administrators (who are about equally involved in both judicial and administrative matters) serve as buffers between the Gilbertese people and the colonial government. Although this "buffer" position allows the Island Council to manage the affairs of their own island freely, without direct interference from Europeans, it also exempts European officials from the difficult task of controlling affairs for which they have little competence or in which they may take only a marginal interest. This arrangement is in effect what sometimes crystallizes in history books as the policy of "indirect rule." It means, in other words, that it may be possible to say that colonization has resulted in the *addition* of two new legal-political levels to the existing or traditional political structure. Each legal and political level includes the allocation of authority to some select members who are the primary actors in economic decision making, political activity, or adjudication.

I have described four of the five major levels of legal and political authority in Gilbertese society. Although these "levels" do not exactly correspond to Pospisil's notion of a cultural "subgroup," it is evident that the Household, Village District Assembly, and the Island Council do in fact represent significant local subgroups within the broader framework of Gilbertese social organization. Levels 4 and 5 come closer to representing institutions than social groups. I will proceed to examine the activities at each of the four lower levels of organization. The analysis of these activities will focus on the "processes of adjudication" (i.e., legal phenomena) and on an evaluation of Pospisil's four attributes of law (i.e., legal concepts).

My central hypothesis may now be briefly restated as follows: *The concepts of law or legal process can be selectively applied to social phenomena at the household, village, island, and colony levels of organization.*

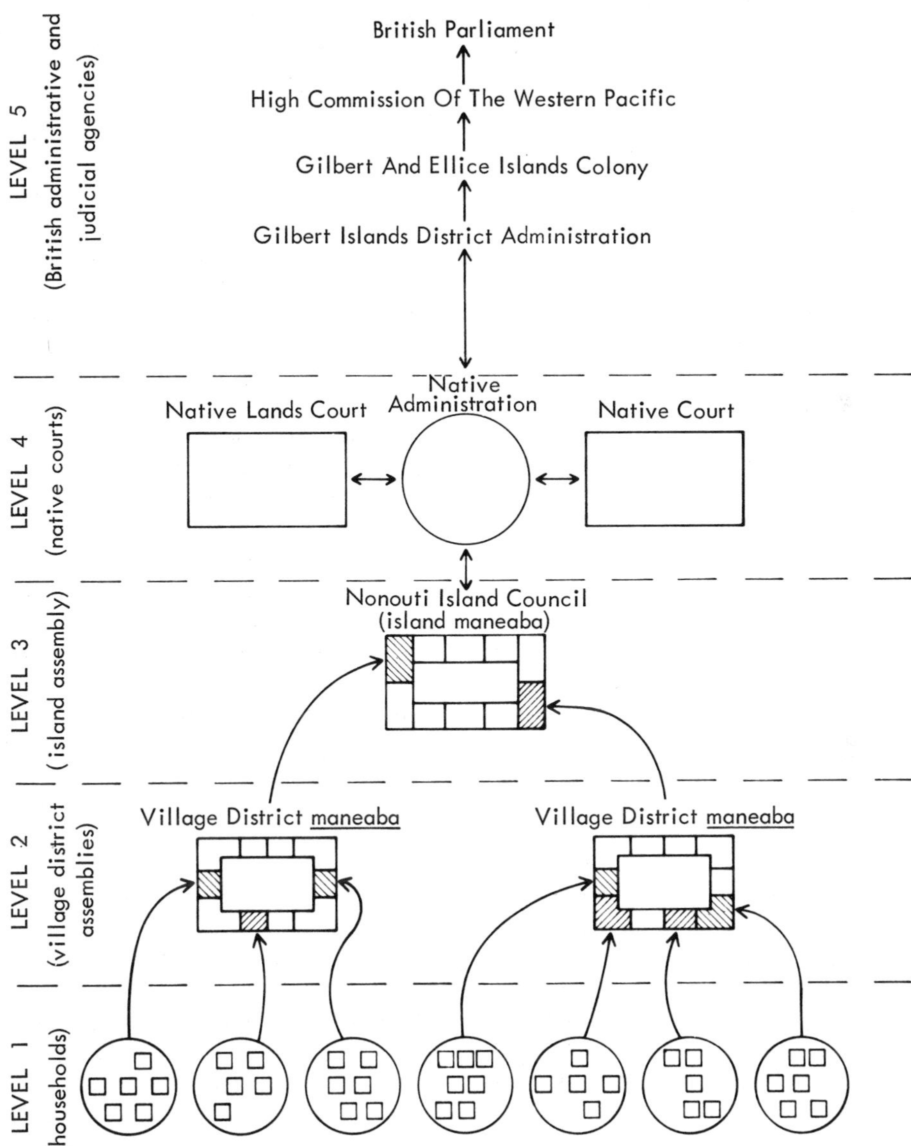

Figure 2. Legal and Political Levels.

Level 1—The Household

The Gilbertese household is not a family unit. It is a very special kind of social group which, for most purposes, represents the smallest residential and legal unit in Gilbertese society. Household members are either recruited on the basis of consanguine kinship ties or by contractual arrangements like marriage, fosterage, or adoption. The Gilbertese household is not a "family" in our own sense of the term because only "blood relatives" are regarded as members of the Gilbertese family, or *utu*.[1] A typical household may, for example, be composed of two brothers, a wife of one of the brothers, and an adoptive child. A slightly different household arrangement may involve a man and his wife, their unmarried daughter, and the daughter's child born out of wedlock. A household may even be composed of a single person who may, of course, have a family and who most certainly has consanguine relatives.

The important point, however, is to understand what a household is and what it does: *a household is a group of persons who share the same domestic facilities and who cooperate in the achievement of economic goals.* The size, composition, and location of a particular household is determined by many different factors. Some of these include a consideration of kinship ties, economic advantage, or—as the case may be—necessity. The household, and not the family, is the smallest "functioning subgroup" in Gilbertese society.

It is obvious that any individual who is identified as a member of a particular household also can be identified as a member of other kinds of groupings. For example, the man who assists his kinsman with the construction of a canoe is performing a duty expected of kinsmen. The same person is not bound by a duty to officiate a public *maneaba* event. Also, if asked to serve as a witness on behalf of a defendant in a case at law, he may possibly decline to serve unless the authorities formally request him to do so (*subpoena* is too precise to be applied to the Gilbertese context).

As an example of the legal relationships involved in membership in a household unit, I shall now briefly outline the legal status of a person who can be described as the head of household or householder. A householder is defined by *Webster's Dictionary* as "The master or head of a family; one who occupies a house with his family or alone . . . one who occupies such a dwelling as to qualify him to exercise the franchise." The Gilbertese themselves define a householder as *te atu n te mwenga,* or "the head of the household." But it is neither surprising nor sufficient to acknowledge the fact that the Gilbertese concept of householder has a parallel in English usage. We need to know what a person has to be or do in order to exercise his franchise as a householder.

The minimal conditions that must be satisfied before a person can become a householder are as follows: he must own or have legal access to a parcel of land on which he can build his house, he must have sufficient economic assets to construct his house or be able to enter a lessor-lessee arrangement with a landowner, and he must be able to protect his residence privileges from the possible claims of others.

Because the Gilbertese generally do not purchase land from each other (native lands cannot be sold to Europeans or other non-Gilbertese), they must primarily rely on succession to an estate through direct inheritance from parents. Parents, who separately hold title to land parcels, usually do not distribute their lands until they reach advanced age. At that time parents *may* distribute their estate to legal heirs if they have abided by the duties attached to the heir-benefactor relationship. What this means, therefore, is that the majority of persons either become independent householders relatively late in life or that a householder enjoys some form of easement arrangement with one or more of his senior kinsmen.

To simplify the situation we can examine some of the circumstances that may affect what might be called the *legal franchise* of a householder. The exact nature of this franchise depends upon two different conditions: (1) if the householder owns the land on which his dwelling is located, or (2) if the householder enjoys some kind of contractual relationship with the legal owner of the land on which the dwelling is located. The first case is relatively simple because the landowner and the householder are the same person.

Many encumbrances that affect an owner-householder are largely determined by factors such as kinship, social status, age, and sex. Although these factors are of considerable importance they do not pertain directly to a person's legal franchise as a householder. Such a person has a series of legal rights, privileges, powers, and immunities *vis-à-vis* other members of his society. Such rights may be spoken of as paucital and multital rights.[2] An owner-householder has certain specific paucital rights with respect to other members of his household; i.e., he may hold the right to evict anyone who does not contribute to the economic maintenance of the household or he may prevent members of his household from inviting other persons to live with his residential unit. An owner-householder may, for example, prevent a junior member of his household from bringing a spouse or an adopted child into his household. There is no way in which a household member can effectively challenge the owner-householder's right to exclude others or to demand that members contribute to the household unit as a whole.

On the other hand, the householder also enjoys many different kinds of multital rights with respect to all other persons on the island. He is, so to speak, immune from trespass by others, and he has the power to take legal action against anyone who fails to respect the sanctity of his household. An owner-householder, therefore, has two basic assets: (1) he can exercise certain paucital rights *vis-à-vis* other members of his household, and (2) he can exercise certain multital rights *vis-à-vis* members of society at large.

The situation is quite different for a person who does not own the land on which his dwelling is located. He is a tenant-householder and this can be a liability. The tenant-householder can exercise the same paucital rights over his household members as an owner-householder may wish to do. However, he is also party to a contractual relationship with the landowner. This relationship, which is treated as a legal obligation between the landowner and his tenant-householder, provides the landowner with certain rights and the tenant-householder with certain duties. These rights and duties are spelled out in Paragraph 17 of the Native Lands Ordinance of 1956, which reads as follows:

> (i) A householder is free to remain in occupancy of his house site provided that he will do one of the things shown below. The landowner may not refuse to allow this and he may only claim to evict the householder from his house site if the householder refuses to do the things prescribed. The landowners and

the householders should signify their mutual agreement before the Lands Court. If they have not made any such agreement then the Lands Court shall decide on what should be done. The Lands Court may also decide the amount of rent or the price of the land or the amount of anything that should be exchanged with the house site in the event of there being no agreement.

(ii) *Things that may be done:*

(a) The householder may lease a house site from the landowner and in so doing will pay rent for such land monthly or yearly.

(b) The householder may allow the use of his land, pit, or pond by the landowner who agrees to him living on his site by way of an exchange for the mutual use of their property during the time the householder uses the landowner's site.

(c) The householder may agree to a permanent exchange whereby he receives a house site, the latter to be regarded as his own property, in exchange for one of his lands, pits, or ponds.

(d) The householder may buy a house site from the landowner. (GEIC 1963: 15.)

It must be noted and emphasized, however, that these statutory provisions are treated as guidelines only and not as immutable principles that must be followed in all lessor-lessee arrangements. The codification of the reciprocal rights and duties between the lessor and lessee may be referred to in cases where it is difficult to achieve a settlement between two litigants by any other means than court litigation. If a lessor-lessee dispute reaches a point where mediation, persuasion, or arbitration cannot settle the conflict the only method left is adjudication before the Lands Court. It is very seldom, however, that any case of this kind ever reaches the court. I know of only one example from Tamana Island in which a landowner attempted legally to evict people from a public *maneaba* building on his estate.

It is now possible to summarize some of the salient facts concerning the legal aspects of the Gilbertese household. First, of course, the householder normally will make many decisions pertaining to the successful operation of his household that are not immediately legal in nature. Second, some of the decisions that a householder, by virtue of his franchise, can make are legal in nature, because they fit the theoretical paradigm outlined in the Introduction.

The most common kinds of conflict situations that call for an authoritative decision by a householder include (1) the decision about household membership (i.e., who will reside in a particular household and who may be denied such residence); (2) the decisions concerning the distribution of economic duties among household members (i.e., who is to be responsible for carrying out primary food-producing activities, who is to be responsible for the maintenance of the household site itself, and who is to contribute what labor to the group effort); (3) the decision to allocate rights and duties to individual members in a way that is acknowledged as being "just" or "fair" (i.e., the recognition of mutual obligations between individual household constituents); and (4) the decision pertaining to any relationships between household members and other persons in general.

A householder's franchise thus can be seen to include a limited but specific set of rights, privileges, powers, and immunities that affect relations within the household itself, and between household members and society at large. In terms of the four attributes of law, as applied to the decisions that are made at the household level, we can note the following relationships.

An owner or tenant householder is recognized as the final authority in all matters directly pertaining to the day-to-day operation of the dwelling complex. His decisions, as these affect his subordinate household members, are generally intended to incorporate the notion of intent to apply the same "reasoning process" to all future and broadly similar circumstances. This means that ideally a householder is expected to treat all like cases alike and treat all different cases differently (see Hart 1961:115). However, it must be noted that the decisions of Gilbertese householders are far less informal than is implied by these fine and sometimes meaningless theoretical distinctions. What is implied here is simply that the authority is expected to exhibit some degree of fairness and consistency with respect to exercising his authority.

If, for example, a householder rules that his son and daughter may not bring an adopted child to reside with them in the household it is to be expected that, other things remaining equal, other married children will be treated in a similar fashion. It is the householder's right to prohibit household members from adding adopted children to the household and it is their duty to abstain from doing so.

If now a person decides to ignore such an obligation he may expose himself to some form of sanction. In an extreme case, a householder may sanction a person who ignores his decision concerning a particular situation by evicting that person from the household. However, if household members abide by the decisions of the authority it is likely that they may benefit from the application of a positive sanction, i.e., a larger share of the inheritance.[3]

If we take the Gilbertese household to represent the smallest "functioning subgroup" in the society it is possible to treat the household unit as a legal entity. But despite the fact that we can thus accommodate Pospisil's four attributes of law at this level, it would be erroneous to interpret any conflict or settlement procedure among household constituents as in any way resembling what might be called the formal processes of adjudication. However, the emphasis on legal process increases as we pass from one legal and political level to another.

Level 2—The Village District Assembly

Any comprehensive analysis of the legal activities of the Village District Assembly inevitably leads to a broader consideration of *maneaba* organization. To simplify matters I will attempt to answer three specific questions relating to governmental activities of the assembly. First, what is the history and social purpose of the *maneaba;* second, what rules are followed in recruiting members and distributing authority within the membership; and, third, what activities of the *maneaba* council may substantiate the hypothesis that the assembly forms a distinct legal entity?

The Gilbertese *maneaba,* as an institution, has a long and complex history. According to H. E. Maude, the first *maneaba* was established on Beru Island by Tematawarebwe who came to the Gilberts from Samoa sometime during the last part of the fourteenth century. In the words of Maude:

Tematawarebwe landed at the south end of Beru with his parents, two of his brothers named Koruabi and Buatara, and a number of followers, and decided to settle at Teakiauma. . . . Beru was already inhabited by the descendants of Tabuariki and Nainginouati, but these appear to have been few in number; at all events there was no war, the island was amicably partitioned and the three groups proceeded to intermarry. . . .

The autochthones had a meeting house on Beru even before the arrival of Tematawarebwe, but tradition asserts that it was merely a centre for social functions and was without any of the essential hallmarks of a properly constituted *maneaba*. For a time Tematawarebwe shared this building, but on his grandson Teweia . . . coming of age, he told him to choose a suitable place for a *maneaba* which was to be a copy of the one they had left behind on Samoa. The site finally selected was a Tabontebike . . . and here Teweia erected the prototype of all Gilbertese *maneaba*, incorporating timber actually brought from the former edifice on Samoa . . . in (the *maneaba*) were held all discussions concerning peace and war or any of the other innumerable concerns affecting the common weal; *it was the Law Court, where offenders against customary norms were tried, and disputes heard and arbitrated by the Old Men; and* the centre for the many ceremonies and feasts of a formal character, as well as the more dignified community recreations and dances.

The *maneaba* was all that to the Gilbertese, and much more: the traditional club-house of the aged; a *pied à terre* for the stranger; and a sanctuary for those in flight. All behavior under its roof had to be seemly, decorous, and in strict conformity with custom, lest the *maneabe* be *matauninga* (offended) and the culprit *maraia* (accursed.) (Maude 1963:10–11; italics added).

This *maneaba* organization eventually spread from Beru Island to all the southern Gilberts including Nonouti Island. Although many of the customs formerly associated with *maneaba* organization are no longer practiced it is still possible to observe some of its more important social and judicial functions in the modern setting. Of particular interest here is the fact that the *maneaba* still serves as a focus for local governmental activities and that *unimane* still mediate, arbitrate, and in some instances adjudicate disputes that affect members within their *maneaba* district.

Although, as illustrated in Maude's (1963) treatment of the Gilbertese *boti* (bos), the formality of many *maneaba* activities has been abandoned (or been displaced to other areas such as the native courts or the local island administration), it is still evident that *boti* or seating arrangements within the *maneaba* itself serve two important purposes: first, the *boti* seating position within the *maneaba* is assigned to persons on the basis of their rights, by descent, to occupy a specific location; second, *boti* members act as one political unit (through its representative) in all matters related to public welfare or community decision-making processes.

The *boti* denotes a seating division within the *maneaba*. Each division is named after its founder, a mythological ancestor, or a spiritual being. Membership in a particular *boti* is for life, and any native Gilbertese may, by right of birth, sit in either his father's or mother's *boti*. Although a person may also sit in the *boti* claimed by his spouse, he cannot publicly speak as a representative of that *boti*. This means that the members of any given household often can claim membership in several different *boti* (e.g., a woman may be entitled to sit in the *boti* of her father, her mother, her husband's father, or her husband's mother). It would, however, be more accurate to say that a person can claim membership only by right of descent or by affiliation with a particular *boti* by means of a contractual relationship with a bona fide *boti* member (i.e., through marriage or adoption).

Several different household units may thus be represented within one *boti*. Each *boti* selects from among its most senior and competent male elders one man who will represent the members of the *boti* in the *maneaba*. This person was and is today spoken of as *te atu n te boti* (lit. "the head of the *boti*"). It is a person of this high status (hereafter referred to as the *boti* representative) who links the household and the village levels of social organization.

The *boti* representative fulfills two distinctive but obviously interrelated roles. On the one hand, he is expected to act as the senior mediator in conflict situations that may arise among *boti* constituents, and, on the other hand, he may speak on behalf of his *boti* on all matters concerning social, political, or juridical problems parleyed by the Village District Assembly. If the *boti* representative is called upon to decide a dispute among his *boti* members he can only mediate or arbitrate rather than directly adjudicate. If a dispute reaches a point at which some kind of legal decision must be made in favor of one party and against another it is up to the *boti* representative to take the case before the *maneaba* council of elders.

The *kabowi n unimane* ("assembly of Old Men") is composed of all *boti* representatives entitled to be seated in the village *maneaba*. The members of this gerontocratic assembly were, in the past, invested with the authority to adjudicate all matters pertaining to traditional law (civil and criminal) and any unanimous decision did in fact become equivalent to the western notion of a statute. One such statutory rule is exemplified by the traditional Gilbertese family law concerning murder. According to Maude:

> On an individual killing another he must be killed in return by some member of the murdered man's Utu (his consanguine kinsmen). If he fled and could not be found the following payments were customary:
>
> 1. *Nuna* = *Te Buangui* = A whale's tooth necklace "His Shadow." This was buried with the murdered man.
> 2. *Baona* = A canoe (if the murderer had one).
> 3. *Te Kieni Kaiti* = All the murderer's personal belongings, together with various additional presents from his *Utu*.
> 4. *Te Nenebo* = Two pieces of land —one from the murderer's *mwini mane* [land parcels transferred to a person from his father's estate] and one from his *mwin aine* [land parcels transferred to a person from his mother's estate]. The same rules apply should a woman be the murderer or murdered. Should the murderer be strong enough to resist payment of his *Nenebo* the fight will go on until the Old Men stop it. The Old Men will enforce the payment. No *Nenebo* passes if the murderer is killed in expiation of his offence (Maude 1963: 47).

This brief example shows that the assembly of elders, before the introduction of British laws and judicial procedures, did in fact have the authority to adjudicate and rule on most serious offenses. Today, however, the assembly of elders does not adjudicate criminal offenses, and it is only rarely that it can do more than mediate disputes between different kin groups. The authority to rule on all law cases now resides in either of the two native courts or with the British colonial authorities. This transference of authority from traditional assembly of elders to a Western-type court organization does not mean that *boti* representatives or assembly elders have been removed *ipso facto* from their authoritative roles in local governmental organization. It simply means that many absolute legal powers, formerly held by such high-status elders, have been placed in different hands. The influence of the Village District Assembly on all matters related to modern Gilbertese law is still manifest in many ways. For example, it is within the power of the assembly of elders to decide if and when a person from their district should take his case before either of the two island courts; it is the assembly which sends representatives to the Nonouti Island Council, and it is the assembly that is largely responsible for selecting police constables from within their own districts. In very simple terms this means that any dispute, wrong, or breach of the Native Laws that may occur on Nonouti Island will become a law case when the *unimane* of the Village District Assembly decide that the situation calls for formal process. The formal legal process is thus most frequently initiated and executed by Gilbertese authority figures themselves.[4]

Level 3—The Island Council

The Nonouti Island Council, referred to by the Gilbertese as *te kabowi n abamakoro,* very much resembles the Village District Assembly. It is, however, an institution that has been created by the British colonial government to facilitate the administration of each island in the colony. It is easy to appreciate why the British found it more convenient to deal with whole islands as political units than to recognize the traditional political autonomy of the *maneaba* district. But, in addition to noting that the Island Council was created by motives of political and administrative expediency, it is of primary interest to understand how the Gilbertese have adapted the traditional *maneaba* organization to work on an all-islands basis. For example, one may still find the island *maneaba* representatives sitting in specific *boti* locations, and we find that many of the legal powers formerly vested in the "assembly of Old Men" have been transferred directly to the village district representatives who now sit on the Island Council.

Although the Island Council does not hear or adjudicate trouble cases, it nevertheless serves two distinct legal functions: (1) the council is responsible for creating, ratifying, or nullifying legal ordinances or regulations pertaining to their island; and (2) the council largely controls the activities of the two island courts by appointing jurors, police constables, and the island magistrate. (*N.B.,* the island magistrate is formally appointed and can be formally dismissed only by the Resident Commissioner for the colony, but the Island Council usually recommends a person for the office of magistrate or it may recommend that the magistrate be dismissed.)

According to Sections 12–16 of the Native Governments Ordinance, the formal establishment, composition, and powers of the Island Council are as follows:

> 12. There is hereby established on each island an Island Council, which shall consist of the magistrate . . . the chief of *kaubure* [jurors], the scribe, the chief of district police, the *kaubure,* the senior native member of the medical department resident in the island, the native members elected in accordance with the provisions of subsection (2) of this section and not exceeding in number half the total number of *kaubure* appointed in respect to the island. . . .
> (2) A native member of the Island Council shall be elected in respect of each electoral district in each island, the boundaries of the electoral districts being fixed by the administrative officer of the district. The native members of the Island Council may be either men or women; and all men and women over the age of thirty years shall have the right to vote in the election of the native member for the electoral district in which they habitually reside. The native members of the Island Council shall automatically retire annually but may offer themselves for re-election (Bryce 1952:123–124).

It is again necessary to emphasize that the formal appearance of this ordinance only approximates actuality. For example, the mention of "the electoral district" may easily give the false impression that Island Council members are actually elected by popular vote and that men or women have about equal chances to serve their district. Although balloting has been introduced (in the late 1960's), it is quite clear that Island Council members are usually selected from among the senior members of the Village District Assemblies and that they are primarily chosen by the council of elders from each village *maneaba* assembly. Also, despite the fact that women theoretically can serve on the Island Council they usually neither seek office nor are they chosen to serve in the capacity of council member. The recruitment procedures for the Island Council—contrary to the formal Native Governments Ordinance—by and large follow traditional and locally controlled modes of selection. Selection is based on kin-group seniority, social status, and relative rank within the village *maneaba* organization. It should be noted, however, that women can and often do serve as jurors in the courts and that some men may serve on the Island Council without having reached the position of *unimane.*

The specific legal powers of the Island Council are spelled out in the following paragraphs:

> 14. The Island Council shall consider reports made to it by members of the council relating to the peace, order and good government of the people in the island . . .

and, concerning the powers of the Island Council to enact and enforce island regulations:

> 16.1. The Island Council may enact, amend, or repeal island regulations relating to any of the following matters:
> (a) the keeping clean of the island and the promotion of public health;
> (b) the maintenance of peace, order and public safety;
> (c) the social and economic betterment of the native population;
> (d) the performance of communal works and other communal activities;
> (e) the control of livestock;
> (f) the prevention or removal of public nuisances;
> (g) the care of children and aged persons;
> (h) the conservation of food supplies;
> (i) fishing and fishing rights;
> (j) the island hospitals, prisons, and schools;

(k) the promotion of the general welfare of the native inhabitants; and
(l) the prescription of fees to be charged in connection with proceedings, other than those in respect of which fees are specifically prescribed in this Ordinance, in the Native and Lands Courts, and to be charged for the issue of true copies of entries in the island registers of births, marriages, and deaths.

The enactment, amendment or repeal of all such regulations shall be subject to the prior approval of the Resident Commissioner.

16.2. The penalties imposed under such regulations shall not exceed a fine of ten shillings nor a term of imprisonment in excess of one month (Bryce 1952:124; italics added).

Although it is clear that the notions of "intention of universal application" and "sanction" are embodied in the jurisdictorial powers of the Island Council, it is not readily apparent how the criteria of "authority" and "*obligatio*" apply to decisions by the Island Council. I do not question the fact that the Island Council has some kind of "authority" to enforce its views, but, unlike the authority of a householder to decide on most matters relating to the successful operation of the household, the authority of the Island Council is diffuse. The Resident Commissioner for the colony holds the ultimate authority in *any* decision promulgated by the Island Council, and most legal decisions are made in the two island courts and not in the Island Council.

Similarly, although council members may decide on the rights of one person and the duties of another, they do not directly adjudicate law cases. What the Island Council does, in fact, is to formulate the principles or rules which the magistrate ideally should follow in cases of land disputes, the neglect of civil duties, or, more specifically, minor questions of equity. The Island Council, therefore, primarily resolves questions relating to traditional morality, determination of acceptable standards of social conduct, and to political control of the magistrate and the island courts.

Level 4—Native Courts

Since the advent of British colonial rule in the Gilbert Islands, most serious disputes have been adjudicated by local island courts. The Native Court is composed of the island magistrate (who acts as judge), a chief of *kaubure* (crown prosecutor or deputy magistrate), and at least four jurors. The Native Court can hear and adjudicate all cases pertaining to matters which, in our society, would be termed the law of persons. All matters of equity, property settlement, and land utilization are handled by a separate Lands Court. The Lands Court, which is also presided over by the island magistrate and his assistants, thus adjudicates most cases that may be classified as belonging in the sphere perhaps best termed *the law of property* and *the law of obligation*. It is significant to note that the same personnel sit on both courts and that these persons embody the legal powers held by the colonial government.

Although both of these courts thus seem to parallel the lower courts in our own society, it is essential to emphasize that the codification of various laws, the establishment of official functionaries, and the introduction of rudimentary court procedures only represent one part—and a small one at that—of the total processes of adjudication.

The distinction between "procedural"

and "positive" law is significant in the context of modern Gilbertese society: (1) procedural law here refers to all those principles, rules, and methods of adjudication prescribed and formulated by British colonial officials (e.g., the composition and powers of the Island Courts, the machinery for conducting trials, or the "official behavior" to be observed by all officers of the courts); and (2) positive law or "law" as it is actually applied to cases that come before the courts. I have chosen to emphasize the distinction between procedural and positive aspects of modern Gilbertese law to avoid some of the pitfalls that could result from an application of such labels as "civil law," "tort law," "criminal law," "lawsuit," "plea," "trial," or "jury." The use of these terms would be misleading because, on the one hand, it would give us the false impression that Gilbertese court procedures nominally follow the prescriptive rules manifest in statutes, ordinances, or written codes and, on the other hand, it would lend an artificial formality to the Gilbertese legal system, which is far more flexible *in practice* than it may appear on paper. This does not mean that either codification of laws or specification of legal powers and procedures are ignored by the Gilbertese magistrate and the local courts.

To exemplify these points I will now analyze the roles played by the Nonouti Island magistrate in his capacity as judge and member of the Protestant London Missionary Society. At age 38, Ten Kirabuke Maio from the Temaanoku Village District was appointed by the Resident Commissioner to succeed Ten Itaaka Ata as magistrate of Nonouti Island on December 11, 1963. The former magistrate and his local staff were suspected of embezzlement of government funds. Although the magistrate himself was not directly involved in the alleged acts of embezzlements, he was dismissed from office on grounds that he had failed to report on this situation to his superiors at Tarawa. Kirabuke Maio thus assumed office under circumstances that conditioned his efforts to meet the responsibilities of his new office. He decided from the outset, on the one hand, to impress the colonial officials responsible for his appointment and, on the other hand, to win the confidence of the senior members of the Island Council.

The new magistrate was well known to government officers because of his important post as manager of the only cooperative store on Nonouti Island. He was well educated (a graduate of the London Missionary Society school on Beru Island) and obviously competent as a store manager. Although Kirabuke's command of English was poor, it was not regarded as a liability by his superiors. His apparent drive, his ability to get things done, and his businesslike manner were regarded as assets for the new task. As every appointment at the level of magistrate carries an automatic probation period of two years one may readily understand why Kirabuke wanted to do his job well.

The colonial officials who appointed Kirabuke were well aware, as was Kirabuke himself, that his age could be a liability in his dealing with members of the Island Council. Traditionally, magistrates were chosen from the *unimane* rank (at which most have reached at least the age of fifty) and, also traditionally, magistrates had prior experience in government service. Because anyone not yet of *unimane* status is by custom expected to defer to the decisions of the elders, it was clear from the very beginning that something had to be done to offset these disadvantages. The solution was quite ingenious. The new Chief of Kaubure, who had prior experience in government and who was of *unimane* status, in some ways could make up for the magistrate's youth and inexperience. The additional fact that the Chief of Kaubure was a Catholic and had been a lay missionary made the appointment of a Protestant magistrate more acceptable to the Catholic faction than it would have been otherwise.

The two major problems facing Kirabuke in his new office can now be seen to involve two conflicting alliances: (1) his alliance with the officials responsible for his appointment to the high and coveted position of island magistrate, and (2) his alliance with his authoritative elders in the Island Council who could either help or hinder his ambitions to prove himself and, perhaps, advance even further within the colonial government.[5]

The strategy followed by Kirabuke during his first year in office has a familiar parallel in the "law-and-order" approach of politically ambitious district attorneys and city mayors. It is a simple strategy and it may be related, as we shall see, only incidentally to high ideals of justice or reform. I can speak more specifically about the period between March 19 and August 16, 1964. During these five months spent on Nonouti Island I witnessed an almost steady stream of islanders going to and from the court sessions presided over by Kirabuke.

Although the Gilbertese, under normal circumstances, are a litigious people (Lundsgaarde 1968a), it is not customary for the courts to hear cases on an almost weekly basis. In fact, the Native Governments Ordinance specifies that the two courts shall each convene only once a month. Kirabuke, however, was of a different opinion and did not tolerate any slackening in the number of people to appear before his "tribunal" nor did he see much advantage in letting things go the way they had in the past. In the brief period between January and June 1964 he managed to convict 132 persons for breach of island regulations and colony laws. The number of convictions for this six-month period represents a 46-per-cent increase in convictions over the total number of convictions between 1955 and 1963! Surely, the Nonouti "crime rate" did not skyrocket because Kirabuke took office, and the Nonoutians did not deliberately quarrel over lands because they thought their chances of winning a desirable land parcel from a neighbor were improved with the new magistrate.

It should be noted, perhaps in Kirabuke's favor, that the prison sentences and fines imposed on convicted persons were of short duration and reasonable. Kirabuke did not create a "kangaroo court," nor did he necessarily make a mockery of justice. He simply followed the letter of the law, as he interpreted it, and prosecuted islanders for breach of local ordinances to which few magistrates before him had paid much attention. For example, he convicted 112 people for failing to clean up the rubbish accumulated around their dwellings, he convicted a 12-year-old girl for violating an ordinance pertaining to the "careless use of fire" (the girl was released with a warning), and he convicted 13 persons for failing to properly manage their pigs.

One cannot deny that the magistrate's decisions were legal, nor can it be denied that his decisions were sanctioned by statutory regulations. Although it is clear that Kirabuke used the office of magistrate to achieve long-term political ends, it would not be correct to say that he deliberately usurped the legal authority of his position. In fact, without the implicit approval of both the government officials and the council of elders the Nonouti magistrate could not have "dispensed justice" in his rather high-handed fashion.

To appreciate why and how a Gilbertese magistrate can sustain his legal authority despite his selective application of legal sanctions, as was clearly the case in the brief example from Nonouti Island, it is essential to enlarge the discussion to include a brief mention of the important interplay between authority and the attributes of both "*obligatio*" and "intention of universal application." The former is particularly relevant in the analysis of the magistrate's personal relations with other members of his community, and the latter is important only insofar as it affects his superficial relations with outside colonial officials. Let me discuss the notion of "intention of universal application" because it is the most simple attribute to apply at this particular level. For example, it mattered less that the magistrate manifested what might be called "legal harassment" as long as his fines, prison sentences, and treatment of litigants more or less followed the specifications of the Native Laws and the Island Regulations. It was the Island Council which, in the first place, helped formulate these laws and regulations (including any penal sanctions established for various offences), and it is the Island Council—not the magistrate—which is responsible for lending moral support to the legal decisions of "their" courts. In the eyes of the Island Council, therefore, the Nonouti magistrate was merely following a prescribed course of action, and, as seen from the vantage point of colonial officials, the magistrate was upholding the basic, if vague, notion of British law that "like cases be treated alike" and "different cases be treated differently."

The attribute of *obligatio* is not as readily perceived because it links the decision process with the traditional social structure. It is quite clear that the magistrate is performing his duty to his government and to his people when he hands down a legal decision. The magistrate's duty to follow "the letter of the law" is complicated in many cases in which he must decide between his rights and duties as a magistrate and the rights and duties of fellow islanders. If, for example, he favors his kinsmen over other islanders in a case involving a disputed parcel of land, he lays himself open to criticisms from members of the Island Council. Because the Island Council controls the appointment of jurors to both courts the council indirectly controls some of the activities of the magistrate; i.e., a *kaubure* can oppose the way in which the magistrate is handling a particular case by voicing his views in court *and* before the Island Council. The magistrate thus knows that he must accommodate the wishes of the Island Council in any case involving "public opinion."

The attribute of *obligatio* and "precedent" thus may be regarded as important feedback mechanisms which influence the magistrate's legal decisions and his powers to apply negative sanctions. The Gilbertese conceptions of right versus wrong or guilty versus not guilty frequently clash with established and statutory procedures for settling a conflict situation. If the magistrate adjudicates a case involving such conflicts he must and does wear two hats. He follows the opinions expressed on the case by his seniors in the Island Council and he nominally follows the procedures spelled out by British officials. The outcome of all this may not spell out "law" and "justice" as we tend to understand these terms, but the fact remains that the magistrate's decisions are regarded by the Gilbertese as both legal and, to a lesser extent, fair.

Any decision that is not regarded as fair may be appealed to a higher authority. For example, a convicted person may appeal his case to the District Officer or a dissatisfied heir may appeal his claim to a touring Lands Commissioner. Although colonial officials generally uphold the decisions of local island magistrates (and thereby sustain their authority), they occasionally reverse a verdict or change a decision relating to a land claim. It must also be noted, however, that the magistrate can manipulate his courts in such a way that appeal becomes a superfluous act. He may hold court sessions immediately after a District Officer has visited his island, he may base decisions on the known fact that District Officers are likely not to visit his island before the expiration of a person's prison sentence, or he may by one method or another prevent any potential appellant from seeing the District Officer who, as a rule, spends only a few days on the island or who has such a busy schedule of activities before him that he simply cannot hear all appeals.

Level 5—The Colonial Government

It would be inappropriate to conclude the discussion of Gilbertese law and politics without considering the relationships between the Gilbertese people and the British colonial administration. May it suffice here to briefly restate some previous conclusions concerning the historical processes and modern outcome of the interplay between Gilbertese and British conceptions of law and government (see Lundsgaarde 1968b:117–130).

The primary areas in which British influence has most profoundly affected precontact or aboriginal legal processes may be seen in the following: (1) the introduction and acceptance of written regulations, ordinances, codes, and formal legislative procedures for the administration of law on the local island and colony levels of organization; (2) the transfer of legal authority from traditional political units (e.g., village and island councils) to colony representatives (Gilbertese and British officials); (3) the imposition of a federal legal and political machinery in the form of District Administrations, Colony Government, and Colony Courts; (4) the gradual systematization of island court procedures as witnessed in the multiple activities of the Native Lands Court, the Native Court, and the Island Administration; and (5) the federalization of hitherto independent island societies into the national unit now known as the Gilbert and Ellice Islands Colony.

The areas in which the British influence has been least successful, in effecting lasting changes include (1) the allocation of political and legal authority to persons in accordance with the traditional Gilbertese social status hierarchy favoring respected male elders over females and all junior members of society; (2) the continuation of multiple and varied "legal levels" as seen in the applicability of "legal attributes" to the decisions of householders, kin group representatives, and village or island councils; (3) the acceptance of social status, kin-group membership, public opinion, or—in more general terms—traditional custom as legitimate elements in the formation of legal decisions; (4) the reliance on customary notions of morality, justice, and fairness in preference to official and statutory settlement procedures; and (5) the frequent recourse to mediation, arbitration, and (in a few cases) adjudication processes within the local *maneaba* assemblies or settlement of law cases outside the colonial court system.

To analyze law at this level (5) we need a broader conceptual framework than the one provided in the introduction to this article. That is to say, one cannot speak of legal phenomena at the household level in the same way that one speaks of law on the colonial level. The two phenomena are just about as different as the conceptions that must be employed in their description and analysis. Bohannan's paper on "The Differing Realms of Law" makes this point quite clear:

> Colonial law is marked by a unicentric power system, with greater or lesser problems conjoining the colonial government with the local government, and the more overt theories (such as the British "indirect rule") of accomplishing the conjunction . . . In colonial law, the problem of disengaging a problem case from the milieu in which it arises is often complicated by the existence of directly opposed ideas about the motives and goals to be achieved in resorting to court action. Once disengaged, the culture of the court officials may be completely different from that of the principals and witnesses in the cases, so that the outcome at best may seem arbitrary. Once "settled" in this more or less arbitrary way, the re-engagement in the institutions of society may be very imperfect, because of lack of consensus about what was decided or lack of agreement about the binding qualities and the justice of it (Bohannan 1965:38–39).

The formal legal activities of the Nonouti Island magistrate and, in fact, all Gilbertese functionaries working on islands outside Tarawa (the administrative center of the colonial government) illustrate the predominance of Gilbertese ideas of law and justice over those represented by the colonial government. The Gilbertese situation thus seems to contradict Bohannan's notion that "the culture of the court officials may be completely different from that of the principals and witnesses in the cases." The contradiction is not a serious one, however, because Bohannan's statement applies to court proceedings on Tarawa Island where most cases are heard by British officials. We could term this Level 6 and extend the discussion to include the legal process as it affects the Gilbertese people who are directly confronted with a Western-type court system and with totally foreign conceptions of procedure, legitimacy, power, and justice. It is at this level of colonial legal and political organization that the anthropologist, the political scientist, and students of comparative jurisprudence most need to cooperate (see Wallerstein 1966).

Conclusions

I have examined five distinctive legal and political levels on Nonouti Island.

The concept of law, if broadly defined, is applicable to the analysis of all these levels of social organization. However, it is necessary to qualify this generalization by stating that law, as a social phenomenon, cannot be easily separated from its cultural matrix. To study legal phenomena outside the more conventional context of courts and legislatures necessarily requires a broadening of theoretical perspectives to include elements that may not appear to be immediately legal in nature.

One cannot speak of Gilbertese law, therefore, as a phenomenon that is either isolated from or unaffected by sociological, political, or historical factors. These have significant influences on all the levels of organization described here. I would, however, now prefer to speak of these "levels" as part of *a complex jurisdictional hierarchy*.

The small household unit and the British colonial government represent the base and apex, respectively. Such attributes as legal authority and legal sanction naturally represent different degrees and kinds of social reality at each level. Thus, the authority exercised by a householder is very different from the kind of authority exercised by the Resident Commissioner. Also, the decisions that may be made in a village *maneaba* assembly are different from the kinds of decisions made by court functionaries. But such differences in both kind and degree—which may be manifest as a difference between a decision founded on mediation versus one based on adjudication—are overshadowed in importance by fundamental similarities.

These similarities derive from the the cultural fact that all decisions, to a greater or lesser extent, involve people who are bound to each other in a network of common obligations and cultural goals. Analytical concepts help to focus attention on isolated elements within this network but they should never be mistaken for the unified phenomenon that we define as reality.

PART V
Religion

INTRODUCTION

It seemed to Sir Edward B. Tylor, one of the principal founders of the anthropological study of religion, that Polynesian myths were intended as explanations of the natural and cosmic orders; such mythic creations were the work of primitive man as philosopher. Tylor's intellectualist approach to religious belief and myth was subsequently criticized and then largely abandoned by a group of scholars who developed a different view of religion because, in part, they held a different view of primitive man: he was less a philosopher than a social creature whose beliefs and concepts reflected social realities. In elaborating magicoreligious beliefs, men seek to rationalize and affirm the social order; solidarity rather than knowledge is the function of religion.

The sociological approach to religion has been dominant in anthropology for a half-century. This is no less true of studies of the religious life of Pacific peoples than of other areas. In our first essay, however, Peter Lawrence, a noted Australian anthropologist and an authority on New Guinea cargo cults, suggests that the prevailing emphasis on the social functions of religion precludes an objective and comprehensive understanding of religious phenomena. His penetrating discussion of the European intellectual roots of the sociological theory exposes its theoretical limitations in certain culture-bound assumptions concerning the place of religion in society—assumptions that many non-Western peoples manifestly do not share. Lawrence urges not that we abandon the sociological perspective, but rather that we consider afresh the cognitive aspects of magic and religion. In addition, he emphasizes the practical importance of appreciating the continuing intellectual role of traditional religious belief for the Pacific-Asian-Australian community.

The remaining essays—Lawrence's on the magicoreligious system of the Ngaing of New Guinea, Stanner's on the world view of the Australian Aborigines, and Firth's on the Polynesian *mana* concept—exemplify the cognitive approach to religion outlined in the introductory essay.

CHAPTER

20

Daughter of Time

PETER LAWRENCE

It is an old proverb that "truth is the daughter of time," and many of you will realize that I am a plagiarist. Josephine Tey (1955) has already used the proverb for the title of a detective story. She interprets its meaning in the way we should automatically assume: in the long run, factual truth must triumph. It may be usurped for centuries but, in the fullness of time, it is bound to come into its own. Miss Tey makes her point by delving into the history of King Richard III of England. Fact by fact, she assembles what she regards to be the truth—that he was brazenly slandered by his enemies—and then reinters him, as it were, a vindicated man.

Yet the proverb is capable of other meanings. We may regard what is often presented to us as "truth" somewhat as Napoleon regarded history: as "agreed-upon fiction," as something socially, politically, and culturally conditioned, and relative to a particular period of time, but by no means universal or perennial. The fiction may be deliberate or unconscious. On the one hand, people may cynically dress up falsehood to take the place of truth because a quick lie may be necessary to establish, for instance, a new sociopolitical order. Miss Tey's argument is that Richard's enemies had to blacken his name to legitimize the fraudulent Tudor regime they established after his defeat at Bosworth Field in 1485. On the other, in virtually every situation, even if there is no immediate imperative of this kind,

From *Daughter of Time,* the inaugural lecture delivered at the University of Queensland, July 11, 1967. Brisbane: University of Queensland Press, 1968. By permission of the author and publisher.

The text of this paper is substantially the same as that of the lecture delivered on 11 July 1967. In this version, I have merely expanded the ethnographic and other illustrative material, and cited book references. I have not altered the argument itself. I should like to thank my friend and colleague Dr. E. H. R. Dowdy for invaluable advice and criticism. I hope later to revise, enlarge, and republish the paper in fulfilment of an earlier undertaking (Lawrence 1964: 5, n. 2): a fuller critical survey of the approaches of other scholars and myself to religion and cargo cults in New Guinea.

people will always select those threads of fact they see to be important and weave them as *their* tapestry of truth. The main determinants of their choice will be their own preoccupations and knowledge—or, more precisely, their socially (that is, artificially) induced anxieties about, and understanding of, the world around them.

I shall now concentrate on this last aspect of the proverb: that people's involuntary, albeit honest, constructions of "truth"—their attitudes towards, assumptions about, and interpretation of the facts they see—are relative to the circumstances in which they live. I shall consider the proposition in the general context of Australia's immediate need to solve the problem of her Aboriginal minority and particularly to come to terms with her nearest neighbours, the emerging nations of Oceania and Asia—an issue of the greatest moment to Queenslanders because of their geographical position. I suggest that social anthropologists and sociologists have a special responsibility in this field and should examine their position critically. Admittedly somewhat tardily, they are now being accepted as useful for the explanation of the new kinds of international relations that have developed in the post-colonial era. If their analyses rest on unsound assumptions, obviously they negate rather than contribute to rapprochement and understanding.

Social anthropologists and sociologists, of course, regard cultural and temporal relativism as a truism, a basic axiom of faith. Their judgments, they believe, are always neutral. Yet they often take their probity for granted. The frequency of their departure from principle would horrify them. Let me begin with a simple example. The New Guinea cargo cult is based on the people's belief that European goods are made *not* by human beings but by a deity and are delivered to men by the spirits of the dead. The people try to discover the identity of the cargo god and the ritual techniques that will induce him to send them supplies of the new wealth, which only Europeans have hitherto enjoyed. I have recently written about cargo cult in the southern Madang District (Lawrence 1964). I show that it represented a continuation into the colonial era of the traditional belief that men had to have the cooperation of gods and ancestors for success in the production of wealth, and that it was stimulated by the failure of the German and especially Australian administrations, before 1942, to help the people take their place in the modern commercial and industrial world. Little was done to develop their economy so that they could buy more Western goods and to educate them to comprehend the leviathan with which they were confronted. Administrative emphasis was on preserving traditional culture and tapping villages for reasonable supplies of labour for plantations and goldmines.

I still support this as a valid part of the explanation of cargo cult but, in other ways, it misrepresents the situation in New Guinea during the 1930's. As a distinguished District Officer of the period[1] has commented to me, my analysis is based on problems which were not visible until after 1945 and overlooks those which the prewar administration understandably regarded as vital. At that time, nobody could see, or be expected to see, cargo cult as the serious political danger it has now become. The bogey then was the threatened depredation of native populations by commercial concerns which, for economic reasons, could not be controlled. The Commonwealth government paid no subsidy to the Territory, and the annual budget depended on royalties from European-produced copra and gold. The administration had no funds for native development, and planters and miners called the political tune. Although there were both blunders and abuses, it can be argued cogently that, under the circumstances, the administration did well to protect the people's traditional sociocultural system so that they were not entirely at the mercy of the labour market. During a period notorious for its commercial rapacity, they were at least guaranteed their own way of life if they preferred it to that offered them by the European recruiter. It is interesting that this approach was endorsed by contemporary anthropologists—not least the great Malinowski—for whom all change was regrettable in that it destroyed what they believed to be the perfect integration of traditional cultures and social structures. In short, as in any administrative situation, you solve one problem only at the expense of another.

This example is hardly grave. It means only that the social anthropologist and sociologist, like the historian, may judge the past unfairly from the vantage point of the present. Yet it is symptomatic of a potentially more dangerous situation when we consider the two major issues now facing social scientists in this country: the computer and, with the loss of the imperialist curtain, Australia's inevitable alignment with Oceania and Asia. Especially for the next generation of Australian social scientists, both issues offer the most exciting prospects, but only if certain conditions obtain. We must be prepared to review and, if necessary, revise our approach to our subject.

In the computer, we have an instrument which, as its devotees continually assert, can analyse and process in a few minutes more facts than an army of human beings in as many months. It can sort out and enumerate more patterns and correlations in the everyday world than was feasible in the past. Yet ultimately it is no substitute for human mental effort. We must know what we are feeding into it. In the present context, social anthropologists and sociologists must know what human social life is—or, especially when aspects of it seem abnormal to them as Europeans, what the social life of a particular group of humans is—before they can assess the particular patterns and correlations that are important. Otherwise, at best they will be pedestrian technicians or at worst make fools of themselves. They should remember Hayek's admonition (1964:51):

> What a distinguished philosopher recently wrote about psychology is at least equally true of the social sciences, namely that it is only too easy "to rush off to measure something without considering what it is we are measuring, or what measurement means. In this respect some recent measurements are of the same logical type as Plato's determination that a just ruler is 729 times as happy as an unjust one."[2]

I am *not* attacking the computer or the principle of measurement. Every field worker must count and analyse frequencies in the patterns of human behaviour and thought he studies. But he will never derive benefit from the computer, which can do the job more efficiently than himself, unless he fully understands the people's sociocultural system. Without this system, human actions and thoughts are so many isolates. If it is ignored, the computer can hardly be blamed if it returns next morning what I have heard one expert describe as "a heap of garbage." In other words, for Australian anthropology and sociology to progress, and contribute to the country's integration with the new geographical and political environment she is beginning to recognize, there must be, together with improved skills in enumerating facts, greater critical awareness of the nature of human cultures and societies, the institutions of which they are composed, and the attitudes and assumptions that underlie them. This will demand a return, in some way, to the old liberal education (including history, and ancient and modern classical literature), which went out of fashion thirty years ago, for which Jacques Barzun (1959) has made an eloquent plea, and to which some American schools and universities are now redirecting their best students. It will demand careful study of our own culture, society, and history from an intellectualist as well as a strictly sociological point of view, and comparative studies of Aboriginal Australia, Oceania, and Asia. Above all, comparative study must ensure that each of the many different sociocultural systems found in these other regions—especially when some aspects of it seem to us bizarre—is examined in its own right: in terms of its own underlying attitudes and assumptions, and not on the basis of definitions derived from attitudes and assumptions which are specifically the products of Western society. To ignore this will be not only to commit the academic sin of confounding the computer but also to risk placing a barrier of misrepresentation between our immediate neighbours and ourselves—a barrier all the more impregnable because of its bogus statistical facade. Moreover, unlike the ex-imperialist British, we do not have the shock absorber of other European nations between the Afro-Asian world and Australia. Our mutual incompatibilities confront each other at almost point-blank range.

This brings me to my central theme: an illustration of the way in which a particular social anthropological approach to the study of religion based on European attitudes and assumptions that crystallized at a certain point in our history seriously falsifies our interpretation of religious phenomena in another society. First, I cite a passage on New Guinea cargo cults written by a distinguished English scholar. Second, I suggest that his approach is heavily influenced by ideas that became anthropologically fashionable—even axiomatic—in France and then Britain during the nineteenth and early twentieth centuries. Third, I try to examine the conditions in which these ideas originated and developed during the last eight hundred years, showing how religion has gradually been relegated to a small part of our conceived cosmic order. Fourth and last, I suggest that these conditions have not obtained in Oceania and much of Asia, so that religion in these areas must be studied differently. Religion is thought to impinge on—indeed, to be inseparable from—parts of the conceived cosmic order that for us have been secularized.

I take the passage on cargo cults, as the example to introduce my argument, from Worsley's well-known *The Trumpet Shall Sound* (1957:236–239). I remind you that in a cargo cult New Guineans perform religious ritual—

prayer meetings, church services, dances, food offerings, and so forth—to induce a deity to send the ancestors with supplies of the new wealth. Worsley asks: ". . . why do the movements take a religious form?" He comments that many colonial peoples and peasants have resisted their rulers in a purely secular way. He goes on:

> The answer lies in the divisions within this type of [i.e., New Guinea] society. In a society split into numerous component units, jealous of each other but seeking to unite on a new basis, a political leader must avoid identification with any particular section of that society. He must avoid being seen as the representative of the interests of any one group, particularly, of course, his own. He must therefore show that he seeks to establish his movement on the basis of a higher loyalty. By projecting his message on to the supernatural plane, he clearly demonstrates that his authority comes from a higher sphere, and that it transcends the narrow province of local gods and spirits associated with particular clans, tribes or villages. He is thus able to build upon existing social foundations, to use the small units of village and clan as elements in his organizational scheme whilst at the same time transcending the cramping limitations of these units by incorporating them in a wider framework.

A little later Worsley says:

> There are other corollaries to the low level of political organization which we find in societies of the types which we have shown to be predisposed to millenarism. These are not so much structural resemblances as cultural, for these societies also lack advanced technological and scientific knowledge. . . . These deficiencies in scientific knowledge and practice, especially knowledge of European society and above all European factory production, provide ample room for the elaboration of fantastic "explanations" in animistic or other supernaturalistic terms, and for the use of magic to try to solve practical problems.

Worsley then states that New Guinea religion is concerned essentially with the provision of material wealth. Gods invented food plants and artefacts, gave them to men, and revealed also the ritual techniques ("magic") essential to produce them. The idea was carried over into cargo cult.

It is clear that Worsley attributes the religious nature of cargo cult *primarily* to secular sociopolitical causes ("The answer lies in the divisions within this type of society") and *only secondarily* to intellectual factors (the nature of belief)—which, indeed, he introduces merely as a corollary, defined in the *Oxford English Dictionary* as "an immediate consequence." This, I contend, puts a modern Western and quite erroneous construction on cargo cult. Although sociopolitical as well as intellectual elements are important in the movement, the facts reverse rather than support Worsley's interpretation. There is ample evidence that intellectual causes have primacy in the particular field under consideration. Although the people's attempt to acquire cargo is clearly motivated by their desire for economic and sociopolitical equality with Europeans, the cults themselves assume a religious form precisely because New Guineans, who think deeply about religion but regard it as a mundane technology rather than an otherworldly theology, cannot in their present circumstances conceive any means of getting the new wealth other than ritual. Their behaviour is intellectually directed: they hold certain religious beliefs as logical and act on them to achieve their ends. The sociopolitical features Worsley describes are only secondary: they are the effects and not the cause of cargo cult. Because certain religious beliefs are accepted and rituals performed, new social formations emerge. But the cultists are not sophisticated, professional revolutionaries: there is little to suggest that they consciously adopt these beliefs to create sociopolitical solidarity, as Worsley appears to indicate. New Guinea leaders have always had recognized techniques for patching over cleavages between their respective groups: military and marriage alliances, and trade and exchange ties. But they do not manipulate religion in this way. As indicated, they accept or reject a belief on pragmatic intellectual grounds: it will or will not lead to tangible benefits, such as making crops grow and pigs breed, and nowadays producing cargo. So little do the people use religion deliberately for political ends that several Madang cult leaders before the war abandoned a cargo belief that was based on Christianity and hence included followers from the whole converted area, in favour of another which was centred on a coastal pagan deity, even though this seriously diminished their following. They were convinced that Christianity was intellectually false because it was economically useless—it had not brought them wealth—and were unconcerned that their new belief eliminated the bulk of the population, the inland natives who had no rights to the coastal god they were now invoking for cargo (Lawrence 1964:260–261).

I turn now to my second point. If there is no ethnographic evidence for Worsley's interpretation, what is its source? In my view, there is only one possible source: his own European background. He is following what has now become an academically respectable—indeed, prescribed—tradition, as is demonstrated by the general anthropological prejudice against accepting belief as sociological fact, and predilection to examine religious phenomena almost exclusively as indices of human social relationships—in the case of cargo cult, of racial tension and conflict. Worsley's interpretation is typical of the kind of argument nearly all social anthropologists, myself included, have unthinkingly used at one time or another. The general approach is a mixture of the Marxist and Durkheimian definitions[3] of religion, which were formulated in the nineteenth and twentieth centuries—although their ancestry goes back at least to the eighteenth—and which have dominated and, I believe, distorted anthropological work in this field for the last forty years.

In this context, Marx (1818–1883) and the French sociologist Durkheim (1858–1917) were opposite sides of the same coin. Whatever the other issues on which they disagreed, they had this in common: as Marx (1962:363) put it, it was not the consciousness of men that determined their being but their social being that determined their consciousness. In more specific terms, Marx (1964:41) said: "*Man makes religion,* religion does not make man." In short, both Marx and Durkheim regarded religion as the reflection of the social order. They differed here only in that, while Marx (1964:41) saw religion as the "existence of error" and an obstacle to human progress, Durkheim saw it as essential for unifying human collectives. Thus for Marx (1964:135), "The religious world is but the reflex of the real world", and (1964:42) "Religion is the sigh of the oppressed creature, the heart of a heartless world, just as it is the spirit of a spiritless situation. It is the opium of the people." For Durkheim (1954:418), the "reality, which mythologies have represented under so many different forms, but which is the universal and eternal objective cause of these sensations out of which religious experience is made, is society." He defines (1954:47) religion as ". . . *a unified system of beliefs and practices which unite into a single moral community called a Church, all those who adhere to them.*" He stresses that religious beliefs symbolize and religious practices reaffirm the solidarity of society, man's collective life. Religion reflects a society's own ideal of itself, which its members strive to achieve and perpetuate by worship. Durkheim (1954:416) concludes that:

> . . . the real function of religion is not to make us think, to enrich our knowledge . . . but rather . . . to make us act, to aid us to live. The believer . . . is not merely a man who sees new truths of which the unbeliever is ignorant; he is a man who is *stronger*. He feels within him more force either to endure the trials of existence or to conquer them.

The stress is clear: religion's sole referent is the secular social order, and its role, for Marx (to borrow Metternich's phrase) "to bolster up a mouldering edifice" or, for Durkheim, to ensure social cohesion. It is not concerned initially with man's ideas about his universe. Its intellectual function is really to engender common sentiments that, for Marx, enable man to live as best he can in "a heartless world" or that, for Durkheim, represent a sanctified moral system helping him approximate to life in that perfected society, which is the focus of all religious interest.

The influence on British social anthropology of the predominantly social, nonintellectualist approach to religion can be seen in many studies by English scholars since the 1920's. On religion, they have adopted the position typified by Radcliffe-Brown, who was Durkheim's first British disciple and who wrote (1952:155) as late as 1945: "My suggestion is that in attempting to understand a religion it is on the rites rather than on the beliefs that we should first concentrate our attention." Religion becomes an oblique reflection of social structure, like Plato's shadows in the cave. In 1959, Fortes of Cambridge (1960:47) wrote: "Ever since . . . Durkheim's great work on *The Elementary Forms of the Religious Life*, anthropologists have known that the springs of religion and ritual lie in kinship and social organization." This is a generalized version of Worsley's statement that cargo cults are religious because of the structure of New Guinea society: their religious nature springs from the need of the different groups concerned to emerge as a unified whole. I suggest that we *know* nothing of the kind. We have accepted it as a convenient formula with minimal scrutiny.

The predominantly social, nonintellectualist approach to religion is now under attack. Scholars such as Voegelin (1952), Evans-Pritchard (1956), Horton (1960), Hayek (1964), Jarvie (1964), and O'Dea (1966) have criticized it variously on the grounds that it provides a totally incomplete picture of a religious system and is an expression of naïve positivism. Because its interest is restricted to the secular social order, it is only the part parading as the whole. It can provide valid explanations for only a limited range of problems. Its tendency to dismiss belief about the wider universe as "not sociological fact" is a crude attempt to "physicalize" enquiry and reduce every proposition, in the words of Comte (one of the fathers of positivism), "to a simple enumeration of fact." As Hayek (1964) has cogently argued, by jettisoning belief we are expected to understand phenomena in terms of less than we actually know about them. Yet perhaps more illuminating—and, in a public lecture, easier to understand—than criticism of the logical inadequacies of the approach will be an attempt to examine it in its historical perspective: the stages by which, and the circumstances in which, it appeared in Western society.

This introduces my third point: the changing role of religion in Europe since the Middle Ages. What impresses an anthropologist most is that, by the middle of the thirteenth century, Christianity impinged on every aspect of man's conceived cosmic order, in which it had pronounced economic, sociopolitical, and intellectual functions. Yet progressively thereafter its influence disappeared from all except the sociopolitical field.

At the height of the Middle Ages, the cosmos was believed to consist of three realms: Heaven, earth, and Hell. Man saw himself as involved in three particular systems: economic, sociopolitical, and religious. The economic system involved his exploitation of material resources and shaded over into the sociopolitical system, the system of relationships between human beings: the ecclesiastical and secular hierarchies of Pope and Church dignitaries, and of emperors, kings, nobles, knights, and commoners. The religious system represented man's putative relationships with the Companies of Heaven and Hell respectively—with the one, if he were properly adjusted, and with the other, if he were not.

Christianity had to be understood in the context of its three roles, economic, sociopolitical, and intellectual. The Church's concern with the economic and sociopolitical fields was determined by the need for stability after the disintegration of the Roman Empire. It had to replace chaos with order. It did so in the Durkheimian manner by explaining, legitimizing, and ritually buttressing a rigid structure of classes whose positions were irrevocably fixed by God and between which there could be no equality, and by banning activities such as usury likely to upset it. It acknowledged that this was not social perfection but stated that, after Adam's sin, man was capable of no better way of life. Although there were dissenters, it regarded this life as a qualifying course for the Kingdoms of Heaven and Hell in the next.

In addition, Christianity was seen as the intellectual system par excellence. It enshrined all knowledge. Yet it had to come to grips with two distinct epistemological traditions, one of them the key to its eventual destruction: the Judaic and the Graeco-Roman. The Judaic tradition was based on the assumption of divine revelation: that all knowledge came to man from God. It was typified, in its Christian form, by the orthodox scholar St. Bonaventure and the heterodox millenarian scholars. The Graeco-Roman tradition was that man had to amass earthly knowledge by his own secular intelligence. It was typified, in its Christian form, by St. Thomas Aquinas and the alchemists. As the struggle between the two traditions was so important for future European intellectual history, I discuss briefly those of their representatives I have mentioned.

In the Judaic tradition, St. Bonaventure (1221–1274)[4] was Franciscan Professor of Theology at the University of Paris. He continued the Augustinian view that all knowledge, all truth, originated in God,[5] being borne into man by divine Ideas residing in Him and expressing His essence. Secular reason unenlightened by faith was bound to fail. The human mind, on its own and unsustained by grace, was unimportant because, after Adam's sin, man could no longer contemplate God directly. The soul was the medium of grace: it had to perfect the natural body and illuminate the secular mind.

The heterodox millenarians, the dissenters to whom I referred earlier, refused to accept the official view of the Church that imperfect feudal society was the best men could expect in this life and that Christ's Kingdom was already established, but only in the next. Generally the underprivileged, they were convinced that the terrestrial sociopolitical order could be perfected. Before the Day of Judgment and the Ending of the World, there would be a thousand years (the millennium) in which God would appoint his Saints (chosen from the underprivileged) to rule the earth with peace, plenty, and justice for all. Millenarian religion was not only concerned with the economic and sociopolitical orders. It was still essentially the intellectual system. The Scriptures would reveal to man his future.

The belief was typified by a Calabrian Abbot, Joachim of Fiore (1145–1202), who has been described as one of the most influential prophetic millenarians before Marx.[6] Having studied *The Book of Revelation,* he elaborated his interpretation of human history. He divided history into three stages, each presided over by one Person of the Trinity. The first stage was that of the Father or of the Law: its rules were contained in the Old Testament, and were based on fear and servitude. The second was that of the Son or of the Gospel: its laws were contained in the New Testament, and were based on faith and filial submission. The third would be that of the Spirit, the culmination of human history, the final revelation of all knowledge, the everlasting gospel, a period of love, joy, and freedom, the resting time of mankind. Men would contemplate God until Judgment Day.

In the Graeco-Roman tradition, St. Thomas Aquinas (1225:6–74)[7] was Dominican Professor of Theology at the University of Paris. Like St. Bonaventure, he saw God as the ultimate *fons et origo* of the total cosmic order. But, unlike him, he tried to *assimilate* to his theology the Aristotelian science that was beginning to find its way back into Europe. For this he had to base his explanatory system on a separation, if still a complementary relationship, between human reason and faith. He let out the human intellect on a long rein. Faith came from revelation and dealt with divine truths inaccessible to reason, which had to start with what could be known through experience and demonstration. Human reason was handicapped by human nature. Unlike the angels, who, as purely spiritual beings, were higher intelligences and could know God's reality without long, discursive thought, man, part material and part spiritual, was a lower intelligence and had to struggle towards understanding. In this struggle, man's mind, although ultimately illuminated by the faintest glimmer of God's grace vouchsafed him because of his spiritual soul, appears to assume at least some of the characteristics of the secular human intellect that was to dominate the world in later centuries.

In alchemy (Holmyard 1957), the attempt to transmute base metals into gold, there was a similar separation, if complementary relationship, between reason and faith, reason being finally subject to the Divine Will. Reason and faith presided over the technical and theological aspects of alchemy respectively. Technical procedures were based on the Aristotelian division of the world into four primary elements—fire, air, water, and earth—which were combined in various proportions to make up all matter. By discovering the correct formula, symbolized by the Philosopher's Stone or Elixir, the alchemist could change the combinations of the elements in the base metals into that of gold. The search for the Stone or Elixir led to much quasichemical experiment. Yet God was ultimately in control: He would grant the final illumination for hastening the cosmic process of transmutation only to the alchemist who had the Christian virtues of sobriety, piety, and unwavering belief.

At its peak, with St. Bonaventure, I should suggest, mediaeval Christianity had gained almost complete ascendancy over economic, sociopolitical, and intellectual life. Yet, as I have hinted, it had to assimilate forces which compelled it to retreat from this position. The trend was fostered, if not begun, by St. Thomas and the alchemists, who attracted to Europe what became known as the New Learning—Greek, especially Aristotelian, manuscripts from Byzantium and science from the Arab world. By separating reason from faith, both had, probably unwittingly, re-established the fact, if not the principle, of the secular human intellect. From 1274 —when both St. Bonaventure and St. Thomas died—until the beginning of the fifteenth century, there was continual struggle between the Judaic and Graeco-Roman intellectual traditions. Duns Scotus (c. 1266 or 1270–1308) and William of Ockham (c. 1300–1349) criticized and moved beyond the Thomist position. Then followed an Augustinian-Bonaventurian reaction. But, by about 1400, the Graeco-Roman tradition had won. Although the Judaic ideal hung on wherever it could, from now on the new humanism directed the world's affairs. The movement had its first impetus in the Italian Renaissance but, after 1500, under the influence of Leonardo, Galileo, and especially the great minds thrown up by the Reformation in northern Europe, it was dominated by what we now call the Scientific Revolution and Enlightenment. The crucial period for us now is the seventeenth and eighteenth centuries.

For the moment, I shall gloss over the relation between religion and the socioeconomic order. Especially during the seventeenth century, although there were certain differences, the official principle was still the same: God had mapped out the system by which man was to live. The immediate importance of the Scientific Revolution lay in the radical changes brought to European intellectual life. Against the intentions of the movement's early leaders, the old theocentric cosmic order gave way to one that became progressively more anthropocentric. Formally, God was still the First Cause, Creator, and Architect of the cosmos. But such were the rapidity and nature of scientific discoveries, it could no longer be maintained that God had given all knowledge to man. Rather He had given man a mind of his own—not the feeble tool allowed him by St. Thomas, but a fine, keen-edged instrument—with which to examine and comprehend the material world. Thus, the relatively unfettered human intellect—a phenomenon unknown since the decline of the classical world—was free to roam the earth, gather fact, and analyse and interpret it according to secular logic.

The Scientific Revolution was not confined to England but, after the foundation of the Royal Society in 1660, it achieved there its greatest glories, culminating in the publication of Newton's *Principia* in 1687.[8] At this time, therefore, English attitudes and achievements were of profound significance. The founders of the Royal Society were extreme Protestants, whose devotion to science did not impair their Christian convictions. They saw their work as consecrated to the greater glory of God. As God was orderly and logical, He had therefore created an orderly and logical cosmos. It would be to His glory to proclaim that order and logic through the instrumentality of the God-given mind and the medium of science. The great discoveries were celebrated in church. Dr. Bentley of Trinity College, Cambridge, preached a sermon on Newton's Law of Gravity as God's final plan for the universe, and Addison eulogized the *Principia* in his famous hymn about the heavenly bodies proclaiming "their Great Original."

Nevertheless, just as in the thirteenth century, there were, in the new compromise between Christianity and science, fissures of doubt. The more people tried to seal them, the wider they became. Man—I mean here intellectual man—now knew too much and too little for his own good, and could no longer be constrained or comforted by a God, Who had ceased to be a close and personal Father but had become a vague First Cause or Architect, distantly removed to the edges of the conceived cosmos—on the outer, looking in.[9] The new science posed too many questions which it could not itself answer, which were outside the scope of Holy Writ, and which even challenged the validity of Holy Writ. For instance, it was now realized that gold did not turn to powder under high temperatures. How, then, did Moses calcinate the Golden Calf? Men such as Sir Thomas Browne, a physician and sincere Christian, took the candidly ostrich-like view that Scripture and reason must be separated: Scripture had to be assigned to the region of faith and kept safe from enquiring intellect. Others argued that Holy Writ was only allegory. It was impious to believe that God had literally planted a Paradise in Eden. He had merely planted terrestrial virtue in men (Willey, 1962*a*:58 ff.).

But the enquiring intellect could not be silenced. Even God Himself became so nebulous that His existence was questioned by some and had therefore to be proved. Most important were the arguments of the philosophers, Descartes and Locke. For Descartes, the idea of God represented the qualities of omniscience, eternity, immutability, omnipotence, and perfection—qualities which had to originate in a conscious mind. They obviously could not be projections from the human mind about man himself and had, therefore, to stem from God. Locke claimed God's existence as a mathematical certainty. He started with the certainty of human existence. As we know that we exist and it is evident that bare nothing could not have produced us, some being must have done so. As we are intelligent beings, an intelligent being must have created us. Hence God, greater than man, exists.

My present interest in these philosophical proofs of God's existence has nothing to do with their internal logic. Their importance here is that they represented the swansong of Christianity as an intellectual force. As Basil Willey (1962*a*:82 ff.) has commented, "At first sight it may seem inexplicable that a philosophy in which God and the soul are the first certainties should prove an enemy of religion." Yet God was no longer an unquestioned conviction. He existed now only by grace and favour of the secular human intellect. Once man began to make God consciously in his own image, as the eighteenth century or Age of Enlightenment wore on, he began to assume that he could dispense with Him altogether. About the time of the French Revolution, he settled for a somewhat impersonal deity whom Durkheim was later to call the ideal society worshipped by its actual approximation.

A probable reason for this trend was that, at the end of the seventeenth century, the savants' main, although not entire, intellectual interest began to shift from the wider material universe to the social order. Especially in monarchical countries such as Britain and France, the official relationship between God and the constitution was maintained. But the philosophers, who were often at odds with governments, now saw society as a fitting object of study. The contemplation and analysis of the vast material universe had, for a time (especially during the seventeenth century), kept man's pretensions in check. He could turn its laws to his advantage, as in navigation, but it was too huge and complex for him to change its structure radically or become its complete master. If he were to feel secure, he had to approach it with humility and keep God in it somewhere.

These considerations did not temper man's attitude towards the social order, which now began to be seen increasingly as a secular and discrete phenomenon. As Hobbes had suggested as early as 1651, it could be treated as artificial or man-made (Hobbes, 1937: 110):

> The skill of making and maintaining Commonwealths, consisteth in certain Rules, as doth arithmetique and geometry; not (as Tennisplay) on Practise onely: which Rules, neither poor men have the leisure, nor men that have the leisure, have hitherto had the curiosity, or the method to find out.

The social order was small enough for man to master and reconstruct. The eighteenth century attitude was summoned up by de Tocqueville writing in the 1850's (de Tocqueville 1959:33–34):

> The general idea of the greatness of man, of the omnipotence of his reason, of the limitless powers of his intelligence, had penetrated and pervaded the spirit of the century. Yet this lofty conception of mankind in general was coupled with a particular contempt for contemporary society.

Even kings, hitherto the Lord's anointed, were no longer sacrosanct. Frederick the Great of Prussia described himself as a man, the first servant of the state. Voltaire wrote his *Henriade*, depicting Henry IV of France as a human being rather than a demigod.

It would be impossible in a few minutes to unravel the many strands in eighteenth century religious thought. It is essential to select. There were those who, like Dr. Johnson and Boswell, maintained orthodox faith. There were those who retained their faith out of respect for scientific achievement. But the philosophers who concentrated their attention on the social order hovered between deism (the acceptance of a primal creator who had little interest in human affairs) and total unbelief. In 1774, Joseph Priestley, a scientist and Unitarian minister, reported that, during a visit to Paris (the centre of the proto-sociological movement), "all the philosophical persons" he met were "unbelievers in Christianity, and even professed atheists" (Willey 1962*b*:165). What was most significant was that the social philosophers prised loose human society from the rest of the material universe (the realm of the natural scientists) and treated it as their own private domain; and those who still regarded religion as important could see no referent for it other than the social order. As man's intellectual self-importance increased, God ceased to be invoked as an explanation of the nature of the world and the events within it. He was reduced to a moral sanction—what we now call social cement.

This was an academic tradition established by Montesquieu and endorsed by Gibbon in their studies of Roman pagan religion.[10] The Roman pontiffs, wrote Gibbon (1960:31) in a famous passage, "knew and valued the advantages of religion, as it is connected with civil government." It was also the militant philosophical position adopted by Rousseau, whose *The Social Contract* appeared in 1762 and whose influence, according to Georges Sorel, was still powerful a hundred years later;[11] although I should argue that, through Durkheim, it is still a living force. His ideas about society and religion were of direct importance during the French Revolution and have lasted, in many forms, into the twentieth century.[12]

Rousseau's problem was: How can man retain his individual freedom and yet live in society? His answer was to propose an ideal form of society with individual citizens moulded into it so harmoniously that they would automatically regard their existence as the only kind of freedom. For this they must have a uniform behavioural system, the General Will: a perfect ideology which they could not work out for themselves but must be taught by a Legislator or Dictator and legitimized by religion. Rousseau is specific that he wants a social, non-intellectualist religion (Rousseau 1960:437–38):

> . . . a purely civil profession of faith, the articles of which it behoves the Sovereign [people] to fix, not with the precision of religious dogmas, but treating them as a body of social sentiments without which no man can be either a good citizen or a faithful subject. . . . The dogmas of this civil religion should be few, clear, and enunciated precisely, without either explanation or comment. The positive clauses are:—the existence of a powerful, intelligent, beneficient, and bountiful God: the reality of the life to come: the reward of the just, and the punishment of evildoers: the sanctity of the Social Contract and the Laws.

There is no suggestion that religion should have a cognitive function.

The religious history of the next century was merely a variation on this theme. For good reason, Durkheim (1960) hailed Rousseau as one of the twin founders of social anthropology and sociology. In 1789, twenty-seven years after the publication of *The Social Contract*, the Revolution broke out in France. Its initial credo, expounded mainly by atheist or agnostic renegade nobles, was that man by his own reason would free himself from the shackles of feudal society and live on terms of equality and brotherhood with his fellows. The Catholic Church was virtually destroyed and exiled. In 1793, middle class extremists took charge and, with Robespierre as Legislator instilling the General Will by severing the heads of those who would not conform, tried to implement the reign of Rousseauist philosophy. By 1794, to use Lenin's phrase, the machine (symbolized by the guillotine) was out of control. The last resort was to civil religion—Rousseau called it "religion, viewed in reference to Society"—which would stabilize the situation by legitimizing revolutionary ideology. In May 1794, the Government issued a decree strikingly similar to the passage quoted from Rousseau:

> The French people recognize the existence of the Supreme Being and the immortality of the soul.—It recognizes that the worship worthy of the Supreme Being is the practice of the duties of man.—It places in the front rank of these duties to detest bad faith and tyranny, to punish tyrants and traitors, to aid the unfortunate, to respect the weak, to defend the oppressed, to do unto others all possible good and to be unjust to no one. There shall be instituted fêtes in order to remind man of the Divinity and of the dignity of his being.—These fêtes shall take their names from the glorious events of our Revolution, the virtues most cherished and most useful to man, and the great gifts of nature.—The French Republic shall annually celebrate the fêtes of the 14th July, 1789 [destruction of the Bastille], the 10th August, 1792 [attack on the Tuilleries], the 21st January, 1793 [death of Louis XVI], and the 31st May, 1793 [rise of the Montagnards].—It shall celebrate every tenth day the fêtes which are hereby enumerated.[13]

Society had at last been told that, in religious exercises, it was projecting and worshipping its perfected image.

After the Revolution came Napoleon, who admired Rousseau, realized the need for a civic religion, regarded himself as the Legislator and incarnation of the General Will but, being a parvenu, wanted only the best—legitimacy. His obvious and immediate need was to reintroduce law and order. He brought back the Catholic Church, but strictly for pragmatic ends. "In religion," he said, "I do not see the mystery of the Incarnation but the mystery of the social order." It was Rousseau again—but with bell, book, and candle.

The post-Napoleonic period after 1815 was war-weary and confused. Above all, people wanted social and political stability. In France, the Bourbon Restoration failed to bring peace. In Germany, the Napoleonic administrative reforms and War of Liberation sowed the seeds of nationalism. Britain was threatened by social and political upheaval as a result of rapid, unplanned industrial expansion. Some, like Metternich, trusted in renovated conservatism. Others looked forward to ever new revolution to create the millennium. Some, like Robert Owen, Blanqui and, of course, Marx, condemned religion as the cause of all evil. Others saw it as a condition of social regeneration.

Those who still placed their faith in religion held orthodox Christian or their own eccentric beliefs. Yet they all had one thing in common. Because of the final establishment of natural science, they could no longer pretend that religion had a primarily intellectual function. Darwin delivered the coup de grâce in 1859. In view of the political disturbances facing them, they concentrated on religion as a social coagulant. This was the only remaining field in which religion could make a seemingly constructive contribution. J. S. Mill (1962:148) writing in 1859, summed up the view:

> In the present age—which has been described as "destitute of faith, but terrified of scepticism"—in which people feel sure, not so much that their opinions are true, as that they should not know what to do without them—the claims of an opinion to be protected from public attack are rested not so much on its truth, as on its importance to society.

Orthodox Christians—de Maistre, de Bonald, Lamennais, Coleridge, Arnold, and Newman—saw the value of their religion not in intellectually deduced truth, but, in Arnold's words, its "efficacy for moral good."[14] Church hymns written in this period were focused on social conditions.

There were many who held eccentric religious views: Buonarroti, Fourier, and Mazzini, to mention but a few. I shall complete my argument by discussing briefly two prominent Frenchmen, who founded sociology as a discipline and were Durkheim's immediate intellectual forebears: Saint-Simon and Comte. Saint-Simon (1760–1825)[15] recognized early in the nineteenth century that European society needed further change than that achieved by the French Revolution. The idea of individual liberty, a basic tenet of the Revolution, had led to anarchy. Society had to be restored, not by reason, but by science in the hands of experts. There should be a science of society which would produce a scientifically based morality. Moreover, since the French Revolution, European society had to face a new challenge, the Industrial Revolution. Saint-Simon realized that industrialism would govern the emerging social order. He proposed a Council of Industrials to administer society on the basis of scientifically worked out knowledge. His Council would implement a new version of the General Will, which would be legitimized and reinforced by yet another Rousseauist civic religion, the New Christianity. This religion would emphasize one cardinal principle: *Love thy neighbour.* It would stress, not the intellect, but the moral order and social cohesion:

> . . . the doctrine of morality will be considered by the new Christians as the most important; creed and dogma will be envisaged by them only as ascessories whose principal purpose is to fix the attention of the faithful of all classes upon morality.[16]

One is tempted to add to this Durkheim's phrase, "*a single moral community* called a Church," for the language is essentially the same.

To discuss Comte in detail would be, from our present limited point of view, to cover essentially the same ground. He was born in 1798 and died in 1857, a year before Durkheim's birth. For a while he was Saint-Simon's secretary. He, too, saw the need to reform European society but believed that it should first be studied scientifically. Reformed society must be legitimized by religion. In the past, men had worshipped imaginary gods. He now offered a new God, Humanity. In the Religion of Humanity, creed and dogma were no less than the discovered laws of positive science, but the principal stress was once again on morality and social solidarity.

Comte wrote: "Love, then, is our principle; Order our basis; and Progress our end."[18] It was yet another version of Rousseau's "religion, viewed in reference to Society." It was the *European* coin of which Marx and Durkheim were the reverse and obverse. It was the tradition that Durkheim accentuated in his work and carried into our own century as an antidote to its turbulence (he died towards the end of the First World War), and that Worsley used to explain cargo cult: that sociopolitical ferment, and the need for unity and brotherly love, make the emergence of a new religion inevitable.

I come now to my fourth and last point. I remarked at the outset that social anthropologists and sociologists regard cultural and temporal relativism as an axiom of faith. Especially in the field of secular culture, we have conditioned ourselves to expect differences between ourselves and other peoples—in our particular case, the Aborigines, Oceanians, and Asians. We know that kinship, birth, family, and personal dignity ("face") are more important for these peoples than for us. We recognize that Aborigines were traditionally nomadic hunters, and Oceanians and South-East Asians peasant agriculturalists, with a low level of technology. Clearly, their outlook, understanding of the world, and history during the last few centuries—despite the coming of the Europeans—differ radically from those of Western society and are not in themselves homogeneous. Even in economically advanced China and Japan, the all-important Scientific and Industrial Revolutions did not occur separately and gradually, as in Europe, but were imported together in their developed form.

Yet there is a special, hidden danger, implicit in my quotation from Forts: that we assume uncritically that we possess definitions of, or approaches to, *some* social phenomena so scientific, so universally valid, that they make cultural differences irrelevant, whereas in truth they are only artifacts of our own limited environment and experience. The predominantly social, nonintellectualist approach to religion is in this category. It is not an eternal and universal concept but a recent and regional European development that was made possible by the sudden growth of secular knowledge and arose to meet the needs of a politically chaotic situation. It has only limited relevance to the peoples to our north, whose backgrounds are dissimilar to our own and in whose lives religion is still a crucial, focal theme. We should be naïve—indeed, guilty of cultural imperialism—to use the approach as our sole or main analytical tool in the area and computerize the results. In some cases, it may be adequate: for instance, Confucianism sees the primary function of ritual as the maintenance of social order. But in most other cases it would either distort or blot out the meaning of religious activity because the societies concerned have not yet passed into the necessary stage of secularism. I have no time to detail it here, but we must adopt a new approach to these religions. I suggest that we begin by viewing them with flexibility, humility, and respect, and by returning to the panoptic outlook of the Middle Ages. We must examine their impingement on all aspects of human life, economic, sociopolitical, and above all intellectual. We must analyse Aboriginal and New Guinea religions, and Hinduism, Buddhism, and Islam—especially in rural areas—in the same sort of terms as I have tried, however amateurishly, to present to you mediaeval Christianity and the philosophies that succeeded it in Europe. These religions must still satisfy anxieties and needs other than the purely socio-political. They are thought to be important in economic production and technology. They are, therefore, also cognitive systems explaining vital events and relationships outside the social structure in the wider cosmic order. We must be prepared for infinite cultural variety and for special meaning in what seems commonplace. For instance, I once asked a New Guinean what qualities a particular cargo cult leader possessed. "*Emi gat tingting bilong God*," came the reply in pidgin English: "He has (*emi gat*) thinking (*tingting*) of God (*bilong God*)." We should automatically translate the phrase as, "He has holy thoughts/thinks about God"—and be wrong. It means: "He holds God's thinking in his power," "He can make God think on him," or "He can make God do what he wants." Clearly this is not the interpretation of the relationship between God and man that the missionaries thought they had imparted. Thirty years of teaching had been misrepresented, often with great personal tragedy. I have told the story of Yali of New Guinea elsewhere (Lawrence, 1964). He returned from war service in 1945 determined to help his people achieve a better way of life. He was encouraged and given authority by administration officers who, quite naturally, assumed that, because he had visited Queensland, he had adopted a secular Western outlook. They did not realize that his mind still worked on the basis of the popular assumption that Europeans acquired their wealth by controlling the *tingting* of the cargo god by means of ritual—a concept the officers had probably not encountered and could not have interpreted had they done so. The result for Yali was seduction into cargo cult, imprisonment, and now deep bitterness.

There are many comparable examples from elsewhere in Oceania and especially Asia: the New Guinea Medical College student who was bewildered by Shakespeare's *Hamlet* because the missionaries had taught him that Europeans did not believe in ghosts; Asian businessmen who have their account books blessed; the Minister of Education who recommended a particular astrologer in the daily press; sportsmen who publicly invoke their gods before a match; Ph.D.'s and government officials who consult palmists before undertak- major scientific or administrative ventures; and medical practitioners and politicians afraid to work or campaign among traditional enemies for fear of sorcery. Technical experts who help Asian peasants in their struggle for development have to learn that these people do not always believe that their lives are governed by secular laws of cause and effect. Thus, in Negri Sembilan, Malaya (Swift 1965:41–42), irrigation and dam-building are important for agriculture. When dams break and water is lost, "there is a suspicion of supernatural malevolence or irritation." The spirits of the river, rice land, and the rice have to be placated. Progressive village headmen wanting to introduce practical improvements, which would seem obvious to Europeans, may meet with great opposition from those who refuse to think beyond their religious beliefs. Even the comparatively Westernized Japanese made a film, *The Harp of Burma*, in which a soldier became a Buddhist monk in Burma at the end of the war. He won merit not by helping his living comrades, as his European counterpart might have done, but by burying the corpses of the fallen. Spirits of ancestors are important for the Japanese in ways that we cannot at once understand. The same is true in the case of the Burmese. Melford E. Spiro (1967:33–34) tells us that the souls of dead Burmese, unless propitiated and properly escorted from their human habitats, are thought to remain to haunt the living.

> The souls of deceased government officials are believed to be especially attached to their positions; to prevent them from remaining in their offices, a special document is prepared, signed, and sometimes recited by the superior officer of the deceased, discharging the soul from all connections with his erstwhile position.

Our immediate response, as "science-minded" Europeans, is to dismiss such incidents as examples of spurious, primitive superstition. Yet we are ourselves too ill-informed to recognize that all these actions, however strange to us, are based on intellectual and logical systems—are conceived to take place within cosmic systems—for which there are no longer, or perhaps have never been, counterparts in our culture. From a practical point of view, with the rise of self-conscious nationalism in Oceania and Asia, it could spell disaster for us to ignore them. The diplomatic impasse in a Southeast Asian kingdom caused by American ignorance of the importance locally attached to astrology, although presented as fiction in Lederer and Burdick's *The Ugly American*, has the ring of authenticity.

In conclusion, what I have said amounts to this: We Australians stand on the threshold of a brave new Pacific world, but we shall neither understand nor survive in it if we cling to outmoded Western assumptions and concepts. We must be prepared to look for new ones. But we should not suppose that even this will provide a final answer to our problems. For a start, one should wish that our own efforts at rapprochment will be matched by the peoples of the northern countries to which I have referred. If there is to be goodwill, they too must tolerate cultural differences in us. Moreover, we should be mistaken if we supposed that what we and they variously see as important *now* had perennial relevance. It is only the product of a specific period, the postcolonial era. Our successors in each generation will have to discover new answers to new problems. Time, after all, will keep on breeding, and her daughters growing up. Only occasionally will we get a thoroughbred: final, absolute truth. The most we can hope for the majority of her progeny is that they will be progressively wiser as they become progressively less parochial.

CHAPTER

21

The Ngaing of the Rai Coast

PETER LAWRENCE

The Ngaing are a linguistic group of between eight and nine hundred people near Saidor on the Rai Coast. They live mainly on the subcoast between the Nankina and Mot rivers, although they have two settlements west of the Mot—Maibang and Kilang. Towards the coast, their territory is bounded by the narrow plain (at most about four miles deep) and low foothills inhabited by the Sengam, Gira, Som, and Neko; and inland, by a line running from Aiyawang to Langani. In the hinterland there are two little known groups: the M'na on the east bank of the Mot and the N'dau on the west.[1]

In this essay I attempt to give a general account of Ngaing religion. It must be remembered, however, that in the native vernacular there is no single word corresponding to this term. Religion, as a special part of the culture, is something which we must abstract for ourselves, looking at the people's total way of life and emphasizing the aspects of it most resembling those connoted by the term *religion* in our own.

The Ngaing implicitly regard their cosmos or world order as a logically integrated system. It consists of the land area known to them, which is inhabited, in their view, not only by human beings and animals but also by deities, totems and spirits of the dead. For our present purposes, we must consider three aspects of the cosmos: the physical environment and economic resources; the social structure (actual relationships between human beings); and what we should call religion (the people's beliefs

---

From *Gods, Ghosts and Men in Melanesia,* Peter Lawrence and M. J. Meggitt, eds., pp. 198–223. Melbourne: Oxford University Press, 1965. By permission of the authors and publisher.

My thanks are due to the Australian National University for providing funds for my fieldwork among the Ngaing (eight months in 1953 and six months in 1956); and to the Department of Territories (Canberra) for enabling me to revisit the area during January 1958, when I was on the staff of the Australian School of Pacific Administration, Mosman, N.S.W.

about, and putative interaction with, deities, totems and spirits of the dead). I shall describe, first and very briefly, the physical environment and social structure, and second and in greater detail, religion. I shall then discuss the part played by religion in the natives' economic and social life, and its importance for understanding their epistemological system. The study is limited by two factors: cultural heterogeneity and the effects of European contact.

First, the Rai Coast terrain allows a high degree of local variation in dialect, custom, and belief. In the space available, such idiosyncrasies must be treated as of only secondary importance. Although they are not ignored entirely, the primary concern is with the fundamental homogeneity underlying all Ngaing religion. Even so, some of the available material has had to be omitted.

Second, Ngaing religion has been modified by administration and mission influence. The people were brought under political influence by the Germans by 1914 and full control by the Australians by 1936. This led to the complete suppression of warfare, cannibalism, and associated religious ceremonies. After 1923 the Rai Coast was subjected to pressure from the missions. Although the first arrivals, the Lutherans, quickly won over the beach peoples, the Ngaing (except in the inland Sibog region) resisted conversion for ten years. But after 1933 they formally adopted the Roman Catholic Mission (Society of the Divine Word), which had recently moved into the area. The Catholics seem to have acted with extreme caution and tolerance. Yet the effects of their work, and of the Japanese invasion and its aftermath, left their mark. By 1945 many of the younger generation knew little about traditional mythology and ritual.

During 1948, however, the Ngaing revolted against the Catholic Mission and made a determined effort to revive their religion.[2] This was five years before my first visit to the field. Thus, although some aspects were inevitably irrecoverable, I was able, by first-hand observation and from second-hand accounts given by reliable informants,[3] to record the people's most important religious beliefs and practices, and analyse the intellectual assumptions underlying them.

The Physical Environment and Social Structure

Ngaing territory is a series of sharp ridges which reach down from the Finisterres towards the sea, like the fingers of an outstretched hand, flattening out on the coastal plain. Between these ridges are deep gorges and swift-flowing rivers. Movement in the area is relatively easy along the ridges, which are trade routes linking the Ngaing to the peoples of the beach and Madang. The Ngaing exchange their betel nut, wooden bowls, and bark cloth for salt, fish, clay pots, Siasi beads, and other marine or overseas products.[4] Movement across the ridges, however, is very difficult. This probably accounts for the development of the wooden slit-gong not only as a musical instrument but also as an efficient means of communication. Each adult male has his personal call-sign, and elaborate messages can be sent over long distances in a short time.

The people's staple crops are taro, yams, bananas, sugar cane, sweet potatoes, and various types of indigenous green vegetables. The most important is taro, of which there are two main kinds—the "red" (*ḳapa*) and the "white" (*ḳaḳ*).[5] "Red" taro is grown in the central uplands of Ngaing territory. It is regarded as superior to "white" taro, which is planted in the area near the Coast and the hinterland of Sibog (inland Nankina region). Pigs, dogs, and fowls are domesticated in the settlements. There are various types of game —wild pig, marsupials, and birds—in the bush and grasslands. In the rivers there are fish and crustaceans.

Ngaing social structure is based on double unilineal descent. Four groups must be considered: the bush group (*masowa* or *mijowa*); the patriclan (*ya*); the patrilineage; and the totemic matriclan (*sapud* or *supud*). Each is described in turn.

Ngaing territory is divided into about twenty named bush areas. The inhabitants of each are a political unit and are here referred to collectively as a *bush group*. They maintain peaceful relations with each other, and combine for offense and defense. Except in two cases to be discussed later, they have a common war god. Bush groups are allied or linked in either of two ways: first, by formal trade relationships, which create permanent alliances between those inhabiting the same ridge; and second, by marriages between even hostile bush groups. In the past, these two factors governed traditional warfare. Fighting had to cut across the trade routes but its severity was often mitigated by interpersonal affinal and kinship ties.

Each bush group consists of a number of smaller named groups (*ya*). Each of these contains several unnamed patrilineages of shallow depth (from three to five generations). The *ya* can be described as a pseudopatriclan. Although individual membership is determined primarily by patrilineal descent, the component patrilineages themselves do not claim a further putative common ancestor. But in other ways they have the corporate identity of a patriclan.

The distinguishing characteristics of the patriclan are as follows: It is the basic unit of local organization. In the past, it formed either a settlement on its own or part of a settlement within its bush area. Nowadays these smaller settlements have come together as composite villages.[6] The patriclan is strictly exogamous. It has exclusive rights to a tract of land for cultivation and hunting, and to certain ritual property.

There are two kinds of ritual property: esoteric formulae; and that used in the main ceremonies honouring the dead. Esoteric formulae are of little significance in the present context. They are usually fairly uniform over wide areas, although occasionally a patriclan may claim rights to minor variations in the performance of a particular spell. Their content is described later on. Ritual property used for honouring the spirits of the dead, however, is extremely important for the social structure. In each settlement there is a central cult house (*tōta*), around which the dwelling houses are grouped. Each patriclan has sole rights over either the whole cult house (in a single patriclan settlement) or a section of it (in a multiclan settlement). It may decorate the end walls, or end wall of its section, with its own carved ornaments (*buyang* or *tōra*) and erect its own special bamboo poles (*silasila*) through the roof. It has its own slit-gong, gourd trumpets (*ḳanggut*) and sacred melodies (*nigul-ing-totō*), from the gong beats of which its members take their personal call-signs. Finally, it has its own sacred pool (*musurukteng* or *waiteng*), where its trumpets are washed and the spirits of its dead members invoked on ceremonial occasions.

Cutting across the patrilineal structure are a number of named totemic matriclans. The matriclan is a true clan, for its component matrilineages (again from three to five generations deep) recognize a common totemic ancestress (*sapud* or *supud*)—a bird, animal, plant, or other object.

The matriclan has little common property and cannot be defined in terms of group activity. In most cases, it has no joint possession other than its totem. (The only exceptions to this rule are the two bush groups Sor and Paramus, whose members do not claim war gods in their own areas but associate each of their totems with a war god of one of the neighbouring bush groups. They regard rights to these deities as part of matriclan inheritance.) Moreover, those belonging to a matriclan never assemble for any specific task. Because residence after marriage is normally viripatrilocal and a woman is the sole transmitter of the totem, they are always dispersed, often in different bush groups. The members of both patriclan and patrilineage are differentiated in terms of totemic allegiance.

Common recognition of the totem, however, imposes certain rules of behaviour. The matriclan is exogamous: a marriage between two of its members is said to result in death. A man should never maltreat or kill not only his own totem[7] but also other members of his matriclan, even if they belong to otherwise hostile bush groups. If a person knows that his totem[8] or one of his matriclan members has been killed, he must protect himself from evil by putting ginger to his nose. When someone has been killed, not only the members of his patriclan and bush group but also his matriclansmen elsewhere must be compensated. These dispersed totemic links are important in three ways. They guarantee a man protection when he is away from home. He may always call on individual matriclansmen for help in important activities. Finally, totemic relationships augment affinal and kinship ties which, as mentioned, used to limit violence in warfare.

Apart from food production, the most important events in social life are a series of ceremonial exchanges associated with marriage, birth, initiation and burial. A man must marry a true or classificatory cross-cousin—the daughter of a mother's brother who should be husband of a father's sister. Likewise, his male cross-cousins must marry his true or classificatory sisters. Marriage payments take the form of exchanges of pigs, food, and valuables (mainly dogs' teeth and Siasi beads) between the husband's patriclan and that of his affines (i.e., his mother's brothers and cross-cousins). These exchanges occur at least three times during the first six years of marriage.

The children of the marriage have important exchange relationships with their mother's brothers and father's sisters. A boy is initiated by his mother's brothers and the event is celebrated by an exchange between their respective patriclans. When a man dies, his initiatory services are reciprocated by his sisters' sons, who prepare his corpse for burial and later dispose of his bones. Thereafter there is an exchange between them and the sons of the dead man. Girls have similar relationships with their mothers-in-law and other fathers' sisters, who perform certain duties for them when they marry. The first marriage exchange is partly in recognition of this. When a woman dies, her daughters-in-law and other brothers' daughters reciprocate by preparing her corpse for burial. This is also the occasion for an exchange.

These exchanges are important for both social structure and religion. They periodically bring together many of a person's kinsmen. The close parallel between a man's relationships with his mother's brothers and a woman's with her father's sisters, in reciprocal services and prestation, stresses a dominant theme in Ngaing life: the recognition of near equality between the sexes. The exchanges are also invariably associated with ritual honouring the spirits of the dead, which is described later on.

It is in the context of the above structural form and important activities that leadership must be considered. There is no single political authority over the whole of Ngaing society but within each patriclan there are several important men (*eik̨ tandabi* or *eik̨ utiring*). These men are neither hereditary nor elected officials, nor do they have any true judicial authority. They achieve their positions by their own prowess—in warfare, agriculture, the organization of exchanges and so on—and by their monopoly of sacred knowledge. This also is discussed later on.

Religion

As stated, Ngaing religion can be defined as the people's beliefs about, and putative interaction with, the extrahuman beings thought to inhabit the physical environment—deities, totems, and spirits of the dead. I shall describe it from two points of view: first, beliefs which explain the origin of the traditional cosmos and the nature of life after death; and second, ritual which is assumed to establish contact between man and these extrahuman beings.

DEITIES AND TOTEMS: THE CREATION OF THE COSMOS

The beings said to be responsible for the origin of the cosmos are the deities (*tut*[9]) and totems (*sapud* or *supud*). As the totems are ordinary animals, birds, and plants existing in the visible world, no further description of their nature is necessary.

The nature of the deities, however, must receive some attention. Except in one case, which appears below, they are highly personalized. They are believed either always to have existed as deities or to have been originally men and women who became deities under special circumstances. They are conceived to be the same as human beings in one sense, having similar physical attributes and emotions, but different in another, having infinitely superior powers. Although normally human in form, they can turn into birds, animals, fish, or insects at will; and they can travel long distances and do things far beyond human capabilities. Yet they live on the earth with men, generally in their own special sanctuaries within striking distance of human settlements.

The Ngaing believe that their cosmos came into being in two stages: the emergence of the basic physical environment followed by that of human beings and their culture. For the first stage, when asked how their world began, the people reply: "Parambik put (*riring*) everything." By this they mean that Parambik "put" the earth, bush, mountains, rivers, wild animals, birds, and plants (including the totems), and the war gods in the bush areas. They make no mention of sun, moon or stars. Parambik is described as a god (*tut*) but, unlike the other deities, is said to be very remote. He is all-pervasive and has no fixed sanctuary. Even his name is merely the general word for myth. Although held responsible for the primary elements of the Ngaing cosmos, he is not thought to take further interest in it and no ritual is performed in association with him.[10]

For the second stage—the emergence of human beings and their culture—there are many explanatory myths (*parambik*). One set tells how men and women came into the world as the result of totemic births or transformations. Birds, animals and so on either brought forth human offspring or turned into human beings, and so founded the matriclans. Normally, all members (both male and female) of a matriclan know their own totemic myth, which is subject to no taboos. Children may learn it from either their mothers or any older matrilineal kinsmen.

Another set of myths tells how, more or less at the same time as the appearance of human beings, the deities created the important parts of the material culture. Bows and arrows were invented by the war gods of Gabumi and Saing, who passed on their knowledge to their followers and to war gods elsewhere. Slit-gongs, wooden bowls, and hand drums were created when two brothers felled a tree, which took wing and flew to another part of the country. When it fell to earth, different sections of it were used for making the abovementioned artefacts. It also scattered seeds of the trees from which they are made nowadays. The two brothers who felled the tree are regarded as the joint deities of the slit-gong. In the Aiyawang, Sindama and Sibog region—and also among the M'na and N'dau—myths describe how local deities discovered the art of making dogs' teeth and Siasi beads, which they send to human beings via the spirits of the dead. Again, in the inland region below the cloud belt, which often blots out the higher peaks of the Finisterres, there are elaborate myths explaining the origin of techniques for controlling the weather. In the area nearer the coast, however, there are no myths for the creation of valuables and those associated with weather control are little emphasized.

The most prominent myths are those for taro and other staple crops, pigs and the Male Cult ceremonies, and the bullroarer. The Ngaing have two taro myths. In the first, a woman called Meanderi invented taro, sugar cane, and other vital foodstuffs at Asang (west of Ngaing territory). These she secreted under her skin. In the guise of a hideous old crone she journeyed east through what is now the "red" taro belt—to Maibang, Kilang, Sereng, Saing, Gabumi, Aiyawang, Sindama and Sibog—intending to give her plants to the people of the inland Nankina region. But she was insulted there and returned in the direction from which she had come. To those along her route who had shown her kindness she gave her best crops, especially "red" taro, and all knowledge necessary for growing them. But the inland people who had insulted her and those near the coast, who lay off her route, (at Amun, Sor and Paramus) received only the inferior "white" taro.[11] Eventually Meanderi became a taro goddess and settled with the inhabitants of Wabing near Maibang, where she has her sanctuary today.

In the second myth, a man was transported to a cloud world above the earth, where he discovered "red" taro and other important crops. He married a daughter of the cloud people and later returned to earth with his wife, child, and the crops he had learnt to cultivate. He settled near Gabumi, where he passed on his knowledge to ordinary men and women, and where he and his wife are regarded as alternative joint taro deities. There are separate but similar myths for yams.

Pigs and the ceremonies of the Male Cult were invented by the deity Yabuling, whose sanctuary also is near Gabumi. Initially he created pigs and hence, by implication, the pig exchange. He then created the gourd trumpets used in the worship of the spirits of the dead. The women were the first to get hold of these trumpets and play them in a cult house, but they and their children defiled them with menstrual blood and excreta. They were supplanted by the men, who washed the trumpets and cleaned out the cult house. The men's music was infinitely superior. Thus men have exclusive rights over the trumpets, although adult women, because of the circumstances described, are allowed to know that they exist and that music is produced from them.[12] Women, however, may never see the trumpets.

There are at least two myths explaining the origin of the bullroarer. In the inland, it is said that Gab'me of Yakierak (N'dau) is its creator deity. He first placed a bullroarer in the netbag of an old woman. She tried various methods of whirling it but they all failed. Then her grandson was taught the secret by Gab'me in a dream. Hence women may see the bullroarer as a piece of black palm, without its rope attached, but may never see it whirled. In the coastal area, there is a different myth based on a different local deity.

The above deities are believed to have their sanctuaries in various places on the Rai Coast but their distribution has no great social or political significance. Except in the cases of Sor and Paramus, war gods are regarded as belonging exclusively to the inhabitants of the bush areas in which they reside, and are inherited patrilineally. Otherwise allegiance to deities does not correlate rigidly with group membership. Some myths and deities are common to all Ngaing—such as the Parambik creation myth, the first taro myth, and those for the slit-gong and the Male Cult. Others are more restricted—such as the second taro myth (which is known only in Gabumi, Saing and, to some extent, Aiyawang), the bullroarer myths for the inland and coastal areas, and the myths (which are found only in the inland) for dogs' teeth and Siasi beads. Again, rights to myths and deities can cut across linguistic borders. The inland bullroarer deity is believed to live in N'dau territory and the slit-gong deities outside Ngaing territory to the west. Meanderi originally came from Asang, west of Ngaing territory. In the same way, Yabuling is accepted as the inventor of the Male Cult ceremonies not only by the Ngaing but also by the M'na, N'dau and Neko, and nowadays even by the Sengam, Gira and Som.[13] But there is a recognized area to which each myth and deity belong. It is said that any attempt by outsiders to use religious secrets which they have not purchased formally—especially those associated with important ceremonial and economic undertakings (such as the secret names for Yabuling, Meanderi, the Cloud Man, the bullroarer deities, and the inland deities for Siasi beads and dogs' teeth)—are regarded as theft and met with strong opposition.

THE SPIRITS OF THE DEAD: LIFE AFTER DEATH

The spirits of the dead (*kabu* or *asapeng*) are not regarded as creators of any part of the culture but as the protectors of their living descendants. Their role as such is discussed in a later context. Here we are concerned only with their conceived nature and mode of existence.

The Ngaing do not distinguish terminologically between distant ancestors and spirits of the recently dead. They call both *kabu* or *asapeng* (which are only local dialectical variants). But they concentrate their interest almost exclusively on spirits of the recently dead: of men and women whom they can still place in their known genealogical structure. Although they admit that distant ancestors are able to intervene in human affairs, they dismiss the idea as quite improbable. They forget the names of individuals above the third (and very often the second) ascending generation and hence do not expect the spirits of such persons to show much concern for remote descendants. Nor do they conceive of a pool of generalized or undifferentiated ancestral spirit power. Distant ancestors, therefore, are ignored in the present account.

There are, however, two issues about which there is no uniformity of belief. First, some Ngaing claim that the breath (*kitang*) and shadow (*ananuang*) are manifestations of a living person's soul, which after death continues as an immaterial being unless it wishes to appear as a *kabu* or *asapeng*—that is, assume visible corporeal form as a human, bat, rat, snake, or glowworm. Others deny this belief. They claim that it is a Christian importation and that after death there is no immaterial soul but only a corporeal *kabu* or *asapeng,* which either remains invisible or assumes any of the forms listed above.

Second, there is no general agreement about where spirits live after death. Variations in belief correlate with differences in burial custom. In the past, bodies were left to rot in old slit-gongs or bamboo coffins. The bones were removed when dry. In some areas (Aiyawang and Sibog), they were placed in the sanctuary of the dead man's patrilineally inherited war god; in others (Gabumi and Saing), near his patriclan sacred pool, believed to be guarded by a minor deity; and in others (Sor and Paramus), somewhere on his hunting land, from which the spirit was thought to find its way to the sanctuary of its matriclan war god.

These differences of belief, however, are not of fundamental importance. The spirits are always associated with a deity of some kind, either a war god or the guardian of a sacred pool. They can be invoked at the sacred pools, even when they are not supposed to be living near them, and they are said to roam the bush and visit human settlements. They are seen by their living relatives, especially in dreams but also during waking hours. Furthermore, although their way of life is only vaguely conceived, they are invariably thought to be interested in material goods. In view of this, argument about the exact nature of the dead is largely academic. In the past, personal property was placed with the corpse for the spirit's use. Even now, whenever spirits are said to have practical dealings with the living, they are consistently described both as corporeal—with the normal human attributes of flesh, blood, bone and hair—and as wearing ordinary clothes and ornaments, and carrying ordinary tools and weapons. (From now on, therefore, the term *spirit* or *spirit of the dead* refers primarily to the *kabu* or *asapeng* conceived as a corporeal being.)

RITUAL: THE CONTROL OF THE COSMOS

In Ngaing ritual, the important beings are the deities (other than Parambik) and the spirits of the dead. The people believe that they can achieve full control over the world around them only by ensuring their support, although occasionally they use pure sympathetic magic as an alternative. The secrets of ritual are revealed to boys when they are initiated into the ceremonies of the Male Cult. The totems are unimportant in this context except for the purely protective ritual already mentioned.

Ritual to the Deities and Sympathetic Magic. The Ngaing say that during the creation of the culture each deity, either through a dream or personal association, gave human beings all the vital information about his or her particular invention. The deity taught both secular and ritual techniques of production. Ritual techniques (*pananak* or *mana*) involved two principles: the symbolic repetition of certain actions performed by the deity; and knowledge of an esoteric formula based on the secret name (*wawing buingna*) of the deity or of the part of the culture he or she introduced.

The distribution of rights to ritual correlates with that of the myth with which the ritual is associated. Thus ritual may be used in areas far distant from the sanctuary of the relevant deity. The members of each patriclan have rights to ritual for the following: warfare; manufacture of slit-gongs; bullroarers, and hunting; weather control; agriculture; pig-raising and Male Cult ceremonies; and sorcery. Inland groups, as noted, claim special ritual for dogs' teeth and Siasi beads.

Correct performance of ritual is assumed to grant automatic success in any important undertaking. The deity must give immediate aid unless the human operator bungles the formula. Ritual procedures are illustrated here for warfare, hunting, agriculture, and sorcery.

In the past, the leader of a raiding party took certain leaves from the sanctuary of his war god,[14] breathed a spell over them and fed them to his warriors, who also shouted the god's name as they attacked. This ensured that the deity would give them strength for battle.

The bullroarer is used mainly before hunting expeditions not associated with feasts in honour of the spirits of the dead. On these occasions, the leader breathes a spell over the bullroarer and whirls it in the bush, out of sight of women and children. The deity will drive the game towards the hunters. When the dead are to be honoured, the bullroarer is carried in a net bag as a hunting talisman but must never be whirled.

For agriculture there are three forms of ritual. They are used with extreme care in gardens planted specially for an exchange, although the procedure is more perfunctory for crops intended solely for household consumption. Only the full forms of the ritual are described.

The first form is associated with the Meanderi myth and is used in the "red" taro belt. The garden leader makes a shrine of stones (*sijik*) in his own plot. He then performs a purely magical act, rubbing a *galip* nut on the shrine and digging sticks so that its flavour will permeate the crops. He next plants outside the shrine an *atatagat* branch to symbolize the staff carried by Meanderi on her journey. Finally, he plants in or near the shrine shoots of the crops she gave to human beings. At the same time he silently breathes a spell to the goddess[15] and audibly invokes the spirits of departed kinsmen who worked the land in the past. (Their role is discussed later.) Occasionally food offerings are left at the shrine for the goddess and spirits, although this is not regarded as essential.

The second form of ritual is used in the areas where there is only the inferior "white" taro. Although people there regard Meanderi as the creator of both kinds of taro, they have never had her secret name for ritual purposes but only spells based on sympathetic magic. The visible ritual techniques are exactly the same as above but the silent spells are addressed to the mango and *galip* trees so that the crops will be as prolific as their fruit and nuts.

The third form of agricultural ritual is performed in Gabumi, Saing and Aiyawang on the basis of the second taro myth. Again, the visible ritual is much the same as described but the silent spells incorporate the secret names of the Cloud Man and his wife.

Finally, there are sorcery and love magic. They are exceptional in that they have no specific myths of origin. Moreover, although all Ngaing are aware of the techniques involved, they do not consider them of very great importance.[16] The techniques for both are based on sympathetic magic. Sorcery (*nayang*) is of a type very common in Papua and New Guinea. The sorcerer steals something which has been part of, or in contact with, his victim and either burns it or heats it over a fire according to whether he intends to cause death or illness. Similar procedures are used for love magic.

Ritual to the Spirits of the Dead. As the protectors of their living descendants, the spirits of the dead are regarded as extremely important in human affairs. They bring messages about the future, ward off illness, confer special benefits in warfare, hunting, and agriculture, and in the inland give presents of valuables. But their goodwill must be ensured by according them special honour.

Thus all mortuary ceremonies—attendance at a funeral, formal weeping, exchange of property, and disposal of the bones—are designed to show the spirit the sense of loss his relatives feel. Members of hunting and raiding parties, as well as performing the ritual already described, carry with them relics of departed relatives—a lock of hair and finger bone tied to a bullroarer, and the jawbone or skull. The spirits are offered food and invoked before the party sets off. They are thought to accompany their descendants into battle or to the hunt, deflecting enemy missiles or driving up plenty of game and seeing that their kinsmen's arrows reach the mark. Again, as mentioned, part of planting ritual is the invocation of, and offering of food to, the spirits. They are looked upon as the true guardians of the land they worked: they do not actually promote the growth of crops but protect them from disaster, mainly incursions of wild pig.

The spirits of the dead are specially honoured, however, during celebrations of the Male Cult: the Harvest Festival and the Kabu Ceremony. The Male Cult is governed by very strong taboos: women and uninitiated boys are prevented from seeing the inner secrets; the bullroarer may not be whirled but only carried as a hunting talisman; and those participating in the cult must maintain peaceful relations with their enemies or the spirits will be angry.

The Harvest Festival[17] takes place early in the year when the crops in the new gardens are ready for eating. The spirits of the dead, having helped to bring them to maturity, must be thanked. They are formally invited to the settlements and offered part of the first fruits.

In the late afternoon before the festival begins, the men of each patriclan go to their sacred pools, where they wash and decorate their gourd trumpets. They perform ritual to ensure that Yabuling and the deity of the pool[18] will send back the spirits of dead patriclan members, whom at the same time they invoke to follow them to the settlements. As soon as it is dark and they cannot be seen by the women and children, the men return home leading the spirits by playing their patriclan melodies on the trumpets. The appearance of glow-worms and bats is especially auspicious for they are assumed to be incarnations of the spirits.

The spirits are escorted to the cult house. As they enter, their personal call-signs are beaten out on the slit-gongs. Then specially cooked food—including meat and fish—is set out in bowls decorated with dogs' teeth and Siasi beads in each house. Each family head invites the spirits of his immediate patrilineal forebears to eat.

Absolute silence is maintained while the spirits eat and rest. The festival is resumed next day. There are exchanges of food between affines, cross-cousins, and any persons in each other's debt, and for several nights the spirits are kept in the cult house, where music is played in their honour. They are then escorted back to the sacred pools.

The Kabu Ceremony is more elaborate and of longer duration. It is celebrated during the dry season (April–November), when there is plenty of food in the gardens, in conjunction with the pig exchanges solemnizing marriage, birth, initiation, and death.

The ceremony begins when the parties to the exchange, each helped by the members of his patriclan, have assembled sufficient pigs, valuables, food, and game. Members of each group wash their trumpets and bring up their spirits to the settlement in exactly the same way as described above. They also decorate the cult house with their patriclan ornaments and some of the food to be distributed. In the meantime, the women and children remain in hiding. But when the work is finished, they are invited to inspect it.

During the first night of the spirits' appearance, a dance (*ola*) is held in the settlement, both men and women participating. It is concluded at daybreak, often with ritual to help fishermen. The trumpets used as musical accompaniment during the night are returned to the cult house so as not to be seen by the women and children. But the men of one team, wearing head-dresses of carved woden fish, continue to dance, while others from the opposite team shoot arrows at their head-dresses. Successful marksmanship is regarded as an omen that the spirits will ensure large catches of fish.

Thereafter the formal business of the exchange is conducted. Pigs are killed and cooked, and in the late afternoon the rest of the food to be distributed is assembled outside the cult house. After the exchange, the men eat in the cult house and the women either outside it or near their own homes.

Meanwhile, men not involved in the work of the exchange play trumpets and slit-gongs in the cult house. After people have eaten, the music is intensified. No food is offered the spirits at this time but pig fat is rubbed on the trumpets and slit-gongs to please them. From now on music is played every night from sunset to sunrise. Women and children, although debarred from the cult house, are expected to dance to this music outside. The music stops during the day and people are free to go to work. At this time also ritual is performed for the growth of pigs. Yabuling's secret name is breathed over a trumpet, which is played over a bowl of cooked food. This is given the pigs to eat.

The Kabu ceremony concludes with a final dance in the settlement. Early next morning the men escort the spirits back to the sacred pools. In the past, the whole ceremony could last as long as three months, additional exchanges between different principals being held during that period. Today, however, the administration has limited its duration to a month.[19]

Birth and Initiatory Ceremonies. Special ritual for the welfare of human beings is performed at the times of the first and second marriage exchanges and, for males, during initiation into ceremonies honouring the spirits of the dead.

Girls are prepared for marriage during their first menstruation. They are tended by their mothers-in-law and other fathers' sisters, who teach them general marital duties, a few minor garden spells, and probably methods of abortion.[20] They are now told that the music in the cult house is not the voices of the spirits (as they have been led to believe hitherto) but is produced by the men on trumpets and slit-gongs.

The first marriage exchange takes place when a girl has completed her first menstruation and goes to live with her husband, and the second when she has given birth to her first child. On these occasions, the bride or mother and child stand over a fire built under green mango leaves, and are later showered with sparks. The strength of fire and smoke is supposed to enter the woman's breasts and so benefit her children. Together with some of her own and her husband's relatives, she helps break up a green tree trunk so that her children's joints may be supple. Finally, in the Sor, Paramus and Amun area, when the first child is a male, the mother stands with it behind a wooden shield, into which her own and her husband's kinsmen, dressed in war regalia and shouting war god names, shoot their arrows. This is supposed to help the boy become a great warrior. (In the above ceremonies, kinsmen of both husband and wife are always expected to take part.)

Initiation for males takes place in either late childhood or early adolescence.[21] The ceremony is conducted as follows: First, the boys' fathers and maternal uncles bring up their respective patriclan spirits to the cult house of the boys' settlement. Second, the boys are shown the sacred instruments and taught the Yabuling myth by their mothers' brothers. Third, they are segregated for about a month and taught to play the sacred instruments. They are also given a symbolic beating by their mothers' brothers. Fourth, in Amun only, the mothers' brothers perform the operation of penile supraincision on the novices. Other Ngaing settlements do not have this custom, which belongs properly to the peoples of the beach.[22] At the end of the month's segregation, the boys are dressed in fine ornaments and formally presented to the women. Thereafter exchanges are carried out between the patriclans of the novices and those of their mothers' brothers. The spirits are honoured in the usual way.

The ceremony has two aims: first, it is supposed to ensure that the novices become healthy and attract wives. The symbolic beating and, in Amun, the act of penile supraincision give them strength. They are now also under the special protection of the spirits of the dead. Second, it is a period of education. During the month of segregation the boys observe rigid taboos on washing, food cooked in water, and various types of meat. They eat only dry taro, either roasted or cooked in bamboo containers, and a little sugar cane. The taboos are essential for learning not only the secrets of the Male Cult but also the other aspects of religion described. The novices are now introduced to the myths and especially the ritual to which their patriclans have rights. If they ignore the taboos, the teaching will be useless and even dangerous. They will never use the spells successfully, and they will be afflicted with boils and other illnesses should they attempt to use them. When their training is extended into later life, they have to observe the taboos again for their own protection. Those who show the greatest ability in learning, and the greatest prowess in using, the ritual eventually become leaders. Those novices who do not undergo longer periods of training for leadership know their patriclan mythology, the Yabuling myth and the elements of the associated ritual, but never become expert practitioners.

We may summarize the respective importance of men and women in religion thus: Under normal conditions, all adult males have a wide knowledge of mythology (their matriclan totemic myths and those to which they have title through their patriclans) and of the principles underlying the esoteric techniques used by their leaders. They also play a full part in the Male Cult. Women know only their matriclan totemic myths and the special ritual taught them before marriage; and they participate only in the external ceremonies of the Male Cult.

The Meaning of Ngaing Religion

Ngaing religion is analysed from two points of view: its social function and the intellectual assumptions underlying it. The first involves only the objective view of the outside observer. The second involves also the subjective view of the people themselves.

SOCIAL FUNCTION

In this context, we consider the general hypothesis that religion validates and reinforces the cosmic order by means of myth (explanation) and ritual (control or manipulation), and that the degree to which it is used for either of these purposes reflects the value people attach to, or the anxiety they feel about, various aspects of their way of life. From the foregoing account, it can be seen that in Ngaing religion the emphasis on mythology and ritual is uneven. This is illustrated by examining the relationship between religion, on the one hand, and the physical environment, economic resources and the social structure, on the other.

The overall physical environment receives very little attention. The heavenly bodies are completely ignored. The Ngaing feel no need to account for their existence as they are not a seafaring people. Again, the origin of the earth is dismissed in a sentence and no ritual is performed for its continuance. The earth is regarded as changeless: it can be taken for granted.

Economic resources, however, are very heavily emphasized. Their origin is explained in a most detailed mythology. Furthermore, their continuance and exploitation cannot be left to chance. This is an obvious cause of anxiety. Hence ritual must be performed to ensure that gods and spirits protect crops from danger and bring them to maturity; make fish and game abundant; make slit-gongs sound the right note; and so on. Again, the degree of anxiety, and hence of elaboration of ritual, varies according to the degree of hazard and need in any situation. For instance, crops planted specially for an exchange are more carefully protected by ritual than those intended only for household consumption. In the inland, where climatic conditions are uncertain, weather ritual is more important than on the coast, where they are more stable. In the inland also, where the flow of marine valuables can fail to meet the demand, the people claim to make good the deficiency by means of special ritual, which the coastal Ngaing, being nearer the source of actual supply, do not possess.

The relationship between Ngaing religion and society is more complex. There is no single myth explaining the origin of the structure in its totality. This is satisfactory for a people who, like others in the Madang District, do not conceive that there can be forms of society other than their own. They take its overall pattern for granted.[23] Furthermore, there is little correlation between allegiance to deities and group membership.

This does not mean, however, that there is no recognition that key parts of the social structure must be validated and reinforced. Thus, in the first place, some myths explain the origin of separate aspects of the total system. Parambik created the war gods, in most cases the symbols of the bush groups. Each totemic myth accounts for a dispersed matriclan and hence important relationships between patrilocal groups. Yabuling, by creating pigs and gourd trumpets, indirectly validated important groups and relationships within the structure: the patriclan, the group which cooperates in the Male Cult ceremonies; the affinal and kinship relationships which provide the framework for exchanges solemnizing marriage, birth, initiation, and death; and the recognition of near equality between the sexes. The Yabuling myth subtly reflects the limited but real participation of women in the Male Cult. In the myth, women were the first to use the trumpets and were forced to surrender them only because they defiled them with menstrual blood. In real life, although they may never see the trumpets, adult women are allowed to know of their existence; they are an integral part of the dance (*ola*) team; and they dance in the settlement while the men play music in the cult house.[24] Again, they must always be invited to inspect the cult house after it has been decorated.

In the second place, ritual directly or indirectly reinforces the structure at its weakest points. The health and fertility of human beings generally are guaranteed by birth and initiatory ceremonies. Localized groups are maintained and perpetuated by means of ritual: the bush group by war ritual and sorcery; and the patriclan by joint rights to ritual property and cooperation in the work of honouring the spirits of the dead. A man's ties with other members of his matriclan are stressed when he receives initiatory services from, and performs mortuary services for, his mother's brothers. He and they are reminded of their common totemic allegiance. Cross-cutting relationships between patriclan and patriclan within the bush group, and between bush group and bush group within the wider structure, are strengthened by the emphasis on cooperation between husband's and wife's kin in birth ceremonies, the necessity of avoiding conflict during celebrations of the Male Cult, and the reciprocal and equivalent duties between mothers' brothers and sisters' sons, and fathers' sisters, and brothers' daughters, in initiatory, menstrual, and mortuary rites.

INTELLECTUAL ASSUMPTIONS[25]

Within the Ngaing epistemological system, we may define two broad categories of knowledge: secular or empirical knowledge, which is actually possessed; and sacred knowledge, which has no empirical foundation but is believed to have been revealed by the deities.

In relation to the resources at their disposal, the Ngaing have accumulated a modest but sound body of secular knowledge, which they use with considerable efficiency. This is exemplified by their practical knowledge of agriculture, and their skill in the manufacture and use of the slit-gong as a means of communication. Using our own analytical concepts, we may say that this knowledge is the result of human endeavour. For what it is worth, it is the people's own intellectual achievement.

The Ngaing themselves, however, do not interpret and evaluate their secular knowledge in this way. Except in minor matters, they dismiss the principle of human intellectual discovery. All the most valued parts of their culture are believed to have been invented by the deities, who taught men not only the ritual but also the empirical techniques for utilizing them. Thus in the two taro myths, Meanderi and the Cloud Man actually showed men how to plant crops (secular knowledge) and to perform the proper ritual (sacred knowledge). It was the bullroarer deity who placed the sacred instrument in the old woman's net-bag but prevented her from finding the right method of whirling it. He gave this knowledge to her grandson as well as teaching him the relevant esoteric formulae.

This concept of revelation by deities dominates all discussions about knowledge. Even pure sympathetic magic is explained in this way. Birth ceremonies, because of their emphasis on strength and prowess in battle, are said to have been invented by the war gods. Sorcery and love magic, which have no myths of origin and are regarded as of little importance, and the ordinary sympathetic techniques used for agricultural ritual at Sor, Paramus, and Amun are conveniently ignored in general conversation. But when challenged, the people attribute their existence to Parambik.

Furthermore, not only is the whole complex of knowledge believed to be derived from the gods but also within the complex it is sacred knowledge that is emphasized as paramount. Secular techniques are, indeed, described as *knowing,* but only at a very elementary level—as something which, given time, everyone can assimilate. The hard core of knowledge is regarded as the mastery of esoteric formulae and symbolic actions associated with them. This can be seen in the traditional processes of education and in leadership.

In the first place, by Western standards, a boy's upbringing is very informal. After an initial period of instruction in basic social usages, he is left to do much as he pleases. He is frequently indulged and rarely disciplined. Many of his amusements at this time, however, are directly imitative of his elders' activities: mock dancing, hunting expeditions, football games, and so on. Often, out of boredom, he accompanies his parents to work in the gardens, at a house site or elewhere, and copies them in what they are doing. He is never discouraged and, as he grows older, comes to be accepted as a member of adult work teams. By the time he has reached adolescence, with a minimum of formal instruction, he has mastered a large part of the secular knowledge of his society.

This, however, is not rated as a high intellectual achievement. True knowledge is acquired only during and after initiation. But what a boy learns at this time has little to do with secular techniques. He is introduced to mythology and ritual: the knowledge which guarantees help from the deities and spirits of the dead, and mastery over occult forces.

In the second place, although personal pre-eminence in important activities is the cornerstone of leadership, it is derived from the mastery of sacred rather than secular skills. The leaders are those who are believed able to ensure success by the performance of ritual. They are the men who *know.* They can direct the activities of others—those who do *not know*—to the best possible advantage. Physical inferiority and temporary poverty are not necessarily handicaps. Attainment of the position depends primarily on talent and patience to learn, and courage to accept responsibility. Otherwise the greatest obstacle is failure in an undertaking because of unforeseen circumstances. Thus in any set of novices, factors of ability, personality, and chance eliminate all but the steadfast and lucky. In each generation, such men are relatively few. There are normally no more than one or two leaders in each patriclan so that rivalry tends to limit the geographical and social range of their influence. But there is no feeling that membership in one group completely precludes following the leader of another. A really energetic man, whose consistent success has demonstrated his complete mastery of sacred knowledge, may attract followers from outside his own patriclan. They may join him because they have no leaders of their own or even because of his obvious superiority over those whom they have.[26]

This predilection for sacred knowledge might suggest a high degree of mysticism in Ngaing thinking. But this would be an interpretation in Western terms. In fact, Ngaing thinking is extremely mundane, as can be seen by reconsidering the spatial and temporal dimensions of their cosmos.

The Ngaing are typical of those nonliterate peoples who, as Bidney (1949: 333) has pointed out, make no distinction between the realms of what we call the natural and supernatural. Gods and spirits are human in character and emotions, and are part of the ordinary physical world. Man sees himself as the focal point of the two systems of relationships described: between himself and other human beings, and between himself and gods and spirits.

The pragmatic quality of both systems of relationships is understood and expressed in roughly the same terms. A man fulfils his social obligations in order to make other persons with whom he has human relationships "think on him" (*inahok ra-*) and fulfil their obligations towards him in their turn. Similarly, the aim of ritual is to make deities and spirits "think on" human beings and confer benefits on them.[27] But the activities of gods and spirits in helping mankind have no mystical quality. They are believed to take place on the same plane of existence and are, therefore, just as real as those of human beings working together at any joint task. Thus although the Ngaing regard work in any important undertaking as a compound of secular and ritual techniques, they assume that both have the same validity. Both derive from the same source (the deities) and both involve cooperation between beings who inhabit the same geographical environment.[28]

In its temporal dimensions, the cosmic order is conceived as essentially fixed and static. There is no historical tradition. Adapting Evans-Pritchard's terms (Evans-Pritchard 1940:94), we may define two kinds of time: ecological time and cosmic time. The former represents the annual succession of the seasons but has no real chronological utility. Time depth can be measured only in relation to the recognized age of the cosmos. Thus cosmic time may be regarded as known genealogical time plus the period of antiquity: the period of the emergence of the physical environment, totemic ancestors, human beings, and their culture.

Even cosmic time, however, has little chronological utility. The depth of empirically recordable genealogies is not only very shallow (no more than five generations even when informants' children are included) but also kept more or less constant. With each new generation distant forebears are forgotten. The period of antiquity is in a sense timeless: there is no clear concept of any order of creation. Although the basic physical environment is assumed to have come into being at the very beginning, thereafter no one event is described as having preceded another. Food plants, artefacts, domesticated animals, ceremonies, and human beings emerged at random.[29]

Again, not only the overall mythology but also the individual myths reflect the absence of the concept of time depth. There is no tradition of a gradual advance from a rudimentary to a more elaborate way of life. This can be seen in two ways. First, each part of the culture is described at the time of its invention in exactly the same form as it is now. Second, each myth depicts the people's culture during the period of antiquity as quite recognizably up to date and complete except for that part of it the relevant deity has to introduce and explain. In short, the way of life of antiquity is the way of life of today and will be the way of life of tomorrow as well. Therefore, the relationships between men, gods, and spirits within the cosmos are finally established: all have their unalterable roles to play towards each other.

By the same token, the body of knowledge, as the people see it, is as static and finite as the cosmic order within which it is contained. It was brought into the world ready made and ready to use. It can be augmented only by further acts of revelation by old or new deities. Moreover, it is hardly surprising that the epistemological system has fossilized in this way. The religion is intellectually satisfying for it operates within a framework which normally guarantees its validity. Because of the relatively monotonous repetition of economic and social life, there is hardly any event which cannot be explained by or attributed to it. The whole visible world—the annually ripening crops, and the fertility of pigs and human beings—far from allowing it an aura of mysticism, proclaims that it is solidly based on empirical fact. There is no need—indeed, no room—for an independent human intellect.

Conclusion

The material presented can be summed up as follows: The Ngaing see their cosmos as an integrated physical whole, in which the existence of gods, spirits of the dead and totems is real in exactly the same sense as that of human beings and animals. Religion—man's beliefs about, and conceived interaction with, gods, spirits, and totems—can be interpreted in two ways. From the outside objective point of view, it is a system which validates the cosmic order. From the people's own subjective point of view, it provides a body of knowledge which completely overshadows the principle of human intellectual inquiry and is regarded as absolutely reliable for explaining the existence of the cosmos and controlling its affairs. The criterion of true knowledge is the mastery of ritual, which is rendered effective by the observance of taboos and which ensures for men beneficial relationships with gods, spirits, and totems. This is the basis of leadership.

From either point of view, however, Ngaing religion does not represent a fully worked out system. It is not concerned equally and impartially with all aspects of the cosmos but only with those of primary and practical importance. It is essentially a working religion. Whatever the people regard as changeless (the basic physical environment and the overall form of the social structure) and whatever does not impinge on their way of life (the sun, moon, and stars), they either gloss over or ignore. They feel no need of detailed knowledge by which to explain and control these things. Religious belief and action are elaborated only for those parts of the culture which cause anxiety: affairs in which there is a considerable degree of risk, in which setbacks cause social disruption and of which, therefore, man must satisfy himself that he has complete understanding. Thus the themes which the religion emphasizes most clearly and consistently are the successful exploitation of economic resources, the acquisition of scarce valuables, the welfare of human beings and pigs, and the strengthening of specific relationships vital for the continuance of society.

Nevertheless, in spite of this limitation of intellectual interest, the attitudes and assumptions underlying Ngaing religion are very tenacious and can be adapted to suit new situations. Fifty years of European contact (direct and indirect) have made virtually no impression on them. During this period the two main changes in the people's way of life have been the importation of steel tools and cotton cloth, and the introduction of Christianity. In common with other peoples of the southern Madang District, the Ngaing reacted to the changes in terms of their traditional values and concepts. Dominant themes similar to those already described emerged in their new way of life. European goods were highly valued. They were a great cause of anxiety: the people wanted larger supplies than those which they enjoyed. But being ignorant of the processes by which these goods were made, they again interpreted their source in terms of creation by a deity and their acquisition in terms of ritual. God and the spirits of the dead in Heaven made the new wealth. Church services, rendered effective by the observance of new taboos (against polygyny and sorcery), would guarantee delivery. Furthermore, as Heaven was believed to be in Australia, the cosmos, although enlarged, still retained its essential physical unity. Dealings between God and man were believed to have a completely pragmatic reality.

The interest in Christianity, however, did not mean the elimination of the old gods. They remained powerful in their own sphere (the traditional culture). Thus when it was recognized that Christianity would not bring them the new wealth, the Ngaing were able to revert to their own religion with a minimum of intellectual dislocation. Although some secrets had been forgotten, the fundamental attitudes and assumptions were unimpaired. It was only a matter of reinstating old gods who had been temporarily neglected. This subject has been analysed more fully in a separate publication.[30]

CHAPTER

22

The Dreaming

W. E. H. STANNER

I

The blackfellow's outlook on the universe and man is shaped by a remarkable conception, which Spencer and Gillen immortalised as "the dream time" or *alcheringa* of the Arunta or Aranda tribe. Some anthropologists have called it The Eternal Dream Time. I prefer to call it what the blacks call it in English—The Dreaming, or just Dreaming.

A central meaning of The Dreaming *is* that of a sacred, heroic time long long ago when man and nature came to be as they are; but neither "time" nor "history" as we understand them is involved in this meaning. I have never been able to discover any aboriginal word for *time* as an abstract concept. And the sense of "history" is wholly alien here. We shall not understand The Dreaming fully except as a complex of meanings. A blackfellow may call his totem, or the place from which his spirit came, his Dreaming. He may also explain the existence of a custom, or a law of life, as causally due to The Dreaming.

A concept so impalpable and subtle naturally suffers badly by translation into our dry and abstract language. The blacks sense this difficulty. I can recall one intelligent old man who said to me, with a cadence almost as though he had been speaking verse:

White man got no dreaming,
Him go 'nother way.
White man, him go different,
Him got road belong himself.

In their own dialects, they use terms like *alcheringa, mipuramibirina, boaradja*—often almost untranslatable, or meaning literally something like "men of old." It is as difficult to be sure of the objective effects of the idea on their lives as of its subjective implications for them.

Although, as I have said, The Dreaming conjures up the notion of a sacred, heroic time of the indefinitely remote

From *Australian Signpost,* T. A. G. Hungerford, ed. Melbourne: F. W. Cheshire Publishing Pty, Ltd., 1956, pp. 51–65. By permission of the author and publisher.

past, such a time is also, in a sense, still part of the present. One cannot "fix" The Dreaming *in* time: it was, and is, everywhen. We should be very wrong to try to read into it the idea of a Golden Age, or a Garden of Eden, though it was an Age of Heroes, when the ancestors did marvellous things that men can no longer do. The blacks are not at all insensitive to Mary Webb's "wistfulness that is the past," but they do not, in aversion from present or future, look back on it with yearning and nostalgia. Yet it has for them an unchallengeably sacred authority.

Clearly, The Dreaming is many things in one. Among them, a kind of narrative of things that once happened; a kind of charter of things that still happen; and a kind of *logos* or principle of order transcending everything significant for aboriginal man. If I am correct in saying so, it is much more complex philosophically than we have so far realised. I greatly hope that artists and men of letters who (it seems increasingly) find inspiration in aboriginal Australia will use all their gifts of empathy, but avoid banal projection and subjectivism, if they seek to borrow the notion.

Why the blackfellow thinks of "dreaming" as the nearest equivalent in English is a puzzle. It may be because it is by *the act* of dreaming, as reality and symbol, that the aboriginal mind makes contact—thinks it makes contact—with whatever mystery it is that connects The Dreaming and the Here-and-Now.

II

How shall one deal with so subtle a conception? One has two options: educe its subjective logic and rationale from the "elements" which the blackfellow stumblingly offers in trying to give an explanation; or relate, as best one may, to things familiar in our own intellectual history, the objective figure it traces on their social life. There are dangers in both courses.

The first is a matter, so to speak, of learning to "think black," not imposing Western categories of understanding, but seeking to conceive of things as the blackfellow himself does.

In our modern understanding, we tend to see "mind" and "body," "body" and "spirit," "spirit" and "personality," "personality" and "name" as in some sense separate, even opposed, entities though we manage to connect them up in some fashion into the unity or oneness of "person" or "individual." The blackfellow does not seem to think this way. The distinctiveness we give to "mind," "spirit," and "body," and our contrast of "body" *versus* "spirit" are not there, and the whole notion of "the person" is enlarged. To a blackfellow, a man's name, spirit, and shadow are "him" in a sense which to us may seem passing strange. One should not ask a blackfellow: "What is your name?" To do so embarrasses and shames him. The name is like an intimate part of the body, with which another person does not take liberties. The blacks do not mind talking about a dead person in an oblique way but, for a long time, they are extremely reluctant even to breathe his name. In the same way, to threaten a man's shadow is to threaten him. Nor may one treat lightly the physical place from which his spirit came. By extension, his totem, which is also associated with that place, and with his spirit, should not be lightly treated.

In such a context one has not succeeded in "thinking black" until one's mind can, without intellectual struggle, enfold into some kind of oneness the notions of body, spirit, ghost, shadow, name, spirit-site, and totem. To say so may seem a contradiction, or suggest a paradox, for the blackfellow can and does, on some occasions, conceptually isolate the "elements" of the "unity" most distinctly. But his abstractions do not put him at war with himself. The separable elements I have mentioned are all present in the metaphysical heart of the idea of "person," but the overruling mood is one of belief, not of inquiry or dissent. So long as the belief in The Dreaming lasts, there can be no "momentary flash of Athenian questioning" to grow into a great movement of sceptical unbelief which destroys the given unities.

There are many other such "onenesses" which I believe I could substantiate. A blackfellow may "see" as "a unity" two persons, such as two siblings or a grandparent and grandchild; or a living man and something inanimate, as when he tells you that, say, the woolybutt tree, his totem, is his wife's brother. (This is not quite as strange as it may seem. Even modern psychologists tend to include part of "environment" in a "definition" of "person" or "personality.") There is also some kind of unity between waking-life and dream-life: the means by which, in aboriginal understanding, a man fathers a child, is not by sexual intercourse, but by the act of dreaming about a spirit-child. His own spirit, during a dream, "finds" a child and directs it to his wife, who then conceives. Physical congress between a man and a woman is contingent, not a necessary prerequisite. Through the medium of dream-contact with a spirit an artist is inspired to produce a new song. It is by dreaming that a man divines the intention of someone to kill him by sorcery, or of relatives to visit him. And, as I have suggested, it is by the act of dreaming, in some way difficult for a European to grasp because of the force of our analytic abstractions, that a blackfellow conceives himself to make touch with whatever it is that is continuous between The Dreaming and the Here-and-Now.

The truth of it seems to be that man, society and nature, and past, present and future, are at one together within a unitary system of such a kind that its ontology cannot illumine minds too much under the influence of humanism, rationalism and science. One cannot easily, in the mobility of modern life and thought, grasp the vast intuitions of stability and permanence, and of life and man, at the heart of aboriginal ontology.

It is fatally easy for Europeans, encountering such things for the first time, to go on to suppose that "mysticism" of this kind rules *all* aboriginal thought. It is not so. "Logical" thought and "rational" conduct are about as widely present in aboriginal life as they are on the simpler levels of European life. Once one understands three things—the primary intuitions which the blackfellow has formed about the nature of the universe and man, those things in both which he thinks interesting and significant, and the conceptual system from within which he reasons about them, then the suppositions about prelogicality, illogicality, and nonrationality can be seen to be merely absurd. And if one wishes to see a really brilliant demonstration of deductive thought, one has only to see a blackfellow tracking a wounded kangaroo, and persuade him to say why he interprets given signs in a certain way.

The second means of dealing with the notion of The Dreaming is, as I said, to try to relate it to things familiar in our own intellectual history. From this viewpoint, it is a cosmogony, an account of the begetting of the universe, a story about creation. It is also a cosmology, an account or theory of how what was created became an orderly system. To be more precise, it is a theory of how the universe became a moral system.

If one analyses the hundreds of tales about The Dreaming, one can see within them three elements. The first concerns the great *marvels*—how all the fire and water in the world were stolen and recaptured; how men made a mistake over sorcery and now have to die from it; how the hills, rivers, and waterholes were made; how the sun, moon and stars were set upon their courses; and many other dramas of this kind. The second element tells how certain things were *instituted* for the first time—how animals and men diverged from a joint stock that was neither one nor the other; how the blacknosed kangaroo got his black nose and the porcupine his quills; how such social divisions as tribes, clans and language groups were set up; how spirit-children were first placed in the waterholes, the winds and the leaves of trees. A third element, if I am not mistaken, allows one to suppose that many of the main institutions of present-day life were *already ruling* in The Dreaming, e.g., marriage, exogamy, sister-exchange, and initiation, as well as many of the well-known breaches of custom. The men of The Dreaming committed adultery, betrayed and killed each other, were greedy, stole, and committed the very wrongs committed by those now alive.

Now, if one disregards the imagery in which the verbal literature of The Dreaming is cast, one may perhaps come to three conclusions.

The tales are a kind of commentary, or statement, on what is thought to be permanent and ordained at the very basis of the world and life. They are a way of stating the principle which animates things. I would call them a poetic key to Reality. The aborigine does not ask himself the philosophical-type questions: What is "real"? How many "kinds" of "reality" are there? What are the "properties" of "reality"? How are the properties "interconnected"? This is the idiom of Western intellectual discourse and the fruit of a certain social history. His tales are, however, a kind of answer to such questions so far as they have been asked at all. They may not be a "definition," but they are a "key" to reality, a key to the singleness and the plurality of things set up once-for-all when, in The Dreaming, the universe became man's universe. The active philosophy of aboriginal life transforms this "key," which is expressed in the idiom of poetry, drama, and symbolism, into a principle that The Dreaming determines not only what life *is* but also *what it can be*. Life, so to speak, is a one-possibility thing, and what this is, is the "meaning" of The Dreaming.

The tales are also a collation of *what is validly known* about such ordained permanencies. The blacks cite The Dreaming as a charter of absolute validity in answer to all questions of *why* and *how*. In this sense, the tales can be regarded as being, perhaps not a definition, but a "key" of Truth.

They also state, by their constant

recitation of what was done rightly and wrongly in The Dreaming, the ways in which good men should, and bad men will, act now. In this sense, they are a "key" or guide to the norms of conduct, and a prediction of how men will err.

One may thus say that, after a fashion —a cryptic, symbolic, and poetic fashion—the tales are "a philosophy" in the garb of a verbal literature. The European has a philosophic literature which expresses a largely deductive understanding of reality, truth, goodness, and beauty. The blackfellow has a mythology, a ritual, and an art which express an intuitive, visionary and poetic understanding of the same ultimates. In following out The Dreaming, the blackfellow "lives" this philosophy. It is an implicit philosophy, but nevertheless a real one. Whereas we hold (and may live) a philosophy of abstract propositions, attained by someone standing professionally outside "life" and treating it as an object of contemplation and inquiry, the blackfellow holds his philosophy in mythology, attained as the social product of an indefinitely ancient past, and proceeds to live it out "in" life, in part through a ritual and an expressive art, and in part through nonsacred social customs.

European minds are made uneasy by the facts that the stories are, quite plainly, preposterous; are often a mass of internal contradictions; are encrusted by superstitious fancies about magic, sorcery, hobgoblins, and superhuman heroes; and lack the kind of theme and structure—in other words, the "story" element—for which we look. Many of us cannot help feeling that such things can only be the products of absurdly ignorant credulity and a lower order of mentality. This is to fall victim to a facile fallacy. Our own intellectual history is not an absolute standard by which to judge others. The worst imperialisms are those of preconception.

Custom is the reality, beliefs but the shadows which custom makes on the wall. Since the tales, in any case, are not really "explanatory" in purpose or function, they naturally lack logic, system and completeness. It is simply pointless to look for such things within them. But we are not entitled to suppose that, because the tales are fantastical, the social life producing them is itself fantastical. The shape of reality is always distorted in the shadows it throws. One finds much logic, system, and rationality in the blacks' actual scheme of life.

These tales are neither simply illustrative nor simply explanatory; they are fanciful and poetic in content because they are based on visionary and intuitive insights into mysteries; and, if we are ever to understand them, we must always take them in their complex context. If, then, they make more sense to the poet, the artist, and the philosopher, than to the clinicians of human life, let us reflect on the withering effect on sensibility of our pervasive rationalism, rather than depreciate the gifts which produced the aboriginal imaginings. And in no case should we expect the tales, *prima facie,* to be even interesting if studied out of context. Aboriginal mythology is quite unlike the Scandinavian, Indian, or Polynesian mythologies.

III

In my own understanding, The Dreaming is a proof that the blackfellow shares with us two abilities which have largely made human history what it is.

The first of these we might call "the metaphysical gift." I mean the ability to transcend oneself, to make acts of imagination so that one can stand "outside" or "away from" oneself, and turn the universe, oneself and one's fellows into objects of contemplation. The second ability is a "drive" to try to "make sense" out of human experience and to find some "principle" in the whole human situation. This "drive" is, in some way, built into the constitution of the human mind. No one who has real knowledge of aboriginal life can have any doubt that they possess, and use, both abilities very much as we do. They differ from us only in the directions in which they turn their gifts, the idiom in which they express them, and the principles of intellectual control.

The blacks have no gods, just or unjust, to adjudicate the world. Not even by straining can one see in such culture heroes as Baiame and Darumulum the true hint of a Yahveh, jealous, omniscient, and omnipotent. The ethical insights are dim and somewhat coarse in texture. One can find in them little trace, say, of the inverted pride, the self-scrutiny, and the consciousness of favour and destiny which characterised the early Jews. A glimpse, but no truly poignant sense, of moral dualism; no notion of grace or redemption; no whisper of inner peace and reconcilement; no problems of worldly life to be solved only by a consummation of history; no heaven of reward or hell of punishment. The blackfellow's afterlife is but a shadowy replica of worldly life, so none flee to inner sanctuary to escape the world. There are no prophets, saints or *illuminati*. There is a concept of goodness, but it lacks true scruple. Men can become ritually unclean, but may be cleansed by a simple mechanism. There is a moral law but, as in the beginning, men are both good and bad, and no one is racked by the knowledge. I imagine there could never have been an aboriginal Ezekiel, any more than there could have been a Job. The two sets of insights cannot easily be compared, but it is plain that their underlying moods are wholly unlike, and their store of meaningfulness very uneven. In the one there seem an almost endless possibility of growth, and a mood of censoriousness and pessimism. In the other, a kind of standstill, and a mood which is neither tragic nor optimistic. The aborigines are not shamed or inspired by a religious thesis of what men might become by faith and grace. Their metaphysic assents, without brooding or challenge, to what men evidently have to be because the terms of life are cast. Yet they have a kind of religiosity cryptically displayed in their magical awareness of nature, in their complex totemism, ritual and art, and perhaps too even in their intricately ordered life.

They are, of course, nomads—hunters and foragers who grow nothing, build nothing, and stay nowhere long. They make almost no physical mark on the environment. Even in areas which are still inhabited, it takes a knowledgeable eye to detect their recent presence. Within a matter of weeks, the roughly cleared camp-sites may be erased by sun, rain, and wind. After a year or two there may be nothing to suggest that the country was ever inhabited. Until one stumbles on a few old flint-tools, a stone quarry, a shell-midden, a rock painting, or something of the kind, one may think the land had never known the touch of man.

They neither dominate their environment nor seek to change it. "Children of nature" they are not, nor are they nature's masters." One can only say they are "at one" with nature. The whole ecological principle of their life might be summed up in the Baconian aphorism—*natura von vincitur nisi parendo*: "nature is not to be commanded except by obeying." Naturally, one finds metaphysical and social reflections of the fact.

They move about, carrying their scant possessions, in small bands of anything from ten to sixty persons. Each band belongs to a given locality. A number of bands—anything from three or four up to twelve or fifteen, depending on the fertility of the area—make up a "tribe." A tribe is usually a language or dialect group which thinks of itself as having a certain unity of common speech and shared customs. The tribes range in size from a few hundred to a few thousand souls.

One rarely sees a tribe as a formed entity. It comes together and lives as a unit only for a great occasion—a feast, a corroboree, a hunt, an initiation, or a formal duel. After a few days—at the most, weeks—it breaks up again into smaller bands or sections of bands: most commonly into a group of brothers, with their wives, children, and grandchildren, and perhaps a few close relatives. These parties rove about their family locality or, by agreement, the territories of immediate neighbours. They do not wander aimlessly, but to a purpose, and in tune with the seasonal food supply. One can almost plot a year of their life in terms of movement towards the places where honey, yams, grass-seeds, eggs, or some other food staple, is in bearing and ready for eating.

The uncomplex visible routine, and the simple segmentation, are very deceptive. It took well over half a century for Europeans to realise that, behind the outward show, was an inward structure of surprising complexity. It was a century before any real understanding of this structure developed.

In one tribe with which I am familiar, a very representative tribe, there are about 100 "invisible" divisions which have to be analysed before one can claim even a serviceable understanding of the tribe's organisation. The structure is much more complex than that of an Australian village of the same size. The complexity is in the most striking contrast with the comparative simplicity which rules in the two other departments of aboriginal life—the material culture, on the one hand, and the ideational or metaphysical culture on the other. We have, I think, to try to account for this contrast in some way.

Their creative "drive" to make sense and order out of things has, for some reason, concentrated on the social rather than on the metaphysical or the material side. Consequently, there has been an unusually rich development of what the anthropologist calls "social structure," the network of enduring relations recognised between people. This very intricate system is an intellectual and social achievement of a high order. It is not, like an instinctual response, a phenomenon of "nature"; it is not, like art or ritual, a complex type of behaviour passionately added to "nature," in keeping with metaphysical insight but without rational and intelligible purposes which can be clearly stated; it has to be compared, I think, with such a secular achievement as, say, Parliamentary Government in a European society. It is truly positive knowledge.

One may see within it three things: given customs, "of which the memory of man runneth not to the contrary"; a vast body of cumulative knowledge about the effects of these customs on a society in given circumstances; and the use of the power of abstract reason to rationalise the resultant relations into a system.

But it is something much more: it has become *the source of the dominant mode of aboriginal thinking*. The blacks use it to give a bony structure to parts of the world outlook suggested by intuitive speculation. I mean by this that they have taken some of its fundamental principles and relations and have applied them to very much wider sets of phenomena. This tends to happen if any type of system of thought becomes truly dominant. It is, broadly, what Europeans did with "religion" and "science" as systems: extended their principles and categories to fields far beyond the contexts in which the systems grew.

Thus, the blacks have taken the male-female social principle and have extended it to the non-human world. In one tribe I have studied all women, without exception, call particular birds or trees by the same kinship terms which they apply to actual relatives. In the same way, all men without exception use comparable terms for a different set of trees or birds. From this results what the anthropologist calls "sex totemism." The use of other principles results in other types of totemism. An understanding of this simple fact removes much of the social, if not the ritual, mystery of totemism. Again, the principle of relatedness itself, relatedness between known people by known descent through known marriages, is extended over the whole face of human society. The same terms of kinship which are used for close agnatic and affinal relatives are used for every other person an aborigine meets in the course of his life: strangers, friends, enemies and known kin may all be called by the same terms as one uses for brother, father, mother's sister, father's mother's brother, and so on. This is what an anthropologist means when he says "aboriginal society is a society of kinship."

It might even be argued that the blacks have done much the same thing with "time." Time as a continuum is a concept only hazily present in the aboriginal mind. What might be called *social* time is in a sense, "bent" into cycles or circles. The most controlled understanding of it is by reckoning in terms of generation-classes, which are arranged into named and recurring cycles. As far as the blackfellow thinks about time at all, his interest lies in the cycles rather than in the continuum, and each cycle is in essence a principle for dealing with social inter-relatedness.

IV

Out of all this may come for some an understanding of the blackfellow very different from that which has passed into the ignorance and vulgarity of popular opinion.

One may see that, like all men, he is a metaphysician in being able to transcend himself. With the metaphysic goes a mood and spirit, which I can only call a mood and spirit of "assent": neither despair nor resignation, optimism nor pessimism, quietism nor indifference. The mood, and the outlook beneath it, make him hopelessly out of place in a world in which the Renaissance has triumphed only to be perverted, and in which the products of secular humanism, rationalism and science challenge their own hopes, indeed, their beginnings.

Much association with the blackfellow makes me feel I may not be far wrong in saying that, unlike us, he seems to see "life" as a one-possibility thing. This may be why he seems to have almost no sense of tragedy. If "tragedy is a looking at fate for a lesson in deportment on life's scaffold," the aborigine seems to me to have read the lesson and to have written it into the very conception of how men should live, or else to have stopped short of the insight that there are gods either just or unjust. Nor have I found in him much self-pity. These sentiments can develop only if life presents real alternatives, or if it denies an alternative that one feels should be there. A philosophy of assent fits only a life of unvarying constancy. I do not at all say that pain, sorrow and sadness have no place in aboriginal life, for I have seen them all too widely. All I mean is that the blacks seem to have gone beyond, or not quite attained, the human *quarrel* with such things. Their rituals of sorrow, their fortitude in pain, and their undemonstrative sadness seem to imply a reconciliation with the terms of life such that "peace is the understanding of tragedy and at the same time its preservation," or else that they have not sensed life as baffled by either fate or wisdom.

Like all men, he is also a philosopher in being able to use his power of abstract reason. His genius, his *métier,* and—in some sense—his fate, is that because of endowment and circumstance this power has channelled itself mainly into one activity, "making sense" out of the social relations among men living together. His intricate social organisation is an impressive essay on the economy of conflict, tension and experiment in a life situation at the absolute pole of our own.

Like all men, too, he pays the price of his insights and solutions. We look to a continuous unfolding of life, and to a blissful attainment of the better things for which, we say, man has an infinite capacity. For some time, nothing has seemed of less consequence to us than the maintenance of continuity. The cost, in instability and inequity, is proving very heavy. Aboriginal life has endured feeling that continuity, not man, is the measure of all. The cost, in the world of power and change, is extinction. What defeats the blackfellow in the modern world, fundamentally, is his transcendentalism. So much of his life and thought are concerned with The Dreaming that it stultifies his ability to develop. This is not a new thing in human history. A good analogy is with the process in Chinese poetry by which, according to Arthur Waley, its talent for classical allusion became a vice which finally destroyed it altogether.

A "philosophy of life," that is, a system of mental attitudes towards the conduct of life, may or may not be consistent with an actual way of life. Whether it is or is not will depend on how big a gap there is, if any, between what life *is* and what men think life *ought to be.* If Ideal and Real drift too far away from one another (as they did at the end of the Middle Ages, and seem increasingly to do in this century) men face some difficult options. They have to change their way of life, or their philosophy, or both, or live unhappily somewhere in between. We are familiar enough with the "war of the philosophies" and the tensions of modern life which express them. Problems of this kind had no place, I would say, in traditional aboriginal life. It knew nothing, and could not, I think, have known anything of the Christian's straining for inner perfection; of "moral man and immoral society"; of the dilemma of liberty and authority; of intellectual uncertainty, class warfare, and discontent with one's lot in life—all of which, in some sense, are problems of the gap between Ideal and Real.

The aborigines may have been in Australia for as long as 10,000 years. No one at present can do more than guess whence or how they came, and there is little more than presumptive evidence on which to base a guess. The span of time, immense though it may have been, matters less than the fact that, so far as one can tell, they have been almost completely isolated. Since their arrival, no foreign stimulus has touched them, except on the fringes of the northern and northwestern coasts. To these two facts we must add two others. The physical environment has, evidently, not undergone any marked general change, although there has been a slow desiccation of parts of the centre into desert, and some limited coastline changes. The fourth fact is that their tools and material crafts seem to have been very unprogressive.

If we put these four facts together—an immensely long span of time, spent in more or less complete isolation, in a fairly constant environment, with an unprogressive material culture, we may perhaps see why sameness, absence of change, fixed routine, regularity, call it what you will, is a main dimension of their thought and life. Let us sum up this aspect as leading to a metaphysical emphasis on abidingness. They place a very special value on things remaining unchangingly themselves, on keeping life to a routine which is known and trusted. Absence of change, which means certainty of expectation, seems to them a good thing in itself. One may say, their Ideal and Real come very close together. The value given to continuity is so high that they are not simply a people "without a history": they are a people who have been able, in some sense, to "defeat" history, to become ahistorical in mood, outlook and life. This is why, among them, the philosophy of assent, the glove, fits the hand of actual custom almost to perfection, and the forms of social life, the art, the ritual, and much else take on a wonderful symmetry.

Their tools and crafts, meagre—pitiably meagre—though they are, have nonetheless been good enough to let them win the battle for survival, and to win it comfortably at that. With no pottery, no knowledge of metals, no wheel, no domestication of animals, no agriculture, they have still been able, not only to live and people the entire continent, but even in a sense to prosper, to win a surplus of goods and develop leisure-time occupations. The evidences of the surplus of yield over animal need are to be seen in the spider-web of trade routes criss-crossing the continent, on which a large volume of non-utilitarian articles circulated, themselves largely the products of leisure. The true leisure-time activities—social entertaining, great ceremonial gatherings, even much of the ritual and artistic life—impressed observers even from the beginning. The notion of aboriginal life as always preoccupied with the risk of starvation, as always a hair's breadth from disaster, is as great a caricature as Hobbes' notion of savage life as "poor, nasty, brutish, and short." The best corrective of any such notion is to spend a few nights in an aboriginal camp, and experience directly the unique joy in life which can be attained by a people of few wants, an other-worldly cast of mind and a simple scheme of life which so shapes a day that it ends with communal singing and dancing in the firelight.

The more one sees of aboriginal life the stronger the impression that its mode, its ethos and its principle are variations on a single theme—continuity, constancy, balance, symmetry, regularity, system, or some such quality as these words convey.

One of the most striking things is that there are no great conflicts over power, no great contests for place and office. This single fact explains much else, because it rules out so much that would be destructive of stability. The idea of a formal chief, or a leader with authority over the persons of others in a large number of fields of life—say, for example, as with a Polynesian or African chief—just does not seem to make sense to a blackfellow. Nor does even the modified Melanesian notion—that of a man becoming some sort of a leader because he accumulates a great deal of garden wealth and so gains prestige. There are leaders in the sense of men of unusual skill, initiative and force, and they are given much respect; they may even attract something like a following; but one finds no trace of formal or institutionalised chieftainship. So there are no offices to stimulate ambition, intrigue, or the use of force; to be envied or fought over; or to be lost or won. Power—a real thing in every society—is diffused mainly through one sex, the men, but in such a way that it is not to be won, or lost, in concentrations, by craft, struggle, or coup. It is very much a male-dominated society. The older men dominate the younger, the men dominate the women. Not that the women are chattels—Dr. Phyllis Kaberry in her interesting book *Aboriginal Woman* disposed of that Just-So story very effectively, but there is a great deal of discrimination against them. The mythology justifies this by tales telling how men had to take power from women by force in The Dreaming. The psychology (perhaps the truth) of it is as obvious as it is amusing. If women were not kept under, they would take over!

At all events, the struggle for power occurred once for all. Power, authority, influence, age, status, knowledge, all run together and, in some sense, are the same kind of thing. The men of power, authority, and influence are old men—at least, mature men; the greater the secret knowledge and authority the higher the status; and the initiations are so arranged (by the old men) that the young men do not acquire full knowledge, and so attain status and authority, until they are too are well advanced in years. One can thus see why the great term of respect is "old man"—*maluka,* as in *We of the Never-Never*. The system is self-protective and self-renewing. The real point of it all is that the checks and balances seem nearly perfect, and no one really seems to want the kind of satisfaction that might come from a position of domination. At the same time, there is a serpent in Eden. The narrow self-interest of men exploits The Dreaming.

Power over things? Every canon of good citizenship and common sense is against it, though there are, of course, clear property arrangements. But what could be more useless than a store of food that will not keep, or a heavy pile of spears that have to be carried everywhere? Especially, in a society in which the primary virtues are generosity and fair dealing. Nearly every social affair involving goods—food in the family, payments in marriage, intertribal exchange—is heavily influenced by equalitarian notions; a notion of reciprocity as a moral obligation; a notion of generously equivalent return; and a surprisingly clear notion of fair dealing, or making things "level" as the blackfellow calls it in English.

There is a tilt of the system towards the interests of the men, but given this tilt, everything else seems as if carefully caculated to keep it in place. The blacks do not fight over land. There are no wars or invasions to seize territory. They do not enslave each other. There is no master-servant relation. There is no class division. There is no property or income inequality. The result is a homeostasis, far-reaching and stable.

I do not wish to create an impression of a social life without egotism, without vitality, without cross-purposes, without conflict. Indeed, there is plenty of all, as there is of malice, enmity, bad faith, and violence, running along the lines of sex inequality and age inequality. But this essential humanity exists, and runs its course, within a system whose first principle is the preservation of balance. And, arching over it all, is the *logos* of The Dreaming. How we shall state this when we fully understand it I do not know, but I should think we are more likely to ennoble it than not. Equilibrium ennobled is "abidingness." Piccarda's answer in the third canto of the *Paradiso* gives the implicit theme and logic of The Dreaming: *e la sua volontate è nostra pace,* "His will is our peace." But the gleam that lighted Judah did not reach the Australian wilderness, and the blacks follow The Dreaming only because their fathers did.

CHAPTER

23

The Analysis of Mana: *An Empirical Approach*

RAYMOND FIRTH

Despite sixty years of discussion and a bulky literature the controversies that have raged round the meaning of the Oceanic term *mana* and its related concepts are still far from settled. Much of the obscurity and confusion has arisen through the fact that elaborate theoretical discussions have been constructed on the basis of inadequate factual data.

In examining the meaning of the native term the investigators have tried to arrive at their results by varying combinations of the following three methods:

a. By attempting an exact "translation" of the word concerned and trying to get a precise verbal equivalent for the native idea.

b. By examining the relationship in native thought between the "*mana*-idea" and other concepts of the same native community; that is, by obtaining linguistic explanations of the "*mana*-concept" from the natives themselves.

c. By studying the actual usage of the word as employed in the course of normal behaviour and activities, and obtaining native linguistic comments on such usages.

The difficulty of obtaining any reliable empirical data in the last two categories makes it inevitable that nearly all armchair discussion has centered round the dictionary definitions supplied by the first category. The results have been unfortunate.

Certainly in past discussions concerning *mana* nearly all the initial emphasis has been laid on trying to find some European verbal equivalent for the Oceanic concept. The diversity of the resulting translations may be an indication of the confusion that has arisen in fixing the meaning of the term. But it may also be a reflex of

From *Journal of the Polynesian Society,* 40:483–510, 1940. By permission of the author and publisher.

the assumption that there is in fact any general *mana* concept that is common to all Oceanic communities. Such an assumption may be quite unjustified; there may be genuine significant differences of connotation between different communities.

The following selection from the various meanings (not all exclusive) that have been attributed to *mana* shows the confusion; it also illustrates the theoretical preconceptions of the various authors. *Mana* has been translated as:

Supernatural power; influence (Codrington);
Magical power; psychic force (Marett);
Impersonal religious force; totemic principle (Durkheim);
Divine force (Handy);
Effective; miracle; authority; prestige, etc. (Tregear);
True (Hocart).

Lehmann in his useful collection of material on the subject gives numerous other examples. More recently, Handy and Driberg have sought an analogy for *mana* in electricity,[1] while Hogbin has compared it with luck.[2]

The difficulty of describing the concept exactly is brought out by Hubert and Mauss,[3] who characterize it as "not only a force, a being; it is also an action, a quality, and a state. In other words the term is at once a noun, an adjective and a verb." This seeming grammatical confusion has been responsible for much laborious theorizing. The elaborate arguments that seek to determine whether the nature of *mana* is "personal" or "impersonal" seem to turn largely on the question as to whether it is more nearly correct to say that an object "is *mana*" or "has *mana*," though as Lehmann has pointed out this distinction is not material in many Oceanic languages. By some writers the notion of *mana* as "a vague and impersonal fluid" has been represented as in opposition to assertions that it is derived from spirit entities.

The type of inference drawn for anthropological theory from the material on *mana* has been almost as varied as the differences in translation. A. M. Hocart has made an important contribution to the study of *mana* by stressing that the Polynesian conception is a practical one connoting prosperity and success, and he has also drawn attention to the fact that *mana* tends to be attributed particularly to the leaders of the community, their chiefs and priests. His inferences, however, are essentially of an ethnological order. He is concerned to show the archaic character of the Polynesian idea and its place in the history of religion as intimately connected with the doctrine of the divinity of kings.[4] A. Capell, again, in a recent article has attempted to trace the linguistic history of the word, taking its primary meaning as "effective," with the general implication that the efficacy goes beyond that encountered in everyday life. With this one agrees. His conclusion is that *mana* is a prevailing Polynesian concept, but that "exactly similar ideas prevail amongst the American Indians, but naturally under a different name." He holds that the Polynesians brought the word *manan* with them from Indonesia, its incidence in Borneo and the Celebes being of particular significance here. He agrees also with Pater Schmidt that *mana* had its origin in and with mythology, developing in dependence upon an ancestor cult.[5]

R. R. Marett, who by his own statement is entitled to rank among the "prophets of the gospel of *mana*," has stressed the view that *mana* and allied notions constitute the category that most nearly expresses the essence of rudimentary religion. His thesis that *mana* is the nearest expression of the positive emotional value which is the raw material of religion is too well known to need further discussion.[6]

Recently Ruth Benedict has revived this view in another form by stating that *mana, wakanda,* etc., have as their fundamental concept the idea of the existence of "wonderful power, a voltage with which the universe is believed to be charged," and always the manipulation of this wonderful power and the beliefs that grow out of it are Religion.[7]

In contrast to these latter views is that of B. Malinowski. He argues cogently that on the empirical material the *mana*-concept is too narrow to stand as the basis of Magic and Religion, and holds that the concepts of *wakan, orenda,* and *mana* are simply "an example of an early generalisation of a crude metaphysical concept, such as is found in several other savage words also." He adds the very necessary warning that we have hardly any data at all showing just how this conception in Melanesia enters into religious or magical cult and belief.[8] As will be seen, the argument of this article agrees in essentials with Malinowski's position. Controversy over the meaning of the term started soon after Codrington had published his somewhat abstract rendering of Melanesian ideas on the subject. This was a set of statements which he might never have given in this form if he had known that they would be treated as a classical text by distant scholars, subjected to microscopic analysis, and made the foundation of a system of primitive philosophy. The theoretical structures of Marett, Durkheim, Hubert, and Mauss on this basis have in fact added much more to our understanding of primitive religion in general than to the clarification of the concept of *mana* itself.

Indeed, treated in this manner, the word *mana* becomes something of a technical term describing a specialized abstraction of the theoretical anthropologist and, as such, may have little in common with the same term as used in native phraseology. This fact indeed is appreciated[9] but it is still assumed without serious enquiry, even by the latest writers on the subject (e.g., Radin "Primitive Religion," p. 13), that, quite apart from the technical usages of Anthropology there is in fact a *mana*-concept that is common to all parts of Oceania.

Scientifically speaking, any such general connotation of the term could only arise by inference as the result of the careful comparison of material from different communities; but in point of fact little adequate material exists. It is true that the term *mana* had been known from Polynesia long before it had received attention from the neighbouring Melanesian area.[10]

In the Maori literature in particular there are some data available which have received less than their due.[11] F. R. Lehmann and E. S. C. Handy have analyzed the concept of *mana* from the available literary material on Polynesia.[12] But while this material is important, it is unfortunate that specific research into this problem was not carried further in the original field work. Moreover, too often it is the European's own conception of the meaning of the term that has been placed on record and not an exact translation of texts spoken by the natives themselves. Again, the observation and analysis of actual native behaviour in situations where *mana* has been used as an explanatory concept is at a minimum. It is particularly to be regretted that Codrington, who knew his Mota people well, did not base his exposition on the analysis of examples which he actually recorded or observed, but instead composed some of them for his purpose. There always remains a doubt whether a native would really have thought out and performed an experiment in the way he describes.

The aim of the present article is to supply a body of empirical material from one particular area, Tikopia. By giving a contextualized description of the native usage of the *mana* concept I hope to clarify its precise meaning at least for this particular community. By implication the material here put forward will also set certain negative limitations to the *mana* concept in its more general connotation.

To my mind the proper understanding of the general notion can only emerge out of a careful consideration of particular usages such as are here recorded, and I would add that for our final appreciation of this general notion, if it exists, particular factual details may be irrelevant.[13] Thus for example the elaborate discussions that have been carried on by Codrington, Lehmann, Hocart and others as to whether or not *mana* is in the last resort dependent upon a spirit agency appears to me to be marginal to our understanding of the concept of *mana* itself.

I am concerned here first with the problem of definition of the term, and then with some other problems of the relation of the concept of *mana* to the economic and religious structure of the Tikopia.

In defining the meaning of the term I present material of three kinds: formulations obtained from men with whom I was specifically discussing the term, and to whom I put questions about it; citation of ritual formulae in which the term *mana* appeared incidentally as a standardized item in another context; and examples of the exercise of *mana* given in discussion of the behaviour and qualities of chiefs, comparison of past and present prosperity, illness, other events in the life of individuals.

In presenting this material I give in translation the statements of my informants, as recorded in my notebooks in the original, and in addition, three long texts and several short ones as samples of the original material. Comparison of the translations with the texts will allow the accuracy of my rendering to be judged. It will be obvious that definition of such a term as *mana*, which is not the direct description of an act of behaviour or of a material object, must rely primarily on linguistic data. But it is important to note that this linguistic material is of varying value for interpretation. Statements given in response to direct questions of the order of "What is *mana*?" are acceptable only when reinforced, as in this case, by material of the other types mentioned above, where the formulation arises from the interest of the native himself in explaining or discussing another topic, and so is much more part of a standardized attitude than an abstraction.

Mana and *Manu* in Tikopia

It may be noted in the first place that the Tikopia use two words, *mana* and *manu,* for the one idea. The problem of definition is complicated by the fact that the sets of phonetic combinations giving *mana* and *manu* in Tikopia have a number of different equivalents according to the context in which they are used.

Mana may mean:

1. Thunder;
2. Father (a short for *tamana*);
3. For him, her, or it (pronounced with first vowel long);
4. Efficacious (equivalent to *manu* in the sense discussed in this article).

Manu may mean:

1. An animal, particularly a bird (the first vowel being stressed but short);
2. Efficacious, etc. (as here discussed, the stress on the second vowel);
3. The name of an *atua,* a spirit-being resident in the heavens, identified with a star, and forming the subject of an important myth-cycle concerning storms.

As a preliminary explanation it may be pointed out that most of the Tikopia explanations of *mana* or *manu* are given by reference to the behaviour of their chief, and to prosperity, success, and welfare. A Tikopia chief is regarded as having a peculiar responsibility toward his people. He is considered to be able through his relations with his ancestors and gods to control natural fertility, health, and economic conditions, in the interests of his dependants.[14] Material evidence of his powers is given in native belief by the condition of the weather, of crops, of fish, and of sick persons whom he attempts to cure. Success or failure in these spheres are symptoms of his *mana.*

I give now a series of statements in detail from natives to illustrate the empirical presentation of the idea by Tikopia. The views expressed by Pa Rangifuri, eldest son of the chief of Tafua, may be first considered. The subject arose between us during our discussion of initiation-ritual prompted by a case then in progress. He said that initiation originated with the god of his clan and that in olden times if the sun had shone fiercely for a long time then the rite was performed to induce rain to fall—"to seek *manu.*" I enquired "what is this *manu* that is sought for?"

He replied "If something is to be done indeed for the seeking of *manu* (for example) you speak for the rain to fall; the rain falls you sought *manu* by it; great is your *manu*; speech of Praise is that, praise for the man (to have it said 'great is your *manu*'); he (the man seeking *manu*) speaks to his deity as my father is used to speaking to the deity of Tafua, thus:

I eat ten times your excrement, Rakiteua,
Drench down upon the land.

"That means the rain to fall; thereupon when we see that the rain has come we say: 'the *manu* chief.' If we say also 'the chief is *manu*' it is correct. If he asks for the breadfruit to come, for it to fruit, and then it fruits, we say 'he has been *manu*'; the asking of the chief has been made *manu.*' If no breadfruits fruit it is *mara.* He is termed a *manu* chief, a *manu* man. He asks for different things, *manu!*

"When we look at the land to which food comes constantly then we say 'the land is *manu.*' But when we see that no food comes that is the *mara.*"

I wished to find out if my informant regarded *manu* as something generally distributed, and inquired if it were to be found in rocks and trees everywhere. He answered, "O! It is not there in stones. It is not there in trees. It is there only in food and in fish. We who dwell here, when we desire food, the chief requests the god to give hither food for us. When we look upon the *taro* and the yam which are living, and the breadfruit which has fruited there, it has become *manu,* the *fakamanu* has come. It is not there in all things, it is only in food and fish. When the fleet goes to sea and brings hither fish that is the reef has risen (figurative expression for the rising shoals of fish), it has risen and is *fakamanu.*"

Somewhat later Pa Rangifuri and I returned to the subject of *manu* and he began by discussing it in relation to the position of a newly elected chief. He said (see Text 1 in appendix at end of article), "The new chief beseeches the chief who has gone for some *manu* for himself, that he may crawl to the gods and the assemblage of ancestors. Indeed it is! That *manu* may come for him whatever may be done for him, the orphaned person cast down on that spot." (This is a technical phrase used of himself by a chief in addressing the gods to signify his humility and need.) "The chief who has departed, listens to the new chief, beseeching him indeed, calling out to him:

I eat ten times your excrement
You crawl to the gods
For some *manu* for me
My hand which touches a sick person may it heal
(When he touches, that his hand may be *manu*)
When I wail for anything that it may be *manu*

"Then the chief who has departed goes, performs his crawling to the god, and stretches out his hand to him 'Here! Give me some *manu* that I may go and give it to my next-in-line (successor).' It is given him by the god, whatever it may be, a bundle of leafage or the fruit of the coconut or a fish, or whatever be the desire of the chief who is beseeching him. Thereupon he comes again to sit in his place. He stretches out his hand to the new chief who is sitting among men (in the world of men). 'Here! There is your *manu.*' The *manu* is given hither after the fashion of gods; not a man looks upon it; he observes only the food which has become good, the *taro*, the yam, the coconut, all food has fruited well indeed."

Pa Rangifuri stated that when an old chief dies his *manu* goes with him —the sun shines, water dries up, food is scarce, and so on. This is the "parting of a chief." Hence the new chief whose vegetable resources have been cut off sends a request for *manu* for himself.

I put a question as to whether there could be *manu* alone independent of these material things. He said, "there is no *manu* alone of itself, there is *manu* of the rain, *manu* of the food, but no *manu* only. We look at the rain which has fallen, that is the *manu* which will come, come to the new chief" ("*Siei se manu mosokoia, te manu o te ua, te manu o te kai, kae siei se manu fuere. Ono ko tatou ki te ua ka to, tera te manu ka u, au ki te ariki fou*").

Some other explanatory material, obtained in other contexts, shows also this essential pragmatic aspect of the concept. Pa Rangifuri on another occasion gave me a formula used in a net rite which I had just seen. It appealed to a spirit, Kere-tapuna, to turn to the net, to act as sea expert, that the net might be filled with fish, and ended

"*Ke manu ko te kupenga.*" When I asked for the meaning of the term *manu* he said "The *manu* canoe, the *manu* net, are those which catch fish. The canoe which has no fish for it, is not *manu*" ("*Te vaka manu, te kupenga manu, e au te ika ki ei; te vaka sise ni ika mana, sise manu*").

Pa Motuangi, of Kafika, said of his mother's brother the Ariki Tafua, "*Toku tuatina, matea na mana; ka fai te kava, ka to te ua; ka fai te kava kite ika, ka tari mai; tari mai te ika*" ("My uncle, great is his *mana*; if he makes the *kava,* the rain will fall; if he makes the *kava* for fish, they will be carried hither; carried hither are the fish").

Again, I was discussing with Pa Tarairaki of Kafika the canoe-rites of the Work of the Gods, and the celebration of what is termed "Evil Things," and offering to the gods of the fish secured. He said, "*Ka tu te vaka i te toki, au mai te ika e toto i te tunga te toki; ena na tunga toki. Tena e manu. Ko te toki e tu e manu, kae siei se tunga toki, e manu foki; te ika fuere e au mai te atua ke kai*" "When the canoe is cut with the adze, the fish comes hither bleeding from the cut of the adze; there is its adze-cut. Now (it) is *manu*. The adze which cuts is *manu*, but if there is no adze-cut, it is also *manu*; the spirit simply brings hither the fish for food").

On another occasion, at a yam-rite in the Work of the Gods, I heard the Ariki Kafika ask for *manu* from the gods Pu-ma, that the breakfruit might "run," that is, that the fruit might be properly formed.

The term *manu* is used in a variety of ritual formulae in which spiritual beings are asked for practical results. Pa Rangifau gave the formula recited when the noose method of fishing for *para* is used; in this he is an acknowledged expert.

Tou soa Ariki tautai
Fatia tou mangai
Ke rere o kai manu
I tou raro vaka
Inu tau poa

Thy friend, sea expert chief,
Let thy tail be broken
To dash and eat in *manu* (fashion)
Below thy canoe
Eat thy bait

To explain here the significance of "friend," used in a special context implying that damage is sought, or the identification of spirit and fish, would demand a lengthy discussion. But the significance of the term *manu* is clearly the production of a practical result of securing the fish.

Again from Pa Vainunu I received the formula recited by a chief in investing a person with a cordyline-leaf necklet to secure his welfare

Te rau ti ka tutaki atu
Ki a ke, Pa e!
Tutaki manu
Motusia ki atea ko te fefea
Ma te urungaruru . . .

The cordyline leaf is being joined
To you, Father (his ancestor)
Join with *manu*
Be parted away things of whatever kind
And headaches . . .

"Things of whatever kind" refer here to the various types of illness or misfortune that might afflict a person. Karakiua of Taumako gave me the formula used by a chief to cure sickness. The chief calls on his father

"Au o fakamana i oku rima Pa e,
Ma te tauru rakau
Takina ki atea
Ko te kafo . . ."

"Come and make effective my hands,
  Father,
And the bunch of leaves
Be dragged away
The fever . . ."

Pa Fenuatara, eldest son of the Ariki Kafika explained *manu* as follows (Text 2): "In this land *manu* is there in the lips of the chief. In his speech whatever he may ask for, if a chief is *manu* then when he asks for fish, they will come; when he speaks requesting a calm it falls. That is a *mana* chief. But a chief who is *mara* there is no *mana* for him. The chief whose *kava* is wrong is *mara*. There is no *manu* for him. If he asks for a calm, no calm falls; if he asks for rain, no rain arrives; that is because his things (rites) are wrong."

I asked if *mana* lay simply in the chief as a man. My question made him laugh. He replied:

"No, friend. His *manu* is given hither by the spirits. When he asks it of the spirits, if the spirits wish to give it hither, they give it, and therefore I say that the chief is *manu*. A chief who is *manu*—the spirits just continually rejoice in their desire towards the chief."

I asked also if *mana* lay simply in the words recited. He replied:

"There is no *manu* in speech, it is simply asking. Now if I bewitch a man, I sit and look as to what may be his day upon which he may fall. If he is not ill that is the spirits are not turning to him, they do not wish my speech that I uttered. I am not *manu*." This too shows the dependence of *manu* on the will of the gods.

Several problems of definition are raised by these texts. The first is that of linguistic usage, as to whether *manu* and *mana* represent the same or different ideas. It will be seen in the texts above *manu* is used more frequently, but that *mana* sometimes occurs side by side with it. I asked Pa Rangifuri about this, and his reply was "A *manu* man, a *mana* man; a *manu* chief, a *mana* chief; great is his *mana* and great is his *manu*—such speech goes just the same; it is praising speech indeed." And Pa Fenuatara and Pa Motuangi also said that the two words meant the same thing.

A simple native assertion about the identity in meaning of the words could not be accepted without question. But I found that in actual usage by my range of informants, as can be seen from the texts, that either term is uttered with apparent indifference. The speaker switches from one to the other, obviously using them an synonyms.

A word closely allied in meaning to *manu* is *mairo*, though I heard it used mostly in reference to the healing of the sick. In discussing the "laying-on of hands" on a sick person the Ariki Kafika said "The hand of a chief is *mairo*; it touches and it heals. *Mairo* is *mana*. He is a *mana* man." He explained further that if the invalid rallied at the touch of the chief but then died when the chief had gone, the people would say, "Indeed, the hand of the chief, of course, was *fakamairo*," meaning that it was this touch alone which had given the invalid sustaining power for the time being. Another statement points also to the equivalence of *mairo* with *mana*. "The hand of a chief is *mairo*; it touches a sick person, he gets well. He (the chief) calls to the gods to *fakamairo* his hand since he is going to the sick person."

Further material on the linguistic usage was obtained from Pae Sao. Our discussion began on the *kava* ritual, which as an important elder he himself regularly performed. He spoke of chiefs and elders making appeals in set phraseology to their gods and ancestors to give them *manu*. He then proceeded to explain "The *manu*—that calm may come and rain may come, that the *kava* made to the gods may be *mairo*. The *fakamairo* indeed of the *kava* are the tokens of the *kava*. That is, it has become calm and it has rained." Later he added, "A ritual elder, a chief, is *mana*, is *manu*; the name of a chief is *manu* and *mana*."

The position in Tikopia thus is that *manu* is the general term with *mana* as a synonym of it and *mairo* used less commonly, mostly in connection with healing. The usage of *manu* in Tikopia instead of or additional to the common Polynesian *mana* is puzzling. It is possible that the use of *manu*, in the sense we are discussing, is due to the fact that in this island *mana* is the ordinary abbreviation for *tamana*, father, with equal stresses also. This is speculation and I have no native opinion to support it.

Both *manu* and *mana* are quite flexible in syntax. Either can stand as a substantive or an adjunct, and can suffer some verbal modification. Some simple examples of the usage of *manu* may be given, extracted from the material quoted in this chapter.

Te manu ena i te ngutu te ariki.
The *manu* is there in the lips (of) the chief.

Na manu e sori mai i nga atua.
His *manu* is given hither from the gods.

Muna atu kuou te ariki e manu.
Speak away I the chief is *manu* (I say that . . .)

E faia toku mana ne manu, ne nofo ko ia, manu rei.
Because my father was *manu*, did live he, *manu* then.

Ku manutia ko te kaisianga a te ariki.
The request by the chief has been *manu*.

Ono iatou ki te mei kua fua, tera ku manu, ku au te fakamanu.
When we look on the breadfruit which has borne fruit, there it has become *manu*, the making-*manu* has come.

An interesting verbal modificaton of the term *mana*, which has a similar range, came from the spirit medium Pa Tekaumata, who after giving me a formula he was in the habit of using said: "*Tena tenea nokofakamana ki oku nea*" (That is the thing used to give *mana* to my affairs"). Here both frequentative and causative prefixes have been attached to the word.

To students of Oceanic dialects this flexibility of the grammatical function of the word will be no novelty.

There has been some discussion as to whether it can be properly said that a man "*has mana*" or he "*is mana*." In Tikopia both types of translation would be valid. If the flexibility of the word in syntax be borne in mind an analagous situation in English would be of a man "having" success and "being" successful.

From the descriptive statements given above it can be seen that *manu* covers a category of socially approved phenomena. It signifies positive results attained. So when a man is said to possess or to be *manu*, this is a judgment in his favour. As Pa Rangifuri said, this is "speech of praise."

Standing in opposition to this active and socially welcomed sphere of interest is the term *mara* which connotes absence of visible results and is not a judgment of approval. A chief who is *manu* is regarded as fulfilling his duty to his people and deserving their praise. A chief who is *mara* incurs their tacit censure because the visible lack of fertility reacts upon their well-being, which is his charge, and this is regarded as being due to some defect in his relations with his ancestors and gods. No action of any kind is taken against such a chief; his people merely grumble and speculate among themselves.

The alignment of *manu* with these positive effects might seem as if *manu* signifies the activity principle in nature. But it is correlated always with concrete situations, falling of rain, growth of food, advent of calms, relief of sickness. In fact its very existence is inferred by such concrete results. Again and again I hammered away at my informants trying to find what was the meaning of *manu* itself apart from the evidence of it in crops, fish, and the like. But all my inquiries for the *Ding an Sich* came to nothing. Always it was insisted that the crops and the fish *were manu*. Now obviously my informants were not facing the logical and metaphysical issues squarely here, but their indifference to the existence of such issues is extremely significant. To the Tikopia, *manu* I am sure has not the connotation of an isolatable principle, a force, a power, or any other metaphysical abstraction—though it may be conceived of as a specific quality. The interpretation in terms of such abstraction can only be the work of the anthropologist. The Tikopia is content with concrete description of the results of activity and does not pursue the intellectual problem as to the nature of that activity.

It is well to reinforce this point by consideration of more material obtained not as the result of questions about *manu* but volunteered in an entirely different context.

When the seasonal dances were being performed in Marae, I participated in them. The songs chanted dealt mostly with the gods. When I asked why the dances were performed, the answer was given: "They are performed for the *manu* of the gods. All the chiefs sing to the gods that they may perform hither the *manu* for the land to be well." It might seem here that we are dealing with a native concept of the physical activity of man giving a stimulus to the activity of nature and using the theme of appeal to the gods as a medium of expression. But reference to the tradition of origins of the dances and to the beliefs about the gods show that though this be true as a sociological abstraction it is unjustifiable if put forward as a native idea. In Tikopia belief the gods give *manu* when the dances are performed because they see that the traditional ways of behaviour which they instituted are being faithfully followed; and they are pleased. Moreover, dancing is their primary amusement in the heavens and they are moved to interest and approval—and even to active participation when they see this practice being observed on earth.[15]

Another linkage of the idea of *manu* with physical activity is given in the formula which is recited when a sacred adze is being used on a new canoe being built by a chief. From the Ariki Taumako and from a number of other people at different times, I was given texts of the formula and the explanation of it.

Manu! for your *marie*
Manu! for your *para*
Manu! for your *varu*
Manu! for your bonito
Manu! for your flying fish
Manu! for all your fish on the starboard side

> *Manu!* may an orchard stand for you on the reef
> *Manu!* let them rise from the foam of the ocean
> *Manu!* flick behind harmful things.

Here again the pragmatic context of the term *manu* comes out very forcibly. The primary function of the canoe is to be an aid in securing fish and the kinds of most important fish are mentioned. The *marie* is a species of shark, while the *para* and *varu* are also types of highly prized large fish. The 'orchard' is a metaphor for the fishing bank, and again it is fish which are adjured to rise from the ocean foam. The last line is an exhortation to ward off those spirits of the ocean which are evilly disposed. Although it is not stated in the formula, this is an invocation to the tutelary deities of the vessel and of the sacred adze. The best translation of *manu* here is "be effective" or "be efficacious." His example illustrates the use of the term *manu* in practical association with the citation of its material manifestation, the belief in the spiritual beings who vouchsafe it and a manual act of canoe-making—all this in a ritual context.

Another manual act believed to be accompanied by *manu* was described to me by Pa Fenuatara in connection with the initiation of a boy of rank. The chief of his clan pours some oil into his hand, announces it to one of his deities and then rubs it on the boy's chest. This is to take away his fear of the approaching operation. Pa Fenuatara said of his own case "I felt his hand strike my vitals. I was frightened but I felt as though he had given me food and that I was full. Great is his *mana*. Then my fear quite left me." In this case the Kafika chief was a very old man and so did not attend the lad's initiation. The ceremony was performed by the Ariki Fangarere instead.

Other material was obtained in discussing traditional events. Pa Torokinga, an old man, was telling me about his ancestors, the chief of the ancient group of Na Faea, who were driven off to sea by their enemies. He said, (Text 3): "Great was the weight of my ancestor the chief. His hand pointed to a man, the man slept down below (in death). His god indeed abode in his hand. He was *manu*. When he went down to the reef-waters and called to the fish to come to land they came—the *ature* (mackerel, which are netted on the reef). Long was the abiding of the fish; the land ate and ate and ate. He went and waved his hand at them to go; they went. Great was his weight. He spoke to a tree, the tree died. He spoke to the breadfruit, it came, it fruited." Pa Torokinga told me that this ancestor, on the day he went out to sea (driven away) loaded his canoe with food, took down a length of bark-cloth, beat the sea with it, and tied it trailing to the stern of his canoe. "The drawing away of the fish to go out to sea. The fish went completely. The reef was bare, there were no fish."

From Pa Motuangi of Marinoa I was told of the time when two rivals both occupied the ritual position of elder of the house at the one time. In this dual reign both performed their own *kava* ceremonies and both sacralized their canoes for sea-fishing. When the rival fleets went to sea, fish were caught by the vessels of one elder named Vaiangafuru (my informant's ancestor) while those of the other caught nothing. "He made fish for his own fleet but not for the fleet of Pu Fangatafea which came in bare from the ocean. That is, Vaiangafuru was *manu*." I asked what was this *manu* and got the answer "A man who is not slept upon by the gods, that is a man who is not *manu*. It is exactly alike (*tau fangatasi*), the *mana*, the *manu*."

Pa Vainunu of Kafika was one day describing to me various types of ritual chant, and gave as example one composed by his father, a former chief. The song referred to the "making bitter" of the lake. At certain times, apparently, the lake-waters became affected so that the fish rose to the surface in large numbers, died, and were collected by the people who carried them home to cook. Pa Vainunu with filial loyalty maintained that this did not happen nowadays, whereas in former times it occurred, because his father was *manu*. "The lake which stands there is not bitter in these after days because another chief has dwelt. When my father used to live it was bitter, from time to time it was bitter, because my father was *manu* as he dwelt, he was *manu* then. When he disappeared among the gods he disappeared with his own *manu*, and the land which stands here has become different. Because he called to his god; but they who dwell here do not know. The two of them, he and his god, have the same name. The name of the god is Mourongo, and my father has Mourongo as his second name. My ancestor Mourongo sat at the *kava* bowl as an *atua*, and prepared the *kava*. He listened to my father calling out among men but he himself heard him from the realm of spirits. My father called out:

'You Mourongo,
I eat your excrement
Turn hither to me who am calling out
Shake the *kava* pith into the lake
To be bitter that the land may eat.'

Then the *kava* bowl was prepared and shaken into the lake; it was shaken in the realm of spirits. And my father the chief called upon the god and therefore his calling was *manu*. The fish went and sucked the *kava* pith, went to drink of it, sucked, were poisoned, and died."

Pa Vainunu gave another incident after this to illustrate his father's *mana*. He said, "My father, great was his *manu*. He called out to the gods and his words were true. Look you upon me; I will tell you. It was his building of the sacred canoe which is drawn up there, Tafurufuru. As his building was going on the people went to hew out the vessel and he called for the fish to run hither. They ran then on the day on which the vessel was hewn out. The fish ran hither and the canoe was hewn while people went to bring hither the fish from the sea. They awoke on another day and brought them hither, awoke on another day and brought them hither, while the vessel continued to be hewn. The canoe was finished, but the fish continued still to stand. But when the chief who dwells here stood in his place he did not act thus and the fish did not run hither."

Here we have the recital of a miracle performed as an accompaniment to an important act of a chief—for the hewing of one of his sacred vessels is one of the marks of his career.

In the above text reference is made to the *truth* of the words of a chief when he called upon the god. The meaning of this is that his appeals to them were validated by results, not falsified by lack of results. The association hinted at here is between correctness of the formulae used, influence with the gods, and validity of one's case. Such association was illustrated by a discussion I had with Pa Motuata and Kavakiua who spoke of their father's brother the late chief of Taumako. They said: "Great was his *mana,* because he did not speak in lying fashion. He used to speak truly only; he spoke for calm—it fell; he spoke for rain—it rained at that moment." From the first part of the sentence it seems as if the possession and exercise of *mana* were contingent upon the practice of truth and the leading of a virtuous life. From the remainder, however, the actual position is clear that the truth is an inference from the results of the appeal and not a prior condition to those results.

This series of examples, drawn from a range of informants in different social groups, show how any Tikopia explanation of *mana* is presented in concrete terms, and on the other hand how concrete results which are more than those produced by ordinary efforts are interpreted in terms of *mana.* In all these examples as mentioned already the reference to *manu* was introduced in the course of explanation of the particular circumstances.

One question which arises is that of the origin of *manu.* From some remarks of the Tikopia it might appear that they believe that it was essentially an attribute of human beings. Pa Rangifuri said "The *manu* is there in you, there in your hand which touches and your outer lips." And, as mentioned earlier, Pa Fenuatara said "in this land the *manu* is there in the lips of the chief."

The statement that *manu* resides in the lips and hands is an explanation of its immediate location. It is there for the time being because these are the agencies through which it is liberated. It is the lips which utter the formulae, the hand which is laid upon a sick person.

To the Tikopia the only real source of *Manu* is in the spirit world. *Manu* does not mean the exercise of human powers but the use of something derived from gods or ancestors. One further example is the case of an ancestor of the Fangarere people named Rakeimaitafua. He was a *tama tapu,* sacred child, of Tafua clan, that is, his mother was of that group. One of his descendants Pa Fenumera described him to me thus: "The coconuts came through him, his *manu;* the breadfruit and the chestnut. Things of the earth, the *taro* and yam, rose up above by his *manu.* He was *manu,* he sprang hither from Tafua, therefore the breadfruit and the coconut rose through the *atua* of Tafua; he made *mana* for his sacred child." This point of the origin of *mana* from the gods was made over and over again in different ways by my informant. Pa Porima, for instance, asked the question, "Kafika is *mana* through what?" And answered himself immediately, "It is *mana* through Tafaki and Karisi who used to be chiefs among men, who used to be chiefs formerly in Kafika." These two are the principal deities of the clan. The statement of Pa Rangifuri about *manu* being handed over by a dead chief to his successor has already been quoted. Pae Sao discussing the same point from another angle, that of the relation between a dead elder and his son, said that sometimes the father out of pique would withhold his *mana.* It is clenched in his fist, the *manu* of the *ḳava* is denied to his son. The *manu* is clasped by his father and diverted away by him that it may not enter to his son." This, Pae Sao pointed out, is proven by the fact that no rain falls and the sea remains rough, hence the son knows that his father is displeased with him and so addresses him in deprecatory fashion to induce him to relent. The *manu* of the *ḳava* may be affected in other ways, as by some imperfection in the form of the invitation or in the list of names invoked. It is held that an ancestor or deity whose name is omitted turns his back in anger upon the performer of the *ḳava* which is thus rendered ineffective. In other words he refuses *manu* to it. Pa Rarovi complained to me that when his father died he was only a child. He got his *ḳava* from the Ariki Taumako and Pae Avakofe. But he was not sure if he received it rightly or not. He imagined that certain names were hidden from him because at first his *ḳava* was not satisfactory. Later, on the advice of Pae Sao he inserted other names into his lists and received good results in the shape of rain, or clear skies, when he demanded them.

When we were discussing the relation of a chief's activities to the state of the wind and of the weather Pa Fenuatara said "A chief who is wrong in his *ḳava* is *mara;* there is no *manu* for him. He requests a calm, but none falls; he requests rain but no rain arrives. That is because his things are wrong." The expression "to be wrong in the *ḳava*" means to omit from the list of deities invoked some important names, or to use expressions incorrectly. A reason given for this is that before his election the future chief has not listened properly to the instruction given him by the reigning chief or other elders. He may have been too intent on fishing, or on work in the cultivations. Then, when he performs his *ḳava* and omits a name, the spirit concerned is offended, turns his back and refuses to hand on *manu* to him—that is, to give any practical results to his invocations.

An example of a chief calling upon his dead father for *mana* arose when Pa Rangifuri gave me a formula used by the Ariki Tafua in cases of illness:

> *"Foḳimainiteni!*
> *Koḳe ono mai ḳi toḳu rima,*
> *Ke fakamana i toḳu rima,*
> *Ka po ḳi te naenae*
> *Ke tu faḳamaroi*
> *Ke laui ḳi te naenae."*

> "Fokimainiteni!
> You look on my hand
> To give *mana* from my hand
> When it touches the sick person
> That he may stand firmly
> That the sick person may be well."

The method whereby *mana* is conveyed to a chief is described thus: "The gods take and place it on the head of him who has asked for the *mana* to be given to him." Hence according to this theory the *mana* lodges in the top of the head of the man. According to the Tikopia it never resides in the belly.

But the native ideas are not very clear on the matter of the relation of *manu* to the spoken word. On the one hand it is said that *manu* resides in the lips and might thus be expected to go out in speech, to exercise its effect. On the other hand, as just stated, it is held that the spoken word which invokes the gods is only a request for them to give *manu.*

This position can be resolved by the thesis that a man first asks his gods for *manu* which, vouchsafed to him, he then emits on other occasions to do its work.

A summary of the native statements quoted will help to bring the Tikopia concept of *manu* into relation with the points discussed in anthropological theory. To the Tikopia nature does not work independently of man; fertility is not merely a concatenation of physical factors but depends on the maintenance of a relationship between man and spiritual beings. *Manu* is discussed largely in terms of concrete results, natural phenomena such as crops, fish, and recovery from disease. Not only is its presence judged by material tokens, but at times it is represented as being in itself a material object—as when a dead chief hands it over to his successor or keeps it clenched in his fist. On the other side *manu* is connected with the personality of human beings, and is exercised through human agencies. It is not spoken of as a universal force inhering in all natural objects. The native view of *manu* may be regarded as an element in a theory of human achievement. Its thesis is that success above a certain point, the "normal," is spirit-given. It connects an end-product empirically observed with a set of human desires by a theory of spirit-mediation and a technique of verbal utterance. To the Tikopia the end-product is frequently equated in summary statements with the means whereby that product is obtained. "We look at the rain which is about to fall, that is, the *manu* which will come." But the separation of means from ends is also done. "The *manu* of the rain," "the *manu* is given after the fashion of gods; no man sees it," "one observes only that the food has become good."

The difficulty of rendering a term such as *manu* in translation is that of comprising under one head a number of categories which we ordinarily separate. Uncertainty in natural phenomena, differential human ability, dependence upon spirit entities, are the three primary factors in the *manu* situation. A possible translation of *manu* or *mana* in Tikopia would then appear to be "success" or "successful," which can embody reference both to the ability of man and to tangible results. This term is valid only if it be remembered that for the Tikopia success is not merely a matter of human effort. It is essentially success in certain spheres, those which affect human interests most vitally—food, health, and weather-control, but in ways with which ordinary technique cannot cope. Another possible translation of *manu* is "efficacy" or "to be efficacious."[16] Here the emphasis again is on the fact that the activity works, that it performs the function for which it was intended. But since the efficacy is believed to be only partly due to human endeavour, any translation must also by implication embody a reference to the extrahuman causes of the result. The difficulty lies in comprising in the one term both the result of activity and the native theory of the reason for it. Any single word in English cannot therefore express the fullness of the native concept.

Most of the translations proposed for *mana* fail to give the reality of the native attitude, because of their abstract nature, and their introduction of categories which may have no counterpart in the native system. "Supernatural power," for instance, does represent one aspect of the concept but it leaves out of account the essentially material evidence of such power, and directs attention to the means rather than to the end-product. It ignores also the vital factor that such power does not exist in vacuo but is exercised by human beings or personified material objects, for human benefit. "Psychic force" is a highly intellectualized rendering of the same idea and neglects the native theory of origins.

I could not find in Tikopia any secular connotation of *mana* as "authority" or "influence." Where this meaning occurs, as it apparently does among the Maori, it appears to be secondary, an inference from the more basic significance already discussed. The possible difference of meaning of *mana* in the various Polynesian communities may lead some critics to the conclusion that the *mana* or *manu* of Tikopia is a typical concept. But this is not a justifiable view until a body of empirical evidence comparable with that here presented has been analyzed for these other communities. From the material already available it seems to me that the same factual definition of *mana* of Tikopia probably could be applied elsewhere in Polynesia, though in some cultures there is an extension of meaning into the social sphere. However this be, it is clearly inappropriate to talk of *mana* at this stage as if it represented an identical system of ideas for the Oceanic field.[17] So far as Tikopia is concerned however, we have now arrived at a factual definition of *mana* (*manu*) in terms of the following characteristics.

1. *Material events, e.g.,* crops, fish, death of bewitched persons, cure of sickness, relief from fear.
2. As a *personal attribute* of chiefs; though by way of illustration an informant may refer to himself.
3. The *volition* of spiritual beings who grant to or withhold the *manu* from the chiefs.
4. *Value*. In contrast to *mara, manu* and *mana* always have a positive connotation.

The concept of *manu* as being a personal attribute only of chiefs raises the problem of the relation of the concept to political and religious organization. To what extent does currency of this concept tend to maintain the organization and in particular the role and status of chiefs?

Viewed from one angle the linguistic concept of *manu* is a means of formulating the responsibilities and privileges of chiefs; it gathers into a single concept a series of disparate occurrences: material events, and the acts and influence of chiefs. The *manu* theme is thus part of the definition of a chief's job.

But the metaphysical control said to be exercised by the chief over goods and production by virtue of his *manu* must be correlated with the factual control exemplified by the chief's receipt of first fruits and baskets of food, and with the ritual control exemplified in his priestly functions.

On the one hand the concept of *manu* tends to sustain the role and status of chiefs and to exaggerate their actual power: it is associated essentially with chiefs, it is there in his lips and in his hands, it is given to him (and not to others) by his chiefs and ancestors. In this manner economic and social results which in a great part at least arise from natural phenomena (e.g., seasonal change, recuperative powers of the human body, etc.) are concentrated upon the person of the chief and thus redound to his credit.

But, on the other hand, in contrast to this, material failure as well as success is projected on to the person of the chief and his reputation may suffer through events entirely outside his control. Thus though a man may be, from the outsider's point of view, an effective chief, with a sense of responsibility to his people, hard working and keen to give a lead to the economic affairs of the clan, and assiduous in the performance of ritual, yet so far as the possession of *manu* is concerned he may be put at a disadvantage merely through a succession of bad seasons. Thus from the practical point of view the *manu* of a chief is no thorough test of his efficiency. I say no *thorough* test because, as with the Ariki Tafua, attribution of *manu* to him by reason of large catches of fish may well be based in reality on his better powers of organization, or his superior judgment of place and time for fishing.

It may be noted also that even where a chief is rated low in *mana* this value judgment is not implemented in economic terms; there is no refusal, for instance, to give him the customary first fruits or other food acknowledgments. One reason for this is that his condition is not necessarily permanent; he may become *manu* again soon. Another reason is undoubtedly the social repercussions which any such refusal would involve. Thus projection of failure on to the person of a chief does not endanger the institution of chieftainship as a whole; all chiefs are not suspect because one is *mara.* It may be postulated that a breakdown of chieftainship in Tikopia from this angle would need a fairly thorough demonstration that success in agriculture, fishing, and medicine could be obtained on a wide scale in the face of resort to gods and ancestors.

Appendix

TEXT 1

"Te ariki fou e tangi ki ni manu mona ki te ariki ko ia ne lavaki, ke nai torofia ko nga atua ma te kau firifiri. So ko ia! ke au ko se mana mona, pe nia ko ia ke faia mai ki tenea fakaarofa ne peia ki te ngangea na. Fakarongo ko te ariki ku lavaki ki te ariki fou e tangi atu ki ei, so ko ia, o karanga atu ki ei

'Kau kaina fakaangafuru ko ou tae
Koke totoro atu ki nga atua
Ki ni manu moku
Toku rima ka po ki te ngaengae ke maroro'
(. . . ke po atu ke mana ko na rima)
'Kau tangi atu kuou ki nia, ke manu.'

"Tera poi ko te ariki ku lavaki, fai torofanga ki te atua, kae ropa atu ko tona rima ki ei. 'Ia! Sori mai ko ni manu moku kau poi o sori ki toku tau tafanga.' Sori mai e te atua, pe sea, te tauru rakau, pe te fua o te niu, pe tefea te fifia o te ariki e tangi ki ei. Tera au foki o nofo i tona ngangea. Ropa atu ko na rima ki te ariki fou o nofo i a tangata: 'Ia! ou manu kora.' Te manu e sori fakangatua mai; sise ono se tangata ki ei; mataki fuere ki te kai ku laui, te taro, te ufi, te niu, te kai katoa ku fua laui ko ia."

TEXT 2

"I fenua nei te manu ena i te ngutu te ariki. Tana taranga ka muna pe ki nia, te ariki e manu, tera kaisi ki te ika, au; muna rei kaisi ki te ngaio, to rei. Tera te ariki mana. Ka te ariki mara, siei se mana mona.

"Te ariki e sara tana kava e mara; siei ni manu mona; kaisi ki te ngaio, siei se ngaio ke to; kaisi ki te ua, siei se ua ke oko; tera e faia e sara ko ana nea."

(In laughing answer to the question whether *mana* lay simply in the chief as a man) "Siei, soa soa e! Na mana e sori mai e nga atua. Kaisi ki nga atua, fifia nga atua ka sori mai, sori mai; tera muna atu kuou te ariki e manu. Te ariki ka manu, nga atua e vakai mau fuere fifia ki te ariki."

(In answer to the question if *mana* could lie simply in the words recited) "Siei se manu ena i te taranga, te kaisi fuere. Tera ka tautuku kuou ki te tangata, nofo o ono pe tefea na aso ka to, sise e ngaengae, tera nga atua sise tafuri mai, sise e fifia ki toku taranga ne fai. Kuou sise manu."

TEXT 3

"Matea te mafa toku puna te ariki. Na rima e tusi ki te tangata, ku moe ki raro ko te tangata. Na atua tonu e fare i tana rima. E manu.

"E fakato ki roto tai, karanga ki te ika ke au ma te fenua, au rei-te ature. E roa te nofo o te ika; ka kai, kai, kai ko te fenua. Ka poi o pui atu ki tana rima ke poi, poi rei.

"Matea na palasu; e muna ki te rakau, maro ko te rakau; e muna ki te mei, au, fua rei ko te mei."

PART VI
Aspects of Change

INTRODUCTION

Only parts of New Guinea, Borneo, the Philippine Islands, and the deserts of Western Australia still harbor groups of primitive or near-primitive peoples, and it seems clear that these few descendants of tribesmen will not remain immune from alien cultural influences for very long. In the Pacific, as in the rest of the world, tribal peoples living in small kin-based societies make up a minute fraction of the area's peoples. Most Pacific Islanders today are peasant farmers, dependent for their livelihoods on the production of cash crops and the import of industrial products. Many are proletarian laborers, working on plantations or in mines and towns. Many aspire to higher technical and professional training, and during the next few years the new University of Papua-New Guinea in Port Moresby and the University of the South Seas in Suva, Fiji, will be preparing their first graduates.

The rapid contraction of the tribal world means that few anthropologists will devote their careers to investigations of exotic primitives. But apart from this, anthropologists have long been interested in culture change, particularly in changes in simple societies resulting from Western cultural penetration. For many, along with the commitment to understanding change and development goes a commitment to help promote desired changes when and where the opportunities and existing knowledge permit.

In the first essay Charles Valentine analyzes in broad areal terms the cultural responses of Pacific societies to European colonial rule. He finds that the characteristics of the indigenous political systems and discrimination on ethnic grounds are among the most important determinants of the varying responses. The subsequent essays by Sharp, Guiart, and Spoehr discuss, respectively, the erosive impact of technological innovation, missionization and cargo cults, and urbanization. Finally, in discussing contemporary problems of development in Papua-New Guinea, Margaret Mead suggests that rather than dwell upon the degree to which non-Western societies are prepared to learn from the advanced countries, we should ask how well prepared we are to teach.

CHAPTER

24

Social Status, Political Power, and Native Responses to European Influence in Oceania

CHARLES A. VALENTINE

Introduction

The purpose of this essay is to make a contribution toward explaining the striking contrasts displayed by recent movements of social, political, and religious change among different island peoples of the Pacific region. The approach will be comparative, covering the culture areas of Polynesia, Micronesia, and Melanesia. Comparisons will be made first in terms of selected aspects of indigenous social and political systems. The approach will be extended to relevant aspects of colonial history in Oceania and contemporary plural societies in the islands. Then the native movements of the contact scene will be analyzed with respect to their regional similarities and differences. The analysis will seek to make recent social and cultural developments intelligible in terms of their aboriginal and historical backgrounds. A major aim will be to offer an interpretation of the development, distribution, and functions of cargo cults as compared with other types of movements. As this is a comparative analysis, the discussion will rely heavily on the existing literature, including secondary sources where appropriate. When it is germane to the purpose of the analysis, however, new data from New Guinea will also be offered.

Indigenous Systems of Prestige and Power

The social and political systems of indigenous Oceania have certain fea-

From *Anthropological Forum,* 1:3–55, 1963. By permission of the author and publisher. This paper has profited from readings of earlier drafts and constructive criticism by several colleagues, particularly James B. Watson and Lewis Langness. Of course, no one is responsible for the ideas set forth here but myself.

tures in common. They all show the characteristics of what Sahlins (1958:-2–3) calls "kinship societies" as opposed to "market-dominated societies." In the kinship societies of Oceania, differentiation of status levels and attribution of power are associated with principles of descent and seniority, corporate group membership, genealogical affiliation, or progress through age grades.

We shall have occasion to note that individual effort and enterprise are of major importance in some of these systems. However, such hallmarks of status and power in market-dominated societies as distinctions based on private wealth, or superordination and subordination based on the relationship between owner and worker, are absent or unimportant in the indigenous societies of the Pacific.

In addition to these similarities, there are also important distinctions between the sociopolitical systems of different areas within Oceania. The present discussion will be focused upon such differences, particularly some of those which distinguish Melanesia from other Pacific areas. Polynesian and Micronesian systems are characterized by relatively high degrees of social stratification and centralization of political authority. These features tend to overshadow the segmentary or other divisive characteristics of kinship systems. The same may be said of many Indonesian societies, as well as other non-Western systems further afield from Oceania, but these are all beyond the scope of this essay. In Melanesia, on the other hand, relative egalitarianism and lack of specialized political institutions make for societies which generally are highly segmented, largely unstratified, and uncentralized.

STRATIFICATION AND CENTRALIZATION IN POLYNESIA AND MICRONESIA

The great importance in Polynesian and Micronesian societies of graded status levels and centralized authority, both including emphasis on hereditary succession, has long been recognized by students of Pacific ethnology. The classical work of Williamson (1924) is largely a study of stratification and centralized power structures in Polynesia. Among more recent scholars, Hocart (1950:74–126) uses Polynesian and Polynesian-influenced societies as prime examples in a comparative study of highly stratified social systems. Sahlins (1958) has contributed an analytical study of Polynesian stratification in relation to ecological adaptation. Suggs (1960) reviews the archaeological and historical evidence for the development of ranked status groups and central political authority in one Polynesian society after another.

In the latest survey of Oceanic cultures, Oliver (1961:73–74) notes the historical Polynesian trend that "the principle of *rank* became generalized throughout the populations, with all the highest-ranking members of all descent groups constituting a distinct upper caste. In such instances the ideology of kinship was apt to be superseded by that of *class*" (italics in original). The same authority (1961:80) writes that in Micronesia, also, "rank and caste were important social and political determinants . . . in general Micronesian society was based on fixed relationships between groups and resources, and on status determined by birth rather than by individual effort." In spite of differences in terminology and emphasis, these and other authorities agree that indigenous Polynesian and Micronesian societies in general were stratified and centralized systems.[1]

These systems range in elaboration from the two status levels of some Polynesian groups to the nine distinct social strata of Yap in Micronesia. These societies are typically described in terms of three levels commonly referred to as chiefs (high chiefs or even kings), nobles (subchiefs or middle classes), and commoners (or the lower class). Some writers, like Firth (1959:105–110) in his description of the New Zealand Maori, also call attention to the existence of slaves.

An early generalized description of Polynesian hierarchies by Williamson (1924: Vol. 3, 138) remains fairly representative: "The different classes of society may be divided roughly into what writers call chiefs, middle classes and common people. I do not treat the priesthood as a class, as they appear to have belonged to all classes, though many of the more important priests were related to the upper classes; and I do not mention the slaves as they, to whatever class or classes of society they may have belonged, were I think, as a rule Polynesian prisoners of war . . ."

In each of these systems, status is ascribed through descent as validated by genealogies and mythologies. Varying degrees of control over economic production, distribution, and consumption are held by chiefly and noble groups. Social relations are conditioned by greater or lesser preferences for intrastatus marriage and more or less elaborate canons of intergroup etiquette. The political preeminence of the higher levels ranges from overlapping petty chieftainships to autocratic paramount chieftainships which evolved into native kingdoms under European influence. Some of these systems of social distinction and power differential even had ethnic overtones, such as the identification of the mythical *menehune* with lower social strata of supposedly distinctive physical type (Luomala, 1951).

In economic affairs generally in Polynesia, "the distinction between producers and distributors corresponds precisely to that between nonchiefs and chiefs" (Sahlins 1958:5). The higher strata control production through supervision of communal labour, overseeing of planting, inspection of productive activities, prohibitions of resource use, and even dispossession of title. Occupational specialization characterizes at least some of these hierarchies. In Tonga, for example, craftsmen cannot belong to the highest stratum, and some crafts are restricted to specific statuses. In general, chiefs do not engage in subsistence activities but depend upon the labour of others. Moreover, "throughout Polynesia rank confers differential prerogatives in the consumption of goods" (Sahlins 1958:8). Fine houses, choice foods, special clothing, ornaments, mats, and insignia of rank are all reserved to the higher statuses.

Status-level endogamy reached its extreme in the well known cases of brother-sister marriage within the ruling groups of Hawaii. Although less extreme elsewhere, "in all Polynesian societies there was a preference, among chiefs, for intrastatus marriages" (Sahlins 1958:9). Social intercourse between members of different status groups is regularly characterized by elaborate forms of obeisance and honorific usages. These customs also had their greatest development in Hawaii, where extreme humility on the part of commoners was accompanied by prohibitions against entering the houses of chiefs, touching their possessions, or eating with them. In some systems, particularly, gods could be worshipped only by high chiefs, and everywhere chiefly life crisis rituals were more elaborate than those of commoners. All these prerogatives were associated with the sanctification of the *mana* and *tabu* complex.

The political specialization and superiority of the higher status groups is described by Sahlins (1958:11) as "control of socioregulatory processes by high chiefs [and] marked difference by status in ability to inflict secular punishments on wrongdoers." In Hawaii, Tonga, and Tahiti, particularly, the extremes of centralized authority were reached. Here chiefs held sway over wide areas, decided questions of war and peace, mobilized armies, exercised arbitrary use of force, settled many disputes, and meted out punishments including confiscation of goods, banishment, and death.

Throughout Polynesia and Micronesia there was a strong tendency for political organization to be centralized in the sense that power was concentrated in the hands of titled men, authority was vested in individuals or groups of high rank, and community decisions were made and carried out through the operation of specialized political institutions organized in terms of social stratification, such as chieftainships and chiefly councils. This did not necessarily mean that there was permanently stable political integration beyond the local level, that the political hierarchy was static in the alignment of subgroups, that the power of any individual or the authority of any office was unlimited, or that there was no scope for factional manoeuvring within the system.

In precontact Samoa, for example, the whole island group was never politically unified so far as we know, there was no paramount chieftainship, intervillage alliances were impermanent, chiefly councils at both village and district levels exercised authority through a rule of unanimous decision, and the power of individual chiefs was limited by the workings of the kin group system (Ember 1962). Indeed, on the basis of all these features of Samoan society Ember (1962:964) concludes that "political authority in aboriginal Samoa was centralized neither on the society level nor on the local level." It nevertheless remains true that the typical Polynesian tendency toward centralization is evident in the Samoan concentration of power in specialized offices and bodies which are defined by the system of social ranking.

Similarly, in New Zealand before the coming of Europeans, the Maori did not develop institutions of intertribal political unity or autocratic authority. Maori chiefs had to consult with elders or other influential persons before making political decisions (Firth 1959). In some atoll societies with a lesser degree of stratification than most Polynesian or Micronesian groups, chiefs had even less absolute political authority. In Pukapuka, Ontong Java, and Tokelau, for example, chiefs and priest-chiefs shared power with councils of elders open to all men of mature years (Sahlins 1958:-92–106).

EGALITARIANISM AND SEGMENTATION IN MELANESIA

Melanesia is an area of great social and cultural heterogeneity, certainly far more varied than either Polynesia or Micronesia. It is thus more difficult to make valid general statements about aboriginal Melanesian social and political systems, and the problem of exceptional cases is correspondingly greater. Nevertheless, anthropological students of the area are agreed that certain features are shared by nearly all Melanesian societies thus far investigated. Among these near-universal features are those which enable us to compare the societies of Melanesia with the aspects of Polynesian and Micronesian systems just summarized.

Describing precontact Melanesia as a whole, Hogbin (1958:84–85) writes that "except in one or two areas there were no social classes, and the whole population carried out the same kind of tasks." In order to distinguish the general Melanesian pattern from a few exceptional cases, Worsley (1957:15–16) gives the following description: "Normally, there were no hereditary political authorities, not even hereditary ranks or statuses . . . . It was largely open to any man to advance himself socially by his own endeavours . . . political and legal security depended upon support by relatives and kin, and the impermanent authority of the 'big-men'."

Reed (1943:70–71) sets forth a similar summary, with particular reference to New Guinea, the Bismarck Archipelago, and the northern Solomon Islands: "We note also proliferation of ethnocentric social units whose fragmented political character is maintained through extreme linguistic diversity and narrow margins of sovereignty. . . . In most of the societies, moreover, there is a notable absence of class and caste stratification . . . individual ability is of more moment than hereditary office or line of descent . . . the traditional equalitarian norms militate against a persons' rising —in wealth, in religious powers, or in political authority—much above the general status level." Another passage by Worsley (1957:227) characterizes Melanesians as "peoples divided into small, separate, narrow and isolated social units . . . societies which have no overall unity, which lack centralized political institutions . . . . They often have no chiefs . . . no army and no administrative officials."

With but few exceptions, then, Melanesian societies are egalitarian in Sahlins' (1958:1–2) sense that the principal or only fixed qualifications for status are the universal ones of "age, sex, and personal characteristics," and that "given these qualifications, every individual has an equal chance to succeed to whatever statuses may be open." Moreover, most indigenous Melanesian societies are characterized by "uncentralized" political systems in the broader sense of that term as defined by Middleton and Tait (1958:2). These are also highly segmented societies, though by virtue of a considerable variety of descent and kinship principles they do not necessarily correspond with the "segmentary lineage systems" described by Middleton and Tait and by Fortes and Evans-Pritchard (1940). As stateless societies, most of them have political systems which correspond generally with what Mair (1962:61–77) has recently termed "minimal government." Some, like the New Hebrides groups with their elaborately ranked secret societies, resemble what Mair (1962:78–107) calls systems of "diffused government." (The Melanesian graded societies in which the standing of the individual is achieved through enterprise and effort differ in mode of recruitment from the African age-set systems instanced by Mair, but the element of authority diffused through the membership of ranks is not dissimilar.)

The typical traditional Melanesian headman or "big-man" achieves prestige and power through hard work in the gardens, prowess in warfare, a reputation as a magician, shrewdness in trading, a commanding personality, or skill in attracting and organizing followers. He must constantly validate his status and humble his rivals by financing and organizing feasts and ceremonies within a context of complex mutual obligations. He has no official hierarchy or sanctified office on which to base his claims of social ascendancy. His control of the economic activities of others is far less than of Polynesian or Micronesian chiefs. He is not exempt from subsistence tasks, and he does not work within a system of graded occupational specialties. He achieves little or nothing in the way of privileged consumption, and any surplus which he controls must be expended in further competitive activities if he is to maintain his position.

There is no equivalent within these Melanesian systems of the status-level endogamy found in Polynesia. Typical Melanesian societies show only the faintest reflections of the obeisance behaviours and honorific usages referred to earlier. Differential access to the supernatural among Melanesians generally occurs in the form of individual and corporate ownership of rites without implications of stratification, essentially nonhierarchical totemic distinctions, or secret societies open to all men on a more or less competitive basis.

The limited political influence which the individual can achieve in most Melanesian societies is as impermanent and open to rivalry as the other forms of privilege noted. Narrow in scope, the authority of the "big-man" does not extend to unilateral decisions of peace and warfare or confiscation of property. These leaders have little power to settle disputes or inflict punishments. Social control depends principally on kin-group responsibility for vengeance and on supernatural sanctions, not on any authority of individuals or offices.

These characteristic patterns take their most typical form in western Melanesia from New Guinea through the Bismarck Archipelago to the Solomons. Even here, however, a few exceptional cases require attention. The best known of these is that of the Trobriand Islanders, with their ranked kin groups and hereditary chiefly leadership. Indeed, the special features of this society have been made so famous by the classical descriptions of Malinowski (1922; 1935) that occasional mention has been made of the fact that it is not at all typical of Melanesia at large (e.g., Worsley 1957:15). It is also true, of course, that Trobriand society is by no means as highly stratified and centralized as many Polynesian and Micronesian systems. In this connection it is interesting to note that, in contrast to the Polynesian societies where stratification was maintained and where political unification expanded under European influence, hereditary leadership appears to be in decline among the Trobrianders (Hogbin 1958: 196–197).

Another famous Melanesian people with a small degree of social stratification, but without precontact political centralization, is the Manus (Mead 1930; 1956). Here we have a mixed system of hereditary rank and egalitarian competitiveness. As Mead (1956:-60–61) puts it: "In times of peaceful economic functioning, actual wealth and economic leadership overshadowed these status relationships based on kinship. . . . In times of crisis clan and rank would come to the fore. . . . So, while the absoluteness of rank and clan membership did provide a little security, a little tempering of manners, and a slight basis for responsibility to kin and village, it became important mainly in personal or communal emergencies. Between the emergencies, people formed their alliances along economic and practical lines." Owing to the geographic position of the Admiralty Islands, together with other evidence of contact between the two regions, it seems likely that this mixed system may reflect Micronesian influence (Nevermann 1934).

As attention is shifted toward the more easterly reaches of Melanesia, the typical features of sociopolitical organization in this culture area are gradually modified, particularly in the existence and elaboration of chieftainships. There are sporadic instances of weakly developed chiefly statuses in certain localities within the larger islands to the east of New Guinea, including New Ireland, New Britain, and Bougainville. Most of these would fit Hogbin's (1935:218) description of the clan leader in the smaller Schouten Islands as "more than a headman, but less than a chief" (see also Hogbin 1939; 1951). Minor chiefs become somewhat more common in parts of the Solomon chain and in the New Hebrides, particularly the southern portions of the latter group. It is possible that Polynesian influence may have been at work here. The institution of chieftainship is much more elaborate and highly structured in New Caledonia, and it reaches its most conspicuous Melanesian elaboration at the eastern border of the area in Fiji. There is little or no doubt that contact with Polynesia played a major role in these easternmost developments, most notably in Fiji.

The situation in the Solomon Islands and the New Hebrides has been summarized by an early authority (Codrington 1891:46–58): "It has been shown that the social structure in these Melanesian islands is not tribal, and it will have been observed therefore that there can be no political structure held together by the power of tribal chiefs; but chiefs exist, and still have in most islands important place and power, though never perhaps so much importance in the native view as they have in the eyes of European visitors, who carry with them the persuasion that savage people are always ruled by chiefs. . . . As a matter of fact the power of chiefs has hitherto rested upon the belief in their supernatural power derived from the spirits or ghosts with which they had intercourse" (p. 46). "The hereditary element is not absent in the succession of chiefs . . . though it is by no means so operative as it appears to be" (p. 51). In order to ensure the succession of their heirs to positions of leadership, chiefly fathers must strive in rivalry with others to see to it that their sons inherit both wealth and ritual skills.

A more recent survey confirms this description and summarizes the somewhat different New Caledonian systems as well (Belshaw 1950*a*:23–36): "In the New Hebrides leaders were men high in the ranks of the [graded secret] societies. In the Solomons leaders seldom controlled more than a village, though there are cases on record of the emergence of temporary leaders whose military prowess attracted the adherence of groups of villages" (p. 34). In New Caledonia "there were large tribal units, in which the chiefs held sway over lesser chiefs who controlled village units, and in which the division of functions was marked by the appointment of special officials" (p. 34). Belshaw also notes the parallel between "the Polynesian islands and the tribes of New Caledonia" where "men turned first to the son of the deceased chief for their new leader. . . . In such cases wealth for distribution was acquired through presents received from the people by virtue of the leader's status" (p. 33).

The islands of Fiji stand at the border between Melanesia and Polynesia, and the culture of their indigenous peoples is compounded of elements from both areas. Buck (1938/39:311) has summarized the developments which led to this situation: "The western triangle of Samoa, Tonga, and Fiji became an important area for exchange and diffusion. Commercial relationships were favoured by intermarriage, and Fijian customs that were of use to the Polynesians were readily adopted. Intermixture took place between chiefly families and as a result a higher Fijian culture that absorbed certain Polynesian elements was developed at the places of contact. This mixed culture was marked by patrilineal descent, powerful chiefs, and much elaborate ceremony which contrasted with the earlier Melanesian culture retained in those parts of Fiji that did not come under Polynesian trade influence."

Thus important local differences in social and political structure developed within Fiji. Stanner (1953:172–173) has summarized the resulting distribution of contrasting forms: "In the west again the conceptions of chieftainship and rank are not stressed as strongly as in the east. . . . There would seem to be little question that, over a long period of time, Fiji has been changing from simpler, less stratified local societies of mainly matrilineal emphasis to those of high stratification and patrineal emphasis, and that this was due to intrusive Polynesian influence." Hocart (1950:74–75) indicates that stratification and centralization are "more definite and well developed" among coastal Fijians and less so among the inland hill tribes. This presumably also reflects a gradient of Polynesian influence from the coast to the interior.

Thus the Fijian social and political systems in the west and the interior of the islands approach those which are typical of Melanesia as a whole. The other and more prominently known form of indigenous Fijian society, however, was characterized by ranked kin groups and hereditary chieftainships holding stewardship over the communally owned land, with political and economic as well as ceremonial functions. Compared with some of the highly structured Polynesian societies, this system was rather flexible. Nevertheless, it was certainly more highly stratified and centralized than other indigenous systems in Melanesia.

Multiracial Systems of Colonial Societies

Since the discovery of the Pacific by mariners from Europe in the sixteenth century, all the indigenous societies of Oceania—save a few as yet uncontacted groups in the interior of New Guinea—have been integrated into colonial systems controlled by European states. As alien control was consolidated, not only did Europeans become resident in every island group, but sizeable Asian populations were brought to most areas as well. These historical developments produced ethnically stratified multiracial or plural societies under the political authority of colonial powers. Thus throughout the Pacific new forms of social stratification and political centralization were superimposed upon the indigenous societies.

As Oliver (1961:367) puts it, the native islanders "were brought out of their isolation into contact with larger polities; in the process, however, they were invariably placed in subordinate caste roles . . ."; and (p. 363): "Except in Japanese Micronesia, whites occupied the highest caste positions and usually gained most economically." These colonial systems are typically composed of three main ethnic strata: Europeans or Americans composing the upper level, Asians holding middle rank, native peoples at the bottom of the structure. In the majority of island areas there are also variable groups of mixed origin, generally known as mixed-bloods or half-castes.

Owing to Euro-American domination, the recent contemporary societies have many special features of European origin. Two of these are particularly important. In the first place, these are market-dominated systems rather than kinship societies, even though their market economics are not as fully developed as those of the controlling metropolitan powers. Thus islanders have been introduced to the special relationship between entrepreneur and hired labourer, and island economics have become subject to the vagaries of world markets. Secondly, the ethnic hierarchies are supported by attitudes and values of exclusiveness and discrimination on the basis of race. Pride of race and belief in racial superiority or inferiority constitute dimensions of stratification which were no more than faintly foreshadowed in traditional Polynesian cultures. Along with these distinctive characteristics, the new sociopolitical systems also share many elements that are analogous to features which we have seen to be typical of aboriginal Polynesia and Micronesia but not of native Melanesia.

The economic affairs of the islands, particularly the productive activities beyond subsistence level and the wider realms of economic policy, are heavily dominated by alien interests. By far the larger share of this control is vested in the European status group, with a lesser degree of economic power accruing to Asian entrepreneurs in most areas. Ultimate economic authority is generally in the hands of European administrations, and may be exercised in such forms as taxation (functionally analogous to tribute levied by Polynesian and Micronesian chiefs), compulsory work of various kinds (comparable to chiefly requisitioning of communal labour), and alienation of land or other resources (like dispossessions of title by indigenous chiefs). Occupational specialization is more highly developed than in any of the native economies, with the most prestigious and powerful occupations generally reserved to Europeans. It is particularly conspicuous that Europeans are exempt from subsistence activities and shun practically all forms of manual labour. Not only do Europeans, and to a lesser extent Asians, generally possess and consume quantities of wealth far greater than those available to native islanders, but whole categories of expensive manufactured goods or luxury items are often owned only by the higher status groups.

Social intercourse between different status levels is regularly limited and conditioned by the privileges of higher groups and disabilities of others. Variations in this respect will be discussed below. Here it can be noted that commanding and humble behaviour between groups is common and often includes deferential usages and honorific patterns. The colour bar, in one form or another, generally inhibits interdining, informal meetings, and equal access to public facilities and services. Status endogamy is of variable strength but present everywhere, at least in the form of an upper-level preference. Particularly as the numbers of Europeans and Asian women in the islands gradually increased, interstatus marriage has generally become more rare.

Writing of the period between the two World Wars, Keesing (1945:55–56) describes this trend as follows: "Over the South Seas as a whole, indeed, social influences of the general character just mentioned have been at work in the past quarter century to limit new intermixture . . . with fuller transplanting of social customs from the homelands have been brought the attitudes of racial exclusiveness and prejudice. . . . The tendency has been, therefore, for new marriages between white and native to be frowned on increasingly, and for those so married, along with their part-native descendants, to be edged subtly or otherwise out of the inner circle of the non-native society. When outsiders still marry persons of native ancestry, their choice usually falls among part natives with small fractions of island blood rather than within the full or predominantly native group."

In the development of colonial regimes, political unity was greatly widened and centralization of authority was imposed on a scale previously unknown in the islands. Whether by indirect rule, or more directly, supreme power was securely placed in the hands of the dominant ethnic group. Thus European governments make war and establish peace, legislate and implement the legal constitutions of their territories, establish systems of justice, and enforce all the more important secular punishments. Commonly, the system of ethnic stratification is officially sanctioned by provisions which assign separate legal statuses to Europeans, Asians, and indigenous peoples.

Within this widespread general framework, there are also significant contrasts between the colonial societies which are typical of Polynesia and Micronesia, on the one hand, and those which have developed in Melanesia on the other. In the former regions we find plural societies characterized by comparatively tolerant, variable, and flexible ethnic stratification, together with relatively mild élite political authority frequently functioning through indirect rule or even multiracial representative institutions. In Melanesia, however, the common pattern is one of comparatively rigid and static ethnic hierarchies accompanied by strong and direct central political control.

PLURAL SOCIETIES IN CONTEMPORARY POLYNESIA AND MICRONESIA

The considerable softening of white-dominated stratification in Micronesia, and especially Polynesia, shows particularly in the relatively tolerant race relations of these areas and the comparative frequency of interstatus marriages or informal liaisons. Though there are some differences of interpretation among qualified observers, nevertheless there can be no doubt that all this exists within a context of ethnic stratification, and popular and official versions of interracial amity are often exaggerated.

Hawaii and New Zealand are best known for relatively amicable inter-group relations. Of all the Pacific islands, these are the areas in which alien settlement has been on the largest scale and most stable. They are also the only areas where Euro-American culture has become sufficiently well rooted to establish fully developed Western societies, one as a member nation of the British Commonwealth, the other as a state of the United States. Hawaii certainly is justly famous as a racial melting pot produced by a high frequency of intermarriage among European, Asian, and Polynesian elements (Adams 1937). Especially in recent decades, some Maoris have played important roles at many levels of national life in New Zealand (Beaglehole and Beaglehole 1946).

Oliver (1961:259–260) sums up the Hawaiian situation as it had developed by 1939: "Almost daily, editorials in the local newspapers commented upon the happy state of interracial relations, and for such a complex racial conglomeration there was, in fact, a surprisingly small amount of racial antagonism. There was, nevertheless, a distinct class system along ethnic lines in spite of a large number of interracial marriages." Furnas (1946:191) presents a similar summary. "It was never true, though the *haole* [island resident of Euro-American descent] still piously tells the outsider so, that racial friction has never existed in the Islands. . . . And there are few signs that the marked social cleavage between the *haole* and everybody else that always characterized the Islands . . . is yet starting to break down. But on the whole a mutual tolerance . . . has kept trouble to a gratifying minimum, certainly less than most mainland communities would have shown under the same circumstances."

The same author (Furnas 1946:392) appraises the New Zealand scene similarly. "The *pakeha* [white New Zealander] likes to tell himself and anybody else who will listen, that New Zealanders feel no anti-Maori prejudice. I could get no intelligent Maori to agree. True, in this respect the New Zealander behaves much better than an Englishman or American probably would . . . but prejudice is still there, cropping up in some employments, in hotel accommodations, among children . . ." The continued existence of widespread ethnic discrimination in present-day New Zealand has recently been documented (Harre, 1962). Both Hawaii and New Zealand are special cases in which the general Pacific pattern nevertheless remains discernible in particular local forms. Another region in which European-native marriages have occurred in substantial numbers is Tahiti and neighbouring parts of French Oceania (Oliver 1961:207).

Hawaii and New Zealand are also unusual in their modern political circumstances. Following a series of intervening political developments which will be noted below in a section on native responses to European influence, both Hawaiians and Maoris have become internal minorities within modern Western nations. In both cases, the descendants of indigenous islanders participate in representative institutions on a basis more or less similar to that of other ethnic groups.

In most of the remainder of Polynesia, the pattern of European domination has been one of more or less indirect role. This was not necessarily the simple result of official policies systematically worked out by metropolitan powers and conscientiously implemented in the islands. Thus the affairs of nineteenth century Tonga, for example, were influenced by the interplay of such factors as a determined traditional native leadership, little European settlement or alienation of land to outsiders, the predominant exercise of Westernizing influence by politically active Methodist missionaries, rather weak German commercial and political influences, and only relatively and latterly stronger British imperial interests (Morrell 1960:48–53, 310–329). Out of all this developed a British protectorate over an autonomous Tongan kingdom with a separatist Methodist establishment which approached the status of a state church. Such are the essentials of the Tongan policy today.

The early interplay between competing external imperial powers and internal native factions in Samoa led to the creation of a short-lived island "kingship." Following the partition of this island group, first German and then New Zealand administrators in Western Samoa wrestled for decades with indigenous factionalism expressed through vigorous forms of traditional leadership which have persisted up to the recent granting of political independence to this territory. In American Samoa, traditional political institutions were encouraged to function as long as they did not constitute a threat to public order as defined by a paternalistic naval administration. During the last few years this general pattern has been continued within a framework of American constitutional forms and under a civil administration (West 1961:129–136).

Although French policy in Tahiti later became increasingly oriented toward assimilation to European political patterns, the early contact history of the Society Group saw a local chieftainship metamorphosed into an island kingdom largely through the influence of the London Missionary Society (Morrell 1960:39–43; West 1961:73–86). Most of the more outlying sections of French Polynesia, where European populations are small, seems to have long been governed rather lightly by a few far-flung representatives of the central authority in Papeete. In the Cook Islands, early Protestant theocratic regimes ruled by missionaries through converted chiefs later developed into a more secular polity in which chiefly roles changed but remained politically significant, first under Britain and then under New Zealand (Morrell 1960:280–297). The comparatively isolated islanders of the Gilbert and Ellice chains have been allowed by Britain to retain a large share of authority over their local affairs (Grimble 1952).

Turning to Micronesia, the development of modern Guam is too complex for summary here, and the resulting cultural transformation is probably more complete than that of any Pacific area which has not become an integral part of a Western nation. Under Spanish and American hegemony there have been various periods and tendencies of absolutism, paternalism, and indirect rule, but the original native patterns of stratification and chiefly power have long since disappeared. In the rest of the Mariana Islands when they became part of the German Empire, as in the Carolines and the Marshalls, "The Germans preferred to work through the local chiefs and restricted their authority only to the extent of abolishing their feuding and their privilege to inflict the death penalty. . . . Native institutions were left alone, except those that obstructed industry and commerce" (Oliver 1961: 348, 350).

Under Japan, massive Asian immigration and alien economic domination tended to overwhelm native interests in these same areas, although the Japanese continued some degree of indirect rule and, according to Oliver (1961:354), "caste lines between natives and non-natives were not so rigidly drawn here" as in most British and French island dependencies. The ultimate intentions of the United States in its postwar retention of practically the entire Micronesian culture area are not altogether clear. Nevertheless, the American administration, transferred from the navy to civil authorities after 1950, appears to be following a general policy of indirect rule which makes some use of surviving native authority patterns.[2]

IMPOSED ETHNIC STRATIFICATION IN MODERN MELANESIA

While the phenomena of modern ethnic stratification have hardly been investigated exhaustively elsewhere in the Pacific, they have received very little systematic scholarly attention in Melanesia. Data will therefore be presented here from one illustrative Melanesian area: the Australian Territory of New Guinea. Though a rather full unpublished analysis of social stratification in modern New Guinea has been carried out (Valentine 1958: 254–330), only one fairly extensive discussion is available in print (Reed 1943:243–252). Reed describes a "caste system" based on a doctrine of "white prestige." His analysis is confined mainly to European values and attitudes and to patterns of interaction between groups as they affect relations between aliens and natives. He attempts little in the way of structural definition and gives little attention to the Asian group.

Various scholarly critics of the Australian record in New Guinea (e.g., Mair 1948; Worsley 1957) have described race relations within the territory in loosely similar terms, without, however, employing the concept of ethnic stratification as such. These views of Reed, Mair, and others have been characterized by Stanner (1953:42–44) as "impressionistic," as being based on a "formula of criticism [which] was shallow," and as reducing "human problems" to "a preposterous simplicity." Stanner nevertheless found these criticisms "extremely difficult to meet, [for] there was altogether too much in the factual grounds of complaint to allow simple denial."

One of the most striking structural features of ethnic stratification in New Guinea is the endogamy of status groups. Statistical data which would provide meaningful indices of this phenomenon have not been published in recent years. Nevertheless, analysis of the 502 marriages registered by Europeans, Asians, and mixed-bloods during the decade 1928–38 provides an indication of a long-established pattern which undoubtedly persists in its essentials today. During the stated period, 96 per cent of European marriages were with Europeans. Among Asians, 62 per cent of registered unions were with Asians, with marriages to native Melanesians accounting for an additional 27 per cent and unions with mixed-bloods for almost all of the remainder. Persons of mixed ancestry were married, in almost equal proportions, to other mixed-bloods, to Asians, or to members of all other groups. Though marriages between Melanesians were not recorded, the indigenous population was, of course, virtually 100 per cent ethnically endogamous (see Table 1).

These figures reveal a system in which the highest and lowest status groups maintain the strictest endogamy in practice. Marriages between members of these two groups are extremely rare. The rather different proportions for Asians probably are due principally to a relative shortage of Asian women, but also in part to a less rigid ethnic consciousness within this mainly Chinese group. The small group of mixed-bloods, accounting for less than 7 per cent of the registered sample, are exceptions to the system of stratification by their very origin and parentage. Their marital patterns reflect their equivocal position with respect to the system. It is notable, however, that only 1 per cent of European marriages involved mixed-bloods.

Another prominent index of ethnic separation and stratification in this system is occupational specialization. Data permitting a meaningful comparison of European and Asian occupations have been published only from the census of 1921. At this time there was a total nonindigenous population in the Territory of slightly under 3,200. Of these, a little more than one half were Chinese, and there were a few other Asians as well, so that the Europeans

Table 1

Marriages Registered in the Territory of New Guinea, 1928–1938

Ethnic Groups	Marriages No.	%	Ethnic Groups	Marriages No.	%
European (Pop. 1933: 3,191)			Melanesian (Pop. 1933: 401,129)[b]		
Endogamous			Endogamous		
European/European	334	96	Melanesian/Melanesian	[c]	[c]
Nonendogamous			Nonendogamous		
European/Asian	2	0.5	Melanesian/European	4	[c]
European/Melanesian	4	1.5	Melanesian/Asian	33	[c]
European/half-caste	4	1.5	Melanesian/half-caste	2	[c]
European/other[a]	2	0.5	Melanesian/other[a]	0	0
Total European	346	100	Total Melanesian	[c]	[c]
Asian (Pop. 1933: 1,772)			Half-caste (Pop. 1933: 195)		
Endogamous			Endogamous		
Asian/Asian	76	62	Half-caste/half-caste	11	33
Nonendogamous			Nonendogamous		
Asian/European	2	1	Half-caste/European	4	12
Asian/Melanesian	33	27	Half-caste/Asian	11	33
Asian/half-caste	11	9	Half-caste/Melanesian	2	7
Asian/other[a]	1	1	Half-caste/other[a]	5	15
Total Asian	123	100	Total Half-caste	33	100

Grand Total: 502 registered marriages

[a]Other=Polynesians, Micronesians, etc.
[b]Partial census only; actual total probably more of the order of 1,000,000.
[c]Unknown, because marriages of Melanesians were not registered unless they involved members of the other groups. Obviously, Melanesian marriages were more than 99 percent endogamous.
Data from Australia, 1930:97; 1931:107; 1932:105; 1933:95; 1934:115; 1935:104; 1936:98; 1937:100; 1938:127; 1939:130.

were in a minority even within the non-Melanesian population. It is a striking statistic that approximately 98 per cent of all the more than 500 positions classified as professional were held by Europeans. At the opposite end of the nonindigenous occupational scale, well over 90 per cent of the nearly 200 positions in the building trades were held by Asians. A major occupational area of overlap between these two non-native groups was commerce, where more than a third of the total was made up of Asians, most of them Chinese small traders (see Table 2).

Further inferences from these data can be presented briefly, though neither the reasoning behind these conclusions nor other supporting evidence can be given in detail here because of limitations of space. (Full details can be found in Valentine 1958:283–294.) The major groups within the professional classification are government officials,

Table 2

Occupations of the Non-indigenous Population in the Territory of New Guinea, 1921

Occupations	Chinese No.	Chinese %	Non-Chinese[a] No.	Non-Chinese[a] %	Total No.
Professional	11	2	544	98	555
Domestic	128	76	40	24	168
Commercial	304	63	171	37	475
Transport and communications	87	47	99	53	186
On seas and rivers	80	52	74	48	154
On roads	6	86	1	14	7
Post and telegraph	1	4	23	96	24
Other	1	50	1	50	2
Industrial	382	79	101	21	483
Manufacturing	139	72	54	28	193
Building	185	93	13	7	198
Earthworks	33	73	12	27	45
Undefined	25	53	22	47	47
Primary production	138	28	352	72	490
Agricultural	114	25	346	75	460
Fisheries	8	73	3	27	11
Forestry	15	100	—	—	15
Other	1	25	3	75	4
Dependents	361	46	424	54	785
Unspecified	13	—	18	—	31
Totals	1,424	45	1,749	55	3,173

[a]Occupational data are available only in this form, comparing Chinese with all other groups. Population figures for the nonindigenous inhabitants of the Territory in the same year are as follows:

	No.	%
Europeans	1,288	41
Asians	1,780	56
Chinese 1,424 (80% of the Asian total)		
Other Asians 356 (20% of the Asian total)		
Mixed-bloods	69	2
Others	36	1
Total	3,173	100

Data from Australia, 1923:120,140.

the military, and missionaries. At the time when these figures were gathered, the public service was restricted to natural-born British subjects, the military officers were Australians, and the senior missionaries were mainly Germans and all Europeans. Thus Asians were entirely excluded from these occupations. The few Chinese in the professional category were probably engineers (Rowley 1958:77).

Of all persons classified as following domestic occupations, about three-quarters were servants and the remainder engaged in the business of board and lodging for hire. There was no European servant class in New Guinea. This, together with other evidence, indicates that all the nonindigenous servants were Asians and, apart from a handful of Asian establishments in the Chinatown of Rabaul, Europeans were the hotel and restaurant keepers.

The categories of industrial and manufacturing occupations are somewhat misleading, for the Territory had no large-scale modern industry. The kinds of establishments referred to here were small-scale enterprises in boat building, tailoring and dressmaking, saw-milling, and blacksmithing. In these activities, the Chinese are by far in the majority over other groups. If craftsmen from other Asian groups could be isolated within the "non-Chinese" category, this majority would grow still larger, for practically all artisans in the alien population were Asians. Together with small commercial operations, these trades were by far their most important occupations (*Official Handbook* 1937:135, 151).

The control of primary production in New Guinea was clearly in the hands of Europeans. In the agricultural classification, which refers mainly to those engaged in running coconut plantations, the Chinese constitute one quarter of the total, and this would be increased slightly by the addition of other Asians. Some of the Asians engaged in agriculture were market gardeners, and apart from a small area set aside for leases to Chinese in New Ireland few Asians owned, leased, or managed plantation estates. These were the characteristic occupations of Europeans outside the professional groups. All aliens on plantations were in managerial or supervisory positions, for earlier experiments in Chinese coolie labour had failed (Rowley 1958:72 ff.), and all unskilled or general labour was performed by Melanesian workers. Somewhat more recent figures indicate that by 1938 this pattern had become even more definite, for of the non-indigenous personnel employed on plantations in that year 81 per cent were Europeans, 14 per cent Asians, and the remaining 5 per cent half-castes (Australia 1939:93).

The perpetuation of this system of ethnic occupational stratification into the last decade can be seen from official statistics compiled for the year 1955 (Australia 1955:112–125, 179–181). These figures also enable us to make a direct comparison of European and native Melanesian occupations. In 1955, some 90 per cent of the approximately 44,000 indigenous employees in New Guinea were engaged as manual labourers, domestic help, and similar kinds of unskilled or slightly skilled workers. In the same labour force only about 5 per cent were employed as drivers, carpenters, clerks, or in similar jobs. Barely 2 per cent of indigenous employees worked as junior teachers, medical assistants, or mission helpers. There were essentially no other positions approaching professional status held by

Melanesians, with the possible exception of about a dozen masters of small coastal vessels. It appears that no Melanesian held a post which could be classified as executive or administrative.

These figures can only be compared with data on the Europeans who worked for the administration, since no information applying to nonofficial Europeans gainfully employed has been made available. Of the almost 850 Europeans in the public service within the Territory in 1955, nearly 5 per cent were classifiable as administrative and executive personnel, a little over 70 per cent as professional or technical specialists, approximately 10 per cent as clerical employees, and about 15 per cent as "other," presumably lower-status job holders. Comparing the two sets of figures, we find that at least 90 per cent of Melanesian employees followed occupations at which Europeans certainly rarely, and probably never, worked. Likewise, approximately three quarters of all officially employed Europeans held positions which were not occupied by any Melanesians. There can be no doubt that these proportions would be essentially unaffected if quantitative data were available on nonofficial Europeans, self-employed or working for private employers.

This stratified division of labour is only part of a wider economic system characterized by an ethnic hierarchy. Resident Europeans and overseas European interests control the overwhelming preponderance of territorial wealth and property involved in the market economy. Not only do members of the highest status group hold all important professional and executive posts in the local society, but they also occupy most of the strategic commercial positions and hold a completely dominant interest in the plantation economy and mining enterprises. They do not engage in subsistence activities, unskilled manual labour, or other forms of low-status work. Asians are primarily small traders, artisans, and craftsmen, though individuals among them are quite successful commercially.

The historical role of the Melanesians has been that of a labouring group without any capital wealth which is immediately usable within the the market economy, even though most of the land remains unalienated and thus constitutes a great potential resource in native hands. The principal role of the indigenous population has been to provide the unskilled workers and servants of the island economy, in addition to a few skilled and semiskilled workers. Since 1949 there has been a small development of Melanesian commercial enterprises, in the form of cooperative societies established and supervised by the Territory government. By 1957 there were nearly 100 such societies producing copra and cocoa (Australian Institute of Political Science 1958:239). Their membership, however, amounted to only 42,000 in an estimated indigenous population of more than a million and a quarter. For the year 1956–57, the combined production of these cooperatives was valued at a little over £A308,000 but this must be compared with the total of the same major agricultural products exported from the territory, valued at about £A8,900,000 (Australian Institute 1958: 214). This means that native cooperative production accounted for only about 3 per cent of territorial exports of plantation products. It should be noted that the cooperative movement has continued to expand, and that there are a few individual Melanesian entrepreneurs with small private businesses in favoured regions like the Tolai area around Rabaul. Nevertheless, the Melanesian share in the modern market economy of New Guinea obviously remains extremely small.

The New Guinea system of stratification includes various special patterns of social intercourse and communication among the three major ethnic groups. A high degree of social separation prevails, including both residential and educational segregation and a general colour bar in multiracial communities. Nevertheless, there are of course many individual and group contacts and interactions across status lines. The nature and atmosphere of these contacts are governed by a rather clearly defined code of intergroup etiquette. The strictness and rigidity of this code are most evident in European-Melanesian contacts and least so for interactions between Europeans and Asians, but the entire system symbolizes the relative positions of all three groups. The present description will be limited to certain prominent aspects of European-native relations, but further details can be found elsewhere (Valentine 1958:294–309).

The major distinctive element of etiquette between these two groups is that it requires overtly obeisant, submissive, and self-effacing behaviour on the part of Melanesians. This pattern takes somewhat different forms in different social contexts which cannot be fully described here. Relations between official administrators and natives are often characterized by regimentation. Ordinary natives are formed into lines or queues and have to stand at attention in the presence of an officer, who often adopts a commanding and brusque attitude, and barks abrupt orders. Native headmen have to salute all officers. The relations between private employers and native labourers or servants embody some of the most direct expressions of alien supremacy. In addition to rather regimented forms of discipline commonly exercised by authoritarian superiors, it is in these contexts that the subservience of the lower status group is most often enforced by kicks and cuffs, even though private corporal punishment is illegal.

Melanesians must generally address Europeans by appropriate honorific titles, such as the pidgin equivalents of "master" and "missus," while natives are customarily addressed as "boy" or "mary." In most circumstances, proper behaviour for a Melanesian wishing to speak to a European who may be otherwise occupied is to stand quietly and unobtrusively by until the object of his attention notices him and invites, or orders, him to state his business. Natives are not normally admitted to alien homes for any purpose except labour or service as directed by their employers. In the last few years some of these customs have been mitigated in certain institutional contexts, particularly by government officers in their official relations with Melanesian public servants and their dealings with native village (now local government) councils. Of course, there are variations in the behaviour of individuals, especially those who belong to the upper status levels. Nevertheless, the general system of social intercourse remains one which stresses superordination and subordination to a marked degree.

The ethnic hierarchy which characterizes New Guinea society is supported and validated by a set of European beliefs, attitudes, and values. For the sake of brevity, the present discussion will again be confined to European-Melanesian relations. Although there have been shifts in emphasis and variations in mode of expression, the essential elements here have remained the same through the history of the Territory, and are generally consistent with ideas held by Europeans who have dominated ethnically diverse peoples in many other parts of the colonial world. The essence of these beliefs can be summed up in two corollary propositions. The first is a stereotype as to the nature of the Melanesian: the native is inferior. The second is the doctrine of white prestige: the European group must remain dominant.

At the same time, certain other European ideas and sentiments have been partially inconsistent with these and have contributed to historical shifts within the general pattern. From the beginnings of European influence in New Guinea, missionaries have had faith that Melanesian souls can be saved, planters have assumed that native men can be made to labour for alien interests, administrators have believed that indigenous communities can be brought under British law. An early tendency to regard the inferiority of the Melanesian as immutable gave way, during the period of the Mandate, to a concept of "gradual evolution."

The "evolutionary" development of which the indigenous peoples were thought to be capable was somewhat vaguely and variously defined by different sections of alien opinion. It was assumed that firm guidance and discipline by Europeans would continue to be required. While admitting the principle that natives might someday achieve some of the standards which distinguish aliens, this position remained nearly as inflexible as ever as to the privileges and prerogatives that go with these standards. It placed the day of possible achievement conveniently in the distant future and tacitly supported attitudes of superiority in the meantime At the same time, however, there was a discernible growth of incipient humanitarianism, particularly at the official level, in a growing refusal to countenance such gross abuses as arbitrary use of military measures, forced labour, and corporal punishment. The official governmental version of this complex of ideas which developed during the period between the World Wars was the policy of "dual development" (Legge 1956:3–4, 85–86; Valentine 1958:647–666). According to this doctrine, alien and native interests are expected to advance in parallel fashion without conflict.

It was during the period just described that the system of ethnic stratification was fully developed and stabilized. In the more recent postwar period of the Trust Territory this system and the beliefs supporting it have undergone some further liberalization, chiefly through developments in governmental attitudes and policies. Within the last few years, official opinion has begun to challenge the assumption of innate Melanesian psychological inferiority, to stress the educability of indigenous groups, and to emphasize cultural inadequacy as opposed to biological inferiority (Gunther 1958). Along with this goes a stated policy that the Melanesians should be granted some improvements in education and opportunities, so that they will be content to remain amicably dependent upon European authority for the foreseeable future (Gunther 1958; Hasluck 1958). For the most part, general nonofficial opinion and sentiment appear to have lagged well behind these developments Meanwhile the broad outlines of government action continue to be consistent with the policy of dual development.

The expression of European status ideas in their most fully developed form can now be documented briefly for each of the major segments of the alien population. The principal organ of opinion for the planter and merchant are the island newspapers such as the Rabaul *Times*. The following extract from an editorial reaction to a government proposal for improving native education expresses views commonly heard among this group, especially during the period of the Mandate (Rabaul *Times*, 25 January 1929, quoted in Reed 1943):

> The local native has very small intelligence, and in the greater number of cases what little intelligence he has is used for criminal purposes. . . .
>
> Left to their own resources the natives are so lazy that it would be only a matter of very little time before every inch of ground would be overgrown. . . .
>
> We must realize that it is no use trying to make a white man of the native. A native is a native, and if God Almighty is content to put the native on earth as such, it is up to us to leave it that way.

A clergyman, who through many years of experience in the islands rose to the head of one of New Guinea's principal missions, published some ten years ago a manual for his missionaries (Scharmach, 1953). This document includes a great deal of material on the characteristics of Melanesians, from which only a few relevant and representative passages can be quoted here:

> The native is not predominantly a creature of strong will or intelligence. Impulsive rather than imaginative, his actions are prompted by instinct (p. 2).
>
> However natives who receive a protracted education in our schools develop favourably. They are able to follow a course of studies similar to those of European children (p. 3).
>
> Principal faults are the following: Egoism, Pride, Greed for wealth, Sensuality and Laziness.
>
> EGOISM manifests itself in the motives of fear and selfish interest.
>
> These two motives constitute the main power by which all the native's actions are driven; they give us the key to his strange mentality (p. 9).

The "principal good qualities" of native character are adumbrated somewhat more briefly under the rubrics "friendliness," "code of good manners," "hospitality," "filial and clan love," and "respect for authority" (pp. 19–22).

While governing the islands under a League of Nations Mandate, the Australian government issued an *Official Handbook of the Territory of New Guinea* (1937), which can be taken as an authoritative expression of the views and policies of officialdom at that time. The section on employment is introduced with these words:

> It has been truthfully written that: "the function of the white man in a tropical country is not to labour with his hands, but to direct and control a plentiful supply of native labour and assist in the government of the country, or to engage in opportunities for trade and commerce from an office desk in a bank or mercantile firm" (p. 328).

The *Handbook* also includes a description of native administration. It is first stated that the administration adheres to League of Nations principles, including concern for native welfare. Then governmental policy is further specified:

> In considering any matter directly or indirectly bearing on the native inhabitants of the Territory, the primitive nature of these people must never be lost

> sight of. Any idea of endeavouring to force a policy of rapid development upon them is foredoomed to failure.
>
> The ultimate aim of the Administration is, by means of a gradual progressive policy, to fit the native to participate in the economic and social life of his country (p. 279).

This brings us to the political structure of contemporary New Guinea. The administration of the Trust Territory is unified with that of the Territory of Papua under a single Australian governing power. Within this combined area, the process of establishing central political authority is still going on, for as late as 1958 there were some 38,000 square miles inhabited by perhaps 300,000 people still outside effective government control (Australian Institute 1958:208; Hasluck 1958:91). Nevertheless, in the greater part of the country over which the territorial government holds sway, Europeans have imposed a high degree of political unification and centralized authority which have neither precedent nor parallel in indigenous Melanesian systems.

As one might expect from the status system described earlier, the establishment of European power has been a paternalistic enterprise, frequently authoritarian, and, in the early stages particularly, often physically forceful. Through a system of essentially direct rule, often backed by strong police measures, warfare is suppressed, taxation is imposed,[3] legal authority is proclaimed, and the central power is thus established. Physical or military resistance has seldom occurred on a large scale or for long periods.

Because of the general absence of indigenous chiefly authorities, attempts at indirect rule have been largely unsuccessful. Ever since the early days of the German protectorate, native headmen (*luluais*) with assistants or interpreters (*tultuls*) have been appointed by European officers, and made responsible to the administration, in each village as it is brought under control. On the whole, the connection between these native officers and the quite fluid indigenous systems of leadership has been unreliable or equivocal at best, and frequently their power is entirely dependent upon the central European authority. When these men do acquire greater power within their own communities, it is usually in the context of changing native authority patterns which often involve anti-European movements.

Beginning in 1950, the system of appointed *luluais* and *tultuls* has been replaced in selected areas by elective native local government councils with modest powers over Melanesian communities which can be vetoed by the central Administration. By the end of 1960, there were 40 such councils in Papua and New Guinea, 24 of them in the Trust Territory (Robson 1961: 10). In the combined territories at this time some 300,000 people, or approximately 15 percent of the native population, were represented by such local councils (Lynch, 1961). Each of the nine districts into which the Trust Territory is divided has an advisory council, made up mainly of Europeans appointed by the Administration. In 1960 the membership of these district councils ranged from seven to fourteen, and nearly all of them included either two or three Melanesians each (Robson 1961:9). The combined Territory of Papua and New Guinea also has a legislative council, which has included token Melanesian representation during the postwar years. The legislative council is chaired by the Administrator, who heads the territorial government. Until recently, the remaining membership of this body has been made up of 25 Europeans, three of them elected by European voters, plus three natives, all appointed by the Administration.

This political structure is buttressed by a system of group legal status which mirrors the ethnic hierarchy. Since Australia has been the administrating authority, the vast majority of Europeans have been British subjects, with the remainder having the option of becoming naturalized subjects by applying for Australian citizenship. The traditional status of Asians has been that of aliens without the privilege of becoming citizens. In the last few years, Asians have been allowed to apply for citizenship; but in the early stages, at least, less than 15 percent of those eligible to make such application actually did so (Gunther 1958:66). The official status of Melanesians is the special one of "Australian Protected Person." The people in this category are governed by special regulations for the administration of native groups and special courts for native affairs, with the administration of justice entirely in the hands of Europeans.

Certain aspects of the territorial political structure were altered significantly in 1960 (Lynch, 1961). The legislative council was enlarged, its composition was changed so that nonofficial members rather than the Administration are now in the majority, the number of native members was increased, and some of the latter were made elective for the first time. Through an electoral system involving the local councils and other intermediate groups, some 500,000 indigenous people or roughly 25 percent of the native population have been granted a form of indirect representation by members of their own ethnic group in the legislative council. These are major changes that appear to give a larger voice in governmental affairs both to Europeans outside the Administration and to Melanesians, which would be in line with the overall policy of dual development.

It is, of course, too early to judge how the new system will work in practice. However, it does appear that Lynch (1961) is correct in emphasizing that it means a considerable step in the direction of internal political authority as opposed to external administrative rule. The remaining question is, who will wield this growing internal political power; and the new arrangement appears to guarantee that the European minority will continue to hold its control for the foreseeable future. Melanesians, including appointed as well as elected members, make up less than one third of the legislative council membership. Moreover, this new council with its nonofficial majority has now been given the authority to make future changes in the system of election and representation. The Australian government has phrased its intentions in terms of evolution toward an eventual common-role electorate with wider suffrage, but it can hardly be assumed that the increasingly decisive power of nonofficial Europeans will be used in this direction.

The effects on the wider political future of New Guinea of the very recent change of sovereignty over the former Netherlands territory remain to be seen. As far as the area controlled by Australia is concerned, the minister responsible for territorial affairs in the Australian government said as recently as 1958: "It would be quite safe to predict that for the next thirty years at the very least a large part of the task of the Administration of the Territory will still be the establishment and maintenance of law and order among the people, whose habits or whose memories are still closely tied to primitive savagery" (Hasluck 1958:92). Schemes for the political future of the Territory which have been discussed range from integration into Australia, under a white settler government, to merging with neighbouring colonies in a Melanesian federation organized as a dominion within or outside the British Commonwealth. The Australian Minister for Territories has been widely quoted as enunciating the policy that New Guinea and Australia will continue to be united in "a partnership which will be free, close and permanent." The Prime Minister is said to have stated the proposition somewhat more bluntly, saying that Australia was in New Guinea to stay and that it did not regard its presence there as temporary or provisional (Kerr 1958:142).[4]

COMPARISON OF THE DIFFERENT AREAS

It certainly cannot be maintained that ethnic stratification and political centralization in contemporary New Guinea are perfectly representative, in all respects, of the entire Melanesian region. Nevertheless, in its general outlines at least, the sociopolitical system which had developed in New Guinea appears to be reasonably typical of western Melanesia as a whole. Within this framework, there are both demographic and structural differences of detail from one colonial territory to another. Each hierarchy accords highest status to the European population, which is both the smallest group numerically and the least stable group in terms of migration to and from the islands. The indigenous Melanesians invariably occupy the lowest position, with the possible exception of New Caledonia, and the native islanders constitute an overwhelming numerical majority everywhere except in Fiji. The middle-rank Asian group is more variable: Indians in Fiji; Tonkinese, Javanese, and Japanese in New Caledonia; Chinese in Australian New Guinea and elsewhere; Malays and Indonesians in what was formerly Netherlands New Guinea. Papua has no significant Asian population. Indians are the largest ethnic group in Fiji, and this colony is also exceptional for other reasons which will be noted below. European attitudes appear to be somewhat unusual in the one important area under the undivided authority of France, New Caledonia, where upper status exclusiveness is said to be directed particularly against Asians (Oliver 1961: 329).

A basic index of the greater degree of contemporary ethnic stratification in Melanesia as opposed to the rest of the Pacific is the comparative incidence of interracial mating. On the basis of a comprehensive survey, Keesing (1945: 54–55) found that: "The Melanesians, on the whole, are much less marked proportionately by modern racial crossing than either the Polynesians or the Micronesians." After considering the possible influence of other factors, Keesing concludes that the most important reason for this contrast is "the fact that unions between whites and the dark Melanesians have not received the stamp of approval . . . in contrast to the situation among the brown-skinned groups. In British jurisdictions at least [covering by far the majority of both territory and population in Melanesia], legal marriages have been virtually out of the question, so that alien strains have come almost wholly through what are counted unorthodox unions." This accords well with the evidence which we have reviewed from New Guinea.

When we compare occupational stratification in Melanesia with that of other areas, similar contrasts emerge. Polynesians in particular never played the Melanesian role of supplying large quantities of inexpensive labour for European interests. This does not mean that Polynesians and Micronesians generally have occupational opportunities equal to those of Europeans. Nevertheless, possibilities for gaining and practising higher status skills have generally been comparatively greater outside Melanesia. The extremes of this tendency are represented by wealthy Chamorros in the Marianas and the many Hawaiians and Maoris who are more or less economically assimilated. With respect to native production for the market economy, Keesing (1945:117) makes the following comparison between Melanesia and other regions: "No figures specifically on native production are available for the larger Melanesian dependencies, but when figures for the types of products which natives sell are placed against population totals, the per capita income from such sources is seen to be obviously much less."

The same survey by Keesing (1945) shows that a greater centralization of power and a greater tendency to ignore indigenous authority systems, so that the latter disintegrate rapidly, is typical of Melanesia as a whole in comparison with other Oceanic areas: "Direct rule, which keeps responsibility mainly in the hands of the controlling group, is most marked in the large dependencies of western Melanesia" (p. 160). In Melanesian communities, "the traditional forms of power and authority have largely broken down. . . . In the new order, effective authority lies only with more or less external agencies as represented in the district officer, the government-sponsored headman, the constabulary, and, to some extent, the mission. This represents an extreme but apparently widespread condition along the more recently pacified frontiers of Melanesia. In a sense, it telescopes and exaggerates a process that has been much more drawn out in areas of longer contact, especially in Polynesia and Micronesia. These places usually had an interim period of fairly stable leadership and polity of the reorganized kinds reviewed above before the more recent forces of individualism and egalitarianism began to show marked effects" (p. 158).

In our review of the evidence from New Guinea, we found that an instance of the general situation described by Keesing has come about through the application of largely direct rule in the absence of stable chieftainships (cf. Hogbin 1951). In the islands of central Melanesia, between New Guinea and the easternmost groups of the region, native administration differs from this in small degree only, by virtue of a slightly greater indigenous development of chiefs and a slightly greater European use of indirect rule. Thus in the Solomons and the New Hebrides several categories of headmen and chiefs are charged with various duties in administering the law imposed by Europeans. As Belshaw (1950*a*:63) points out, however, "It is important to note that these native officials were in all cases appointed . . . *De jure* leadership became an unpopular job, for it involved a middle position between European and native. . . . The appointed headman was often the "cover" for a man more powerful in village affairs. . . . In all areas popular control of leaders was made more difficult than before: once appointed they could only be removed by administrative action."

In a later work on the same areas, Belshaw (1954:79–80) sums up the results of these processes in the following words: "In early Melanesian society, political authority was an aspect of local groupings. In the present situation the position is much more confused. Previously there was conflict between individuals for power: now there is conflict between both individuals and groups. What is more, the groups owe their allegiance not solely to the small political units of yesterday, but to wider ones such as the State and the Church. Standarization of values is less complete than in the early society" (see also Hogbin 1939).

While conditions appear to have changed little in the New Hebrides in recent years, there have been significant political innovations in the Solomons since the Second World War (Belshaw 1950*a*; 1954). Stemming in part from prewar experiments, both native local government councils and native courts have been established with indigenous personnel. The councils are broadly similar to those established later in New Guinea, as described above. In the Solomons, however, there seems to have been a somewhat greater attempt to enlist traditional leadership, to follow indigenous custom, and to allow for local differences in organization. The Solomons councils also involve a much larger proportion of the total indigenous population.

Contemporary New Caledonia has behind it a complex history, involving several thousand convicts and political exiles from France as well as more thousands of Asian labourers. Indigenous military insurrections occurred on a sizeable scale late in the nineteenth century and early in the present century. The policy of the French administration was one of paternalistic indirect rule, which relied heavily on police powers but allowed a substantial degree of internal self-government by indigenous authorities. As Belshaw (1950*a*: 116) puts it, the French "found themselves administering a people with a strongly developed tribal organization. . . . The policy has been to support this organization and to rule through it; so much so that the chief is solely responsible for the internal administration of the tribe. . . ." Beginning in the 1930's, this policy has been increasingly augmented by one of introducing limited enfranchisement of the Melanesians. This process was furthered by the establishment of a common electoral roll for the colonial legislature in the 1950's. On this basis New Caledonia now has a considerable measure of home rule within the French Union.

Located between the poles of our overall regional comparison, Fiji not only was aboriginally transitional between Melanesia and Polynesia but has also been more recently intermediate in a number of significant respects. After early experiments it soon appeared that most Fijians, like Polynesians, were unwilling to labour on European plantations, though much later in the 1930's they did make up 80 percent of the unskilled work force in local gold mines (Oliver 1961:294). At the same time, Fijians have been much more successful in commercial productive enterprise than other Melanesian peoples. Thus, in sharp contrast to the New Guinea situation described earlier, native-owned coconut groves produced between one half and two thirds of the copra exported from Fiji between the World Wars (Oliver 1961:288–289). Of course, in interpreting such figures it must be remembered that Fiji's principal crop is not copra but sugar, and that this industry is controlled entirely by Europeans and worked mainly by Indians.

The general pattern of political affairs in modern Fiji has been, with some significant exceptions, one of expanding chiefly authority followed by indirect rule. The pre-European process by which chieftainships had been developing for some time was accelerated first by the influence of Tongans and then through the earliest European contacts. The acquisition of firearms made possible conquests which led to the formation of wide confederations among the coastal tribes. Thakombau, high chief of one of these realms, was even accorded the title King of Fiji by Europeans, although he had rivals of roughly equal power and his authority did not extend to the hill tribes of the interior.

It was through voluntary cession by Thakombau that Fiji became a British dependency in 1874. A system of indirect rule through the chiefs and customary law, which was unusually liberal for its time, was then established (Legge 1958:202 ff.), and has continued with modifications from that time forward. Warfare and cannibalism were abolished, but the rank and power of chiefs were otherwise confirmed. Other European influences seem to have undermined the religious and economic powers of indigenous authorities, but within the framework of British rule the chieftainships have been preserved as territorially based centres of secular power. In the early years these developments were confined to coastal areas, and for some time the hill tribes remained under direct rule by European officers.

All this has been greatly complicated, however, by the influx of Indians, first as a minority of indentured labourers in the sugar fields, later as an expanding, upward-mobile numerical majority. Indians have gone into tenant farming, taken over most of the craft and service positions in the local economy, and with more recent increases in education are now beginning to move into the upper-status occupations previously reserved to Europeans. Most of the land continues to belong to Fijians. As might be expected, Indians are beginning to demand both land rights and political suffrage. Meanwhile, Fijians continue to exercise much power over their own affairs under an elaborate form of indirect rule (devised by a Fijian statesman) which preserves chiefly authority and conservatism, partly by separating Fijian politics somewhat from the general government of the colony (West 1961:12–66; *cf.* Sahlins 1962:370–395).

The mixed conditions of Fiji thus point up the general regional contrast to which attention is being called here. The development of these wider regional differences can be understood, in considerable part at any rate, as stemming from contrasts in physical type, social structure, and cultural configuration, between indigenous Melanesia and the surrounding Oceanic areas. Objective social and cultural differences between the different island regions are certainly important. Equally important, however, is the perception of differences by the Europeans who dominate modern life in all these areas; and this subjective factor is particularly significant with respect to the contrasting physical appearance of different native island populations. Within Euro-American value systems, Polynesians and Micronesians have been regarded ever since their discovery as being among the most physically and sexually attractive peoples of the world, whereas Melanesians are commonly regarded as more or less repulsive. There can be no doubt that these contrasting evaluations constitute a major basis for the comparative regional incidence of racial mixture and the closely associated social, economic, and political differences.

Along with the attribution of unattractive appearance, Europeans typically ascribe extreme mental and moral inferiority to the innate nature of Melanesians, while corresponding stereotypes of other islanders are relatively mild. Such conceptual constructs are supported by selective observations of behaviour and perceptions of social and cultural forms, again bolstered by reference to some objective contrasts in degree of resemblance to European institutions or customs. These ideas too, of course, carry inherent value judgments, and they are influenced by implicit cultural evolutionist assumptions. So we have the essentially universal European beliefs that, whereas all the native peoples in question are primitive, the Polynesian and Micronesian ways of life are relatively "high" and the Melanesian cultures comparatively "low." The cases of Fiji and New Caledonia, however, demonstrate that racial stereotypes have not alone determined European political behaviour.

The objective differences in degree of social stratification and political centralization between Melanesian and other indigenous Oceanic systems are particularly important here. From the beginnings of contact, Europeans were able to see Micronesian and Polynesian social and political institutions as resembling certain contemporary or historical features of their own class-structured societies. They could and did deal with chiefly groups as a kind of nobility, and with high chiefs as local royalty. In the process, they exerted an influence on the island systems which led to developments in the direction of class societies ruled by monarchies. In Melanesia, apart from Fiji, New Caledonia, and other partial exceptions mentioned earlier, the indigenous societies could not be perceived, approached, or influenced in these ways.

Native Responses to Imposed Stratification and Centralization

Thus far we have surveyed certain facets of the indigenous sociopolitical systems of the Pacific, and considered selected aspects of the contemporary societies established in Oceania under European domination. We turn now to further consideration of reactions on the part of native islanders to European influence in general and, in particular, to the imposition of ethnic stratification and centralization. Here again we will find a contrast between Polynesia and Micronesia on the one hand and Melanesia on the other.

In the first-named regions, native reactions have been varied; but they are typically recognizable as the predominantly secular responses of stratified societies, operating through the instrumentality of pre-existing and sometimes revitalized organs of central authority. For the most part, Polynesians and Micronesians have not responded through primarily religious means, using ritual sanctioned by sacred mythology to bring about supernatural results. In Melanesia, on the other hand, the principal movements in response to European influence have developed forms of new leadership and expanded sociopolitical unity which have relatively little continuity with the precontact past. Moreover, the most characteristic Melanesian movements of contact times have been the supernaturalistic, millenarian, cargo cults which, together with more recent secular movements, include important themes of protest against ethnic stratification.

COOPERATION, RESISTANCE, AND NATIONALISM IN POLYNESIA AND MICRONESIA

Probably the most characteristic Polynesian-Micronesian form of development under contact conditions is one which has already been mentioned: the perpetuation and strengthening of traditional chiefly groups in one guise or another. The ever-present European power behind such developments led to syncretistic changes which incorporated many alien elements. Land tenure changed in the direction of feudal or other Western models, tribute tended to evolve into taxation, warrior groups became more like standing armies, and paramount chieftainships developed into constitutional monarchies manipulated by Europeans.

Keesing (1945:152–153) has summarized the process which led to these developments: "The influences pictured here have tended to bring to the forefront a dominant and leisured élite in native societies—a class of people more or less isolated from the masses, yet living upon their labour. . . . The most spectacular examples, however, are provided by native royalty and nobility. Replicas of the thrones, crowns, titles, uniforms, and other appurtenances of rank in Europe were transplanted to Hawaii, Tonga, Samoa, Tahiti, and a number of other islands."

Many of these systems were not very stable, and they did not long remain unchallenged. Both native and European intrigue, rebellions by island populations, royal attempts to overthrow alien influence, European suppression of growing native powers, and rivalry among Western imperial interests, all threatened the stability of these systems. Nevertheless, the net result in many areas has been to preserve, in more or less altered form, native or mixed élites.

Not long after the discovery of Hawaii by Cook in the last quarter of the eighteenth century, the conquests of Kamehameha united this entire island group, with a population in excess of 300,000, under a divine monarchy. This regime persisted through various vicissitudes until the last decade of the nineteenth century, when it was overthrown by Euro-American commercial interests just prior to American annexation (Furnas, 1946). Hawaiian or part-Hawaiian descendants of the former ruling group are still accorded a certain eminence in the social affairs of what is now the fiftieth American state. During the intervening decades, however, most of the indigenous culture has been entirely lost. Today the Hawaiians are a Westernized minority within a part of the United States which is dominated by American business interests but, of course, has a common electoral roll including descendants of islanders.

The Pacific monarchy which can make the strongest claims to aboriginal authenticity, and which has been best preserved to the present, is that of the Tonga Islands: "The Tongans . . . have developed a degree of political centralization unequalled by any of their neighbours and essentially unchanged even today, after a century of westernization" (Oliver 1961:179–180). Semi-feudal kings ruled as representatives of the traditional gods with little outside interference until the influx of Methodist missionaries in the early nineteenth century. By 1865 Tonga was ruled by a Christian king, George I Tubou, with a British missionary in the dominant position of principal royal adviser. Twenty years later this had become a constitutional monarchy with a legislature dominated by chiefs, Tongan Methodism was established as an independent Free Church, and the same missionary held all the more important posts in the government. After the latter individual was removed, a British protectorate was proclaimed at the turn of the century, and since then Tonga has been a peaceful autonomous kingdom with an English consular agent attending to financial and foreign affairs.

European attempts to stimulate parallel developments elsewhere in Polynesia were not quite so successful. Schemes of this sort, promoted by the commercial and political agents of imperial interests in Samoa, foundered because of Samoan conservatism and factionalism, European misunderstanding of indigenous institutions, and rivalry among the imperial powers. In the nineteenth century, European interests mistakenly recognized the ceremonial high chief as a sovereign monarch. For the last decade of the century Germany, Britain, and the United States even jointly guaranteed a so-called Independent Kingdom of Samoa, which had little relation to the complexities of actual power relations and succession to leadership in Samoan society. This rather artificial structure was abandoned after Samoa was divided between Germany and the United States (Keesing, 1934).

Protestant missionaries from England arrived in Tahiti at the close of the eighteenth century. Although there was in fact no single paramount chieftainship here, the British clergymen soon elevated to royal rank a chiefly family who were early converts. Thus the Pomares were proclaimed the monarchs of Tahiti, with powers over the Society Islands and some neighbouring groups. This arrangement might have evolved into an independent Protestant native kingdom somewhat like Tonga, as the missionaries evidently intended that it should. However, the Pomare regime did not long survive the annexation of the area by France which began with the establishment of a Protectorate shortly before 1850 (West 1961:78–86). French colonial policy set in motion changes leading eventually to a quite different kind of political development, which will be touched on below. Various lesser "kings" and "queens" were recognized from time to time elsewhere in Polynesia, but none were as powerful as those just described.

French Oceania outside the Society Group accounts for virtually all the remaining inhabited areas of eastern Polynesia. Throughout this large region, a number of special circumstances militated against the development of strong native stratification or centralization as a response to European influence. In some atoll areas, as in the Tuamotu Archipelago, neither resources nor population were plentiful, and aboriginally there seems to have been rather little development of the characteristically Polynesian patterns of strong leadership. Depopulation during the early stages of contact reached its most savage extremes in parts of the region, such as the Marguesas Islands and Rapa in the Tubuai chain, where whole native societies were destroyed, leaving only a few hundred souls and the merest fragments of native culture. During most of their modern history, the outlying parts of French Polynesia have drifted along under a rather remote form of indirect rule, with few European settlers and less pressure for social change than most other Pacific areas.

Much the same has been true of the British administration in the Ellice Islands of western Polynesia, and the Gilbert Islands in neighbouring southeastern Micronesia (Grimble 1952). New Zealand maintained a rather similar regime in the Cook Group, beginning at the opening of the present century. Strongly centralized indigenous political institutions were generally lacking in the Cooks (outside Rarotonga and Mangaia), and British Protestant missionaries again established a large measure of theocratic control here, though without any strong development of local monarchs. Recent political developments have been in the direction of greater local autonomy but closer over-all ties with New Zealand (Oliver 1961:201; Hooper 1961).

The one remaining area of importance in Polynesia is New Zealand, where the Maoris have had to cope with a form of European influence which has no Pacific analogue with the partial exception of Hawaii. Being nearly the largest and certainly the most temperate land area in Oceania, New Zealand became the scene of large-scale European invasion for purposes of permanent settlement. Alien expansion, and particularly the increasing European occupation of the land, created a situation more akin to the frontiers of Australia and North America than to most island conditions. The Maori polity which faced this situation had little traditional intertribal unity; and by the middle of the nineteenth century, when the threat had become acute, the indigenous people were already demoralized by depopulation, tribal conflicts, and defeatism. Out of this situation arose a militant nationalism which included the Maori King movement and the Hauhau religion, and which led to the Maori wars of the 1860's (Sinclair 1957). A man of chiefly rank was elected king by traditional leaders and an imitation of British governmental forms was set up. The Hauhau movement employed syncretisic rituals, invoking both Jehovah and traditional Maori deities, to provide invulnerability against the *pakeha* bullets and strength to drive the Europeans out of the land (Winks 1953).

After a decade of military resistance, the Maoris were decisively defeated and retired into passive avoidance of things European. In recent decades they have re-emerged to experience a resurgence of population and a kind of cultural renaissance within the general framework of modern New Zealand society. The Maoris have not been culturally assimilated as have the Hawaiians. Although there is no longer a significant nationalist movement, a somewhat more diffuse ethnic identity remains. Meanwhile, the indigenous population has had direct representation in the New Zealand parliament for nearly a century, and not a few individual Maoris have achieved positions of respect and power in national life. At the same time, however, *pakeha* administration of

Maori affairs remains paternalistic in some respects, and the alienation of land still continues apace. The current position has been summed up by a recent commentator in New Zealand (Pearson 1962:148): "The most striking feature of the Maori situation seventeen years after the end of the war is the continued existence, within the welfare state, of rural enclaves of material poverty and, in city and country, spiritual insecurity."

In Micronesia, one of the most thoroughgoing metamorphoses of any Pacific people occurred among the Chamorros under the former Spanish regime in the Mariana Islands. Here indigenous chiefs with traditional stewardship over clan lands became feudal landlords and mixed racially with both Spaniards and Filipinos. They held autocratic political power for a time as well, since the colonial regime encouraged the development of a mestizo aristocracy in the islands. During much of the complex subsequent history of the Marianas these Hispanized, Catholic, landed families consorted socially with European officialdom. In Guam, especially, they remained important politically until the American naval administration displaced them from all higher power positions and excluded them from its social circles. In 1950 the Guamanians received United States citizenship and a measure of local autonomy.

Social change has been less radical in the rest of Micronesia. Spanish influence was not as strong in the Caroline and Marshall groups as in the Marianas, and the later German administration practised indirect rule. Except under the Japanese, alien settlement was never a major factor here, and there is today no class of white settlers in these islands. The indigenous chiefly powers survived the Japanese period, and now are recognized and encouraged to play a part in the governing of local affairs under the American administration. Units of local government are patterned after native political divisions and headed by magistrates some of whom, at least, are hereditary chiefs. There are also regional advisory congresses, several of which include houses of nobles or chiefs. Although under earlier colonial regimes some Micronesian groups had to be subdued by force of arms, there has apparently been no significant opposition to alien rule in recent years.

The remaining American possession of importance in the Pacific is Eastern Samoa. Here there has never been any substantial European settlement, and the traditional social order, including politically significant stratification, has been preserved more fully than in most parts of Micronesia. Local government at village, county, and district levels is largely indigenous in structure, though it has been given modern functions as well as traditional ones. A central legislation of two houses, modelled on the metropolitan institutions of the United States in form, developed after the Second World War and was granted the powers of a real law-making body, with some limitations, in 1960. Within this formal structure, the election of representatives, the conduct of debate, and the general spirit of the proceedings, are all dominated by indigenous authorities, the *matai* or titled heads of extended families, and the various ranks of higher chiefs (West 1961:137–170). There are no political parties, few conflicts between older and newer forms of leadership, and no nationalistic successors to the early Mau movement, which became much more important in the neighbouring territory to the west.

Modern anticolonial nationalism in the sense of a movement for complete political independence has had its only major success among Pacific peoples in Western Samoa. This movement has been in part an expression of cultural conservatism, and here again traditional forms of leadership have been of central importance right up to the present. Agitation for self-government first gained prominence with the rise of the Mau or "Opinion" movement during the 1920's in both Western and Eastern Samoa. Led by Samoan *matai* chieftains, and aided by part-Samoans and European dissidents, the Mau adopted "Samoa for the Samoans" as its slogan, carried out mass anti-European demonstrations together with a widespread campaign of civil disobedience, and organized a native government in opposition to the colonial authorities. Both New Zealand and American administrations first suppressed the movement and then later gave it limited recognition, though it was not allowed to assume governing authority in either territory.

After World War II, pressure for self-determination was renewed. Western Samoa became a United Nations trust territory administered by New Zealand. In 1959 this territory gained internal self-rule under a Samoan government, and at the beginning of 1962 Western Samoa became an independent nation (McKay 1962). The new state has a constitution which combines important features of the traditional power structure with Western representative forms. The franchise is limited to persons of chiefly status, some 6,000 *matai* who make up about 12 percent of the adult population. The leaders of the government are from the highest-ranking Samoan families.

The closest approach to a nationalist movement of major proportions elsewhere in the islands has occurred in recent years in Tahiti (West 1961:100–122). Here the French policy of social and political assimilation has largely destroyed the indigenous power structure and replaced it with central representative institutions closely modelled on those of France. In this context, local political parties became important soon after the Second World War. By 1953, a distinctively Tahitian party had won a large majority in the Representative Assembly. This organization, led by the part-Tahitian Pouvanaa, advocated local autonomy within the French Union. By the time of the de Gaulle referendum in 1958, Pouvanaa had adopted the slogan "Tahiti for the Tahitians and the French into the sea." However, Tahiti—and indeed French Polynesia as a whole—voted by a little over 60 percent to remain under the rule of France, Pouvanaa was imprisoned, and the legislative majority which he had controlled disintegrated. Thus nationalism in this part of the Pacific has been at least temporarily defeated.

As far as their contemporary political conditions are concerned, the peoples of Polynesia and Micronesia can now be seen to fall into four rather distinct groups. The first category is made up of Tonga and Western Samoa, where native independence has succeeded through adaptive modifications of indigenous political institutions, and by virtue of the conditions that their territories have contained only small numbers of European or Asian residents, have attracted relatively minor alien economic interests, and have been of little strategic value to metropolitan powers. These areas were among those which had the mostly highly stratified and centralized sociopolitical systems in precontact Oceania (Sahlins 1958). The second group consists principally of Hawaii and New Zealand, although Guam and perhaps Tahiti may be on their way to joining this classification. These are the areas where the opposite of the postcontact conditions just listed have applied most strongly, with the result that indigenous populations are becoming mixed or assimilated, native power structures have been most completely destroyed, and the island polities have been absorbed into world powers. These are also areas with highly developed aboriginal stratification and (apart from New Zealand) centralization; but through the processes indicated above these native institutions have been more completely lost or metamorphosed here than elsewhere, and native nationalism has existed but has been defeated.

The third group is constituted by American Micronesia, apart from Guam, together with American Samoa. These are areas where primarily strategic considerations have motivated the United States to keep firm control of the islands, but the absence of large European populations or substantial European economic stakes has helped to allow the perpetuation of indigenous politics under indirect and, until recently, military rule. Nationalism has been unsuccessful in Eastern Samoa and has not yet appeared in the US trust territory. Finally, French Polynesia, the Gilbert and Ellice group, the Cook Islands, and various smaller Polynesian dependencies, make up a class of areas where European control has been maintained for less clear-cut and more diversified reasons, alien populations have remained small, isolation from modern developments has been generally greater than in the other areas, and central political authority has often been but lightly exercised. The potentiality for nationalism here has shown itself chiefly in Tahiti and the rest of the Society Islands, which again was an area of maximum Polynesian stratification and centralization aboriginally.

Although the largely secular political developments just reviewed constituted the dominant expression of Polynesian and Micronesian ambivalence in accepting some aspects of European influence and resisting others, there has also been a more minor theme of religious response in the modern history of these areas. Today, virtually all of Oceania outside Melanesia is more than nominally Christian. A good deal of the conversion process leading to this situation was marked only by the initial (sometimes violent) resistance, the competition between different mission bodies, and the compromises with indigenous religious patterns, which are common to many mission fields.

During the early stages of religious acculturation there have been more or less nativistic and sometimes revivalistic developments associated with cultural conservatism and resistance to European influence in general. These include the syncretistic Hauhau religion of the Maori, already referred to, and the royal Hawaiian revival of traditional religious roles and practices (Keesing 1945:236). There have also been convulsive movements of mass conversion from traditional religious systems to Christianity, some of them occurring surprisingly late in long-isolated areas (Monberg 1962). Another kind of development familiar from other parts of the world where Christianity has been introduced is the growth of schisms within local Christian bodies and the establishment of native churches. Among the less heretical examples of this sort are the separate establishment of the Free Church of Tonga, as well as the creation of a Maori Branch of the Episcopal Church.

A number of schismatic Christian sects have been decidedly more heterodox. Thanks to recent scholarship (Gunson 1962), the best known of these is the Mamaia heresy of Tahiti in the Society Islands. The Mamaian leaders progressed from preaching the wrath of God to teaching that the millennium had already commenced so that there was no more evil in the world and thus no more need for secular law or supernatural punishment. Gunson shows that the essentials of these beliefs were taken over selectively or reinterpreted from the mission doctrines of the time. They were supported by dreams which harked back to the role of traditional Polynesian spirit mediums, and they were used to justify lapses from the moral code imposed by the missions. Supernatural curing was also prominent in this sect. The movement took over one church in a locality without resident European missionaries, but elsewhere it seems to have been mainly a tendency within Protestant flocks. It was generally opposed by Tahitian chiefs as a threat to their position, but it had complex relations with the political intrigues of the time, and it supported one major rebellion. The heresy was first proclaimed in 1826, had a checkered career of some fifteen years before its demise as an organized movement, and still has a minor place in Tahitian mythology today.

A century after the rise of the Mamaia, a much more explosive and shortlived Christian heretical movement erupted on one of the Gilbert Islands in Micronesia. In 1930 this was a quiet, somewhat neglected, area where Christian missions had long held sway but there were very few European settlers and the British administration indulged in a light form of indirect rule. It was at this time that what we may call the God the Father movement appeared (Gilbert and Ellice Colony 1930; Grimble 1952:127–139). It occurred at the climax of a conflict between a Protestant Gilbertese community and a Catholic native magistrate. Several prophets arose and predicted the coming of God with a tidal wave which would wipe out both the Catholics and the Government. Violence ensued, and the movement was suppressed by European authorities.

In addition to these schismatic but basically Christian sects, there have been one or two recorded instances of religious movements in Polynesia which display elements that are suggestively similar to the typical Melanesian responses to contact conditions which will be reviewed below. The general nature of these movements can be defined in terms of four principal interrelated characteristics. None of these thematic elements is by any means unique, but together they make possible at least a rough delineation of a recurrent type within the broad category of revitalization movements as defined by Wallace (1956). In the context of the present discussion, the most obvious examples of this type are the many cargo cults and related phenomena of Melanesia and a small number of Polynesian and

Micronesian cases. Numerous movements of the contact scene in other parts of the world could undoubtedly be similarly classified, but they lie outside the scope of this paper.

One characteristic of these movements is that they are syncretistic, in the sense that they combine elements from diverse cultural contexts. The elements combined include most prominently Christian and indigenous religious beliefs and practices, but other aspects of European and native cultures are often brought together as well. Closely related to this is the second characteristic that these movements are avowedly acculturative in their goals. That is, they are not culturally nativistic or revivalistic but rather aim at the achievement by native populations of everything that is regarded as desirable in the European way of life. In the third place, doctrine and policy in these movements are revealed and leadership is provided through individuals possessed or inspired by indigenous or Christian supernatural beings, often both. Thus the leaders express the syncretistic and acculturative aspects of the movements through roles which range from native spirit mediumship to Christian prophecy, and frequently combine elements from both. Finally, the central tenet of movement doctrine is a belief in an imminent millennium which will accomplish the purposes of the movement through the same supernatural agencies. This belief generally shows the influence of Christian adventism, and it is often supported by parallel elements in native tradition as well. Thus the related themes of cultural syncretism, acculturative purpose, prophetic mediumship, and millenarian faith, are integrated to form a distinct type of movement.

The best known Polynesian movement which clearly exemplifies this type is the Siovili cult, which arose in Samoa in 1830. At this time Christian ideas were already known in Samoa, although European missionaries were only just about to begin their work there, and the Samoan "kingdom" referred to earlier had not yet been set up. The prophet Siovili had been exposed to the Mamaia heresy in Tahiti before he returned to his native Samoa and founded the cult. The account of this movement by Freeman (1959) clearly shows a syncretistic combination of Christian and Samoan religious belief and behaviour harnessed to acculturative motives, especially the acquisition of European material culture by worshipping the white man's gods. Siovili was probably a spirit medium earlier in his life, but if not he certainly became one when he founded the movement. A millennial dawn, to be signalled by the second coming of Christ, was prophesied by two lesser leaders of the movement. Many Samoans became followers of Siovili, and the cult remained strong through the 1840's.

The other Polynesian movement of this kind occurred in the Cook Islands approximately one hundred years later, as a brief and apparently minor flare-up which may be called the Kapuvai cult after its prophetess. It will be remembered that this island group remained rather isolated and neglected for some time after its populace was converted to Protestantism in the 1820's. After a boom in the 1930's the island economy suffered a decline in the 1940's, and by 1947 a native movement with secular economic and political aims had been founded in Rarotonga and spread to other parts of the group, including

Atiu in the Lower Cooks. In the same year, the woman Kapuvai received a revelation while living in Rarotonga and returned to her home in Atiu, where she founded the cult. Although the existing report of this movement is tantalizingly brief (Crocombe 1961), it is clear that the prophecy involved the coming of a supernatural ship loaded with European goods and manned by traditional Tahitian gods. Ritual included the building of a *marae* and a baptismal ceremony in the name of Satan but also a number of indigenous elements. Apparently only some thirty individuals joined this movement; it collapsed soon after the prophecy failed to materialize, and as of 1959 it had not been revived.

One particular set of ideas which appeared early in the contact history of these western Polynesian areas is especially relevant to a later stage of our discussion below. This is the belief that Christian deities are responsible for the marvels of European material culture and wealth, and that these coveted objects can be obtained by human beings—including native islanders—if they worship the white man's gods. That these ideas were common in Samoa from the 1830's onward is made clear by the contemporary accounts of John Williams and others (quoted in Keesing 1945:230 and Freeman 1959: 186–187). The same beliefs were present in the Tahitian Mamaia heresy (Gunson 1962:226). They reappeared in the Siovili movement, and apparently have survived to recent years in syncretistic form in the Cook Islands as shown by the Kapuvai cult. In each of these cases there is the added element that European riches are visualized as coming in great ships.

As Freeman (1959:186) has emphasized, these ideas are readily derivable from traditional Polynesian beliefs: "To the Samoans their own material culture was god-begotten and god-given, and so, when they came to learn of the white man's religion they readily concluded that the great God Jehovah was the fount of all the *papalangi's* [European's] riches and cleverness." It is doubtful that missionaries did anything to discourage such beliefs as long as they promoted conversion, and indeed missionary writings make it clear that they often emphasized to potential converts that the spiritual and material blessings of European culture go together (e.g., Brown 1908).

In Polynesia these ideas represent but one theme among many in religious movements, which were mostly on a minor scale, mainly early in the contact process, and all outside the mainstream of Polynesian reaction to European influence. The dominant Polynesian responses were, as we have seen, secular, political, and nonmillenarian. In Melanesia, on the other hand, religious beliefs strikingly similar to those just reviewed were greatly elaborated and became the central doctrinal theme in the typical Melanesian supernaturalistic reaction to contact with Europeans. The possibility of connections between the Polynesian beliefs and their Melanesian analogues can be left for the discussion of Melanesia below. The point which emerges as relevant in the present context is that the ideas in question remained only a minor theme in the general picture of modern Polynesian development.

It might be argued that the Hauhau religion of the Maoris should be included as one more non-Melanesian movement which belongs in the same category as the Siovili and Kapuvai cults. The principle reasons for not including Hauhau here are that it was essentially anti-acculturative in spirit and it did not offer much in the way of a positive millennium apart from the defeat and disappearance of Europeans. It should perhaps also be noted that West (1961:108) has written of Pouvanaa's Tahitian nationalism that it "had many of the elements which elsewhere in the Pacific would be called a cargo cult." However, this movement was certainly not primarily religious in nature, and it does not seem to have had a highly developed millenarian theme. Although it is possible that future research will reveal other relevant cults, the available literature does not seem to contain reports of such developments in Polynesia or Micronesia.

REJECTION, MILLENARIANISM, AND PROTO-NATIONALIST MOVEMENTS IN MELANESIA

It has been implicit in the work of several authorities (especially Worsley 1957), and has recently been made clearly explicit by Fogelson (1962), that the social movements of the Melanesian contact scene fall into three rather definite types. The present survey will employ the rephrasing of Fogelson's typology proposed above.[5] The first of these types includes a rather small number of known religious movements which are contra-acculturative in orientation. They probably involve relatively little innovation or syncretism, relying on what appear to be largely or completely indigenous forms of prophetic spirit mediumship. Particularly when the disrupting effects of contact have as yet been minor, these movements envision no great changes, and if they have a millennial dream it pictures a revival, perpetuation, or intensification of the good life in its traditional form. This kind of movement typically occurs early in the contact process, and in coastal or near-coastal areas it appears to have arisen mainly before the end of World War I.

The second type is that of the partially acculturative religious movement. This is the most characteristic form of Melanesian response to contact conditions, and its typical manifestation is the classical cargo cult. Here the Christian—indigenous syncretism is highly developed, and the acculturative aims of the cults are quite explicit. The prophets now proclaim elaborate innovative millennia which typically include, among other things, the return of the dead, the arrival of the Cargo, and radical changes in the social and political order of plural societies in the islands. These movements are also associated with extensive changes in leadership and power relations within native communities, and wider forms of native unity. This is by far the most numerous class of Melanesian movements, the number which can be documented probably exceeding seventy-five. These cults are more uniform than those which make up the first category, and they show a greater tendency to diffuse from one people to another along both traditional trade routes and modern networks of transport and communication. They have developed principally since the First World War, probably had their greatest manifestation since 1930, but have by no means disappeared today.

The third type is that of the more recent, thoroughly pro-acculturative, movement which is much more secular in emphasis than either of the preceding classes. These organizations are variously termed "sophisticated" (Inglis

1957) or "programmatic" (Schwartz 1962), to indicate that they rely more heavily on economic and political programmes and involve a cognition of the relations between means and ends which is more "valid" (Stanner 1953) in the sense of approaching European standards. In such movements the prophetic visionary and the supernatural revelation have a smaller role or appear in more secular guise. The vision of the future has become more "practical" or "realistic" and less millenarian. These movements are typically more cooperative in their relations with European administering authorities than the other types. At the same time, however, they frequently express some kind of demand for limited or local self-determination. This gives them a kind of proto-nationalist character, though they have not yet shown the full-blown nationalism which demands complete political autonomy. Although some of these movements have succeeded in uniting different tribal and linguistic groups, none has yet brought unity to a whole district, much less a territory-wide organization. Reported movements of this type are as yet few in number. With some exceptions, such as the Rabaul strike of 1929, the Chair and Rule movement in the Solomons of the 1930's (Belshaw 1950*b*), and one or two Kwato mission movements also in the thirties (Guiart and Worsley 1958), they have had their main proliferation since World War II.

Typical examples of the early contra-acculturative religious movements are the Milne Bay prophet cult of 1893 (Abel 1902), the Baigona movement beginning in 1912 (Williams 1928), and the various Taro cults from about the same time (Chinnery and Haddon 1917), all in Papua. In all three cases, doctrine was concerned principally with traditional supernatural beings and with preserving or enhancing the indigenous way of life, the idea of Cargo was absent, and only in the Milne Bay movement was it predicted that the dead would return in a ship. The antiacculturative spirit is exemplified by the Milne Bay prophet's ban on all European goods.

Many examples of the full-blown cargo cult could, of course, be cited. Only a few which are relatively well reported and to which further reference will be made in discussion below need be mentioned specifically. Apart from some of the earliest manifestations of Mansren in Biak (Kamma 1954), and early Fijian developments to be discussed later, the first reported cargo cult was the German Wislin movement of 1913–14 in the Torres Straits (Chinnery and Haddon 1917). The most famous of the early cults is the Vailala Madness, which was first reported in 1919 in the Gulf Division of Papua (Williams 1923; 1934). Among the rash of cargo cults in Australian New Guinea during the thirties were the Black King movements of Aitape and Wewak, and the Marifi Satan movement of the Markham Valley (Lommel 1953); the Mambu movement (Burridge 1960), the Letub cult (Inselmann 1944), and other movements (Lawrence 1954; 1955), all in the Madang District; and the Pako and Sanop cults of Buka (Worsley 1957:114–122). Papuan movements of the 1940's include the Assisi cult (Cranswick and Shevill 1949) and the Filo cult (Belshaw 1951).

The principal cargo-oriented organization in the New Hebrides has been the John Frum movement, which has persisted for many years and included developments in the direction of the third type of movement (Guiart 1951; 1956). At the opposite end of the region are a series of rather recent cults in the New Guinea Highlands which show the close connection between cargo movements and traditional, indigenous, cult forms in areas where European influence has been minimal (Berndt 1952; Salisbury 1958). So ubiquitous have cargo cults been in the Melanesian scene that they have been reported from virtually every district in New Guinea, and from all other major island groups except New Caledonia.

It will be remembered that the tribes among which these movements arose were peoples without indigenous social stratification or political centralization who were experiencing the imposition of ethnic stratification and European political control. Whether through administrative design or through the lack of amenable native elites, the establishment of central political authority came about mainly through direct rule. Worsley (1957:221–256) has ably emphasized that the cargo movements embodied the creation of new forms of leadership and wider sociopolitical unity within Melanesian societies. He argues convincingly that, since these peoples had no centralized political institutions, they had no way to respond in a unified fashion to European influence. He goes on to show that the cults functioned to reduce this disadvantage by producing new unifying structures. This occurred partly through the decline of the traditional leaders serving competitive, atomistic interests, together with the rise of newer leadership based on the wider appeal of competence in manipulating the white man's world in a plural society.

However, Worsley's analysis lays greatest stress on the importance of allegiance to broadly conceived extrasegmental, supralocal, supernatural agencies. The pronouncements of prophets speaking in the name of the departed ancestors or Christian deities or both can arouse an interest, command a faith, and form an organization which overrides segmental, sectional, and even linguistic boundaries. This analysis points to a principal reason why the typical Melanesian response to European domination, unlike that which is characteristic of other Oceanic areas, is supernaturalistic and ritualistic, that is, religious rather than secular. Because of a lack of experience with stratification or centralization, Melanesians, unlike Polynesians and Micronesians, have been able to succeed in responding to the contact situation in an organized and unified way only by turning to religious instrumentalities. In this connection, it is interesting and perhaps significant that one of the few areas in western Melanesia from which cargo movements have not been reported is the Trobriand Islands. The Trobrianders are, of course, the one famous case of a western Melanesian society which does have ranked kin groups and power concentrated in hereditary chiefs.

The work of several investigators (e.g., Lawrence 1954; Salisbury 1958) has provided evidence that most of the basic religious elements employed by Melanesians in their typical response to contact conditions were already present in the precontact indigenous cultures of the region. Such elements include the prophet medium, the cult mechanism, the belief that material wealth and social success can be achieved through expert manipulation of the supernatural, and even ready-made myths of departed culture heroes or creators whose return might be hoped for. Christian themes are easily taken over, reinterpreted, and grafted on to indigenous concepts: particularly beliefs in European supernatural beings, Biblical narratives, and the chiliastic idea of the millennium.

As Salisbury (1958) has argued, the common indigenous religious patterns mentioned probably functioned normally in precontact times to preserve the social and cultural status quo against recurrent threats inherent in the social structure or way of life. The early anti-acculturative movements which have been referred to, and such developments as the Highland cults reported by Salisbury, indicate that these religious instrumentalities may continue to have the same function at the beginning of contact when the disruption of native society is not yet serious. As the crisis brought on by European influence deepens, however, old supernaturalistic means are combined with new ones to deal with the unprecedented problems of a rapidly changing world. It seems probable that Melanesians have responded to other kinds of radical (not normally recurrent) crises in the past, also, through similar innovating religious movements. For example, there is evidence (Valentine, n.d.) that the Lakalai of New Britain responded with an innovative prophet cult when faced with a devastating natural disaster which occurred before significant European contact.

This is not the place to discuss in detail the elaborate syncretistic adoptions and reinterpretations of Christian teachings which have played such an important part in many cargo movements. Nevertheless, it should be noted that very much the same Christian beliefs to which the Polynesians were exposed were also made available to Melanesians. Indeed, some of the same missionaries worked in both areas, such as the Methodist George Brown who carried out his ministry for some time in Samoa before becoming the first missionary in New Britain and New Ireland (Brown 1908). Thus the same potentially millenarian idea of the advent, and the same coupling of Christian spiritual blessings with European material welfare, were offered to Melanesians. It is quite clear that in New Britain (Valentine 1958), and probably elsewhere as well, Melanesians became Christians in the first instance at least partly because they believed that practising the new faith would bring them not only the material riches but also the privileges and power of Europeans.

One aspect of the progress of Christianity from Polynesian to Melanesian mission fields which has received little notice is the fact that early labour recruits from western Melanesia were taken to work on planations in both Samoa and Fiji. According to old informants among the Lakalai of New Britain, who remember the return of such plantation hands, these men came back to their homes early in the present century with news of Christianity well before missionaries arrived in their territory. These returnees are said to have brought word that the seemingly new faith had once belonged to natives (a common idea in later cargo cults), and that if the people would embrace it again their worldly and spiritual welfare would be assured.

Another relevant circumstance of the introduction of Christianity into Melanesia which seems to have been largely overlooked is the fact that such pioneers as Brown made much use of Samoan, Tongan, and Fijian pastors in their early contacts with Melanesians (Brown

1908; Danks 1899). These first teachers of the new faith to Melanesians were men whose Christian faith had been nurtured in the schismatic and sometimes heretical situation of western Polynesia which has been described. With all these avenues for exposure to potentially millenarian and otherwise heterodox forms of Christianity, the typical Melanesian religious developments of the contact period become more understandable. Indeed, in some areas at least, people turned to cargo cults only after being converted and becoming disillusioned with Christianity because it did not bring the wealth, status, and power which they hoped for from it. The fact which is of particular interest from our comparative point of view is that the same doctrinal seeds which flowered so comparatively modestly in Polynesia bloomed with such luxuriance in the more hospitable soil of Melanesian cultural and historical conditions.

Another relevant interpretation has received brief notice from a number of analysts of cargo movements and is also mentioned by Worsley (1957:251–252), although he too does not develop it. He notes that "defiance of authority" is one significant theme in the cults, and then remarks that: "The extreme expression of this defiance and the most positive rejection of the present way of life is the *inversion* of the existing social order." This observation provides the essential clue to another key difference between Melanesian and other Pacific movements in the contact world. We have seen how Polynesians and Micronesians have been able to preserve and strengthen their own indigenous institutions of stratification and centralization, and we have found among these peoples few protests against hierarchical structures as such. The typical Melanesian movement, on the other hand, is just that: a protest against the unfamiliar stratification of rank and centralization of power, a rejection and defiance of these principles, and a myth-dream (Burridge 1960) in which the millennium explicitly includes either the reversal or the destruction of such hierarchical structures.

Since it may be that the importance and ubiquity of this theme in cargo doctrines has not been fully recognized, this can be documented briefly here. In one Mansren movement after another, the inversion of the sociopolitical order was prophesied: Papuans would become whites, the Europeans would have to clear gardens while their erstwhile subjects ate rice in comfort, the whole cosmos would be inverted, Christ would turn out to be a Papuan, and Christianity would be revealed as originally the Papuan faith. Some followers of the German Wislin believed that the Millennium would bring equality between Europeans and natives, others that the Europeans would be slaughtered while the natives prospered. The Vailala doctrine included beliefs that Papuans would change their skin colour to white, that the Europeans would be driven away and their possessions would pass to the rightful Papuan owners.

The idea of the Black King symbolizes the reversal of ethnic group roles, while the Marafi worship of Satan expresses an inversion of the whole Christian cosmology as presented by Europeans. The Mambu movement held that taxes should go to the Black King rather than the Government, that the white man should clear his own roads and carry his own loads, that all obedience and submission to Europeans should be renounced. The Letub cult combined many of these beliefs with the Biblical imagery of a black people descended from Ham. All the Madang movements included the belief that skin colours would be exchanged, and there were also prophecies that the Japanese would return and drive out the Europeans. The exchange of skins was also an article of faith in the Assisi movement and the Highland cults. Followers of both the Filo movement and a cult on Karkar Island believed that the entire universe would be turned upside down. Part of the doctrine of John Frum is that the Europeans will be expelled and black Americans will come to rule the islands for the benefit of the native inhabitants.

The principal examples of the third category of recent secular developments are Masinga Rule in the Solomon Islands (Allen 1951), the Paliau movement of Manus (Mead 1956; Schwartz 1962), and the Tommy Kabu Kampani in the Purari Delta (Maher 1961). Masinga Rule had many cargo-oriented ideas, particularly early in its career before it turned more to agitation for native local government, economic progress, and educational opportunities. Paliau has had to struggle with competing and intercurrent cargo doctrines to keep his movement directed toward succeeding with native councils, cooperative enterprise, and a native church. The Kabu Kampani is mainly an economic cooperative run by the same people who clung for many years to the Vailala movement. Each of these movements has accomplished much of a practical nature, and developed an impressive secular organization patterned after available European models. The Paliau organization and Masinga Rule lay great emphasis on racial equality and the brotherhood of man, both as religious principles and as practical goals. These two movements have both cooperated extensively with the local government councils recently established in their respective territories.

As Fogelson (1962:54) has pointed out, evidence is accumulating that long-term developments in particular areas have occurred which include all three types in chronological order. Some such sequence can now be partly or wholly documented for Biak in Netherlands New Guinea (DeBruyn 1949; Kamma 1954), Malaita and neighbouring parts of the Solomons (Allen 1951; Belshaw 1950*a*), Espiritu Santo and Tanna in the New Hebrides (Guiart 1956), the Admiralty Islands (Mead 1956; Schwartz 1962), the Purari Delta of Papua (Maher 1961), and the Lakalai area of New Britain (Valentine 1958; 1960). It is tempting to regard this as an evolutionary sequence, though Fogelson properly suggests that we be cautious in this regard because genetic connections between successive phases cannot always be convincingly demonstrated.

Such linkages can be demonstrated by ethnohistorical research in some areas. This can be briefly illustrated for the Lakalai area in New Britain, although this is not the place to offer extensive documentation, much of which is available elsewhere (Valentine 1958; 1960). In their first fleeting contacts with Europeans, beginning before the end of the last century, the Lakalai identified what they saw with certain traditional supernatural beings, reacted with traditional ritual means of protection, and invoked traditional mythology to account for the new beings. A major tendency of this response was avoidance of the Europeans, and it amounts to an early form of contra-acculturative movement. Soon, however, Lakalai men were captured and taken to work on plantations in eastern Melanesia and western Polynesia as noted earlier. When some of these men returned home with news of Christianity, as described above, Lakalai acculturation began.

In the second decade of the present century it became impossible for the Lakalai to avoid governmental as well as commercial contacts with Europeans, and by the beginning of the 1920's European missionaries were residing in the Lakalai area. By this time European culture was greatly admired, its benefits were coveted, and there were vague beliefs that all this had once belonged to natives long ago but been lost to the white man. Lakalai eagerly participated in plantation labour and Christianity, in the belief that these were the means to securing all the advantages of the European way of life. During the 1930's the Lakalai heard about cargo movements in numerous other areas, including a number that have not been reported in the literature.

Thus the stage was set for a typical Melanesian partial-acculturative movement. At the end of the 1930's it came in the shape of the cargo cult known by the name of its Lakalai prophet, Batari. This movement incorporated the beliefs which had been developing since the beginning of contact. It was violently antimission, and it identified the wartime Japanese invaders as the returning ancestors. A subsequent movement which the Lakalai call the Kivung (pidgin for "council") was organized in 1946, and still existed in 1956. The charter of the Kivung remained a newly elaborated version of the cargo doctrine and associated syncretistic mythology, including the same beliefs brought back decades earlier by early labour returnees. At the same time, however, this movement has been strongly promission and avowedly Christian, it has striven to maintain peaceful relations with the Territory administration (even though covertly opposing many of its key policies), and it has engaged in cooperative economic enterprise. Both these movements produced new forms of leadership and greatly expanded sociopolitical unity, which eventually spread across linguistic boundaries and well outside the Lakalai area. There has also been a substantial continuity of leadership from the Batari cult to the Kivung.

The latter movement is clearly transitional from the partial-acculturative cult to the fully pro-acculturative type of development, while at the same time elements which go back to a much earlier stage of contact are also discernible. Another contemporary faction in Lakalai society has participated in Government-sponsored cooperatives and looks forward to the establishment of local government councils in the area. Although this is a minority organization, it exemplifies more fully the increasingly secular approach of recent pro-acculturative movements.

There is much evidence that this Lakalai sequence constitutes a developmental microcosm of modern Melanesia. There are indications from many areas that initial native responses seeking to preserve or re-establish the status quo by avoidance, withdrawal, or anti-acculturative behaviour, were quickly overwhelmed by the march of events. This phase is repeatedly succeeded by cargo movements which incorporate earlier themes but also develop new religious and secular means for dealing with the changing historical situation. New economic developments and political movements are on the rise, but few of these have been entirely free of cargo themes derived from the immediate past of the same societies.

New Caledonia stands out as an area where this typical Melanesian evolution does not appear to have occurred. The available literature contains no report of a cargo cult from this territory. The principal anti-European movements among New Caledonians were the armed revolts of some years ago, and these were not primarily religious movements, nor do they appear to have included millenarian doctrines. According to Belshaw (1954:82), these rebellions "were tribal in compass and had immediate grievances rather than a change in status as their aim." This situation seems quite consistent with the analysis presented in preceding pages. It would appear that because of relatively strong chiefly powers and tribal organizations, the resulting ability to organize major military resistance, the perpetuation of indigenous authority through indirect rule, and the recent opportunities for political activity, native New Caledonians have not needed millenarian religious movements to enable them to adapt to the conditions of European domination.

It will be recalled that the general sociopolitical conditions just noted for New Caledonia apply also, with even greater force in some respects, to Fiji. It may therefore seem paradoxical that Fiji was the scene of what may fairly be described as the earliest known cargo movement (with the possible exception of early Mansren cults in Netherlands New Guinea). This is the Tuka religion, which appeared in 1885 (Brewster 1922; Sutherland 1910). The movement was founded by a prophet who predicted an acculturative millennium in which the ancestors would return bringing vast quantities of European wealth. The prophet also proclaimed a complex syncretistic doctrine which gave prominent places both to Jehovah and to traditional Fijian deities. Included in the prophecy were the familiar projections of a world reversed, in which Europeans would serve Fijians and, significantly, chiefs would become inferior to commoners.

The apparent paradox is resolved by the fact that the Tuka movement occurred only among the interior hill tribes. Its members were thus the Fijians among whom rank and chieftainship were least developed and probably most recent, who were not ruled by Thakombau's coastal "kingdom," and who had been subjected to direct rule by the British authorities in the years immediately preceding the movement. Thus of all Fijians these Tuka followers were least prepared, by either background or circumstances, to react like their Polynesian-influenced coastal cousins under indirect rule, and their condition was most similar to that of central and western Melanesians among whom so many subsequent cargo cults have erupted. It is noteworthy that the Tuka prophecy envisaged the overthrow of chiefly ranking as part of the millennium. This apparent symbolic expression of protest against pre-European forms of social stratification and political centralization can be interpreted as an older Melanesian type of response, breaking through the veneer of Polynesian influence just where the latter is thinnest.

Modern Fiji has also had other kinds of social movements, all essentially nonmillenarian. The Luveniwai or Water Babies arose at about the same time as Tuka, involved a cult of traditional spirits, and also offered its members opportunities for gaining status by religious qualifications outside the traditional chiefly hierarchy. The Apolosi cult, beginning at the time of World War I, was a religio-political movement which proclaimed its leader King of Fiji, and which was strongly resisted by the chiefs as a threat to their position (Worsley 1957:29). The Kelevi movement of 1946 was essentially a Christian separatist sect with some syncretistic but nonapocalyptic elements. While these minor movements have occurred from time to time, the majority of Fijians have participated peacefully in the modern sociopolitical system described earlier, and some of them have recently turned especially to labour union activities.

Thus on the basis of those social, cultural, and historical features which have been employed for comparative purposes here, there are what we may term two sociological regions which appear to overlap somewhat the traditional division of Oceania into culture areas. Considering indigenous sociopolitical structure, contact history, and recent reactions to European rule alone, the conventional boundary between Polynesia and Melanesia in particular seems irrelevant to the results of the present survey. In very broad terms we seem, rather, to have one large region consisting of Micronesia, Polynesia, Fiji, and New Caledonia, plus a second region made up of the remainder of Melanesia. Although it may be mainly a reflection of relatively recent Polynesian influence to the west, this finding is of possible interest in connection with current work tending to revise linguistic boundaries and affiliations in Oceania (Goodenough 1961; Grace 1961; Capell 1962).

Summary and Conclusions

If we examine the structuring of rank and the management of power in the aboriginal societies of Oceania, two broad sociological provinces emerge. The first of these regions consists of the conventional culture areas of Polynesia and Micronesia, together with Fiji and New Caledonia (see map, Figure 1). For convenience of reference this can be called Area 1. It is characterized by well-developed social stratification, considerable centralization of power, and a range of political unification stopping just short of true states. While in each of these respects there are differences of degree from one Area 1 society to another, there is a much more striking contrast between these and the sociopolitical systems in the remainder of Oceania.

The second sociological province extends from New Guinea through the Bismarck Archipelago and the Solomon Islands to the New Hebrides (see Figure 1). This can be labelled Area 2. The predominant sociopolitical characteristics of this region are egalitarianism, segmentation, fluid loci of power, and small, narrow sovereignties. There are indications of precontact movement and diffusion into this region from neighbouring parts of Area 1. The central Melanesian groups of the Solomons and the New Hebrides show some development of features which resemble Polynesian patterns, and this is also the area of the Polynesian outliners. This phenomenon becomes more pronounced further east toward the boundary between the two provinces, and New Caledonia and especially Fiji exhibit so many traits which strongly indicate derivation from neighbouring Polynesia that they belong in Area 1.

Manus to the north and west shows some evidence of relatively minor Micronesian influence. The only prominent internal exception to the prevailing pattern of Area 2 is the sociopolitical system of the Trobriand Islanders.

A survey of the history and structure of modern multiracial colonial societies in the Pacific reveals significant differences between the same two regions. In Area 1 we find relatively tolerant, somewhat variable, often rather flexible, systems of ethnic stratification, accompanied by comparatively mild forms of European political domination generally operating through indirect rule and, in some cases, evolving toward either assimilation by Euro-American societies or native nationalism. Area 2 is characterized by relatively rigid and static ethnic hierarchies, together with forceful and direct control by European political authorities. These contrasts are partly the result of the aboriginal distinctions between the two regions, and partly due to differences in the approach of Europeans to their contact situations. Especially after the early part of the contact period, and partly as a result of historical trends within this period, Fiji and New Caledonia can now be seen as belonging even more definitely to Area 1.

The same regional contrast appears when we compare the responses to European influence of native islanders in the two areas. The typical response of indigenous peoples in Area 1 has been predominantly secular, mediated principally by indigenous political institutions, largely nonmillenarian, strongly acculturative, often at least passively accepting ethnic stratification, and increasingly oriented toward one of the alterna-

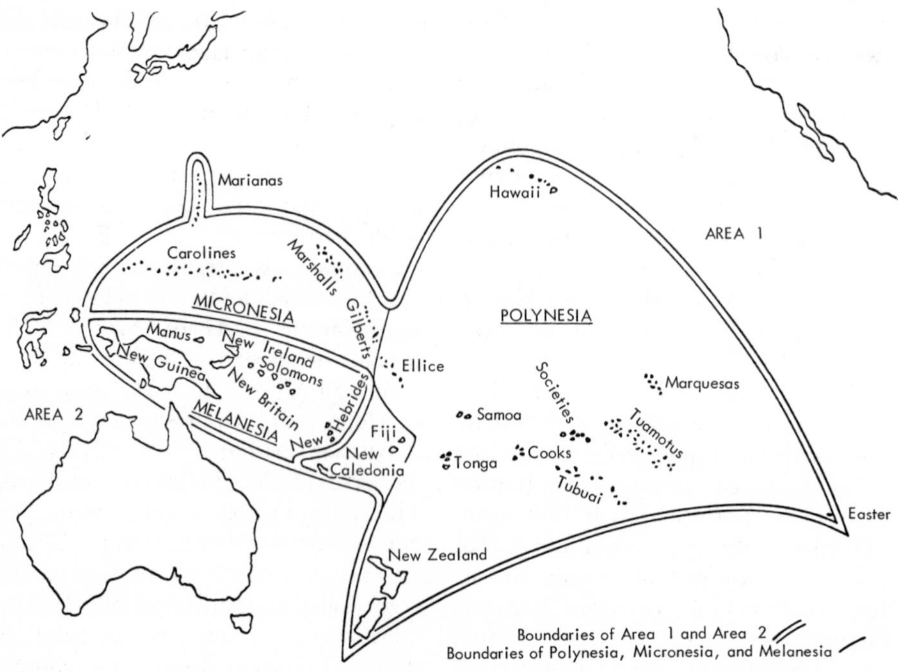

Figure 1. Boundaries of Polynesia, Micronesia, and Melanesia.

tives of assimilation or nationalism. The only major exceptions are the Hauhau religion and the Siovili movement, and these both belong to early phases of contact now a century or more in the past. The characteristic reaction in Area 2 has been supernaturalistic, expressed through modified indigenous religious instrumentalities, definitely apocalyptic, syncretistically acculturative, distinctly and often violently anti-European, strongly opposed to ethnic stratification, politically innovative for native polities, but no more than proto-nationalist. The major exceptions are a few recent developments, such as the Paliau movement and Masinga Rule, which are more secular, less chiliastic, and less anti-European, but otherwise similar to the movements just described.

Again, the regional differences are understandable in terms of the contrasting cultural and historical backgrounds of the two areas. The dominion of the Europeans over Area 1 peoples was established through social and political institutions which, in spite of their alien origin, were both structurally and functionally analogous, in many features of stratification and centralization to the indigenous systems. Thus the islanders of Area 1 have been able to adjust to European influence through adaptive modifications of their own institutions, a process encouraged by European approaches ranging from indirect rule to granting national independence. In sections of the region where indigenous systems were overwhelmed because of the nature of European settlement, such as Hawaii and New Zealand, the native peoples have been more or less successfully absorbed into the polities of modern world powers. Elsewhere, native nationalism or traditional autonomy has succeeded where the strongest indigenous stratification and centralization have been combined with the weakest European determination to maintain direct control, as in Tonga and Samoa.

In Area 2 there were no such parallels between European and Melanesian concepts or institutions of status and power. Indigenous sociopolitical instrumentalities were ineffective and inappropriate as vehicles of response to European invasion and domination. Furthermore, European control was established more directly and often more forcefully in Area 2, partly because Europeans became aware of the lack of native institutions corresponding to their own. Melanesians reacted by employing adaptive modifications of traditional religious means, mainly cargo cults, which enabled them to meet the cognitive and emotional threats of contact with Europeans and to counter the unprecedented sociopolitical domination and economic inequality of the contact world. In the course of these movements, Melanesians have forged new sociopolitical systems which are more appropriate to the contemporary circumstances in which they find themselves. They are now showing themselves increasingly able to assimilate and reintegrate in their own fashion functional elements of Western culture, and to proceed in their adaptation to the modern world through secular as well as supernaturalistic means.

It might be added as a final note that these Pacific peoples are again demonstrating that the Euro-American conceit of ethnic superiority is based on a profound misunderstanding of human capacities. The cultural and historical record reviewed here makes an absurdity of the prevalent Western assumption that the light skinned Polynesians and Micronesians, being more like Europeans, somehow represent a higher form of humanity than the dark Melanesians. The sociological and cultural boundaries which are significant for differences in developmental style cut across the groupings of physical type in Oceania. Furthermore, the cognitive creations and organizational innovations produced by contemporary specimens of "primitive man" in New Guinea are in no sense inferior to what has been achieved through cultural conservatism, adaptive persistence, or acculturative assimilation, by the "noble savage" of Polynesia. Indeed, the success of Pacific peoples of both regions in meeting the almost overwhelming challenges of their modern existence is a salutary reminder, in this day of unprecedented world problems, that there are important human capacities for dealing with situations that have never been faced before.

CHAPTER

25

Steel Axes for Stone-Age Australians

LAURISTON SHARP

Like other Australian aboriginals, the Yir Yoront group which lives at the mouth of the Coleman River on the west coast of Cape York peninsula originally had no knowledge of metals. Technologically their culture was of the old stone age or paleolithic type. They supported themselves by hunting and fishing, and obtained vegetables and other materials from the bush by simple gathering techniques. Their only domesticated animal was the dog; they had no cultivated plants of any kind. Unlike some other aboriginal groups, however, the Yir Yoront did have polished stone axes hafted in short handles which were most important in their economy.

Towards the end of the nineteenth century metal tools and other European artifacts began to filter into the Yir Yoront territory. The flow increased with the gradual expansion of the white frontier outward from southern and eastern Queensland. Of all the items of western technology thus made available, the hatchet, or short handled steel axe, was the most acceptable to and the most highly valued by all aboriginals.

In the mid-1930's an American anthropologist lived alone in the bush among the Yir Yoront for thirteen months without seeing another white man. The Yir Yoront were thus still relatively isolated and continued to live an essentially independent economic existence, supporting themselves entirely by means of their old stone-age techniques. Yet their polished stone axes were disappearing fast and being replaced by steel axes which came to them in considerable numbers, directly or indirectly, from various European sources to the south.

What changes in the life of the Yir Yoront still living under aboriginal conditions in the Australian bush could

From *Human Organization,* 11:17–22, 1953. By permission of the author and The Society for Applied Anthropology.

be expected as a result of their increasing possession and use of the steel axe?

The Course of Events

Events leading up to the introduction of the steel axe among the Yir Yoront begin with the advent of the second known group of Europeans to reach the shores of the Australian continent. In 1623 a Dutch expedition landed on the coast where the Yir Yoront now live.[1] In 1935 the Yir Yoront were still using the few cultural items recorded in the Dutch log for the aboriginals they encountered. To this cultural inventory the Dutch added beads and pieces of iron which they offered in an effort to attract the frightened "Indians." Among these natives metal and beads have disappeared, together with any memory of this first encounter with whites.

The next recorded contact in this area was in 1864. Here there is more positive assurance that the natives concerned were the immediate ancestors of the Yir Yoront community. These aboriginals had the temerity to attack a party of cattle men who were driving a small herd from southern Queensland through the length of the then unknown Cape York Peninsula to a newly established government station at the northern tip.[2] Known as the "Battle of the Mitchell River," this was one of the rare instances in which Australian aboriginals stood up to European gunfire for any length of time. A diary kept by the cattle men records that ". . . 10 carbines poured volley after volley into them from all directions, killing and wounding with every shot with very little return, nearly all their spears having already been expended. . . . . About 30 being killed, the leader thought it prudent to hold his hand, and let the rest escape. Many more must have been wounded and probably drowned, for 59 rounds were counted as discharged." The European party was in the Yir Yoront area for three days; they then disappeared over the horizon to the north and never returned. In the almost three-year long anthropological investigation conducted some seventy years later—in all the material of hundreds of free association interviews, in texts of hundreds of dreams and myths, in genealogies, and eventually in hundreds of answers to direct and indirect questioning on just this particular matter—there was nothing that could be interpreted as a reference to this shocking contact with Europeans.

The aboriginal accounts of their first remembered contact with whites begin in about 1900 with references to persons known to have had sporadic but lethal encounters with them. From that time on whites continued to remain on the southern periphery of Yir Yoront territory. With the establishment of cattle stations (ranches) to the south, cattle men made occasional excursions among the "wild black-fellows" in order to inspect the country and abduct natives to be trained as cattle boys and "house girls." At least one such expedition reached the Coleman River where a number of Yir Yoront men and women were shot for no apparent reason.

About this time the government was persuaded to sponsor the establishment of three mission stations along the 700-mile western coast of the Peninsula in an attempt to help regulate the treatment of natives. To further this purpose a strip of coastal territory was set aside as an aboriginal reserve and closed to further white settlement.

In 1915, an Anglican mission station was established near the mouth of the Mitchell River, about a three-day march from the heart of the Yir Yoront country. Some Yir Yoront refused to have anything to do with the mission, others visited it occasionally, while only a few eventually settled more or less permanently in one of the three "villages" established at the mission.

Thus the majority of the Yir Yoront continued to live their old self-supporting life in the bush, protected until 1942 by the government reserve and the intervening mission from the cruder realities of the encroaching new order from the south. To the east was poor, uninhabited country. To the north were other bush tribes extending on along the coast to the distant Archer River Presbyterian mission with which the Yir Yoront had no contact. Westward was the shallow Gulf of Carpentaria on which the natives saw only a mission lugger making its infrequent dry season trips to the Mitchell River. In this protected environment for over a generation the Yir Yoront were able to recuperate from shocks received at the hands of civilized society. During the 1930's their raiding and fighting, their trading and stealing of women, their evisceration and two- or three-year care of their dead, and their totemic ceremonies continued, apparently uninhibited by western influence. In 1931 they killed a European who wandered into their territory from the east, but the investigating police never approached the group whose members were responsible for the act.

As a direct result of the work of the Mitchell River mission, all Yir Yoront received a great many more western artifacts of all kinds than ever before. As part of their plan for raising native living standards, the missionaries made it possible for aboriginals living at the mission to earn some western goods, many of which were then given or traded to natives still living under bush conditions; they also handed out certain useful articles gratis to both mission and bush aboriginals. They prevented guns, liquor, and damaging narcotics, as well as decimating diseases, from reaching the tribes of this area, while encouraging the introduction of goods they considered "improving." As has been noted, no item of western technology available, with the possible exception of trade tobacco, was in greater demand among all groups of aboriginals than the short handled steel axe. The mission always kept a good supply of these axes in stock; at Christmas parties or other mission festivals they were given away to mission or visiting aboriginals indiscriminately and in considerable numbers. In addition, some steel axes as well as other European goods were still traded in to the Yir Yoront by natives in contact with cattle stations in the south. Indeed, steel axes had probably come to the Yir Yoront through established lines of aboriginal trade long before any regular contact with whites had occurred.

Relevant Factors

If we concentrate our attention on Yir Yoront behavior centering about the original stone axe (rather than on the axe—the object—itself) as a cultural trait or item of cultural equipment, we should get some conception of the role this implement played in aboriginal culture. This, in turn, should enable us to foresee with considerable accuracy some of the results stemming from the displacement of the stone axe by the steel axe.

The production of a stone axe required a number of simple technological skills. With the various details of the axe well in mind, adult men could set about producing it (a task not considered appropriate for women or children). First of all a man had to know the location and properties of several natural resources found in his immediate environment: pliable wood for a handle, which could be doubled or bent over the axe head and bound tightly; bark, which could be rolled into cord for the binding; and gum, to fix the stone head in the haft. These materials had to be correctly gathered, stored, prepared, cut to size and applied or manipulated. They were in plentiful supply, and could be taken from anyone's property without special permission. Postponing consideration of the stone head, the axe could be made by any normal man who had a simple knowledge of nature and of the technological skills involved, together with fire (for heating the gum), and a few simple cutting tools—perhaps the sharp shells of plentiful bivalves.

The use of the stone axe as a piece of capital equipment used in producing other goods indicates its very great importance to the subsistence economy of the aboriginal. Anyone—man woman, or child—could use the axe; indeed, it was used primarily by women, for their's was the task of obtaining sufficient wood to keep the family campfire burning all day, for cooking or other purposes, and all night against mosquitoes and cold (for in July, winter temperature might drop below 40 degrees). In a normal lifetime a woman would use the axe to cut or knock down literally tons of firewood. The axe was also used to make other tools or weapons, and a variety of material equipment required by the aboriginal in his daily life. The stone axe was essential in the construction of the wet season domed huts which keep out some rain and some insects; of platforms which provide dry storage; of shelters which give shade in the dry summer when days are bright and hot. In hunting and fishing and in gathering vegetable or animal food the axe was also a necessary tool, and in this tropical culture, where preservatives or other means of storage are lacking, the natives spend more time obtaining food than in any other occupation—except sleeping. In only two instances was the use of the stone axe strictly limited to adult men: for gathering wild honey, the most prized food known to the Yir Yoront; and for making the secret paraphernalia for ceremonies. From this brief listing of some of the activities involving the use of the axe, it is easy to understand why there was at least one stone axe in every camp, in every hunting or fighting party, and in every group out on a "walk-about" in the bush.

The stone axe was also prominent in interpersonal relations. Yir Yoront men were dependent upon interpersonal relations for their stone axe heads, since the flat, geologically-recent, alluvial country over which they range provides no suitable stone for this purpose. The stone they used came from quarries 400 miles to the south, reaching the Yir Yoront through long lines of male trading partners. Some of these chains terminated with the Yir Yoront men, others extended on farther north to other groups, using Yir Yoront men as links. Almost every older adult man had one or more regular trading partners, some to the north and some to the south. He provided his partner or partners in the south with surplus spears, particularly fighting spears tipped with the barbed spines of sting ray which snap into vicious fragments when they penetrate human flesh. For a dozen such spears, some of which he may have obtained from a partner to the north, he would receive one stone axe head. Studies have shown that the sting ray barb spears increased in value as they move south and farther from the sea. One hundred and fifty miles south of Yir Yoront one such spear may be exchanged for one stone axe head. Although actual investigations could not be made, it was presumed that farther south, nearer the quarries, one sting ray barb spear would bring several stone axe heads. Apparently those people who acted as links in the middle of the chain and who made neither spears nor axe heads would receive a certain number of each as a middleman's profit.

Thus trading relations, which may extend the individual's personal relationships beyond that of his own group, were associated with spears and axes, two of the most important items in a man's equipment. Finally, most of the exchanges took place during the dry season, at the time of the great aboriginal celebrations centering about initiation rites or other totemic ceremonies which attracted hundreds and were the occasion for much exciting activity in addition to trading.

Returning to the Yir Yoront, we find that adult men kept their axes in camp with their other equipment, or carried them when travelling. Thus a woman or child who wanted to use an axe—as might frequently happen during the day—had to get one from a man, use it promptly, and return it in good condition. While a man might speak of "my axe," a woman or child could not.

This necessary and constant borrowing of axes from older men by women and children was in accordance with regular patterns of kinship behavior. A woman would expect to use her husband's axe unless he himself was using it; if unmarried, or if her husband was absent, a woman would go first to her older brother or to her father. Only in extraordinary circumstances would she seek a stone axe from other male kin. A girl, a boy, or a young man would look to a father or an older brother to provide an axe for their use. Older men, too, would follow similar rules if they had to borrow an axe.

It will be noted that all of these social relationships in which the stone axe had a place are pair relationships and that the use of the axe helped to define and maintain their character and the roles of the two individual participants. Every active relationship among the Yir Yoront involved a definite and accepted status of superordination or subordination. A person could have no dealings with another on exactly equal terms. The nearest approach to equality was between brothers, although the older was always superordinate to the younger. Since the exchange of goods in a trading relationship involved a mutual reciprocity, trading partners usually stood in a brotherly type of relationship, although one was always classified as older than the other and would have some advantage in case of dispute. It can be seen that repeated and widespread conduct centering around the use of the axe helped to generalize and standardize these sex, age, and kinship roles both in their normal benevolent and exceptional malevolent aspects.

The status of any individual Yir Yoront was determined not only by sex, age, and extended kin relationships, but also by membership in one of two dozen patrilineal totemic clans into which the entire community was divided.[3] Each clan had literally hundreds of totems, from one or two of which the clan derived its name, and the clan members their personal names. These totems included natural species or phenomena such as the sun, stars, and daybreak, as well as cultural "species": imagined ghosts, rainbow serpents, heroic ancestors; such eternal cultural verities as fires, spears, huts; and such human activities, conditions, or attributes as eating, vomiting, swimming, fighting, babies and corpses, milk and blood, lips and loins. While individual members of such totemic classes or species might disappear or be destroyed, the class itself was obviously ever-present and indestructible. The totems, therefore, lent permanence and stability to the clans, to the groupings of human individuals who generation after generation were each associated with a set of totems which distinguished one clan from another.

The stone axe was one of the most important of the many totems of the Sunlit Cloud Iguana clan. The names of many members of this clan referred to the axe itself, to activities in which the axe played a vital part, or to the clan's mythical ancestors with whom the axe was prominently associated. When it was necessary to represent the stone axe in totemic ceremonies, only men of this clan exhibited it or pantomimed its use. In secular life, the axe could be made by any man and used by all; but in the sacred realm of the totems it belonged exclusively to the Sunlit Cloud Iguana people.

Supporting those aspects of cultural behavior which we have called technology and conduct, is a third area of culture which includes ideas, sentiments, and values. These are most difficult to deal with, for they are latent and covert, and even unconscious, and must be deduced from overt actions and language or other communicating behavior. In this aspect of the culture lies the significance of the stone axe to the Yir Yoront and to their cultural way of life.

The stone axe was an important symbol of masculinity among the Yir Yoront (just as pants or pipes are to us). By a complicated set of ideas the axe was defined as "belonging" to males, and everyone in the society (except untrained infants) accepted these ideas. Similarly spears, spear throwers, and fire-making sticks were owned only by men and were also symbols of masculinity. But the masculine values represented by the stone axe were constantly being impressed on all members of society by the fact that females borrowed axes but not other masculine artifacts. Thus the axe stood for an important theme of Yir Yoront culture: the superiority and rightful dominance of the male, and the greater value of his concerns and of all things associated with him. As the axe also had to be borrowed by the younger people it represented the prestige of age, another important theme running through Yir Yoront behavior.

To understand the Yir Yoront culture it is necessary to be aware of a system of ideas which may be called their totemic ideology. A fundamental belief of the aboriginal divided time into two great epochs: (1) a distant and sacred period at the beginning of the world when the earth was peopled by mildly marvelous ancestral beings or culture hreoes who are in a special sense the forebears of the clans; and (2) a period when the old was succeeded by a new order which includes the present. Originally there was no anticipation of another era supplanting the present. The future would simply be an eternal continuation and reproduction of the present which itself had remained unchanged since the epochal revolution of ancestral times.

The important thing to note is that the aboriginal believed that the present world, as a natural and cultural environment, was and should be simply a detailed reproduction of the world of the ancestors. He believed that the entire universe "is now as it was in the beginning" when it was established and left by the ancestors. The ordinary cultural life of the ancestors became the daily life of the Yir Yoront camps, and the extraordinary life of the ancestors remained extant in the recurring symbolic pantomimes and paraphernalia found only in the most sacred atmosphere of the totemic rites.

Such beliefs, accordingly, opened the way for ideas of what *should be* (because it supposedly *was*) to influence or help determine what actually *is*. A man called Dog-chases-iguana-up-a-tree-and-barks-at-him-all-night had that and other names because he believed his ancestral alter ego had also had them; he was a member of the Sunlit Cloud Iguana clan because his ancestor was; he was associated with particular countries and totems of this same ancestor; during an initiation he played the role of a dog and symbolically attacked and killed certain members of other clans because his ancestor (conveniently either anthropomorphic or kynomorphic) really did the same to the ancestral alter egos of these men; and he would avoid his mother-in-law, joke with a mother's distant brother, and make spears in a certain way because his and other people's ancestors did these things. His behavior in these specific ways was outlined, and to that extent determined for him, by a set of ideas concerning the past and the relation of the present to the past.

But when we are informed that Dog-chases-etc. had two wives from the Spear Black Duck clan and one from the Native Companion clan, one of them being blind, that he had four children with such and such names, that he had a broken wrist and was left handed, all because his ancestor had exactly these same attributes, then we know (though he apparently didn't) that the present has influenced the past, that the mythical world has been somewhat adjusted to meet the exigencies and accidents of the inescapably real present.

There was thus in Yir Yoront ideology a nice balance in which the mythical was adjusted in part to the real world, the real world in part to the ideal pre-existing mythical world, the adjustments occurring to maintain a fundamental tenet of native faith that the present must be a mirror of the past. Thus the stone axe in all its aspects, uses, and associations was integrated into the context of Yir Yoront technology and conduct because a myth, a set of ideas, had put it there.

The Outcome

The introduction of the steel axe indiscriminately and in large numbers into the Yir Yoront technology occurred simultaneously with many other changes. It is therefore impossible to separate all the results of this single innovation. Nevertheless, a number of specific effects of the change from stone to steel axes may be noted, and the steel axe may be used as an epitome of the increasing quantity of European goods and implements received by the aboriginals and of their general influence on the native culture. The use of the steel axe to illustrate such influences would seem to be justified. It was one of the first European artifacts to be adopted for regular use by the Yir Yoront, and whether made of stone or steel, the axe was clearly one of the most important items of cultural equipment they possessed.

The shift from stone to steel axes provided no major technological difficulties. While the aboriginals themselves could not manufacture steel axe heads, a steady supply from outside continued; broken wooden handles could easily be replaced from bush timbers with aboriginal tools. Among the Yir Yoront the new axe was never used to the extent it was on mission or cattle stations (for carpentry work, pounding tent pegs, as a hammer, and so on); indeed, it had so few more uses than the stone axe that its practical effect on the native standard of living was negligible. It did some jobs better, and could be used longer without breakage. These factors were sufficient to make it of value to the native. The white man believed that a shift from steel to stone axe on his part would be a definite regression. He was convinced that his axe was much more efficient, that its use would save time, and that it therefore represented technical "progress" towards goals which he had set up for the native. But this assumption was hardly born out in aboriginal practice. Any leisure time the Yir Yoront might gain by using steel axes or other western tools was not invested in "improving the conditions of life," nor, certainly, in developing aesthetic activities, but in sleep—an art they had mastered thoroughly.

Previously, a man in need of an axe would acquire a stone axe head through regular trading partners from whom he knew what to expect, and was then dependent solely upon a known and adequate natural environment, and his own skills or easily acquired techniques. A man wanting a steel axe, however, was in no such self-reliant position. If he attended a mission festival when steel axes were handed out as gifts, he might receive one either by chance or by happening to impress upon the mission staff that he was one of the "better" bush aboriginals (the missionaries definition of "better" being quite different from that of his bush fellows). Or, again almost by pure chance, he might get some brief job in connection with the mission which would enable him to earn a steel axe. In either case, for older men a preference for the steel axe helped change the situation from one of self-reliance to one of dependence, and a shift in behavior from well-structured or defined situations in technology or conduct to ill-defined situations in conduct alone. Among the men, the older ones whose earlier experience or knowledge of the white man's harshness made them suspicious were particularly careful to avoid having relations with the mission, and thus excluded themselves from acquiring steel axes from that source.

In other aspects of conduct or social relations, the steel axe was even more significantly at the root of psychological stress among the Yir Yoront. This was the result of new factors which the missionary considered beneficial: the simple numerical increase in axes per capita as a result of mission distribution, and distribution directly to younger men, women, and even children. By winning the favor of the mission staff, a woman might be given a steel axe which was clearly intended to be hers, thus creating a situation quite different from the previous custom which necessitated her borrowing an axe from a male relative. As a result a woman would refer to the axe as "mine," a possessive form she was never able to use of the stone axe. In the same fashion, younger men or even boys also obtained steel axes directly from the mission, with the result that older men no longer had a complete monopoly of all the axes in the bush community. All this led to a revolutionary confusion of sex, age, and kinship roles, with a major gain in independence and loss of subordination on the part of those who now owned steel axes when they had previously been unable to possess stone axes.

The trading partner relationship was also affected by the new situation. A Yir Yoront might have a trading partner in a tribe to the south whom he defined as a younger brother and over whom he would therefore have some authority. But if the partner were in contact with the mission or had other access to steel axes, his subordination obviously decreased. Among other things, this took some of the excitement away from the dry season fiesta-like tribal gatherings centering around initiations. These had traditionally been the climactic annual occasions for exchanges between trading partners, when a man might seek to acquire a whole year's supply of stone axe heads. Now he might find himself prostituting his wife to almost total strangers in return for steel axes or other white man's goods. With trading partnerships weakened, there was less reason to attend the ceremonies, and less fun for those who did.

Not only did an increase in steel axes and their distribution to women change the character of the relations between individuals (the paired relationships that have been noted), but a previously rare type of relationship was created in the Yir Yiront's conduct towards whites. In the aboriginal society there were few occasions outside of the immediate family when an individual would initiate action to several other people at once. In any average group, in accordance with the kinship system, while a person might be superordinate to several people to whom he could suggest or command action, he was also subordinate to several others with whom such behavior would be tabu. There was thus no overall chieftanship or authoritarian leadership of any kind. Such complicated operations as grass-burning animal drives or totemic ceremonies could be carried out smoothly because each person was aware of his role.

On both mission and cattle stations, however, the whites imposed their conception of leadership roles upon the aboriginals, consisting of one person in a controlling relationship with a subordinate group. Aboriginals called together to receive gifts, including axes, at a mission Christmas party found themselves facing one or two whites who sought to control their behavior for the occasion, who disregarded the age, sex, and kinship variables of which the aboriginals were so conscious, and who considered them all at one subordinate level. The white also sought to impose similar patterns on work parties. (However, if he placed an aboriginal in charge of a mixed group of post-hole diggers, for example, half of the group, those subordinate to the "boss," would work while the other half, who were superordinate to him, would sleep.) For the aboriginal, the steel axe and other European goods came to symbolize this new and uncomfortable form of social organization, the leader-group relationship.

The most disturbing effects of the steel axe, operating in conjunction with other elements also being introduced from the white man's several sub-cultures, developed in the realm of traditional ideas, sentiments, and values. These were undermined at a rapidly mounting rate, with no new conceptions being defined to replace them. The result was the erection of a mental and moral void which foreshadowed the collapse and destruction of all Yir Yoront culture, if not, indeed, the extinction of the biological group itself.

From what has been said it should be clear how changes in overt behavior, in technology and conduct, weakened the values inherent in a reliance on nature, in the prestige of masculinity and of age, and in the various kinship relations. A scene was set in which a wife, or a young son whose initiation may not yet have been completed, need no longer defer to the husband or father who, in turn, became confused and insecure as he was forced to borrow a steel axe from them. For the woman and boy the steel axe helped establish a new degree of freedom which they accepted readily as an escape from the unconscious stress of the old patterns—but they, too, were left confused and insecure. Ownership became less well defined with the result that stealing and trespassing were introduced into technology and conduct. Some of the excitement surrounding the great ceremonies evaporated and they lost their previous gaiety and interest. Indeed, life itself became less interesting, although this did not lead the Yir Yoront to discover suicide, a concept foreign to them.

The whole process may be most specifically illustrated in terms of totemic system, which also illustrates the significant role played by a system of ideas, in this case a totemic ideology, in the breakdown of a culture.

In the first place, under pre-European aboriginal conditions where the native culture has become adjusted to a relatively stable environment, few, if any, unheard of or catastrophic crises can occur. It is clear, therefore, that the totemic system serves very effectively in inhibiting radical cultural changes. The closed system of totemic ideas, explaining and categorizing a well-known universe as it was fixed at the beginning of time, presents a considerable obstacle to the adoption of new or the dropping of old culture traits. The obstacle is not insurmountable and the system allows for the minor variations which occur in the norms of daily life. But the inception of major changes cannot easily take place.

Among the bush Yir Yoront the only means of water transport is a light wood log to which they cling in their constant swimming of rivers; salt creeks, and tidal inlets. These natives know that tribes forty-five miles further north have a bark canoe. They know these northern tribes can thus fish from mid-stream or out at sea, instead of clinging to the river banks and beaches, that they can cross coastal waters infested with crocodiles, sharks, sting rays, and Portuguese men-of-war without danger. They know the materials of which the canoe is made exist in their own environment. But they also know, as they say, that they do not have the canoes because their own mythical ancestors did not have them. They assume that the canoe was part of the ancestral universe of the northern tribes. For them, then, the adoption of the canoe would not be simply a matter of learning a number of new behavioral skills for its manufacture and use. The adoption would require a much more difficult procedure; the acceptance by the entire society of a myth, either locally developed or borrowed, to explain the presence of the canoe, to associate it with some one or more of the several hundred mythical ancestors (and how decide which?), and thus establish it as an accepted totem of one of the clans ready to be used by the whole community. The Yir Yoront have not made this adjustment, and in this case we can only say that for the time being at least, ideas have won out over very real pressures for technological change. In the elaborateness and explicitness of the totemic ideologies we seem to have one explanation for the notorious stability of Australian cultures under aboriginal conditions, an explanation which gives due weight to the importance of ideas in determining human behavior.

At a later stage of the contact situation, as has been indicated, phenomena unaccounted for by the totemic ideological system begin to appear with regularity and frequency and remain within the range of native experience. Accordingly, they cannot be ignored (as the "Battle of the Mitchell" was apparently ignored), and there is an attempt to assimilate them and account for them along the lines of principles inherent in the ideology. The bush Yir Yoront of the mid-thirties represent this stage of the acculturation process. Still trying to maintain their aboriginal definition of the situation, they accept European artifacts and behavior patterns, but fit them into their totemic system, assigning them to various clans on a par with original totems. There is an attempt to have their myth-making process keep up with these cultural changes so that the idea system can continue to support the rest of the culture. But analysis of overt behavior, of dreams, and of some of the new myths indicates that this arrangement is not entirely satisfactory, that the native clings to his totemic system with intellectual loyalty (lacking any substitute ideology), but that associated sentiments and values are weakened. His attitudes towards his own and towards European culture are found to be highly ambivalent.

All ghosts are totems of the Head-to-the-East Corpse clan, are thought of as white, and are of course closely associated with death. The white man, too, is closely associated with death, and he and all things pertaining to him are naturally assigned to the Corpse clan as totems. The steel axe, as a totem was thus associated with the Corpse clan. But as an "axe," clearly linked with the stone axe, it is a totem of the Sunlit Cloud Iguana clan. Moreover, the steel axe, like most European goods, has no distinctive origin myth, nor are mythical ancestors associated with it. Can anyone, sitting in the shade of a *ti* tree one afternoon, create a myth to resolve this confusion? No one has, and the horrid suspicion arises as to the authenticity of the origin myths, which failed to take into account this vast new universe of the white man. The steel axe, shifting hopelessly between one clan and the other, is not only replacing the stone axe physically, but is hacking at the supports of the entire cultural system.

The aboriginals to the south of the Yir Yoront have clearly passed beyond this stage. They are engulfed by European culture, either by the mission or cattle station sub-cultures or, for some natives, by a baffling, paradoxical combination of both incongruent varieties. The totemic ideology can no longer support the inrushing mass of foreign culture traits, and the myth-making process in its native form breaks down completely. Both intellectually and emotionally a saturation point is reached so that the myriad new traits which can neither be ignored nor any longer assimilated simply force the aboriginal to abandon his totemic system. With the collapse of this system of ideas, which is so closely related to so many other aspects of the native culture, there follows an appallingly sudden and complete cultural disintegration, and a demoralization of the individual such as has seldom been recorded elsewhere. Without the support of a system of ideas well devised to provide cultural stability in a stable environment, but admittedly too rigid for the new realities pressing in from outside, native behavior and native sentiments and values are simply dead. Apathy reigns. The aboriginal has passed beyond the realm of any outsider who might wish to do him well or ill.

Returning from the broken natives huddled on cattle stations or on the fringes of frontier towns to the ambivalent but still lively aboriginals settled on the Mitchell River mission, we note one further devious result of the introduction of European artifacts. During a wet season stay at the mission, the anthropologist discovered that his supply of tooth paste was being depleted at an alarming rate. Investigation showed that it was being taken by old men for use in a new tooth paste cult. Old materials of magic having failed, new materials were being tried out in a malevolent magic directed towards the mission staff and some of the younger aboriginal men. Old males, largely ignored by the missionaries, were seeking to regain some of their lost power and prestige. This mild aggression proved hardly effective, but perhaps only because confidence in any kind of magic on the mission was by this time at a low ebb.

For the Yir Yoront still in the bush, a time could be predicted when personal deprivation and frustration in a confused culture would produce an overload of anxiety. The mythical past of the totemic ancestors would disappear as a guarantee of a present of which the future was supposed to be a stable continuation. Without the past, the present could be meaningless and the future unstructured and uncertain. Insecurities would be inevitable. Reaction to this stress might be some form of symbolic aggression, or withdrawal and apathy, or some more realistic approach. In such a situation the missionary with understanding of the processes going on about him would find his opportunity to introduce his forms of religion and to help create a new cultural universe.

CHAPTER

26

The Millenarian Aspect of Conversion to Christianity in the South Pacific

JEAN GUIART

Much has been written about "cargo cults," the best known form that millenarism has taken in Oceania. Yet none of the synthetic studies that have been attempted to date has been entirely satisfactory. If one maps the emergence of the cults, it will be seen that they have occurred in a curiously irregular pattern. The question thus arises: why is there a cargo cult here and not there? This has been one of the problems on which I have pondered during my nine years of field work in Melanesia.

Studies have often been based on so restricted a concept of cargo cults as to make it difficult to discern the common features of the different movements. The many different aspects and variations of religious structures as they appear in contact conditions have too seldom been viewed as a whole. Up to now, few anthropologists have troubled to analyze Christianity in the area as it has evolved over nearly two centuries. We talk of missionization as an external factor which plays havoc with traditional society. We look for the remnants of heathenism inside the existing Christian society. We rarely think of Christianity as a living factor inside the social structure, as being in many ways an entirely new phenomenon: the reinterpretation of occidental traditional religious ideas and structures by people who have chosen to make use of them as their own.

I am presenting here not any final analysis, but simply a working hypothesis for future research. Existing

From *Millennial Dreams in Action,* Sylvia L. Thrupp, ed. (*Comparative Studies in Society and History,* Supplement 2). New York: Cambridge University Press, 1962, pp. 122–138. By permission of the author and the publisher.

data are very self-justifying in nature; only field work of both an extensive and intensive kind can allow us to understand the precise value of such and such detail. I am persuaded that further research could ultimately in many ways deepen our understanding of culture change in the area. The cooperation of members of the new generation of islanders in the area could be of immense help.

I start with the question: how did the indigenous people react to their initial contacts with Christian missions? For an answer to this question we must turn first to the mission literature. Unfortunately this is rather poor for our purpose. Early mission reports were written for home congregations, in the hope of stirring enthusiasm and obtaining badly needed financial help. Only occasionally were missionaries given to social analysis. Nevertheless they always give some clues to the reaction of the people. Their evidence leads me to the hypothesis that from the beginning the people tended to view everything new that was offered them by the missionaries as a whole, as a "package deal."

With us, it took a whole generation of work in social anthropology to gain acceptance for the functional approach (that is, for the notion that each element of a culture has a function to perform within an integrated whole), then to supersede the first general ideas of the "patterning" of culture by the more precise concept of structure. I suggest that Melanesians and Polynesians discovered functionalism and structuralism for themselves through being confronted with the white man's culture and society. Among other fine points, they grasped that religion had a definite function inside our world. They realized that if they were ever to come to our level they would have to accept our religion. At first they ascribed to white men a kind of godlike status; but this view passed. The native people were soon trying to think out how they might become the equals of these pale-skinned, rich, powerful, at times naïve or ruthless mortals. The simplest way appeared to be the adoption of their religion.

The best evidence we have on this point is in some quite recent Lutheran Mission reports stating that converts had expressed disappointment with the mission's attitude toward them. The reports attempt to analyze "from the inside" the converts' reaction to their disappointment. E. F. Hanneman and R. Inselmann have drawn on this material in studies that confirm each other with rare intellectual honesty.

The "inside analysis" was made through an interesting use of symbols at the 1937 annual conference of the New Guinea Lutheran Mission. In the brand new hut built for the Conference, a bush vine was placed so as to represent the moral division between the Mission and the people, created when the latter separated themselves from their pastors in following the local variant of a cargo cult, the Letub. The Church Assembly expressed its regret that such a division had occurred and explained that it had arisen because the missionaries had kept for themselves the material wealth which should accrue to the Church membership as a whole from its acceptance of Christian faith. The missionaries agreed to patch up the apparent quarrel, but suspended sacraments as long as they were not sure of the community's will to follow a wholly Christian way of life. The following year the natives took the initiative of drawing a vine through the hall, as symbolic of continuing division between them and the missionaries; they were openly accusing the latter of hiding from the native members of the Church the secrets of European wealth.

This feeling was not new. It had already been expressed in 1933 in a pidgin address to Rev. R. Hanselmann, beginning, *"Bilong wonem mifela no sawe kisim as billing cargo? . . ."*, which may be translated as follows:

> How is it we cannot obtain the origin of wealth? You hide this secret from us. What is ours is only rubbish, you keep the truth for yourselves. We know that all that is the white man's work is forbidden to us. We would like to progress, but the white man wants to keep us in our state of Kanakas. The Mission, it is true, has given us the word of God, but it does not help us black men. The white men hide from us the secret of the Cargo . . .

Speaking of a still earlier time just after 1914, Hanneman tells how, after a period of active and passive resistance to European control and after a series of prolonged discussions among themselves, the Madang area people finally decided to obey administrative regulations and accept the Mission's teaching. For a time there were many happy collective conversions to Christianity. In Hanneman's view, more than half the population of the Madang district thought that through acceptance of European civilization and religion they would gain automatic access to the white man's food, tools, money, clothes, domestic comfort, mental faculties and strength of character. The Christian God was to give them the white man's riches and abilities, in the same way as their former gods gave them success in their ceremonial exchange expeditions or protected their warlike incursions into enemy territory.

Hanneman goes on to show how this hope of access to the cargo could influence outwardly Christian developments. The Kukuaik (beware) movement was born in 1940 on the island of Karkar, north of Madang, after the local missionary had preached about the return of Christ. Phenomena of quaking, glossolalia, and hysterics appeared, all in hope of hastening the coming of Christ and of the cargo. In the same way, after the last war, it was said around Finschhafen that Christ had died again here and that his bones were being assembled to be sent to the U.S.A. Ten years earlier, at the village of Biliang, near Madang, the people celebrated an outwardly Christian ritual, in Sunday clothes, to request from God the coming of the cargo.

Today, in this area, cargo-cult leaders denounce over and over again what is in their eyes the falsity of missionary preaching, as the cargo has never come. The respective attitudes of natives and Europeans on the matter are shown in a poetic exchange of symbolic discourse between natives of the area and a patrol officer: "A father has two sons; one inherits from his father a cargo ship, the other only gets a canoe," said the natives. The European officer replied, "The dove flies upwards, finding its food on various trees, but the duck's habit, when seeking food, is to stick its head in the mud." This was an unhappy answer, although not untruthful in the context of segregational attitudes which persist among the European population in New Guinea. Another remark made to missionaries in this area was: "What the Mission has given us is good. We like the word of God. But they have given us only one part, merely the shell. The kernel they keep for themselves." Such declarations are to my mind the most important evidence of the trend of native thought in the South Pacific.

How widely diffused are these attitudes? I do not propose to examine here the whole of the missionary literature, but will present only some of the evidence that it contains for areas that I know best, beginning with Tanna, in the New Hebrides. Mission reports are almost our only source for early European contacts in this area. We lack any first-hand record of the attitudes of the earliest converts.

Missionary work in Tanna was not always easy. Frank Paton quotes a serious catechism listener who asked to be paid for his attendance. This is by no means an isolated case; the first London Missionary Society people had the same experience in the Loyalty Islands. In some villages of North Tanna the missionary was told, *"Me fella want copra man, me fella no want missionary."*

This materialistic attitude was noted and partly satisfied through the organization of commercial stations by lay Presbyterians of good standing, by Forlong at Loanbakël, Bates on Aniwa, Carruthers at Lenakel. These men did good business at the same time as they tried to impress a Christian way of life upon their customers. This did not last, the traders on Tanna soon dropping evangelization and sticking simply to business. But the early missionaries had certainly realized that the natives had urges which were not merely spiritual. Outside Tanna missionaries were not always adverse to trading direct. Well-known cases are those of Samuel Marsden in New Zealand, Pitman in Rarotonga, Pritchard in Tahiti, and some of the members of the Boston Mission in Hawaii.

The needs of the natives at their first contacts with our culture, though very small if measured in terms of money, were in some ways desperate, so deeply did their envy of the wealth of their new masters bite. The missionaries of the last century were overdressed and by the standards of the time lived in conditions of near luxury, their stipends being £200 a year. Judging by material remains of L. M. S. Mission Stations, for example, they displayed in Oceania the way of life of the English or Scottish Victorian middle classes. To the natives they appeared immensely rich.

The early missionaries were moreover responsible for creating the hope among the natives that they in turn could become rich through Christianization, for they doled out material goods as rewards for conversion and religious zeal. Buzacott has left us a record of presents given to the people in Rarotonga as a reward for their building a missionary college in 1844:

Piece goods and cloth from mission stocks, value £11.8.9
24 dozen knives (the gift of a friend)
4 bundles of children's dresses (gift of English friends)
Piece goods and cloth supplied by Buzacott, value £25.2.3
3 large bullocks, value 30 dollars each value £18.0.0
5 boxes of American glass, value £10.0.0
50 hogs
Presents of bolts, hasps, white lead

These presents represented good wages for the time. The published letters of Mrs. Watt, wife of the Kwamera missionary, on the south coast of Tanna, tell of rewarding promising pupils with clothing that was sent out around 1870 by the Glasgow Foundry Boys' Religious Society. Frank Paton also used gifts of clothing as a way of paying for work done for his mission. Most photographs published in the missionary literature of the time show converts of long standing as well dressed.

Material rewards could however be distributed only so long as converts remained a small minority of the population. As the body of converts grew, the material given them inevitably diminished, and when collective conversions occurred, the flow dried up altogether. This circumstance goes far to explain the later sense of disillusionment. Some missionaries I know have latterly tried to get converts to work for them without pay. This situation is accepted with less and less good grace and is apt to be met with flat refusal.

Another material way of rewarding early converts may be discerned in the mission literature. The best help F. Paton got in Lenakel was from a man called Loohmae, who, with his friend Yawus, used the Mission to cover up his landgrabbing at the expense of a vanquished tribe; there were enough Old Testament texts to justify his attitude. Loohmae could thus count the rewards of his conversion in terms of coconuts and copra. He also however counted on going to heaven. When friends tried to persuade him to leave the mission to go to work for a nearby trader at a better salary he told them, *"Very good you work along money, by and by you go along big fire: Me work along Misi, we want go to heaven."*

The doctrine of hell fire was indeed a very significant element of mission teaching in this area, the Presbyterians insisting that everything heathen was from the devil. Satan came thus inadvertently to play as large a role as Jehovah. A man called Nabuk, just before he died, saw in a dream the people of the Lomwanyan group burn in hell and cry aloud for oranges. His friend Yawus then went to Lomwanyan and explained to the members of this group what would be their fate if they remained pagan. F. Paton gives the following story:

> While we were (on furlough) in Victoria a report got about among the Heathen that Jesus was coming on a certain day to take the worshippers to heaven, and burn up Tanna and all the Heathen. Some of the Heathen gathered their pigs together, and sat up all night watching; others began to kill and eat them lest they should be destroyed by the fire. Others again turned fiercely upon the Worshippers as the cause of all the trouble. In the midst of all this excitement, a labour vessel came. The Heathen told the recruiter of the report that Tanna was to be burned, and asked him if it was true. The recruiter, being a long headed man, replied: "I don't know about Tanna, but I know that Queensland is not going to be burned," and hinted that it would be as well to make sure by recruiting for Queensland.

The doctrine of a vengeful God proved to be a dangerous one. Gordon, who preached in this vein on Eromanga in 1861, at the time that an epidemic of measles was running through the island, was murdered there a week later. It is a well attested fact that native people frequently blamed epidemics on the Christian God and on the inroads of Christianity in their traditional way of life. Turner and Nisbet in 1843, and in 1860 the famed John G. Paton, had to abandon Tanna because of this attitude.

With their narrow-minded theology, such nonconformist Protestant missionaries unwittingly transformed Christianity into a form of Monism. They themselves, did not realize how they had oversimplified their faith. They were convinced that the natives of the Pacific area were in the main mere children who had to be given a simple choice between good and evil. Almost every aspect of the customary life was condemned as the work of the Devil.

Their simple presentation laid great stress on the Apocalypse. Over and over again I have seen Presbyterian and Seventh Day Adventist teachers walking about the hills in Espiritu Santo and Malekula to show the heathen sets of brightly coloured pictures of the life of Jesus. The last picture of the set, by contrast in tones of black and red, always depicted the Day of Judgment according to the Book of Revelation of St. John.

We have thus isolated two aspects of how early native converts understood Christian doctrine as brought to them by nineteenth century missionaries: (a) the Kingdom to come, glowing with happiness, material wealth, and, not to be forgotten, the promise of the resurrection of the dead; (b) the fiery doom held out to nonbelievers. Both these elements appear in most of the cargo cults or other so-called nativistic movements that are described in the literature. Both occur in those I had the opportunity of studying personally in the field. The only change might be the replacement of Jesus' name by some other.

Let us now turn to the New Caledonia area, where there were both Catholic and Protestant missionaries. The initial reaction to the missionaries here was clearly to believe that they had godlike powers, even power over death. Catholic sources in New Caledonia tell us how in Balade, a district Captain Cook had already described as poor and desolate, the natives pleaded with the very first Marist fathers reproachfully, "Why are you miserly with us? You do not give us rain. Your brothers the white men keep it away from us in their country. Come and see our crops. They are dying so very much, the ground is dry." People would also come and ask the priests for the "water which called away death."

Later there was a hostile reaction, aroused in part by envy of the abundance of food in the mission stations. Brother Blaise Marmoiton was martyred in Balade after it became known that his dog had been trained to attack natives who trespassed on Mission premises.

The hostility soon turned to fear, when a wave of epidemics swept the islands. In Rarotonga, an epidemic of dysentery in 1830 killed a seventh of the population. In two districts "which had manifested much opposition to the advancement of Godliness," nearly everyone died. Ernest Beaglehole observes that "the sickness swept away all the leaders of the opposition and completely crushed the numerous parties which had set themselves against the establishment of Christianity and of law." The missionaries encouraged the belief that this was a punishment. Buzacott inquires:

> Are we wrong in coming to the conclusion which all the natives have come to: "This visitation is from God?" . . . For many years afterwards this judgement was used as a text, from which class leaders exhorted their inattentive schol-

> ars; parents were wont to warn their refractory sons and daughters by reference to it; and occasionally the voice of the missionary pleaded tenderly with ungodly youth, and entreated them to believe lest they too should fall into the hands of the living God.

Thus prophetism of a wrathful kind, in the Old Testament tradition, became part of missionary teaching in the area. It was strongest among the Protestants but competition between Catholics and Protestants probably made it fairly general. It is easy to understand how anathema were transferred from the heathen creed to the other new creed. With the arms trade flourishing, and new political ambitions governing at times the choice of Church, wars of religion became cruel, particularly in Fiji and the Loyalty Islands (Ouvéa, Maré).

The phenomenon that we must try to understand, however, is that of the many instances of mass conversion to Christianity. What were the underlying forces at work?

A modern myth collected on the Isle of Pines, south of New Caledonia, may give us a clue. It deals with the land of the dead, thought to be in the Bay of Oro, in the district of Tuete, north-east of the Island:

> It was the time of "Queen Hortense" and her consort chief Samuel. The whole island was Catholic since a generation. A group of people from Tuauru on the island of New Caledonia proper had come to visit the paramount chief's court at Gadji. Some young men of this group went to fetch wood in the forest. One of them disappeared and was only found in the morning, as he tumbled half dead inside one of the village huts. Once he regained consciousness, he explained how he had followed an old woman and her granddaughter and got lost. In fact, the two women were not living beings but goddesses and they took him all the way to the bay of Oro. He found there a stockade, at the entrance of which was a French soldier on one side, and a black warrior on another side. In the fenced area were the dead, white and black being mixed, without any discrimination. . . .

The old myth of the land of the dead and the Catholic teaching that every one is equal before God had come together in this pathetic fashion. It must be noted that the period this myth recalls is one which saw the native population losing half of its land in favour of a political deportees' settlement and a strong army garrison. A few years later the greater part of this land was restored to the people. This favourable turn of events may have prevented a recurrence of such myth-making. The myth has nevertheless been handed on until today.

Somewhat similar feelings explain curious happenings around 1940 in the mountainous area of Northern New Caledonia. A traditional diviner named Pwagatch had been working for some years in the region, being called in from village to village to discover and eradicate newly introduced forms of witchcraft referred to by the name *doki*. His activity was frowned upon by both the administration and the missions. But the people seemed so glad to see their villages purified of sorcery, the men accused being purified through drinking a vegetable brew, that there were no disturbances. Pwagatch was therefore left at liberty. He ended his ten years' purification campaign by transferring his former very lax allegiance to the Catholic faith to the native Protestant Church, under the influence of Maurice Leenhardt. Then, during the war, when the island administration and the missions were distracted with other troubles, the old man became the unhappy tool of a visionary woman, self-appointed prophetess of a new variant of Christianity. She decided that Pwagatch was Jesus Christ reincarnated, and that there should be a great feast and dance. People assembled to eat all the food they had been able to collect. Henceforth, "Jesus was to feed them, the law of the mission and of the white man was ended." At this point, however, the principals of the affair were arrested.

The meaning of this story, which I have told elsewhere with fuller detail, appears to be complex. What is of particular interest here is that, in a matter of a few months, the regular procedure of conversion in small groups, with public baptism, spontaneously transferred itself to a new Messianism. This Messianism was more in line with the feelings of the people at the moment about the colonial administration and about the mission's apparent complicity with it. The procedure of conversion was adapted to a deviant form of Christianity. It is typical of the New Caledonians that the movement collapsed quite peaceably. They are too realistic a people to persist in a course that has lost efficacy.

Both the myth of the black and white dead and the hailing of Pwagatch as Jesus represent attempts to evade a situation which was felt to be oppressive. The personality of Maurice Leenhardt, a great upholder of the native cause in his time, was equal in native eyes to that of the Old Testament prophets, at least with those of kindlier and more humane vein. Leenhardt gone, none of the local missionaries, who were afraid of him, could fill this place. In their anxiety, the people had to resort to a living Messiah. This does not say much for their understanding of Catholicism, which they had accepted for over half a century. Yet actually they did nothing extreme; every action was on a symbolic plane, as though they were seeking a way of obliging Fate to comply with their wishes. Most manifestations of cargo cults show a similar tendency to organize spectacular symbolic and collective series of actions, which it is hoped will be automatically efficacious.

Were mass conversions to Christianity then undertaken in the same kind of spirit? And if so, in what way did people hope the action would be efficacious? Two texts written by native informants from the district of Canala in New Caledonia will help us answer this question. The older text was collected by Maurice Leenhardt and is contained in his unpublished notes:

> A clod of earth thinks and opens up in the figure of a man. This figure talks, a body appears. He pulls out a flower in the form of a bell, presses on the petals which separate themselves slightly, adds a leaf, and this is then a second body born from the word of the first, the woman after the man. They give birth to sons who are the heads of clans. The parents having died and the children being jealous of one another, they dream, one of a sea snake, the other of a lizard. The children die, their totems remain. The children are bodies, their totems spirits who reveal the useful stones: yam cultivation stones, fishing stones. The dead parents help with all their heart the totem who receives the prayers of the children, because of the parents. Parents and totems work together to answer the son's prayers. Spells, wicked charms, yam or fishing stones, war magic, everything comes from them.

> The origin, the clod of earth, is now hidden; the children have eaten men and committed crooked deeds. So the heart, the love which stayed inside the clod, has remained closed in. The fluid does not go to them, the children, and they remain alone with their totems and their dead parents; but Jesus has taken away the fence, the fence which fell after the ill was done, to separate the names and hide the origin where love stayed away.

This text came out of half a century of resistance to Christianization in the region of Canala. Late conversion meant that in this case people kept a certain pride in their past. How in fact traditional beliefs coexisted with participation in the life of a Christian Church, is shown by the following story:

> During the year 1951, Sasine Boiso fell sick. He was a member of the clan named Thupira. On a morning of that year, he called pastor Tomedy and told him: "Pastor, I want to talk to you about Kodu, our ancestral God. I know he is responsible for my illness. See, I dreamed this night and in my dream, Kodu appeared to me in human form, saying that if we do not hunt or fish for him, he will eat us all. I call you today to show you my thoughts before I tell them to my fathers: I want Kodu's life to end with the past. I shall ask my fathers to present you Kodu so that you shall pray on him and that his power ceases." The Pastor answered: "Sasine, if your fathers accept, I shall pray on Kodu."
>
> Boiso spoke again and said: "Pastor, I shall do this for my children. My sickness becomes worse every day. I have only a few days left to live amongst you. But I shall die after having seen you take Kodu and pray over him, so that my children shall worship one God only, Yahve. You must bring to an end the time of Kodu and his power."
>
> Sasine Boiso called his fathers. They were four brothers. Three of them were Christians of the Protestant faith. The last one had remained heathen. He was the servant of Kodu, their God. It was in the eve of a day that Sasine decided to talk to his fathers. Their discussion lasted one night, a day and another night. The Christians accepted their son's proposal. The pagan resisted, saying: "Who is the man who will come and destroy Thupiras?"
>
> Sasine Boiso's suffering was increasing. He said to his father, the heathen one: "Father, have pity upon me. My pain is too great in waiting for the Pastor to do his work." The morning of the second night of discussion, Korobani told his son: "I accept your proposal." He fasted, then called his brothers: "Go and call the Pastor so that we can go and fetch grandfather."
>
> They called the Pastor who went off with Korobani and one of the latter's brothers called Albert. They followed a mountain trail for about three kilometers. They crossed the summit of a mountain and reached a waterfall. Behind this waterfall were high cliffs overhanging caves. Old man Korobani showed the Pastor and Albert one of the cliffs where dwelt Kodu and told them: "Let us not walk, but run, lest he escapes." They ran and when they came to the spot, Kodu was not there. The old Korobani did not talk, but grew pale and shivered. Then he told his two companions: "Let us run towards the second cliff; it seems Grandfather is escaping upwards." When they got close to the cliff, Korobani climbed towards the top, while Albert and Tomedy were searching all round the cliff.
>
> Korobani discovered the ancestor. He jumped towards his companions and said: "I have seen Grandfather up there." The Pastor spoke and said to the two brothers: "Do not speak, I am going up." He climbed the rock and discovered on the top the mysterious stone. He asked then his two friends to keep their peace and prayed. Korobani climbed the cliff meanwhile to be present at the end of Kodu, the wild and fierce ancestor of the clan Thupira, who so many times

> during the ages gave proof of his superior power.
>
> The Pastor took hold of the stone Kodu and they returned to the village where they showed it to Sasine. After having thanked the Pastor, Sasine called all his children and family and said: "Behold our God Kodu. He was in the past a warring God. He hunted men for his food. Today we dwell in the peace of Christ and our heathen wars have ceased. If we keep Kodu, he will eat us all. I am his last victim, do not count me any more. My sickness is worsening and I shall soon die. I was to be his last victim amongst us. Today everything comes to an end with the life of Kodu. From now on, he will no more be our God. You shall worship one God only, Yahve; listen to his word and follow his bidding which the Pastor shall teach you."
>
> Having said these last words, Sasine Boiso passed away. The pastor took the stone to the sea and threw it away there.

This story, dating from only a few years ago, shows how the Pastor himself is integrated in a mythical world, where the stone God Kodu is a worthy rival of Yahve; how the priest of the clan remained heathen because of his function, while his brothers became Christians. It is nevertheless valuable to note that in the long run the continuance of both rituals was thought not to be conceivable and that the choice would be a Christian one. After fifty years of hesitation, acceptance of Christianity came to be considered as a total choice, adherence to the more important aspects of paganism inevitably spelling death.

This brings us to an essential aspect of the symbolism of conversion in Oceanian thought: life versus death. Maurice Leenhardt has on this point published some interesting descriptions of native dreams centering around the dangers of conversion in a specific context. We cannot analyze them further here. But the origin of the conversion of one dreamer, Kapea, who became a deacon, is of particular interest to us. In his dream, as he related it, "One day fishermen at Houailou saw a canoe coming from the south. They hailed the man in the canoe, who told them: 'I bring you the word of life.' Kapea, who was one of the fishermen, answered: 'The word of life! That is what we have been waiting for.'" This laconic conversation was the real beginning of Protestant evangelization on New Caledonia proper. Mathaia, the evangelist, came from Ouvéa, the northermost island of the Loyalties, at the time Christian since nearly half a century. This contact with Houailou followed the pattern of traditional relationships between this district and Ouvéa. The details of the methods then evolved spontaneously by native pastors hailing from Mare, Lifou, and Ouvéa make a fascinating story, unhappily too long to tell here.

"The word of life" has remained the key word in all religious discourse in the Protestant Churches of New Caledonia. Thus Maurice Leenhardt writes: "I only noted two sayings marking the stages of natives coming to Christianity. The first: 'I do not drink any more.' The second, and never has this order been reversed: 'I want to be alive.'"

According to the Journal of Taunga, London Missionary Society evangelist in Tuauru around 1844, the zest of his teaching lay in the message that the true God only was capable of giving salvation. The notion of salvation must have been very vague at this time. There had been little direct contact with whites except through some distribution of firearms to warring parties.

The term "alive" had later a very precise connotation. The tribes which accepted Protestantism around 1900 were those at the time the most in danger of losing their land to European settlers. The new form of Christian faith, brought by native evangelists, offered both a rallying point and a new hope for people who were being thrown out from their ancestral lands and regrouped in Reserves. Only a few had land rights there and kept relations with the old gods and totems. The new religion was the more appealing in that it was less authoritative than Catholicism. To desperate people it was a haven, a frame within which social cohesion could be reestablished. This "word of life" had for them exactly the meaning we would have put in it. It meant the refusal of social death, the hope of a better deal, and the will to be considered something other than ignorant savages. Such deeply rooted ideals gave native pastors and deacons courage to oppose, with dignity, any measures that they considered to be unjust. Some were deported; Pastor Setefano of Maré was murdered. In this case, early Christianization was definitely a subtle, in many ways efficient, and at times overt, form of resistance to the worst aspects of colonial rule.

Moreover, the insistence of the very first native pastors on learning to read, write and count, gave the people the means to a better understanding of European procedures, and particularly of checking on the more or less straight deals offered to them by the local European traders. Consequently many European settlers hated the native leaders of the church and charged them with being dangerous political agitators. From 1867, when a Catholic Father was brought to judgment for "incitement to rebellion," to 1917, when Pastor Maurice Leenhardt was accused of having fostered a native uprising, it was a byword that colonization could thrive only when missions had been destroyed.

It cannot always be demonstrated that conversion was due to such circumstances. Partly this is for lack of documentation, and partly it is because the situation has not always been so clear-cut.

On Espiritu Santo, in the northern New Hebrides, the coastal groups converted to Presbyterianism were extremely aggressive towards the unconverted natives of the interior. As I have shown elsewhere, their attitude was determined by the aim of becoming powerful enough to resist the inroads of the white man on their land rights and on their society generally. On the other hand, the unconverted feared that the Presbyterians would simply oppress them in ways that the coastal natives had often practised before. The local missionaries never realized that they were mere pawns in a complex game of power between Melanesian groups differing in their judgment about the imminence of European pressure. In short, conversion on Espiritu Santo was a means of establishing a generalized cohesion of a native society confronted by a dominant alien group.

Conversion in these circumstances had to be total. The whole of the native society was to be reorganized according to the pattern of the church; it was to be governed by its hierarchy of pastors, teachers and deacons, secular chiefs being there only as a "front" in case of administrative interference. Reorganization, to the native leaders, would mean strength; in many cases this was as far as their thinking went. Missionaries were not always responsible for the militant aspect of the work and planning of their converts. But there was something of the old temptation which gave rise to the Jesuit "reductions" in Paraguay. The Marist Fathers tried various forms of this type of Christian social organization in New Caledonia. It had a certain appeal to Catholic natives in assuring them of the protection that the mere presence of a white missionary gave. At the Melanesian mission on Mota Lava, in the Banks group, "Jarawia . . . came to the Bishop with a plan of his own, of which he had already spoken to his countrymen [while] at Norfolk Island, and which amounted to a request to buy some land near the station on which he and others might settle and form a Christian village, to which all the group could come and live their own native lives, but giving up all that was distinctly heathen." Such collective conversions have occurred over the whole of the Banks group, and not only around Catholic or Melanesian Mission Stations.

It is notorious, however, that these large Christian villages are today the seat of numerous quarrels, particularly about land. The early missionaries had thought that it would be easier to establish the Kingdom of God in the Pacific than in suburban Scotland. How curious a Rousseauism, how curious a neglect of the Calvinist doctrine of grace! The naïve and triumphant Presbyterian or L.M.S. missionary of the years around 1900 was sitting on the very tensions he thought he had eradicated.

But for the time being there was some reason to be pleased. Everything was outwardly quiet and orderly in a Christian way. Teachers and deacons in the church were the real power inside the villages, traditional authority having disappeared or become subservient to them. Some of the methods used were the subject of numerous confidential dispatches between the British Government and the High Commission in Suva (Fiji).

On Tanna, the early years of the century were marked by the rapid conversion, to the Presbyterian Church, of the greater part of the population. Native informants refer to this time as the period of the "Tanna law." Administrative archives tell us how local courts had been organized, and how flogging or fines were inflicted upon Christian and heathen alike for immoral conduct, or simply for the carrying of kava roots on a path close to a Christian village. Informants who had experienced the "Tanna law" explained in recent years that if the "School," i.e., the Mission, had worked "straight," and had used progressive methods, "gone small small," everybody would have become Christian in course of time. They say that a general wish for peace, at a time of a severe death toll taken by internecine wars fought with firearms supplied by European traders, was responsible for earlier conversions. Then floggings expedited the process.

Missionaries of the time accepted the responsibility for having encouraged the setting up of the courts. The abuses of these courts seem to have been in many ways the work of the local zealots; this attitude recalls the aggressiveness of Christian groups already noted on Espiritu Santo. It seems to be a fact that these courts were at the time popular, in so much as they furnished a means of cohesion, under the patronage and protection of the mission, a means of organization of the native coastal society against other abuses against which feeling ran strongly, those of European traders and recruiters. That is the reason why the period which official reports refer to as the one of the "native courts" is for native informants the time of the "Tanna law," when no European presided over their courts.

It should be noted here that in May of 1941 the majority of the Tanna Christians returned to paganism. They became and have remained staunch members of the sect of John Frum. This sect has revived the worship of Karapenmun, the god with whom John G. Paton had to contend in Tanna.

Mass conversions were stimulated also by more materialistic motives. They were followed by far-reaching changes in everyday life: changes in clothing, the learning of new building methods (using lime), by the appearance of European furniture and household implements in the converts' homes, and the acquisition of cattle and horses. Money economy was introduced through encouragement of coconut planting and copra production. There is abundant evidence of these changes in the mission reports, this aspect of mission work being easy to describe to home congregations.

The missionaries aimed at far more than improving the material conditions of life. A whole reorientation of the native society was envisaged. Consider, for example, the part of the New Hebrides where social recognition, prestige and control were functions of acquired rank inside a graded hierarchy generally known under the name of *Namangi,* grades of rank being paid for with pigs. The complex pattern of symbols and behaviour which this graded hierarchy justified, disappeared overnight with conversion. Leaders now had to be experienced not in pig rearing, but in the Work of God Teachers and deacons were, naturally enough, the new men of authority in the new world of Christianity that had been accepted, with its promise of a glowing future. Later missionaries tried to install Christian chiefs so as to separate lay and religious functions. It is then that they found themselves in trouble with governments.

It has to be realized that a native group can of itself, with relative ease, decide to shed what would once have seemed to us anthropologists the most important and functional elements of its culture: on Espiritu Santo even such things as exogamy or bride price. There were dozens of such instances in New Guinea. The process of Christianization often involved sudden and radical changes, for which the missionary does not bear the sole responsibility. Usually kinship and matrimonial structures persisted unchanged; there would otherwise have been anarchy in social life, even among Christians. But so far as outward and spectacular aspects of their traditional culture were concerned, native converts have always been fairly ready to relinquish anything that in their eyes was inconsistent with adherence to Christianity.

Recalling Williams' information, E. Beaglehole describes in this way the last stages of Aitutaki's formal conversion, under the sole influence of a Polynesian evangelist, Papeiha:

> On the Sabbath on which he had the delightful satisfaction of seeing the whole of the inhabitants convene to worship

> the one living and true God, he [Papeiha] announced an important meeting to be held on the next day. At this meeting, he made two propositions: "That all the *maraes* in the island should be burned, and that all the remaining idols should be brought to him" . . . the second proposition was: "That they should commence immediately building a house in which to worship Jehovah." To both of these proposals, the assembled multitude yielded their cordial assent. As soon as the meeting broke up, crowds set off to burn up the *maraes*. District after district came in procession, chief and priest leading, to place their rejected idols at the teacher's feet, receiving in return a few copies of the gospels and elementary books.

In the same way, in each of the Loyalties, mass conversions preceded the coming of European missionaries and were due to the untiring and selfless efforts of Polynesian teachers. After a difficult beginning, it took less than two years to convert four fifths of the island of Lifou. Once a civil war in the district of Lösi had come to an end, the teachers were recalled from the nearby island of Maré where they had taken refuge, and the island opened itself up to the work of Fao and his companions. The material results were shown by the building of monumental churches in every village.

There is still a better case in the records of the Methodist Mission, that of the spontaneous conversion of Ono i Lau, related by the Rev. Calvert. After a disastrous epidemic, it was decided that the priest should offer prayers not to the old gods but to the god known to be worshipped on another island as the only god, Jehovah. The providential arrival of a Tongan canoe, the crew of which were Christians, enabled these people to learn the authentic ritual. They then became zealous Christians. A few years later, they refused to allow Tui Nayau, the polygamous King of Lakemba, to take one of the local Christian girls as a wife. After this crisis, they developed revivalist symptoms. Loud weeping broke out and continued for some months despite the presence of a missionary who was sent in to try to control the excitement. The Rev. Calvert, who had at first doubted the reports he had heard, wrote that "The effect upon my poor frame was thrilling, but very enlivening."

Similar cases of spontaneous conversion are known from Tubuai and Manua. They give rise to the plan of the London Missionary Society, and of other Protestant bodies, of sending native evangelists to open up new mission fields, before any European missionary was stationed. The native teachers interpreted Christian teaching in terms of symbolic phrases and spectacular acts, promising to save and to give a new life, and demanding sweeping changes in the habits of the people. Because of its integrated aspect, this total approach was exceedingly successful.

We must remember that the people of Oceania were confronted with a terrifying experience, that of their first contact with Europeans. The Europeans cheated, abused and kidnapped them and brought death through new diseases and new weapons. In the absence of any administrative structure to protect them, is it astonishing that the natives sought help and protection through conversion?

Is it astonishing, in the face of the prophecies made by the evangelists and confirmed by the missionaries, that wild hopes should be entertained about the golden and happy future reserved to

Christian converts? Christianity was originally millennial. My contention is that, in its Pacific expansion, there has been in most cases an authentic revival of early Christian expectations, and that this relatively recent historical experience explains many aspects of the later falling away from the faith. Thus cargo cults and other nativistic movements should not be studied outside the frame of reference given by the early Christian history of the people. The manner of their contact with Christianity, whether direct or indirect, has been one of the principal sources of all their religious reinterpretations of the past and of the Christian faith itself.

CHAPTER

27

Port Town and Hinterland in the Pacific Islands

ALEXANDER SPOEHR

The current scene in the Pacific islands is the product of the contact—extending over a century and a half—of island peoples with Europeans, Asiatics, and Americans. It has involved the migration and settlement of non-indigenous peoples in the area—particularly during the period of colonial development, the transformation of New Zealand and Hawaii, and the great impact of World War II. The literature of the Pacific includes a number of comprehensive works by anthropologists which portray the historical changes either for the area as a whole, or for certain of its significant parts. Outstanding among the former are Keesing (1941) and Oliver (1951). Among the latter are to be noted studies by Belshaw (1954) on Melanesia, Stanner (1953) on the British dependencies, Keesing (1934) on Samoa, Guiart (1957) on the French possessions, and Beaglehole (1957) on the Cook Islands.

A perusal of these works would raise doubts in the mind of any careful reader whether, in the face of change in the Pacific, there still exist isolated, self-sufficient societies outside the web of administration, trade, and missionary influence. The answer is that, with the possible exception of certain areas of New Guinea, while some islands are indeed geographically remote and contacts with the outside world few, the Pacific islands as a whole are divided into a number of subregions, each consisting of one or more towns or small centers, surrounded by a hinterland. The town is generally a port, the hinterland usually an assemblage of islands, except where a large land mass such as New Guinea provides a less aqueous setting. Port town, hinterland, the subregion which encompasses them both, the totality of these subregions, and

From *American Anthropologist,* 62: 586–592, 1960. Reproduced by permission of the author and The American Anthropological Association.

finally the forelands beyond the sea to which these subregions are linked by transportation and communication combine to form the geographic framework of contemporary culture change in the Pacific islands. The purpose of this paper is to comment on port town and hinterland, for within this geographic framework the relation between the two is crucial for an understanding of the changes taking place in the Pacific today.

If we set aside Hawaii and New Zealand, there are no cities in Polynesia, Micronesia, or Melanesia. There is instead a series of port towns, varying in size from less than a thousand to some 30,000 people, together with a number of smaller centers which are essentially embryonic towns and which serve similar functions. These towns and centers —Papeete, Apia, Suva, Noumea, Rabaul, Port Moresby, to name the larger and more familiar ones—are the creation of alien influences. They owe their establishment and subsequent growth to European enterprise. They came into existence as commercial, administrative, and missionary centers. In the nineteenth and early twentieth centuries these towns were focal points of colonization within European and to a lesser extent American territories. As a result, the Pacific islands became fragmented into a series of colonial subregions, each subregion or territory with at least one major center, and sometimes several subsidiary ones.

These port towns today reflect the national cultural differences of the colonizing powers. Noumea and Suva are different not only in the languages spoken, but in other cultural ways that are either characteristically French or British. Furthermore, these towns vary in their racial composition, with some having a much higher indigenous component than others. Finally, one cannot ignore the effect of World War II. Rabaul and Lae were completely destroyed. Due to Australian energy, they have been just as completely rebuilt. In the U.S. Trust Territory, one of the circumstances with which American administration has had to cope is the destruction during World War II of literally all the port towns of the area. These towns had grown up during the Japanese regime. When conducting field work in the Marshalls after the War, I found that the people compared their current living standard unfavorably with that which had prevailed in Japanese times; but I suspect that the real lack which they felt was the obliteration of the small ports which were their link with the sophistications of the outside world. These former port centers are very slowly reconstituting themselves around the various administrative headquarters of the districts into which the U.S. Trust Territory is divided. If the policy of excluding foreigners continues, they will come to be composed of islanders rather than migrating aliens.

Pacific port towns continue to serve as commercial, administrative, and church centers. As a result, they are communication and transportation centers as well. Economically, they live primarily by organizing the trade between the hinterland and the foreland. Apart from the processing of extractive products, there is either no industry, or only a modest development in the production of locally consumed goods. In his book on medieval cities, Pirenne (1925) notes that the Roman meaning of the word *portus* was simply "a storehouse or transfer point for merchandise," a meaning which lasted at least until Carolingian times in Europe. Pacific port towns economically still tend to conform to the Roman meaning of *portus*.

The relation of foreland to hinterland is crucial in the development of all ports. In the words of Weigend (1958): "Forelands are the land areas which lie on the seaward side of a port, beyond maritime space, and with which the port is connected by ocean carriers." The forelands of Pacific island ports are in some degree the other parts of the Pacific, but more dominantly they are metropolitan countries, to which is shipped a limited variety of exports: agricultural products such as copra, cacao, and coffee, some marine products such as trochus, and those particular to a given territory such as nickel ore from New Caledonia, sugar from Fiji, and canned fish from American Samoa. In return, virtually all manufactured products are imported from metropolitan foreland countries into the port towns. The economic relation between foreland and port is still organized by national interests and influenced by national trade agreements—though broadened since World War II—so that each Pacific territory or subregion is greatly affected by its tie to the administering metropolitan power.

This tie between subregion and metropolitan power, mediated through the port town, also extends into noneconomic spheres. Thus, for example, the formal educational systems prevailing in the Pacific territories reflect in a striking manner the national differences of their metropolitan countries of origin (Keesing 1934).

In regard to the hinterland, Pacific port towns are so widely dispersed that competition among them for trade is minimized. This is in contrast with the competition which has characterized the history of European port towns, which are not so far apart and which have the great resources of a productive continent behind them. An interesting exception has recently been reported by Bennett (1957) in a study of Vila and Santo in the New Hebrides, where Vila, the older, retains most of the import trade and its administrative functions, but Santo, due to the greater productivity of its hinterland, has captured more than half of the export trade.

A postwar development affecting Pacific ports is commercial aviation and with it the growth of tourism in areas with exotic scenery and no malaria. It is still too early for the pattern of commercial aviation finally to crystallize, but in some areas it will play an increasing role as an agent of change and will add a new dimension to the concept of Pacific port towns as primarily maritime shipping points.

Given the continuation of their established economic, administrative, and mission functions, the principal interest of Pacific port towns lies in the dynamics of their growth. In his review of social anthropology in Polynesia, Keesing (1953) points out that, whereas even twenty-five years ago these towns were composed mainly of Europeans, part-islanders, and Asiatics, there subsequently has been a steady movement of islanders from the hinterland into the towns, which "serve as magnets, drawing from the outer areas for permanent and temporary residence the ambitious, the adventurous, the discontented, the curious, as well as many concerned with official, mission, and other business." As a result the towns are changing in racial and ethnic composition. A recent study by Belshaw (1957) of a

Melanesian village which has become part of Port Moresby illuminates the manner in which islanders have been incorporated into town life and the social problems which have resulted. In a previous article, Belshaw (1952) described the development of a purely Melanesian canoe trade in the marketing of fresh fish in Port Moresby—a response to the continuous shortage of fresh food which the town experiences.

As these Pacific towns and smaller centers have changed from being creations of necessity, or for the convenience of administering metropolitan nations, to an ethnically integral part of the Pacific scene, they have become focal points in a melange of relations among the different racial groups which inhabit the Pacific islands. Long-established Chinese merchants and shopkeepers impress one with how little historical literature there is on the movement of Chinese into the islands and the cultural effect of this movement. Saturday soccer games in Rabaul, where Melanesian participants are drawn from all over the Territory of Papua and New Guinea, are a reflection of the manner in which European demand for labor has changed the total social system of New Guinea. It is certain that the social position of resident Europeans as a minority group throughout the Pacific islands will become increasingly complex, and in all the islands the question of the status and the future of persons of mixed racial ancestry will come to the fore.

With his wide experience of the Pacific, Keesing has pointed out that the serious study of Pacific towns is handicapped by a lack of basic descriptive information. In terms of anthropological interest, they have been by-passed for field studies of hinterland societies. This situation is now changing. Davidson and Guiart (1959) have recently published under South Pacific Commission auspices a memorandum on the significance of town studies, enumerated a number which are in process or about to be initiated under various institutional auspices, and included a topical outline of the investigation which Guiart is now conducting in Noumea.

Granted the practical need of the territorial administrations for information on Pacific port towns, what kinds of anthropological problems are involved? It can be anticipated that they will relate to two principal subjects: the significance of port towns in culture history; and the comparative study of urbanization.

The history of port towns is a major chapter in the growth of cities. Ports have been the organizing centers in the development of the world's trade routes. They have been transmission points in the transfer of ideas, as well as goods. They have been the meeting point of men from different lands and societies. They have served as breeding grounds and as a point of origin of cultural change. In consequence, their study holds much of interest for the historically minded anthropologist. Pacific port towns are still small enough to be amenable to traditional techniques of anthropological investigation, and they offer opportunity for observing the kinds of changes which in general terms have occurred in the past in a number of much older and now much larger ports in other parts of the world.

Pacific island ports also offer the opportunity for observing early stages of urbanization. It must be emphasized that these towns are not cities and it is unlikely that they ever will be. Quite possibly New Guinea will one day support one or more cities, but the resources of the island hinterlands of most of these towns are so limited that the towns may never grow to major size. But they do provide contemporary examples of the urbanization process in an island setting which can be related to a similar process in continental areas and hence can contribute to the comparative study of urbanization as a world-wide phenomenon.

The usual goal of anthropologists conducting field work in the Pacific islands has been the hinterland, for it is there that the flavor and character of island life are most apparent. It is from hinterland studies that the corpus of Pacific ethnological literature has been derived, from Codrington to the present day.

These hinterland studies themselves reveal the changes which are taking place in communities removed though tributary to ports. Hogbin's *Transformation Scene* and Mead's *New Lives for Old* document the extent of changes in what were once isolated communities. Danielsson's (1955) study of Raroia in the Tuamotus is a similar example from Polynesia, and others have been made in different parts of the Pacific. It is true that there are still plenty of remote islands. Rennell and Tikopia and a score of others are accessible only a few times a year. Yet throughout the Pacific a trend is discernible, long established in some parts, more recent in others, and still to take full effect in uncontrolled parts of New Guinea. This trend is based on the relationship of hinterland to port town and the transformation of hinterland society into a kind of modern Oceanic peasantry.

As anthropology has broadened its field of investigation beyond studies of primitive or tribal societies, partly because such societies are disappearing from the earth, it has concerned itself with exploring other types of societies, of which one is modern peasantry. The nonautonomous nature of peasant society and culture and its requirement for continued communication with an outside culture which generally is associated with a relatively more complex social center, such as town or city, seem to be characteristic. In what ways are these Oceanic hinterland societies nonautonomous, in the sense that they depend on a connection, however tenuous, with the port town? Three examples follow.

A first characteristic of the independence of Pacific islanders, which has been aptly described by Firth (1953), is that they are now "without exception, committed to the material civilization which is the hallmark of the West." Tools, cloth, sewing machines and other manufactured goods are imported into the ports and from there find their way to the hinterland, largely in return for agricultural products. As Firth notes, the world increase in raw material prices has supported this trend. Yet there is no doubt of an increasing desire on the part of the islanders to participate in an international economy, whether or not they understand its ramifications. With this has gone the penetration into the hinterland of a money economy. There is great variability in the extent to which this penetration has taken place, and as Firth (1954) points out, its effects may be markedly different where it is associated with wage labor for Europeans as opposed to local commodity production for export and trade. But there is no doubt of an increasing sophistication in the use of money and familiarity with the concept of capital. The recent growth of credit unions in Fijian villages is a case in point.

A second characteristic is the development out of the contact milieu of new forms of leadership and a changing elite group. Thus there is the emerging figure of the entrepreneur, granted that in his struggles and aspirations he is often to be identified as much by his failures as his successes. The pastor, the school teacher, elected or appointed local officials, and increasingly the medical aid all play important roles. These roles are differentiated to a large degree in accordance with the training and educational experience received in town centers. It is probably true that emerging indigenous leadership groups are even more characteristic of the towns than the hinterland, but in this respect there is a common thread of social change which ties the two together. In this connection, the most penetrating study of elites in a Pacific island area, examined in the context of the formalized traditional social system of Samoa, has been published by the Keesings (1956).

Finally, there is the dependence of hinterland on town for implementing those lines of transportation and communication which link the hinterland community with a larger world. Partly this is a matter of travel. In his book on Raroia, Danielsson includes information on how this Tuamotuan atoll is linked to Papeete. He shows that Raroians visit Tahiti more than they do closer atolls and that they use it as a common meeting ground, though Tahitians in return seldom visit their country cousins in the Tuamotus.

Partly also the dependence of hinterland on port town is a matter of communication, whether or not travel and transportation are involved. The transistor radio may become one of the major technological developments in the Pacific, for it is cheap and easy to maintain in a tropical climate. Out of the port towns is broadcast not only the price of copra, but news of the world and many other items. Printed matter, and with it bilingualism, is still principally characteristic of towns, but is becoming more common in the hinterland (F. M. and M. M. Keesing 1956). The port town, more than ever before, is the source of the dissemination of the kind of mental content which is shaping the world view of the hinterland.

In these and in other ways, the forces of the modern world are being channelled through the port towns to the hinterland and, at least in the more acculturated parts of the Pacific, particularly parts of Polynesia and Micronesia, are producing a similar type of hinterland society. Beaglehole (1957) has remarked on this in his recent book on the Cook Islands, in comparing Aitutaki, Rarotonga, Pangai, and Micronesian Majuro. I would submit that a closer examination than is possible here would reveal that this social type conforms in many ways to what has come to be thought of as a peasantry. There is no question but that the marked cultural and social diversity in traditional background found through the Pacific will greatly affect the specific character of future culture change, as one island group is compared with another. New Britain and Fiji are still culturally far apart. Yet the form of this change will be equally conditioned by the common geographic framework in which it takes place, based as I have suggested here on the relation of hinterland to port town.

A final point concerns the scale of the system within which specific social and cultural change in the Pacific islands is examined. The analysis of a particular situation of change may require the isolation of a social system limited to one small island community, or even to a fragment thereof. But in future studies, such a small isolated system must in the end be related to larger and more inclusive ones if the changes examined are to be fully comprehended. In the Pacific islands the nature and scale of these systems need to be made more explicit. This paper is a preliminary attempt at such clarification.

CHAPTER

28

The Rights of Primitive Peoples

MARGARET MEAD

I

In the contemporary climate of opinion, all peoples of the world are claiming the right of nationhood, with all its perquisites—sovereignty, economic self-sufficiency, and membership in the United Nations. Within this situation, the condition of "primitive peoples"—peoples who only recently lived a self-sufficient life without script or any relationship to script—occupies a peculiar place.

The world may be roughly divided into: modernized nations, some of which are also new nations, in the sense that they were colonized from Europe within the last five hundred years and are dependent upon a European tradition—for instance, the United States, Australia, Argentina; old, traditional or exotic peoples with traditions antedating those of the high cultures of Europe, currently struggling with problems of absorbing new economic and political forms—China, India, Burma, Thailand; and new nations within which the earlier forms of cultural life, while often elaborate and highly organized, lacked script and depended upon an oral tradition—for example, many of the countries of Africa south of the Sudan, Tonga, Samoa, etc., where political power has now passed or is passing to the immediate descendants of peoples who were substantially primitive until they came in contact with modern European or Asian cultures.

Furthermore, within many of the countries dominated by a European or Asian tradition there are minorities which have preserved in their present-

---

From "The Rights of Primitive Peoples, Papua-New Guinea: A Crucial Instance," *Foreign Affairs,* January, 1967, pp. 304–318.

day forms of life considerable traces of the unsatisfactory compromise relationships worked out when they encountered the high cultures of Europe, Asia, or Africa and were pushed into undesirable land, isolated in special occupations, made dependent and deteriorated wards of the state or were converted into an uneasy peonage, peasantry, or proletarian labor force. The word loosely applied to such groups is "tribe," a catchall term for ethnic groups that preserve an internal organization which is both somewhat independent of and indifferent to the superordinate forms of organized state government with which they come in contact.[1] They continue to rely on a spoken form of their own language; if they attain literacy in the superordinate culture it is usually of a very limited kind; in values and expectations they are turned inward toward their own "tribal" cultures. World attitudes toward such primitive or tribal peoples are heavily influenced by differential knowledge of or contacts with nomadic tribes of the Middle East, Eskimos in Greenland, Australian Aboriginals, the Maori of New Zealand, Indian populations in Mexico or Peru, Gypsies, Navajo Indians in North America, and so on.

In such encounters the extent to which these decendants of former primitive people have preserved forms of their earlier cultures, or insist on new distinctive costumes and manners, is conspicuous; and the ways in which they have adapted to the technologies, ideologies or social customs of the states within which they live are less conspicuous. The fact that they continue to live in tents or hogans or igloos, or dress their women in long skirts, and that they cling to their native tongue and speak it to their children, sets them apart. Furthermore only those primitive peoples who have maintained such a separate and tribal status are visible at all; for ten thousand years comparable groups have become the peasantry and the proletariat of complex societies, speaking the language and following the customs of the state of which they are a part. They may often constitute quite special regional groups and give the special style to a region of a modern state; they may, also, like the Welsh, the Scots and the Irish, the Basques, the Croatians, the Ukrainians, still provide the cultural background for various sorts of irredentism. What is forgotten is the circumstance that they and also those against whom they are rebelling were once the descendants of peoples with an exclusively oral tradition, living in self-contained tribal groups. So, whether the primitive peoples in question have been living in uncomfortable symbiosis with an organized state for a thousand years or five hundred years or only a decade, the emphasis is upon the groups which have not consented to assimilation, and it is to experience with these groups that all new encounters are referred.

The standard expectation is that "primitive peoples" when they encounter "civilized" peoples react by refusal to become assimilated, and after various efforts by missionaries and government, revert to their primitive styles of life. Then, according to the ethic of the period of encounter, they may be hunted like game, have a price set on their heads like vermin, be relegated to reservations or subjected to elaborate plans for education, rehabilitation and welfare. When an account of a new African state is prefaced by remarks of how recently the majority of the citizens lived (or still live) in a tribal state, the expectations of the future fate of the country are pessimistic in spite of the fact that it may have large modern cities and a sizable university-educated and sophisticated urban population. Or in the case of new states like the Philippines or Indonesia, the continued existence of some relatively unassimilated pagan tribes on some of the smaller islands compromises the national image of the country, and we hear derogatory phrases that include references to "savage" or "heathen" customs. The centuries of sophisticated contacts with Asia and Europe are not allowed for; the primitive minorities come temporarily to stand for the whole.

II

Within this setting, the process of nation-building in the eastern half of the immense island of New Guinea does, nevertheless, present very complicated problems. In this area,[2] governed by Australia, live some 2,000,000 Melanesians and Papuans, a dark-skinned people with a superficial resemblance to Africans and a physical appearance that evoked the racial exclusiveness of their European discoverers. They had been cut off from the rest of the world for thousands of years and at the time of discovery lacked any knowledge of script, metals, the wheel, the plough, or of any form of political organization capable of uniting originally disparate peoples into political units larger than congeries of hamlets of a few hundred people and occasional temporary larger alliances for purposes of raiding or warfare. Their backward state can be reasonably attributed to their isolation. They had not, as have many other so-called tribal peoples, lived cheek by jowl in uncomfortable symbiosis with more civilized neighbors with whom they did not choose to amalgamate, or who, for various religious, racial or political reasons, refused to incorporate them—as is the case, for instance, with alien groups within China, India, and parts of Southeast Asia and some countries of the Middle East and Africa. They can therefore be regarded, in the contemporary ethic of the mid-twentieth century, as having been treated unfairly by history, as having lacked a location on the earth's surface that would have given them an opportunity to accept the culture of more advanced civilizations, and so prove their superiority, or to reject or be rejected by it and so prove their inferiority. As the exploration and pacification of the interior of New Guinea is a post-World War II phenomenon, it has involved the most striking discrepancy in recorded history between the newly discovered and the discoverers, men who lived in a stone-age horticultural state of technology confronting members of an airborne society. The relevant Metropolitan powers—Germany, Great Britain, Australia, the Netherlands, and Indonesia—can all be saddled with responsibility for the continued backwardness of the peoples whom they have ruled under various colonial mandates and trusteeship arrangements.

The forms of social organization in the Territory of Papua-New Guinea, although differing in detail, can be characterized for the entire area as clusters of hamlets, the inhabitants of which have ties of common or claimed descent, common language and territory, and intermarriage. Between the clusters there occur trade, warfare, headhunting and, less frequently, intermarriage. Hereditary positions of authority hardly exist: those who organize large-scale feasts, exchanges and war parties are "Big-Men" who emerge briefly and who cannot pass on their power directly. Absent are the institutions or practices on which state-like forms have been based, such as rank, conquest, tribute and annexation. Instead, the principal value of an enemy group has been that it provided a means to attain honors and prizes for bravery. Expanding populations did sometimes drive neighboring groups from their land, sometimes permanently, or sometimes exterminated, another group, but the type of social organization did not lend itself to the development of complex stratified societies. There is a tremendous premium upon differentiating one group from another, the smallest details of dialect being seized upon and elaborated; there is great specialization of crafts and materials for trade, with various forms of compulsive barter to stimulate trading partners to fish, hunt, make baskets, net bags, spears, wooden bowls to provide for the needs of those who lack particular foods or objects or manufacturing skills.

Contact took place under such conditions that missionizing and governing groups had minimum estimates of the potentialities of the people. Before World War II efforts to educate the peoples of Papua-New Guinea were very limited indeed. Training as clerks, catechists and elementary schoolteachers was just sufficient to staff local establishments at the lowest levels. There was no tertiary education and very little secondary education of any kind. Those trained within the missions were not admitted to ordination. Intermarriage with the colonists, from which slightly more socially advanced groups elsewhere have produced a native elite, was almost totally lacking.

When the trusteeship power, Australia, was confronted in the post-World War II climate of world opinion with demands that Papua-New Guinea be given early independence, the enormity of the problem became evident. Other new nations are less viable in terms of size and economic resources than Papua-New Guinea, but none faces the prodigious problem of governing a territory in which the people to whom authority within the country would fall have all come so recently—some within the last ten years—directly out of stone-age cultures. For this is a country in which cannibalism and headhunting are in some parts only just coming under control, where old feuds over land and fishing rights simmer beneath the surface even in fully missionized villages, and in which no educated élite has been built up.

In the debates which will undoubtedly quicken in tempo and intensity over the future of Papua-New Guinea, many of the perennial questions of the relationships between isolated tribal peoples and the civilized peoples who attempt to conquer, enslave, convert, pacify, or improve and elevate them come to the fore. If the progress toward independence and if the attainment of independence itself are accompanied by violence and disorder, this will have repercussions in discussions around the world regarding the political competence of peoples emerging from early states of technical and political development. It will also reinforce arguments that confuse the consequences of racial discrimination with an attributed lesser capacity of peoples with darker pigmentation of the skin.

III

The principal questions that are already coming up for review are: Do civilized people have a right to destroy, by overwhelming power, the specific particular cultures of groups of people who owe the persistence of these local styles to their isolation? Do civilized people have an obligation to bring such people as rapidly as possible up to the standard of their own citizens by spending large amounts of money, time, and manpower on education, health, and economic and political development? If civilized people have this obligation, should it fall on those particular modern or modernizing nation-states which are, often through some unrelated historical event, in a position of suzerainty, or is this an obligation of the entire industrialized world? What is known about the capacity for political development of individuals whose grandparents or parents lived a culturally isolated, primitive life—as individuals, as whole communities and as members of a recent aggregation of communities which have historically been inimical to their close neighbors and unaware of the existence of the more remote neighbors with whom they are now asked to identify themselves? What political models, old or new, can appropriately be invoked to create conditions in which political independence can be made viable?

The question of the right of any people to the particular style of culture which they have developed over time has multiple origins in European theories of human rights, self-determination of ethnic groups within the European setting, the tendency to identify language and the right to political autonomy; there also are confusions between race and culture, so that those with different customs were thought of as being intrinsically different as a group and therefore substantially unsuitable for complete assimilation. As there developed a society based on contract rather than status, the exclusion of certain groups who were physically distinguishable and culturally very diverse became a way of begging the question of their rights as individuals. Indians in the United States and Canada, the Aboriginal population in Australia, could be protected—as groups—and denied status as individual citizens. Forcing and bribing a primitive group to live on assigned territory—a reservation (the term is uncomfortably reminiscent today of the phrase "preservation of game")—and sentimentalizing their way of life was the outcome of this mixed position, reinforced in the latter part of the nineteenth century and the early part of the twentieth by the testimony of anthropologists as to the destructiveness of forcible acculturation and by missionization. Artists and humanitarians both responded to the intrinsic appeal of traditional culture, with its internal consistency and sense of harmony, and claimed that interference was wrong. These attitudes became variously expressed in policy toward native peoples within large states, in colonial policies like the Netherlands' respect for local customary law, and in the protective policies of colonial and trust-territory governments which kept native peoples attached to their villages or districts, prevented the alienation of land, limited recruitment, and otherwise promoted the preservation of local cultures and retarded any development of wider allegiances and sophistication.

Since World War II, it has ceased to

be ethically respectable to advocate cultural preservation except in those cases, like that of North American Indians, where the indigenous people are deeply imbedded within a historical ethic and a contemporary expanding economy. Those who argue today for the preservation of local languages and for slow change are identified with those who wish to prevent an indigenous people from receiving the benefits to which they are entitled. The emphasis has shifted from language, religion and customary law to the standardized categories of schooling, public health and political democracy. Attempts to perpetuate local identity or local ethnocentrism are identified as "tribalism"—ethically based factionalism which retards the development of modern states.

But aside from the demands for more education and for externally supported economic development, the tendency has been to rely on the development of types of nationalism, the intensity of which depends on enmity toward some outside power—the ex-colonial or neocolonial power, or neighboring states with a different political ideology (as when citizens of Papua-New Guinea fear "infiltration" from the inhabitants of West New Guinea) or difference in physique—which may be a matter of stature or skin color or small traces of previous disallowed ancestry. Alternatively, reliance may be placed upon religion as the basis of a wider identity.

If tribalism can be defined as a form of political self-identification which places all ties within the group above ties to any wider group, then the forms of nationalism which are current in emerging states are in fact simply an attempt to produce a larger unit with the characteristic ethnocentrism of the component smaller units. Just as tribalism—whether it be of the Yoruba in Nigeria, the Uzbeks in the Soviet Union, the Pathans in Pakistan, or the German sects living in isolation within the United States—can be seen as essentially incompatible with the demands of a modern state for individual responsibility and autonomy, so the forms of nationalism which are emerging in the formation of the new nations can be seen as the exportation onto the world scene of this kind of exclusive, ethnocentric self-identification. Nazism was of course an extreme example of an overweening sense of identity that was both ethnic and national.

So the question of the rights of indigenous and culturally backward people to the benefits of the modern world has become almost inextricably combined with their right to political autonomy—within a variety of historically accidental units—as the necessary condition of their obtaining their proper share of education, health and economic well-being. Questions of the superiority of regional economic and political arrangements become submerged under the discussion of what are essentially magnified "tribal" claims to all the trappings of nationalism.

There is little recognition of the contribution that those peoples who have stubbornly maintained their cultural differences, clung to their languages, and insisted on their separate identities have made to our understanding of the extent of possible variety in human cultures. It is, none the less, important; and vital issues remain, such as whether many of these passionately preserved local languages are to be swept away by the expansionism of the great powers or preserved through the timely adoption of some secondary world language. But they have less salience in world public opinion than the importance of a higher standard of living and greater political autonomy.

When a culturally isolated people come into contact with the modern world, the question arises of how fast they can learn, as individuals and in groups. Learning, whether to behave like a stone-age primitive man, or like a member of a submerged urban proletariat, or like the heir of a royal family, or like a future physicist, has, as an essential component, the question of self-identification and expectancy. There are, of course, great innate differences among individuals in primitive groups quite comparable to the differences between members of civilized societies. But for the individual who has the original endowment to become a statesman or a scientist, an artist or a scholar, an organizer or an inventor, the sociocultural environment within which he is reared is crucial. Thus the question of the educability of *individual* members of a primitive group is significant only when—as a method of bringing them into step with the modern world—individuals are taken from their villages and educated in boarding schools or as residents in communities of the dominant culture. If individuals are taken entirely away from their primitive villages, to whatever extent they successfully assimilate the different culture of those among whom they live, they may become too alienated from their culture of birth to play a useful role when they return to it. On the other hand, in boarding schools with partly acculturated indigenous teachers drawn from a variety of local cultures, pupils tend to lose their local identity while gaining a very inferior, watered-down, partial version of the majority culture into which they hope to move. The graduates of such schools tend to cluster in the growing towns, unable to deal either with the full representatives of the dominant culture or with their own kin and fellow villagers.

A third method of bringing a primitive people into the modern world is by community development, in which the entire community, from grandparent to grandchildren, participates in learning new forms of political and economic behavior.[3] In such cases, it is possible to introduce new behavior models in the form of village teachers and technical assistance leaders through whom the children, supported by their active and aspiring elders, can move on into forms of education that need not become alienating. Even though the elders in many cases may attain only a caricature of modern behavior, the self-identification and progress of the children is much easier provided what they learn is of a sort to support change. But this kind of wide cultural progress of a community is dependent upon a large amount of genuine spontaneity and a sense of intrinsic potentiality and dignity, which most modernization activities inhibit. The educated villager who has embraced a different way of life looks down on his past, while the foreign technical-assistance expert, or in contemporary jargon the "change agent," is usually too intent on change to respect those who are changing. Contact with those who feel either humiliation or contempt does not promote rapid learning of a new set of cultural forms.

So while it may be said that there is no inherent reason either in the genetic constitution of primitive peoples or in their primitive social structure which would prevent them from skipping the intervening cultural forms in which they have not participated, current political inventions are so unfavorable that the results are likely to suggest that such learning is in fact impossible because of some intrinsic characteristic of race or level of culture. In actual fact, it is probably easier to move from membership in an isolated, proud, indigenous culture to full citizenship in a modern state than to reach the same level starting from membership in a culturally deprived group within a modern state, where generations of low status have created an expectation of inferiority and failure. Comparisons between the achievements of regions of New Guinea which have been within close and denigrating contact with Europeans for over half a century, and those which have had an opportunity to come straight into a world where they were treated with more dignity, are very illuminating. Although mission education has provided some linguistic sophistication and familiarity with European ideas of democracy and responsibility, those who are its product contrast disadvantageously with the individuals of the highland areas which are forging ahead very rapidly. The most primitive and latest entrants to the world scene may be those most able to learn, least encumbered with previous learnings, if they are presented either with a complete model of a viable modern culture —as immigrants are—or with a specially devised system capable of encompassing their divergences.

IV

In the light of these considerations, we may examine New Guinea more closely, with a primary emphasis on Papua-New Guinea. The merger of the administrative apparatus of Papua and the Australian Trust Territory after World War II has saddled the country with a conflict between the allegiances of former Papuan officials and former Trust Territory officials. Inevitably, this has produced repercussions among the indigenous peoples and heated attempts to find a name and national identity for the merger of the two divisions. This rivalry and hostility are a conspicuous example of the way in which external governmental powers have so often created artificial tribes, districts, and kingdoms as part of their governing apparatus.[4]

Within these two recently merged territories, there exist between five hundred and seven hundred languages spoken by the some two million people. Along with the diversification of language there is a bewildering degree of cultural diversity, of such a nature that an attempt by a government official or teacher to understand a local culture will qualify him to deal with perhaps five hundred or a few thousand people but often absolutely disqualify him from dealing with every other group he may encounter. There are no indigenous political chiefdoms or tribal organizations which could or can be used as the basis of political organization. The administration's practice of dealing with villages individually and restricting citizenship and political identity to registration in the village census books was both a consequence and a reinforcement of the low level of political organization.

If the trusteeship power had wished to educate those who would possibly inherit leadership roles, it would have been impossible to identify them without detailed study of particular small groups. Since World War II, a phenomenon called "cargo cults" has created a small amount of native leadership, in which individuals with outstanding charismatic powers have combined organizational skills and imagination with apocalyptic promises of an immediately transformed world. Most of these cults crumbled, either because the leaders could not realize the promise or because the administration looked on them as subversive. In Manus (Admiralty Islands) a genuine political movement developed out of a set of very local conditions in the late 1940's.[5] A highly gifted political leader, Paliau, now in late middle age, has been elected to the House of Assembly, established under pressure from the United Nations,[6] and has become chairman of a set of local councils within the Manus archipelago. But he does not speak English, and under the pressure for education and wider experience which may foster a young elite group he is being passed by. Most of the elected members of the assembly have scant influence in their often artificial home constituencies.

In the face of such conditions there is a temptation for analysts to emphasize only deficiencies in the cultures of New Guinea and despair of ever building a viable nation state. Yet at the same time events are inexorably moving towards its creation. The same pressure which works toward the establishment of a nation-state—pressure from the other recently emerged nations, anticolonialism, antineocolonialism, reverse racist thinking—works simultaneously in a case like New Guinea to promote indigenous nationalism and discourage trusteeship. The Australians do not feel that they have tremendous sins to atone for; in fact they have thought of themselves in a colonial predicament *vis-à-vis* the mother country. Their preference for a white Australia was predominantly a desire to keep other racial groups out rather than any interest in extending dominance over them. A large number of Australians disinterestedly administered Papua and New Guinea between the two world wars, when this was a lifetime career; but today, when the policy is to transform all services rapidly so that they will be staffed by indigenous personnel, there is no career line. Contracts have replaced career commitments. Idealism close to the Peace Corps type did produce a large crop of diverse and dedicated young teachers, but recruitment has been discontinued. Aside from defense—and here experts are divided on the advantage of continued responsibility for New Guinea—there is little incentive for Australia to continue to pour money and energy into New Guinea only to be abused as an exploitative colonial power.

Some form of authority as an alternative to the continuing demands on Australia would not necessarily solve the problem. If the responsibility were transferred to the United Nations the issues might shift somewhat from the repetitive reproaches that have become the style when the backwardness of any group of people is concerned. But the sense of national responsibility which is a strong element in Australia's commitment of funds and personnel to the process of nation-building in New Guinea would then be lost.

There does seem to be good reason, however, to shift the question from how much can a primitive people learn —to which the answer is, under the right conditions as much as any other kind of people can learn and sometimes more—to the question of how much are the present administrators and planners in New Guinea likely to be able to *teach,* given present conditions of ideology, funds and personnel.

The pages of *New Guinea,* a quarterly published in Sydney, indicate the extent to which the characteristics of a democratic nation-state are being thrust upon perhaps the least prepared group in the entire world. In a single recent issue the subjects dealt with included the fears expressed by a 32-year-old member of the House of Assembly from the Upper Sepik River that infiltrations from West Irian will bring disease, spies, and Communists into the Territory; the right of asylum of primitive inhabitants of the interior; wildcat strikes; whether or not to outlaw card playing and problems of restoring wives and children lost in "lucky games" to their rightful husbands and fathers; gloomy prospects for coffee growing, money incomes and traditional standards of diet, clothing and housing; Australian responsibilities in connection with UN trusteeship decisions; and the advantages of maintaining local customary law with a right of appeal to national courts. The list is one small indication of the bewildering set of political and other problems confronting two million people emerging from tiny clusters of population, without definite territorial or linguistic boundaries and with only a handful of very recently educated political leaders.

There seems reason to suggest that the way to deal with these peoples of Papua-New Guinea is to adopt more modern and more rationalized methods than those used in education situations where the students are more sophisticated. There is always a tendency, however, to use methods which are less rather than more rationalized—for example, to send technologically obsolete machinery to underdeveloped countries, when we should be sending teaching models based on the very most advanced machinery, possibly specially simplified for learning by the inexperienced.

The question of the handling of names, birth registrations, health treatments, electoral rolls, etc., in Papua-New Guinea is an example. Conventional names differ greatly from one linguistic and local group to another and are intricately related to the local forms of social organization. The names delineate clan membership, relationship to other clans, claims to land; relate an individual to particular ancestors, define reincarnation, memorialize the number of "mother's brothers" who contributed to a birth feast. During the early days of pacification the custom grew and spread of giving the census-taker names that were either false or little used among a number of names which an individual could claim. In our own history, the question of acquiring a stable surname was often solved in a variety of ways on the insistence of tax officials or others; in many cases names were simply assigned arbitrarily. The same kind of unsystematic process is now going on in New Guinea as insistence on the same name, on two names, on a surname, on using the "father's name" undefined, are being indiscriminately urged in different regions. Meanwhile, it is more urgent than ever before to identify individuals and locate them in an increasingly complex system of relations between citizen and state. A number assigned at birth and printed on a metal tag which could be replicated, plus a computerized retrieval system, would at one stroke set up a workable system. Such a rationalized system of names is more needed in New Guinea than in, for example, the United States because none of the intermediate conventions which make our system intelligible and workable, even if not fully rational, are present there. In the same way, it may be convenient to teach Australian school-children, who have grown up on lessons on pounds, shillings and pence, to treat the new Australian dollars as if the dollars belonged in the pounds column and the cents in the shillings, and omit any reference to the decimal system. But for New Guinea schoolchildren, immediate recourse to the decimal system would be more intelligible.

A further advance could also be made if instead of looking at New Guinea as a long list of lacks and defects—no complex social organization, no hierarchical system of authority, no clear boundaries, no hereditary positions, no technical experience beyond the stone age, no common language, no calendar, no currency, no educated elite to undertake leadership—some attempt were made to look for unsuspected strengths. It is true that the largest completely effective political unit is about five hundred people and that small adjacent communities are frequently bitter enemies. But this also means that people do not have extended enmities. Regional loyalties and indeed loyalties to any group at all likely to be large enough to be troublesome are all artifacts of the present system of administration. People without strong loyalties to large groups might much more easily become citizens of a nation-state than those who have been bound by centuries of experience (either indigenous or colonial) of factionalisms based on such loyalties. Furthermore, the people of New Guinea have a long tradition of hereditary networks of trade friendships and show great adaptability both in maintaining these ties across enemy lines and in adjusting them to modern conditions like common service in the police. This cultural skill might be utilized in building groups of New Guineans who would be loyal to each other. It might be a feasible basis of an army which in turn might contribute the best form of order to a country where the maintenance of order will be a pressing necessity for a long time to come. But such steps require a willingness to use highly technical help to identify a real cultural strength. In the present state of opinion, such efforts are only too likely to be treated as subversive, or to become the target of political attack.

Primitive peoples are our contemporaries, no matter how isolated they have been from the ongoing stream of civilization or how much they have been damaged by contacts with civilizations which threw them back into reactive and self-defeating isolation. Their histories are as old as ours; their innate capacities are those of the same species. The more primitive they are, the less wounded by various forms of compromise and conflict, the more unspoiled intelligence and curiosity they can bring to the modern world. The one obligation which we may be said to have is to take the trouble to use every skill and invention we have to make the advanced cultures of the modern world possible to teach, and so possible to learn.

Notes and References

Chapter 1. Island Cultures

Birdsell, Joseph B.
1957 "Some Population Problems Involving Pleistocene Man," *Cold Spring Harbor Symposia in Quantitative Biology*, 22:47–68.
1958 "On Population Structure in Generalized Hunting and Collecting Populations," *Evolution*, 12:189–205.

Danielsson, Bengt
1956 *Love in the South Seas* (F. H. Lyon, tr.). London: Allen and Unwin.

Dobzhansky, Theodosius
1965 "Biological Evolution in Island Populations," in *Man's Place in the Island Ecosystem*, F. R. Fosberg, ed. Honolulu: Bishop Museum Press.

Firth, Raymond
1936 *We, the Tikopia*. London: Allen and Unwin.
1939 *Primitive Polynesian Economy*. London: Routledge.
1957 "A Note on Descent Groups in Polynesia," *Man*, 57:4–8.

Fischer, John L.
1958 "Folktales, Social Structure, and Environment in Two Polynesian Outliers," *Journal of the Polynesian Society*, 67:11–36.

Fischer, John L., and Ann M. Fischer
1957 *The Eastern Carolines*. New Haven, Conn.: Pacific Science Board and Human Relations Area Files.

Ford, E. B.
1960 "Evolution in Progress," in *Evolution After Darwin*, Sol Tax, ed., Vol. 1, pp. 181–196. Chicago: University of Chicago Press.

Foster, George M.
1960 *Culture and Conquest: America's Spanish Heritage*. Viking Fund Publication in Anthropology, 27. New York: Wenner-Gren Foundation for Anthropological Research.

Goodenough, Ward H.
1955 "A Problem in Malayo-Polynesian Social Organization," *American Anthropologist*, 57:71–83.

Gumplowicz, Ludwig
1899 *The Outlines of Sociology* (Frederick Moore, tr.). Philadelphia: American Academy of Political and Social Science.

Lorimer, Frank, *et al.*
1954 *Culture and Human Fertility*. Paris: UNESCO.

Mason, Leonard E.
1950 "The Bikinians: A Transplanted Population," *Human Organization,* 9:5–15.
1957 "Ecologic Change and Culture Pattern in the Resettlement of Bikini Marshallese," in *Cultural Stability and Cultural Change,* Verne F. Ray, ed., pp. 1–6. Seattle: American Ethnological Society.
1958 "Kili Community in Transition," *South Pacific Commission Quarterly Bulletin,* 8(2):32–35, 46.

Maude, H. E.
1952 "The Colonization of the Phoenix Islands," *Journal of the Polynesian Society,* 61:62–89.

Mayr, Ernst
1954 "Change of Genetic Environment and Evolution," in *Evolution as a Process,* Julian Huxley, A. C. Hardy, and E. B. Ford, eds., pp. 157–180. London: Allen and Unwin.

Mead, Margaret
1958 "Cultural Determinants of Behavior," in *Behavior and Evolution,* Anne Roe and G. G. Simpson, eds., pp. 480–503. New Haven, Conn.: Yale University Press.

Munch, Peter A.
1946 "Sociology of Tristan da Cunha," in *Results of the Norwegian Scientific Expedition to Tristan da Cunha,* 1937–1938, Vol. 2, No. 13, Erling Christophersen, ed. Oslo: Det Norske Videnskaps-Akademi.

Sahlins, Marshall
1957 "Differentiation by Adaptation in Polynesian Societies," *Journal of the Polynesian Society,* 66:291–300.
1958 *Social Stratification in Polynesia.* Seattle: University of Washington Press.

Schneider, David M.
1955 "Abortion and Depopulation on a Pacific Island," in *Health, Culture and Community,* Benjamin D. Paul, ed., pp. 211–235. New York: Russell Sage Foundation.

Shapiro, Harry
1936 *The Heritage of the Bounty.* New York: Simon and Schuster.

Sharp, Andrew
1956 *Ancient Voyagers in the Pacific.* Polynesian Society Memoir 32. Wellington, New Zealand.

Swadesh, Morris
1959 "Linguistics as an Instrument of Prehistory," *Southwestern Journal of Anthropology,* 15:20–35.

Vayda, Andrew P.
1958 "A Voyage by Polynesian Exiles," *Journal of the Polynesian Society,* 67: 324–329.
1959a "Native Traders in Two Polynesian Atolls," *Cahiers de l'Institut de Science Economique Appliquée,* Series V, No. 1, pp. 119–137.
1959b "Polynesian Cultural Distributions in New Perspective," *American Anthropologist,* 61:817–828.

Wagley, Charles
1951 "Cultural Influences on Population: A Comparison of Two Tupí Tribes," *Rev. Mus. Paulista* (n.s.) 5:95–104.

Williamson, Robert W.
1939 *Essays in Polynesian Ethnology,* Ralph Piddington, ed. Cambridge: Cambridge University Press.

Chapter 2. Polynesian Navigation to Distant Islands

1. Sharp 1956, 1957.
2. Cook 1784:202.
3. Gatty 1958:32–41, 76–86.
4. Gatty 1943.
5. Duff 1960:55–56.
6. Suggs 1960:83–85.
7. Cook 1784:167–170.
8. Henry 1928:401–402.
9. Smith 1910:185–186.
10. Gatty 1943:85–86.
11. Duff 1959:127–144.
12. Suggs 1960:83–85.
13. Sharp 1956:50–54.
14. Goodenough 1957:153, 155.
15. Gladwin 1958.
16. Hilder 1959.

Cook, J.
1784 *A Voyage to the Pacific Ocean,* Vol. 1. London: Nicoll and Cadell.
Duff, R.
1959 "Neolithic Adzes of Eastern Polynesia," in *Anthropology in the South Seas.* New Plymouth: Avery.
1960 "The Coming of the Maoris," in *New Zealand Junior Encyclopaedia.* Wellington: New Zealand Educational Foundation.
Gatty, H.
1943 *The Raft Book.* New York: Grady Press.
1958 *Nature is Your Guide.* London: Collins.
Gladwin, T.
1958 "Canoe Travel in the Truk Area: Technology and Its Psychological Correlates," *American Anthropologist,* 60:893–899.
Goodenough, W. H.
1957 "Controls in the Study of Cultural and Human Evolution," *Journal of the Polynesian Society,* 66:146–155.
Henry, T.
1928 *Ancient Tahiti.* Bulletin No. 48. Honolulu: Bishop Museum.
Hilder, B.
1959 "Polynesian Navigational Stones," *Journal of the Institute of Navigation,* 12:90–97.
Sharp, A.
1956 *Ancient Voyagers in the Pacific.* Polynesian Society Memoir No. 32. Wellington, New Zealand.
1957 *Ancient Voyagers in the Pacific.* Harmondsworth: Penguin Books. Reprint.
Smith, S. P.
1921 *Hawaiki.* Wellington, New Zealand: Whitcombe and Tombs.
Suggs, R. C.
1960 *The Island Civilizations of Polynesia.* New York: Mentor.

Chapter 3. Austronesian Linguistics and Culture History

Collingwood, R. G.
1956 *The Idea of History.* (Galaxy Books.) New York: Oxford University Press.
Dyen, Isidore
1949 "On the History of the Trukese Vowels," *Language,* 25:420–436.
Grace, George W.
1955 "Subgrouping of Malayo-Polynesian: a Report of Tentative Findings," *American Anthopologist,* 47:337–339.
1959 "The Position of the Polynesian Languages Within the Austronesian (Malayo-Polynesian) Language Family," *Indiana University Publications in Anthropology and Linguistics. International Journal of American Linguistics Memoir 16 and Bernice P. Bishop Museum Special Publication 46.*
Sharp, Andrew
1956 *Ancient Voyagers in the Pacific.* Polynesian Society Memoir 32. Wellington, New Zealand.

Chapter 4. The *Kon-Tiki* Myth

1. See T. Heyerdahl, *Kon-Tiki,* London: Allen and Unwin, 1950; *American Indians in the South Pacific,* London: Allen and Unwin, 1952.

2. For a report of this work, see R. T. Simmons and J. J. Graydon, "A Blood Group Genetical Survey in Eastern and Central Polynesians," *American Journal of Physical Anthropology,* Vol. 15, No. 3, 1957.

3. T. Heyerdahl, *Aku-Aku.* Chicago: Rand McNally, 1958, p. 376.

4. T. Heyerdahl, "The Voyage of the Raft Kon-Tiki," *Geographical Journal,* 115:23, 1950.

5. Heyerdahl, *op. cit.,* 1952.

6. Heyerdahl, *op. cit.,* 1950, p. 20.

7. S. Ryden, "Did the Indians in Chile Know the Use of Sails in Pre-Columbus Times?", *Southwestern Journal of An-*

thropology, Vol. 12, No. 2, 1956. Also for a typical rejoinder, see T. Heyerdahl, "Guara Navigation: Indigenous Sailing off the Andean Coast," *Southwestern Journal of Anthropology,* Vol. 13, No. 2, 1957.

8. B. Danielsson, *The Happy Island—Kon-Tiki Isle.* London: Panther Books, 1956, p. 40.

9. See E. D. Merrill, "The Botany of Cook's Voyages," in *Chronica Botanica,* Vol. 14, Nos. 5/6, 1954, pp. 263–70; R. Heine-Geldern, "Some Problems of Migration in the Pacific," in *Kultur und Sprache Wiener Beiträge zur Kulturgeschichte und Linguistik,* IX, Vienna: 1952; and R. Firth, review of Thor Heyerdahl's "American Indians in the South Pacific," *Nature,* 171:713–714, 1953.

10. Heyerdahl, *op. cit.,* 1958, plates between pp. 304 and 305.

11. *Ibid.,* p. 352.

12. *Ibid.,* p. 352.

13. *Ibid.,* pp. 334–335.

14. J. A. Mason, *The Ancient Civilizations of Peru.* Harmondsworth, England: Penguin Books, 1957, pp. 90, 113, 114, 131, 202, 203, 213, 214, 220, 232, 233.

Chapter 5. Origins of the Melanesians

Avias, J.
1950 "Potéries canaques et Potéries préhistoriques en Nouvelle-Calédonie," *Journal de Société d'oceanistes,* p. 6.

Barrau, J.
1965 "Witness of the Past: Notes on Some Food Plants of Oceania," *Ethnology,* 4:3.

British Newsletter
1967 British Residency, Vila, New Hebrides, Anglo-French Condominium, 8:1.

Bulmer, S.
1964 "Radiocarbon Dates from New Guinea," *Journal of the Polynesian Society,* 73:3.

Bulmer, S., and R. Bulmer
1964 "The Prehistory of the Australian New Guinea Highlands," *American Anthropologist,* 66:4, pt. 2.

Capell, A.
1962 "Oceanic Linguistics Today," *Current Anthropology,* 3:4.

Casey, D. A.
1936 "Ethnological Notes," *Memoirs of the National Museum of Melbourne,* p. 9.

Coon, C. S.
1965 *The Living Races of Man.* New York: Alfred Knopf.

Dyen, I.
1962 "The Lexicostatistical Classification of the Malayo-Polynesian Languages," *Language,* p. 38.

1965 "A Lexicostatistical Classification of the Austronesian Languages," *International Journal of American Linguistics,* Memoir 19.

Garanger, J.
1966 "Recherches archéologiques aux Nouvelles-Hébrides," *L'Homme,* 6:1.

Gifford, E. W.
1951 "Archaeological Excavations in Fiji," *Anthropological Records,* 13:3, University of California Press.

Gifford, E. W., and D. S. Gifford
1959 "Archaeological Excavations in Yap," *Anthropological Records,* 18 (2), University of California Press.

Gifford, E. W., and R. Shutler, Jr.
1956 "Archaeological Excavations in New Caledonia," *Anthropological* Records, 18:1, University of California Press.

Goodale, J. C.
1966 "Blowgun Hunters of the South Pacific," *National Geographic Magazine,* 129:6.

Grace, G. W.
1964 "Movement of the Malayo-Polynesians: 1500 B.C. to A.D. 500: The Linguistic Evidence," *Current Anthropology,* 5:5.

Green, R. C.
1963 "A Suggested Revision of the Fijian Sequence," *Journal of the Polynesian Society,* 72:3.

Hébert, B.
1965 "Nouvelles-Hébrides. Contribution à l'étude archéologique de l'île d'Efaté et des îles avoisinantes," *Etudes Mélanésiennes,* nouvelle série, nos. 18–20.
Heine-Geldern, R.
1932 "Urheimat und fruheste Wanderungen der Austroeisier," *Anthropos,* 27.
Kraus, B. S.
1945 "Preliminary Report on the Discovery of Surface Sherds on Mono Island, Treasury Group, Solomon Islands," *American Antiquity,* 2:2.
Lenormand, M. H.
1948 "Découverte d'un Gisement de Poteries Indigènes a l'Ile des Pins," *Etudes mélanésiennes*, n.s., 3.
Macintosh, N. W. G.
1965 "The Physical Aspect of Man in Australia," in *Aboriginal Man in Australia,* R. M. and C. H. Berndt, eds. Sydney: Angus & Robertson.
Mulvaney, D. J.
1964 "The Pleistocene Colonization of Australia," *Antiquity,* 38.
Murdock, G. P.
1964 "Genetic Classification of the Austronesian Languages: A Key to Oceanic Culture History," *Ethnology,* 3:2.
Oliver, D. L.
1961 *The Pacific Islands.* Garden City: Doubleday.
Shutler, M. E., and R. Shutler, Jr.
1965 *A Preliminary Report of Archaeological Explorations in the Southern New Hebrides, 1963–1964.* Honolulu: Bishop Museum.
Shutler, Jr., R., and M. E. Shutler
1964 "Potsherds from Bougainville Island," *Asian Perspectives,* 8:1.
Solheim II, W. G.
1958 "Some Potsherds from New Guinea," *Journal of the Polynesian Society,* 67:2.
1964 "Pottery and the Malayo-Polynesians," *Current Anthropology,* 5:5.
Speiser, F.
1946 "Versuch einer Siedlungsgeschichte der Südsee," *Denkschauer d. Schweiz. Naturfor. Gesell.*, 77, abh. 1.
Spoehr, A.
1957 "Marianas Prehistory," *Fieldiana: Anthropology*, 48, Chicago Natural History Museum.
Watson, J. B.
1964 "Introduction: Anthropology in the New Guinea Highlands," *American Anthropologist,* 66:4, pt. 2.

Chapter 7. Agricultural Technology of the Pagan Gaddang

1. A survey of slash-and-burn farmers in Southeast Asia reveals significant ecological and technological variation from region to region. Probably the single most useful bibliographic source on shifting cultivation in Southeast Asia is Spencer (1966).

2. *Swidden* is a general term which in recent years has come to be used by anthropologists in place of the more traditional designations of "shifting cultivation" or "slash-and-burn farming" (cf. Spencer 1966; Conklin 1961; Ekwall 1955). The Gaddang term for a swidden is *uma.*

3. In earlier times the Pagan Gaddang constructed some of their houses in trees.

4. Fallowing is practiced in certain northern Pagan Gaddang communities.

5. Other factors were also involved. Most important, the man had an illicit sexual affair with a married woman of the community.

6. One old widower remained in Pakak but he is not farming. He gains his livelihood by fishing and gathering and occasionally by working in the lowlands as a day laborer. When I asked him why he did not go with the others to a new area, he said that he had no family and that Pakak was as good a place as any to die.

Census
1960 *Census of the Philippines, 1960.* Manila: Bureau of Statistics.
Conklin, Harold C.
1957 *Hanunóo Agriculture in the Philippines.* Forestry Development Paper No. 12. Rome: FAO.
1961 "The Study of Shifting Cultivation," *Current Anthropology,* 2, 1:27–61.
Dobby, E. H. G.
1954 *Southeast Asia.* London: University of London Press.
Ekwall, E.
1955 "Slash-and-Burn Cultivation: A Contribution to Anthropological Terminology," *Man,* 55:135–136.
Freeman, J. D.
1955 *Iban Agriculture.* Colonial Research Studies No. 18. London: Her Majesty's Stationery Office.
Galang, Ricardo E.
1935 "Ethnographic Study of the Yogads of Isabela," *Philippine Journal of Science,* 56, 1:81–94.
Geddes, W. R.
1954 *The Land Dayaks of Sarawak. Colonial Research Studies* No. 14. London: Her Majesty's Stationery Office.
Geertz, Clifford
1963 *Agricultural Involution: The Processes of Ecological Change in Indonesia.* Berkeley: University of California Press.
Huke, Robert E.
1963 *Shadows on the Land: An Economic Geography of the Philippines.* Makati: Carmelo and Bauermann.
Lambrecht, G.
1959 "The Gaddang of Isabela and Nueva Vizcaya: Survivals of a Primitive Animistic Religion," *Philippine Studies,* 7, 2:194–218.
1960 "Anitu Rites Among the Gaddang," *Philippine Studies,* 8, 3:584–602.
Reed, Robert R.
1963 "The Tobacco Industry," in *Shadows on the Land,* Robert E. Huke. Makati: Carmelo and Bauermann.
Spencer, J. E.
1966 *Shifting Cultivation in Southeastern Asia.* University of California Publication in Geography 19.
Troyer, M.
1960 "Gaddang Phonology," *Philippine Journal of Science,* 88, 1:95–102.
Wallace, Ben J.
1967a "Gaddang Rice Cultivation: A Ligature Between Man and Nature," *Philippine Sociological Review,* 15, 3–4:114–122.
1967b *Gaddang Agriculture: The Focus of Ecological and Cultural Change.* Unpublished Ph.D. dissertation, University of Wisconsin.
1968 "A Preliminary Report on the Yogad of Northern Luzon," Mimeographed report to the Agricultural Development Council, Inc.
1969 "Pagan Gaddang Spouse Exchange," *Ethnology* (*in press*).
Wernstedt, Frederick L., and J. E. Spencer
1967 *The Philippine Island World: A Physical, Cultural, and Regional Geography.* Berkeley and Los Angeles; University of California Press.
Yengoyan, Aram A.
1960 "Survey Reports on Some Tribal Communities in Davao, Surigao and Agusan." Mimeographed.

Chapter 8. Production, Distribution, and Power in a Primitive Society

1. The system of kerekere may thus be termed an "optionally reciprocal" system. As such, it is a variant of Professor Polanyi's "reciprocal form of economic integration" (Karl Polanyi, *The Great Transformation,* New York, 1944, Chap. IV).

2. As such, kerekere may be contrasted with the redistributive mechanisms in Polynesia where control of the distributive

system is an inherent right of chieftainship. See Marshall Sahlins, *Social Stratification in Polynesia,* University of Michigan Microfilms, 1954, Ann Arbor (Columbia University Ph.D. dissertation).

Chapter 9. Ponapean Prestige Economy

1. In the transcription of Ponapean words, : indicates vowel length; ĕ is pronounced as the vowel in *bet* and ă as the vowel in *but; i* is pronounced as the vowel in *bit,* except in the final position and in diphthongs, when, like *i*: it represents the vowel in *beat.* IPA symbols have been used elsewhere with the exception of *p* and *pw,* which seem to be separate phonemes.

2. Ponape is divided politically into five autonomous districts, each with its own district chiefs. The districts are subdivided into sections, equivalent to local communities, with subordinate section chiefs. Each section in turn is composed of a number of farmsteads, inhabited by individual households.

3. A recently introduced system of prestige competition resembling that in Western society, however, is directly related to the commercial economy. In this new system, prestige is based on the ownership of wealth in the form of money, coconut trees (the primary source of money), and imported goods (purchased with money). This paper is limited to a consideration of the traditional prestige competition associated with feasting.

4. Japanese figures for the Ponape Branch Bureau in 1937 show the production of 3,404.6 tons of breadfruit as against 792.7 tons of yams. Considerable quantities of breadfruit were produced on Kusaie, but presumably most of the yams were grown on Ponape.

5. See M. J. Herskovits, *The Economic Life of Primitive Peoples,* New York, Knopf, 1940.

6. For an example of its application, see Bascom, *Ponape: a Pacific Economy in Transition, Anthropological Record,* vol. 22. Berkeley: University of California Press, 1965.

7. See Bascom, *op. cit.*

Chapter 10. Trading in Northeast New Guinea

1. The items exchanged were taro, yams, sweet potatoes, bananas, sago, coconuts, *Canarium* almonds, and other foods; fish and salt in various forms; *Areca* nut, lime, and tobacco; axes of stone and clamshell; obsidian, bows and arrows, woven net bags, baskets, clay pots and wooden bowls of several kinds; bark cloth, drums, betel mortars, lizard skins, and sewn mats, raincapes and sails of pandanus leaf; canoes, timber, creepers for lashings, and bark fiber for nets; pigs and dogs; curved boars' tusks and imitation tusks of clamshell; headbands, belts, and breastplates of dogs' teeth; strings and ornaments of *tambu* shell; disc beads, eggshell cowries, gold-lip shell, and turtle-shell bracelets; red ochre and black pigment.

Belshaw, Cyril S.
1955 *In Search of Wealth.* American Anthropological Assoc. Memoir No. 80.

Bulmer, Ralph
1960 "Political Aspects of the Moka Ceremonial Exchange System Among the Kyaka People of the Western Highlands of New Guinea," *Oceania,* 31:1–13.

Evans-Pritchard, E. E.
1951 *Social Anthropology.* Glencoe, Ill.: The Free Press.

Firth, Raymond, ed.
1957 "The Place of Malinowski in the History of Economic Anthropology," in *Man and Culture, An Evaluation of the Work of Malinowski,* pp. 209–277. London: Routledge & Kegan Paul.

Fortune, Reo
1963 *Sorcerers of Dobu*. New York: Dutton.

Freedman, Michael P.
1967 *The Social and Political Organization of the Siassi Islands, New Guinea.* Doctoral dissertation, University of Michigan. Ann Arbor: University Microfilms.
1968 Personal communication.

Hannemann, E. F.
1949 *Village Life and Social Change in Madang Society*. Madang.

Harding, Thomas G.
1967a *Voyagers of the Vitiaz Strait.* Seattle and London: University of Washington Press.
1967b "Ecological and Technical Factors in a Melanesian Gardening Cycle," *Mankind,* 6:403–408.

Harding, Thomas G., and Peter Lawrence
In press. "The Mainland North-East Coast: Karkar to Finschhafen," in Papua-New Guinea Election Study of 1968. Canberra: Australian National University Press (*forthcoming*).

Malinowski, Bronislaw
1961 *Argonauts of the Western Pacific.* New York: Dutton.

Murdock, George
1964 "Genetic Classification of the Austronesian Language: A Key to Oceanic Culture History," *Ethnology,* 3:117–126.

Powell, H. A.
1965 Review of J. P. Singh Uberoi, *Politics of the Kula Ring, Man,* 65:97–99.

Sahlins, Marshall D.
1965 "Exchange-Value and the Diplomacy of Primitive Trade," in *Essays in Economic Anthropology,* June Helm, ed. pp. 95–129. Proceedings of the 1965 Annual Spring Meeting of the American Ethnological Society, Seattle.

Seligman, C. G.
1910 *The Melanesians of British New Guinea.* Cambridge: Cambridge University Press.

Uberoi, J. P. Singh
1962 *Politics of the Kula Ring.* Manchester: Manchester University Press.

Weber, Max
1947 *The Theory of Social and Economic Organization* (A. M. Henderson and Talcott Parsons). Glencoe, Ill.: Free Press.

White, Leslie A.
1959 *The Evolution of Culture.* New York: McGraw-Hill.

Chapter 12. Male-Female Relationships in the Highlands of Australia

1. The ethnographic present tense here covers the periods of field work of the anthropologists to whom I refer, that is, between about 1950 and 1960.

2. In this paper "Central Highlands" refers to the region in the Highlands of Australian New Guinea lying between the Chimbu divide and the Hagen Range.

3. I carried out field work among the Enga in 1955–1957, 1960, and 1962 under the auspices of the University of Sydney; I thank the University for its financial support. The situation I describe in this paper refers mainly to the period 1955–1957 and earlier. Since then, as a result of mission teaching, the employment of young men for wages and the widening of the range of affinal choices following the imposition of a general peace, Mae attitudes towards sex have changed considerably. Such changes are intelligible in the light of the analysis I make in Section IV.

4. Fuller accounts of various aspects of Enga societies and cultures appear in R. Bulmer 1960a, 1960b, n.d.; Bus 1961; Elkin 1953; Goodenough 1953; Meggitt 1956, 1957, 1958a, 1958b, 1958c, 1962a, 1962b, n.d.a, n.d.b; and Wirz 1952a.

5. Women marry when they are about 15 or 16 years old, but men do not marry until they are about 25 or so.

6. In such contexts the Mae are re-

ferring to mental, as well as physical, growth and maturity; in particular they are concerned with the development of such characteristics as aggressive self-confidence and commercial acumen.

7. The Mae have no ceremonies to mark the menarche or otherwise indicate that a girl has attained puberty.

8. Thus, one Taro man who divorced his wife for this reason announced that he would take stronger action. At the time, I pointed out to him the probable consequences of such behavior (arrest and imprisonment) but later learned that he killed the offending wife with his axe.

9. Women warn young sons not to play near forest trees lest they inadvertently uncover old menstrual moss.

10. If a young woman ate such meat, the clan ancestral ghosts would be angered and cause her to bear a deformed child.

11. A Mae man would rarely, if ever, copulate with his wife in her house, partly for lack of privacy, partly for fear of contamination. Nor should they have intercourse in the gardens, lest the crops die. The proper place for coitus is in the bush-covered fallow.

12. A woman may stretch vines around the perimeter of her gardens and hang from them portions of old skirts, whose emanations then create a barrier against male trespass. Similarly, a man preparing for intercourse would not touch the woman's skirt nor let her touch his apron.

13. Men keep their own hair-cuttings to make wigs but do not use women's hair in their wigs for fear it might weaken them.

14. Mae place in the category of "vital juice" semen, vaginal secretions, milk, sap, rendered fat, and the "grease" that is thought to exist in fertile soil.

15. Most Mae are right-handed in their use of tools and weapons; nobody comments on the occasional left-handed person.

16. Mae men who have visited Mount Hagen are shocked by the sexual freedom of Medlpa youths, the style of their courting ceremonies, and the early age at which they marry. "Don't the Medlpa care about their skins?" they ask. On one occasion, when a Mae girl actually seduced a young Mae man of good family in her fowl-house, he was so worried about his "skin" that next day he publicly demanded that she wed him so he could quickly acquire the married man's protective magic. His agnates, who did not favor the union (her family was poor), could persuade him to drop the idea only by promising to give him the magic he sought. Naturally enough, prostitution was not a feature of the pre-European culture; but of late some married or divorced women have begun to solicit around the cantonments of the immigrant native policemen. Even so, they have to rely on gambling to eke out their small takings.

17. The interval may have been longer in the recent past when interclan warfare was rife.

18. The age at first seclusion may have been somewhat higher in the past.

19. I know of one instance in which, following the confessed fornication of a bachelor, all the irises in his subclan plot were found dead; his comrades were able to buy only one replacement, which cost four netbags, three cowry headbands, one stone axe, four Astrapia bird-of-paradise plumes, one decorated waistbelt, and three hanks of axe lashing. Should plants die when there is no evidence that any of the bachelors has transgressed, the men assume that some unclean trespasser has seen the plot; they have no way of identifying the putative culprit to exact a fine. If a clan loses the land containing its irises in a military defeat, the bachelors can do nothing but try to buy new plants.

20. One such festival was a dreadful fiasco because the bachelors had been too fearful for their "skins" to visit many of the girls of neighboring clans. When the young men emerged from seclusion, only a handful of outsiders were present and the prestige of the host clan suffered a damaging blow.

21. Senior bachelors must, of course, occupy their own subclan houses, and usually the other men follow suit. Occasionally a young man may spend a sanggai seclusion in the house of another subclan in order to be with a good friend. A co-resident nonagnatic bachelor in the clan

parish is part of the subclan of his sponsor. Any visiting bachelor who is a close cognate is also invited to join in the seclusion, and a few men regularly participate in the sanggai of their mother's brother's subclan as well as their own.

22. Most sanggai songs refer to plants and trees with desirable qualities; for instance, certain mosses *(Lycopodium* and *Polytricum* spp.) are brightly colored and grow rapidly, the pine (*Podocarpus* sp.) has a smooth skin; the beech (*Nothophagus* sp.) is tall and strong. Some songs also mention particular birds, such as the black and white chat (*Saxicolla* sp.) and the six-plumed bird of paradise (*Parotia* sp.), whose glossy plumage is much admired.

23. In this context there is an interesting variation of the equation of right hand–left hand and male-female. A bachelor should use only his left hand to rub his body with sanggai and to hold his penis when urinating, and his right hand to take food that has at some time passed through women's hands. In this way he prevents an indirect contamination of his skin or his genitals. A conscientious young man also takes care never to let a woman stand on his left lest by accident her body or skirt brush his left hand.

24. The plants of some clans are reputedly so powerful that they may only be touched lightly and briefly against the head or chest; otherwise the user would suffer an unsightly growth of hair. I know several exceptionally hirsute men whose condition is attributed to incautious use of strong iris leaves.

25. To guard against a rebuff, a girl who is uncertain of the feelings of a young man may perform love magic beforehand. She recites spells (acquired from her mother or elder sister) into fern leaves which she wears in her armbands. Sometimes, in order to induce many girls to come to the sanggai festival and so raise clan prestige, the bachelors may employ similar techniques at the end of their seclusion.

26. See, for instance, Faron 1962; Needham 1960a, 1960b, 1962; and, of course, Hertz 1960.

27. In asserting that the presence of a system of prescriptive alliance is neither necessary nor sufficient for the existence of a system of symbols of dual opposition, I am, of course, also implying that the symbolic classification is neither necessary nor sufficient for the alliance system. It is worth noting here Needham's own remark that a dualistic classification is not necsssarily found only with prescriptive alliance (1960a:103), an admission that destroys much of the force of his argument.

28. See Meggitt 1962c, n.d.c.

29. As a social anthropologist I am not concerned here to speculate about individual psychological dynamisms operative in such a set of transformations. It may be, for instance, that, because one's male affines are simultaneously military enemies and ceremonial exchange partners, the attitude towards them is awkwardly ambivalent and therefore, for "economic" reasons, the anxiety this induces is displaced onto female affines; but only sophisticated analysis in depth of mental processes could test assertions of this kind.

30. It should be noted that I do not attempt here to "explain" the reported Kuma hostility between the sexes by relating it in any specific way to other variables in the society, for the available ethnography does not permit this.

31. I do not wish to deny the possibility that Highlands field work may discover societies in which intersexual relations are neutral or relatively free from tensions; indeed, Dr. J. B. Watson informs me that Gadsup on the eastern edge of the Highlands may fall into this category.

Berndt, Ronald M.
1962 *Excess and Restraint: Social Control Among a New Guinea Mountain People*. Chicago: University of Chicago Press.

Bulmer, R. N. H.
1960a *Leadership and Social Structure Among the Kyaka*. Ph.D. thesis, Australian National University, Canberra.
1960b "Political Aspects of the Moka Ceremonial Exchange System among the Kyaka People," *Oceania,* 31:1–13.

n.d. "Kyaka Religion," in *Symposium on New Guinea and Melanesian Religions,* Lawrence and Meggitt, eds. (*in preparation*).
Bus, G. A. M.
1951 "The Te Festival or Gift Exchange in Enga," *Anthropos,* 46:813–824.
Elkin, A. P.
1953 "Delayed Exchange in Wabag Subdistrict," *Oceania,* 23:161–201.
Faron, L. C.
1962 "Symbolic Values and the Integration of Society Among the Mapuche of Chile," *American Anthropologist,* 64: 1151–1164.
Glasse, R. M.
n.d. "Huli Religion," in *Symposium on New Guinea and Melanesian Religions,* Lawrence and Meggitt, eds. (*in preparation*).
Goodenough, W. H.
1953 "Ethnographic Notes on the Mae People," *Southwestern Journal of Anthropology,* 9:29–44.
Hertz, R.
1960 *Death and the Right Hand.* Glencoe, Ill.: Free Press
Meggitt, M. J.
1956 "The Valleys of the Upper Wage and Lai Rivers," *Oceania,* 27:90–135.
1957 "Housebuilding Among the Mae Enga," *Oceania,* 27:161–176.
1958a "The Enga of the New Guinea Highlands," *Oceania,* 28:253–330.
1958b "Mae Enga Time Reckoning and Calendar," *Man,* 58, No. 87.
1958c "Salt Manufacture and Trading in the Western Highlands," *Australian Museum Magazine,* 12:309–313.
1962a *Desert People: a Study of the Walbiri Aborigines of Central Australia.* Sydney: Angus & Robertson.
1962b "Dream Interpretation Among the Mae Enga," *Southwestern Journal of Anthropology,* 18:216–229.
1962c "Growth and Decline of Agnatic Descent Groups Among the Mae Enga," *Ethnology,* 1:158–165.
n.d.a. *The Lineage System of the Mae Enga of New Guinea.* Edinburgh: Oliver and Boyd (*forthcoming*).
n.d.b "Mae Enga Religion," in *Symposium on New Guinea and Melanesian Religions,* Lawrence and Meggitt, eds. (*in preparation*).
n.d.c "Marriage among the Walbiri of Central Australia: a Statistical Analysis," in Festschrift for Professor A. P. Elkin, R. M. Berndt, ed. (*forthcoming*).
Needham, R.
1960a "A Structural Analysis of Aimol Society," *Bijdragen tot de Taal, Landen Volkenkunde,* 116:81–108.
1960b "The Left Hand of the Mugwe," *Africa,* 30:20–33.
1962 *Structure and Sentiment.* Chicago: University of Chicago Press.
Nilles, J.
1950/53 "The Kuman of the Chimbu Region, Central Highlands, New Guinea," *Oceania,* 21:25–65; 24:1–27, 119–31.
Read, K. E.
1952 "Nama Cult of the Central Highlands, New Guinea," *Oceania,* 23:1–25.
1954 "Cultures of the Central Highlands, New Guinea," *Southwestern Journal of Anthropology,* 10:1–43.
Reay, Marie
1959 *The Kuma: Freedom and Conformity in the New Guinea Highlands.* Melbourne: University Press for the Australian National University.
Salisbury, R. F.
n.d. "Political Organization in Siane Society," in *Political Systems of Papua-New Guinea,* K. E. Read, ed. (*forthcoming*).
Vicedom, G. F., and H. Tischner
1943/48 *"Die Mbowamb: die Kultur der Hagenberg Stämme im Östlichen Zentral-Neuguinea* (3 Vols.). Hamburg: de Gruyter.
Wirz, P.
1951 Über die alten Steinmörser und die andere Steingaräte des nordöstlichen Zentral-Neuguinea und die heilige Steinschale der Minembi. *Südeseestudien, Gedenkenschrift zur Erinnerung an Felix Speiser.* Basel: Museum für Völkerkunde.

Chapter 13. Sociocentric Relationship Terms and the Australian Class System

1. Since this paper was written, an article by Romney and Epling has been published which mentions essentially the same distinction between class terminology and kinship terms (among the Kariera tribe) that I am here trying to establish: ". . . kinship terms are in large part *relative* in the sense that the term used depends upon the relation between two persons, while the section terms are *absolute* in the sense that every individual is assigned to a section by birth and he retains this affiliation throughout life" (Romney and Epling 1958:64).

2. For purposes of this paper, I am granting the existence of recognized descent lines. Actually, I am in accord with the suggestions of A. L. Kroeber (1952), Paul Kirchhoff (1955), A. M. Hocart (1955:193), and Radcliffe-Brown (1930–1931:100, 107) that unilineal descent lines are probably not in fact recognized, but exist only implicity as an aspect of postmarital residence customs. An additional argument against the Murdock-Lawrence theory could be made on this basis.

3. There seems to be no appropriate word for this distinction. The usual "consanguineal" and "affinal" are inadequate because in primitive society affinal relatives are ordinarily consanguineal relatives as well.

4. A further, but rather parenthetical, remark is relevant here. Many anthropologists have regarded Australian social organization as very complex because of the presence of the class system, and they have used this as an argument against the theory of cultural evolution; that is, they argue that evolutionists assume that a simple technology must be accompanied by a simple social organization, but technologically primitive Australians have an "advanced" (complex) kinship system: hence, evolutionist assumptions are wrong. But I hope this paper has shown that the class nomenclature is a *substitute* for the kinship nomenclature in particular contexts (and a simplification of it, in fact), and is in no way an added dimension to the social organization itself, which remains equally simple whether or not a sociocentric class terminology is used.

Davidson, D. S.
1926 "The Basis of Social Organization in Australia," *American Anthropologist,* 28:529–548.
1928 "The Chronological Aspects of Certain Australian Social Institutions as Inferred from Geographical Distribution," Ph.D. dissertation, University of Pennsylvania, Philadelphia.

Deacon, A. B.
1927 "The Regulation of Marriage in Ambrym," *Journal of the Royal Anthropological Institute,* 57:325–342.

Durkheim, E.
1897 "La prohibition de l'inceste et ses origines," *L'Année sociologique,* 1:1–70.

Elkin, A. P.
1932 "Social Organization in the Kimberly Division, Northwestern Australia," *Oceania,* 2:296–333.
1950 "The Complexity of Social Organization in Arnhem Land," *Southwestern Journal of Anthropology,* 6:1–20.
1954 *The Australian Aborigines,* 3rd ed. Sydney and London: Angus and Robertson.

Galton, F.
1889 "Note on Australian Marriage Systems," *Journal of the Anthropological Institute*, 18:70–72.

Hocart, A. M.
1955 "Kinship Systems," in *Readings in Anthropology,* E. A. Hoebel, ed., pp. 189–193. New York: McGraw-Hill.

Howitt, A. W.
1889 "Further Notes on the Australian Class Systems," *Journal of the Anthropological Institute,* 18:31–68.

Kirchhoff, P.
1955 "The Principles of Clanship in Human Society," *Davidson Journal of Anthropology,* 1:1–10.

Kroeber, A. L.
1952 "Basic and Secondary Patterns of Social Structure," in *The Nature of Culture,* pp. 210–218. Chicago: University of Chicago Press.

Lawrence, W. E.
1937 "Alternating Generations in Australia," in *Studies in the Science of Society,* G. P. Murdock, ed., pp. 319–354. New Haven, Conn.: Yale University Press.

Murdock, G. P.
1940 "Double Descent," *American Anthropologist,* 42:555–561.
1949 *Social Structure.* New York: Macmillan.

Radcliffe-Brown, A. R.
1913 "Three Tribes of Western Australia," *Journal of the Royal Anthropological Institute,* 43:143–194.
1927 "The Regulation of Marriage in Ambrym," *Journal of the Royal Anthropological Institute,* 57:343–348.
1930–1931 "The Social Organization of Australian Tribes," *Oceania,* 1:34–63, 206–246, 426–456.
1951 "Murngin Social Organization," *American Anthropologist,* 53:37–55.
1952 "The Study of Kinship Systems," in *Structure and Function in Primitive Society.* Glencoe, Ill.: Free Press.

Romney, A. K., and E. J. Epling
1958 "A Simplified Model of Kariera Kinship," *American Anthropologist,* 60:59–74.

Seligman, B. Z.
1927 "Bilateral Descent and the Formation of Marriage Classes," *Journal of the Royal Anthropological Institute,* 57:349–375.

Spencer, B., and F. J. Gillen
1899 *The Native Tribes of Central Australia.* New York: Macmillan.

Thomas, N. W.
1906 *Kinship Organisations and Group Marriage in Australia.* Cambridge: Cambridge University Press.

Warner, W. L.
1937 *A Black Civilization.* New York: Harper.

Chapter 14. Social Organization of a Siassi Island Community

1. For recent summary discussions consult Phyllis M. Kaberry's "The Plasticity of New Guinea Kinship," in *Social Organization, Essays Presented to Raymond Firth.* Maurice Freedman, ed., Chicago: Aldine, 1967 and Marie de Lepervanche, "Descent, Residence and Leadership in the New Guinea Highlands," *Oceania,* Vol. 38, Nos. 2–3, 1967–1969.

Chapter 15. The Iban of Western Borneo

1. The Iban are also known as Sea Dayaks. In Sarawak it so happened that the first Iban with whom the British came into contact, in the early 1940's, were inhabitants of the Lupar and Saribas Rivers who, in league with Malays, had taken to coastal piracy. The British called them Sea Dayaks. From an ecological point of view, however, the term *Sea Dayak* is misleading; the vast majority of the Iban have always been a hill people living many miles from the coast with an economy based on the cultivation of dry rice. Today, among the tribes of the interior, the name *Iban* (a borrowing from the Kayan) is in general use; it was first introduced into ethnographic literature by Haddon (1901: 325).

My first period of field work among the Iban was carried out under the auspices of the Colonial Social Science Research Council of Great Britain, and the second from the Australian National University. I wish to express my thanks to both these institutions.

3. Freeman 1958. This published paper,

prepared before my second period of field research among the Iban, incorporates much of the material which I presented at the symposium in Bangkok.

4. *Bilek* is a term used by the Iban to refer to the living room of a long-house apartment; the same term is also used to refer to the family which owns and occupies the whole of such an apartment. The other main sections of an apartment are the *ruai* or gallery and the *tanju* or open platform. When a series of family apartments are joined together they form what is, in effect, a terrace of attached houses. The *ruai* and *tanju* have no side walls and so run the full length of the long-house.

5. In the event of a marriage not producing a child, the usual course is for the child of a close cognate to be adopted. Many families follow this course to ensure their survival. Such adopted members acquire full parcenary rights in the *bilek* estate, and in the account which follows adoption should be regarded as jurally equivalent to descent based on consanguinity.

6. This statement is based on the assumption that the marriage of the affine concerned is a stable and enduring one. An out-marrying member does retain the contingent residual right to return to his (or her) natal *bilek* should a marriage end in divorce.

7. From the Latin, *uter,* "either of two," "one or the other," "one of two." I prefer "utrolocal" to "bilocal" on the ground that for Iban society it is more precise etymologically. Similarly, the Iban system of filiation is best described by the term *utrolateral;* to call the Iban system "bilateral" is to invite misunderstanding, for filiation is always to one side or the other, never to both.

8. See Freeman (1958) and note 7 above.

9. Goodenough, in a recent discussion of Malayo-Polynesian social organization, points with perspicacity to the feasibility of a solution to the problem of forming corporations in cognatic societies which is, in essence, the same as that reached by the Iban. "Kindreds," he writes (Goodenough 1955:71), "cannot . . . function as land-owning bodies. Bilocal extended families could so function, but this would require that all out-marrying members of a family lose membership in the land-owning group while all in-marrying spouses acquire such membership."

10. I.e., the long-houses of the districts of Pengulu Jenggut and Pengulu Grinang, during the year 1948.

11. For a fuller account of Iban land tenure and usage see Freeman (1955).

12. According to Radcliffe-Brown, "Kith were one's friends by vicinage, one's neighbors; kin were persons descended from a common ancestor" (Radcliffe-Brown and Forde 1950:15).

13. E.g., Nadel 1947:17.

14. *Cf. Oxford English Dictionary;* Pollock and Maitland, 1952, Vol. 2, p. 241; Phillpotts 1913:2; Rivers 1924:16; Evans-Pritchard 1940:193; Murdock 1949:46.

15. According to Pollock and Maitland (1952, Vol. 2, p. 242), "there were as many blood-feud groups as there were living persons; at all events each set of brothers and sisters was the centre of a different group." The term "personal kindred" was introduced to the literature by Leach (1950:62).

16. In Iban society, in which the marriage of cognates is preferred, it frequently happens that a married pair are close collateral kin, i.e., first, second, or third cousins. In many cases, however, the cognatic relationship of spouses is either more remote than this or is nonexistent.

17. I have not the space in an outline paper of this kind to discuss the changes in kinship terminology and relationship which are adopted when cognates of different generations do marry. Because of the marked generational emphasis of the Iban kinship system these changes always result in incongruities which cause resentment and irritation among many of the other cognates involved. Indeed, I would hypothesize that Iban marital prohibitions beyond the *bilek* family are chiefly concerned with the avoidance of this sort of dysnomia.

18. In 1936, when a section of the *adat* of the Third Division Iban was codified under the authority of the Third Rajah, this fine was set at $15. In 1952 it was in-

creased to $30. A Malay dollar is valued at 2s. 4d. sterling. See *Sea Dayak Fines,* 1940; *Tusun Tunggu Iban,* 1955.

19. If first cousins marry there is an overlap of 50 per cent, but this will be increased if they are related on more than one side, as sometimes happens. Theoretically, universal first-cousin marriage (i.e., in all generations) would result in the complete coincidence of the two categories *Kaban namdal* and *kaban tampil.*

20. At Rumah Nyala, for example, the linkage of *bilek* families to the rest of the long-house community was traced either exclusively or predominantly from a natal *bilek* member in 62 per cent of instances, and from an in-married *bilek* member in 38 per cent

21. This statement applies only to pioneer areas, like the Baleh, where land is not in short supply. In some parts of Sarawak, such as the Second Division, the adverse population-land balance prevents or severely inhibits the movement of *bilek* families from one long-house to another. In the Baleh region rubber is now becoming widely established as a cash crop, and already the population has become more sedentary than under the traditional subsistence economy based on shifting cultivation.

22. As early as 1889, for example, Starcke (1889:207) wrote: "A consideration of the whole series of our researchers . . . will show that . . . the nomenclature was in every respect the faithful reflection of the juridical relations which arose between the nearest kinsfolk of each tribe. Individuals who were, according to the legal point of view, on the same level with the speaker, received the same designation. The other categories of kinship were formally developed out of this standpoint."

23. Hence Ego, in Figures 1 through 3, may be either male or female. This has been indicated by superimposing a circle (the symbol for a female) on a triangle (the symbol for a male).

24. *Petunggal* is the classificatory term applied to all cousins of whatever degree. It is applied, only to collateral cognates on the same generation level as Ego; the Iban have no concept comparable to "cousin once removed" in the English kinship system. First cousins are more exactly described as *petunggal diri menyadi* (cousins sprung from siblings) or *petunggal se kali* (cousins for the first time). More remote degrees of cousin-ship are indicated by numerical phrases, e.g., *petunggal dua kali,* second cousins; *petunggal tiga kali,* third cousins.

25. It often happens that differential ease of communication results in an individual becoming more closely associated with one side of his (or her) kindred than the other. This, however, does not alter the fact that, beyond the *bilek,* both sides are *de jure* equally available for all the purposes of kinship.

26. As a term of address *menyadi* is commonly extended to include all cousins. Alternative terms of address for cousins are *petunggal* and *unggal.* Again, both siblings and cousins (male and female) may be addressed by the terms *aka and adi,* the former for siblings and cousins older than oneself and the latter for those younger. These terms of address have about them a tone of affection associated with the sentiments that arise from the interdependence of siblings and cousins who grow up together. The vocatives *aka* and *adi* are in no way related to jural rights; during disputes between siblings, for example, they are dropped in favor of the more formal term *menyadi.*

27. In its terms of address, however, the Iban system conforms to Murdock's Hawaiian type, for as a vocative the term *menyadi* may be used in a classificatory way to address any cousin on either side of the personal kindred.

28. This term may be used in addressing cognates of Ego's own generation and, in joking, those of the second ascending or second descending generations, but it is not permissible between cognates of adjacent generations. Personal names are interdicted only for cognates of the first ascending generation, but they are not commonly used for those of the second ascending generation.

29. The term of reference for a great-grandchild is *ichit.* This term, however, is never used as a vocative; instead, great-

grandchildren are always addressed as *ucho*.

30. *Ipar* is also used as a term of address. Alternatively, an *ipar* may be addressed as *ika* if older than Ego's spouse, or as *adi* if younger. *Duai* refers to the relationship between the spouses of a pair of siblings, i.e., a double affinal relationship.

31. In many respects the kinship system of the Iban resembles that of the contemporary United States (*cf.* Parsons 1943).

32. Of the world ethnographic sample of 565 societies compiled by Murdock (1957), 247 have patrilineal descent, 85 have matrilineal descent, 29 have double descent, and 204 have bilateral descent.

33. Radcliffe-Brown and Forde 1950; Fortes 1953.

Evans-Pritchard, E. E.
1940 *The Nuer.* New York: Oxford University Press.

Fortes, M.
1953 "The Structure of Unilineal Descent Groups," *American Anthropologist,* 55:17–41.

Freeman, J. D.
1955 *Iban Agriculture.* Colonial Research Studies No. 18. London: Her Majesty's Stationery Office.
1958 "The Family System of the Iban of Borneo," *Cambridge Papers in Social Anthropology,* I:15–52.

Goodenough, W. H.
1951 "Property, Kin, and Community on Truk," *Yale University Publications in Anthropology,* 46:1–192.

Haddon, A. C.
1901 *Head-Hunters: Black, White and Brown.* London: Methuen.

Leach, E. R.
1950 *Socal Science Research in Sarawak.* Colonial Research Studies No. I. London: Her Majesty's Stationery Office.

Murdock, G. P.
1949 *Social Structure.* New York: Macmillan.
1957 "World Ethnographic Sample," *American Anthropologist,* 59:664–687.

Nadel, S. F.
1947 *The Nuba.* Oxford.

Parsons, T.
1943 "The Kinship System of the Contemporary United States," *American Anthropologist,* 45:22–38.

Phillpotts, B. S.
1913 *Kindred and Clan.* Cambridge: Cambridge University Press.

Pollock, F., and F. W. Maitland
1952 *The History of English Law,* 2nd ed. (1st ed., 1895). Cambridge.

Radcliffe-Brown, A. R., and D. Forde, eds.
1950 *African Systems of Kinship and Marriage.* London: Oxford University Press.

Starcke, C. N.
1889 *The Primitive Family in Its Origin and Development.* New York: D. Appleton & Co.

Chapter 16. Poor Man, Rich Man, Big-Man, Chief: Political Types in Melanesia and Polynesia

1. The present paper is preliminary to a wider and more detailed comparison of Melanesian and Polynesian polities and economies. I have merely abstracted here some of the more striking political differences in the two areas. The full study—which, incidentally, will include more documentation—has been promised the editors of *The Journal of the Polynesian Society,* and I intend to deliever it to them some day.

The comparative method so far followed in this research has involved reading the monographs and taking notes. I don't think I originated the method, but I would like to christen it the "Method of Uncontrolled Comparison." The description developed of two forms of leadership is a mental distillation from the method of uncontrolled comparison. The two forms are abstracted sociological types. Anyone conversant with the anthropological literature of the South Pacific knows there are important variants of the types, as well as exceptional political forms not fully treated here. All would agree that consideration of the variations and exceptions is necessary and desirable. Yet there is pleasure, too, and some intellectual reward, in discovering the broad patterns. To (social-) scientifically justify my pleasure, I could have referred to the pictures drawn of Melanesian big-men and Polynesian chiefs as "models" or as "ideal types." If that is all that is needed to confer respectability on the paper, may the reader have it this way.

I hope all of this has been sufficiently disarming. Or need it also be said that the hypotheses are provisional, subject to further research, etc.?

2. Since Rivers' day, the Pacific has provided ethnographic stimulus to virtually every major ethnological school and interest. From such great landmarks as Rivers' *History of Melanesian Society;* Radcliffe-Brown's *Social Organization of the Australian Tribes;* Malinowski's famous Trobriand studies, especially *Argonauts of the Western Pacific;* Raymond Firth's pathmaking *Primitive Economics of the New Zealand Maori,* his functionalist classic, *We, the Tikopia;* and Margaret Mead's *Coming of Age in Samoa,* one can almost read off the history of ethnological theory in the earlier twentieth century. In addition to continuing to provision all these concerns, the Pacific has been the site of much recent evolutionist work (see, for example, Goldman 1955, 1960; Goodenough 1957; Sahlins 1958; Vayda 1959). There are also the outstanding monographs on special subjects ranging from tropical agriculture (Conklin 1957; Freeman 1955) to millenarianism (Worsley 1957).

3. This question, however, is presently in debate. See Grace (1955, 1959); Dyen (1960); Suggs (1960); Golson (1961).

4. There are notable bumps in the geographical gradient. The Trobriand chieftainships off eastern New Guinea will come to mind. But the Trobriand political development is clearly exceptional for western Melanesia.

5. Hogbin and Wedgwood (1952–1953, 1953–1954). On New Guinea Highland political scale see among others, Paula Brown (1960).

6. See the summary account in Sahlins (1958), especially pp. 132–133.

7. Kirchhoff 1955; Firth 1957; Goldman 1957; Bacon 1958; Fried 1957.

8. The big-man pattern is very widespread in western Melanesia, although its complete distribution is not yet clear to me. Anthropological descriptions of big-man leadership vary from mere hints of its existence, as among the Orokaiva (Williams 1930), Lesu (Powdermaker 1933), or the interior peoples of northeastern Guadalcanal (Hogbin 1937–1938a), to excellent, closely grained analyses, such as Douglas Oliver's account of the Siuai of Bougainville (Oliver 1955). Big-man leadership has been more or less extensively described for the Manus of the Admiralty Islands (Mead 1934, 1937); the To'ambaita of northern Malaita (Hogbin 1939, 1943–1944); the Tangu of northeastern New Guinea (Burridge 1960); the Kapauku of Netherlands New Guinea (Pospisil 1958, 1959–1960); the Kaoka of Guadalcanal (Hogbin 1933–1934, 1937–1938); the Seniang District of Malekula (Deacon 1934); the Gawa' of the Huon Gulf area, New Guinea (Hogbin 1951); the Abelam (Kaberry 1940–1941, 1941–1942) and the Arapesh (Mead 1937a, 1938, 1947) of the Sepik District, New Guinea; The Elema, Orokolo Bay, New Guinea (Williams 1940); the Ngarawapum of the Markham Valley, New Guinea (Read 1946–1947, 1949–1950); the Kiwai of the Fly estuary, New Guinea (Landtman 1927); and a number of other societies, including, in New Guinea Highlands, the Kuma (Reay 1959), the Gahuka-Gama (Read 1952–1953, 1059), the Kyaka (Bulmer 1960–1961), the Enga (Meggitt 1957, 1957–1958), and others. (For an overview of the structural position of New Guinea Highlands' leaders, see Barnes 1962.) A partial bibliography on Polynesian chieftainship can be found in Sahlins 1958. The outstanding ethnographic description of Polynesian chieftainship is, of course, Firth's for Tikopia (1950, 1957); Tikopia, however, is not typical of the more advanced Polynesian chiefdoms with which we are principally concerned here.

9. Gifford 1929:124.

10. Thus the enclavement of the big-man pattern within a segmented lineage

organization in the New Guinea Highlands appears to limit the leader's political role and authority in comparison, say, with the Siuai. In the Highlands, intergroup relations are regulated in part by the segmented lineage structure; among the Siuai intergroup relations depend more on contractual arrangements between big-men which throws these figures more into prominence. (Notable in this connection has been the greater viability of the Siuai big-man than the native Highlands leader in the face of colonial control.) Barnes' (1962) comparison of Highland social structure with the classic segmentary lineage systems of Africa suggests an inverse relation between the formality of the lineage system and the political significance of individual action. Now, if instances such as the Siuai be tacked on to the comparison, the generalization may be further supported and extended: among societies of the tribal level (see Sahlins 1961; Service, *in press*), the greater the self-regulation of the political process through a lineage system, the less function that remains to big-men, and the less significant their political authority.

11. Hogbin 1943–1944:258.

12. Oliver 1955:408. Compare with the parallel statement for the Kaoka of Guadalcanal in Hogbin (1937–1938:305).

13. Pospisil 1958:81.

14. It is difficult to say just how important the military qualifications of leadership have been in Melanesia, since the ethnographic researchers have typically been undertaken after pacification, sometimes long after. I may underestimate this factor. Compare Bromley (1960).

15. Landtman 1927:168.

16. Indeed it is the same people, the Siuai, who so explicitly discover themselves eating their leader's renown who also seem able to absorb a great deal of deprivation without violent reaction, at least until the leader's wave of fame has already crested (see Oliver 1955:362, 368, 387, 394).

17. "In the Paniai Lake region (of Netherlands New Guinea), the people go so far as to kill a selfish rich man because of his 'immorality.' His own sons or brothers are induced by the rest of the members of the community to dispatch the first deadly arrow. *'Aki to tonowi beu, inii idikima enadani kodo to niitou'* (you should not be the only rich man, we should all be the same, therefore you only stay equal with us) was the reason given by th Paniai people for killing Mote Juwopija of Madi, a *tonowi* [Kapauku for 'big-man'] who was not generous enough (Pospisil 1958:80, *cf.* pp. 108–110). On another egalitarian conspiracy, see Hogbin (1951:145), and for another aspect of the Melanesian contradiction note, for example, Hogbin (1939:81); Burridge (1960:18–19); and Reay (1959:110, 129–130).

18. Aside from the transitional developments in eastern Melanesia, several western Melanesian societies advanced to a structural position intermediate between underdeveloped Melanesian politics and Polynesian chiefdoms. In these western Melanesian proto-chiefdoms, an ascribed division of kinship groups (or segments thereof) into chiefly and nonchiefly ranks emerges—as in Sa'a (Ivens 1927), around Buka passage (Blackwood 1935), in Manam Island (Wedgwood 1933–1934, 1958–1959), Waropen (Held 1957), perhaps Mafulu (Williamson 1912), and several others. The rank system does not go beyond the broad dual division of groups into chiefly and nonchiefly: no pyramid of ranked social-political divisions along Polynesian lines is developed. The political unit remains near the average size of the western Melanesian autonomous community. Sway over the kin groups of such a local body falls automatically to a chiefly unit, but chiefs do not hold office title with stipulated rights over corporate sections of society, and further extension of chiefly authority, if any, must be achieved. The Trobriands, which carry this line of chiefly development to its highest point, remain under the same limitations, although it was ordinarily possible for powerful chiefs to integrate settlements of the external sector within their domains (*cf.* Powell 1960).

19. Malo 1903:257–258.

20. Goldman 1955; 1957; 1960.

21. The great Tahitian chiefs were traditionally enjoined not to eat the power

of government too much, as well as to practice open-handedness towards the people (Handy 1930:41). Hawaiian high chiefs were given precisely the same advice by counselors (Malo 1903:255).

22. Buck 1938:70–77, 160, 165.

23. The Hawaiian traditions are very clear on the encouragement given rebellion by chiefly exactions—although one of our greatest sources of Hawaiian tradition, David Malo, provides the most sober caveat regarding this kind of evidence. "I do not suppose," he wrote in the preface to *Hawaiian Antiquities,* "the following history to be free from mistakes, in material for it has come from oral traditions; consequently it is marred by errors of human judgment and does not approach the accuracy of the word of God."

Malo (1903:258) noted that "Many kins have been put to death by the people because of their oppression of the *makaainana* (i.e., commoners)." He goes on to list several who "lost their lives on account of their cruel exactions," and follows the list with the statement, "It was for this reason that some of the ancient kings had a wholesome fear of the people." The propensity of Hawaiian high chiefs for undue appropriation from commoners is a point made over and over again by Malo (see pp. 85, 87–88, 258, 267–268). In Fornander's reconstruction of Hawaiian history (from traditions and genealogies) internal rebellions are laid frequently, almost axiomatically, to chiefly extortion and niggardliness (Fornander 1880:40–41, 76–78, 88, 149–150, 270–271). In addition, Fornander at times links appropriation of wealth and ensuing rebellion to the provisioning of the chiefly establishment, as in the following passage: "Scarcity of food, after a while, obliged *Kalaniopuu* (paramount chief of the island of Hawaii and half broth of Kamehameha I's father) to remove his court (from the Kona district) into the Kohala district, where his headquarters were fixed at Kapaau. Here the same extravagant, *laissez-faire,* eat-and-be-merry policy continued that had been commenced at Kona, and much grumbling and discontent began to manifest itself among the resident chiefs and cultivators of the land, the 'Makaainana.' *Imakakaloa,* a great chief in the Puna district, and *Nuuampaahu,* a chief of Naalehu in the Kau district, became the heads and rallying points of the discontented. The former resided on his lands in Puna [in the southeast, across the island from Kohala in the northwest], and openly resisted the orders of *Kalaniopuu* and his extravagant demands for contributions of all kinds of property; the latter was in attendance with the court of *Kalaniopuu* in Kohala, but was strongly suspected of favouring the growing discontent" (Fornander 1880:-200). Aside from the Mangarevan uprising mentioned in the text, there is some evidence for similar revolts in Tonka (Mariner 1827:80; Thomson 1894:294ff.) and in Tahiti (Henry 1928:195–196, 297).

24. Or see Handy (1923) and Linton (1939).

25. On the difficulty of provisioning the Hawaiian paramount's large establishment, see the citation from Fornander above, and also Fornander (1880:100–101); Malo (1903:92–93), *et passim.* The Hawaiian great chiefs developed the practice of the circuit—like feudal monarchs—often leaving a train of penury behind as they moved in state from district to district of the chiefdom.

Bacon, Elizabeth E.
1958 *Obok.* Viking Fund Publication in Anthropology No. 25. New York: The Wenner-Gren Foundation.

Barnes, J. A.
1962 "African Models in the New Guinea Highlands," *Man,* 622:5–9.

Blackwood, Beatrice
1935 *Both Sides of Buka Passage.* Oxford: Clarendon Press.

Bromley, M.
1960 "A Preliminary Report on Law Among the Grand Valley Dani of Netherlands New Guinea," *Nieuw Guinea Studien,* 4:235–259.

Brown, Paula
1960 "Chimbu Tribes: Political Organization in the Eastern Highlands of New Guinea," *Southwestern Journal of Anthropology,* 16:22–35.

Buck, Sir Peter H.
1938 *Ethnology of Mangareva.* Bernice P. Bishop Museum Bulletin 157.
Bulmer, Ralph
1960–1961 "Political Aspects of the Moka Exchange System Among the Kyaka People of the Western Highlands of New Guinea," *Oceania,* 31:1–13.
Burridge, Kenelm
1960 *Mambu: A Melanesian Millenium.* London: Methuen.
Conklin, Harold C.
1957 *Hanunóo Agriculture.* FAO Forestry Development Paper No. 12. Rome: Food and Agricultural Organization of the United Nations.
Deacon, A. Bernard
1934 *Malekula: A Vanishing People in the New Hebrides,* C. H. Wedgwood, ed. London: Routledge.
Dyen, Isidore
1960 Review of *The Position of the Polynesian Languages within the Austronesian (Malayo-Polynesian) Language Family,* by George W. Grace. *Journal of the Polynesian Society,* 69:-180–184.
Firth, Raymond
1950 *Primitive Polynesian Economy.* New York: Humanities Press.
1957 *We, the Tikopia,* 2nd ed. London: Allen and Unwin.
Fornander, Abraham
1880 *An Account of the Polynesian Race,* Vol. II. London: Trübner.
Freeman, J. D.
1955 *Iban Agriculture.* Colonial Research Studies No. 18. London: Her Majesty's Stationery Office.
Fried, Morton H.
1957 "The Classification of Corporate Unilineal Descent Groups," *Journal of the Royal Anthropological Institute,* 87:1–29.
Gifford, Edward Winslow
1929 *Tongan Society.* Bernice P. Bishop Museum Bulletin 61.
Goldman, Irving
1955 "Status Rivalry and Cultural Evolution in Polynesia," *American Anthropologist,* 57:680–697.
1957 "Variations in Polynesian Social Organization," *Journal of the Polynesian Society,* 66:374–390.
1960 "The Evolution of Polynesian Societies," in *Culture and History,* S. Diamond, ed. New York: Columbia University Press.
Golson, Jack
1961 "Polynesian Culture History," *Journal of the Polynesian Society,* 70: 498–508.
Goodenough, Ward
1957 "Oceania and the Problem of Controls in the Study of Cultural and Human Evolution," *Journal of the Polynesian Society,* 66:146–155.
Grace, George
1955 "Subgroupings of Malayo-Polynesian: A Report of Tentative Findings," *American Anthropologist,* 57:337–339.
1959 *The Position of the Polynesian Languages within the Austronesian (Malayo-Polynesian) Family.* Indiana University Publications in Anthropological Linguistics 16.
Handy, E. S. Craighill
1923 *The Native Culture in the Marquesas.* Bernice P. Bishop Museum Bulletin 9.
1930 *History and Culture in the Society Islands.* Bernice P. Bishop Museum Bulletin 79.
Held, G. J.
1957 *The Papuas of Waropen.* The Hague: Koninklijk Instituut Voor Taal-Land-En Volkenkunde.
Henry, Teuira
1928 *Ancient Tahiti.* Bernice P. Bishop Museum Bulletin 48.
Hogbin, H. Ian
1933–1934 "Culture Change in the Solomon Islands: Report of Field Work in Guadalcanal and Malaita," *Oceania,* 4:233–267.
1937–1938 "Social Advancement in Guadalcanal, Solomon Islands,' *Oceania,* 8:289–305.
1937–1938a "The Hill People of Northeastern Guadalcanal," *Oceania,* 8:62–89.
1939 *Experiments in Civilization.* London: Routledge.

1943–1944 "Native Councils and Courts in the Solomon Islands," *Oceania,* 14:-258-283.

1951 *Transformation Scene: The Changing Culture of a New Guinea Village.* London: Routledge and Kegan Paul.

Hogbin, H., and Camilla H. Wedgwood

1952–1954 "Local Groupings in Melanesia," *Oceania,* 23:241–276; 24:58–76.

Ivens, W. G.

1927 *Melanesians of the Southeast Solomon Islands.* London: Kegan, Paul, Trench, Trubner.

Kaberry, Phyllis M.

1940–1941 "The Abelam Tribe, Sepik Districk. New Guinea: a Preliminary Report," *Oceania,* 11:233–258, 345–367.

1941–1942 "Law and Political Organization in the Abelam Tribe," *Oceania,* 12:79–95, 209–225, 331–363.

Kirchhoff, Paul

1955 "The Principles of Clanship in Human Society," *Davidson Anthropological Journal,* 1:1–11.

Landtman, Gunnar

1927 *The Kiwai Papuans of British New Guinea.* London: Macmillan.

Linton, Ralph

1939 "Marguesan Culture," in *The Individual and His Society,* A. Kardiner, ed. New York: Columbia University Press.

Malo, David

1903 *Hawaiian Antiquities.* Honolulu: Hawaiian Gazette.

Mariner, William

1827 *An Account of the Natives of the Tonga Islands* (John Martin, compiler). Edinburgh: Constable.

Mead, Margaret

1934 "Kinship in the Admiralty Islands," *American Museum of Natural History Anthropological Papers,* 34:-181–358.

1937 "The Manus of the Admiralty Islands," in *Cooperation and Competition among Primitive Peoples,* M. Mead, ed. New York and London: McGraw-Hill.

1937a "The Arapesh of New Guinea," in *Cooperation and Competition among Primitive Peoples,* M. Mead, ed. New York and London: McGraw-Hill.

1938 "The Mountain Arapesh I. An Importing Culture," *American Museum of Natural History Anthropological Papers,* 36:139–349.

1947 "The Mountain Arapesh III. Socio-Economic Life," *American Museum of Natural History Anthropological Papers,* 40:159–232.

Meggitt, Mervyn

1957 "Enga Political Organization: A Preliminary Description," *Mankind,* 5:133–137.

1957–1958 "The Enga of the New Guinea Highlands: Some Preliminary Observations," *Oceania,* 28:253–330.

Oliver, Douglas

1955 *A Solomon Islands Society.* Cambridge, Mass.: Harvard University Press.

Pospisil, Leopold

1958 *Kapauku Papuans and Their Law.* Yale University Publications in Anthropology No. 54. New Haven: Yale University Press.

1958-59 "The Kapauku Papuans and their Kinship Organization," *Oceania,* 30:188–205.

Powdermaker, Hortense

1933 *Life in Lesu.* New York: Norton.

Powell, H. A.

1960 "Competitive Leadership in Trobriand Political Organization," *Journal of the Royal Anthropological Institute,* 90:118–145.

Read, K. E.

1946-47 "Social Organization in the Markham Valley, New Guinea," *Oceania,* 17:93–118.

1949–50 "The Political System of the Ngarawapum," *Oceania,* 20:185–223.

1952–53 "The Nama Cult of the Central Highlands, New Guinea," *Oceania,* 23:1–25.

1959 "Leadership and Consensus in a New Guinea Society," *American Anthropologist,* 61:425–436.

Reay, Marie

1959 *The Kuma.* Melbourne: Melbourne University Press.

Sahlins, Marshall D.

1958 *Social Stratification in Polynesia.*

American Ethnological Society Monograph. Seattle: University of Washington Press.
1961 "The Segmentary Lineage: An Organization of Predatory Expansion," *American Anthropologist,* 63: 322–345.
Service, Elman R.
1962 *Primitive Social Organization: An Evolutionary Perspective.* New York: Random House.
Suggs, Robert C.
1960 *Ancient Civilizations of Polynesia.* New York: Mentor.
Thomson, Sir Basil
1894 *The Diversions of a Prime Minister.* Edinburgh and London: William Blackwood.
Vayda, Andrew Peter
1959 "Polynesian Cultural Distributions in New Perspective," *American Anthropologist,* 61:817–828.
Wedgwood, Camilla H.
1933–34 "Report on Research in Manam Island, Mandated Territory of New Guinea," *Oceania,* 4:373–403.
1958–59 "Manam Kinship," *Oceania,* 29:239–256.
Williams, F. E.
1930 "Orokaiva Society." London: Oxford University Press (Humphrey Milford).
1940 *Drama of Orokolo.* Oxford: Clarendon Press.
Williamson, Robert W.
1912 *The Mafulu: Mountain People of British New Guinea.* London: Macmillan.
Worsley, Peter
1957 *The Trumpet Shall Sound.* London: Macgibbon and Kee.

Chapter 17. A Leader in Action

1. To any reader interested only in the general account of rank-acquiring, this chapter may be passed over without risk of loss of continuity.

2. Some readers may object to the use of the word "history" in this context since there is no written documentation behind it. In defense it can only be said that the "history" presented covers a relatively recent time span and that the events in question were independently described by several informants. Moreover, even if this "history" were not "true" it nevertheless possesses ethnographic significance (see D. Oliver, *A Solomon Island Society*, Cambridge, Mass., Harvard University Press, 1955, pp. 411–412).

3. See Oliver, *op. cit.*, p. 319.

4. *Iibid.*

5. For the cultural anthropologist some more detailed information about this period of uncertainty and change would be of great interest, but unfortunately such information is not available.

6. See Oliver, *op. cit.*, p. 328.

7. Identity unknown.

8. See Oliver, *op. cit.,* p. 328.

9. The average size of 64 Siuai line villages was 70 in 1938; the average size of Turuŋom during 1938–1939 was 95.

10. See Oliver, *op. cit.,* pp. 424–425.

11. Reraka, and not the Ronoro creek, as was erroneously reported in my "Land Tenure in Northeast Siuai, Southern Bougainville," Peabody Museum Papers, 29(4):62. Cambridge, Mass., 1949.

12. See Oliver, *A Solomon Island Society, op. cit.,* p. 111.

13. Maimoi was a loyal adherent of Soŋi's although a resident of Rennu village.

14. See Oliver, *op. cit.,* p. 171.

15. See Oliver, *op. cit.*, p. 391.

16. Because of the nature of death in childbirth it cannot be postponed by "life-tying." (see Oliver, *op. cit.,* p. 89).

17. A visitor from Mi'kahna village.

18. After the feast, when there was no need for his full-time services at the clubhouse, Ho'oma slipped back into his usual routine, slept at home and worked industriously in his garden. He no longer directed fellow villagers as they worked at their more prosaic tasks, and his two sons resumed their customary roles as the village laggards.

19. By October 1939, the social merger of the two villages had become so complete that the Australian patrol officer officially recognized it and persuaded Soŋi to become Headman (*kukerai*) of both villages. This merger was not a mere verbal political alliance, it was effected by the closer associations among natives of the two villages and by the direct authority which Soŋi began to exercise over all of them—an authority, moreover, which did not refer through Tukem. At first Tukem did not behave as though he objected to being supplanted. He appeared to share in the renewed *esprit de corps* just as all the other natives did, with one exception. The exception was Soŋi's enemy in Rennu, who used to sit alone in Tukem's club-house while his friends flocked to Turuŋom. He even forbade his wife and daughter to attend a memorial feast given on behalf of Soŋi's deceased wife. Later on, he moved out of Rennu in disgust and returned to his birthplace at Mataras.

20. Tukem's authority was weakened so considerably by this merger that he later became involved in an argument with one of his former adherents and was threatened with an ax. He became so resentful he expressed intention of returning—along with the old man—to Mataras.

21. The principal Defender.

Chapter 18. Political Organization, Supernatural Sanctions, and the Punishment for Incest on Yap

Schneider, D. M.
1953 "Yap Kinship Terminology and Kin Groups," *American Anthropologist,* 55:215–36.

Chapter 19. Law and Politics on Nonouti Island

1. For a detailed discussion of the Gilbertese *utu* see, for example, Lundsgaarde (n.d.), Maude (1963), and Silverman (1966).

2. The concepts of right, privilege, power, and immunity—as well as their opposite and correlative concepts of no-right, duty, disability, and liability—have been adapted from the work of W. N. Hohfeld (in Cook 1964). Hohfeld's use of the terms "paucital" and "multital" to describe relations *in personam* and *in rem* have also been used; e.g., "A paucital right, or claim (right *in personam*), is either a unique right residing in a person (or group of persons) and availing against a single person (or a single group of persons); or else it is one of a *few* fundamentally similar yet separate rights, actual and potential, against a few definite persons. A multital right, or claim (right *in rem*), is always *one* of a large *class* of *fundamentally similar*, yet separate, rights availing respectively residing in a *single* person (or single group of persons) but availing *respectively* against persons constituting a very large and indefinite class of people" (Cook 1964:72). For a more detailed discussion of these points, see Stone (1950) and Lundsgaarde (n.d.).

3. The legal aspects of Gilbertese adoption practices have been described in Lundsgaarde (n.d.).

4. See, for example, Goldschmidt's (1966) extended treatment of legal sanctioning processes and his analysis of the "official behavior" by legal authorities.

5. When I revisited the Gilberts in 1965 I learned that Kirabuke had been chosen for a newly developed program for the training of "Island Executive Officers." These officials will exceed island magistrates in authority.

Barwick, D. R.
1965 *Island Courts in the Gilbert and*

Ellice Islands Colony. Tarawa, Gilbert Islands (mimeographed).

Bohannan, P.

1965 "The Differing Realms of the Law," *American Anthropologist* (special publication), 67:33–42.

Bryce, W. G.

1952 *The Laws of the Gilbert and Ellice Islands Colony* (Rev. ed.), London: H.M.S.O.

Cook, W. W., ed.

1964 *Fundamental Legal Conceptions as Applied in Judicial Reasoning*. New Haven: Yale University Press.

Gilbert and Ellice Islands Colony

1963 "Gilbert and Phoenix Islands Lands Code," *Western Pacific High Commission Gazette* (suppl.), 3:6–17.

1965 *Local Government Policy*. Tarawa, Gilbert Islands (mimeographed).

Gluckman, M.

1965 *Politics, Law and Ritual in Tribal Society*. Chicago: Aldine.

Goldschmidt, V.

1966 "Primary Sanction Behavior," *Acta sociologica,* Vol. 10, Fasc. 1–2, 173–190.

Hart, H. L. A.

1961 *The Concept of Law*. London: Clarendon Press.

Lundsgaarde, H. P.

1968a "The Strategy and Etiology of Gilbertese Property Disputes," *American Anthropologist,* 70:86–93.

1968b "Some Transformations in Gilbertese Law: 1892–1966," *Journal of Pacific History,* 3:117–130.

n.d. "Some Legal Aspects of Gilbertese Adoption: Tamana Island, Southern Gilbert Islands," in *Adoption in Eastern Oceania,* V. Carrol, ed. Honolulu: University of Hawaii Press (*forthcoming*).

n.d. *Persons, Property, and Obligations in Gilbertese Society* (ms.)

Maude, H. E.

1963 *The Evolution of the Gilbertese Boti: An Ethnohistorical Interpretation*. Polynesian Society. Memoir No. 35. Wellington, New Zealand.

McArthur, N., and J. B. McCaig

1964 *A Report of the Results of the Census of the Population 1963*. Suva, Fiji: Government Printer.

Pospisil, L.

1952 *Nature of Law*. (Unpublished M.A. thesis) University of Oregon.

1958 *The Kapauku Papuans and Their Law*. Yale University Publications in Anthropology No. 54.

Radcliffe-Brown, A. R.

1952 *Structure and Function in Primitive Society*. Glencoe, Ill.: Free Press.

Redfield, R.

1967 "Primitive Law," in *Law and Warfare: Studies in the Anthropology of Conflict,* P. Bohannan, ed. New York: Natural History Press.

Silverman, M. G.

1966 *Symbols and Solidarities on Rambi Island, Fiji*. Unpublished Ph.D. dissertation, University of Chicago.

Stone, J.

1950 *The Province and Function of Law*. Cambridge: Harvard University Press.

Vansina, J.

1965 "A Traditional Legal System: The Kuba," in *African Law: Adaptation and Development,* H. and L. Kuper, eds. Berkeley: University of California Press.

Wallerstein, I., ed.

1966 *Social Change: The Colonial Situation*. New York: Wiley.

Chapter 20. Daughter of Time

1. The late Commander Eric Feldt, R.A.N.

Hayek's quotation is from Cohen (1964:305).

3. It is important that Worsley (1957: 266) states expressly that his "analytical tools" "are those forged by Marx." For reasons of space, in my summary of Marx's and especially Durkheim's definitions of religion below, I have deliberately selected only those aspects that have had the most direct influence on British social anthropology (*cf.* Evans-Pritchard, 1956; Horton, 1960; and Jarvie, 1964). I shall present a

more rounded account in the publication suggested in n. 1 above.

4. For general accounts, see Leff (1958: 197 ff.) and Taylor (1962:432 ff.).

5. *Cf.* Hazard (1965:37), writing of the pre-Enlightenment period generally: "In the eyes of the religiously minded, reason was a divine spark, a particle of truth vouchsafed to mortals until the time should come when, having passed through the gates of the tomb, they would see God face to face."

6. The best general account of millenarian cults in mediaeval Europe is by Cohn (1962). For Joachim of Fiore, see Cohn (1962:99 ff.).

7. For general accounts, see Leff (1958:211 ff.) and Taylor (1962:463 ff.).

8. For general accounts, see Bronowski (1960:18–46) and Merton (1959:574 ff.).

9. *Cf.* Fenelon (1651–1715): "Two conceptions of Godhead lie before you—the one of a Ruler, good and vigilant and wise, who will be loved and feared by men, the other a First Cause, so high that he cares nothing for souls he made, for their virtue or their vices, their disobedience or their love. Examine well these two conceptions. I defy you to prefer the second to the first." Quoted from Martin (1963:40).

10. For a general account, see Gay (1967).

11. See Talmon (1960:vi).

12. See Talmon (1961), a seminal work in this field of enquiry.

13. Quoted from Becker (1960:157–158). It is noteworthy that Durkheim (1954:428) expressly recognizes the role of these fêtes and the civic religion during the French Revolution.

14. For a general account, see Willey (1964).

15. See Durkheim (1962) and Hayek (1964).

16. Quoted from Durkheim (1962:229).

17. For a general account, see Willey (1964).

Barzun, J.
1959 *The House of Intellect.* New York: Harper.

Becker, C. L.
1960 *The Heavenely City of the Eighteenth Century Philosophers.* New Haven: Yale University Press (paperback).

Bronowski, J.
1960 *The Common Sense of Science.* Harmondsworth: Pelican Paperback.

Cohen, M. R.
1964 *Reason and Nature.* Glencoe, Ill.: Free Press.

Cohen, N.
1962 *The Pursuit of the Millennium.* London: Mercury Paperback.

Durkheim, E.
1954 *The Elementary Forms of the Religious Life.* London: Allen and Unwin.
1960 *Montesquieu and Rousseau.* Ann Arbor: University of Michigan Press.
1962 *Socialism.* New York: Collier Paperback.

Evans-Pritchard, E. E.
1956 *New Religion.* London: Oxford University Press.

Fortes, M.
1960 "Oedipus and Job in West African Religion," in *Anthropology of Folk Religion,* C. Leslie, ed. New York: Vintage Paperback.

Gay, P.
1967 *The Enlightenment.* London: Weidenfeld and Nicolson.

Gibbon, E.
1960 *The Decline and Fall of the Roman Empire,* Vol. I. London: Dent (Everyman).

Hayek, F. A.
1964 *The Counter-Revolution of Science.* Glencoe, Ill.: Free Press Paperback.

Hazard, P.
1965 *European Thought in the Eighteenth Century.* Harmondsworth: Pelican Paperback.

Hobbes, T.
1937 *Leviathan.* London: Dent (Everyman).

Holmyard, E. J.
1957 *Alchemy.* Harmondsworth: Pelican Paperback.

Horton, R.
1960 "A Definition of Religion, and Its

Uses," *Journal of the Royal Anthropological Institute,* 90:201–226.
Jarvie, I. C.
1964 *The Revolution in Anthropology.* London: Routledge and Kegan Paul.
Lawrence, P.
1964 *Road Belong Cargo.* Manchester: Manchester University Press; and Melbourne: Melbourne University Press.
Lederer, W. J., and Burdick, E.
1958 *The Ugly American.* London: Transworld Paperback.
Leff, G.
1958 *Mediaeval Thought.* Harmondsworth: Pelican Paperback.
Martin, K.
1963 *French Liberal Thought in the Eighteenth Century.* New York: Harper Torchbooks.
Marx, K.
1962 "Preface to a Contribution to the Critique of Political Economy," in *Marx and Engels, Selected Works,* Vol.I. Moscow: Foreign Languages Publishing House.
1964 "Contribution to the Critique of Hegel's Philosophy of Right," and extracts from "Capital, Book I," *Marx and Engels on Religion,* R. Niebuhr, ed. New York: Schocken Paperback.
Merton, R. K.
1959 *Social Theory and Social Structure.* Glencoe, Ill.: Free Press.
Mill, J. S.
1962 "On Liberty," in *Utilitarianism,* M. Warnock, ed. London: Fontana Paperback.
O'Dea, T. F.
1966 *The Sociology of Religion.* Englewood Cliffs, N.J.: Prentice-Hall Paperback.
Radcliffe-Brown, A. R.
1952 "Religion and Society," *Structure and Function in Primitive Society.* London: Cohen and West.
Rousseau, J. J.
1960 "The Social Contract," in *Social Contract,* Sir E. Barker, ed. London: Oxford University Press.
Spiro, M. E.
1967 *Burmese Supernaturalism.* Englewood Cliffs, N.J.: Prentice-Hall Paperback.
Swift, M. G.
1965 *Malay Peasant Society in Jelebu.* Bristol: Athlone Press.
Talmon, J. L.
1960 *Political Messianism.* New York: Praeger.
1961 *The Origins of Totalitarian Democracy.* London: Mercury Paperback.
Taylor, H. O.
1962 *The Mediaeval Mind,* Vol. II. Cambridge, Mass.: Harvard University Press.
Tey, J.
1955 *The Daughter of Time.* London: Peter Davis.
Tocqueville, A. de
1959 *The European Revolution and Correspondence with de Gobineau.* New York: Doubleday, Anchor Paperback.
Voegelin, E.
1952 *The New Science of Politics.* Chicago: University of Chicago Press.
Willey, B.
1962a *The Seventeenth-Century Background.* Harmondsworth: Peregrine Paperback.
1962b *The Eighteenth-Century Background.* Harmondsworth: Peregrine Paperback.
1964 *Nineteenth-Century Studies.* Harmondsworth: Peregrine Paperback.
Worsley, P. M.
1957 *The Trumpet Shall Sound.* London: Macgibbon and Kee.

Chapter 21. The Ngaing of the Rai Coast

1. Approximate population figures for the other groups mentioned are: Sengam 600; Gira 220; Som 150; Neko 180; M'na and N'dau unknown. I am indebted to the Administration of Papua and New Guinea for this information.

2. During the so-called Yali Movement of 1948; see Lawrence (1954; 1955; 1964).

3. My material on war ritual and sorcery was given entirely by informants. I have also indicated other statements drawn from the same source.

4. The Nankina-Mot section of the Rai Coast has no clay deposits. Pots have to be imported. Siasi beads are small shells pierced with holes so that they can be strung on thread. The trading system mentioned here once linked Siasi, Madang, the Rai Coast, the Huon Peninsula, and probably the coast north of Madang. Between Madang and the Rai Coast it is now largely defunct, the last exchange having taken place in 1953, although the network of relationships survives. I use the present tense when discussing the system (and also warfare) for reasons of consistency and space. For a somewhat fuller description of the trading system between Madang and the Rai Coast, see Lawrence (1964); and for references see Neuhauss (1911: *passim*) and Hannemann (n.d.a: 10 and n.d.b:4).

5. The terms "red" and "white" refer to the colours of the layers immediately beneath the outer rinds of the two types of taro.

6. In most cases, each modern Ngaing village consists of the inhabitants of a named bush area concentrated into a single settlement. For the beginning of this process, see Aufinger (1940–1941).

7. Except for the Pig and Betel-nut matriclans, whose members are said to have relaxed the taboos for obvious reasons.

8. Except of course, for the Pig and Betel-nut matriclans.

9. Translated as *masalai* in pidgin English.

10. Informants were quite unable to explain the significance of Parambik's name. They merely reiterated the vagueness of his identity, although they claimed that he was always somewhere within Ngaing territory. For this reason, and also because he is not given a separate designation by the people themselves, I class him as a deity (*tut*) rather than as a culture hero, as his present lack of interest in Ngaing affairs might suggest. In contrast, among the Sengam and Som, the primal god (Barnun and Balauau = myth)is far more positively conceived. He has an esoteric name, which is used in agricultural ritual.

11. Meanderi's distribution of "red" and "white" taro as described in the myth correlates exactly with their actual distribution in Ngaing territory today.

12. In contrast with other societies in Papua and New Guinea, in which women are not supposed to know that music emanates from sacred instruments. *Cf.* Read (1952a:6).

13. Hannemann (n.d.b:6–8 and 9–10) quotes separate origin myths for the Male Cult among the Sengam. Nowadays the Sengam invariably refer to Yabuling as the creator of the Male Cult. This may be due to losses from Sengam religion under mission influence.

14. Except in Sor and Paramus because of the distance of the sanctuaries of their war deities. In this area, materials for war ritual are taken from the bush. They include bark of a black palm said to have been made to grow by the war god of Saing, one of the creators of the bow and arrow.

15. In Maibang and Gabumi Meanderi's secret name is used; in Aiyawang, the secret name of the *wirijabi* creeper, which she is said to have planted there; and in Sibog, the secret name of her daughter, who is believed to have remained there on the return journey

16. During my fourteen months with the Ngaing I witnessed only one accusation of sorcery. In contrast, among the Garia of the Bagasin Area sorcery accusations were a regular occurrence.

17. I was unable to observe a celebration of the Harvest Festival. The following account, apart from the section on the washing of the trumpets at the sacred pools, was taken from informants.

18. In Gabumi, Maibang and Kilang, Yabuling's secret name is used; in Aiyawang, that of the *rombong* shrub, said to have been planted there by Yabuling. In Sor and Paramus, the people have no secret name for Yabuling but claim that the performance of the other ritual at the sacred pools will cause him to send up the spirits.

19. Owing to its close association with

the cargo movement during and after 1948; see Lawrence (1954; 1955; 1964).

20. I could not fully confirm this statement in the field. Men claim that women have the monopoly of methods of abortion. Women are unwilling to give away information. My informants, however, believed that the secrets were passed on to a girl just before marriage.

21. I was unable to witness an initiation ceremony. The following account was taken from informants.

22. For accounts of circumcision in the southern Madang District, see Aufinger (1941) and Bodrogi (1953).

23. This is typical of native parochialism in the southern Madang district. Garia and Ngaing were quite unable to accept differences between their two cultures, and even the Ngaing were unaware of the considerable variations in their own.

24. Men often complain that they are not allowed to rest from playing music in the cult house because the women are so keen to dance outside.

25. I have discussed this subject generally in Lawrence (1959; 1964).

26. This is especially true today. The temporary eclipse of the traditional religion between 1933–1948 left many patriclans without leaders or with leaders of very little status.

27. See Lawrence (1954:10–11), where similar concepts among the Garia are discussed.

28. In the same way, sympathetic magic unleashes forces which are essentially parts of the physical environment.

29. See Evans-Pritchard (1940:108) for a discussion of the same problem among the Nuer.

30. See Lawrence (1964).

Aufinger, A.
1940–1941 "Siedlungsform und Häuserbau an der Rai Küste Neu Guinea," *Anthropos,* 35–36.
1941 "Einige ethnographische Notizen zur Beschneidung in Neu Guinea," *Ethnos,* 6.

Bodrogi, T.
1953 "Some Notes on the Ethnography of New Guinea," *Acta ethnographica,* 3.

Evans-Pritchard, E. E.
1940 *The Nuer.* Oxford: Clarendon Press.

Hannemann, E. F.
n.d.a. "Village Life and Social Change in Madang Society" (mimeographed), Madang.
n.d.b. "Papuan Dances and Dancing" (mimeographed), Madang.

Lawrence, P.
1954 "Cargo Cult and Religious Beliefs Among the Garia," *International Archives of Ethnography,* 47.
1955 "The Madang District Cargo Cult," *South Pacific,* 8.
1959 "The Background to Educational Development in Papua and New Guinea," *South Pacific,* 10.
1964 *Road Belong Cargo.* London: Manchester University Press and Melbourne University Press.

Neuhauss, R.
1911 *Deutsch Neu-Guinea,* Vol. I. Berlin: Reimer.

Read, K. E.
1952 "Nama Cult of the Central Highlands, New Guinea," *Oceania,* 23.

Chapter 23. The Analysis of *Mana:* An Empirical Approach

1. Handy, *Polynesian Religion,* 28; J. H. Driberg, "The Secular Aspect of Ancestor Worship in Africa," *Journal of the Royal African Society,* 35:4, 8, 1936.

Driberg likens *mana* to "an abstract Power of natural potency, formless as ether. . . . It has been likened in its manifestations to electricity (though perhaps radium would provide a better analogy). . . ." "Like radium it gives out energy indefinitely without diminishing its own extent or potency, and each spark is capable no less of infinite subdivision without loss of potency." This sounds like a denial of the second law of thermodynamics, but even if the proposition could be defended by modern physics I doubt if it very much helps us to appreciate the meaning of *mana*.

2. H. Ian Hogbin, *Oceania,* 6:265.

3. H. Hubert and M. Mauss, "Théorie générale de la Magie," *L'Année Sociologique,* 1902–1903, 108 *et seq*. Their otherwise excellent analysis is, however, obscured by a mystical element which they bring into it, thus:

"L'idée de mana est une de ces idées troublés, dont nous croyons être débarrassés, et que, par conséquent, nous avons peine à concevoir. Elle est obscure et vague et pourtant d'un emploi étrangement déterminé. Elle est abstraite et générale et pourtant pleine de concret. Sa nature primitive, c'est à dire complexe et confusé, nous interdit d'en faire une analyse logique; nous devons nous contenter de la décrire. . . ." (p. 109); and again:

"L'idée de mana se composé d'une série d'idées instables qui se confondent les unes dans les autres. Il est tour à tour et à la fois qualité, substance et activité." The confusion and instability, however, seem to be the result of the anthropologists' analysis rather than a property of the native idea; indeed as this article will show, the concept in Tikopia at least is entirely nonmystical, has always a concrete referent, and is quite capable of being handled in a nonintellectual way. The complexity of the concept begins to arise only when anthropologists insist that mana—"c'est également une sorte d'éther, impondérable, communicable, et qui se répond de lui-même" (*op. cit.,* p. 112).

4. Mana Again, *Man,* 1922, 79. It may be remarked that such attempts at recovery of the "original notion" from which others have been derived rests implicitly upon a projection of a sequence in the mind of the analyst into the phenomena analyzed. This sequence may or may not have been followed historically.

5. "The Word Mana: A Linguistic Study," *Oceania,* 9:89–96, 1938.

6. *The Threshold of Religion,* 2nd ed., 1914, pp. xxiii–xxvii, xxxi *et passim.*

7. In *General Anthropology,* F. Boas, ed., 1938, p. 630.

8. "Magic Science and Religion," in *Science, Religion and Reality,* J. A. Needham, ed., 1926, pp. 72–73.

9. Marett, *Threshold,* p. 99; Hocart, *Progress of Man,* p. 185.

10. W. Williams, *Dictionary of the New Zealand Language,* Paihia, 1844, where it is translated as "power, influence." A later edition by Bishop H. W. Williams (1917) gives "authority, control, influence, prestige, power, psychic force," and verbally "to take effect"; the causative *whakamana,* "to give effect to, to give prestige to."

11. For example, see W. E. Gudgeon, "Mana Tangata," *Journal of Polynesian Society,* 14:49–66, 1905.

12. Lehmann, *Mana,* Leipzig, 1922; Handy, *Polynesian Religion,* 1927, pp. 26–34. Some pertinent observations are also given in R. W. Williamson's "Religion and Social Organisation in Central Polynesia," edited by R. Piddington, p. 110.

13 Note . . . ". . . if it exists"; Hogbin's material from Ontong Java and Wogeo suggests that the *mana-* concept is far from being common to the whole of Oceania, and hence he questions the validity of attempting to build up any general theory of primitive religion on concepts of the *mana* type (*Oceania,* 6:274).

14. See my *We, the Tikopia* and *Primitive Polynesian Economy, passim.*

15. See my *Work of the Gods in Tikopia,* Vol. 2, London School of Economics Monographs in Social Anthropology, No. 2, 1940.

16. The translation given by Bishop Williams (*Maori Dictionary*) "to take effect" appears to be an appropriate one; his *whakamana* is also apt.

17. My recent research in Kelantan, Unfederated Malay States, has shown that a very similar factual definition can be given to the Malay word *keramat,* translated by R. J. Wilkinson as "saintly; working miracles . . ." (*A Malay-English Dictionary,* Mytilene, 1932). That it also can bear meaning akin to *mana* is shown from the remark of a Malay friend of mine to me: "I think Tuan must be *keramat*—Tuan said, 'Tomorrow you will get fish'; and I did."

Chapter 24. Social Status, Political Power, and Native Responses to European Influence in Oceania

1. Except when quoting the words of others, in the present paper I have deliberately used the more general concepts of "ethnic stratification" and "status groups" rather than the more specific term *caste* with reference both to indigenous social structures and to colonial societies. This is done here to avoid immediate involvement in the controversies among Indianists, American sociologists, and others over the use of the caste concept, controversies which do not seem particularly germane to the principle problems of the present discussion. Nevertheless, some readers may be interested in the issues involved here.

The term *caste* has been applied to indigenous social stratification in Polynesia and Micronesia, somewhat loosely and impressionistically by Oliver (1961) and more elaborately by Hocart (1950). Oliver also uses the concept of caste rather informally in describing the colonial systems of the Pacific in general. Reed (1943:243–252) applied the term to modern Australian New Guinea in an extended discussion, and I have argued at length elsewhere that the ethnic hierarchy of contemporary New Guinea shows many structural and functional analogies to the classical caste structure described by Indianist scholars (Valentine 1958:254 ff.). Authorities on the Indian system include Ghurye (1950), Hutton (1946), and Srinivas (1957), some of whom, notably Hutton (pp. 133–147), take the position that the special term should be applied only to the Indian institution. Many anthropologists have applied the term much more broadly around the world, e.g., Rivers (1924), Linton (1936), Lowie (1948), Coon (1948). One school of thought within American sociology regularly applies the concept to race relations in American society (e.g., Dollard 1937; Warner 1936; Warner and Davis 1939; Wagley and Harris 1958), while another group opposes this usage (e.g., Berry 1951; Simpson and Yinger 1953; Frazier 1957; Cox 1945, 1948). The discussion has recently been continued through the republication in translation of a classical analysis (Bougle 1958) and in contributions by contemporary Indianists (Berreman 1960; Dumont and Pocock 1958a, 1958b; Dumont 1961).

Somewhat similar questions could be raised as to the use of the term *class* in reference to status groups in precontact Oceania.

2. Since these lines were written, a statement of United States government policy has been issued in the form of a speech by an Assistant Secretary of State. According to the *New York Times* (Western Edition, 30 March, 1963), this official stated that "from time to time groups of islanders have expressed an interest in becoming permanently associated with the United States." It was suggested by the Assistant Secretary that this was indeed a possible future for the American islands in Micronesia. At the same time, however, he is also quoted as saying that these ideas are "premature" at present, and that the islanders should exercise their "right of self-determination" after they have "acquired a first-hand knowledge of both the benefits and the responsibilities of 20th-century civilization."

3. Head tax for natives was abolished after 1945 until 1958, when it was reintroduced for natives not paying taxes direct to their Native Local Government Councils. These Councils use taxes levied for native development projects in their own areas. (R. M. Berndt.)

4. Sketchy press reports available in the United States indicate that, beginning in 1962, European opinion in New Guinea was considering the possibility that the Territory might gain some form of independence under an elected Melanesian-dominated government within a matter of years rather than decades. This evidently coincided with an increase in official Australian expenditures for development of the Territory, particularly in the matter of native education. The editor of this journal [*Anthropological Forum*] informs

me that public announcements by the Minister for Territories within the last few months suggest that self-determination for the peoples of Papua and New Guinea is now officially anticipated much earlier than the statements quoted above would indicate. It may well be that the pressure of events both internal and external to the Territory is rapidly creating a situation which few would have predicted even a year or two ago.

5. Although typological problems are not a matter of primary concern in this paper, the definition of a movement type here prompts a reference to related typologies in the literature. These have recently been carefully reviewed by Fogelson (1962). The classification proposed here is a result of what Fogelson calls "a limited comparative approach," which seems appropriate since my purpose is a comparison of different areas within Oceania. The category which I have described corresponds to the class which Fogelson labels "partial-assimilative movements," and which he distinguishes from both "contra-assimilative" and "pro-assimilative movements." This type is defined by Fogelson (p. 50) in the following words: "These movements contain a mixture of both native and white elements. There is partial acceptance and rejection of segments of both cultures. In Melanesia this type corresponds to the typical cargo cults. It is comparable to what have been termed syncretistic or vitalistic movements in other parts of the world. . . ." Particularly since I have used the term *assimilation* in another sense, which seems to me closer to its normal usage, I would prefer to call these movements "partially acculturative" rather than "partial-assimilative." Rephrasing Fogelson's classification, then, I am proposing that there is an Oceanic variant of the partially acculturative type which includes both cargo cults and a few Polynesian movements.

The defining characteristics which I ascribe to this type have all been employed by other students of social movements. The concept of syncretism, together with the closely related notion of cultural reinterpretation, was elaborated years ago by Herskovits (1937) and has more recently been reapplied by Smith (1959), Voget (1959), and Köbben (1960), among others. The distinction between acculturative and contra-acculturative movements was also made explicit at a rather early stage by Herskovits (1948:531–532) and has likewise been employed, in somewhat varying terminology, by later students including those just cited, as well as Stanner (1953), Wallace (1956), Inglis (1957), Worsley (1957), Ames (1957), Adelman (1960), and Newman (1961). The roles of prophets in many kinds of movements have been given attention by most of these authorities, particularly Wallace (1956), Worsley (1957), Burridge (1960), and Schwartz (1962). The element of millenarian faith has also received much attention, again particularly from the last series of writers cited. Freeman (1959) has also identified the four elements which I emphasize here, albeit in somewhat different terms from mine, as being common to cargo cults and the Siovili movement in Samoa.

Assuming that Fogelson's typology represents a continuum rather than a set of perfectly discrete units, his scheme can also be paraphrased to cover the other kinds of movements dealt with here. In order to do this, however, the secular-religious continuum which has been more or less explicit in the preceding discussion must also be taken into account. The predominantly religious contra-acculturative movements of Oceania would then include Hauhau and the Hawaiian revival in Polynesia, together with such Melanesian developments as the Milne Bay movement, the Taro cult, and the Baigona cult. Because of its many Christian-derived elements, Hauhau would have to be placed on the continuum closer to the intermediate partial-acculturative type than the other examples just cited, in spite of the anti-assimilation Hauhau attitudes. Religious pro-acculturative moments would take in the normal process of conversion wherever it is relatively smooth and undisturbed, as well as the formation of native churches which are not very markedly heterodox or anti-European, as in Tonga. In the secular realm, the category of contra-acculturative reactions would presumably apply principally to military resistance or avoidance of Europeans early in the contact process wherever it has occurred in the Pacific. Partial-acculturative secular movements are the native kingdoms of Polynesia (with Tonga closest to the pro-acculturative type), the nationalism exemplified by the Samoan Mau, and the Maori King movement. Secular pro-acculturative developments in Micronesia and Polynesia would be exemplified by Guamanian, Hawaiian, and Maori participation in American and British institutions including citizenship, in Melanesia by the Paliau and Tommy Kabu movements, with Masinga rule in the same category but probably somewhat closer to the partially acculturative type.

Abel, Charles W.
1902 *Savage Life in New Guinea.* London: London Missionary Society.
Adams, Romanzo
1937 *Interracial Marriage in Hawaii.* New York: Macmillan.
Adelman, Fred
1960 *Kalmyk Cultural Renewal.* Unpublished Ph.D. dissertation, University of Pennsylvania.
Allen, C. H.
1951 "Marching Rule: A Nativistic Cult of the British Solomon Islands," *Corona,* 3:93–100.
Ames, M. M.
1957 "Reactions to Stress: A Comparative Study of Nativism," *Davidson Journal of Anthropology,* 3:17–30.
Australia, Governor General (later Prime Minister's Department)
1921–1939 Reports to the League of Nations on the Administration of the Territory of New Guinea. Melbourne (later Canberra): Government Printer.
Australia, Department of External Territories (later Department of Territories)
1947–1955 Reports to the General Assembly of the United Nations on the Administration of the Territory of New Guinea. Canberra: Government Printer.
Australian Institute of Political Science
1958 *New Guinea and Australia.* Sydney: Angus and Robertson.
Beaglehole, Ernest and Pearl
1946 *Some Modern Maoris.* Wellington: Whitcombe and Tombs, for New Zealand Council for Educational Research.
Belshaw, Cyril S.
1950a *Island Administration in the South West Pacific.* London: Royal Institute of International Affairs.
1950b "The Significance of Modern Cults in Melanesian Development," *Australian Outlook,* 4:116–125.
1951 "Recent History of Mekeo Society," *Oceania,* 22:1–23.
1954 *Changing Melanesia: Social Economics of Culture Contact.* Melbourne: Oxford University Press.
Berndt, Ronald M.
1952–1953 "A Cargo Movement in the Eastern Central Highlands of New Guinea," *Oceania,* 23:40–65, 137–158, 202–234.
Berreman, Gerald D.
1960 "Caste in India and the United States," *American Journal of Sociology,* 66:120–127.
Berry, Brewton
1951 *Race Relations.* New York: Houghton-Mifflin.
Bougle, C.
1958 "The Essence and Reality of the Caste System," *Contributions to Indian Sociology,* 2:7–30.
Brown, George
1908 *George Brown, D.O., Pioneer-Missionary and Explorer: An Autobiography.* London: Hodder and Stoughton.
Brewster, A. B.
1922 *The Hill Tribes of Fiji.* London: Seeley.
Buck, Peter H.
1938–1939 *Vikings of the Sunrise.* New York: Stokes.
Burchett, Wilfred G.
1941 *Pacific Treasure Island: New Caledonia.* Melbourne: Cheshire.
Burridge, Kenelm O. L.
1960 *Mambu: A Melanesian Millennium.* London: Methuen.

Capell, Arthur
1962 "Oceanic Linguistics Today," *Current Anthropology,* 3:371–428.

Chinnery, E. W. P., and A. C. Haddon
1917 "Five New Religious Cults in British New Guinea," *Hibbert Journal,* 15:448–463.

Codrington, R. H.
1891 *The Melanesians: Studies in Their Anthropology and Folklore.* Oxford: Clarendon.

Coon, Carleton S.
1948 *A Reader in General Anthropology.* New York: Holt.

Cox, Oliver C.
1945 "Race and Caste: A Distinction," *American Journal of Sociology,* 50: 306–308.
1948 *Caste, Class, and Race: A Study in Social Dynamics.* New York: Doubleday.

Cranswick, George H., and Ian Shevill
1949 *A New Deal in Papua.* Melbourne: Cheshire.

Crocombe, R. G.
1961 "A Modern Polynesian Cargo Cult," *Man,* 61:40–41.

Danks, Benjamin
1899 *A Brief History of the New Britain Mission.* Sydney: Methodist Missionary Society.

De Bruyn, J. V.
1949 "The Mansren Cult of Biak," *South Pacific,* 5:1–10.

Dollard, John
1937 *Caste and Class in a Southern Town.* New Haven, Conn.: Yale University Press.

Dumont, Louis
1961 "Caste, Racism, and Stratification: Reflections of a Social Anthropologist," *Contributions to Indian Sociology,* 5:20–43.

Dumont, Louis, and D. Pocock
1958a "Commented Summary of the First Part of Bougle's *Essais,*" *Contributions to Indian Sociology,* 2:31–44.
1958b "A. M. Hocart On Caste—Religion and Power," *Contributions to Indian Sociology,* 2:46–63.

Ember, Melvin
1962 "Political Authority and the Structure of Kinship in Aboriginal Samoa," *American Anthropologist,* 64:964–971.

Firth, Raymond
1959 *Economics of the New Zealand Maori* (rev. ed.). Wellington, New Zealand: Government Printer.

Fogelson, Raymond D.
1962 "Recent Issues in the Study of Social Movements." Unpublished ms.

Fortes, Meyer, and E. E. Evans-Pritchard, eds.
1940 *African Political Systems.* London: Oxford University Press.

Frazier, E. Franklin
1957 *Race and Culture Contacts in the Modern World.* New York: Knopf.

Freeman, J. D.
1959 "The Joe Gimlet or Siovili Cult: An Episode in the Religious History of Early Samoa," in Freeman and Geddes, eds. (1959).

Freeman, J. D., and W. R. Geddes, eds.
1959 *Anthropology in the South Seas.* New Plymouth: Avery Press.

Furnas, J. C.
1946 *Anatomy of Paradise: Hawaii and the Islands of the South Seas.* New York: Sloane.

Ghurye, G. S.
1950 *Caste and Class in India.* Bombay: Popular Book Depot.

Gilbert and Ellice Islands Colony
1930 Annual Report on the Social and Economic Progress of the People of the Gilbert and Ellice Island Colony, 1929–1930. London: H. M. Stationery Office.

Goodenough, Ward H.
1961 "Migrations Implied by Relationships of New Britain Dialects to Central Pacific Languages," *Journal of the Polynesian Society,* 70:112–136.

Grace, George
1961 "Austronesian Linguistics and Culture History," *American Anthropologist,* 63:359–368.

Grimble, Sir Arthur
1952 *We Chose the Islands: A Six-Year Adventure in the Gilberts.* New York: Morrow.

Guiart, Jean
1951 "Forerunners of Melanesian Nationalism," *Oceania,* 22:81–90.

1956 "Un siècle et demi de contacts culturels à Tanna, Nouvelles-Hébrides," *Publications de la Société des océanistes,* 5.

Guiart, Jean, and Peter Worsley
1958 "La repartition des mouvements millenaristes en Mélanésie," *Archives de sociologie des réligions,* 71:209–243.

Gunson, Niel
1962 "An Account of the Mamaia or Visionary Heresy of Tahiti, 1826–1941," *Journal of the Polynesian Society,* 71:209–243.

Gunther, John T.
1958 "The People," in Australian Institute of Political Science, 1958.

Harre, John
1962 "A Case of Racial Discrimination in New Zealand," *Journal of the Polynesian Society,* 71:257–260.

Hasluck, Paul
1958 "Present Tasks and Policies," in *New Guinea and Australia,* Australian Institute of Political Science. Sydney: Angus and Robertson.

Herskovits, Melville J.
1937 "African Gods and Catholic Saints in New World Religious Belief," *American Anthropologist,* 39:635–643.
1948 *Man and His Works: The Science of Cultural Anthropology.* New York: Knopf.

Hocart, A. M.
1950 *Caste: A Comparative Study.* London: Methuen.

Hogbin, H. Ian
1935 "Native Culture of Wogeo," *Oceania,* 5:308–337.
1939 *Experiments in Civilisation: The Effects of European Culture on a Native Community of the Solomon Islands.* London: Routledge.
1951 *Transformation Scene: The Changing Culture of a New Guinea Village.* London: Routledge.
1958 *Social Change.* London: Watts.

Hooper, Antony
1961 "Cook Islanders in Auckland," *Journal of the Polynesian Society,* 70:147–193.

Hutton, J. H.
1946 *Caste in India: Its Nature, Functions, and Origins.* Bombay: Oxford University Press.

Inglis, Judy
1957 "Cargo Cults: The Problem of Explanation," *Oceania,* 27:249–263.

Inselmann, Rudolph
1944 *Letub: The Cult of the Secret of Wealth.* M.A. thesis, Hartford Seminary Foundation.

Kamma, F. C.
1954 *De Messiaanse Koreribewegingen in het Biaks-Noemfoorse Culturgebied.* The Hague: J. N. Boorhoeve.

Keesing, Felix M.
1934 *Modern Samoa.* London: Allen and Unwin.
1945 *The South Seas in the Modern World* (rev. ed.). Institute of Pacific Relations, International Research Series. New York: John Day.

Kerr, J. R.
1958 "The Political Future," in Australian Institute of Political Science.

Kobben, A. J. F.
1960 "Prophetic Movements as an Expression of Social Protest," *International Archives of Ethnography,* 49: 117–164.

Lawrence, Peter
1954 "Cargo Cult and Religious Beliefs Among the Garia," *International Archives of Ethnography,* 47:1–20.
1955 "The Madang District Cargo Cult," *South Pacific,* 8:6–13.

Legge, John D.
1956 *Australian Colonial Policy: A Survey of Native Administration and European Development in Papua.* Sydney: Angus and Robertson.
1958 *Britain in Fiji, 1858–1880.* London: Macmillan.

Linton, Ralph
1936 *The Study of Man: An Introduction.* New York and London: Appleton-Century.

Lowie, Robert H.
1948 *Social Organization.* New York: Rinehart.

Lommel, Andreas
1953 "Der 'Cargo-Kult' in Melanesian: ein Beitrag zum Problem der 'Europaiserung der Primitiven," *Zeitschrift für Ethnologie,* 78:17–63.

Luomala, Katherine
1951 "The Menehune of Polynesia and Other Mythical Little People of Oceania," Bernice P. Bishop Museum Bulletin 203, Honolulu.

Lynch, C. J.
1961 "A New Constitution for Papua and New Guinea," *Journal of the Polynesian Society,* 70:243–246.

McKay, C. G. R.
1962 "Western Samoa's Independence," *Journal of the Polynesian Society,* 71: 107–109.

Maher, Robert F.
1961 *New Men of Papua: A Study in Culture Change.* Madison: University of Wisconsin Press.

Mair, Lucy P.
1948 *Australia in New Guinea.* London: Christophers.
1962 *Primitive Government.* Baltimore: Penguin.

Malinowski, Bronislaw
1922 *Argonauts of the Western Pacific.* London: Routledge.
1935 *Coral Gardens and Their Magic.* London: Oxford University Press.

Mander, Linden A.
1954 *Some Dependent Peoples of the South Pacific.* Leiden: Brill.

Mead, Margaret
1930 *Growing up in New Guinea.* New York: Morrow.
1956 *New Lives for Old: Cultural Transformation—Manus, 1928–1953.* New York: Morrow.

Middleton, John, and David Tait, eds.
1958 *Tribes Without Rulers: Studies in African Segmentary Systems.* London: Routledge and Kegan Paul.

Monberg, Torben
1962 "Crisis and Mass Conversion on Rennell Island in 1938," *Journal of the Polynesian Society,* 71:145–150.

Morrell, W. P.
1960 *Britain in the Pacific Islands.* London: Oxford University Press.

Nevermann, Hans
1934 *Admiralitäts-Inseln.* Hamburg: de Gruyter.

Newman, Paul
1961 *Cargo Cults.* Unpublished M. A. thesis, University of Pennsylvania.

Official Handbook of the Territory of New Guinea
1937 Compiled under the authority of the Prime Minister. Canberra: Government Printer.

Oliver, Douglas L.
1961 *The Pacific Islands* (rev. ed.). New York: Doubleday (Anchor Book) and American Museum of Natural History.

Pearson, Bill
1962 "New Zealand Since the War: The Maori People," *Landfall,* 16:148–180.

Reed, Stephen W.
1943 *The Making of Modern New Guinea, with Special Reference to Culture Contact in the Mandated Territory.* Philadelphia: American Philosophical Society.

Rivers, W. H. R.
1924 *Social Organization.* New York: Knopf.

Robson, R. W.
1956 *Pacific Islands Yearbook* (7th ed.). Sydney: Pacific Publications.

Robson, R. W. (compiler)
1961 *Handbook of Papua and New Guinea* (3rd ed.), J. Tudor, ed. Sydney: Pacific Publications.

Rowley, Charles D.
1958 *Australians in German New Guinea, 1914–1921.* Melbourne: Melbourne University Press.

Sahlins, Marshall D.
1958 *Social Stratification in Polynesia.* Seattle: University of Washington Press.
1962 *Moala: Culture and Nature on a Fijian Island.* Ann Arbor: University of Michigan Press.

Salisbury, Richard F.
1958 "An 'Indigenous' New Guinea Cult," *Kroeber Anthropological Society Papers,* 18:67–78.

Scharmach, Bishop Leo
1953 *Manuale Missionariorum.* New Britain: Vunapope Catholic Mission.

Schwartz, Theodore
1962 *The Paliau Movement in the Admiralty Islands, 1946–1954.* New York: Anthropological Papers of the American Museum of Natural History, 49:207–422.

Simpson, George E., and J. Milton Yinger
1953 *Racial and Cultural Minorities.* New York: Harper.
Sinclair, Keith
1957 *The Origins of the Maori Wars.* Wellington: New Zealand University Press.
Smith, Marion J.
1959 "Towards a Classification of Cult Movements," *Man,* 59:8–12.
Srinivas, M. H.
1957 "Caste in Modern India," *Journal of Asian Studies,* 16:529–548.
Stanner, William E. H.
1953 *The South Seas in Transition: A Study of Post-War Rehabilitation and Reconstruction in Three British Pacific Dependencies.* Sydney: Australasian Publishing Co.
Suggs, Robert C.
1960 *The Island Civilizations of Polynesia.* New York: New American Library.
Sutherland, William
1910 "The Tuka Religion," *Transactions of the Fijian Society, 1908–1910,* pp. 51–57.
Valentine, Charles A.
1958 *An Introduction to the History of Changing Ways of Life on the Island of New Britain.* Unpublished Ph.D. dissertation, University of Pennsylvania.
1960 "Uses of ethnohistory in an Acculturation Study," *Ethnohistory,* 7: 1–27.
n.d. "The Lakalai," in *Melanesian Religious Systems,* M. Meggitt *et al.* (*to be published*).
Voget, Fred W.
1959 "Towards a Classification of Cult Movements: Some Further Contributions II," *Man,* 59:26–28.
Wagley, Charles, and Marvin Harris
1958 *Minorities in the New World: Six Case Studies.* New York: Columbia University Press.
Wallace, Anthony F. C.
1956 "Revitalization Movements," *American Anthropologist,* 58:264–281.
Warner, W. Lloyd
1936 "American Class and Caste," *American Journal of Sociology,* 42: 234–237.
Warner, W. Lloyd, and Allison Davis
1939 "A Comparative Study of American Caste," in *Race Relations and the Race Problem,* Thompson, E. T. ed., Durham, N.C.: Duke University Press.
West, Francis J.
1961 *Political Advancement in the South Pacific: A Comparative Study of Colonial Practice in Fiji, Tahiti and American Samoa.* Melbourne: Oxford University Press.
Williams, F. E.
1923 "The Vailala Madness and the Destruction of Native Ceremonies in the Gulf Division," *Papuan Anthropology Report,* 4, Port Moresby.
1928 *Orokaiva Magic.* London: Oxford University Press.
1934 "The Vailala Madness in Retrospect," in *Essays Presented to C. G. Seligman,* Evans-Pritchard, E. E., ed., London: Kegan-Paul.
Williamson, Robert W.
1924 *The Social and Political Systems of Central Polynesia.* Cambridge: Cambridge University Press.
Winks, Robin W.
1953 "The Doctrine of Hau-hauism," *Journal of the Polynesian Society,* 62:199–236.
Worsley, Peter
1957 *The Trumpet Shall Sound: A Study of 'Cargo' Cults in Melanesia.* London: MacGibbon and Kee.

Chapter 25. Steel Axes for Stone-Age Australians

1. An account of this expedition from Amboina is given in R. Logan Jack, *Northmost Australia* (2 vols.), London, 1921, Vol. 1, pp. 18–57.

2. R. Logan Jack, *op. cit.,* pp. 298–335.

3. The best, although highly concentrated, summaries of totemism among the Yir Yoront and other tribes of north

Queensland will be found in R. Lauriston Sharp, "Tribes and Totemism in Northeast Australia," *Oceania,* 8:254–275; 439–461, 1939 (especially pp. 268–275); also "Notes on Northeast Australian Totemism," in *Papers of the Peabody Museum of American Archaeology and Ethnology,* Vol. 20, *Studies in the Anthropology of Oceania and Asia,* Cambridge, 1943, pp. 66–71.

Chapter 26. The Millenarian Aspect of Conversion to Christianity in the South Pacific

Armstrong, E. S.
1900 *The History of the Melanesian Mission,* London.

Beaglehole, E.
1957 *Social Change in the South Pacific: Rarotonga and Aitutaki.* New York.

Brainne, Ch.
1854 *La Nouvelle Calédonie. Voyages, missions, moeurs, colonisation,* t. I. Paris.

Guiart, J.
1958 "Espiritu Santo, Nouvelles Hébrides," *L'Homme, cahiers d'ethnologie, de géographie et de Linguistique,* NS No. 2, Paris.
1955 "Maurice Leenhardt, missionaire et sociologue," *Le monde non chrétien,* NS, 33:52–71. Paris.
1959 "Naissance et avortement d'un messianisme. Colonisation et décolonisation en Nouvelle Calédonie," *Archives de sociologie des réligions,* 7:3–44.
1958 "L'Océanie. Histoire universelle," *Encyclopedie de la Pléiade, III: 1747–1799.* Paris.
1956 "Un siècle et demi de contacts culturels à Tanna, Nouvelles Hébrides," *Publications de la Société des Océanistes,* 5. Paris.

Hanneman, E. F.
1948 "Le culte de cargo en Nouvelle Guineé," *Le monde non chrétien,* NS, 8:937–962, Paris.

Inselmann, R.
1948 *Changing Missionary Methods in Lutheran Missions in New Guinea.* Thesis submitted in partial fulfillment of the requirements for the degree of Bachelor of Divinity, Wartburg Seminary, Dubuque, Iowa (mimeographed).
1944 *Letub, the Cult of the Secrets of Wealth.* Thesis submitted in candidacy for the degree of Master of Arts, Faculty of the Kennedy School of Missions, Hartford Seminary Foundation (mimeographed).

Leenhardt, M.
1953 *De la mort à la vie. L'Evangile en Nouvelle Caledonie,* Paris.
1953 "Kapéa," *Le monde non chrétien,* NS, 25:77–91, Paris.

Leenhardt, M., and J. Guiart.
1958 "Notes de sociologie réligieuse sur la région de Canala (Nouvelle Calédonie)," *Cahiers internationaux de sociologie,* NS, 24:18–33, Paris.

Leenhardt, R. H.
1957 *Au vent de la Grande Terre.* Paris.
1953 "La première mission en Nouvelle Calédonie, d'après le journal de Taunga," *Le monde non chrétien,* NS, 28:430–443, Paris.

Murray, A. W.
1874 *Wonders in the Western Isles, Being a Narrative of the Commencement and Progress of Mission Work in Western Polynesia.* London.

Parsonson, G. S.
1956 "La mission presbytérienne des Nouvelles Hébrides. Son histoire et son rôle politique et social," *Journal de la Société des Océanistes,* T. XII; 12:107–137.

Paton, Frank H. L.
1903 *Lomai of Lenakel. A Hero of the New Hebrides. A Fresh Chapter in the Triumph of the Gospel.* London.

Watt, Agnes C. P.
1896 *Twenty-Five Years of Mission Life on Tanna, New Hebrides.* London.

Williams, Th., and J. Calvert
1859 *Fiji and the Fijians.* New York.

Chapter 27. Port Town and Hinterland in the Pacific Islands

Beaglehole, E.
1957 *Social Change in the South Pacific; Rarotonga and Aitutaki.* London: Allen and Unwin.

Belshaw, C. S.
1952 "Port Moresby Canoe Traders," *Oceania,* 23:26–39.
1954 *Changing Melanesia.* Melbourne: Oxford University Press.
1957 *The Great Village: The Economic and Social Welfare of Hanuabada, An Urban Community in Papua.* London: Routledge and Paul.

Bennett, J. M.
1957 "Vila and Santo: New Hebridean Towns," *Geographical Studies,* 4:116–128.

Davidson, J. W., and Jean Guiart
1959 "Research Project in Urbanization and Industrialization in the Pacific Islands," in *Social Development in the South Pacific.* Noumea: South Pacific Commission Technical Paper 122.

Danielsson, Bengt
1955 *Work and Life on Raroia.* Uppsala: Almquist and Wiksells.

Firth, R.
1953 "Social Changes in the Western Pacific," *Journal of the Royal Society of Arts,* 51:803–819.
1954 "Money, Work, and Social Change in Indo-Pacific Economic Systems," *International Social Science Bulletin,* 6:1–11.

Guiart, Jean
1957 *Tahiti, Nouvelle Calédonie, Nouvelle Hebrides.* Paris: Berger-Levrault.

Hogbin, H. I.
1951 *Transformation Scene: The Changing Culture of a New Guinea Village.* London: Routledge and Paul.

Keesing, Felix M.
1934 *Modern Samoa.* London: Allen and Unwin.
1941 *The South Seas in the Modern World.* New York: John Day.
1953 *Social Anthropology in Polynesia.* London: Oxford University Press.

Keesing, Felix M., and M. M. Keesing
1956 *Elite Communication in Samoa: A Study of Leadership.* Stanford, Calif.: Stanford University Press.

Mead, Margaret
1956 *New Lives for Old: Cultural Transformation—Manus, 1928–1953.* New York: Morrow.

Oliver, D. L.
1951 *The Pacific Islands.* Cambridge, Mass.: Harvard University Press.

Pirenne, Henri
1925 *Medieval Cities: Their Origins and the Revival of Trade.* Princeton, N.J.: Princeton University Press.

Stanner, W. E. H.
1953 *The South Seas in Transition: A Study of Post-War Rehabilitation and Reconstruction in Three British Pacific Dependencies.* Sydney: Australasian Publishing Company.

Weigend, G. C.
1958 "Some Elements in the Study of Port Geography," *Geographical Review,* 48:185–200.

NOTE: After this paper was submitted for publication, an important monograph on culture change in the Pacific appeared:

Force, Roland W.
1960 *Leadership and Culture Change in Palau.* Fieldiana: Anthropology 50, Chicago Natural History Museum.

Chapter 28. The Rights of Primitive Peoples

1. Morton H. Fried, "On the Concept of 'Tribe' and 'Tribal Society,'" *Transactions,* New York Academy of Sciences, Series II, 28:527–540.

2. This area constitutes the Territory of Papua-New Guinea, resulting from the administrative merger of Australian New Guinea (Papua) and the Australian Trust

Territory of New Guinea. The latter was established after World War I from the former German colony of Kaiser Wilhelmsland and the Bismarck Archipelago.

3. See the author's *New Lives for Old: Cultural Transformation, Manus, 1928–1953,* New York, Morrow, 1955.

4. Neo-Melanesian, a lingua franca based on Melanesian grammar and a predominantly English vocabulary, was the contact language in the Trust Territory; a little English—with a small smattering of Police Motuan—was that in old Papua. The interchange of Australian officials with different linguistic habits has been disruptive. The influx of New Guinea men and women as laborers into Port Moresby has resulted in the spread of Neo-Melanesian, and the recent ecumenical decision to issue an authorized Neo-Melanesian version of the *New Testament* has given it a new impetus. The United Nations missions, on the other hand, have discouraged its use. Another adverse factor is the increasing dominance of the people of the highlands, whose languages are non-Melanesian.

5. See Theodore Schwartz, *The Paliau Movement in the Admiralty Islands, 1946–1954,* Anthropological Papers of the American Museum of Natural History, New York, 1962, Vol. 49, pt. 2.

6. See F. J. West, "The New Guinea Question: An Australian View," *Foreign Affairs,* April 1961.

Index

Aboriginal Woman (Kaberry), 314
Aborigines, 40, 94–111, 139, 146, 152, 179, 203, 214, 262, 266, 268, 270, 282, 285–315, 340, 365, 369, 381–382, 385–395, 420, 423
Abortion, 296
Absolutism, 348
Abstinence, 64, 131
Acculturation, 373, 374, 382–384, 417, 423, 425
Accumulation of goods, 57, 59, 81, 218
Achievement, 426
Ad hoc law, 244
Adam, 274, 275
Adaptation, 81, 203, 384
Adat, 181
Addison, 277
Adjudicate law, 245, 248, 252, 253, 256, 258, 263, 309
Administration, 161, 286, 348, 349, 354, 357–358, 412–414
Admiralty Islands, 25, 160, 343, 378, 427
Adolescence, 126–128, 132, 300
Adoption, 9, 167, 168, 177, 182, 250
Adultery, 162, 163, 174, 307
Adzes, 42–44
Affinal relationships, 153, 161, 168, 170, 174, 177, 178, 181–186, 188–191, 195–198, 287, 288, 295, 298, 311
Africa, 10, 52, 61, 198, 242, 243, 270, 314, 341, 419, 420, 421
Age, 82, 152, 244, 251, 257, 314, 315, 341, 389–390, 393–394
Age of Enlightenment, 278
Aggression, 93, 163, 234, 235, 396
Agnatic relationships, 159, 161, 165, 167, 170, 174, 185–186, 311
Agnostics, 280
Agriculture, 8, 52–84, 99, 101–104, 114, 204, 211, 282, 289, 293–294, 299, 300, 313, 332, 351–353, 414, 416, 428
Aimol clan, 138
Aitape region, 374
Aitutaki Island, 417
Aiyawang cult, 290, 291, 292, 294
Akapana architecture, 37
Aku-Aku culture, 35–38
Aku-Aku (Heyerdahl), 35
Albert, 405
Alchemy, 276
Alienation, 354, 367, 425
All the Rivers Ran East, 35
Alliances, 207, 272
Alvarado, 32
Ambition, 57
American Anthropological Association, 47
American Anthropologist (Gladwin), 19
American Indians, 7, 30, 33, 35, 85, 317
Amun cult, 296, 297, 300
Anarchy, 108

Ancestry, 7, 31, 32, 167, 177, 205, 254, 271, 301, 317–318, 320, 321, 324, 325, 328, 332, 349, 375, 379, 380, 386, 390, 391, 415, 424, 428
Ancient Voyagers in the Pacific (Sharp), 13
Andalusia, 7
Aneityum Island, 45
Animals, 165, 257, 287, 301, 307, 313, 385
Animism, 271
Aniwa Island, 45
Annexation, 364, 422
Anthropology, 39–40, 47, 113, 116, 198, 201–265, 268, 269, 279, 282, 311, 317, 318, 329–330, 385, 386, 396, 397, 398, 409, 412, 414, 415, 416, 423
Anticolonial nationalism, 368
Anticolonialism, 427
Antineocolonialism, 427
Apia (town), 413
Apolosi cult, 381
Appearance, 131
Appellant, 262
Approval, 85, 88, 245
Arabs, 61, 276
Aramot tribe, 163–164, 174
Aranda tribe, 304–315
Arbitration, 252
Arca artifacts, 44
Archaeology, 1, 43–46
Architecture, 37
Argentina, 419
Argonauts of the Western Pacific (Malinowski), 47
Ariki Kafika, 118, 120, 123, 323
Ariki Tafua, 121, 322, 328, 329, 332
Ariki Taumako, 121, 329
Aristotelian science, 275, 276
Armies, 364, 403, 408
Arnold, 281
Arop Inlanders, 103
Art, 36, 52, 203, 308, 309, 313
Artifacts, 39, 43, 44–46, 52, 271, 282, 290, 301, 353, 387, 392, 395, 396, 429
Artists, 306, 308, 423
Arunta clan, 148, 304–315
Ascending generations, 151, 186, 292, 342
Asia, 10, 30, 31, 33, 39, 42, 46, 266, 268, 269, 270, 282–284, 344–347, 349–353, 358–359, 361, 412, 414, 419–421
Assault, 235, 239
Assemblage, 169–177, 212, 255
Assent, 313
Assimilation, 360, 368, 369, 383, 384, 395, 420, 421, 423, 425
Assisi cult, 374, 378
Astrology, 283, 284
Asylum, 428
Atam system, 101
Atheism, 279, 280
Athens, 102
Atlantic cultures, 6
Atlantis, 38
Atoll cultures, 8, 9, 11, 29, 246, 340, 365, 417
Attractiveness, 363
Augurs, 184
Australia, 39, 40, 43, 139, 144–158, 201, 203, 217, 222, 265, 266, 268, 270, 284, 286, 303–316, 349, 351, 352, 357–359, 374, 385–386, 395, 413, 418–423, 426–429
Australian New Guinea, 41, 203, 349–363, 381
Australian Trust Territory, 355, 357, 423, 426–428
Australoids, 40
Austro-Melanid race, 42–43
Austronesian Linguistics, 20–28, 40–42, 97
Authority, 78, 84, 194, 205, 210, 213, 214, 217, 238, 243, 244, 245, 253, 255, 256, 258, 261, 262, 264, 271, 313, 314, 317, 331, 337–384, 393, 408, 409, 422, 427, 429
Autocratic control, 81
Autonomy, 108, 181, 184, 194, 204, 213, 233, 234, 236, 256, 367, 368, 374, 383, 416, 423–425
Aviation, 414, 421
Axes, 42–44, 385–386

Bachelorhood, 131–138
Bacon, Roger, 310
Bad luck, 240
Baiame (hero), 309

Baigona movement, 374
Balade district, 402
Baleh region, 184
Bamboo, 65, 66, 69, 75
Bananas, 90–91, 286
Banks Island, 41, 45, 117, 408
Bantu language, 243
Baptism, 118, 219, 372, 404
Bargaining, 108
Barriers
economic, 120
man-made, 5, 7
of misrepresentation, 270
natural, 5, 8, 96–97
social, 120–121, 214, 216, 280, 315, 363
Barter, 105
Barthel, Dr. T., 36
Barton, 201
Barzun, Jacques, 270
Bascom, William R., 49, 85–93
Basketweaving, 52
Basque tribes, 420
Bass Strait, 9
Bastille Day, 280
Batari (prophet), 379
Batari cult, 379
Bates, 400
Bau-Malay tradition, 43
Beads, 386
Beaglehole, Ernest, 402, 409–410
Beauty, 308
Behavior 144, 149, 258, 299, 306, 312, 390–396, 425
Belgium, 90
Beliefs, 53–56, 265, 276, 285, 286, 289, 302, 318, 320, 325, 354, 370, 371, 379, 391, 405
Benedict, Ruth, 318
Bentley, Dr., 277
Bering Straits, 33
Bernice Bishop Museum, 36
Beru Island, 253–254
Betrayal, 307
Bible, The, 275, 376, 378
Bidding, 108
Big-man system, 86–89, 201, 203–214, 341, 342, 422
Bikini Atoll, 6
Bilateral descent, 147, 192, 198
Bilek family, 181–200
Bilibili Islanders, 95, 96
Bilingualism, 417
Birth, 129–131, 182, 226, 258, 282, 288, 295–299, 428
control of, 9, 10-11, 366
Bismarck Archipelago, 41, 203, 341, 342, 381
Black King movements, 374
Black men, 32, 40, 42–43, 304–315
Blades, 44
Blanqui, Jérome Adolphe, 280
Boats, 42
Body, 275, 305, 306, 331
Boiso, Sasine, 405–406
Bolivia, 37
Bonald, Louis Gabriel Amboise de, 281
Bonaventure, St., 274, 275, 276
Book of Revelation, The, 275, 402
Borneo, 41, 64, 114, 180–200, 317
Boston Mission, The, 400
Boswell, James, 279
Bosworth Field, 267
Botany, 2
Bouganville, Louis Antoine de, 26, 44, 343
Bourbon family, 280
Breadfruit, 86–90, 92, 93, 204, 320, 328
Bridewealth, 101, 102, 104, 106, 110, 169, 176, 179, 208, 224
British Newsletter, 45
British Solomon Islands Protectorate, 117, 245
Brotherhoods, 280
Brown, George, 376
Browne, Sir Thomas, 277
Buddhism, 282, 283
Buecher, C., 51–52, 62
Buka district, 374
Bullroarer cult, 290–295, 299
Buonarroti, 281
Burdick, Eugene, 284
Burial rites, 118, 219, 226, 288, 289, 292, 294, 299
Burma, 283, 419
Burns Philp vessels, 19
Bush cultures, 285–303, 385–396
Buzacott, 400, 402–403

Bwoitalu (village), 61
Byzantium, 276

Calvert, Rev., 410
Calvinism, 408
Canada, 30, 423
Canala district, 404, 405
Canoe trade, 96, 415
Canoes, 33, 56, 95, 98–100, 104, 110, 115, 116, 118, 167, 179, 184, 214, 322, 325–327, 394–395, 399, 406
Capell, A., 317
Capital punishment, 348
Capitalism, 417
Card playing, 428
Cargo cult, 268–273, 282, 283, 337, 364, 370, 373–380, 383, 397–411, 426–427
Caroline Islands, 61, 85, 232, 348, 367
Carolingian times, 414
Carruthers, 400
Carving, 61, 98, 102, 110, 286, 287, 295, 422
Cash cropping, 76, 164
Cassava, 83
Caste system, *see* Class system
Catechists, 422
Catholic Sacred Heart Mission, 247
Catholicism, 118, 221, 247, 260, 271, 274, 275, 280, 281, 286, 348, 361, 367, 402–404, 407
Cattle stations, 386, 387, 392, 396
Caucasians, 32, 36–37, 345, 346, 349, 355, 356, 367, 375, 385–387, 392–395, 398, 399, 404, 406, 407, 427
Cause-and-effect, 283
Celebes Island, 41, 42, 317
Celebrations, *see* Ceremonies; Feasts; Rituals
Celibacy, 64, 131
Central African Bantu region, 205
Central Asia, 205
Central Pacific, 28
Centralization, 97–98, 213, 338–340, 342, 344, 346, 360, 363–384
Ceremonies, 99–101, 105–106, 121, 126, 141, 159, 161, 165, 167, 207, 208, 211, 212, 214, 247, 286–288, 290–297, 299, 301, 313, 325, 326, 342, 344, 372, 387, 389, 393, 394
See also Feasts; Rituals
Chair and Rule movement, 374
Chamorros Indians, 24–25, 41, 360, 367
Change, 20–24, 181, 313, 335–429
Chiefdoms, 207–215, 364
Chiefs, 53, 56–60, 78, 80, 81, 84, 86–88, 91, 94, 117, 118, 121, 122, 204–205, 260, 314, 317, 319–321, 323–332, 339, 340, 342, 345, 348, 351, 360–365, 367, 368, 375, 380, 381, 409, 410
Child labor, 66, 82
Childbirth, *see* Birth
Childhood, 126–128, 140, 257
Children of the Sun, 38
Chimbu clan, 127, 142
China, 32, 42, 180, 205, 282, 312, 350–352, 359, 415, 419, 421
Chomskiam culture, 243
Christian Gaddang, 63, 64
Christianity, 117–119, 121, 272, 274, 276–280, 283, 303, 313, 365, 369–371, 373, 375–379, 381, 397–411, 420–422
Church, the, *see* Catholicism; Protestantism
Circular trading, 62
Circuses, 212
Citizenship, 314, 358, 367, 423, 428, 429
Civil administration, 348, 349
Civil law, 255, 258, 259
Civil religion, 279, 280, 281
Claims, 428
Clans, 88, 128, 130, 131, 138, 141, 143–158, 163, 169, 178, 197, 271, 307, 320, 331, 342, 367, 390, 391, 395, 396, 404, 405, 428
Class systems, 143–158, 197, 214, 311, 313, 338, 341, 345, 349, 350, 363, 364, 367, 400
Climate, 82, 155–156, 298, 417
Cloth, 303, 416
Clothing, 85, 115–116, 339, 399, 401, 409, 420, 428
Cloud Man (god), 291, 292, 294, 299
Club-houses, *see* Men's club-houses
Codes, 258, 259, 262

Codrington, 317, 318, 319, 416
Coercion, 217
Coffee, 414, 428
Co-gardeners, 171, 172
Cognatic relationships, 159, 170, 177, 178, 181, 184, 187–198, 204
Cognitive approach, 266, 279, 283, 384
Cogon grass, 64–67, 70, 73, 74, 76
Coitus interruptus, 10, 11
Coleridge, 281
Collaboration, 215
Collateral relationships, 186
Collecting cultures, 42, 165
Collective participation, 169
Colonialism, 13–19, 201, 248, 256, 258, 262–264, 268, 337–384, 403, 404, 407, 413, 419–429
Color, 359–360, 377, 378, 422, 424
Comfort, 399
Commerce, 7, 61, 85, 86, 92, 160, 164, 179, 268, 269, 344, 348, 349, 351, 356, 361, 364, 413
  See also Economy; Trade
Commodities, 85
Commoners, 274, 339
Communal labor, 54, 55, 59, 257, 339
Communication, 97, 214, 286, 299, 351, 390, 413, 416, 417
Communism, 428
Community cultures, 103, 177–178, 190–191, 425
Competition, 85–93, 101, 125, 178, 201, 203–214, 342, 403, 414
Composing, 159, 226
Composting, 128
Compromise relationships, 420, 429
Computer, 269, 270, 428
Comte, Auguste, 281–282
Condemnation, 235
Conduct, *see* Behavior
Confederations, 362
Conflict, 201, 312, 429
Confucianism, 282
Conical clan, 205, 210
Conjugal relationships, 183
Conquest, 422
Consanguine relationships, 153, 177, 183, 186, 249, 250
Conservatism, 280, 362, 365, 368, 369, 384
Constitutions, 159, 346, 348, 364, 368
Construction, 65, 215, 283, 409, 410
Consumption of goods, 62, 78, 85, 86, 165, 167, 208, 214, 294, 298, 339, 342, 345
Contact, 1, 2, 46, 286, 303, 360, 362, 364, 366, 372, 373, 375, 376, 377, 382–383, 386, 400, 412, 419, 420, 426
Continuity, 182, 312, 314, 369
Contra-acculturative religion, 373–375, 378, 379
Contracts, 243, 245, 250, 251, 423
Control
  economic, 80, 81, 84
  political, 258, 375
  religious, 211, 298, 341
  social, 201–264
Conus artifacts, 44, 45
Conus millepunctatus, 57
Conversion, *see* Christianity
Convicts, 361
Cook, Captain James, 2, 13, 16, 402
Cook Islands, 8, 348, 364, 366, 369, 371, 372, 412, 417
Cooperation, 364–373
Cooperatives, 378–379
Copra, 86
Coral atolls, 203
Coral Islands, 245
Cordillera Central, 64
Corn, 76, 137
Corporal punishment, 354, 355
Corporate relationships, 113, 181–200, 207, 338
Corroboree, 310
Cosmetics, 230
Cosmic order, 301, 302
Cosmic time, 301
Cosmogony, 307
Cosmology, 307
Cosmos, creation of, 289–292, 293–297, 404
Costumes, 420
Councils, 241, 340, 354, 357, 358, 361, 378, 379, 427
Counsel, 162
Countercurrent, 30

Counter-giving, 56, 57, 60
Courts, 241–243, 246, 252, 254, 256, 258–262, 361, 409, 428
Courtship, 131–138
Cowboys, 386
Crafts, 9, 52, 99, 101, 212, 286, 313, 314, 339, 362, 422
Creation, the, 289–292, 293–297, 404
Credit unions, 417
Creed, 281
Crews, 171, 175
Criminal law, 245, 255, 259
Croatian Indians, 420
Crops, 42, 64, 70–71, 73–76, 78, 82, 83, 90, 103, 128, 162, 164, 165, 177, 181, 204, 286–287, 290, 294, 295, 298, 302, 320, 325, 330, 331
Cult-houses, 130, 287, 291, 295–297, 299
Cultigens, *see* Crops
Cultivation, 42, 44, 49, 63–77, 82, 160, 180, 181, 190, 287, 385, 404
  See also Gardening cultures
Cults, 127, 265, 268–272, 295, 317, 337, 370–378, 380, 381, 383, 396–411, 426–427
Culture, 1, 7, 20–28, 53–56, 95, 102, 109, 113, 125–143, 178, 181, 183, 184, 191, 203, 204, 213, 215, 233, 234, 236, 256, 265, 268–270, 282, 284, 285–303, 309–310, 335–429
Currents, 14, 19, 30
Customs, 39, 62, 120, 167, 242–244, 263, 286, 292, 304, 307, 308, 311, 313, 346, 361–363, 420–424, 428

Dam-building, 283
Dance, 59, 122, 123, 136, 137, 226, 271, 295–296, 299, 300, 314, 325, 404
Danielsson, 417
Darumulum (hero), 309
Darwin, Charles, 281
De facto grouping, 159
De Gaulle, Charles, 368
De jure leadership, 360
Death, 130, 139, 182, 193, 209, 233, 239, 240, 258, 288, 289, 295, 298, 331, 340, 395, 407, 408, 410
Death penalty, 348
Debts, 166, 172, 295
Decentralization, 213
Decisions, 245, 252, 255, 258, 261
Deductive thinking, 306–307
Defender, 223, 225, 226, 230, 231
Defense, 179, 427
Deism, 279
Deities, *see* Gods
Deliberate settlement theory, 14, 15–19
Demand, 102
Democracy, 205, 424, 426, 428
Demography, 10
Demons, 222, 227, 231
Demonstrable relationships, 170
Demonstrations, 275, 368
Dempwolff, 34
Dependency, 392
Depopulation, 366
Descartes, René, 277
Descent, 147, 148, 153, 156–157, 167, 177, 181, 183, 194, 205, 247, 287, 311, 338, 341, 344, 421
  See also Grouping
Destruction of property, 85
Development
  economic, 282, 423
  political, 423–428
  social, 337, 381, 383, 384
Devil worship, 377, 401
Dialects, 286, 324
Dictators, 215
Dictionaries, 243
Diet, 428
Differentiation of cultures, 5, 6, 7, 422
Diffusion, political, 341, 381
Dignity, 282
"Dionysian" Kwakiutl cult, 93
Direct rule, 360, 362, 375, 380, 382
Discrimination
  racial, 344–384, 421, 422, 427
  sexual, 162, 168, 192, 197, 289, 298, 315
  social, 120–121, 156, 214, 216, 280, 315, 363
Disease, 330, 387, 401, 410, 428
Disinheritance, 239
Disputes, 162, 163, 245, 252
Dissemination, 417

Distribution
  of class system, 153–154, 157
  economic, 49
  of food, 161, 167, 168
  of goods, 56, 57, 59, 78–85, 99, 100–102, 104–106, 125, 161, 165, 167, 168, 178, 201, 214, 245, 339–340, 344–345, 393, 414, 416
  of labor, 169–177
  See also Ceremonies
Divination, 229, 233, 234, 238, 275, 317, 403
Divine descent, 210
Divine monarchy, 364
Divine Will, 276
Divorce, 64, 129, 189
Dobuan tribe, 107
Dog-chases-iguana-up-a-tree-and-barks-at-him-all-night (man), 391
Dogma, 281
Domestic labor, 351, 352
Domesticated animals, 301, 313, 385
Dowry, 189
Drama, 307
Dreaming cult, 304–315
Dreams, 386, 406
Driberg, 317
Dualism, 309, 355, 358
Duels, 310
Dues, 208
Duff, Roger, 13, 18
Duns Scotus, 276
Durkheim, Émile, 272–273, 279, 281, 282, 317, 318
Dutch New Guinea, 24–26, 358, 359, 378, 380
Duties
  civil, 193, 245, 250, 258
  economic, 247
Dysentery, 402–403

Ear piercing, 193
Earth, the, 274
Easter Island, 30, 31, 35–36, 203
Ecclesiastical hierarchies, 274
Ecology, 39, 154, 158
Economics, 44, 47–111, 120, 130, 177, 184, 205–206, 208, 211, 213–215, 247, 250, 268, 271, 272, 274, 276, 283, 285, 286, 292, 298, 302, 312, 320, 331, 339, 342–345, 353, 357, 360, 362, 363, 368, 371, 374, 378–379, 385, 389, 409, 414, 419, 422–425
Economics of the New Zealand Maori (Firth), 47
"Economics of the Trobriand Islanders, The" (Malinowski), 47–48
Education, 268, 270, 297, 300, 354, 355, 356, 362, 378, 414, 417, 420–429
Efate Island, 25, 28, 41, 45
Egalitarianism, 84, 201, 203–214, 338, 340–344, 360, 381
Ego, 170, 171, 193, 195, 315
Egocentric kinship system, 144, 145, 156
Einstein, Albert, 38
Elections, 257, 357, 358, 361, 417, 428
Electoral roll, 364
Electricity, 317
Elementary Forms of the Religious Life, The (Durkheim), 273
Élites, 364, 375, 417, 422, 427, 429
Ellice Islands, 245, 262, 348, 366, 369, 370
Ellis, William, 30
Empathy, 305
Emperors, 274
Empirical method, 299, 302, 316–333
Employment, 144, 313, 339, 342, 345, 347, 350–352, 356, 360, 362, 388, 420, 422
Endogamy, 149, 151, 152, 177, 178, 191, 339, 342, 346, 349, 350
Enfranchisement, 252, 361, 368
Enga tribe, 127, 142
English language, 250, 330, 427
Enlightenment, 276
Enmity, 315
Enterprise, 338, 341, 361, 379, 413
Entrepreneurs, 345, 353, 417
Environment, 40, 49, 79, 81, 102, 282, 285–289, 298, 301, 302, 306, 309, 313, 388, 391, 392, 395, 396, 425
Epi Island, 25, 28, 41
Epidemics, 402–403, 410
Episcopal Church, 370
Epistemological system, 299, 302
Equality
  political, 271
  racial, 344–384, 421, 422, 427

Equality (*Continued*)
sexual, 162, 168, 192, 197, 289, 298, 315
social, 120–121, 156, 214, 216, 280, 315
Equity, 245, 258
Erromango Island, 45, 401
Eskimos, 193, 420
Espiritu Santo Island, 26, 402, 407, 408
Eternity, concept of, 277
Ethics, 424
Ethnic stratification, 64, 363–364, 375, 382, 383
Ethnobotany, 41–42
Ethnocentrism, 341, 353, 354, 358, 359, 424
Ethnography, 47–49, 113, 125, 127, 158, 169, 193, 243, 272
Ethnology, 2, 3, 39, 42–43, 51, 242, 317, 338, 414, 416
Etiquette, 117, 123, 167, 339, 354
Etruscans, 102
Europe, 31, 33, 42, 61, 104, 118, 119, 123, 161, 174, 205, 243, 248, 250, 268, 270, 272, 274–276, 281–284, 303, 306, 310, 311, 316, 318, 339, 342–345, 349–358, 360–365, 367–368, 370–377, 380, 382, 383, 385–387, 394, 395, 399, 408–410, 412–415, 419–423, 426, 427
Evangelism, 400, 410
Evil eye, 188
Evisceration, 387
Evolution
cultural, 5–12, 363
human, 6, 43–46, 203
political, 204, 213, 214
Excavations, 45
Exchange
of goods, 60–62, 94–111, 118–120, 160, 207, 288, 291, 294–297, 315, 387–389, 393, 422
spouse, 65
Executioners, 212
Executive posts, 352–353
Exicostatistics, 22
Exiles, 10, 19, 68, 189, 361
Exogamy, 150, 152, 154, 167–169, 178, 182, 188, 197, 236, 287, 288, 307, 409
Expansion, 104, 198, 213, 280, 366, 422, 424
of Christianity, 397–411
Expeditions, 181
Experiments, 312
Exporting of goods, 85, 101, 102, 179, 353, 414–416

Fear, 331
Feasts, 85–90, 92, 100, 104, 106, 110, 161, 162, 179, 207, 216, 218–219, 221, 222–231, 247, 310, 342, 404, 422, 428
Fees, 258
Females, *see* Women
Fertile Crescent civilizations, 203
Fertility
human, 141, 299, 302, 320, 325, 329–330
soil, 82
Fertilizer, 90
Feudalism, 275, 280, 364, 365, 367
Feuds, 161–164, 169, 175, 207, 217, 218, 348
Fiji Agricultural Department, 82
Fiji Island, 25, 28, 41, 43–46, 49, 78, 97, 152, 203–205, 342, 344, 359, 361–363, 374, 376, 380–382, 403, 408, 414, 416, 417
Fila Island, 45
Filo cult, 374, 378
Fines, 117, 189, 258, 408
Firth, Raymond, 47, 84, 115–124, 266, 316–333
Fishing, 52, 56, 75, 99, 100, 106, 121, 160, 161, 164, 165, 169, 175, 179, 211, 245, 257, 286, 287, 296, 298, 320–323, 325, 326, 330–332, 351, 385, 388, 394–395, 404, 406, 414, 415
Flogging, 408
Flores Island, 41
Flutes, 126
Food, 9–10, 39–42, 52, 57–59, 66, 81–83, 85, 92, 99, 100, 103, 105–106, 119, 130, 132–134, 155, 158, 161, 179, 207, 211, 221, 235, 257, 271, 288, 290, 294–296, 301, 310, 315, 320, 321, 330, 331, 339, 399, 415, 422
Forlong, 400
Formal leadership, 162, 163
Formalists, 48
Formosa Island, 42

Fosterage, 250
Foué Peninsula, 44
Founder principle, 6, 7
Fourier, Pierre, 281
France, 29, 31, 32, 270, 278, 280, 347–349, 359, 361, 365, 366, 368, 369, 412, 413
Franciscans, 275
Fratricide, 233, 234, 236, 237
Frederick the Great, 278
Free Church, 365, 370
Freedman, Michael P., 113–114, 159–179
Freedom, 275, 279
  sexual, 142
Freeman, Derek, 113–114, 180–200
French Revolution, 278, 280, 281
Friendliness, 197
Friendship economy, 64, 65, 96, 103, 105, 107, 108, 178, 429
Frum, John, 378, 409
Functionalism, 398
Funds, 211, 212, 427, 428
Funerals, 118, 219, 226, 288, 289, 292, 294
Furneaux Islands, 8
Furniture, 409
Futuna Island, 45
Future, concept of, 305, 306

Gab'me (god), 291
Gabumi cult, 294
Gahuku-Gama cult, 126
Galileo, 276
Games, 298, 415
Gardening cultures, 9, 53–59, 76, 81–83, 90, 99, 103, 104, 118, 125, 128, 138, 141, 160–162, 165, 166, 168, 174, 179, 225, 231, 269, 294–296, 300, 339, 342, 352, 355, 409, 421
Gathering cultures, 42, 44, 188, 388
Gatty, Harold, 13, 14
Genealogical relationships, 168–177, 187–189, 216, 233, 292, 338–339, 386
Generation levels, 145, 146, 151, 180–200, 292, 311, 342
Generosity, 162, 213
Geography, 1, 8, 47–49, 96–97, 101–103, 160, 413, 417
Geology, 1, 21, 388
Germany, 91, 92, 160, 163, 186, 268, 280, 286, 348, 352, 357, 367, 374, 377, 421, 424
Gerontocratic assembly, 255
Ghosts, 130–131, 222, 233–235, 237–240, 283, 306, 343, 390, 395
Gifts, 56–58, 60, 237, 238, 393, 401
Gilbert and Ellice Islands Colony, 262
Gilbert Islands, 6, 201, 242–264, 348, 369, 370
Gira cult, 285, 291
Gladwin, Thomas, 17, 19
Glasgow Foundry Boys' Religious Society, 401
Glossolalia, 399
God, 275–278, 303, 370, 401–403, 405, 406, 410
Goddesses, 403
Gods, 118, 264, 268, 271, 272, 285, 286, 288–295, 298–303, 312, 320–329, 332, 340, 365, 368, 372, 375, 380, 407, 410
Gold, 268, 276, 361
Goodenough, 201
Goodness, concept of, 308, 309
Goods
  accumulation of, 57, 59, 81, 218
  consumption of, 62, 78, 85, 86, 165, 167, 208, 214, 294, 298, 339, 342, 345
  distribution of, 56, 57, 59, 78–85, 99, 100–102, 104–106, 125, 161, 165, 167, 168, 178, 201, 214, 245, 339–340, 344–345, 393, 400, 414, 416
  exchange of, 60–62, 94–111, 118–120, 160, 207, 288, 291, 294–297, 315, 387–389, 393, 422
  exporting of, 85, 101, 102, 179, 353, 414–416, 424
  importing of, 7, 85, 99, 101, 102, 178, 245, 303, 374, 387, 414, 416
  production of, 51–56, 60, 62, 78–85, 96, 99–101, 103, 104, 159, 161, 165–167, 169, 178–179, 207, 209, 211, 212, 214, 242, 258, 261, 268, 271, 283, 288, 313, 331, 339, 351–353, 360, 361, 409, 413–416
  redistribution of, 98
Gordon, 401

Government
  absolute, 348
  autocratic, 81
  colonial, 13–19, 201, 248, 256, 258, 262–264, 268, 337–384, 403, 404, 407, 413, 419–429
  constitutional, 159, 346, 348, 364, 368
  democratic, 205, 424, 426, 428
  direct, 360, 362, 375, 380, 382
  imperial, 269, 270, 282, 308, 348, 364
  indirect, 78, 348, 357, 361, 362, 366, 367, 380–383
  military, 84, 103, 209, 212–215, 343, 352, 355, 357, 361, 364, 369, 380, 403, 408
  monarchical, 274, 363–365
  parliamentary, 310
  proletarian, 214
  self-, 205
  state, 361, 368
  trusteeship, 355, 357, 423, 426–428
Grace, doctrine of, 309, 408
Grace, George W., 20–28
Graeco-Roman tradition, 274, 275
Grammars, 243
Granaries, 66
Grand houses, 212
Great Britain, 78, 201, 245, 255, 256, 258, 261, 262, 267, 269, 270, 273, 278, 280, 347–349, 352, 355, 365, 370, 380, 400, 408, 412, 413, 421
Greater Sunda Islands, 41
Greece, 102, 276
Greed, 307
Green Hell, 35
Greenland, 420
Group marriage, 147, 154
Grouping, 9, 11, 51–62, 78–84, 96, 101, 104, 105, 108, 113, 123, 130–131, 144–148, 159, 161, 167, 169–171, 174, 175, 177, 179, 181, 185–188, 190–200, 203, 204, 212, 213, 220–221, 224, 232–241, 247, 249–251, 263, 273, 282, 286–289, 291, 296, 298, 299, 307, 311, 338, 340, 345, 349, 361, 375, 389–390, 393, 409
  See also types of
Guadalcanal, 26
Guam Island, 348, 367–369
Guiart, Jean, 397–411, 412
Guns, 387
Guya'u, 53
Gypsies, 420

Haggling, 108
Hamlet (Shakespeare), 283
Hand-money, 223
Handy, E. S. C., 317, 318
Hanneman, E. F., 398
Hanselmann, Rev. R., 399
Harding, 49
Harp of Burma, The (film), 283–284
Harrassment, 261
Harvest Festival, 295
Harvesting, 90
Hauhau religion, 366, 369, 372, 383
Hawaii, 14–19, 30, 203, 205, 212–214, 339, 340, 347, 364, 366, 383, 400, 412
Hawaiian Antiquities (Malo), 211–212
Headhunting, 181, 184–185, 421, 422
Head-to-the-East Corpse clan, 395
Health, 193, 257, 299, 320, 330, 423, 424, 428
Heathenism, 118, 121, 397, 401, 405, 406, 408, 420, 421
Heaven, 274, 309
Hegemony, 348
Heirlooms, 166, 181, 218
Hell, 274, 309
Hell fire, doctrine of, 401
Henriade (Voltaire), 278
Henry, Teuira, 16
Henry IV, King, 278
Hereditary authority, 422
Heroes, 308, 309
Hesperonesian-speakers, 41
Heterodox millenarian cults, 275
Heterogeneity, 286, 340
Heyerdahl, Thor, 3, 29–31, 33–37
Hierarchies, 9, 274, 340, 346, 353, 354, 358, 359, 377, 407, 409, 429
High-island cultures, 8, 9
Highland cultures, 43, 44, 113, 125–143, 159, 204, 216, 426
Hilder, Bret, 19
Hinduism, 282
Hinterland cultures, 412–418
Hispanic American cultures, 7

Historia de las Islas Philipinas (de Zuñiga), 30
History, 1, 20–28, 217, 268–270, 275, 282, 304, 307, 312, 381–383, 421, 424
Hobbes, Thomas, 314
Hobgoblins, 308
Hocart, A. M., 317, 319
Hoeing assemblage, 174
Hogan, 416
Hogans, 420
Hogbin, 201, 317, 416
Homeostasis, 315
Hortense, Queen, 403
Horticulture, *see* Gardening cultures
Hospitals, 257
Hostility, 81, 103, 107, 125–143, 163, 288, 402, 426
Hosts, 222–231
Houailou district, 406
Household economy, 56, 64, 81, 82, 85, 92, 160, 165–167, 177–179, 208, 215, 220, 244, 247–253, 255, 258, 263, 294, 298
Housing, 56, 65–66, 69–70, 75, 128–131, 140, 161, 179, 181, 214, 287, 339, 340, 388, 420, 428
Hubert, 317, 318
Huli tribe, 127
Humanism, 306, 312
Humanitarianism, 355, 423
Hunting, 43, 75, 128, 188, 282, 287, 293–295, 300, 309, 310, 385, 388, 422
Hunting-gathering cultures, 8
Hybridization, 40
Hymns, 281

Iban of Borneo, 114, 180–200
Idealism, 159, 427
Ideas, 7, 390, 391, 394–396, 415
Identity, *see* Stratification
Ideology, 338, 390, 391, 394, 395, 420, 424, 428
Igloos, 420
Ile des Pins, 43
Illnesses, 82, 233, 240, 294, 297, 319, 320, 322, 323, 324, 329, 330, 331, 387, 401, 410, 428
Immigration, 349, 426
Immorality, 238, 313
Immunity, 251, 252
Immutability, 277
Imperialism, 269, 270, 282, 308, 348, 364
Impersonal religious force, 317
Importing
of goods, 7, 85, 99, 101, 102, 178, 245, 303, 374, 387, 414, 416
of labor, 86
Inca empire, 37
Incest, 150, 188, 189, 232–241
Income, 69, 74–77, 315
Independence, 179, 181, 383, 385, 422, 423
India, 308, 419–421
Indians, 30, 32, 359, 362, 423, 424
Indigenous culture, *see* Culture
Indirect descent, 148
Indirect rule, 78, 348, 357, 361, 362, 366, 367, 380–383
Individual, 177, 215, 338, 340, 341, 396, 423–425
Individual relationships, 146, 164
Individualism, 360, 361
Indonesia, 41, 42, 52, 180, 317, 359, 420, 421
Industrial Evolution (Buecher), 51
Industrial Revolution, 282
Industry, 56, 162, 268, 280, 281, 349, 351, 352, 413, 423
Inferiority, 363, 383, 421, 426
Infidelity, 162
Inheritance, 165–166, 181, 182, 192, 193, 218, 250, 253, 288, 343
Initiation rites, 117, 118, 125–141, 288, 295–300, 307, 310, 320, 326, 389, 391, 393, 394
In-marriage, 198
Innovation, 373, 382, 384, 392
Inselmann, R., 398
Insights, 312
Institutions, 113
Insularity, 5–8, 9, 11, 198
Insult, 233, 234
Integration, 203, 340, 410
Intellectualism, 271, 272, 275–279, 284, 297, 299–303, 305, 307–310, 313, 325, 330, 395, 398
Interaction, 289
Interdependence, 99

Interference, 419–429
Intergroup relationships, 97, 103, 178, 205
Intermarriage, 96, 140, 152, 157, 169, 189, 190, 344, 421
International relationships, 268, 416
Internecine wars, 408
Interpersonal relationships, 113, 126, 133, 144, 210, 243, 388
Interracial relationships, 346–355
Intertribal relationships, 92, 146–147, 156, 163, 366
Intragrouping, 234, 236, 238–240
Intra-village relationships, 92, 104–105, 177
Ipili clan, 142
Ipso facto, 256
Ireland, 420
Iron Age, 43
Irridentism, 420
Irrigation, 9, 83, 212, 283
Islam, 282
Island Civilizations of Polynesia, The (Suggs), 14
Isle of Pines, 403
Isolationism, 5–8, 9–12, 40, 46, 111, 348, 385, 412, 416, 420–425, 429
Israel, 205
Italian Renaissance, 276

Japan, 43, 86, 88, 90, 91, 282–284, 286, 345, 349, 359, 367, 378, 379, 413
Jarawia (man), 408
Java, 44, 359
Jehovah, 366, 372, 380, 401, 410
Jesuits, 408
Jesus Christ, 275, 371, 377, 399, 402, 404, 405
Jews, 274, 309
Joachim of Fiore, 275
Job (man), 309
Jobs, *see* Employment; Labor
John, St., 402
John Frum movement, 374–375
Johnson, Dr. Samuel, 279
Joint operation, 166
Joking, 194, 196, 391
Journal of Taunga, 406
Joy, 275
Judges, 243, 258
Judgment, 332
Jugos, Mrs. Robert C., 31
Jurisprudence, *see* Law
Jury, 161, 183, 192–193, 243, 256, 259
Justice, 262, 263, 275, 346

Kaberry, Dr. Phyllis, 314
Kabu Ceremony, 295–296
Kadai culture, 41
Kaikai language, 115, 208
Kajang culture, 180
Kalinga, *see* Pagan Gaddang
Kamano clan, 126, 142
Kamehameha (conqueror), 364
Kapauku tribe, 207
Kapea (man), 406
Kapingamarang culture, 25
Kapone culture, 26
Kapuvai (woman), 372
Kapuvai cult, 371–373
Karakiua (man), 322–323
Karapenmun (god), 409
Karisi (chief), 328
Karkar Island, 378, 399
Kava ritual, 86, 90, 92, 118, 323, 325–329, 408
Kayan clan, 180
Kayasa ceremonies, 56, 59
Kelevi movement, 381
Kenyah clan, 180
Kerekere trading, 79–80
Kili Island, 6
Killing, 255, 307
Kingship, 274, 363, 364–365
Kinship grouping, *see* Grouping
Kiowa Rockshelter, 43
Kiriwina region, 60, 61
Kivung cult, 379
Knights, 274
Knowledge, 102, 265, 268, 271, 273, 275, 277, 282, 289, 299–302, 310, 311, 314, 421
Kodu (god) 405
Komba mountaineers, 105–107
Kombani trading, 172, 174
Kon-Tiki (raft), 29–30, 33
Kon-Tiki theory, 3, 29–38

Korobani (man), 405
Kovai tribe, 101, 104
Kuba tribe, 243
Kubu (man), 187
Kukuaik movement, 399
Kula ring, 62, 94, 99, 106–109
Kuma tribe, 127, 140–142
Kunukuntha (woman), 91
Kwameria region, 400
Kwato missions, 374
Kyaka clan, 127, 142

L. M. S. Missions, 400, 408
Labor, 51, 55–56, 64–69, 74, 86, 94, 105, 144, 268, 269, 313, 339, 342, 345, 347, 350–356, 360, 361, 362, 364, 379, 381, 388, 415, 416, 420, 422
  child, 66, 82
  communal, 54, 55, 59, 257, 339
  costs, 98
  distribution of, 169–177
  importing of, 86
  organization of, 51–56
  sexual discrimination and, 54, 82, 90, 164, 168, 171, 197, 227
Lae (town), 413
Lakalai tribe, 376, 378, 379
Lakemba district, 410
Lamennais, 281
Land, 69–70, 73–74, 181, 217, 250, 255, 258, 287, 315, 345, 359, 367, 403, 407, 422, 423, 428
  holding, 53, 69, 82, 86, 160, 166, 244, 250, 252, 262, 364, 367
  rights, 82, 166–168, 239, 362, 407
Land Dayaks, 180, 184
Landmarks, 68
Lands Court, 252, 258
Language, 1, 8, 20–28, 39–42, 97, 117, 146, 204, 243, 285, 304, 307, 316, 319, 323–324, 330, 331, 341, 374, 375, 379, 390, 413, 420, 423, 424, 426–429
Lapita culture, 43–45
Laterality, 177
Latin languages, 243
Lattice structure, 177–179
Lavachéry, 35
Law, 53, 62, 184–185, 242–283, 309, 346, 353, 358–360, 362, 365, 367, 402, 408, 409, 424, 428
  anthropology of, 201–264
Law Courts, 253
Law of Gravity, 277
Lawrence, Peter, 265, 267–303
Lawsuits, 259
Leadership, 162, 163, 205, 210, 216–231, 271, 289, 294, 300, 302, 314, 317, 342–344, 348, 357, 360, 361, 364–366, 371, 375, 379, 393, 394, 399, 417, 425, 427
League of Nations, 356–357
Learning, 300, 425, 426, 429
Leases, 251, 252
Lederer, 284
Leenhardt, Maurice, 403–407
Legislation, 242, 245, 248, 262, 365
  See also Law
Lehman, F. R., 318, 319
Lehmann, 317
Lenin, Nikolai, 280
Leonardo da Vinci, 276
Letub cargo cult, 374, 377, 398
Levity, 56, 59, 194
  See also Joking
Leywota plots, 54, 55
Liberty, 313
Life after death, 277, 289, 292–293
Life expectancy, 152
Lifou Island, 406, 410
Line houses, 221
Lineage, 113, 128, 161, 167–169, 205, 210, 233, 234, 235–241, 341
  See also types of
Linguistics, *see* Language
Linton, Ralph, 36
Liquor, 387
Literacy, 181, 407
Literature, 270, 307, 308, 318, 337, 373, 379, 380, 398, 401, 402, 412, 415, 416
Litigation, 107, 244, 260, 261
Livestock, 165, 257, 287
Living standards, 387
Local trade, 160
Locke, John, 277–278
Logic, 277, 284, 305, 308, 325
Logos, 305, 315

Lomwanyan group, 401
London Missionary Society, 348, 400, 406, 410
Long-house community, 181–200
Loohmae (man), 401
Lookouts, 66
Lösi district, 410
Louis XVI, King, 280
Love, 275, 282
Love magic, 294, 300
Lower Cook Islands, 8
Loyalty, 207, 208, 395
Loyalty Islands, 26, 28, 44, 403, 406, 410, 429
Luck, 240, 317
Lundsgaarde, Henry P., 201, 242–264
Lutheran Mission, 398
Lutherans, 286
Luveniwai cult, 380–381
Luxury, 214, 345

Machinery, 428
Madagascar, 41
Madang District, 268, 303, 378, 399
Mae Enga tribe, 127, 128–143
Magic, 53–56, 58, 59, 60, 62, 122, 128–132, 138, 166, 181, 193, 210, 226, 228, 237, 240, 266, 271, 294, 308, 317, 318, 342, 346, 404
Magistrates, 244, 245, 256, 257, 260, 261
Mairo, 323
Maistre, de, 281
Majuro Island, 417
Makura Island, 25, 45
Malais tribe, 163
Malaya, 20–28, 41, 42, 180, 283, 359
Maldive Islands, 5
Male co-gardeners, 172, 173
Male Cults, 124–143, 290, 291, 293, 295, 298
Malekula district, 402
Malice, 315
Malinowski, Bronislaw, 47, 48, 49, 51–62, 113
Malo, David, 211–212
Malos, 211
Mamaia heresy, 370, 371, 372
Mambu movement, 374, 377
Man, 211, 281, 290, 301, 302, 306, 307, 315, 330, 390
Mana concept, 210, 266, 316–333, 340
Mandak group, 169
Mandate period, 355, 356
Mandok tribe, 105, 160, 164, 168, 170–174, 177
Mangarevan tribe, 213
Manipulation, 80, 84, 298
Man-made barriers, 5
Manpower, 82, 423
Mansren cult, 337, 374, 380
Manu, 319–332
Manua district, 410
Manufacture, 44, 52, 97, 98, 99, 102, 161, 165, 206, 293, 299, 342, 345, 351, 352, 395, 413, 414, 416, 422
Manus Island, 160, 378, 382, 422
Maori tribe, 13, 121, 318, 339, 340, 347, 360, 366, 369, 420
Maré Island, 406, 407, 410
Marett, R. R., 317
Mariana Islands, 28, 348, 360, 367
Marifi Satan movement, 374
Marist fathers, 402, 408
Maritime trading, 96, 99, 102, 103, 160
Market economy, 96, 99, 338, 345, 352–354, 360
Markham Valley, 374
Marmoiton, Brother Blaise, 402
Maron, 161–163
Marquesas Islands, 30, 31, 32, 36, 213, 366
Marriage, 96, 117, 118, 126, 127, 128, 130, 131, 132–140, 141, 146, 147, 148, 150–152, 154, 157–158, 168, 169, 177, 178, 181, 182, 188–190, 193, 194, 196, 197–198, 208, 217, 247, 250, 258, 272, 287, 288, 289, 295, 296, 297, 298, 307, 311, 315, 339, 344, 346, 349, 350, 359–360, 409, 421, 422
  group, 147, 154
Marsden, Samuel, 400
Marshall Islands, 6, 348, 367, 413
Martinique Island, 32
Marx, Karl, 272–273, 280
Masculinity, 125–143, 165, 390
Masinga Rule, 383
Massim culture, 109

Materialism, 125, 271, 274, 398–400, 409, 416
Mathaia (evangelist), 406
Matriclan, 287, 288, 290, 297, 298, 299
Matrilineal relationships, 130–131, 170, 174, 217–222, 233, 236, 344
Mau government, 367, 368
Mauss, Marcel, 47, 317, 318
Mazzini, 281
Mead, Margaret, 416, 419–429
Meanderi (goddess), 290, 291, 292, 294, 299
Meaning, 307
Mediation, 252
Medicine, 221, 283, 332, 417
Mediterranean, 33
Mediums, 370, 371, 373
Medlpa tribe, 127, 142
Meggitt, M. J., 113, 125–143
Melanesia, 24–27, 39–47, 93–111, 113, 116, 117, 119, 125, 203–214, 314, 318, 337, 340–345, 349–384, 398, 407, 408, 412, 413, 415, 421
Melanua clan, 180
Melville, Hermann, 213
Mendi clan, 142
Men's club-houses, 100–101, 161, 167–175, 177, 178, 204, 207, 218–231
Menstruation, 127–130, 131, 138, 139, 291, 296, 298, 299
Merrymaking, 56, 59, 194
Meru clan, 138
Mesolithic period, 40
Messianism, 404
Mestizos, 367
Metals, 276, 313, 385–396, 421
Metaphysics, 310, 311, 325, 331
Methodists, 221, 348, 376, 410
Methodology, 243
Métraux, 35
Metternich, Klemens von, 280
Mexico, 420
Micronesian Islands, 24–26, 28, 42, 85 90, 94, 201, 232–233, 337, 338–340, 345–384, 413, 417
Middens, 45
Middle Ages, 274, 282, 312
Middle classes, 339, 400
Middle East, 420, 421
Migration, 1, 7, 13–19, 30, 37, 39, 180, 359, 412, 413
Militant egalitarianism, 84
Military alliances, 207, 272
Military power, 84, 103, 209, 212–215, 343, 352, 355, 357, 361, 364, 369, 380, 403, 408
Millenarian cults, 275, 364, 371–373, 397–411
Milne Bay movement, 374
Mimunaw rites, 70
Mind, 275, 277, 305
Minimal government, 341
Mini-man system, 101
Mining, 209
Minorities, 268
Miracles, 317, 327
Missionaries, 32, 119, 122, 181, 221, 243, 286, 348, 352, 356, 360, 365, 366, 369, 371, 372, 376, 387, 392, 393, 396, 398–400, 402, 404, 408–410, 412–414, 420, 423, 426
Mitchell River mission, 386, 387, 395, 396
Mitra artifacts, 45
Mixed races, 32
M'na group, 285, 290, 291
Moala Island, 78–84
Moari language, 119
Mobility, 103, 211
Modernization, 419–429
Modesty, 85, 88–89
Moiety, 146, 147, 149, 150, 151, 152, 153–157, 163
Moka system, 109
Mokakaru people, 216–217, 219
Moluccan language, 41
Monarchies, 274, 363, 364–365
Money, 60, 61, 62, 78, 84, 85, 86, 104, 119–120, 207, 217, 218, 219–222, 223, 399, 409, 416–417, 423, 427, 428, 429
Mongoloid race, 32, 40, 42
Monism, 402
Monogamy, 189, 197
Monopolies, 96, 99
Monsoon forests, 64
Montagnard family, 280
Montesquieu, Baron de la Brède, 279

Moon, 302
Morality, 236, 238, 239, 279, 281, 307, 309, 313, 315, 408
Mota Laya Island, 408
Mota tribe, 115, 319
Motivation, 82, 86
Motlav clan, 118
Mourning, 117
Mourongo (god), 327
Movement doctrine, 371
Mu (legend), 38
Mula cultigen, 70–71
Multilingualism, 97
Multiracial systems, 344–384
Muminai Feast, 222–231
Mumiship, 216–231
Murder, 255, 307
Music, 159, 225, 226, 231, 295, 296, 306
Mutual trust, 107
Mysticism, 306
Mythology, 165, 216, 217, 254, 286, 290, 293, 297–298, 300–302, 308, 314, 317, 339, 370, 377, 378, 386, 390, 395, 403, 404

Names, 144–148, 305, 308, 428–429
Napoleon I, Emperor, 267, 280
Narcotics, 387
Nardi district, 82
Nation states, 427, 429
Nationalism, 62, 284, 364–374, 382, 383, 424, 427
Nationality, 144
Native Companion clan, 391
Native Courts, 258
Native Lands Ordinance of 1956, 251–252, 256–258
Natung cultigen, 71
Natural barriers, 5, 8, 96–97
Natural resources, 102, 388
Natural science, 279, 280
Naturalization, 358
Nature, 306, 309, 310, 325, 329
Nature Is Your Guide (Gatty), 13
Navajo Indians, 420
Naval administration, 348, 349
Navatu Phase, 45
Navigation, 13–19, 278
Nazism, 424
N'dau group, 285, 290, 291
Negative sanctions, 245
Negroes, 32, 40, 42–43, 304–315
Neighborhood organizations, 247
Neko cult, 285, 291
Neolithic period, 40, 42, 43
Neolocal residence, 189
Neo-Melanesian culture, 97
Netherlands, 358, 378, 380, 386, 421, 423
New Britain, 25, 40, 44, 61, 95, 96, 102, 160, 174, 175, 343, 376, 378, 417
New Caledonia, 26–28, 40, 43, 44, 204, 343, 344, 359, 363, 375, 380–382, 402, 403, 406, 414
New Guinea, 5, 43, 49, 62, 91, 94–111, 113, 125–143, 146, 152, 159, 160, 203, 204, 207, 265, 266, 268–271, 282, 283, 294, 337, 341-343, 349–352, 354–360, 374, 375, 378, 380, 384, 409, 415, 416, 421, 422, 424, 426–428
New Guinea (quarterly), 428
New Guinea Lutheran Mission, 398
New Guinea Medical College, 283
New Hebrides, 25, 26, 28, 41, 44–46, 343, 360, 361, 374, 378, 381, 400, 407, 409
New Ireland, 44, 343, 352, 376
New Lives for Old (Mead), 416
New Testament, 275
New World, 7, 30, 33
New Zealand, 5, 14–19, 203, 339, 340, 347, 348, 366, 368, 383, 400, 412, 420
Newman, 281
Newton, Sir Isaac, 277
Ngaing culture, 266, 285–303
Nguna tribe, 25
Nigeria, 424
Nisbet, 401
Nobility, 274
Nomadic tribes, 282, 309, 420
Nomenclature, 144–148, 305, 308, 428–429
Nonintellectualism, 273, 274
Nonouti Island, 242, 264
Nonunilineality, 9
Norfolk Island, 408
Norsemen, 36
North America, 32, 420, 424
North American Indians, 32, 424

Northern Islands, 45
Northwest Coast Indians, 30, 36, 85, 205
Norwegian Expedition, 31, 35, 36
Noumea (town), 413, 415
Nuclear settlements, 64, 81, 161, 178, 233, 235
Nuku Hiva Island, 31–32, 36
Nukuoro tribe, 25
Numerical parity, 178

Obligations, 56, 243–245, 258, 261, 264, 342
Obscenities, 131
Occidental tradition, 397
Occult forces, 300
Occupations, *see* Employment
Oceania, 20, 28, 29, 40, 268–270, 282–284, 316–318, 324, 337–384, 397, 400, 406, 410
Oceanography, 1
Offenses, 233, 238, 245
Offerings, 271, 294
Official Handbook of the Territory of New Guinea, 356–357
Old Testament, 275, 401, 403, 404
Old World, 8, 31
Oliver, Douglas L., 201, 216–231
Omens, 68
Omnipotence, 277
Omniscience, 277
Omten politics, 205
Ono i Lau (man), 410
Ontology, 306
Ontong Jaua district, 340
Opportunities, 355
Oratory, 125, 162, 207, 211, 419, 420
Order, 279, 280, 282, 359, 429
Ordinances, 248, 256, 259, 262
Organization, 51–56, 60, 65, 78, 114, 117, 125, 144, 157–179, 191, 203–214, 232–264, 273, 287, 312, 331, 332, 340, 343, 361, 374, 375, 384, 394, 407–409, 412–422, 426–427
"Origins of the Melanesians" (Shutler and Shutler), 2
Ornamentation, 214
Orthodox Eastern Church, 279
Orthography, 119
Out-marriage, 182, 189
Ouvéa Island, 406
Owen, Robert, 280
Ownership, 53, 62, 69, 82, 85, 86, 160, 165–167, 192, 211, 218, 243, 244, 250–252, 255, 258, 262, 287, 288, 315, 338, 342, 353, 364, 367, 394
Oxford English Dictionary, 271

Pa Fenuatara (man), 118, 323, 326
Pa Fenumera (man), 328
Pa Kavakiua (man), 328
Pa Motuangi (man), 322, 323, 325–326
Pa Motuata (man), 328
Pa Porima (man), 328
Pa Rangifau (man), 322
Pa Rangifuri (man), 320, 321, 323, 324, 328, 329
Pa Rarovi (man), 329
Pa Tariaraki (man), 322
Pa Tekaumata (man), 324
Pa Torokinga (man), 326
Pa Vainunu (man), 322, 327
Pae Avakofe tribe, 329
Pae Sao (man), 323, 328–329
Pagang Gaddang culture, 63–77
Paganism, 272, 279, 405–406, 409
Painting, 309
Paired relationships, 392, 393
Pakak Gaddang culture, 63, 64, 67–74, 76
Pakistan, 424, 425
Pako cult, 374
Palaces, 214
Palau culture, 24–25, 28, 41, 97
Paleolithic Age, 20, 385
Paliau (leader), 427
Paliau movement, 378, 383
Palmerston Island, 6
Palmists, 283
Pangai Island, 417
Papeete (town), 348, 413, 417
Papeiha (evangelist), 409–410
Papua, Territory of, 26–28, 40, 94, 99, 125, 208, 294, 357, 374, 377, 378, 415, 421, 422, 424, 426–428
Papuo-Melanesians, 40
Paradiso (Piccarda), 315
Paraguay, 408
Parambik (god), 289–292, 298, 300

Paramus district, 296, 300
Paramus (god), 291, 292
Parceners, 182, 183
See also Inheritance
Parentage, 178, 193–194
Parkinson's Law, 213
Parliamentary government, 310
Partitions, 183
Partnership trade, 98, 101, 105–107, 110, 164, 223, 224, 388–389, 392–393
Past, the, 304, 306
Pastor, 417
Paternalism, 348, 367
Pathans tribe, 424
Paton, Frank, 401
Paton, John G., 401, 409
Patricide, 235, 236, 237
Patriclans, 287, 288, 289, 292, 293, 295, 297, 300
Patrilateral relationships, 177
Patrilineal relationships, 159–179, 204, 233, 235, 236, 239–241, 287, 288, 292, 344, 390
Pa-us, 211
Payments, 55–56, 58–60, 101, 102, 104, 106, 110, 169, 172, 176, 179, 207, 208, 224, 255, 288, 315, 401
Peace, 104, 106, 107, 108, 163, 248, 257, 275, 287, 295, 309, 312, 340, 342, 346, 408
Peace Corps, 427
Peasantry, 416, 420
Penalties, 162, 258
Penile supraincision, 297
Peonage, 420
Perfectionism, 277, 313
Permanency, 306
Person, concepts of, 82, 144, 206, 255, 305, 306
Personal power, 206
Personal relationships, 261
Personality, 305, 306, 308, 330, 342
Personnel, 426–428
Persuasion, 252
Peru, 29–38, 420
Pestle and mortar, 44
Philippine Islands, 30, 41, 42, 63–77, 367, 421
Philosophers, 265, 279, 308, 312, 313
Philosophy, 278, 280, 283, 307, 308, 312, 318
Phoenix Islands, 6
Phonemic change, 21, 22
Photographs, 401
Physical anthropology, 39–46
Physical attractiveness, 363
Physique, 362, 424
Piccarda, 315
Pidgin-English, 115, 116, 172, 208, 219, 354, 379
Piety, 276
Pig-raising, 98–101, 293
Pitcairn Island, 6, 8
Pithecanthropoids, 40
Pitman, 400
Placostylus artifacts, 44
Plantations, 268, 352, 361, 376
Planting, 81–82, 83, 90, 269, 294, 339, 355, 409
See also Gardening cultures
Plato, 269
Pleistocene period, 40, 43, 44
Plow, 76, 421
Plural societies, 180, 345–349, 375
Poetry, 307, 308, 312
Polanyi, Karl, 47
Pole Star, 17
Police, 256, 257, 357, 361, 429
Political scientists, 263
Politics, 84, 97, 101, 104, 108, 109, 110, 140, 161, 167, 177, 178, 271, 280, 283, 286, 287, 291, 332, 337–384, 398, 403, 407, 419–429
anthropology of, 201–264
law and, 242–264
leadership in, 216–231
organization of, 78, 191, 203–214, 232–241, 263, 331, 340, 412–421, 426–427
and social control, 201–264
types of, 203–214
unification and, 239, 282, 289, 303, 306, 340, 341, 346, 357, 364, 366, 374, 375
Politics of the Kula Ring (Uberoi), 109
Polity, 80, 111, 201, 210, 348, 366, 369
Pollution, 125–143
Polygamy, 57, 64, 140, 208, 303

Polynesia, 7–9, 13–38, 40–43, 52, 94, 115–124, 201, 203–214, 265, 266, 308, 314, 317, 324, 331, 337–340, 345–363, 366, 376, 377, 381, 384, 398, 409, 410, 413, 414, 416, 417
Pomares clan, 365
Ponape region, 49, 85–93
Pope, 274
Population, 8, 52, 95, 96, 125, 128, 154, 168, 171, 177, 180, 213, 214, 247, 348, 350, 353, 357–361, 364–366, 369, 408, 413, 414, 420–423, 428
  control of, 9–11, 366
Port Moresby (town), 413
Port towns systems, 412–418
Positions, 144, 342, 345
Positivism, 245, 259, 273
Pospisil, 201
Possessions, 53, 62, 69, 82, 86, 160, 165, 166–167, 211, 218, 243, 244, 250–252, 255, 262, 338, 364, 367, 394
Post-contact period, 6, 268
Posthumous debts, 166
Postwar period, 170, 272, 346, 355, 362, 367, 368, 374, 404, 412–414, 421–423, 426, 427
Potlatching, 85, 100-101, 207
Pottery, 37, 42–46, 52, 98–102, 106, 110, 160, 222, 313
Pouvanaa (man), 368, 373
Poverty, 300
Power, 57–60, 78–84, 103, 162, 201–264, 257, 258, 318, 330–332, 337–384, 396, 398, 402, 403, 407, 408, 414, 419, 421–424, 426
Prayer, 235, 237, 271, 404, 405, 410
Precedent, 244, 261
Precontact period, 381
Prejudice, 272, 346, 347
Preliterate society, 242
Premarital sexual intercourse, 141
Presbyterians, 387, 400, 401, 407, 408
Present, the, 305, 306
Prestige, 58, 81, 84–93, 190, 317, 337–345, 349, 355, 390, 396, 409
Pricing, 104–108, 416
Priest-chiefs, 340
Priestley, Joseph, 279
Priest-mediums, 70
Priests, 212, 317, 331, 339, 406, 410
Principia (Newton), 277
Printing, 417
Prisons, 257, 258, 261, 262, 339
Pritchard, 400
Private trade, 165
Privilege, 57, 58, 59, 211, 250–252, 331, 345, 355, 376
Pro-acculturative religion, 373–374, 379
Probity, 268
Procedural law, 258–259
Production of goods, 51–60, 62, 78–85, 96, 99–101, 103, 104, 159, 161, 165–167, 169, 178–179, 207, 209, 211, 212, 214, 215, 242, 258, 261, 262, 271, 283, 288, 313, 331, 339, 351–353, 360, 361, 409, 413–416
Professionalism, 351, 352–353, 360
Profits, 104–108, 389
Programmatic religion, 374
Progress, 214, 425
Proletarian government, 214
Promiscuity, 141
Property, 53, 62, 69, 82, 85, 86, 160, 165–167, 192, 211, 243, 244, 250–252, 258, 262, 287, 288, 315, 338, 342, 353, 364, 367, 394
Prophetism, 371–376, 380, 403, 404
Proprietorship, 178–179
Prosperity, 319, 320
Prostitution, 393
Protestant London Missionary Society, 247, 259
Protestantism, 247, 260, 277, 348, 365, 366, 370, 371, 402, 403, 405–407, 410
Proto-languages, 1, 22, 24–25, 27–28, 40
Proto-nationalism, 373, 374, 383
Proto-sociological movement, 279
Psychic forces, 317, 330
Psychology, 55, 269, 314, 392–393
Pu Fangatafea (man), 326
Public health, 257, 424
Public opinion, 244, 261, 263, 424
Public welfare, 248
Puhetini, Tahia, 31–32
Puhetini, Tahiaei, 31
Pukapuka Atoll, 9

Pu-ma (god), 322
Punishment, 181, 201, 203, 232-241, 309, 340, 342, 346, 354, 355, 370, 402
Purari Delta region, 378
Putative relationships, 96, 170, 286, 289
Pwagatch (man), 403–404
Pyramidal politics, 205, 210

Queensland, 268, 283, 385, 386, 401

Ra Phase, 46
Rabaul (town), 374, 413, 415
Rabaul *Times,* 356
Race
  determination of, 31–32, 40, 51, 144
  discrimination and, 344–384, 410, 421, 422, 427
  mixed, 32
  relationships, 344–384, 410, 414, 415, 421, 422, 427
  status and, 354
Radio, 417
Raft Book, The (Garry), 13, 16
Rafts, 33, 38
Raiding, 294
Rainfall, 83
Rakeimaitafua (man), 328
Ramage ranking, 205
Ranches, 386, 387
Random connubium, 178
Rank, 58, 80, 204, 205, 207, 210, 215, 244, 338–343, 362, 377, 409, 422
Rapa Island, 366
Rapa Iti Island, 36
Rappaport, Roy A., 2, 5–12
Raroia Atoll, 29, 34, 416, 417
Rarotonga Island, 400, 402, 417
Rataiku people, 216–217, 219
Rationality, 308, 311
Raw materials, 99, 416
Reading, 407
Reality, 307, 308
Reason, 275, 276, 311
Reciprocity, 78–80, 107, 207, 208, 209, 243, 288, 389
Recreation, 208
Recruitment, 423, 427
Red taro, 290, 291, 294
Redemption, 309
Redistribution of goods, 94, 98
Reformation, 276
Regional variation, 82
Regrouping, 209
Regulations, 232, 238, 239, 248, 256, 257, 258, 260, 261, 262, 428
Rehabilitation, 420
Relationships, *see* types of
Relativism, 268, 282
Religion, 62, 117–118, 121, 126, 139, 203, 211, 207, 247, 265–333, 341, 362–364, 366, 369–377, 379–381, 383, 397–411, 424
Renaissance, 311
Rennell (town), 416
Renown, 206, 207, 209, 217
Representation, 358
Reservations, 82, 407, 420, 423
Resiake family, 122
Residence, 125, 140, 181, 182–183, 189, 196, 247, 250, 288, 354
Resistance, 364–373
Resources, 9, 102, 160, 292, 299, 302, 321, 339, 345, 365, 388
Respect, 194
Responsibility, 241, 331, 424, 426
Resurrection, 402
Retrieval system, 428–429
Revivalism, 369, 370, 371, 373
Rhetoric, 162
Rice, 42, 49, 66, 180, 181, 245, 283
Richard III, King, 267
Ridicule, 88–89
Rights, 166, 167, 168, 182, 183, 184, 192–193, 206, 239, 245, 251, 252, 257, 287, 288, 293, 362, 407, 419–429
Ringworm, 240
Rites, 118, 181, 189, 219, 226, 288, 289, 292, 294, 322–324, 389, 351
Rituals, 126, 131–138, 159, 181, 184–185, 193, 196, 237, 268, 270, 271, 282, 286, 287, 289, 290, 293–298, 303, 308 309, 312, 313, 320, 323, 324, 331, 340, 343, 364, 366, 372, 375, 378, 399, 406, 410
Rivalry, 80, 81, 84, 101, 178, 213, 300, 426
Robespierre, Maximilian, 280
Roman Catholic Mission, 286

Roman Empire, 274
Roman pagan religion, 279
Rongorongo boards, 36
Root cultigens, 42, 78
Rot measurement, 71–72
Rotuma district, 25, 28, 41
Rousseau, Jean-Jacques, 279, 280
Rousseauism, 408
Routledge, 35
Royal Society, 277
Ruhuaku people, 217
Rule, 203–215

Sacraments, 398
Sacred knowledge, 299, 300, 301
Sacrilege, 237
Sadness, 312
Safety, 257
Sagali ceremonies, 57, 59
Sahlins, Marshall D., 49, 78–84, 201, 203–216
Sa-Huynh-Kalanay tradition, 43
Sailing, 102, 110, 120, 165, 169–171, 179
Saint-Simon, 281
Salt, 106
Salvation, 406
Samoa Island, 8, 16, 33, 117, 340, 344, 348, 364, 365, 367–369, 372, 376, 383, 412, 414, 417, 419
Samuel, Chief, 403
Sanction, 232–241, 243–245, 253, 258, 261–262, 264, 279, 342, 346, 364
Sanggai rituals, 131–138
Sanop cults, 374
Santa Cruz Islands, 28
Santo Island, 414
Satan, 377, 401, 402
Scandinavia, 308
Schmidt, Pater, 317
Schools, 122, 257, 270, 318, 424, 425
Schouten Islands, 343
Schulterbeil culture, 42
Science, 268, 271, 275, 277, 279, 280, 311, 312
Scientific Revolution, 276, 282
Scotland, 205, 400, 408, 420
Script, 421
Sculpture, 35–36, 37
Sea Dayaks, 180, 200
Seclusion house, 126, 132–134
Secrecy, 86, 89, 90, 92, 93
Secret societies, 169, 342
Section chief, 88
Secularism, 274, 275, 282, 299, 300, 348, 362
Security, 104
Sedentary horticulture, 125, 128
Segmentation, 205, 340–344, 375, 381
Segregation, 297, 354, 399
Self-government, 205
Self-pity, 312
Self-sufficiency, 103, 165, 392, 419, 420
Semen, 130, 131
Semi-moieties, 148, 154, 157
Sengam cult, 285, 291
Seniority, 338
Sentiments, 390, 394, 396, 423
Separatism, 381
Service, Elman R., 113, 144–158
Services, 212, 352–354, 362
Sesake clan, 25
Set, 14–17
Setefano, Pastor, 407
Settlement, 14–17, 28, 64–68, 161, 247, 367, 412
Sex
  labor and, 54, 82, 90, 164, 168, 171, 198, 227
  premarital, 141
  relationships and, 118, 125–143, 150, 188, 189, 194, 196, 232–241, 306
  status and, 113, 125–143, 162, 164, 165, 168, 192, 197, 244, 251, 289, 298, 315, 341, 389–390, 393–394
  totemism, 311
Shakespeare, William, 283
Sharp, Andrew, 2, 13–19
Sharp, Lauriston, 385–396
Shell money, 217, 219, 222, 223
Shepherd Islands, 45
Ships, 33, 120, 372
Shutler, Mary Elizabeth, 39–46
Shutler, Richard, Jr., 39–46
Siane tribe, 126
Siang district, 294
Siassi Island, 95–111, 114, 159–179

Siblings, 183, 188, 192-193, 197, 233, 235–236, 306
Sibog cult, 290–292
Sigatoka Phase, 45
Sindama cult, 290–292
Singing, 225, 226, 314, 325
Sio (village), 102, 107, 109, 110
Siovili (prophet), 371
Siovili cult, 371–373, 383
Sister-exchange, 307
Siuai area, 219, 220
Skills, 82, 92, 102, 103, 207, 314, 360, 422, 427, 429
Slander, 162
Slavery, 188, 339, 422
Small businesses, 352–354
Smith, Percy, 16
Sobriety, 276
Social anthropology, 113, 198, 268, 279, 282, 398, 414, 415
Social barriers, 120–121, 216
Social climbing, 100–101
Social Contract, The (Rousseau), 279, 280
Social discrimination, 120–121, 156, 214, 216, 280, 315, 363
Social organization, 56, 65, 117, 125, 144, 157–179, 248, 255, 273, 312, 394, 407–409, 422, 429
Social relationships, 109, 110, 125, 141, 145, 146, 149, 156, 169–177, 196, 272, 339, 345, 389–390, 392–394
Social religion, 265, 279, 297–299
Social status, 85, 127, 141, 144, 146, 151, 152, 244, 247, 251, 262, 263, 337–384
Social stratification, 57, 114–200, 269, 286, 302, 305, 313, 315, 338, 357, 363, 375, 380, 381
Social structure, 62, 84, 167, 168, 177, 181, 190, 192, 197, 198, 204, 233, 236, 238, 261, 269, 273, 279, 282, 285–289, 298, 302, 307, 310, 343, 344, 346, 362, 398
Society, 177–178, 242, 262, 265, 270, 279–281, 289, 298, 303, 306, 311–315, 337, 353, 363, 395, 397, 422
Society Island, 8, 30, 204, 348, 365, 369, 370
Socioantrism, 144
Sociocentrism, 113, 144–158
Socioculturism, 48, 102, 269, 270, 425
Socioeconomics, 276
Sociology, 264, 265, 268–270, 279, 281, 282, 381, 384
Sociopolitics, 271, 274, 276, 282, 283, 338, 343, 359, 363–364, 369, 379–381
Soil, 68, 73, 82, 90, 246
Solidarity, 214, 235, 239, 265, 281
Solomon Islands, 26, 40, 41, 44, 201, 203, 209, 341–343, 360, 361, 374, 378, 381
Solstices, 33
Som cult, 285, 291
Songs, 325
Soŋi cult, 216–231
Sopol (man), 163–164
Sor (god), 291, 292
Sor area, 296, 300
Sorcery, 106, 107, 130, 162, 163, 166, 222, 283, 293, 294, 299, 300, 303, 306–308, 403
Sorrow, 312
Souls, 275, 276, 278, 292, 355
South America, 29–30, 37, 91
South China, 43
South Equatorial Current, 14
South Pacific Commission, 415
Southeast Asia, 27, 28, 39–43, 180, 198, 284, 421
Southern Cross (ship), 115, 116, 119
Sovereignty, 341, 381, 419
Space, 178
Spain, 7, 91, 348, 367
Spear Black Duck clan, 391
Specialization, 94, 345, 350, 422
Spells, 404
Spirit, the, 275, 400
Spirit-children, 307
Spirits, 121, 130, 161, 222, 227, 231, 238, 239, 254, 268, 271, 284–286, 288, 289, 292–294, 297, 298, 300–303, 305, 306, 317, 321, 323, 327, 330, 331, 343, 370–373, 381
Spoehr, Alexander, 412–418
Sports, 56, 283
Spouse exchange, 65
Stability, 306, 314, 395
Standards, 423

Stanner, W. E. H., 266, 304–315
Stare decisis law, 244
Stars, 14–18, 302
State government, 361, 428
Statistics, 270
Status, 57, 75, 80, 85, 88, 93, 101, 113, 125–158, 162, 164, 165, 168 177, 178, 192, 197, 205, 213, 244, 247, 251, 255, 262, 263, 289, 298, 314, 315, 331, 337–384, 389–390, 393–394, 398, 415, 420, 423, 426
Statutes, 255, 259, 260
Steel axes, 385–386
Steinen, Karl von den, 36
Stem families, 194
Steward, Bishop, 122
Stokes, J. G., 36
Stone axes, 385–388
Stone-age cultures, 385–396, 422, 425, 429
Stone-working, 37
Store-houses, 211–212
Stratification
cultural, 64, 338–340, 346, 349–384, 422, 424, 426
social, 57, 114–200, 269, 286, 302, 305, 315, 338, 357, 363–364, 375, 380, 381–383
Strength, 79–80, 82, 399
Strikes, 428
Structuralism, 62, 84, 167, 168, 177, 181, 190, 192, 197, 198, 204, 233, 236, 238, 261, 264, 273, 279, 282, 285–289, 298, 302, 307, 310, 343, 344, 346, 362, 398
Students, 263, 270, 341, 428, 429
Subgrouping, 7, 8, 20–24, 146, 244, 248, 250, 253, 340, 394
Subordination, 151, 338, 393, 394
Subpoena, 250
Subsistence economy, 76, 78, 85, 89, 90, 92, 100, 103, 180, 339, 342, 345, 353, 388
Substantivists, 48
Success, 320, 324, 330, 341, 375, 399
Sudan region, 419
Suffrage, 257, 358, 362
Sugar, 245, 286, 362
Suggs, Robert C., 3, 14, 18, 29–38
Suicide, 394
Sumba Island, 41
Sun, 83, 302
Sunlit Cloud Iguana clan, 390, 391, 395
Superiority, 356, 383, 421, 424
Supernatural, 122, 127, 196, 232–241, 271, 283, 301, 317, 330, 342, 364, 370, 371, 372, 374, 375, 376, 378, 383
Superordination, 338, 389
Superstition, 284
Supply-and-demand, 98
Suprafamilial institutions, 146
Supralocal organization, 208, 375
Suprapersonal structures, 210
Surpluses, 81, 101, 179, 211, 215, 313, 342
Suva (town), 413
Suzerainty, 423
Sweet potato, 30, 31, 42, 54, 57, 59, 61, 73, 81, 83, 86, 128, 134, 137, 226, 286
Swidden agriculture, 64–68, 70–74, 78–84
Symbolism, 307
Sympathetic magic, 294
Syncretism, 369, 373, 376, 381, 382

Tabalayan house, 64
Tabu, 340
Tafaki (chief), 328
Taķ measurement, 71
Tahiti, 2, 13, 14, 16, 205, 210, 215, 340, 347, 348, 364, 365, 368–370, 372, 373, 417
Taiwan, 41
Talent, 300
Tamana Island, 252
Tami Island, 95, 96, 102
Tanna Island, 45, 408, 409
Tapas, 211
Taro, 81, 83, 87, 90, 100–101, 137, 204, 223, 226, 227, 245, 286, 287, 290, 291, 321, 328
Taro cult, 290, 291, 292, 374
Task force, 169–177
Taxation, 62, 205, 357, 364, 428
Teachers, 407–410, 417, 422, 425, 427
Technology, 47–111, 212, 271, 276, 283, 285, 386, 387, 390, 391, 392, 394, 420, 421, 422, 425, 428
Tematawarebwe (settler), 253–254

Temples, 212
Temporal relativism, 268, 282
Ten Itaaka Ata (man), 259
Ten Kirabuke Maio (man), 259
Tenant farming, 251, 362
Tension, 312, 313
Tents, 420
Tenure, 53, 69, 82, 86, 160, 166, 244, 250, 252, 262, 364, 367
Terebra artifacts, 45
Terei clan, 217
Terminology, 144–158, 191–200, 338
Territorial limitations, 5, 8–11, 12
Tey, Josephine, 267
Thailand, 419
Thakombau (chief), 362, 380
Theft, 233, 234, 292
Theology, 402
Thomas Aquinas, St., 274–275, 276
Thought, 306, 311, 316
Thupira clan, 405
Tiahuanaco period, 37
Tikopia Island, 117, 319–332, 416
Time, concept of, 267–284, 301, 304–315, 423
Tobacco, 64, 70, 74–75, 76, 134, 245, 387
Tokelaus Islands, 8, 340
Toli, 53
Tomedy, Pastor, 405
Tommy Kabu Kampani role, 378
Tonga Islands, 45, 117, 204, 205, 339, 340, 344, 348, 362, 364, 365, 368, 370, 376, 383, 410, 419
Tongoa group, 25
Tonkinese language, 359
Tools, 42–44, 52, 104, 303, 313, 385–396, 399, 416
Tooth paste cult, 396
Torres Islands, 45, 374
Tort law, 259
Totemism, 286, 288, 289–292, 293, 297, 298, 299, 301, 305, 306, 309, 311, 317, 342, 387, 389, 390, 391, 394 395, 396, 404, 405, 407
Towosi, 53–55
Trade, 60–62, 79–80, 92, 94–111, 120, 159, 160, 164, 165, 178–179, 223, 224, 286, 287, 313, 342, 344, 351, 353, 356, 387–389, 392–393, 400, 403, 408, 409, 412–418, 422, 429
Tradition, 177, 243, 255
Tragedy, 312
Transcendentalism, 312
Transformation Scene (Hogan), 416
Transistor radios, 417
Transportation, 56, 105, 214, 351, 394–395, 413, 417
Tree cultigens, 42, 181
Tregear, 317
Trials, 259
Tribalism, 51–62, 191, 209, 271, 380, 420, 424, 426
Tributes, 56, 364, 422
Tridacna artifacts, 45
Trinity College, 277
Tristan da Cunha culture, 6, 8
Trobriand Islanders, 51–62, 107, 342, 375, 382
Trochus artifacts, 44
Truk Islands, 19, 27, 88
Trumpet Shall Sound, The (Worsley), 272
Trusteeship, 355, 357, 423, 426–428
Truth, concept of, 267–284, 308, 317, 327–328
Tuamotu Archipelago, 8, 29, 365, 417
Tuauru region, 406
Tubou, George I., 365
Tubuai Islands, 366, 410
Tudor regime, 267
Tuete district, 403
Tui Nayau, King, 410
Tuilleries, Attack of, 280
Tuka religion, 380
Tulagi (town), 116
Turner, 401
Turuŋom Village, 220
Tylor, Sir Edward B., 265
Typee (Melville), 213
Typhoons, 93

Uberoi, 109
Ugly American, The (Burdick & Lederer), 284
Ukraine, 420
Uli Ai Iban tribe, 180

Umboi Island, 96, 100, 101, 162, 164, 165, 172
Underbidding, 108
Understanding, 268, 302, 305, 308, 310–312, 319, 407
Unicentrism, 263
Unification, 239, 282, 289, 303, 306, 340, 341, 342, 346, 357, 364, 366, 374, 375, 381
Unilineal descent, 113, 114, 159, 198, 287
Union of Soviet Socialist Republics, 424
United Nations, 219, 368, 427, 428
United States, 30, 284, 345, 347–349, 363, 365, 367–369, 399, 412–414, 423, 424, 429
U.S. Navy, 367
Universities, 270
University of Paris, 275
Upheaval, 280
Upper classes, 339
Urbanization, 412–418, 424
Usufructure, 166–167
Utrolateral filiation, 182–183, 198
Utrolocal marriage, 182
Uxorilocal residence, 182, 189
Uzbek tribe, 424

Vahihaloa (guide), 115, 122
Vailala doctrine, 374, 377, 378
Valentine, Charles A., 337–384
Value, 62, 104–108, 288, 290, 294, 298, 302, 331, 361, 363, 390, 394
Vayda, Andrew P., 2, 5–12
Vaygua, 57, 60, 61
Vengeance, 174
Viarcocha (god), 37
Victorian period, 400
Vierkanterbeil culture, 42
Vila Island, 45, 414
Village District Assembly (Nonouti Island), 247, 253–256
Village economy, 160–165, 177
Violence, 103, 106, 162–164, 370, 379, 422
Virilocal residence, 182, 189
Viripatrilocal residence, 288
Viti Levu Island, 45
Vitiaz Strait, 94–111
Volcanoes, 203
Voltaire, 278
Voting, 257, 358, 362
Voyaging, 10, 13–19, 28–38, 95, 97, 99, 170–171, 240
Vunda Phase, 46

Wage labor, 86, 416
Wales, 420
Waley, Arthur, 312
Wallace, Ben J., 49, 63–77
Walzenbeil culture, 42
War, 10, 36, 57, 59, 103–104, 139, 142, 159, 161, 163, 164, 208, 217, 236, 248, 286, 293, 294, 299, 313, 339, 340, 342, 346, 357, 362, 379, 387–389, 399, 403, 404, 406, 408–410, 421, 422
War of Liberation, 280
Wards, 163, 169, 178
Warrior groups, 364
Water, 245, 247
Water Babies, 380–381
Water buffalo, 75, 76
Water craft, 33, 38, 42, 102, 110, 120, 165, 169–171, 179, 372
Watom Island, 43
Watt, Mrs., 400
Wealth, 57–58, 60, 62, 75, 96, 98, 104–108, 162, 165, 190, 213, 217, 268, 271, 272, 275, 283, 288, 290, 294, 298, 302, 303, 331, 341–344, 353, 361, 363, 375, 380, 390, 394, 399, 402
Weather, 290, 293, 298, 320, 330
Weaving, 37, 57, 98, 110, 286, 422
Webb, Mary, 305
Webster's Dictionary, 250
Welfare, 193, 206, 248, 257, 258, 289, 296, 302–303, 320, 322, 342, 367, 376, 420
Western Highlands, 43
Western Islands, 25
Westernization, 47, 48, 95, 117, 282, 284, 349–384, 416
Wet taro, 78, 83
Wewak cult, 374
Wheel, 313, 421
White men, 32, 36–37, 345, 346, 349, 355, 356, 367, 375, 385–387, 392–395, 398, 399, 404, 406, 407, 427

White taro, 294
Wife exchange, 65
William of Ockham, 276
Williams, 409
Williams, John, 372
Winds, 14, 15, 19, 30, 70
Wisdom, 312
Wislin movement, 374, 377
Witchcraft, 331, 403
Women
  labor and, 54, 82, 90, 164, 171, 198, 227
  status of, 54, 82, 90, 113, 125–143, 162, 164, 165, 168, 171, 178, 192, 197, 227, 244, 251, 289, 298, 315, 341, 389–390, 393–394
Wood carving, 52
Work, *see* Labor
World War I, 282, 346, 355, 361, 362, 373, 381, 427
World War II, 170, 272, 346, 355, 362, 367, 368, 374, 404, 412–414, 421–423, 426, 427
Worsley, 270–272, 282
Writing, 407
Written codes, 258, 259

Xanthosoma, 83

Yabuling (god), 292, 295–298
Yahveh, 309, 405, 406
Yalasu language, 27
Yali (man), 283
Yam culture, 57, 59, 83, 86–93, 204, 286, 321, 328, 404
Yap Island, 201, 232–241, 339
Yawus (man), 401
Yir Yoront group, 385–396
Yoruba tribe, 424
Youth, *see* Adolescence; Childhood
Yuku site, 43

Zanzibar, 5
Zuñiga, Father Joacquin M. de, 30